MICHAËL N. VAN DER MEER, Ph.D. (2001) in Theology, [illegible] post-doc fellow Old Testament, teaches religious [illegible] He has published on the Formation and Reformulation of the Book of [illegible] (Brill, 2001) and the Septuagint of Isaiah.

PERCY VAN KEULEN, Ph.D. (1995), Leiden University, is currently attached to the TURGAMA-project as a post-doctoral fellow. He has published on the Deuteronomistic History, the Septuagint, Peshitta, and Targum of Kings, and on Aramaic and Syriac linguistics.

WIDO VAN PEURSEN, Ph.D. (1999) in Semitic Languages, Leiden University, is associate professor of Old Testament at Leiden University. His publications include *The Verbal System in the Hebrew Text of Ben Sira* (Brill, 2004) and *Language and Interpretation in the Syriac Text of Ben Sira* (Brill, 2007).

BAS TER HAAR ROMENY, Ph.D. (1997), Leiden University, is Professor of Old Testament and Eastern Christian Traditions at Leiden University. He has published extensively on Eastern Christianity, Late Antiquity, Syriac literature, and history of biblical interpretation, including *Religious Origins of Nations? The Christian Communities of the Middle East* (Brill, 2010).

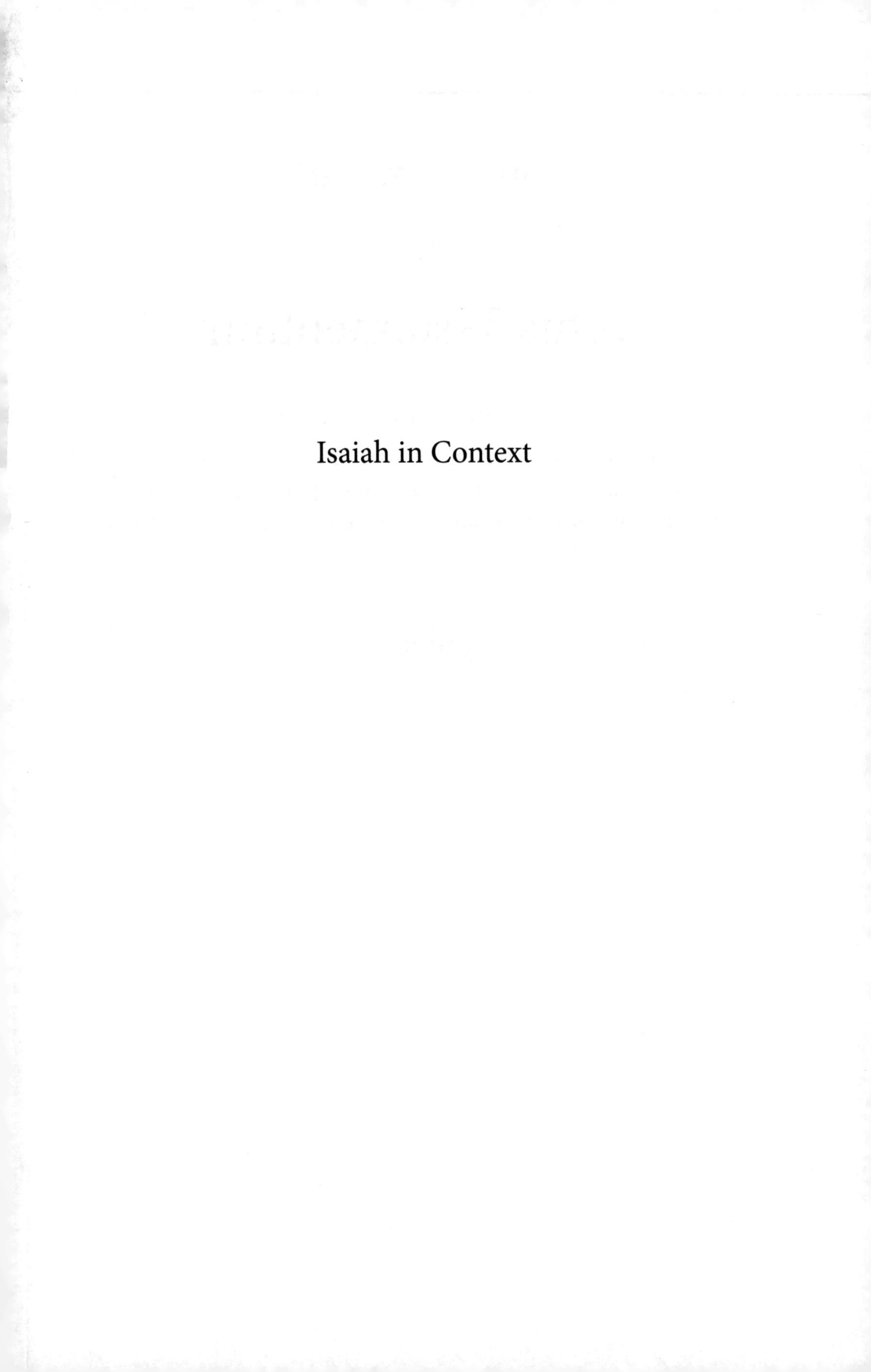

Isaiah in Context

Supplements

to

Vetus Testamentum

VOLUME 138

Prof. Dr. Arie van der Kooij

Isaiah in Context

Studies in Honour of Arie van der Kooij on the Occasion of his Sixty-Fifth Birthday

Edited by

Michaël N. van der Meer
Percy van Keulen
Wido van Peursen
Bas ter Haar Romeny

BRILL

LEIDEN • BOSTON
2010

This book is printed on acid-free paper.

Library of Congress Cataloging-in-Publication Data

Isaiah in context : studies in honour of Arie van der Kooij on the occasion of his sixty-fifth birthday / edited by Michaël N. van der Meer, Percy van Keulen, Wido van Peursen, Bas ter Haar Romeny.
p. cm. – (Supplements to Vetus Testamentum, ISSN 0083-5889 ; v. 138)
Includes bibliographical references and index.
ISBN 978-90-04-18657-6 (hardback : alk. paper) 1. Bible. O.T. Isaiah–Criticism, interpretation, etc. I. Kooij, Arie van der, 1945- II. Meer, Michaël N. van der. III. Keulen, P. S. F. van. IV. Peursen, W. Th. van. V. Haar Romeny, R. B. ter. VI. Title. VII. Series.

BS1515.52.I585 2010
224'.106–dc22

2010015912

ISSN 0083-5889
ISBN 978 90 04 18657 6

PRINTED BY DRUKKERIJ WILCO B.V. - AMERSFOORT, THE NETHERLANDS

CONTENTS

PART TWO

ISAIAH IN THE CONTEXT OF SEPTUAGINT, PESHITTA, AND MODERN INTERPRETATIONS

PREFACE

The following collection of essays on the Book of Isaiah in its Hebrew, Aramaic, Assyrian, Greek, Syriac, and Dutch contexts is a tribute to Arie van der Kooij, offered by his colleagues, friends, and students. This volume is presented to him on the occasion of his sixty-fifth birthday, which coincides with his retirement as Professor of Old Testament Studies at Leiden University. It is intended as a token of appreciation for his outstanding scholarship, his participation in many major international research projects, his academic teaching stretching over a period of more than forty years, and his friendly supervision of numerous dissertations.

Born the son of a minister of the Dutch Reformed Church on 8 March 1945, Arie van der Kooij was brought up on biblical study. After a solid classical training in Latin, Greek, and Hebrew at secondary school, Arie entered Utrecht University in 1963 to study Theology. During his study he was also trained in various Oriental languages and Russian. In 1967 he took up his first academic position there as a teacher of Hebrew and immediately after the completion of his studies in 1969 he became a lecturer in the same theological faculty.

His participation as a colleague of Professor Alexander Hulst in the United Bible Societies' Hebrew Old Testament Text Project introduced him to the world of textual criticism and the ancient versions of the Hebrew Bible, as well as to the circle of scholars, which included Eugene Nida, Dominque Barthélemy and his assistant Adrian Schenker, James Sanders, and Hans Peter Rüger. During the sessions of this group of scholars, his fascination for the ancient versions was aroused, which led him to devote his further doctoral studies to the ancient textual witnesses of the Book of Isaiah (1978). Up to the present, the German translation of his PhD thesis, *Die alten Textzeugen des Jesajabuches* (OBO 35; Fribourg–Göttingen, 1981), has remained a reference work for the history of interpretation of the prophecies of Isaiah in the ancient versions (Qumran, Septuagint, Theodotion, Aquila, Symmachus, Targum, Peshitta, and Vulgate). In particular his emphasis on the need to study the ancient versions 'in their own right', his discovery of the political background of these Bible translations, and his insight that all these ancient translations applied the ancient prophecy by way of 'fulfilment interpretation' to their own respective political and religious contexts, have proven to be a major contribution to Old Testament research.

Before and after the completion of his PhD dissertation Van der Kooij broadened his horizon further by investigating the redaction history of the Pentateuch, the Eden narrative in Genesis and its Mesopotamian parallels, the textual history of the Books of Samuel and Kings, and the history of Old Testament scholarship within the Dutch Reformed tradition of research. The list of Van der Kooij's academic publications placed at the end of the present volume attests to his broad interests. As secretary of the *Verkenningscommissie Godgeleerdheid* he held a major position in the committee that was responsible for the reorganization of the Dutch academic theological landscape in the final decades of the twentieth century.

In 1989 Arie moved to Leiden to occupy the chair of Old Testament studies as the successor to Martin Mulder and his illustrious predecessors, Piet de Boer, Berend Eerdmans, and Abraham Kuenen. One of his first tasks there was to organize an international conference on the legacy of Kuenen. Besides his responsibilities for the Old Testament courses and research programmes, Arie became responsible for the Leiden Peshitta edition, and, together with Adrian Schenker, Yohanan Goldman, Gérard Norton, Stephen Pisano, Richard Weis, and Jan de Waard, for the new edition of the Hebrew Bible, the *Biblia Hebraica Quinta*. In 1995 he succeeded John Emerton as the chief editor of one of the leading journals for Old Testament studies *Vetus Testamentum*. He had numerous other academic activities, including his role as secretary of the International Organization for the Study of the Old Testament, his participation in the supervisory board for the New Dutch Bible translation, his participation in the German translation and annotation project of the Septuagint (*Septuaginta Deutsch*), and other major projects such as the Biblia Qumranica, the International Organization for Septuagint and Cognate Studies Commentary on the Septuagint, and the Hexapla Project. From 2001 to 2004 Arie served as president of the International Organization for the Study of the Old Testament, which he brought back in 2004 to Leiden, the place where it was founded in 1950.

Among Arie's scholarly interests the Book of Isaiah, its historical setting against the background of Assyrian propaganda and politics, and its interpretation in the Greek, Aramaic, Syriac, and Latin versions have remained a central focus over the years. Van der Kooij's publications on the various aspects of this biblical book include not only his dissertation, but also a second monograph, *The Oracle of Tyre*, the proceedings of the Leiden Colloquium on *The Old Greek of Isaiah*, and numerous scholarly articles. It is therefore fitting that a *Festschrift* presented to this highly esteemed mentor, colleague, and friend should be devoted to the Book of Isaiah both in its original Hebrew and ancient near-eastern context and within the context of ancient and modern versions.

The contributions to this volume have been subsumed under two sections. The first section contains essays on the Book of Isaiah in the context of Hebrew and ancient near-eastern writings, that is, within the context of the complex redaction history of the book, and within the context of the books of the Hebrew Bible, Hebrew and Aramaic epigraphic documents, and, in particular, writings from Mesopotamia. The second section focuses on the reception of the book in Greek, Syriac, and Dutch translations.

The first contribution is written by Bob Becking. The essay explores the background of the simile in Isaiah 25:10, 'As Straw is Trodden Down in the Water of a Dung-pit', in the light of a similar sentence from ancient Mari (*šapal tibnim mû illakū*). Becking argues that the two passages can be mutually illuminating and that they should be understood as proverbs rather than riddles.

Pancratius C. Beentjes explores the way the Chronicler presents Isaiah. After discussing the divergent presentations of Isaiah in 2 Kings 18–20 versus 2 Chronicles 29–32, Beentjes examines in depth the rephrasing in 2 Chr 20:20 of a particular Isaianic passage found in Isa 7:9b, in which the negative prophecy has been transformed into a positive summons.

In 'Woe to Powers in Israel that Vie to Replace YHWH's Rule on Mount Zion! Isaiah Chapters 28–31 from the Perspective of Isaiah Chapters 24–27', Willem Beuken explores the intertextual relations between Isaiah 24–27 and the following chapters 28–31. Beuken shows how these blocks in the Book of Isaiah are connected by means of a web of common expressions and how the judgement on the earth, which is formulated in rather general terms in the so-called Apocalypse of Isaiah (Isaiah 24–27), is applied to the concrete situation of Jerusalem (Isaiah 28–31).

Robert P. Gordon revisits the theme of the dying gods in ancient near-eastern literature including the Bible, particularly the Book of Isaiah. Gordon examines this motif in texts such as the Ugaritic Baal Cycle, Enuma Elish, the Myth of Zu, Psalm 82, and Genesis 6, where the theme of the punishment of deities who challenge the supreme authority of the main Deity occurs. Gordon points out that this theme occurs also in texts, where humans aspire to divinity, such as Isaiah 14, 36–37, and 26, Ezekiel 28, Genesis 2–3, and the Gilgamesh Epic.

Holger Gzella critically examines the alleged instances of a *poʿel* or 'conative stem' for the regular verb in Biblical Hebrew (Ps 77:18; Hos 13:3; 1 Sam 21:3; Isa 10:13; 40:24; Ps 101:5; Job 9:15b) and places this pattern into its historical context. Gzella argues that a productive *poʿel* in Hebrew does not exist. Most alleged examples are replete with textual problems, whereas none of the very few serious cases exhibit any sharply identifiable meaning of the *poʿel* as opposed to other verbal stems. Instead, the *poʿel* pattern seems to serve as a rare means for deriving secondary denominal or deverbal by-forms on the spot.

Building upon his ground-breaking study *Isaiah among the Ancient Near East Prophets*, Matthijs J. de Jong studies Isa 10:24–27 in the context of Neo-Assyrian texts. These texts throw new light on the often misunderstood phrase 'the road to Egypt'. De Jong discerns an older layer (10:24–25) dating from the time of Sargon's campaigns in 720 BCE, and a later, seventh-century supplement (10:26–27), reflecting the removal of the yoke of Assyria in the time of King Josiah. In this way Isa 10:24–27 becomes 'A Window on the Isaiah Tradition in the Assyrian Period'.

The following contribution also deals with the Isaianic prophecies in the context of Neo-Assyrian imperialism. Percy van Keulen comments 'On the Identity of the Anonymous Ruler in Isaiah 14:4b–21'. Whereas many scholars believe that this passage refers to the death of the Assyrian king Sargon II, Van Keulen makes clear that the connection between the presumed reference to a humiliating death of this Assyrian ruler without proper burial in 705 BCE and the text of Isa 14:18–19 does not stand close scrutiny. The Isaianic passage should rather be dated to the period after the fall of Nineveh (612 BCE). The tyrant of the poem should not be interpreted as a specific Assyrian monarch, but rather as *typus* of a cruel and arrogant leader. Precisely the anonymous character of this tyrant enabled later readers of the book to identify him as Antiochus IV Epiphanes.

André Lemaire examines the divine epithet *Yhwh ṣᵉbāʾôt* in Isaiah in the light of Hebrew and Aramaic epigraphic evidence. The use of that epithet is typical of the Hebrew Book of Isaiah, as is the transliteration, rather than translation of the same phrase for the Greek translation of Isaiah. Lemaire draws parallels both for the early use of *ṣᵉbāʾôt* (from a recently published Hebrew inscription dating from the eight century BCE) and for the later, second function as a proper name (from Aramaic ostraca from Elephantine).

Johan Lust also deals with divine epithets in the Book of Isaiah. He compares 'The Divine Titles האדון and אדני in Proto-Isaiah … with Ezekiel', with special attention to the intricate literary-critical and text-critical problems related to these titles. The first of these two titles appear to be distinctive for the Book of Isaiah, particularly the oldest literary layers. While אדני could be used interchangeably with the divine name יהוה, at least from the time of the oldest textual witnesses (Qumran and Septuagint) onwards, האדון could not. Whereas the latter title characterizes the Lord as ruler of the world, the former title emphasizes the special relationship between the Lord and his prophetic messenger.

Karel Vriezen examines 'The Wording of "Destruction" in the Latter Prophets'. He points to the fact that recent archaeological theories concerning the emergence of Ancient Israel, such as the theories of peaceful infiltration or gradual sedentarization of indigenous pastoralists, share with the books of the Former Prophets the notion that the destruction of Palestinian cities was relatively restricted: according to the Book of Joshua only the cities of Jericho, Ai and Hazor were completely destroyed. The vocabulary describing destroyed cities is far more widespread in the books of the Latter Prophets. According to Vriezen these observations are best understood in the context of the destructive and aggressive Neo-Assyrian campaigns in Palestine in the times of these Latter Prophets.

In 'Patterns of Mutual Influence in the Textual Transmission of the Oracles Concerning Moab in Isaiah and Jeremiah', Richard D. Weis addresses one of the most complicated issues in the textual criticism of the Hebrew Bible. Adopting a descriptive rather than a prescriptive approach such as that found in earlier editions of the Biblia Hebraica, Weis examines in great detail all the cases of the mutual influence of Jeremiah 48, Isaiah 15–16, as well as Numbers 24 in all their extant textual witnesses. Among his conclusions is the observation that the process of assimilation between these passages increased over time—Targum and Peshitta have more examples of assimilation than, for instance, the Septuagint—culminating in the various proposals of modern critical scholars to 'correct' one of the two texts on the basis of the other.

H.G.M. Williamson closes the first section of this book with a detailed examination of the first verse of Isaiah 30. Whereas almost all commentators on the verse interpret it in the light of the prophet's condemnation of Judah's policy of making an alliance with Egypt against Sennacherib, Williamson offers a fresh interpretation based on a careful philological examination. In his view the second part of the verse does not deal with making plans, but fabricating idols, and belongs to a series of interpolations in Proto-Isaiah by a glossator who interpreted wrong moral behaviour in terms of idolatry.

The second part of this volume contains contributions concerning the reception history of the Book of Isaiah, primarily in the Greek and Syriac translations as well as in the Masoretic tradition, the New Testament, and early modern Dutch interpreters.

Johann Cook combines the focus of his own academic endeavours with that of the honorand. He examines the relatively free translation technique of the Septuagint versions of Proverbs and Isaiah as well as the intertextual relations between the two as detected by Joseph Ziegler. Although literary dependence of the one book on the other cannot be substantiated, the issue of intertextuality between these books remains an area for much future research. Although the Greek Proverbs may not have originated in Leontopolis and does not contain the amount of contemporization detected by Van der Kooij for the Greek Isaiah, it does contain a certain amount of contextualization as far as moral and religious elements are concerned, dating from almost the same period as the Greek Isaiah was produced, that is, the middle of the second century BCE.

Kristin De Troyer opens a window on the New Testament. In Matt 27:43, the Evangelist added a sentence to his source text, for which he found inspiration in the Book of Isaiah. De Troyer argues that his source was not a revised Old Greek text of Isaiah, but the re-interpreted Isaiah text as found in Wisd 2:18, which he combined with Ps 22:9.

The relationship between the Greek Isaiah and other translation units of the Septuagint is also the focus of the next contribution. Cécile Dogniez examines the links between the Septuagint versions of Isaiah and the Dodekapropheton that have been adduced by Isac Seeligmann to argue for a literary dependence of the Greek Isaiah upon the Greek Dodekapropheton. A careful examination of these intertextual links, however, rather demonstrates 'L' indépendance du traducteur grec d' Isaïe par rapport au Dodekapropheton'. Not only are alleged translational borrowings (such as the much-discussed designation of Jerusalem as a hut for orchard-watchers, ὀπωροφυλάκιον) open to different explanations, but there are also quite a number of Hebrew phrases attested in the two Hebrew books that have been rendered in a markedly different fashion by their respective Greek translators.

The question: 'Is there an Antiochene Reading of Isaiah?' is answered affirmatively by the leading expert in the study of the Antiochene Bible,

Natalio Fernández Marcos. On the basis of a detailed examination of the final two chapters of the Book of Isaiah, Fernández Marcos detects examples of small additions and interventions, stylistic improvements, and atticistic corrections in the textual witnesses that were classified by Ziegler as 'Lucianic' readings. This text also contains a few genuine Greek readings, which have been obliterated in the later Greek tradition. Finally, Fernández Marcos discusses the exegesis of Isaiah by the Antiochene church fathers, who despite individual differences can be seen to follow a common set of exegetical principles focusing on the historical rather than on the allegorical interpretation of the Bible.

Cornelis Houtman discusses a much later phase in the reception history of Isaiah, pertaining to the discussion in the Netherlands in the nineteenth century concerning the veracity of Isaiah's prophecies. Houtman selects two opposite voices, namely that of Abraham des Amorie van der Hoeven, who considered the new findings in the Middle East to be valuable illustrations of the traditional view, and Ferdinand Alexander de Mey van Alkemade, spokesman for the opposite, radically critical viewpoint. Houtman places these two interpreters in the context of modern biblical exegesis, thus adding to a field of research to which Van der Kooij himself also has contributed.

Michaël van der Meer revisits another controversy, namely that of the proper context for the study of the Greek Isaiah as a Jewish translation of ancient oracles in the setting of second-century BCE Hellenistic Egypt. He takes the famous Greek version of the Immanuel prophecy (Isa 7:14–17) as a case in point. Whereas some would adduce the Hellenistic mystery cults as the proper context for interpreting the Greek translation, and others the Greek Pentateuch, Van der Meer adduces parallels from the often neglected corpus of Egyptian-Greek prophecies (concerning Nectanebo and the oracles of the Lamb, the Potter, and a priest called Ḥor) to contextualize the Greek version of Isaiah. Besides a number of correspondences on the level of phrases and imagery, he finds parallels for the phenomenon of fulfilment prophecy of an indigenous polemic against Assyrian domination translated and reapplied to the Seleucid period, along with a parallel for the young queen bearing a son.

The contribution of Takamitsu Muraoka also focuses on the Old Greek version of Isaiah. He offers a painstaking and fresh philological commentary to 'Isaiah 2 in the Septuagint'.

Wido van Peursen investigates the text of Isa 26:9–19 as part of the Syriac Odes. The text of the Ode was taken from the Peshitta, but has been revised in the course of its transmission. Van Peursen discerns an early West Syriac recension, a late West Syriac recension, and a Melkite recension. These recensions have some shared readings, but also contain some readings that show their independence. They reflected a development which started from the Peshitta text and which is mainly, but not exclusively, characterized by the influence of the Greek text.

'Of Translation and Revision: From Greek Isaiah to Greek Jeremiah', written by Albert Pietersma, applies the methodology that Joseph Ziegler employed to argue for the inner coherence of the Greek Isaiah to the question of the bisecting of the Greek Jeremiah. Pietersma challenges Emanuel Tov's widely accepted thesis that the second part of the Greek Jeremiah is in fact the result of a revision of an older Greek translation. He pleads for more attention to the variation in translation and contextual accommodation within the two parts of the Greek Jeremiah.

Bas ter Haar Romeny discusses the revision of the Peshitta of Isaiah produced by the West Syrian polymath Jacob of Edessa around 705. He argues against the recent suggestion that Jacob's quotations of the biblical text in the margins of a translation of Severus of Antioch's hymns constituted an earlier phase of the same work. In addition, he deals with the question of whether Jacob used the Syro-Hexapla as a source.

Adrian Schenker studies an interesting textual variant in Isa 66:20 and argues that the reading found in the Masoretic Text mentioning 'a clear vessel' (בכלי טהור) in fact represents a later revision of a more original reading preserved in the Old Greek, mentioning 'with psalms' (μετὰ ψαλμῶν). By the middle of the second century BCE the joyful procession towards the Holy City had given way to concerns for ritual purity.

Emanuel Tov concludes the second section by discussing the personal names in the Septuagint of Isaiah with special attention to the rendering of Assur. Tov concludes that the Greek translator reflects what he calls 'the Septuagint system of representing personal names'. While the translator is far from consistent, he stands out among the various Septuagint translators as someone who contemporized several geographical names.

The volume closes with a list of the academic publications by Arie van der Kooij, and indices of ancient sources and modern authors. The system of abbreviations is based upon Siegfried M. Schwertner (ed.), *Theologische Realenzyklopädie. Abkürzungsverzeichnis, 2., überarbeitete und erweiterte Auflage* (Berlin etc., 1994) and where deficient, *The SBL Handbook of Style for Ancient Near Eastern, Biblical, and Early Christian Studies* (Peabody, 1999). The editors wish to thank Ms Helen Richardson for her assistance in correcting the English texts, Ms Dianne van der

Zande for her editorial corrections and Mr Barry Hartog for his help in compiling the indices, but above all, we wish to thank our mentor, Arie van der Kooij, for his sustained support, scholarship, and gentle guidance.

Leiden, March 2010

Michaël N. van der Meer
Percy van Keulen
Wido van Peursen
Bas ter Haar Romeny

LIST OF CONTRIBUTORS

BOB BECKING is Senior Research Professor for Bible, Religion, and Identity at the Faculty of Humanities of Utrecht University.

PANCRATIUS C. BEENTJES is Professor emeritus of Old Testament and Hebrew at the Faculty of Catholic Theology, Tilburg University.

WILLEM A.M. BEUKEN is Professor emeritus of Old Testament at the Catholic University of Leuven.

JOHANN COOK is Professor of Hebrew and Aramaic at Stellenbosch University.

KRISTIN DE TROYER is Professor of Old Testament and Hebrew Bible at the University of St Andrews.

CÉCILE DOGNIEZ est chercheur au CNRS, Centre Lenain de Tillemont, UMR 8167 « Orient et Méditerranée ».

NATALIO FERNÁNDEZ MARCOS is Research Professor of Biblical Studies in the Centro de Ciencias Humanas y Sociales, CSIC, Madrid.

ROBERT P. GORDON is Regius Professor of Hebrew in the University of Cambridge and Fellow of St Catharine's College.

HOLGER GZELLA is Professor of Hebrew and Aramaic at Leiden University.

CORNELIS HOUTMAN is Professor emeritus of Old Testament at the Protestant Theological University in Kampen

MATTHIJS J. DE JONG is Coordinator for Biblical Studies at the Netherlands Bible Society.

PERCY VAN KEULEN is currently a Post-doc Fellow attached to the TURGAMA project, Peshitta Institute, Leiden University.

ANDRÉ LEMAIRE is Professor of Hebrew and Aramaic at the École pratique des Hautes Études, Paris.

JOHAN LUST is Professor emeritus of Old Testament Studies at the Catholic University of Leuven.

MICHAËL N. VAN DER MEER, formerly Post-Doc Fellow in Old Testament Studies, Leiden University, teaches Religious Education and Latin at the Hermann Wesselink college, Amstelveen.

TAKAMITSU MURAOKA is Professor emeritus of Hebrew Language and Literature, Ugaritic, and Israelite Antiquities at Leiden University.

WIDO VAN PEURSEN is associate professor at the Leiden Institute for Religious Studies and director of the project Turgama: Computer-Assisted Analysis of the Peshitta and the Targum: Text, Language and Interpretation.

ALBERT PIETERSMA is Professor emeritus of Septuagint and Hellenistic Greek, Department of Near and Middle Eastern Civilizations at the University of Toronto.

BAS TER HAAR ROMENY is Professor of Old Testament and Eastern Christian Traditions at Leiden University.

ADRIAN SCHENKER is Professor emeritus of Old Testament at the University of Fribourg.

EMANUEL TOV is J.L. Magnes Professor emeritus of Bible at the Hebrew University, Jerusalem.

KAREL VRIEZEN is retired Senior Lecturer of the Old Testament department at Utrecht University.

RICHARD D. WEIS is Professor of Old Testament Theology and Dean of the Seminary at United Theological Seminary of the Twin Cities, New Brighton, Minnesota, USA.

H.G.M. WILLIAMSON is Regius Professor of Hebrew at Oxford University and a Student of Christ Church.

PART ONE

ISAIAH IN THE CONTEXT OF HEBREW AND ANCIENT NEAR EASTERN WRITINGS

'AS STRAW IS TRODDEN DOWN IN THE WATER OF A DUNG-PIT': REMARKS ON A SIMILE IN ISAIAH 25:10

Bob Becking*

1. *Introduction*

The Book of Isaiah contains many beautiful passages. I will not list them all. One of these passages is the oracle of salvation in the Sub-Canto Isa 25:6–12. This passage has given rise to a beautiful anthem that is incorporated in the hymnbook of the Dutch Protestant Churches.[1] It is interesting to note that in the Book of Isaiah the oracle of salvation for Israel is contrasted by an oracle of doom for Moab, whereas this contrast is absent from the anthem just mentioned. In this paper, I will not ponder on interpretative strategies in modern Dutch church anthems. I would like to focus on a simile that is used in Isa 25:10 to underscore the character of the calamity that will fall upon Moab.

2. *Simile, Text, and Translation*

In Isa 25:10 the Hebrew text reads:

10bA ונדוש מואב תחתיו
10bB2 כהדוש מתבן במי מדמנה

Line 10bB is problematic, since it contains a question of Ketiv–Qere. The Qere proposes to read b^{e}*mô madmēnā*, 'in a dung-pit', while Ketiv seems to favour b^{e}*mê madmēnā*, 'in the waters of a dung-pit'. 1QIsa[a], Symmachus and Targum support the Ketiv, while the other ancient versions

---

* It is with great pleasure that I dedicate this contribution to my former teacher and long year colleague Arie van der Kooij.

[1] 'De Heer richt op zijn berg een maaltijd aan' (The Lord lays on a feast on his mountain); lyrics by Willem Barnard, in *Liedboek voor de Kerken. Psalmen en gezangen voor de eredienst in kerk en huis aangeboden door de interkerkelijke stichting voor het kerklied* ('s Gravenhage–Leeuwarden, 1973), Hymn 27.

are in favour of the Qere.[2] In modern scholarship a tendency is present to accept the Qere as the better reading,[3] although some scholars would prefer the Ketiv.[4] Hans Wildberger writes: 'במו ist zweifellos die richtige Lesung, es entspricht ugar. *bm* und findet sich auch sonst im Alten Testament gelegentlich für einfaches ב'.[5] The main argument against the Ketiv seems to be that this reading does not make much sense.[6] In this contribution, I would like to argue that the reading of the Ketiv makes sense by pointing at

[1] a strophe parallelism within Isa 25:10–11 and
[2] a comparable sentence in the prophetic letters from ancient Mari.

3. *Strophe-Parallelism*

The next Masoretic verse reads as follows:

And he shall spread out his hands in the midst of it	ופרש ידיו בקרבו	11aA
As the swimmer spreads out to swim	כאשר יפרש השחה לשחות	11aB
His pride will be laid low	והשפיל גאותו	11bA
Despite the struggle of his hands	עם ארבות ידיו	11bB

Within this verse a number of parallels can be observed. I would like to refer to two examples: ופרש (11aA) // יפרש (11aB); ידיו (11aA) // ידיו (11bB), but more connections between the lines can be shown indicating that 11aA–11bB can be construed as a coherent unit. Together with 10bA–bB these lines form a strophe and with the strophes Isa 25:9–10aA

[2] LXX ἐν ἁμάξαις, V *in plaustro*; see Arie van der Kooij, 'Isaiah 24–27: Text-Critical Notes', in Hendrik J. Bosman *et al.* (eds.), *Studies in Isaiah 24–27. The Isaiah Workshop-De Jesaja Werkplaats* (OTS 43; Leiden etc., 2000), p. 14.

[3] See, e.g., Marvin H. Pope, 'The Word שַׁחַת in Job 9:31', *JBL* 83 (1964), p. 275; Lambertus A. Snijders, *Jesaja* 1 (Prediking van het Oude Testament; Nijkerk, 1969), p. 253; Otto Kaiser, *Der Prophet Jesaja. Kapitel 13–39* (ATD 18; Göttingen 1973), p. 164; Hans Wildberger, *Jesaja* 2. *Jesaja 13–27* (BK 10.2; Neukirchen–Vluyn, 1978), p. 971; Dan G. Johnson, *From Chaos to Restoration. An Integrative Reading of Isaiah 24–27* (JSOT.S 61; Sheffield, 1988), pp. 104–105.

[4] Hendrik J. Bosman and Harm W.M. van Grol, 'Annotated Translation of Isaiah 24–27', in Bosman *et al.*, *Studies in Isaiah 24–27*, p. 8; Brian Doyle, *The Apocalypse of Isaiah Metaphorically Speaking. A Study of the Use, Function and Significance of Metaphors in Isaiah 24–27* (BEThL 151; Leuven, 2000), p. 236.

[5] Wildberger, *Jesaja*, p. 971.

[6] See, e.g., Wildberger, *Jesaja*, pp. 970–971.

and 25:12 they form the Canticle Isa 25:9–12,[7] which is indicated in the Masoretic tradition with a *petuḥā* before verse 9 and a *setumā* after verse 12.[8] The Sub-Canto Isa 25:6–12 consists of two canticles. This also implies that I do not share the general view that Isa 25:10b–12 is to be seen as a later addition.[9]

Within the unit Isa 25:10bA–11 an interesting strophe parallelism can be detected. The simile in line 11aB כאשר יפרש השחה לשחות, 'as the swimmer spreads out to swim',[10] presupposes on the mental map of the reader a watery environment to swim in. In my view, this watery environment needs to be connected to the Ketiv reading *b^e mê madmēnā*, 'in the waters of a dung-pit', in 10bB. This connection provides the reader with a nice strophe-parallelism and evokes an image behind 10bB that straw is trodden in a watery pit. In other words: Within the co-text the Ketiv reading makes sense.

4. *A Sentence from Ancient Mari*

4.1. *šapal tibnim mû illakū*

In the archives from Ancient Mari a great number of letters were found that contained references to divination and prophetic activity. Soon after their discovery and especially after the publication of the female

[7] Wildberger, *Jesaja*, pp. 970–974; J. Todd Hibbard, *Intertextuality in Isaiah 24–27. The Reuse and Evocation of Earlier Texts* (FAT 2.16; Tübingen, 2006), pp. 26–32, 107–116; Bosman and Van Grol, 'Annotated Translation', pp. 7–8; Hendrik J. Bosman, 'Syntactic Cohesion in Isaiah 24–27', in Bosman *et al.*, *Studies in Isaiah 24–27*, pp. 19–50; Harm W.M. van Grol, 'An Analysis of the Verse Structure of Isaiah 24–27', in Bosman *et al.*, *Studies in Isaiah 24–27*, pp. 68–70, though applying different methodologies, arrive at the same conclusion as regards the delimitation of the unit under consideration.

[8] See also the outline by Konrad D. Jenner, 'Petucha and Setuma. Tools for Interpretation or Simply a Matter of Lay-Out?', in Bosman *et al.*, *Studies in Isaiah 24–27*, pp. 81–117.

[9] With Simon J. de Vries, *Yesterday, Today and Tomorrow. Time and History in the Old Testament* (Grand Rapids, 1975), pp. 305–306; Hibbard, *Intertextuality in Isaiah 24–27*, pp. 107–116; *pace* Kaiser, *Jesaja 13–39*, pp. 164–165; Wildberger, *Jesaja*, pp. 900, 970–974; Johnson, *From Chaos to Restoration*, p. 12; Marvin A. Sweeney, 'Textual Citations in Isaiah 24–27. Toward an Understanding of the Redactional Function of Chapters 24–27 in the Book of Isaiah', *JBL* 107 (1988), p. 47; Sigurdur Ö. Steingrímsson, *Gottesmahl und Lebensspende. Eine literarwissenschaftliche Untersuchung von Jesaja 24,21–23.25,6–10a* (ATSAT 43; St. Ottilien, 1994), pp. 14, 96; Marvin A. Sweeney, *Isaiah 1–39 with an Introduction to Prophetic Literature* (FOTL 16; Grand Rapids, 1996), p. 335; Doyle, *Apocalypse of Isaiah*, pp. 234–240.

[10] On this expression see esp. John Ellington, 'A Swimming Lesson', *BiTr* 47 (1996), pp. 246–247.

correspondence by Dossin in 1967,[11] these texts caught the attention of Old Testament scholars interested in the phenomenon of prophecy.[12] It is not my aim to fully discuss here these texts or to survey the importance of them and other ancient near eastern texts for the understanding of the idea of divination.[13] I would like to draw attention to a proverb that is attested in three of the Mari letters and that might help understanding the simile in Isaiah 25. The proverb-like sentence runs as follows: *šapal tibnim mû illakū*, 'Beneath straw water runs!'. Usually, it is understood as meaning something like: 'things are not what they seem!'.[14] Sasson, however, has challenged this interpretation by remarking that above running water, only moving straw can be found, which would imply that the proverb warns for a real danger.[15] I would like to have a closer look at the three letters in which the proverb is attested looking for its function within the text and afterwards see if this proverb can be of any help when reading Isaiah 25.[16]

---

[11] Georges Dossin, *Archives royales de Mari* 10. *La correspondance féminine* (TCL 31; Paris, 1967).

[12] See, e.g., Herbert B. Huffmon, 'Prophecy in the Mari Letters', *BiAr* 31 (1968), pp. 101–124; Friedrich Ellermeier, *Prophetie in Mari und Israel* (ThOrAr 1; Herzberg, 1968); William L. Moran, 'New Evidence from Mari on the History of Prophecy', *Bib.* 50 (1969), pp. 15–56; James F. Ross, 'Prophecy in Hamath, Israel, and Mari', *HThR* 63 (1970), pp. 1–28; Klaus Koch, 'Die Briefe "Profetischen" Inhalts aus Mari. Bemerkungen zu Gattung und Sitz im Leben', *UF* 4 (1972), pp. 53–77; Ed Noort, *Untersuchungen zum Gottesbescheid in Mari. Die "Mari-prophetie" in der alttestamentlichen Forschung* (AOAT 202; Neukirchen, 1977).

[13] See, e.g., Frederick H. Cryer, *Divination in its Ancient Near Eastern Environment. A Socio-historical Investigation* (JSOT.S 142; Sheffield, 1994); Martti Nissinen, *References to Prophecy in Neo-Assyrian Sources* (SAAS 7; Helsinki, 1998); Karel van der Toorn, 'Mesopotamian Prophecy between Immanence and Transcendence. A Comparison of Old Babylonian and Neo-Assyrian Prophecy', in Martti Nissinen (ed.), *Prophecy in its Ancient Near Eastern Context. Mesopotamian, Biblical and Arabian Perspectives* (SBL.SymS 13; Atlanta, 2000), pp. 71–88.

[14] Ross, 'Prophecy', pp. 17–18; see also Moran, 'New Evidence', p. 54; Angel Marzal, *Gleanings from the Wisdom of Mari* (StP 11; Roma, 1976), pp. 27–31; Simon B. Parker, 'Official Attitudes Toward Prophecy at Mari and in Israel', *VT* 43 (1993), pp. 50–68, esp. 58.

[15] Jack M. Sasson, 'Water Beneath Straw: Adventures of a Prophetic Phrase in the Mari Archives', in Ziony Zevit *et al.* (eds.), *Solving Riddles and Untying Knots. Biblical, Epigraphic, and Semitic Studies in Honor of Jonas C. Greenfield* (Winona Lake, 1995), pp. 599–607, esp. 607.

[16] I am much indebted to the analyses by Sasson, 'Water Beneath Straw', pp. 599–608; Hans M. Barstad, 'Sicut dicit dominus: Mari Prophetic Texts and the Hebrew Bible', in Yairah Amit *et al.* (eds.), *Essays on Ancient Israel in Its Near Eastern Context, A Tribute to Nadav Na'aman* (Winona Lake, 2006), pp. 36–39; Karel van der Toorn, *Scribal Culture and the Making of the Hebrew Bible* (Cambridge, Mass. etc., 2007), pp. 112–113.

4.2. *Inib-šina to Zimrilim*

In this relatively short letter,[17] Inib-šina reminds her brother, King Zimrilim, of the fact that sometime ago Shelebum, the *assinnu*, had delivered an oracle. This introduction most probably functions as some sort of warning to the king to take the following message seriously. A *qammatum* of Dagan of Terqa had spoken to her:

> The peacemaking of the man of Esh[nunna] is false; beneath straw runs water! I will gather him into the net that he knot. I will destroy his city and I will ruin his wealth, which comes time immemorial.[18]

The 'I' in this message is the god Dagan. The content of the message is an oracle of hope for the king of Mari: The inimical Eshnunna will be destroyed! The 'man of Esh[nunna]' most probably is King Ibalpiel II. This king was at war with Mari and had offered a peace-agreement that is scorned to be treacherous by the *qammatum* of Dagan.[19] The prophetic message ends with a warning for King Zimrilim:

> Now, protect yourself! Without consulting an oracle, do not enter the city.[20]

In this context the proverb under consideration functions as an imaginary illustration of the treacherous peace-agreement of Ibalpiel. The

---

[17] A. 1047 = ARM X 80 = ARM 26 197; Martti Nissinen, *Prophets and Prophecy in the Ancient Near East* (SBL.WAW 12; Atlanta, 2003), No. 7 (with literature).

[18] ARM 26 197:11–19; translation by Nissinen, *Prophets and Prophecy*, p. 28, with an exception in line 15 where I—in contrast to Marzal, *Gleanings*, p. 28; Nissinen, *Prophets and Prophecy*, p. 28—construe *ú-kà-aṣ-ṣa-ru* as a 3 m. sg. form. The idea here is that the traitor will be caught by his own net, see Willem H.Ph. Römer, *Frauenbriefe über Religion, Politik und Privatleben in Mari. Untersuchungen zu G. Dossin, Archives royales de Mari X* (AOAT 12; Neukirchen–Vluyn, 1971), pp. 21–22; Jean-Marie Durand, *Archives épistolaires de Mari* 1.1 (ARM 26; Paris, 1988), p. 424; Van der Toorn, *Scribal Culture*, pp. 112–113.

[19] The historical framework is outlined by Römer, *Frauenbriefe*, pp. 44–45; Dominique Charpin, 'Un traité entre Zimri-Lim de Mari et Ibâl-Pî-el II d'Ešnunna', in Dominique Charpin and Francis Joannès (eds.), *Marchands, diplomates et empereurs. Études sur la civilisation mésopotamienne offertes à Paul Garelli* (Paris, 1991), pp. 139–166; Dominique Charpin, 'Histoire politique du Proche-Orient amorrite (2002–1595)', in Dominique Charpin *et al.* (eds.), *Mesopotamien. Die altbabylonischen Zeit* (OBO 160.4; Fribourg–Göttingen, 2004), pp. 25–480. It is interesting to note that Ibalpiel II had received an oracle of salvation from the goddess Kititum, see Maria de Jong Ellis, 'The Goddess Kititum Speaks to King Ibalpiel: Oracle Texts from Ishchali', *MARI* 5 (1987), pp. 235–266; Jack N. Lawson, '"The God Who Reveals Secrets". The Mesopotamian Background to Daniel 2.47', *JSOT* 74 (1997), pp. 66–67; Nissinen, *Prophets and Prophecy*, pp. 93–95 (with literature). It is uncertain whether the two prophecies would refer to the same situation.

[20] ARM 26 197:21–23; translation by Nissinen, *Prophets and Prophecy*, p. 28.

image is taken from the experience of daily life. A path of straw looks like a nice alley to walk in, but it is not trustworthy. The water underneath can make one sink deep and even loose his life. In other words, the message is conveyed that the peace-agreement of Ibalpiel is not what it looks like at the surface, since it contains a hidden trap. Phrased otherwise: 'latet anguis in herba';[21] underneath the appearance of innocence lurks a malicious intention.

4.3. *Sammetar to Zimrilim*

This letter[22]—that makes the impression of being an intelligence report to the king—deals with more or less the same period in the history of ancient Mari. The letter opens with a section on the prophecy of Lupahum, a prophet of Dagan from Tuttul. That section makes the impression of being a collection of pieces of information on the encounter of Zimrilim and Ibalpiel II. The tenor of the information is that the gods are on Mari's side and that the king has to trust the gods meanwhile improving his military power. At the end of that section, Lupahum—via Sammetar—refers the king to a recent prophecy of salvation for the king in connection with the Yaminite tribes. Then Sammetar continues:

> Afterwards, on the following [da]y, a *qammatum* of Dagan of T[erqa] came and spoke [to me]: 'Beneath straw water ru[ns]! They keep on send[ing to you] messages of friendship, they even send their gods [to you], but in their hearts they are planning something else. The king should not take an oath without consulting God'.[23]

The historical circumstances of this oracle are much the same as with the preceding text. The proverb functions in a comparable way: King Zimri-Lim is once more warned not to take the tokens of peace and friendship of Ibalpiel II at face value. Almost certainly both letters refer to the same prophetic event, which is illustrated by a remark in the letter:

> Then she delivered her instructions in the temple of Belet-ekallim to the high pr[iestess In]ib-šina.[24]

---

[21] Vergilius *Ecl.* 3, 93; see Celia E. Schultz, 'Latet Anguis in Herba. A Reading of Vergil's Third Eclogue', *AJP* 124 (2003), pp. 199–224.

[22] A. 925 + A. 2050 = ARM 26 199; Nissinen, *Prophets and Prophecy*, No. 9 (with literature).

[23] ARM 26 199:41–40; translation by Nissinen, *Prophets and Prophecy*, p. 31.

[24] ARM 26 199:52–54; translation by Nissinen, *Prophets and Prophecy*, p. 31; see also Parker, 'Official Attitudes', p. 57.

Here too, the proverb expresses the idea that underneath the appearance of innocence lurks a malicious intention.

4.4. *Kanisan to Zimrilim*

This letter[25] makes the impression of being a reaction to the previous two texts. In this letter, Kanisan quotes a report by a certain Kibri-dagan:

> [Th]is is what [they] spoke to me: 'Be[neath straw] water ru[ns]! The god of my lord has come! He has delivered his enemies in his hands.' Now, as before, the prophet broke out in constant declamation.[26]

In this letter, the proverb is delivered without a clear application. In my view, the letter refers to the same prophetic event as the two letters discussed above. It is interesting to note, though, that where ARM 26 197 and 199 make mention of a *qammatum* of Dagan, this third letter presents a deliverance by a *muḫḫum*, prophet. In my opinion, this difference in indication does not by implication refer to a difference in identity or person.[27] Both words, *qammatum* as well as *muḫḫum*, can refer to an ecstatic. I would like to propose the following general interpretation of ARM 26 202. After receiving the message *šapal tibnim mû illakū*, King Zimrilim felt the need to check the trustworthiness of this oracle, since it would have major implications for his political stand toward Ibalpiel II. The letter under consideration then contains the answer to his request, saying that indeed such a prophecy had been delivered, and, moreover, had been constantly repeated by the ecstatic.

4.5. *Public Proverb or Enigmatic Riddle?*

So far, I have treated the sentence 'Beneath straw water runs' more or less as a proverb. I have to admit that this is a problematical classification. The general definition of a proverb includes that it is a simple and concrete saying. Such a saying is popularly known and repeated. It expresses a truth that is based on common sense and the collective interpretation of reality. Proverbs quite often describe basic rules of conduct, be it descriptive or prescriptive.[28] In this light, it should be noted that

---

[25] M. 11046 = ARM 26 202; Nissinen, *Prophets and Prophecy*, No. 12 (with literature).

[26] ARM 26 202:8–16; translation by Nissinen, *Prophets and Prophecy*, p. 35.

[27] *Pace* Parker, 'Official Attitudes', p. 57.

[28] On the definition of the concept 'Proverb' see, e.g., Archer Taylor, *The Proverb* (Cambridge, 1931); Nigel Barley, 'A Structural Approach to the Proverb and Maxim

- The sentence under consideration is—as far as I can see—not known from Sumerian, Mesopotamian, or Babylonian collections of proverbs.[29]
- The sentence is not easily related to human conduct, be it descriptive or prescriptive.
- The sentence cannot easily be construed as a simple and concrete saying.

On the other hand it should be noted that

- The language of the sentence refers—or seems to refer—to daily life experience: straw and water were part of the general experience of the reality. The exact reference to reality is, however, not quite clear. Most scholars think of an agricultural background, but are not very specific as to the exact agricultural feature the saying would represent.[30] Finet proposed a background in the world of brick-making. In his opinion, straw was poured out in pools to reach the right degree of moistness before clay was added. The image, then, would be that bales of straw seem to be secure to walk on but in fact are not.[31] This view did not receive many followers especially since there is not much evidence to substantiate it.

The problematic part lies in the combination of these two features from reality. Under normal circumstances, straw is laid on the ground, on a floor, or a comparable surface. This observation, together with the uniqueness of the message *šapal tibnim mû illakū*, makes it possible to construe the sentence not as a proverb, but as an enigmatic riddle, to be untied by the recipient.[32] Before arriving at a more definite proposal, I would like to confront the simile in Isaiah with the sentence from Mari, and vice-versa.

---

with Special Reference to the Anglo-Saxon Corpus', *Proverbium* 20 (1972), pp. 737–750; Garreth Byrne, 'The Enduring World of Proverbs', *Contemporary Review* 287 (2005), pp. 285–291.

[29] See, e.g., Edmund I. Gordon, Thorkild Jacobsen, *Sumerian Proverbs. Glimpses of Daily Life in Ancient Mesopotamia* (Philadelphia, 1959); Wilfred G. Lambert, *Babylonian Wisdom Literature* (Oxford, 1960); Bendt Alster, *The Instructions of Shuruppak. A Sumerian Proverb Collection* (Mes. 2; Copenhagen, 1974); Bendt Alster, *Proverbs of Ancient Sumer. The World's Earliest Proverb Collections* (Bethesda, 1997).

[30] See, e.g., Marzal, *Gleanings*, p. 28.

[31] André Finet, 'Citations litéraires dans la correspondance de Mari', *RA* 68 (1974), pp. 41–42.

[32] See Sasson, 'Water Beneath Straw', pp. 206–207.

5. *Light from Mari on the Isaiah-Passage*

Irrespective of the question whether the sentence 'Beneath straw water runs' should be construed as a proverb or as a riddle, the line is of great importance for the interpretation of Isa 25:10. It makes clear that in the figurative language of the ancient Near East the image of water underneath straw existed. By implication, the Ketiv-reading makes sense and leads to the following translation:

And Moab shall be trodden under it	ונדוש מואב תחתיו	10bA
As straw is trodden down in the water of a dung-pit	כהדוש מתבן במי מדמנה	10bB

The question remains, what sense does this reading make? A closer look at the text of Isa 25:10 makes clear that a specific version of the more general image is described. The simile in Isaiah compares the fate of Moab by a comparison to the world of agriculture.[33] Farmers collected the excrements of animals in pits for turning it into dung that could be used for fertilizing the soil. These manure pits probably were in a watery state—as is implied in Job 9:31.[34] As can be imagined, they produced a disagreeable smell, hence they were covered by straw to soften the odour. In Palestine, in the beginning of the twentieth century CE, Dalman had observed comparable ways for fertilizing the soil or heating the houses in colder times:

> Der flüssige Rinderdung wird im Mischung mit grobem Häcksel mit den Füßen getreten und von den Frauen zum Mistkuchen ... geformt.[35]

6. *Can Isaiah be of Help in Understanding the Mari-texts?*

In Isa 25:10 a quite specific image is thus implied. Might it shed light on the interpretation of the message *šapal tibnim mû illakū* discussed above? In my view, the text from Isaiah reinforces the plausibility to read the line from Mari against an agricultural background and not so much against the background of the world of brick-making. Moreover, the text from Isa

---

[33] For different interpretations see, e.g., Snijders, *Jesaja*, p. 253; Doyle, *The Apocalypse of Isaiah*, pp. 238–239.

[34] See Pope, 'Word שַׁחַת', p. 274.

[35] Gustav Dalman, *Arbeit und Sitte in Palästine* 2. *Der Ackerbau* (SDPI 5; Gütersloh, 1932), pp. 139–146; the quotation at p. 140.

25:10 hints at the possibility to read the message *šapal tibnim mû illakū* against a similar background.

In such a reading, the phrase of the message *šapal tibnim mû illakū* has a very specific meaning. The proverb can be formalized in a quadripartite structure as follows:[36]

šapal	*tibnim*
under	straw
−	+
mû	*illakū*
water	runs
+	−

In an agricultural society 'straw' is an important commodity. It can be used for several goals: to feed the animals, to soften the ground to make a bed for sleeping, and also to reduce the nasty smell of dung and mist. 'Under' has the implication that beneath the visible reality something else is hidden. 'Water' as such is a positive element: Without water life would be impossible. The fact, however, that it 'runs' hints at the dark side of water.

Reading the proverb against its historical background reveals the following image:

šapal	*tibnim*		
under	straw	underneath	Ibalpiel's peace offerings
mû	*illakū*		
water	runs	hides	the dung of a pit

This implies that the phrase *šapal tibnim mû illakū* can be construed as a proverb, and not so much as a riddle. It is to be compared with Latin 'Latet anguis in herba'. In uttering these words, the ecstatic warned King Zimri-Lim for the dark side of Ibalpiel II's diplomatic moves. Accepting the peace offerings would make him stand knee high in the dung of history while Ibalpiel II would be the hidden actor in another proverb: **dìm-šáh-gin$_7$ šer$_{10}$-da** KA-KA-**na al-sìg**, 'The dung strikes his face, like a hippopotamus'.[37] In a way his fate would have been comparable to the fate

---

[36] See Barley, 'Structural Approach'; Marzal, *Gleanings*, pp. 28–29.

[37] Alster, *Instructions of Shuruppak*, SP 8 Sec. B 9; Miguel Civil, '"Adamdun," the Hippopotamus, and the Crocodile', *JCS* 50 (1998), pp. 11–14.

of the Moabites as foreseen by the prophet Isaiah.[38] Ironically enough, Zimri-Lim flouted the divine advice and made peace with Ibalpiel II. He, however, made a good thing out it by later gaining forces that eventually helped him to enter into a coalition that devastated Eshnunna.[39]

[38] Or the tradition based on him; see, e.g., Theodoor C. Vriezen and Adam S. van der Woude, *Ancient Israelite and Early Jewish Literature* (Leiden etc., 2005), pp. 312–334.

[39] See Charpin, 'Traité entre Zimri-Lim de Mari et Ibâl-Pî-el II d'Ešnunna'; Sasson, 'Water Beneath Straw', p. 608; Charpin, 'Histoire politique', pp. 192–212.

ISAIAH IN THE BOOK OF CHRONICLES

Pancratius C. Beentjes[*]

1. *Introduction*

The Book of Chronicles has a strong interest in prophets, seers, men of God, and inspired messengers.[1] A detailed scrutiny of the material, however, reveals that the Chronicler—as we henceforth will call the author of the Book of Chronicles—has created a special framework in which these functionaries are presented. Whereas, for instance, in the Book of Kings the narratives on Ahijah, Elijah, Elisha, and other prophetic characters commonly include miraculous elements and are concerned with the efficacy of the prophetic pronouncements, nowhere in the Book of Chronicles is the ministry of the prophets described in terms of ecstasy, miracles, or political dimensions; see, for example, the exhortation to rebellion by Ahija of Silo (1 Kgs 11:29–39) or the anointing of Jehu by one of Elisha's disciples (2 Kings 9). It is quite striking that the entire complex of the Elijah narratives (1 Kings 17–19; 2 Kings 1–2) has been completely skipped over by the Chronicler. In their place only a letter by Elijah is mentioned (2 Chr 21:12–15).

---

[*] With this small contribution I wish to honour my colleague Arie van der Kooij and to thank him for all those hours we spent together in Utrecht teaching both our Protestant and Catholic Masters students the principles of biblical exegesis, a discipline to which we are both so dedicated.

[1] See, for example, Rosemarie Micheel, *Die Seher- und Prophetenüberlieferungen in der Chronik* (BET 18; Frankfurt am Mainz, 1983); Harry van Rooy, 'Prophet and Society in the Persian Period According to Chronicles', in Tamara C. Eskenazi and Kent H. Richards (eds.), *Second Temple Studies 2. Temple and Community in the Persian Period* (JSOT.S 175; Sheffield, 1994), pp. 163–179; William M. Schniedewind, *The Word of God in Transition. From Prophet to Exegete in the Second Temple Period* (JSOT.S 197; Sheffield, 1995); Isac L. Seeligmann, 'Die Auffassung von der Prophetie in der deuteronomistischen und chronistischen Geschichtsschreibung', in John A. Emerton (ed.), *Congress Volume. Göttingen, 1977* (VT.S 29; Leiden, 1978), pp. 254–279; Simon J. de Vries, 'The Forms of Prophetic Address in Chronicles', *HAR* 10 (1986), pp. 15–36; Joel P. Weinberg, 'Die "Ausserkanonischen Prophezeiungen" in den Chronikbüchern', *AAH* 26 (1978), pp. 387–404.

In the Book of Chronicles a total of eighteen prophetic addresses are found, of which no less than fourteen have no parallel in 1–2 Samuel or 1–2 Kings and can therefore be characterized as the creation of the Chronicler himself, a phenomenon which is often referred to by the technical term *Sondergut*.[2] At least ten times these prophetic addresses are put into the mouths of persons who nowhere else in the Hebrew Bible are known as prophets, seers, or men of God.[3] In a number of instances they are expressly presented with the help of a special introductory formula of divine inspiration: 'the spirit clothed ...' (1 Chr 12:19; 2 Chr 24:20); 'the spirit of God came upon ...' (2 Chr 15:1; 20:14).

The majority of the prophets and inspired messengers in the Book of Chronicles have been 'invented' by the Chronicler and should therefore be characterized as 'literary personages' rather than historical persons. Consequently, the speeches delivered by these literary personages are the most appropriate place to look for the Chronicler's own theological convictions and emphases. In these prophetic addresses the fundamental theological notions expressed in 1–2 Chronicles are found.[4]

Before answering the question regarding the way in which the Chronicler presents Isaiah and his book, we need a broad outline of the context in which this prophet is presented in the Book of Kings (which is the Chronicler's source). Therefore, first of all a general overview of 2 Kings 18–20 will be undertaken, which will then be compared with the characteristics of 2 Chronicles 29–32.

2. *Divergent presentations of Isaiah: 2 Kings 18–20 versus 2 Chronicles 29–32*

By far the largest part of 2 Kings 18–20 has been devoted to the story dealing with the siege of Jerusalem by the Assyrian army (2 Kgs 18:9–19:37), followed by the narrative relating to King Hezekiah's illness (2 Kgs

[2] See Rodney K. Duke, *The Persuasive Appeal of the Chronicler: A Rhetorical Analysis* (JSOT.S 88; Sheffield, 1990), pp. 175–176 ('List 8: Prophetic Speech Material').

[3] Jürgen Kegler, 'Prophetengestalten im Deuteronomistischen Geschichtswerk und in den Chronikbüchern. Ein Beitrag zur Kompositions- und Redaktionsgeschichte der Chronikbücher', *ZAW* 105 (1993), pp. 481–497, esp. 487 (Table 4).

[4] As an example, see Pancratius C. Beentjes, 'Prophets in the Book of Chronicles', in Johannes C. de Moor (ed.), *The Elusive Prophet. The Prophet as a Historical Person, Literary Character and Anonymous Artist* (OTSt 45; Leiden, 2001), pp. 45–53.

20:1–11), and the report dealing with the arrival of the Babylonian delegation (2 Kgs 20:12–19). Little attention is paid to Hezekiah's efforts with respect to the reform of the cult (2 Kgs 18:3–7).

Within the narrative cycle of 2 Kings 18–20, the prophet Isaiah plays a prominent role. Three times it is reported that King Hezekiah and the prophet in some way get in touch with each other. In the first case (2 Kgs 19:1–7), we are told that Hezekiah, under threat of a siege by the Assyrian army, in great distress sent messengers to the prophet, who in his turn put the king's heart at rest by saying that YHWH himself would lower the morale of the king of Assyria, so that he would return to his own land.

The second report (2 Kgs 19:20–34) is a circumstantial prophecy sent by Isaiah to Hezekiah, containing God's answer to the king's prayer for deliverance. God would defend his city to save it; the king of Assyria would not come into Jerusalem, nor cast up a siege-ramp against it.[5] The third narrative (2 Kgs 20:1–11) reports the prophet's encounter with King Hezekiah, who had fallen seriously ill and was cured by Isaiah's intervention.[6]

The Chronicler's presentation of King Hezekiah's reign, and the role of Isaiah, however, is completely different. The author of the Book of Chronicles has devoted no less than three chapters (2 Chronicles 29–31) to the religious and cultic reforms King Hezekiah brought into force. Apart from the opening lines (2 Chr 29:1–2), which are more or less identical to 2 Kgs 18:1–3, the remainder of 2 Chronicles 29–31 is completely the Chronicler's own creation ('*Sondergut*'). The confrontation with the Assyrian army (2 Chr 32:1–23) is much less marked here than in the detailed report offered in 2 Kgs 18:9–19:37. Hezekiah's illness has got only three lines (2 Chr 32:24–26), whereas the delegation from Babylon is given no more than one single line (2 Chr 32:31)!

While the Book of Kings draws substantial attention to the prophet Isaiah, in the Book of Chronicles, on the contrary, the prophet is given only marginal notice. As a character within a narrative, he is mentioned

[5] See Arie van der Kooij, 'Das assyrische Heer vor den Mauern Jerusalems im Jahr 701 v. Chr.', *ZDPV* 102 (1986), pp. 93–109.

[6] I deliberately do not take into consideration here the often disputed question of the interrelationship between 2 Kings 18–20 and Isaiah 36–39. See, for example, Brevard S. Childs, *Isaiah and the Assyrian Crisis* (SBT 2.3; London 1967); Brevard S. Childs, *Isaiah* (OTL; Louisville, 2001), pp. 258–266; Christopher R. Seitz, *Zion's Final Destiny: The Development of the Book of Isaiah: A Reassesment of Isaiah 36–39* (Minneapolis, 1991); Jacques Vermeylen, 'Hypothèses sur l'origine d'Isaïe 36–39', in Jacques van Ruiten and Marc Vervenne (eds.), *Studies in the Book of Isaiah* (BEThL 132; Leuven, 1997), pp. 95–118.

only once: 'Then King Hezekiah and the prophet Isaiah son of Amoz prayed because of this and cried to heaven' (2 Chr 32:20). Here the Chronicler has combined two separate reports from his source—the king's request to Isaiah to pray for him (2 Kgs 19:4b) and the prayer of Hezekiah himself (2 Kgs 19:14–19)—and compressed them into one brief sentence.

Nowhere else in the Book of Chronicles is Isaiah presented as a character who appears in the drama. On the contrary, he has been reduced to the book bearing his name: 'The other events of Uzziah's reign, from first to last, are recorded by the prophet Isaiah son of Amoz' (2 Chr 26:22); 'The other events of Hezekiah's reign, and his works of piety, are recorded in the vision of the prophet Isaiah son of Amoz and in the annals of the kings of Judah and Israel' (32:32). It can hardly be a coincidence that the first part of this latter sentence—'the vision of Isaiah son of Amoz'—is found only one more time in the Hebrew Bible, namely, as the opening words of the Book of Isaiah (Isa 1:1)! To me this is solid evidence that the Chronicler is more interested in the (text of the) Book of Isaiah than in the prophet Isaiah as a historical person or even as a literary figure.[7]

3. *The Chronicler's Intention*

If there is such a marked difference between the Chronicler's account of Hezekiah's reign and the role of Isaiah, on the one hand, and the narrative found in the Book of Kings, on the other, then the question might arise as to whether the author of the Book of Chronicles at this point did use the Book of Kings as his source at all. However, it is beyond any doubt that the Chronicler not only knew the Book of Kings in some Hebrew version, but that he frequently made use of it too.

Isaac Kalimi, who is a well-known expert in the study of the Book of Chronicles, is determined in his view: 'Chronicles is the only comprehensive book of the Bible whose sources are, for the most part, available to us. A comparison of Chronicles with other books of the Bible reveals that almost half the text of Chronicles has parallels in the books of Samuel and Kings'.[8] Gary Knoppers, who at present is also one of the leading and inspiring scholars in this field, is quite convinced about the Chronicler's

[7] We will pay attention to this feature in section 4.

[8] Isaac Kalimi, *The Reshaping of Ancient Israelite History in Chronicles* (Winona Lake, Ind., 2005), p. 1.

source: '... the dependence upon Kings is unmistakable in the narration of Solomon and the kingdom of Judah (2 Chronicles 1–36). In each case, the book quotes extensively from earlier materials'.[9]

That the Chronicler indeed did know the Hezekiah section in 2 Kings 18–20 is confirmed, first, by the opening lines of 2 Chr 29:1–2 ('... twenty-five years old; he reigned for twenty-nine years in Jerusalem. His mother's name was Abijah daughter of Zechariah. He did what was right in the sight of YHWH, just as his ancestor David had done'), which are almost identical to 2 Kgs 18:2–3. Second, a more or less literal resemblance can be established between 2 Chr 32:10 and 2 Kgs 18:19 ('Thus says King Sennacherib of Assyria: On what are you relying ...?'). Third, one can point to the common ground between 2 Chr 32:12 and 2 Kgs 18:22 ('Was it not this same Hezekiah who took away his high places and his altars and commanded Judah and Jerusalem ...'), and finally between 2 Chr 32:15a and 2 Kgs 18:29a ('... do not let Hezekiah to deceive you ...').[10]

In fact, the Chronicler has preserved from his source only the *narrative framework*, simplified it and filled it in such a way as to present King Hezekiah as an ideal monarch.[11] It is not by accident, of course, that the Chronicler has given Hezekiah such an extensive section, the majority of it (2 Chr 29:3–32:8) being his own creation ('*Sondergut*').[12] Only David and Solomon get more space in his book.[13]

---

[9] Gary N. Knoppers, *1 Chronicles 1–9* (AncB 12; New York, 2004), p. 66. For detailed information see, for example, Matthias Augustin, 'Beobachtungen zur chronistischen Umgestaltung der deuteronomistischen Königschronik nach der Reichsteilung', in Matthias Augustin and Jürgen Kegler (eds.), *Das Alte Testament als geistige Heimat. Festgabe für Hans Walter Wolff zum 70. Geburtstag* (EHS.T 17; Frankfurt am Mainz, 1982), pp. 11–50; Marc Z. Brettler, 'From the Deuteronomist(s) to the Chronicler: Continuities and Innovations', in David Assaf (ed.), *Proceedings of the 11th World Congress of Jewish Studies, Division A* (Jerusalem, 1995), pp. 83–90; Steven L. McKenzie, *The Chronicler's Use of the Deuteronomistic History* (HSM 33; Atlanta Ga., 1984), pp. 83–188.

[10] For more details see Wido Th. van Peursen and Eep Talstra, 'Computer-Assisted Analysis of Parallel Texts in the Bible. The Case of 2 Kings xviii–xix and its Parallels in Isaiah and Chronicles', *VT* 57 (2007), pp. 45–72.

[11] 'Right from the start it is clear that the Chronicler is concerned to fashion his sources in such a way that Hezekiah appears in the most favourable light'; Childs, *Isaiah and the Assyrian Crisis*, p. 110.

[12] But compare the correspondence between 32:7 and 2 Kings 19:6, discussed in Van Peursen and Talstra, 'Computer-Assisted Analysis of Parallel Texts in the Bible', p. 70.

[13] See Mark A. Throntveit, 'The Relationship of Hezekiah to David and Solomon in the Books of Chronicles', in M. Patrick Graham, Steven L. McKenzie, and Gary Knoppers (eds.), *The Chronicler as Theologian* (JSOT.S 371; New York, 2003), pp. 105–121.

I do agree with Christopher Begg that the Chronicler has an urgent need to present King Hezekiah as being as religious as possible.[14] I also fully agree with him that '[t]he Hezekiah of Chronicles—particularly in the *Sondergut*—is portrayed as himself a prophetic figure'.[15] Paying attention to Isaiah 'would have the effect of obscuring Hezekiah's status as *the* prophet of his time, and accordingly the Chronicler passes over (or rewrites) just these portions' (relating to Isaiah, PCB).[16]

However, I am convinced that Begg's view is only a *partial* solution to the question of why Isaiah has so noticeably been put aside by the Chronicler. For it is not only Isaiah who to a high degree has been silenced by the Chronicler. All the classical prophets were![17] Prophets like Samuel (1 Chr 11:3; 29:29) and Jeremiah (2 Chr 35:25; 36:12, 21, 22) are marginalized too. And the prophet Ezekiel is not even mentioned at all by the Chronicler![18]

This means that there must be a *theological*, maybe even an *ideological*, reason why the author of the Book of Chronicles paid so little attention to the classical prophets as factual characters. In my view, it is William Schniedewind who has convincingly demonstrated that, as far as the Book of Chronicles is concerned, one has to differentiate between speeches by speakers with prophetic titles ('prophet', 'seer', 'man of God') and speeches by speakers without prophetic titles, but who are introduced by 'possession formulas' ('the spirit of God was upon ...', 'the spirit enveloped ...'). Speakers with prophetic titles usually address only the king, whereas so-called 'inspired messengers' generally address the people.[19] After a careful investigation Schniedewind reaches the conclusion that persons with prophetic titles 'often give explanations for past or future events, functioning as *interpreters of events*'.[20] In the speeches of the 'inspired messengers', on the contrary, emphasis is put on another

---

[14] Christopher Begg, 'The Classical prophets in the Chronistic History', *BZ* 32 (1988), pp. 100–107.

[15] Begg, 'Classical prophets', p. 102.

[16] Begg, 'Classical prophets', p. 102.

[17] '... the literary prophets play no part in the Chronicler's narrative'; Sara Japhet, *The Ideology of the Book of Chronicles and Its Place in Biblical Thought* (BEAT 9; Frankfurt am Mainz, 1989), p. 181.

[18] See Kegler, 'Prophetengestalten', p. 487 (Table 5).

[19] There are five 'inspired messengers': Amasai (1 Chr 12:19), Azariah (2 Chr 15:1), Jahaziel (2 Chr 20:14), Zechariah (2 Chr 24:20), and Neco (2 Chr 35:21). On Jahaziel, see Pancratius C. Beentjes, 'Tradition and Transformation: Aspects of Innerbiblical Interpretation in 2 Chronicles 20', *Bib.* 74 (1993), pp. 258–268.

[20] Schniedewind, *The Word of God in Transition*, p. 127 (Italics added).

aspect, viz. 'the *inspired interpretation of authoritative texts* which revitalized the word of God anew for the post-exilic community'.[21] Therefore, it can hardly be an accident that precisely in the final chapter of the Book of Chronicles a clear-cut distinction has been made between 'messengers' and 'prophets' (2 Chron. 36:16)!

I would like to substantiate Schniedewind's thesis with the help of a famous text from the Book of Isaiah, which has been adopted by the Chronicler to emphasize his point of view. We therefore need to take a closer look at a specific line in 2 Chronicles 20.

4. *The Chronicler's Rephrasing of a Particular Isaianic Passage*

There is a remarkable *opinio communis* that the word combination האמינו ... ותאמנו in the first half of 2 Chr 20:20 is a direct allusion to Isa 7:9b, a line which—as is shown by all Bible translations—can hardly be translated adequately.[22] The Chronicler is ascribing to King Jehoshaphat words which, historically speaking, he did not have not at his disposal at all. The prophet Isaiah was supposed to speak this line more than a hundred years *after* Jehoshaphat's death, in a similar situation, when hostile armies threatened Jerusalem.[23]

The *anachronistic presentation* by the Chronicler makes it very plausible that the author of the Book of Chronicles had interests other than purely historical facts. It is striking, for example, that the Chronicler, on the one hand, has transformed the negative form of Isa 7:9 (אם לא תאמינו כי לא תאמנו) into a positive summons; and that, on the other hand, the *hiph'il* conjugation which in the Isaiah text is used in an absolute form—a cause of endless discussion[24]—in the context of 2 Chr 20:20 has been given an unequivocal sense:

---

[21] Schniedewind, *The Word of God in Transition*, p. 127 (Italics added).

[22] RSV: 'If you will not believe, surely you shall not be established'; NEB: 'Have firm faith, or you will not stand firm'; REB: 'Have firm faith, or you will fail to stand firm'.

[23] The same phenomenon occurs in the report of Sennacherib's campaign against Jerusalem: Hezekiah's words in 2 Chr 32:7 are clearly reminiscent of Isaiah's words in 2 Kgs 19:6, which form part of an address of Isaiah to Hezekiah that has been omitted in Chronicles; cf. Van Peursen and Talstra, 'Computer-Assisted Analysis of Parallel Texts in the Bible', p. 70.

[24] See, for example, Rudolf Smend, 'Zur Geschichte von *he'amin*', in Benedikt Hartmann (ed.), *Hebräische Wortforschung. Festschrift zum 80. Geburtstag von Walter Baumgartner* (VT.S 16; Leiden, 1967), pp. 284–290; Hans Wildberger, 'Glauben', in Hartmann

(a) האמינו ביהוה אלהיכם ותאמנו
(b) האמינו בנביאיו והצליחו

Whereas it is obvious that the first part of 2 Chr 20:20 can be considered a remodelling of the famous Isaianic word, in respect of the second half of this verse such a point of view is untenable. For the phrase האמינו בנביאיו והצליחו has no other point of reference to the Isaiah text than the opening verbal form.[25] The most plausible inference therefore would be that the second half of 2 Chr 20:20 is to be considered as the interpretation which the Chronicler himself wants to apply to the remodelled Isaianic text from the first part of his statement.[26] That 2 Chr 20:20b must indeed be understood in this way is certainly proved by the appearance of two elements which can be said to be typically Chronistic:

(1) The statement האמינו בנביאיו exposes and emphasizes the prominent and pointed place which in the Book of Chronicles has been allotted to the prophets.[27] Their connection with and parallel to the summons האמינו ביהוה is undisputable proof for that.
(2) Using the verb צלח *hiphʿil* ('to succeed'), the Chronicler highlights a theme which is near to his heart. For, whereas in the *hiphʿil* conjugation the verb צלח is found thirty times in the Old Testament, 1 and 2 Chronicles have no less than thirteen occurrences, eleven of which

---

(ed.), *Hebräische Wortforschung*, pp. 372–386; Alfred Jepsen, 'אֱמֶת אָמֵן אֱמוּנָה אָמַן', in G. Johannes Botterweck and Helmer Ringgren (eds.), *Theologisches Wörterbuch zum Alten Testament* 1 (Stuttgart etc., 1974), cols. 313–348; Hans Wildberger, 'אמן *ʾmn* / fest, sicher' in Ernst Jenni and Claus Westermann (eds.), *Theologisches Handwörterbuch zum Alten Testament* 1 (München etc., 1971), cols. 177–209; Nico H. Ridderbos, 'Enkele beschouwingen naar aanleiding van *taʾaminu* in Jes. 7:9', in *Schrift en Uitleg. Studies van oud-leerlingen, collega's en vrienden aangeboden aan prof.dr. W.H. Gispen ter gelegenheid van zijn vijfentwintigjarig ambtsjubileum als hoogleraar aan de Vrije Universiteit en ter gelegenheid van het bereiken van de zeventigjarige leeftijd* (Kampen, 1970), pp. 167–178.

[25] Nowhere in the literature on 2 Chr 20:20 have I met a comment on the fact that the Septuagint version renders a singular: ἐν προφήτῃ αὐτοῦ, by which the range of this statement has explicitly been narrowed down to Jahaziel alone.

[26] See Michael Fishbane, *Biblical Interpretation in Ancient Israel* (Oxford, 1985), pp. 386–388.

[27] See, for example, Seeligmann, 'Die Auffassung von der Prophetie', pp. 270–279; Yairah Amit, 'The Role of Prophecy and Prophets in the Book of Chronicles' (Hebr.), *BetM* 28 (1982), pp. 113–133; Mark A. Throntveit, *When Kings Speak. Royal Speech and Royal Prayer in Chronicles* (SBL.DS 93; Atlanta, 1987), pp. 127–129; Duke, *The Persuasive Appeal of the Chronicler*, pp. 128–133, 171–176; Rex Mason, *Preaching the Tradition. Homily and Hermeneutics after the Exile. Based on "Addresses" in Chronicles, the "Speeches" in the Books of Ezra and Nehemiah and the Post-Exilic Prophetical Books* (Cambridge, 1990).

> appear in the so-called 'chronistisches Sondergut'.[28] To the Chronicler, צלח symbolizes the outcome of 'seeking guidance from the Lord' (e.g. 2 Chr 26:5) and 'observing carefully the decrees and ordinances of the Lord' (e.g., 1 Chr 22:13).

The seven (!) words which constitute Jehoshaphat's factual address together build up the most concise summary of the message of the Book of Chronicles. I won't go as far as Mark Throntveit who considers 2 Chr 20:20 to be the exact centre of a number of concentric circles exposing a chiastic structure relating to speeches from the period of the 'Divided Monarchy'.[29] Nor do I go to the other extreme, and agree with Gerhard Von Rad's view that 2 Chr 20:20b is a slap in the face of the Isaianic statement.[30] To my mind, Von Rad in this particular case overlooked that precisely in the Book of Chronicles the prophets were given a crucial role as a sign of God's manifest mercy (2 Chr 36:15–16). Moreover, in determining the specific meaning of the famous Isaianic quotation and its interpretation in 2 Chr 20:20, the synonymous parallelism of this line should have mitigated Von Rad's view. For it is the literary make-up of this parallelism that can bring us a step further. The present writer wants to submit it to the reader as a hypothesis.

Both the sequence and the wording of 2 Chr 20:20 to a high degree have been influenced by and modelled on Exodus 14.[31] Precisely in the final line of that narrative we come across the phrase ויאמינו ביהוה ובמשה עבדו (Exod 14:31b). It is hardly possible to avoid the impression that both the structure and the content of this verse are conducive to the attachment of the famous Isaianic saying within the theological concept of the Chronicler, on the one hand, and its peculiar interpretation, on the other.[32]

The author of 2 Chronicles 20 has exploited the (written) traditions of Exodus 14 relating to Israel's fundamental experience at the Read Sea

[28] See Magne Saebø, 'צלח *ṣlḥ* gelingen', in Ernst Jenni and Claus Westermann, *Theologisches Handwörterbuch zum Alten Testament* 2 (München, 1976), cols. 551–556.

[29] Throntveit, *When Kings Speak*, pp. 115–120.

[30] 'Das Nebeneinander des Mahnens zum Glaubem an Jahwe und an seine Propheten schlägt dem wahren Sinn des Jesajawortes ins Gesicht'; Gerhard von Rad, 'Die levitische Predigt in den Büchern der Chronik', in Gerhard von Rad, *Gesammelte Studien zum Alten Testament* (TB 8; München, 1965), pp. 248–261, esp. 254–255.

[31] See Beentjes, 'Tradition and Transformation'.

[32] For this hypothesis only Kasher is on my side: Rimon Kasher, 'The Saving of Jehosaphat: Extent, Parallels, Significance' (Hebr.), *BetM* 31 (1985), pp. 242–251. He however says not a single word about a relation between 2 Chr 20:20 and Isa 7:9b!

in order to encourage and stimulate the community of his own time. I therefore disagree absolutely with Otto Eissfeldt's statement that YHWH is placed upon the stage as a *deus ex machina*, a situation in which the people have nothing to do but to pray and sing.[33] Did Eissfeldt forget that praying and singing (in a word, liturgy) is always preceded by a fundamental act, that is to say: faith in Him and those sent by Him?

[33] 'Es ist also wirklich an dem, daß Jahwe als ein deus ex machina in Szene gesetzt wird und die Menschen nichts zu tun haben, als zu beten und zu singen'.; Otto Eissfeldt, *Einleitung in das Alte Testament* (2nd ed.; Tübingen, 1956), p. 663.

WOE TO POWERS IN ISRAEL THAT VIE TO REPLACE YHWH'S RULE ON MOUNT ZION! ISAIAH CHAPTERS 28–31 FROM THE PERSPECTIVE OF ISAIAH CHAPTERS 24–27

Willem A.M. Beuken

The composition of Isaiah 28–39 and its place in the first part of the book have been studied from three points of view: (1) The historical background of the prophecies contained in these chapters; (2) The redactional 'bridges' between the two main parts of the Book of Isaiah: chapter 33 and 35 (whether related to chapter 34 or not); (3) The function of chapters 36–39 in the redaction of the book as a whole. Another point of view is my own. Since the preceding chapters 13–23 and 24–27 appear to form a coherent bipartite entity and continue, moreover, the specific events announced in chapters 1–12,[1] the subsequent chapters 28–39 can be studied from the point of view of how they pursue the basic events of chapters 24–27: the break-through of YHWH's kingship on Mount Zion (24:21–23) and its inauguration by the returning exiles at that very place (27:13).

Chapter 28 opens a new subdivision of the first part of the Book of Isaiah but its closure is located differently and might be a shifting end (chapter 32; 33; 34). Many scholars consider chapters 28–33 an autonomous literary composition: 'das Buch der Wehe'.[2] This consists of five woe cries concerning Ephraim, Ariel (i.e. Zion), its leaders and the people (28,1; 29:1,15; 30:1; 31:1), followed by one relating to Assyria (33:1).[3] The latter woe cry ranks as a redactional extension to the five woe cries regarding God's own people in chapters 28–31(32), which would be,

---

[1] Willem A.M. Beuken, *Jesaja 1–12*, *Jesaja 13–27* (HThKAT; Freiburg etc., 2003, 2007). English translations of the Hebrew text are based on RSV.

[2] Franz Delitzsch, *Biblischer Commentar über das Buch Jesaia* (4th ed.; BC 3.1, Leipzig, 1889), p. 311.

[3] Bernhard Duhm, *Das Buch Jesaia* (4th ed.; HK 3.1; Göttingen, 1922; reprint 1968), p. 13, following Delitzsch, considered Isaiah himself to be the original author of chapters 28–32. In the subsequent scholarly discussion the literary autonomy of 29:15–24 remains disputed. After the 'Literarkritik' the schema of the woe cries has been elaborated by Gary Stansell, 'Isaiah 28–33: Blest Be the Tie that Binds (Isaiah Together)', in Roy F. Melugin, Marvin A. Sweeney (eds.), *New Visions of Isaiah* (JSOT.S 214; Sheffield, 1996), pp. 68–103.

in a literary-historical respect, an older composition. The very fact that these five woe cries display a strong coherence has diminished the interest in their relation to the preceding text of the Book of Isaiah. Therefore, we shall now investigate the larger semantic network in which chapters 28–31 follow upon chapters 24–27, in as far as it serves to continue the dominating event of the latter chapters, i.e. the foundation of YHWH's kingship on Mount Zion (24:23).[4]

1. *The First Woe (Isaiah 28) in Light of Isaiah 24–27*

1.1. *Isaiah 28:1–6*

The first question regards the correlation of Isa 28:1 with the immediately preceding context since MT does not offer a *setuma* or *petucha* at this crossing. This sort of question arises often in the Book of Isaiah, especially at the transition of the main sections (from chapter 39 to 40[5] and from chapter 55 to 56),[6] but also within the three main sections the question comes up at the junction of the subdivisions (13:1; 48:22; 57:21).

For that matter, the assumption of a redactional link between chapter 28 and the preceding chapters is endorsed by the compound nature of the former. First of all, verses 1–6 and verses 7–22 are awkwardly connected: 'the drunkards of Ephraim' (vv. 1, 3) are artificially followed by 'these also reel with wine', i.e. the priests, prophets, and leaders of Jerusalem (vv. 7, 14). Secondly, verses 1–6 consist of two parts, verses 1–4 and verses 5–6, connected by the redactional framework formula 'on that day', which is absent at the crossing of chapter 27 to chapter 28 (although present in 27:12, 13), and by the reversal of 'the crown of beauty', from Ephraim (vv. 1, 3) to YHWH (v. 5).

[4] For the concept of dramatic performance in general and in a specific part of the Book of Isaiah, cf. Stefan A. Nitsche, *Jesaja 24–27: ein dramatischer Text. Die Frage nach den Genres prophetischer Literatur des Alten Testaments und die Textgraphik der großen Jesajarolle aus Quman* (BWANT 166; Stuttgart etc., 2006).

[5] Willem A.M. Beuken, 'The Unity of the Book of Isaiah: Another Attempt at Bridging the Gorge Between its Two Main Parts', in J. Cheryl Exum, Hugh G.M. Williamson (eds.), *Reading from Right to Left. Essays on the Hebrew Bible in Honour of David J. Clines* (JSOT.S 373; Sheffield, 2003), pp. 50–62.

[6] Simone Paganini, 'Der Übergang von Deutero- zu Trito-Jesaja: zu Jes 56,9', in Matthias Augustin, Hermann M. Niemann (eds.), *Stimulation from Leiden. Collected Communications to the XVIIIth Congress of the International Organization for the Study of the Old Testament* (BEAT 54; Frankfurt a. M. etc., 2006), pp. 105–111.

These preliminary observations pave the way for the following semantic stock-taking. 'The haughty crown' is a complicated metaphor, because it has an anthropological application ('of the drunkards of Ephraim') and a geographical one ('on the head of the fat valley'). It is not always a royal attribute (2 Sam 12:30; 1 Chr 20:2; Ezek 21:31; Ps 21:4; Cant 3:11; Esth 8:15) but may also be part of a festive attire (Isa 62:3; Jer 13:18; Ezek 16:12; 23:42; Prov 4:9; 16:31). The background of fertile land and excessive enjoyment suggests a ruling class that abuses its position. 'The head of the valley' refers in the context of Ephraim to its capital Samaria. In this way, the elements are on hand for a contrast between the end of chapter 27 and the beginning of chapter 28. There, the returning deportees pay homage to YHWH on his holy mountain in Jerusalem (27:13); here someone who is invested with YHWH's power treads upon the crown of Ephraim's carousing governors (28:2–3). As a consequence, the opening passage of chapter 28 depicts the fall of the first power that contends with the city of YHWH in Isa 27:13.

This fundamental opposition is supported by some semantic connections with Isaiah 24–27:

- The woe cry regarding Ephraim's 'haughty crown / glorious beauty' (28:1: עטרת גאות /צבי תפארתו; cf. v. 4) corresponds to the oracle on Tyrus, 'the bestower of crowns' (23:8: המעטירה), in which it is announced that 'YHWH has purposed it, to defile the pride of all glory' (v. 9: גאון כל צבי).
- The adjunct 'haughty' (גאות) integrates the metaphor 'crown' into the continuous redactional theme of YHWH's 'majesty'. This began in the introduction to the book (2:10, 19, 21: 'from before the terror of YHWH and from the glory of his majesty [גאון]') and was taken up in the first song of the prophet (12:5: 'Sing praises to YHWH, for he has done gloriously [גאות]'). In the so-called Apocalypse of Isaiah (ApcIsa) the call from the first song (Isa 12:5) finds a response (24:14: 'They shout from the west over the majesty [גאון] of YHWH'), whereas in 26:10 ('The wicked do not see the majesty [גאות] of YHWH') we find a reversal of this theme. This isotope gives Ephraim a place among powers who disdain the coming of God's judgement.[7]

[7] For a discussion of the terminology of 'isotopy' and 'antinomy' see Algirdas J. Greimas and Joseph Courtés, *Sémiotique. Dictionnaire raisonné de la théorie du langage* (Paris, 1979, 1986).

- 'The fading flower (ציץ נבל)' of Ephraim (28:1, 4) belongs to the 'withering (נבל) earth' (24:4) and is opposed to Israel which 'shall blossom (יציץ) and put forth shoots, and fill the whole earth with fruits' (27:6).
- The fall and trampling down of Ephraim (28:2–3: 'He will cast down to the earth [הניח לארץ] ... The proud crown of the drunkards of Ephraim will be trodden under foot [ברגלים תרמסנה]') accords with Judah's song of confidence (26:5–6: 'He has brought low the inhabitants of the height, the lofty city. He lays it low to the ground [ישפילה עד ארץ], casts it to the dust. The foot tramples it, the feet of the poor [תרמסנה רגל רגלי עני]'). The ruin of the drunkards (28:3) is the consequence of the judgement on the earth, which will put an end to all enjoyment of wine (24:9–11).
- YHWH's intervention by means of someone who acts 'like a storm (זרם) of hail, a destroying tempest, like a storm (זרם) of powerful, flooding waters' (28:2) and brings revenge like 'the blast of the ruthless like a storm (זרם) against a wall' (25:4).
- In the dramatic performance of chapter 26 the demand of people in Judah to enter the city of YHWH constitutes an important moment: 'Open the gates (שערים), that a righteous nation (גוי צדיק) which keeps faith may enter in' (v. 2).[8] In the sequence to the chapter, this group express their hope of the coming of YHWH's 'judgements' (vv. 8–9: משפטים). Against this background 28:5–6 may be understood. As the capital of Ephraim represents the crown of its drunkards (vv. 1, 3), in the same way YHWH in his city, according to verse 5, is a crown for the rest of his people. He grants there, according to verse 6, 'judgement (משפט) to the one who sits in judgement' and 'valour to those who turn back the battle at the gates (שערים)'.
- In this respect, the reversal of the concept 'remnant' (28:5: שאר) deserves attention. The ApcIsa has prophesied that in 'the city of chaos' (24:10) no life will remain: 'Desolation is left (נשאר) in the city' (24:12; cf. v. 6). This clause summarizes the destiny of the nations mentioned before (cf. שאר or שארית in 14:22: Babylon; 14:30: Philistea; 15:9; 16:14: Moab; 17:3: Aram; 21:17: Kedar). In contrast to this over-all ruin, the prophet foresees a glorious existence for 'the remnant of his (YHWH's) people' (28:5). At the end of this part of the book, this is explicitly situated in Jerusalem (37:4, 32; cf. 4:3).

[8] Beuken, *Jesaja 13–27*, pp. 368–370.

- The peculiar clause construction of 28:2 ('Behold, YHWH has one who is mighty and strong, like a storm of hail, a destroying tempest. Like a storm of mighty, overflowing waters, he will cast down to the earth with the hand')[9] on the one hand, seems to indicate that YHWH used an agent to mete out vengeance on his behalf on Ephraim, whereas on the other hand, it also ascribes the authoritaty to YHWH himself. The twofold mention of 'like a storm' connects the agent to his superior, yet the term 'with the hand' cannot but refer to YHWH's hand.[10] In this way, the oracle concerning Ephraim is on a par with that concerning Moab in 25:10: 'For the hand of YHWH will rest on this mountain, and Moab shall be trodden down in his place' (cf. YHWH's 'hand' in 14:26–27; 19:16, 25; 23:11; 26:11).

Briefly, the oracle about Ephraim in 28:1–6 prepares the ground by means of the theme of drunkenness for the oracle concerning the priests and prophets in Jerusalem (vv. 7–22), but it is also a sequel to Isaiah 24–27. The proud crown of Ephraim, i.e. its capital with its arrogant, spendthrift leaders belongs to the earth which comes to grief (chapter 24). The place does not continue to exist as opposed to the holy mountain in Jerusalem, where YHWH as king of the universe receives the homage of the deportees (chapter 27).

1.2. *Isaiah 28:7–22*

The next passage of chapter 28 constitutes an independently developed composition but some connections with chapters 24–27 can be established, and they shed special light on the passage. The wrong leaders of Jerusalem put in an appearance. They are, firstly, the priests and prophets: reeling with drunkenness (v. 7: תעה) they resemble the earth (24:20: נוע)

---

[9] The construction of לאדני with a subject in a nominal clause occurs seldom (Dan 9:9; cf. Gen 18:30, 32; Mal 1:14; Ps 22:31; 130:6; with regard to ליהוה in the same construction, cf. Ezek 42,13; Zech 14,1). The verse has been interpreted in several ways, cf. Joseph A. Alexander, *Commentary on the Prophecies of Isaiah* (2 vols., 2nd ed.; Philadelphia, 1875; reprint Grand Rapids, 1976), p. 445; Hans Wildberger, *Jesaja* 3. *Teilband. Jesaja 28–39* (BK 10.3; Neukirchen, 1982), pp. 1043, 1048. Most probably, the words 'one who is strong and mighty' refer to the king of Assyria. The fact that he is not mentioned by name, is appropriate after 27:13, where the deportees are gathered from Assyria, and also in anticipation of v. 6, where YHWH is presented as the protagonist. The same anonymity characterizes the portrayal of Cyrus in 41:2.

[10] Delitzsch, *Jesaja*, p. 312; Wildberger, *Jesaja*, p. 1048; Willem A.M. Beuken, *Isaiah 2.2 Isaiah Chapters 28–39* (HCOT; Leuven, 2000), pp. 26–27.

and their destiny is that of its inhabitants under the judgement of YHWH (cf. v. 13b: '... that they be broken, and snared, and caught' in 24:10 ['to be broken', נשבר] and in 24:18 ['to be caught', נלכד]). On a par with them (or maybe the same) are 'you scoffers, who rule (משלי) this people in Jerusalem' (v. 14). They are in sharp contrast to YHWH of Hosts, who 'will reign (מלך) on Mount Zion and in Jerusalem' (24:23) and receive there the homage of the returning deportees (27:13). In brief, against the background of the ApcIsa the malicious governors of Jerusalem appear as insurgents against YHWH's rule.

This contrast between YHWH and the wrong leaders is also predominant in the confrontation with death. While YHWH on his mountain 'will swallow up death for ever' (25:8), the rulers of Jerusalem submit to the dominion of the arch-enemy: 'We have concluded a covenant with death and with Sheol we have made an agreement' (28:15). The context of both prophecies sharpens this contrast. YHWH puts an end to death for the benefit of all people: '... the shroud that is cast over all peoples ... he will wipe away tears from all faces' (25:7–8). Jerusalem's upper class, however, think they can protect themselves against death: 'When the overwhelming scourge passes through it will not come to us' (28:15). YHWH, moreover, is 'a stronghold to the needy in his distress, a refuge (מחסה) from the storm' (25:4), but the rulers of Jerusalem can only state: 'We have made lies our refuge (מחסנו), and in falsehood we have taken shelter' (28:15).

This context clarifies the core of the chapter: 'Behold, it is I who has laid in Zion for a foundation a stone, a massive stone, a cornerstone valuable for a sure foundation' (v. 16).[11] The opening sentence with the words הנני יסד בציון אבן raises two questions: (1) Should the verb form יסד be interpreted as a participle or emended into that? (2) Does the preposition ב in בציון serve as a *beth essentiae* or as a locative? As for the first question, exegetes are more and more inclined to maintain the MT and also the past meaning of יסד ('he has laid'). As for the second question, ambiguity seems to play a role. YHWH does not argue that literally he has put a cornerstone for a house on Zion in order to live there but that metaphorically he has provided Zion with a cornerstone as a solid foundation. In this sense his statement concerns both his own sojourn on Mount Zion and the refuge which, according to chapter 25, he offers the needy (cf. 14:32), as he has in vain summoned the leaders

[11] The present interpretation relies on Jaap Dekker, *Zion's Rock-Solid Foundations. An Exegetical Study of the Zion Text in Isaiah 28:16* (OTS 54; Leiden etc., 2007), pp. 124–144.

of Jerusalem to do: 'This is rest, give rest to the weary, this is repose' (28:12). As opposed to this dwelling on a strong foundation, the refuge of lies of the leading class will be swept away in heavy weather (vv. 17–18). By means of the same imagery YHWH's protection for the destitute has previously been described (25:4; 28:2, 15).

1.3. *Isaiah 28:23–29*

The close of chapter 28 still carries on the important theme of YHWH's 'counsel' or 'plan' which spans Isaiah 1–39: 'This also comes from YHWH of Hosts; he is wonderful in counsel (הפליא עצה), great in wisdom' (v. 29). The song of praise with which the prophet in 24:23 welcomed the proclamation of YHWH's kingship on Mount Zion opens exactly with that topic: 'I will praise thy name, for thou hast done wonderful things, counsels formed of old, faithful and sure' (25:1: עשית פלא עצות מרחוק). This text also forms a continuation of the topic 'counsel' in chapters 13–23 (cf. 14:24–27; 19:17; 23:8–9). YHWH's policies concerning the nations and his own people transcend human expectation and assessment. This also holds true for what follows upon the revelation of his sovereignty in chapters 24–27, i.e. when the refuge of lies constructed by Jerusalem's rulers threatens to overwhelm Zion as it was founded by YHWH (chapter 28).

2. *The Second and Third Woes (Isaiah 29:1–14, 15–24) in the Light of Isaiah 24–27*

These two woe cries can be treated together since the theme of wisdom bridges the end of the former and the beginning of the latter (vv. 13–16). Precisely these 'hinge' verses make it possible to read the two passages as a continuation of chapters 24–27 although they may not have been composed as a sequel to that book part.

2.1. *Isaiah 29:1–8*

From the angle of 'plot', the passage continues the theme of chapter 28. The beginning, the siege of Ariel, 'the city of David' (29:1–2), transfers the reader in time and space to the appearance of 'the overwhelming scourge' (28:15, 18–19) by which YHWH performs his 'strange deed / alien work' (28:21). The surprising event is that YHWH himself lays the siege (v. 3) but also causes the enemies to disappear as 'small dust / passing chaff' (vv. 5–6), so that the siege comes to an end as a nightmare (vv. 7–8). Henceforth the understanding of this event is at stake (vv. 9–14).

Isaiah 24–27 serves as the background to this prophecy. The city under siege is a particular case of the judgement proclaimed in 24:7–13, with the difference that the latter text depicts the situation after its seizure and destruction. Both passages mention the lament: 'moaning and mourning' (29:2: תאניה ואניה)[12] here, 'the merry-hearted sigh' (24:7: נאנחו) and 'outcry in the streets' (24:11: צוחה) there. The passages have in common that YHWH's intervention is mentioned with the characteristic term 'to visit' (פקד: 24:21–22; 26:14, 16, 21; 27:1, 3).

This intervention is nuanced in chapter 24 by veiled language, as if to mask the fact that it was YHWH who was playing a role in the course of events. After the passage in 24:1 ('YHWH will lay waste the earth and make it desolate. He will twist its surface and scatter its inhabitants'), causality is expressed by means of passive verb forms and basically attributed to 'the curse' (24:3, 6). Only in 24:21 do we learn that: 'YHWH will visit (פקד) the host of heaven and the kings of the earth', which is, then again, elaborated by passive verb forms (vv. 21–23: 'they will be gathered ... will be shut up ... will be visited [יפקדו] ... The moon will be confounded and the sun ashamed'). Chapter 29, too, begins with YHWH's personal interference: 'I will distress Ariel ... I will encamp against you round about, and will besiege you with towers and I will raise siege-works against you' (vv. 2–3) but the passive verb form is used as well: 'There will be a visit (תפקד) from YHWH of Hosts with thunder and with earthquake ...' (v. 6).[13] This restrained parlance about YHWH's action only serves highlight the surprising reversal of fortune, firstly for those who war against Ariel but finally for 'the multitude of all the nations that fight against Ariel / Mount Zion' (vv. 7–8). The mention of the latter place-name positions the passage in line with the ApcIsa (24:23; 25:6, 7, 10; 27:13). The outcome of the siege concerns the location, which YHWH has chosen in order to establish there his kingship.

---

[12] The rhyme of the Hebrew expression (further only found in Lam 2:5) has been imitated in this way in the translations of Edward J. Kissane, *The Book of Isaiah* 1. *Isaiah I–XXIX* (Dublin, 1941), p. 322; Avraham J. Rosenberg, *Isaiah* 1. *Translation of Text, Rashi and Commentary* (Miqra'ot Gedolot; New York, 1982), pp. 232–233; Joseph Blenkinsopp, *Isaiah 1–39* (AncB 19; New York etc., 2000), p. 51.

[13] For the interpretation of תפקד as a third person feminine verb form with neutral meaning, cf. Beuken, *Isaiah* 2.2, p. 71.

Verses 7–8 describe the siege as a battle of the nations against Ariel, yet in the preceding verses this is rarely the case. In verse 5, the mention of 'your invaders / the ruthless' (עריצים / זרים) refers to the prophet's song of praise in 25:1–5, in which he sets the fall of the mighty tyrants' bulwark against YHWH's protection of the defenceless. The same word pair turns in verses 2–3 and verses 4–5 the antinomy between nations into a case in which YHWH sides with the needy. In 29:4–6, also, the outcome of the siege of Ariel is depicted less as a military encounter between nations than as a theophany in which 'YHWH of Hosts' demonstrates his superiority. Cosmic phenomena accompany his appearance (v. 6).[14] Indeed, the spectacle of the siege presents just one powerful party: YHWH. The inhabitants of Ariel are described as powerless beings, close to dying: they speak 'like a ghost' (v. 4; cf. 8:19). Even before they can undertake any defensive action, their sojourn is already in 'earth / dust', where according to the ApcIsa the residents of mighty fortresses also end up when they rise against YHWH (ארץ / עפר: 25:12; 26:5; cf. 26:19; 47:1; 49:23; Ezek 24:7; Mic 7:17; Ps 7:6; 22:30; 44:26; Job 14:8; Eccl 12:7). The same, however, holds true for the nations: their aggressive power is as light as that of 'fine dust / passing chaff' (v. 5 cf. אבק: Exod 9:9; Dtn 28:24; Isa 5:24; Ezek 26,10; Nah 1:3; מוץ: Isa 17:13; 41:15; Hos 13:3; Zeph 2:2; Ps 1:4; 35:5; Job 21:18).

In this way, the scene demonstrates that the city of David returns to the exclusive authority of YHWH. Maybe the place-name at the beginning, 'Ariel', expresses this by means of its resemblance to the common noun 'altar hearth'. The cultic connotation characterizes the city as the site where YHWH is worshipped, evoking his right to recognition and his obligation to afford shelter. The name is confirmed by the theophany, YHWH's visit 'with the flame of a devouring fire' (v. 6).

The subsequent verses mention first the reaction to YHWH's intervention in the Ariel event. Verses 7–8 still belong to the description of the siege: the inhabitants of Ariel referred to here see the enemies withdraw quickly and completely 'like a dream, a vision of the night' (v. 7).

[14] The terms employed here can be found elsewhere in the context of theophany: 'thunder', רעם: Ps 77:19; 81:8; 104:7; Job 26:14; 'earthquake', רעש: 1 Kgs 19:11–12; Ezek 3:12–13; 38:19; '(great) noise', (גדול) קול: Dtn 5:22; Jer 10:13; Amos 1:2; Ps 18:14; 29:3–5; 46:7; 68:34; 77:19; 104:7; 'whirlwind', סופה: Isa 17:13; Amos 1:14; Nah 1:3; Ps 83:16; 'tempest', סערה: Isa 40:24; Jer 23:19; 30:23; Ezek 1:4; Zech 9:14; Job 38:1; 40:6; 'flame', להב: Isa 30:30; 66:15; '(devouring) fire', (אוכלה) אש: Exod 3:2; 19:18; 24:17; Dtn 4:11, 24; 1 Kgs 18:24, 38; 2 Kgs 1:10–14; Isa 66:15; Nah 1:6.

Thereupon, a double comparison describes how the hostile nations react to YHWH's appearance: they awake from a deceitful dream, because their desires seemed to be fulfilled but are not (v. 8).

2.2. *Isaiah 29:9–14*

In this section the prophet leaves the Ariel story. Again he addresses the audience of the woe cry (vv. 1–6), accuses them of incomprehension (vv. 9–12) and discloses how YHWH from now on will be dealing with them (vv. 13–14). In this way, the passage constitutes an accompanying commentary on the Ariel prophecy (*metatext*).

The first half, the accusation in verses 9–12, raises many questions, especially because the opening line of verse 9a, with the semantic word-game being played with the four verbs, is highly intricate: 'Tarry and be astounded! Delight yourselves and be blind!' In my interpretation which does not emend but follows the MT,[15] the audience is accused of not taking the message concerning Ariel seriously, due to indecisiveness and absorption with their own pleasures. They are warned that events will overtake them and that they will find themselves in permanent blindness. Subsequently, verse 10 interprets this self-inflicted blindness as a punishment from YHWH. In this way, accusation and the announcement of judgement are closely connected in the sense that unbelief continues as mischief: those who no longer wish to see shall no longer be able to see. Due to the fact that YHWH has closed their eyes, the vision has become a sealed writing (vv. 11–12).

The expression 'the vision of all this' deserves attention (v. 11). According to some, it refers to the revelation entrusted to the prophet in general or at least in as far as he has committed it to writing (cf. 1:1).[16] Others explain it as a function of its context.[17] In that case, the vision concerns not only the discovery that the enemies have suddenly disappeared (vv. 7–8) but the whole course of events, YHWH's bewildering action included ('all this'). This interpretation is supported by the fact that in verse 11 the prophet addresses the audience of verse 9a, in addition to

[15] Beuken, *Isaiah* 2.2, pp. 72–73, 91–93: the first two imperatives are taken to be consonant, the latter pair homonymous.

[16] Michael Friedländer (ed.), *The Commentary of Ibn Ezra on Isaiah* (London, 1873), p. 135; Alexander, *Isaiah*, p. 465; Delitzsch, *Jesaja*, p. 325; Duhm, *Jesaja*, p. 210; Wildberger, *Jesaja*, pp. 116–117; Blenkinsopp, *Isaiah*, p. 405.

[17] Kissane, *Isaiah*, p. 331; Otto Kaiser, *Der Prophet Jesaja. Kapitel 13–39* (ATD 18; Göttingen, 1973), pp. 214–215.

those addressed in verses 3–5 as the object of God's punishment. In this respect, the fact that the adjuncts 'upon you' (v. 10) and 'to you' (v. 11) are placed in front of the clause is remarkable. The preceding prophecy has not met with comprehension by the listeners in as far as YHWH at the same time punishes the city of David by means of a siege by the nations and also protects Mount Zion against that army. This baffling way of acting is only comprehensible in the light of the function that God had allotted to his holy mountain in chapters 24–27 (24:23; 25:6, 7, 10; 27:13).

The divine oracle (vv. 13–14) takes up again in its accusatory role in verse 13, some topics, particularly the contrast between lip service and the service of a sincere heart, that are alien to the ApcIsa and more kindred to indictments in Isaiah 1–12 (especially chapter 1). Nevertheless, the announcement of YHWH's intervention in verse 14, 'I go on doing wonderful things (להפליא)', continues the theme by which the prophet in chapters 24–27 acknowledges God for his action against the ill-disposed city: 'the wonderful things, counsels of old' (25:1: פלא / עצות). The reference is the more cogent if one looks beyond the demarcation of verses 9–14 and takes the beginning of the third woe cry (29:15) into consideration. This is aimed against 'those who, away from YHWH, hide deep their counsel (עצות)'. Obviously, verses 14 and 15 make a sort of connection between verses 9–14 and 15–24 in which YHWH's policy is opposed to the perishable wisdom of his adversaries. This link is sustained by the connecting terms 'to hide' (סתר) in verses 14–15 and 'discernment / no understanding' (לא הבין / בינה) in verse 14 and 16. Moreover, verses 14–15 form a sequel to the end of the first woe cry (see above).

2.3. *Isaiah 29:15–24*

At first sight, the third woe cry contains no other connections with chapters 24–27 than those just mentioned. The divine title 'the Holy One of Israel' (29:19, 23) does not occur in the ApcIsa. Indeed, the name 'Jacob' does occur there (27:6, 9; 29:22–23), but other names such as 'Abraham' (29:22) and 'Lebanon' (29:17) do not. All the same, the opposition between the 'meek / poor' (אביונים / ענוים) and the 'ruthless' (עריץ) in 29:19–20 finds a parallel in the ApcIsa, where 'the palace of the aliens' and 'the city of ruthless nations' yield to YHWH, 'the stronghold to the poor in his distress' (25:2–4; cf. 26:6).

This theme is related to the time-scale. Chapter 26 is dominated by the need for the reprobate to be on the look-out for YHWH's judgements which will overthrow him (vv. 7–11). The third woe cry raises the topic 'when?' in an explicit manner: 'Is it not yet a very little while ...?' (v. 17), and announces what will happen 'on that day' (v. 18). Impatience for the fall of the wicked pervades both passages. The difference lies in the fact that chapter 26 raises the question in a world-wide perspective while the third woe cry deals with it from the point of view of 'Jacob / Israel' as is also the case in the first and second one (chapter 28 and 29:1–14).

At the background of this, another parallel catches the eye. In chapter 26 the prophet has drawn a distinction between two groups: 'When thy judgements are on the earth, the inhabitants of the world learn righteousness (צדק למדו ישבי תבל)' (v. 9) but 'If favour is shown to the wicked, he does not learn righteousness (יחן רשע בל למד צדק). In the land of uprightness he deals perversely' (v. 10). This is elaborated in the third woe cry (29:15–24). In addition to the contrast between the 'meek / poor' and the 'ruthless / all who watch to do evil' (vv. 19–20), the prophet raises the issue of Jacob's shame about his children (vv. 22–24). Henceforth these will acknowledge YHWH: 'They will stand in awe of the God of Israel. Those who err in spirit will know understanding, and murmurers will learn instruction (ילמדו לקח)' (vv. 23b–24). In this way they will be similar to the inhabitants of the earth who learn justice by God's judgement (26:9).

3. *The Fourth Woe (Isaiah 30) in the Light of Isaiah 24–27*

At first sight, this woe cry does not naturally ensue from the ApcIsa. Explanations of chapter 30 as a composition diverge but a partially autonomous development of the chapter which precedes the final redaction of the Book of Isaiah, is generally recognised.[18]

A prophecy of Isaiah ben Amoz announcing that a diplomatic mission to Egypt from a group of Judah's politicians would result in a disastrous flight of the people (vv. 1–17), has been expanded and actualized by a passage concerning a return to Zion (vv. 18–26). In so doing the tradition makes use of the ancient paradigm of a 'journey' under YHWH's leadership: 'Your eyes shall be looking upon your Teacher and your ears shall hear a word behind you saying: 'This is the way, walk in it'' (vv. 20–21). Obedience to God's word and renunciation of the worship of idols

[18] Willem A.M. Beuken, 'Isaiah 30: A Prophetic Oracle Transmitted in Two Successive Paradigms', in Craig C. Broyles and Craig A. Evans (eds.), *Writing and Reading the Scroll of Isaiah: Studies of an Interpretive Tradition* 1 (VT.S 70.1; Leiden etc., 1997), pp. 369–397.

characterize the new relationship between YHWH and his people (v. 22). This journey will lead to a loyal and blessed life in the land (vv. 23–26).

The tradition has further actualized Isaiah's prophecy by a second expansion, which relies on the paradigm of YHWH's appearance on Mount Zion (vv. 27–33). The coming of YHWH, apparently to his mountain (vv. 27–33), forms the sequel to the journey of the refugees back to Jerusalem and the land (vv. 19–22). Terrifying phenomena belonging to a theophany embody the judgement. The nations are removed (v. 28), the people, who again inhabit Zion, go up to the mountain of YHWH and celebrate a holy festival (v. 29). The mighty enemy Assyria comes to an end on the bonfire of Tophet, the symbol of the anti-YHWH liturgy (vv. 30–33). In this way, the paradigm of a theophany addresses questions unanswered in the preceding paradigm of the journey. YHWH's appearance on Mount Sinai (Exodus 19) and his presence in the cloud above the tabernacle during the wandering through the desert (Exod 40:34–38) serve as one theological model for his manifestation of himself on Mount Zion after the people's return to the land.

It is evident that the first paradigm, the return to the land which is also a return to YHWH, forms a prolongation of 27:13 whereas the second paradigm, YHWH's manifestation on Mount Zion, links up with 24:13. Consequently, we should take note of the semantic connections between the three sections of chapter 30 and the ApcIsa.

3.1. *Isaiah 30:1–17*

This section, at least as its core goes, is generally conceived as deriving from the prophet Isaiah himself. Its dramatic development does not appear to ensue from chapters 24–27. The idea of going to Egypt for military help betrays the situation before the exile and it does not fit with the expected judgement of the whole earth. Therefore, points of contact with chapters 1–12 are more compelling, while those with chapters 24–27 remain restricted to some clusters of topics:

- The 'counsel' or 'plan' (v. 1: עצה) of an alliance with Egypt fails to take into account the supremacy of YHWH's 'counsel' (25:1; cf. 29:14, discussed above in section 2.2). In as far as this policy aggravates Israel's 'sin' (v. 1: חטאת; cf. v. 13: עון), it comes under the 'sinfulness of Jacob', whose atonement has been promised in 27:9 (עון / חטאת). When Israel is put to shame in the 'refuge / shelter / shadow (מעוז

/ חסות / צל)' that Egypt cannot offer (30:2–3), he will experience the contrast between 'the fortress (מעוז) of the aliens' (25:2) and the 'stronghold / shelter / shade' (צל / חסות / מעוז) which YHWH prepares for the needy (25:4). Jacob shares this shame (בוש; cf. v. 5) with the celestial bodies at the dawn of YHWH's dominion (24:23) and with the wicked, when the hand of YHWH rises in judgement (26:11).

- Bound up with this is the programme of 'to trust and to be saved' which YHWH has offered to the rebellious Israel but which they have rejected: 'In returning and rest you shall be saved (תושעון), in quietness and trust (בטחה) shall be your strength. But you have refused ...' (30:15; cf. v. 12). This demeanour sharply contrasts with the attitude, which the song of Judah proclaims: 'We have a strong city; he sets up salvation (ישועה) as walls and bulwarks. Open the gates, that the righteous nation, which keeps faith may enter in. Thou dost keep him in perfect peace, whose mind is stayed on thee, because he trusts in thee (בטוח)' (26:1–3; cf. the song in 25:9).

3.2. *Isaiah 30:18–26*

The reversal of the judgement on Israel, which leads to his reconciliation, occurs, of course, only at the end of the ApcIsa (27:3–4, 12–13) because this large composition deals primarily with the victory of YHWH's dominion over all resisting powers. Yet, this reversal is expressed by means of the same terms. With regard to the city that used to be strong, but is now depopulated, it is stated: 'This is a people without discernment. Therefore he who made them will not have compassion (ירחמנו) on them, he that formed them will show them no favour (יחננו)' (27:11). When, however, only a remnant is left once the support of Egypt turned out to be valueless (30:17), the text continues with the same terms as found in 27:11: 'Therefore YHWH waits to be gracious (לחננכם) to you; therefore he exalts himself to show mercy (לרחמכם) to you, for YHWH is a God of justice (משפט)' (30:18). The prophet refers in the motif of YHWH's 'justice, judgement' to what the spokesman of the people in YHWH's city looks forward (26:8–9; cf. 28:6, 17, 26).

The reconciliation takes shape in the new habitation of Zion (30:19) and the land (vv. 23–26), in connection with the guarantee that Israel would go the right way (vv. 20–22). If we compare this loaded text with the short announcement of the gathering and return of the exiles in 27:12–13, then it appears that both passages rely on the paradigm of the exodus, yet this model contains fundamentally different topics in 30:18–

26. Here, moreover, it completes the succinct end of the ApcIsa by its multiplicity. While 27:12–13 is restricted to YHWH's initiative and his being honoured by the returning deportees in Jerusalem, it is explicitly announced in 30:19a: 'Truly, a people shall dwell in Zion, in Jerusalem you shall weep no more' (cf. Ex 15:17).[19] Another element of the exodus story is missing in 27:12–13 but is taken up here, namely that YHWH will hear Israel's cry: 'He will surely be gracious to you at the sound of your cry. When he hears it, he will answer you' (v. 19b; cf. Exod 2:23–25; 3:7).

After the motif that YHWH will provide his people in adversity with bread and water which summarizes the respective miracles in the desert (v. 20a), the instruction of 'your Teacher' concerning the road that Israel has to take, appears as the principal element (vv. 20b–22). The geographical way out of the exile in Egypt and Assyria, depicted in 27:12–13, appears now as a moral way of fidelity to YHWH and renunciation of idols. The word-play of 'your teachers' and 'your Teacher' (v. 20: מוריך in the plural and singular) contains a reference to YHWH's Torah. With that the foundation for a blessed existence on fertile soil has been laid (vv. 23–26). In this way, the instruction in the right way concerns both the journey through the desert and the life in the land.

If we are allowed to interpret the comprehensive text form of the return to the land in 30:18–26 as a supplement to the succinct announcement of this in 27:12–13, some other related texts in chapter 27 become important reference points. In that case, the key question concerning Israel in 27:7: 'Has he (i.e. YHWH) smitten him (i.e. Jacob / Israel) as he (i.e. YHWH) smote those who smote him (i.e. Israel)? Or has he been slain as his slayers were slain?'[20] resounds like an echo in 30:26b: 'when YHWH binds up the injuries (שבר) of his people, and heals the wounds inflicted by his blow (מכתו)'. The cryptic, threefold occurrence of the root 'to smite', נכה *hiph'il*, in 27:7a implies that by inflicting calamity upon Israel YHWH is pursuing another aim than the one he pursues by inflicting calamity on the hostile nations, as becomes evident in God's solicitude for Israel's wounds.[21] In the same way, the parallel term 'to

[19] Beuken, *Isaiah* 2.2, pp. 136, 141–142.

[20] The reading of 1QIsa[a] (LXX) is to be preferred, cf. Henk Leene, 'Isaiah 27:7–9 As a Bridge between Vineyard and City', in Hendrik J. Bosman and Harm van Grol (eds.), *Studies in Isaiah 24–27. The Isaiah Workshop* (OTS 43; Leiden etc., 2000), pp. 199–225, esp. pp. 200–202, 217–219; J. Todd Hibbard, 'Isaiah xxvii 7 and Intertextual Discourse about "Striking" in the Book of Isaiah', *VT* 55 (2005), pp. 461–476.

[21] The term 'injuries' (root שבר, 'to break'), in 30:26 parallel with 'to smite' (נכה), occurs in 27:11 and 30:14 with the same meaning.

slay' (27:1, 7: הרג) at the end of 30:18–26 characterizes the day when these powers taste defeat while Israel enjoys abundant water: 'There will be, on every lofty mountain and every high hill, brooks running with water, on the day of the great slaughter, when the towers fall' (30:25).

With regard to this day, a parallel presents itself between the shame of the 'moon / sun' at the ruin of the powers that are hostile to YHWH's kingship (24:23) and the all-surpassing radiance of these celestial bodies at Israel's restoration (30:26; the word pair לבונה / חמה occurs further only in Cant. 6:10).

3.3. *Isaiah 30:27–33*

The second paradigm of chapter 30, the theophany, exhibits, just as the previous one, not many, yet clear semantic connections with the ApcIsa. Whereas YHWH's action is described as happening soberly there (repeatedly with the term 'to visit', פקד: 24:21–22; 26:21; 27:1, 3), here it happens intensively. Out of the well-known attributes of a theophany only the terms 'indignation' (26:20; 30:27: זעם) and 'fire' (26:11; 29:6; 30:30: אש) occur in both segments.

While ApcIsa avoids stating that YHWH 'comes' (בוא) to his mountain, it does say that he reigns (24:23) and acts (25:6–7, 10; 27:13) there. In 30:27 this want is supplied: 'Behold, the name of YHWH comes from far away'. The remarkable expression 'the name of YHWH' as the subject of the theophany (30:27) builds on the mention of God's name in the ApcIsa, in the song of praise of the nations, which reply to the judgement on the earth (24:15); in the prophet's hymn of thanksgiving as a reaction to the establishment of YHWH's dominion on Mount Zion (25:10); and finally in the plea of the people for God's judgement (26:8, 13; cf. 29:23). The addition 'from far away' can refer to 26:21: 'YHWH is coming forth (יצא) out of his place'.

In the ApcIsa, the returning exiles 'come' to the mountain of YHWH in order to pay him homage (27:13). This is repeated in chapter 30: the addressees, YHWH's restored people, will 'come' to the same place for a holy festival (v. 29). In this way, the *inclusio* formed by the verb 'to come' (בוא) in verse 27a and verse 29b creates a coherent image of movement and place. YHWH comes 'from far away' (v. 27) to an unnamed location from which he removes the nations (v. 28). The addressees go up to 'the mountain of YHWH' and encounter there 'the Rock of Israel' (v. 29). While everything in verse 28 is in motion and the nations have nothing to hold on to, the addressees in verse 29 find firm ground there. The identity of the location in question is only disclosed when the nations are removed and Israel meets its God.

The striking parallelism in verse 29 between 'the mountain (הר) of YHWH' and 'the Rock (צור) of Israel' (further only in 2 Sam 23:3) is an echo of 26:4: 'YHWH is an everlasting rock'.[22] Since from a syntactical perspective verse 30 ('YHWH will cause his majestic voice to be heard') is directly (*wᵉ qāṭal*) linked to verse 27 ('Behold, the name of YHWH comes'), Zion is also the place where YHWH will carry out his judgement against Assyria (vv. 30–33). Nevertheless, the closure of chapter 30 seems to differ from the ApcIsa in one important item, i.e. with regard to 25:6–8. The banquet for 'all peoples / all nations' does not know restrictions, but here their enforced deportation is foreseen: '… to sift the nations with a deceptive sieve, and to place on the jaws of the peoples a bridle that leads them astray' (30:28). Yet, this verse does not hold a repudiation of the universal banquet. It belongs to another topic: the hostile march on Jerusalem (cf. 29:5). The punishment in question forms a contrast with the promise made to the exiles: 'A people will dwell in Zion' (v. 19) since the verb 'to go astray' does not only mean 'to miss the correct path', but also 'to lose the place where one lives' (תעה in this meaning: Gen 20:13; 21:14; Exod 23:4; Isa 35:8; Jer 50:6; Ps 107:4; Prov 21:16). The deportation of the evil nations is part of the delivery of Zion and precedes the universal banquet but is not mentioned in chapter 25.

All these points of contact allow us to read the closure of chapter 30 in *lectio continua* as an elaboration of ApcIsa, more specifically 24:23 en 27:12–13.

4. *The Fifth Woe (Isaiah 31) in the Light of Isaiah 24–27*

Although chapter 31 together with the two passages of chapter 32 (vv. 1–8 and vv. 9–20) makes up a literary composition (cf. the connecting function of the term 'rock' [סלע] in 31:9 and 32:2), it can definitely stand

[22] In the Book of Isaiah and elsewhere, 'rock' stands both for Mount Zion (Isa 17:10; 27:5; 61:3) and for YHWH (Isa 8:14; 26:4; Ps 18:3, 32,47; 31:3; 62:3; 71:3; 94:22; 144:1–2; see Ernst Haag, 'סֶלַע *sælaᶜ*' in G. Johannes Botterweck, Helmer Ringgren, and Heinz-Josef Fabry (eds.), *Theologisches Wörterbuch zum Alten Testament* 5 (Stuttgart etc., 1986) cols. 872–880, here col. 879; Heinz-Josef Fabry, 'צוּר *ṣûr* צֹר *ṣor* I צֹר *ṣor* II', in G. Johannes Botterweck, Helmer Ringgren, and Heinz-Josef Fabry (eds.), *Theologisches Wörterbuch zum Alten Testament* 6 (Stuttgart etc., 1989), cols. 968–983, here 980.

independently.[23] Since chapter 32 derives its contents and place mainly from the over-all redaction of chapters 1–39, we limit our investigation to chapter 31, which seems to belong to the actual collection of the five woe cries (chapters 28–31).

All the same, the fifth woe cry is not as strongly related to the ApcIsa as the preceding woe cries. Chapter 31 is not unique with regard to its core theme, i.e. YHWH's care for Mount Zion, but with regard to the topics used, such as the contrast between Egypt with its horses and 'the Holy One of Israel' (vv. 1–3), and the two comparisons of the growling lion (v. 4) and the hovering birds (v. 5). Therefore the number of semantic connections of this chapter with chapters 24–27 is rather modest. We notice, by way of example, that the divine title 'the Holy One of Israel' frequently occurs in these chapters (29:19, 23 ['Jacob']; 30:11, 12, 15; 31:1; 37:23), and harks back to the programmatic chapter 12 (v. 6), while it is missing in chapters 24–27. Nevertheless, the theme that no earthly power is able to deprive YHWH of his sovereignty over Mount Zion constitutes a sequel to the purport of the ApcIsa: YHWH reigns on his holy mountain (24:23; 25:9–10; 27:12–13). This dominant theme is sustained by a small number of terms which occur in both textual complexes, chapters 24–27 and chapter 31:

- 'YHWH will arise (קום) against the house of evildoers' (31:2) but the earth under judgement and the powers hostile to YHWH 'will not rise again' (24:20; 26:14; 27:9), merely the dead who belong to him will do so (26:19)
- The opposite term, 'to fall' (נפל), characterizes the destiny of God's adversaries (24:18, 20; 26:18–19; 30:13, 15; 31:3, 8)
- 'The hand (יד) of YHWH' is the attribute by which he exerts authority (25:10; 26:11; 31:3)
- Likewise, 'the sword, not of man' which defeats Assyria (31:8) refers back to 'the hard, great and strong sword' by which YHWH annihilates Leviathan (27:1)
- 'Those who go down to Egypt for help and rely on horses, who trust (בטח) in chariots ...' (31:1) are the counterpart of those in Judah who make the appeal: 'Trust in YHWH for ever, for YHWH God is an everlasting rock' (26:3–4; cf. 25:9).

[23] Beuken, *Isaiah* 2.2, pp. 222–228.

This enumeration of parallels between chapter 31 and ApcIsa seems to be exhaustive. As far as chapter 32 is concerned, the themes of protection against heavy weather (v. 2), the abandoned vineyard (v. 12b) and the devastated city (vv. 13b–14) do have parallels in ApcIsa (respectively in 25:4–5 and 24:7, 10–12), yet the way they are related to the acting persons is quite different. 'King / princes' (32:1) and 'women at ease' (32:9) do not occur in chapters 24–27.

5. *Conclusion*

Isaiah 28–31 is connected to Isaiah 24–27 by an extensive web of common expressions. This stems from more than the same prophetic or Isaianic vocabulary, for in Isaiah 28–31 it serves as a dramatic performance, which continues or rather rounds up that of Isaiah 24–27. The latter part of the prophetic book portrays how YHWH's kingship takes dominion over the whole earth; the former part addresses those in Zion who do not agree to that rule. In principle, they fall under the verdict passed on the world in chapters 24–27. These chapters address the nations in their totality; they hardly mention ethnic names (25:10; 27:6, 9) and use the expression 'the children of Israel' for the returning deportees who come to pay YHWH homage (27:12–13). Besides, the names 'Zion' and 'Jerusalem' designate only the seat of YHWH's rule (24:23; 27:13). These proper names, however, denote also another part of reality: the arrogant Ephraim (28:1–4), the reckless rulers of Jerusalem (28:14), the blinded people in Ariel (chapter 29), 'the rebellious children' there (30:1) and 'those who go down to Egypt for help' (31:1). Against this background, Isaiah 28–31 applies the judgement on the earth as it has been announced in Isaiah 24–27 to the concrete situation of Jerusalem. Rulers and people in this city do not hold out against the kingship which YHWH has founded on Mount Zion.

Over the years, research on the Book of Isaiah in the 'Jesaja Werkplaats' has brought me into contact with Professor Arie van der Kooij. His special contribution to our research group was his dedication to the basic task of establishing the Hebrew and Greek texts, which we explored. I dedicate this essay to him in recognition of his communicative expertise and in gratitude for his gentlemanly friendship.

THE GODS MUST DIE: A THEME IN ISAIAH AND BEYOND

Robert P. Gordon

1. *Introduction*

The idea that gods die seems at first to be countercultural in an ancient near eastern context, not least because of well-placed statements that divide the gods and humanity on the very issue of immortality. This is expressed succinctly in the widely quoted lines from the *Epic of Gilgamesh*:

> When the gods created mankind,
> Death for mankind they set aside,
> Life in their own hands retaining. *Gilgamesh* 10.iii:3–5 (ANET, p. 90)

While the popularizing of the 'dying and rising god' theme by Sir James Frazer and others has made the idea of the dying god more familiar, it has little to contribute to the present study. The idea has, in any case, been subjected to periodic attack, and conspicuously in recent times by Jonathan Z. Smith[1] and Mark S. Smith.[2] Mark Smith, for example, seeks to re-describe the Ugaritic Baal Cycle in the light of his premise that gods scarcely ever die. He accepts that there is prima facie evidence for the dying and rising theme in the final two tablets of the Cycle (KTU 1.5–1.6),[3] but he claims that the extant text never recounts Baal's return to life.[4] More significant for his purpose, the corpus of Ugaritic *ritual* texts never mentions the death and rising of Baal.[5] Smith lifts the Baal narrative right out of ritual and argues that it is the royal funerary cult that provides parallels for Baal's death, as in KTU 1.161.[6] Elements from

[1] Jonathan Z. Smith, 'Dying and Rising Gods', *Encyclopedia of Religion*, vol. 4 (ed. Mircea Eliade; New York, 1987), pp. 521–527.
[2] Mark S. Smith, 'The Death of "Dying and Rising Gods" in the Biblical World: An Update, with Special Reference to Baal in the Baal Epic', *SJOT* 12 (1998), pp. 257–313.
[3] M.S. Smith, 'Dying and Rising Gods', p. 264.
[4] M.S. Smith, 'Dying and Rising Gods', p. 289.
[5] M.S. Smith, 'Dying and Rising Gods', pp. 290, 294.
[6] M.S. Smith, 'Dying and Rising Gods', pp. 296, 311.

the discrete worlds of the natural, human, and divine all help account for the existence of the Baal myth, and these include the natural cycle and the royal funerary cult.[7] So if there are one or two cases of 'dying and rising gods' in the ancient Near East, Smith does not recognize Baal as one of them. In West Semitic culture, cosmic divine enemies such as Yamm and Mot, or Tiamat, may die, but gods with active cults seldom do, and Baal's death becomes all the more striking.[8] W. von Soden had previously commented on the absence in Babylonian mythology of the humiliation of a major deity, with the exception of an Assyrian text in which Bel (= Marduk) is subjected to an ordeal and humiliation, but Von Soden concluded that this text is politically motivated and relates to Sennacherib's endeavour to subject Babylon and Marduk to Assur.[9]

More recently, Tryggve N.D. Mettinger has sought to rehabilitate the 'dying and rising gods', claiming that '[t]he world of ancient Near Eastern religions actually knew a number of deities that may be properly described as dying and rising god'.[10] He includes Baal among these, and argues that the *descensus* mytheme may have entered the Baal tradition from the Mesopotamian Dumuzi cults[11] We shall happily bypass the 'dying and rising' issue in this essay, focussing, rather, on texts dealing with the censure and punishment of deities and those who aspire to deity.

The idea of gods, whether formally in council or otherwise, sitting in judgement on erring colleagues is, of course, well attested in Mesopotamian sources. A text from the Mari archive has a prophet reporting a judgement against Tishpak, the tutelary god of Eshnunna, who had fallen into disfavour with members of the pantheon.

---

[7] M.S. Smith, 'Dying and Rising Gods', pp. 308, 311.

[8] M.S. Smith, 'Dying and Rising Gods', p. 296.

[9] Wolfram von Soden, 'Gibt es ein Zeugnis dafür, dass die Babylonier an die Wiederauferstehung Marduks geglaubt haben?', *Zeitschrift für Assyriologie* NF 17 (1955), pp. 130–166 (161). The text in question (KAR 143) comes from Assur and there is a related text from Nineveh (KAR 219), both of which Von Soden sets out in transliteration. Von Soden mentions Tiamat as an exception to the rule that gods do not die, but she is a negative figure and so not regarded as contradicting the basic principle (p. 161).

[10] Tryggve N.D. Mettinger, *The Riddle of Resurrection: "Dying and Rising Gods" in the Ancient Near East* (CBOTS 50; Stockholm, 2001), p. 217.

[11] Mettinger, *The Riddle of Resurrection*, p. 218.

> Dagan spoke to Tishpak as follows: 'From ... you have ruled over the land. Now your day has passed; you will confront your days like Ekallatum' ... Hanat says, 'Do not forget the judgement that you have given.'[12]

This insight into the subtler forms of theomachy in eighteenth century Mesopotamia may reflect some political reality 'on the ground', since the passing of a deity from his position of former authority may indicate a downturn in the fortunes of the city of which he was tutelary deity. Hanat, representing another of the southern Mesopotamian cities in rivalry with Eshnunna, even appears to urge Dagan to make sure that the sentence is followed through. The expression 'your day has passed' may have a parallel in 1 Sam 26:10, where David, urged by Abishai to despatch his enemy Saul, confidently predicts that YHWH would smite him or that 'his day will come and he will die'.[13] Perhaps even more appositely, the same basic expression also comes in Jer 50:31 where YHWH declares to the 'arrogant' city of Babylon, 'your day has come, the time when I will punish you'. Babylon's crime is to have 'defied the Lord, the Holy One of Israel' (v. 29).

More explicit judgements on dissident gods, even involving their elimination, are also found, notwithstanding that one of the differentiae separating gods and humans is the possession or non-possession of immortality. Thus, in *Enuma Elish* the god Kingu, who is Tiamat's consort and her appointee as chief of the gods in her circle (IV:81–82), is arraigned before Ea for inciting Tiamat to rebellion and is adjudged guilty: 'They imposed on him his guilt and severed his blood (vessels). Out of his blood they fashioned mankind' (VI:32–33).

The Myth of Zu recounts a not dissimilar set of circumstances when the bird-god Zu steals the Tablet of Destinies and claims for himself the 'Enlilship', viz. supremacy over the other gods.[14] The gods meet in assembly and Anu challenges 'the gods, his sons': 'Which of the gods shall slay Zu? His name shall be the greatest of all!' (Old Babylonian text; II:9–10).[15] There is hesitation among the gods until one of their

[12] See Jean-Marie Durand, in *Archives épistolaires de Mari* 1.1 (= *Archives royales de Mari* 26; Paris, 1988), pp. 422–423 (text 196 [A.3719], lines 5–10,12–14). Durand (p. 423) tentatively links *ú-ut-ka/ú-ud-ka* with Sumerian *ud*, 'day'.

[13] Jean-Georges Heintz, 'Aux origines d'une expression biblique: *ūmūšu qerbū*, in A.R.M., X/6, 8?', *VT* 21 (1971), pp. 528–540, compares the expression *ūmūšu qerbū* in another Mari text with 1 Sam 26:10; Ezek 21:30; Ps 37:13. The line in the Mari text reads in English translation: 'his days are near; he will not live' (p. 534).

[14] See ANET, pp. 111–113, with additional material on pp. 514–517.

[15] ANET, p. 111.

number, variously identified in the transmission history of the myth, deals with Zu.[16] According to the Assyrian recension, it was while in the service of Enlil, and enjoying the privileged access that went with it, that Zu conceived the idea of arrogating the 'Enlilship' to himself. As an expression of high ambition, Zu's soliloquy has much in common with the first of the biblical texts that we shall discuss below.

> I will take the divine Tablet of Destinies, I,
> And the decrees of all the gods I will rule!
> I will make firm my throne and be the master of the norms,
> I will direct the totality of all the Igigi.
> *Myth of Zu* (Assyrian text) 1.2:12–15 (ANET, pp. 112–113)

2. *Isaianic Texts*

We shall now consider several biblical texts, beginning with three in Isaiah, that exhibit in one way or another the theme 'the god(s) must die'. As we shall see, there is an element of refraction involved in the way that the theme appears in some of the texts—in the sense that humans who aspire to godlikeness come under the same sentence.

2.1. *Isaiah 14:3–23*

In Isa 14:3–23 the downfall of Babylon is celebrated and the archetypal Babylonian monarch is portrayed as an oppressor of nations who sets his sights on the divine mount of Zaphon but finally is brought down to Sheol. The underworld, including the effete spirits of others of earth's rulers already deceased, is depicted as stirring itself to greet the Babylonian monarch's arrival (v. 9). 'Stirring' (*rgz*) is not a welcome experience either for the shades of the dead (see 1 Sam 28:15) or for their tombs,[17] but on this occasion the departed spirits (*rp'ym*) of the world leaders, grotesquely associated with thrones even in the underworld, are happy to be disturbed. It gives them pleasure to know that the Babylonian tyrant

---

[16] In the fuller text published in ANET, pp. 514–517, the account of the battle in which Zu is defeated is still lacking. In this recension it is Ninurta who does battle with Zu, and it may be Ninurta who is credited with his defeat in the line culled from fragmentary descriptions of the battle: 'He routed Zu and cut his throat' (see ANET, p. 517). Such an end for the rebel deity is very much in keeping with the pre-battle instructions delivered to Ninurta: 'Slit his throat, vanquish Zu, Let the winds carry his wings to a secret place …' (Assyrian text; II: 113–114 [ANET, p. 516]).

[17] The word occurs in Phoenician sepulchral texts forbidding the disturbing of tombs.

has become as weak as they are (v. 10). The full force of 'brought down' in verse 11—repeated in verse 15—begins to become evident in the following verse, where the Babylonian king falls down from 'heaven'. So high have been his aspirations that he is given mythological title: 'O Day Star, son of Dawn' (NRSV). He had thought to set up his throne 'above the stars of God', to rule from the 'mount of assembly', from the heights (*yrkty*) of Zaphon, the mount of the gods, and his ambition had been to make himself like Elyon (vv. 13–14). Instead, he has been brought down to the recesses (*yrkty*) of 'the pit' (v. 15). And whereas the departed kings 'lie in state' in Sheol (v. 18), the honour of a decent burial will not be for him (vv. 19–20). While the kings of Babylonia were not considered gods in the way of the divinized kings of, say, Egypt, the arrogance of Babylonian power is hyperbolized in this passage into an attack on the mount of the gods, and the monarch's preoccupation with the heights generates the detailed account of the descent into the underworld. This is expressed most clearly in verses 14–15: '[You said,] I will become like Elyon, but you are brought down to Sheol, to the recesses of the pit.' The language of verses 12–14 strongly suggests that there is some sort of astral myth in the background, though the textual evidence for such is lacking and the verses continue to generate both interest and speculation in good measure.[18]

2.2. *Isaiah 36–37*

The depiction of Sennacherib in Isaiah 36 is also about hubris on the part of a human who challenges the divine order. In his messages to the people of Judah the Assyrian monarch 'blasphemes' YHWH and, for all that his representative claims that Sennacherib was sent by YHWH to punish Judah (36:10//2 Kgs 18:25), the Assyrian speaks as if he is challenging YHWH himself. He presents himself as the one who can bring the Judahites to a land of promise and plenty, using language that elsewhere describes the land to which YHWH had brought his people (36:16–17//2 Kgs 18:31–32). He asks which of the gods of the Levantine states has been able to resist his progress, and he lumps YHWH with them in asking whether 'they' have been able to deliver Samaria from his hand (36:18–20//2 Kgs 18:33–35). As the Chronicler puts it, Sennacherib's officers 'spoke about the God of Jerusalem as they did about the gods

[18] For discussion see John Day, *Yahweh and the Gods and Goddesses of Canaan* (JSOT.S 265; London, 2000), pp. 166–184.

of the other peoples of the world—the work of human hands' (2 Chr 32:19). Thus Hezekiah, in his appeal to the prophet Isaiah, talks of Sennacherib sending his field commander to 'ridicule the living God' (37:4//2 Kgs 19:4). And notwithstanding the Assyrian's claim that he has been commissioned by YHWH to destroy Judah, the mask slips when he warns Hezekiah not to let the god on whom he depends mislead him into thinking that Jerusalem will elude Sennacherib's grasp (37:10//2 Kgs 19:10). Moreover, the Assyrians' contempt for the deities of defeated peoples is seen in their treatment of them. In his prayer, Hezekiah says that 'their gods' were thrown into the fire and destroyed (37:18–19//2 Kgs 19:17–18). The claim is the more significant when it is considered that the Assyrian annals are seldom so explicit about the fate of captured images. The annals of Sargon II mention that, following a revolt by Ashdod, its ruler, together with his gods, his family and his possessions, were declared 'booty', and Sennacherib's annals record that, when the king of Ashkelon did not submit to the Assyrian, he, his gods and all his family were deported to Assyria.[19] Otherwise, the treatment of captured gods does not feature much in the annals. The biblical writers are, then, pitting Sennacherib against YHWH and the gods in such a way that his personal hubris becomes a major feature of the narratives.

The Assyrian ideology of war and conquest, in keeping with a more general tendency in the ancient Near East, would lead us to expect that Sennacherib would assert the supremacy of his own god and attribute his victories to him. Thus, in the report of his third campaign—that is, in the text that includes the account of the siege of Jerusalem—Sennacherib records that he overwhelmed Luli, king of Sidon, with the help of Ashur: 'The awe-inspiring splendour of the "Weapon" of Ashur, my lord, overwhelmed his strong cities Great Sidon, Little Sidon, Bit-Zitti, Zaribtu, Mahalliba, Ushu, Akzib, (and) Akko …' Similarly, when his campaign extended further south and Sennacherib had to go into battle in the plain of Eltekeh, he claims that he did so 'upon a trust(-inspiring) oracle by Ashur, my lord'.[20] On the other hand, there is nothing in the three accounts in Kings, Isaiah, or Chronicles about Ashur or any of the Assyrian deities. Here it is the Assyrian monarch who claims the credit for himself and his predecessors, even when he is deriding the helplessness of the gods of the defeated peoples.

[19] ANET, pp. 286, 287.
[20] See ANET, p. 287.

> Surely you have heard what the kings of Assyria have done to all the countries, destroying them completely.[21] And will *you* be delivered? Did the gods of the nations that were destroyed by my fathers deliver them—Gozan, Haran, Rezeph, and the people of Eden who were in Telassar?
> (37:11–12 // 2 Kgs 19:11–12)

The Chronicler's shorter account of Sennacherib's invasion has a similar slant: 'Do you not know what I and my fathers have done to all the people of the lands? Were the gods of the peoples of [those] lands at all able to deliver their lands out of my hand?' (2 Chr 32:13). We have no way of telling how much the biblical writers knew or cared about Sennacherib's piety, official or otherwise. What is clear is that they leave no room in their accounts for Sennacherib's tutelary god Ashur, as they line up Sennacherib against the gods of the lands to which he aspired. It seems that, in the estimation of the biblical writers, Sennacherib is giving himself the airs of a deity, deriding all other deities, including YHWH, and presenting his victories as evidence of his supremacy over them. The bragging and hyperbolical language attributed to him in Isaiah's prophecy of his downfall leans in this direction.

> With my many chariots
> I have ascended the heights of the mountains,
> the far recesses of Lebanon.
> I have cut down its tallest cedars,
> its choicest pines.
> I have come to its remotest heights,
> the finest of its forests.
> I have dug wells
> and drunk [their] water.
> With the soles of my feet
> I have dried up all the streams of Egypt. (Isa 37:24–25//2 Kgs 19:23–24)

The language and, more particularly, the tone of this passage are evocative of the lament on the king of Babylon in Isaiah 14 where the pines and cedars of Lebanon rejoice because the one who came to cut them down has been laid low (v. 8). Likewise, the claim to have dried up the streams of Egypt encroaches upon activity that is associated with the power of Israel's God (Ezek 30:12; cf. Isa 50:2; 51:10; Jer 51:36; Nah 1:4). There is, therefore, justification for Iain W. Provan's claim that, as far as the biblical writers are concerned, Sennacherib 'thinks of himself as a god'.[22]

---

[21] The reference to the Assyrian kings is picked up in Hezekiah's prayer (Isa 37:18//2 Kgs 19:17).

[22] Iain W. Provan, *1 and 2 Kings* (New International Biblical Commentary: Old Testa-

As a self-appointed deity Sennacherib must fulfil the theme requirements and die, and his death is given due prominence in the biblical text. The prophet Isaiah informs Hezekiah's officials that YHWH will cause Sennacherib to return to his own country where he will have him fall by the sword (37:7//2 Kgs 19:7). The biblical writers are careful to note how, on his return, he was assassinated by two of his own sons while he was worshipping in the temple of his god Nisroch (37:38//2 Kgs 19:37). On the assumption of a 701 dating for Sennacherib's besieging of Jerusalem, he remained king-emperor for another twenty years, but the biblical accounts have telescoped the history in order to bring the prediction and its fulfilment into the closest association.

2.3. *Isaiah 26:13–15*

The theme 'the gods must die' also offers itself as a possible interpretation of Isa 26:13–15, which begins with the confession: 'O Lord our God, other lords besides you have ruled over us' (v. 13). The conventional interpretation is that these are foreign overlords who, when the Judahites defected from their allegiance to YHWH, were able to have political mastery over them. This may be supported by Isa 19:4 where a contrast is drawn between YHWH as 'lord' (*'dwn*) and the 'cruel lord' (*'dwnym*, with plural of rank) whom he would impose upon the Egyptians, though the verse could be pressed in support of either interpretation in 26:13. The attractions of the consensus interpretation of 26:13 are obvious, but there are good reasons for not limiting the 'lords' to human rulers. The description of YHWH as 'our God' may be intended to distinguish him from rival deities and their claims on Judahite allegiance. 'Lords' (*'dwnym*) can refer to human rulers (Isa 19:4 [as above]; Jer 22:18; 34:5), but both as common noun and in the form *adonay* the word is often used for YHWH. Other 'lords' could be gods other than YHWH. The choice of verb for 'rule' is compatible with such an interpretation. The verb *bʿl* is used only here and (possibly) in 1 Chr 4:22 with this sense; otherwise it denotes marrying, which sense indeed has also been suggested for 1 Chr 4:22 (see NRSV). The word would, in a context of rule by non-Yahwistic deities, be suggestive of the god Baal, whose attractions for the Israelites are very evident in the Hebrew Bible—though Baal is not mentioned by name in the Book of Isaiah. Wordplay involving the *bʿl* root would not be unique

ment Series; Peabody, Mass., 1995), p. 262.

in the Hebrew Bible (see Hos 2:18[16]). Again, the several other occurrences of the prepositional phrase 'apart from (you)' (*zwlt*[*k*]), when used in this kind of context, consistently form part of an affirmation that there is no other god apart from YHWH. Finally, the expression 'make mention of your name' connotes allegiance to YHWH as distinct from other possible objects of devotion and worship (Ps 20:8[7]; 45:18[17]; cf. Exod 23:13; Isa 48:1; 62:6). These 'lords', whether human or divine or inclusive of both, are judged. There is no mention of hubris in verse 13, but since the displacement of YHWH comes as the consequence of the rule of the 'other lords' the theme of death is again invoked:

> The dead do not live;
> The departed spirits (*rephaim*) do not rise,
> Because you have punished and destroyed them,
> And wiped out all memory of them. (v. 14)

The section 26:13–15 occurs within the so-called 'Isaiah Apocalypse', and it may therefore be significant that human and divine rulers are clearly associated in another section of the 'Apocalypse'. In 24:21–23 YHWH punishes both the host of heaven and the kings of the earth; they are to be assembled 'like prisoners in a pit' (NRSV) and will be punished after many days (v. 22). The removal of both categories of rulers clears the way for the rule of YHWH on Mount Zion (v. 23).

3. *Non-Isaianic Texts*

3.1. *Psalm 82*

Within the Hebrew Bible, Psalm 82 is the text that most strikingly imposes sentence of death upon non-Israelite gods. In this psalm God simply dispenses with the otiose deities of the Near East. Hereafter not even relegation to angel status remains an option for them.[23] The setting is the 'council of El' (NRSV 'divine council'), where the charge of unjust rule and partiality in judgement is laid (v. 2). God is said to 'take his place' (*nṣb*; cf. NRSV) in the council. Since *nṣb* is not the natural verb to use for someone seated in order to pronounce judgement, it is sometimes inferred that the psalm starts from a position further back than the assumption

[23] See Lowell K. Handy, *Among the Host of Heaven: The Syro-Palestinian Pantheon as Bureaucracy* (Winona Lake, 1994), pp. 153–154, who notes the existence of angelic/messenger figures already in the mythological texts from Ugarit.

that God—by which is meant YHWH in this elohistic psalm—is actually presiding ('God presides', NIV) over the assembly. Rather, he stands forth from among the assembly of gods and acts first as accuser (vv. 2–5) and then as judge (vv. 6–7). It is, in any case, a daring enough hypothetical construct, devised in order formally to serve the gods with their redundancy notices. The requirement of justice administered for the weak and needy is set out (vv. 3–4), but the defendants are themselves in darkness and incapable of delivering justice, and so the basis of social morality has been overthrown: 'all the foundations of the earth are shaken' (v. 5; cf. Ps 11:3). These failing gods are adjudged worthy of death, and formal sentence is pronounced: 'I say, "You are 'gods', children of Elyon, all of you; nevertheless, you shall die like mortals and fall like one of the princes"' (vv. 6–7). Thereafter, the God of Israel is bidden to rise up and 'judge' the earth, doing what the gods of the nations could not do (v. 8). The psalm adopts, therefore, the figure of the divine council in order to disband it, and the gods are subjected to a fate normally experienced by humans.

The older view that the 'gods' in this psalm are human rulers has little to commend it. It rested on the assumption that 'god(s)' in such references as Exod 21:6; 22:7(8), 8(9) denotes human judges or rulers, but, whatever the merits of the explanation for these references, it fits ill in Psalm 82. The description of the addressees in verses 6–7 as 'sons of Elyon' (v. 6) is much more appropriate to deities than to humans, and the pronouncement that they would die 'like humans' (*k'dm*, v. 7) derives its force precisely from their not being human in the first place. Thus does Elhau son of Keret seize on the seeming incongruity of his father's illness and evident mortality when he asks,

> How can it be said, 'A son of El is Keret,
>   An offspring of the Kindly One, and a holy being'?
> Shall, then, a god die,
>   An offspring of the Kindly One not live?
>
> *Legend of King Keret* C i–ii:20–23 (ANET, p. 147)[24]

Moreover, there is no need to assume with Morgenstern that verses 2–4 are secondary, replacing the original indictment against the gods.[25] A

[24] Gerald Cooke, 'The Sons of (the) God(s)', *ZAW* 76 (1964), pp. 22–47, makes the comparison with Keret 'who more nearly approximates a divine figure' and is charged with failure to uphold the cause of the needy (30).

[25] Julius Morgenstern, 'The Mythological Background of Psalm 82', *HUCA* 14 (1939), pp. 29–126 (71 [citing vv. 2–4], 75 citing vv. 2–5ab]).

charge against the gods of failing to maintain justice in the social order is no embarrassment to the majority explanation of the psalm. Part of the contribution of the psalm is its raising of the issue of justice and equity to the upper deck of the gods, as appears also to be the case in Ps 58:2–3(1–2), 12(11).

3.2. *Ezekiel 28*

The theme 'the gods must die' is also present in Ezekiel 28, where, as in a couple of the texts already discussed, kingly hubris is judged. In this chapter, the 'Prince of Tyre' goes so far as to proclaim himself a god; 'I am a god; I sit in the seat of the gods, in the heart of the seas' (v. 2). In the same verse, however, he is declared to be 'a mortal and not a god'. Again there is emphasis on the death of this 'god':

> They shall thrust you down to the pit
> and you shall die a violent death in the heart of the seas.
>
> Will you still say, 'I am a god',
> in the presence of your killer,
> though you are but mortal, and not a god,
> in the hands of those who wound you?
>
> You shall die the death of the uncircumcised
> by the hand of foreigners,
> for I have spoken, says the Lord God. (vv. 8–10)

In the following 'lamentation over the king of Tyre' (vv. 12–19) the god-like nature of the Tyrian king is expressed further. He was in Eden 'the garden of God' (v. 13), and on 'the holy mountain of God' (v. 14), but—in a poem that interleaves ideas of kingship, primal creation and Tyrian trading prowess—his end is to be cast to the ground and turned to ashes (vv. 17–18). This king has, in poetic terms, exceeded even the hubris of his Babylonian colleague in Isaiah 14, in that he imagines that he is actually sitting in the seat of the gods (v. 2; contrast Isa 14:13–14). Mettinger correctly observes that '[t]he fact that the king of Tyre dies is the final proof that he was not a god'.[26] Indeed, it is his arrogation of divine status that ensures that this 'god' too must die.

[26] Tryggve N.D. Mettinger, *The Eden Narrative: A Literary and Religio-historical Study of Genesis* 2–3 (Winona Lake, 2007), p. 93.

3.3. *Genesis 6:1–4*

The judgement of death is also visited upon human aspirations after the wrong sort of godlikeness in the Genesis protohistory. In Gen 6:1–4, the consorting of the 'sons of God' with the 'daughters of men' results in a kind of death sentence. These verses form part of the introduction to the flood narrative that occupies Genesis 6–8. In their present setting they have chapter 5 as background, in which chapter there is a succession of obituary notices on a line of antediluvians broken only by the entry on Enoch, said to be 'no more', because God 'took' him in apparent recognition of his having 'walked with God' (v. 24). Genesis 6, in introducing the 'sons of God', seems to envisage an attempt to circumvent the problem of death and dying of the previous chapter. These 'sons of God' have been variously explained. They have been understood to refer to the 'go(o)dly' line of Seth, born after Abel's murder and Cain's sentence to a life of nomady. In this case, the assumption would naturally follow that 'the daughters of men' are offspring of Cain. This is the view represented by C.S. Lewis in a letter written in January 1952 to his correspondent, Sister Penelope.

> I have, if not thought, yet imagined, a good deal about the other kinds of Men. My own idea was based on the old problem 'Who was Cain's wife?' If we follow Scripture it wd. seem that she must have been no daughter of Adam's. I pictured the True Men descending from Seth, then meeting Cain's not perfectly human descendants (in Genesis vi.1–4, where I agree with you), interbreeding and thus producing the wicked Antediluvians.[27]

Here Lewis, like the older commentators, is working with limited data, in this case being restricted to information internal to Genesis. However, there are other possibilities for which both biblical and extrabiblical support can be adduced. The 'sons of God' have been explained as royal figures, and comparison has been made with King Keret in the already-mentioned Ugaritic text, in which Keret is described as 'son of El'.[28] Comparable language is used in the Hebrew Bible when a Davidic ruler is addressed as a son of YHWH/God (Ps 2:7; cf. 2 Sam 7:14). However, the balance of evidence favours the identification of these 'sons of

[27] Walter Hooper (ed.), *C.S. Lewis: Collected Letters. 3. Narnia, Cambridge and Joy 1950–1963* (London, 2006), p. 157. The crucial words 'descending from Seth, then meeting Cain's not perfectly human' are missing, evidently by *homoioarcton*, in the earlier version in W.H. Lewis (ed.), *Letters of C.S. Lewis* (revised ed.; edited and enlarged by Walter Hooper; San Diego, 1993), p. 417.

[28] *Legend of King Keret* C i–ii: 10, 20 (ANET, p. 147).

God' as divine beings. The term is used in and out of the Hebrew Bible to denote members of the Divine Council (see Job 1:6; 2:1). Whatever the difficulties that such an explanation sets up for a literal interpretation of the section, the claims of 'natural sense' should be paramount. Moreover, the recognition of the 'sons of God' as divine beings may help account for the absence of any mention of the Divine Council in the Genesis flood narrative. The parallels in other respects between the biblical and Mesopotamian flood traditions are clear and various. In the Mesopotamian versions, such a major decision as to destroy humanity by means of a flood is taken in the context of the Council, yet, and despite the other parallels, there is not even a residual hint of the Council in Genesis 6, and it is a reasonable surmise that this may be related to the involvement of the 'sons of God' in the narrative, in which they evidently help bring about the circumstances in which the decision to destroy the earth with a flood was taken.

In the light of the preceding discussion, the imposition of a fixed life-span upon humanity begins to acquire a fuller meaning. In response to the divine-human cohabitation in verses 1–2—which itself constitutes an instance of the 'boundary crossing' that has been observed in the Genesis protohistory (see 3:1–7 and 11:1–9)—God decides to impose a limit on human life-spans: they will not exceed 120 years. The verb form *ydwn* is key to the interpretation of verse 3, at the same time as its translation is less than certain. The derivation from Biblical Hebrew *dyn*, with the sense 'strive' (so AV, RV), may be interpreted in relation to the oncoming flood and the curtailment of the sinful ways that have brought it about: in 120 years the flood will supervene on the human scene. However, the explanation of *ydwn* as cognate with the Akkadian verb *danānu* ('be strong') opens up another possibility that has gained greater currency. The divine spirit will not always 'be strong' in humans: they will not live beyond 120 years, in contrast with the long lives attributed to the antediluvians hitherto. They are, after all, only 'flesh', as verse 3 notes. This is the sense towards which the ancient versions can be seen striving with, for example, 'remain' (LXX) and 'dwell' (Peshitta) for *ydwn*.[29] Such an understanding of the verse fits especially well with the presence of the 'sons of God' in the background. Their involvement with humans opens up the possibility of a superbreed that may be able to avoid the

---

[29] Targum Onqelos is more free: 'this evil generation shall not be established before me forever'. The question whether any of the versions reflect a non-Masoretic reading need not be pursued here.

serial dying that has so far been the experience of humanity but, if this is the thought or intention, verse 3 pronounces a 'life sentence' that is a virtual death sentence upon the idea. The section reflects a tendency in early Genesis towards what John B. Van Seters has aptly described as the 'antiheroic', in that the potential saviours of humanity are deprived of any glory or honourable function.[30] In contrast with Mesopotamian and classical traditions, these 'heroes' are, in the line of causation that is created in 6:1–8, instrumental in bringing the flood upon the earth. The human condition is not enhanced by the mixing of the divine with the human; rather, a life limit is imposed as a judgement on what has taken place. It is phased in gradually, as the subsequent life spans in the Genesis protohistory suggest, but the basic point is established in 6:3 in advance of the flood.

3.4. *Genesis 2–3*

Finally, insofar as Genesis 2–3 describes a human striving after what belongs to God, the 'death' of the aspirants can be read in the light of our theme. When Adam was placed in the garden in Eden he was instructed on pain of death not to eat from the tree of the knowledge of good and evil. The discussion of the precise significance of the expression 'the knowledge of good and evil' has been inconclusive, but some commentary is offered in the serpent's speech in Gen. 3:5: 'For God knows that when you eat of it your eyes will be opened, and you will be like God, knowing good and evil.' What he offers is God-like knowledge, and if his explanation is questioned as an unsafe guide to the general narrative intention, it can be pleaded that it is not in the serpent's interest unnecessarily to pit the woman against God, lest she recoil from taking the forbidden fruit. It is true that, according to verse 6, the woman sees the tree in terms of its physical attractiveness and as a means of acquiring wisdom, but this does not at all exclude the possibility that her true, if unexpressed, desire was to acquire the godlikeness that the serpent held out to her.[31]

---

[30] John B. Van Seters, *In Search of History: Historiography in the Ancient World and the Origins of Biblical History* (New Haven, 1983), pp. 26–27, notes that the whole attitude of early Genesis to culture and civilization is 'antiheroic'. In his *Prologue to History: The Yahwist as Historian in Genesis* (Louisville, 1992), p. 170, Van Seters observes that the idea of a 'heroic' age that was violent and warlike is also represented in Ezek 32:27–28.

[31] Cf. Hugh C. White, *Narration and Discourse in the Book of Genesis* (Cambridge,

What the act of disobedience actually achieved is stated in 3:22, where the Lord God declares that 'the man' has become 'like one of us, knowing good and evil'. The gerundival use of the infinitive in 'to know good and evil' (lit.) expresses the means by which, or circumstances in which, this likeness to deity has come about.[32] Elsewhere, knowledge of this sort is associated with 'the angel of God', as in 2 Sam 14:17 (cf. 19:27). It is reasonable, then, to read the original prohibition in 2:17 in the light of 3:22. 'Godlikeness' in this way was meant to be beyond the reach of humans. Now, it seems, unhindered access to the tree of life meant further encroachment on the divine prerogative, for the humans might eat its fruit and live forever.

Whether the actual sentences on the humans in 3:16–19, 22–24 amount to the instant or imminent death threatened in 2:17 is debated. Instantaneous death would, of course, have meant the end of the human story, since we are not given to understand that Adam and Eve had any children in the Eden garden. The only literal death indicated in the narrative is that of the animals—presumably—whose skins were used to clothe the self-consciously naked humans. Even so; it is the possibility of godlike wisdom, unauthorized and threatening, that gives rise to the mention of death in 2:17, and we may recognize in the story more than a hint of the theme that the aspirant to godlikeness must 'die'.

With their acquisition of the knowledge of good and evil in Genesis 3, the humans have attained to something that was regarded elsewhere in the ancient Near East as a perquisite of the gods. Thus in the story of Adapa, the primal man is endowed with wisdom, but not immortality.

> He perfected him with great intelligence, to give instruction about the ordinance of the earth.
> To him he gave wisdom, he did not give him eternal life.

And again,

> Anu looked at him; he laughed at him:
> 'Come, Adapa, why did you not eat or drink? Hence
> you shall not live! Alas for inferior humanity!' 'Ea my lord

1991), p. 134: 'And, more significantly, the inadmissible desire for god-likeness is carefully concealed behind the more acceptable desire for "wisdom" ... But beneath this is the unspeakable, possible thought: "I desire to be like God".'

[32] See Bruce K. Waltke and M. O'Connor, *An Introduction to Biblical Hebrew Syntax* (Winona Lake, 1990), p. 609.

> told me: “Do not eat, do not dr[i]nk!” ’
> ‘Take him and [retu]rn? him to >his< earth.’ *Adapa* A i:3–4; B:66–70[33]

Gilgamesh 10.iii:3–5, quoted above, agrees that (eternal) life belongs to the gods and not to humans. And so the eleventh tablet of *Gilgamesh*, and probably the epic, concludes with Gilgamesh losing the plant named ‘Man Becomes Young in Old Age’, which was stolen from him by a serpent while he bathed.[34]

In Genesis it is evident that ‘wisdom’ in the sense of ‘knowing good and evil’ is not inherent in the human condition, and comes only with Eve’s eating of the forbidden fruit. In this respect Genesis and Adapa differ. Indeed, Genesis 3 shows the vulnerability of first the woman and then the man to the subtlety of the serpent ‘more crafty than any of the wild animals that the Lord God had made’ (v. 1). That version of Eden, however, that is represented in Ezekiel 28 associates wisdom with the King of Tyre / primal man from the beginning: ‘You were … full of wisdom and perfect in beauty’ (v. 12). This is in partial contrast with the oracle in the earlier part of the same chapter where the wisdom of the Tyrian king is derided: it is he himself who thinks that he is wise as a god (v. 2; ‘Are you wiser than Danel? Is no secret hidden from you?’ v. 3). And although his wisdom and skill have brought him great wealth (vv. 4–5), it is because of this claim to be wise as a god that his nemesis will come (vv. 6–10).

It is debated whether Genesis 2–3 represents immortality as original to the human condition, but subsequently forfeited through an act of disobedience. Clearly, at most it is a contingent immortality that depends for its continuance upon the humans’ acquiescence with the prohibition in 2:17. The expulsion determined in 3:22 appears to assume that the humans can live indefinitely simply by continuing to have access to the tree of life. In the new circumstances, however, the act of taking fruit from the tree of life compounds the original offence. This is perhaps implied phraseologically in the reference to ‘stretching out the hand’, which is more suggestive of a formal, deliberate act than even the taking and eating of 3:6. Any such stretching out of the hand would be an attempt

---

[33] Translation as in Shlomo Izre’el, *Adapa and the South Wind: Language Has the Power of Life and Death* (Mesopotamian Civilizations 10; Winona Lake, 2001), pp. 9–10, 20–21. The conjoining of the themes of wisdom and immortality in Adapa (A:4) and its possible relevance in the interpretation of Genesis 2–3 is very evident, as has most recently been noted by Mettinger, *The Eden Narrative*, pp. 99–122.

[34] ANET, p. 96.

to thwart the fate announced in 3:19, for now it will be the lot of humans to 'return to the dust'. We may even have to suppose that, whereas the humans had availed themselves from time to time of their right of access to the tree of life, now, in their 'wise', godlike condition ('like one of us'), any stretching forth of the hand could be sufficient to bring immortality within their grasp. At any rate, their expulsion from the garden denies them access and therewith immortality.

Arie van der Kooij has greatly illuminated and enlivened the academic study of the Book of Isaiah, and of other parts of the biblical tradition. In making this small contribution to his Festschrift I am most pleased to salute both his achievements and his considerable labours editorially on behalf of the international Old Testament community.

SO-CALLED PO'EL-FORMS IN ISAIAH AND ELSEWHERE

Holger Gzella

1. *Introduction*

The last few years have witnessed a revival of interest in the semantics of the D-stem series—after German *Doppelungsstamm*—in Biblical Hebrew, where it appears as *pi'el*, *pu'al*, and *hitpa'el*, no less than in other Semitic languages. Contributions to the former culminate for the time being in Ernst Jenni's *relecture* of his famous monograph from 1968.[1] Thanks to such extensive work from a descriptive as well as from a more historical-comparative perspective, the finer nuances of the *pi'el* beyond purely lexical meanings and simple translation equivalents are now significantly better known than they used to be half a century ago. Various other phenomena related to it, however, do not normally feature anymore in current contributions to the grammar of Hebrew. Nonetheless, in particular the other, infrequent, derivational categories of the verb somehow connected with the D-stem system still bear many uncertainties regarding their form, function, and history.

For the purpose of this paper, the hitherto mysterious '*po'el*' will serve as a case in point. Although it firmly belongs to the study of Hebrew from medieval times onwards, no comprehensive analysis in the light of recent research has been undertaken for more than six decades. The last attempt, by Henri Fleisch in 1944, has been published one year before the honorand was born—and, to be sure, written before he was conceived. There is thus ample room for a new survey of the available evidence against the background of contemporary Semitic philology. An investigation like the one envisioned here evidently requires methods which in part belong to Arie van der Kooij's

[1] Ernst Jenni, *Das hebräische Pi'el. Syntaktisch-semasiologische Untersuchung einer Verbalform im Alten Testament* (Zürich, 1968). See now the same author's 'Aktionsarten und Stammformen im Althebräischen: Das Pi'el in verbesserter Sicht', *ZAH* 13 (2000), pp. 67–90, reprinted in *idem*, *Studien zur Sprachwelt des Alten Testaments* 2 (Stuttgart, 2005), pp. 77–106.

daily bread; if the results, too, add something to the elucidation of one of his preferred books of the Bible, he may consider the latter as a fitting encore.

2. *The Semitic Background*

Any contribution to the Hebrew *poʿel*-stem sensibly departs from its alleged sister category (or, according to some, even its *alter ego*), that is, the *polel*. Within frameworks geared towards Comparative Semitics, it is often referred to as L-stem, after German *Längungsstamm*. There can be little doubt that, at least from a synchronic point of view, the *polel* serves as the obvious counterpart to the *piʿel* for verbal roots which were at first not capable of further lengthening their middle radical—the distinctive feature of the D-stem and perhaps iconically related to its principal function as a marker of verbal plurality in the most general sense[2]—either because this radical is a long vowel, as with the so-called 'hollow roots' (*mediae infirmae*), or, in the case of the *mediae geminatae*, a long consonant. For verbs belonging to either class, the root is subsequently reanalysed as a triconsonantal pattern and instead of the middle radical, the vowel between the first and the second radical becomes long.[3] This is a fairly natural principle often applied in order to integrate biconsonantal bases[4] into a, synchronically, by and large triconsonantal system. In all likelihood, lexical by-forms of nouns such as לֵבָב next to לֵב, reflecting original */libb-/,[5] follow a similar strategy. If the lengthening of the middle radical iconically reflects the D-stem meaning which consists in verbal plurality, as Bert Kouwenberg and others suggest, the reduplication of the last radical is indeed the most straightforward alternative

[2] See N.J.C. Kouwenberg, *Gemination in the Akkadian Verb* (SSN 23; Assen, 1997) for a revival of the theory of iconicity within Semitics.

[3] Hans Bauer and Pontus Leander, *Historische Grammatik der hebräischen Sprache des Alten Testamentes* (Halle an der Saale, 1922), § 58w. Vowel and consonantal length are structurally equivalent in the phonetics of Semitic languages in general, see Shlomo Izreʾel, 'Segmental Length: A View from Akkadian', in Tali Bar and Eran Cohen (eds.), *Studies in Semitic and General Linguistics in Honor of Gideon Goldenberg* (Münster, 2007), pp. 13–28.

[4] The present writer thinks it is the easiest solution to interpret the 'hollow roots' and the *mediae geminatae* as originally biconsonantal, see Holger Gzella, 'Morgenländische Sprachen und die europäische Grammatiktradition', *Wiener Zeitschrift für die Kunde des Morgenlandes* 95 (2005), pp. 63–85, esp. 67–70, for a somewhat more detailed discussion.

[5] Joshua Fox, *Semitic Noun Patterns* (HSS 52; Winona Lake, Ind., 2003), pp. 215–216.

for cases where lengthening of the middle radical is excluded on phonetic grounds. Unfortunately, the exact way in which both verbal classes adopted this pattern cannot be determined with certainty. The prevailing view seeks the origin of this pattern in the *mediae geminatae*, thereby assuming, and quite reasonably so, that it has spread from them through analogy to the 'hollow roots'.[6]

Since the *Tiefenform* of the 'perfect' of the D-stem underlying both its Hebrew and Aramaic reflexes clearly has to be reconstructed as */qattila/,[7] the vowel melody of the *polel* in the Tiberian pointing can be easily explained with the help of sound changes well known throughout the history of Hebrew: the compensatory lengthening of the */a/ in the first syllable results in */ā/ which then, via the 'Canaanite Sound Shift', becomes /ō/,[8] whereas etymological */i/ in the second one appears as [ẹ] (written with *ṣērē*, which can also indicate a short vowel) when it carries the stress.[9] An alternative approach chiefly associated with Theodor Nöldeke and others, by contrast, derives the /ō/ in the *polel* from an original */aw/ and consequently relates the entire pattern to the *pawlel*-stem of 'hollow roots' in Aramaic,[10] where it is supposed to chronologically precede the use of the normal D-stem (*paʿel*) in analogy with the sound verbs.[11] The problem of the origin of the /ō/ in Hebrew is still unsolved, and perhaps insoluble,[12] but in any case both the 'hollow roots' and the *mediae geminatae* for the D-stem series clearly adopt a different pattern in place of the *piʿel* used for sound roots or verbs III-ī (*ultimae infirmae*) under circumstances on the whole not too difficult to understand.

---

[6] Bauer and Leander, *Historische Grammatik*, § 58w. However, Bernhard Stade, *Lehrbuch der hebräischen Grammatik. Erster Teil: Schriftlehre, Lautlehre, Formenlehre* (Leipzig, 1897), § 155c–d, thought this process took place the other way round, while others posit the workings of reciprocal analogy.

[7] John Huehnergard, 'Historical Phonology and the Hebrew Piel', in Walter R. Bodine (ed.), *Linguistics and Biblical Hebrew* (Winona Lake, Ind., 1992), pp. 209–229.

[8] So, among many others, Stade, *Lehrbuch*, § 155c.

[9] Bauer and Leander, *Historische Grammatik*, § 14d.

[10] See Theodor Nöldeke, review of Hartmann, Pluriliteralbildung, *ZDMG* 30 (1876), pp. 184–188, esp. 184, and especially the discussion in Jacob Barth, 'Die Pôlēl-Conjugation und die Pôlāl-Participien', in George A. Kohut (ed.), *Semitic Studies in Memory of Rev. Dr. Alexander Kohut* (Berlin, 1897), pp. 83–93; Hans Bauer and Pontus Leander, *Grammatik des Biblisch-Aramäischen* (Halle an der Saale, 1927), § 46t. Note that in their earlier *Historische Grammatik*, the same authors explained the /ō/ in Hebrew as a result of compensatory lengthening (< */ā/).

[11] Klaus Beyer, *Die aramäischen Texte vom Toten Meer* 1 (Göttingen, 1984), p. 488.

[12] Joshua Blau, 'Studies in Hebrew Verb Formation', *Hebrew Union College Annual* 42 (1971), pp. 133–158, esp. pp. 147–151.

As to the meaning, the *polel* רוֹמֵם 'he exalted', for instance, thus relates to the *qal* רָם 'he is exalted', or סוֹבֵב to סָבַב respectively, much the same way as the *pi'el* קִדַּשׁ 'he sanctified' relates to the *qal* קָדַשׁ 'he is holy'. Generally speaking, there is no observable semantic or functional difference, although in a number of verbs *mediae geminatae polel* forms coexist with true *pi'els* in analogy with sound verbal roots. Secondarily, both develop distinct nuances (like סבב *pi'el* 'to transform' vis-à-vis *polel* 'to go round')[13] or serve in order to distinguish homonymous roots (such as הלל$_2$ *pi'el* 'to praise' as opposed to הלל$_3$ *polel* 'to make look foolish'). Furthermore, some 'hollow roots' also adopt the *pi'el*-pattern. More often than not, these occur in later texts like Ben Sira, presumably an analogical development reinforced at a subsequent stage of the language by Aramaic influence.[14] It is therefore hardly surprising that the same tendency is carried still further in Rabbinic Hebrew.[15] This might also imply that a number of *pi'els* in the Tiberian pointing in fact conceal original *polels*.[16]

Intriguingly, however, roots which do have a productive *pi'el*, or at least would be expected to have one if there were sufficient evidence, are in a few instances attested in yet another verbal stem carrying the same vowel melody as the *polel*. According to the time-honoured nomenclature of Hebrew morphology, this pattern is often called *po'el*, with a passive counterpart *po'al* and a reflexive *hitpo'el*, but scholars differ as to its actual status within the language system. While numerous shorter grammars, notably those with a practical rather than a scholarly purpose, do not mention this phenomenon at all, most comprehensive descriptions from David Qimchi onwards do acknowledge the *po'el* as a category in its own right. Carl Brockelmann, who had studied the correlations between the individual Semitic languages more thoroughly than most of his predecessors, argued that the *polel* is, from a historical point of view, nothing else than the *po'el* used instead of the *pi'el* for *mediae geminatae* because of phonetic reasons;[17] a similar idea already emerges, though a bit less explicitly, from Heinrich Ewald's discussion of the topic.[18] Despite the identical template, however, Hans Bauer and Pontus Leander as well

---

[13] Bauer and Leander, *Historische Grammatik*, § 58x–y.

[14] Bauer and Leander, *Historische Grammatik*, § 56l.

[15] Moshe H. Segal, *A Grammar of Mishnaic Hebrew* (Oxford, 1927), §§ 191–192.

[16] Perceptively remarked by Blau, 'Studies', p. 147, n. 63.

[17] Carl Brockelmann, *Grundriß der vergleichenden Grammatik der semitischen Sprachen* 1 (Berlin, 1908), p. 513.

[18] Heinrich Ewald, *Ausführliches Lehrbuch der hebräischen Sprache des alten Bundes* (8th ed.; Göttingen, 1870), § 125a.

as Rudolf Meyer postulated a systematic distinction between the *poʿel* and the *polel.*[19] Gotthelf Bergsträsser, who eliminated the major part of the examples under discussion by means of textual criticism, and Klaus Beyer, by contrast, even explicitly denied the existence of an independent *poʿel*-pattern.[20] Since this paper will focus on the meaning of the *poʿel,* the controversial question whether both stems are actually identical or not plays no major role here, although one can at least say that a clear differentiation between both emerged gradually in the history of Hebrew grammar without a satisfactory conclusion being reached so far.

For the matter to be investigated, it is therefore more important to note that seemingly cognate forms of the Hebrew *poʿel* occur abundantly in the form of the Arabic *Zielstamm* (or *Beziehungsstamm*) and the Ethiopic 'influencing stem' (or 'L-stem', 'I 4' etc.). They are absent in the rest of Semitic, with the exception of some possible 'Hebraizing' pseudo-corrections in Aramaic Targums having Babylonian pointing,[21] although the consonantal writing system of most older, epigraphic, languages may of course conceal some relevant facts. Usually, this stem is supposed to have a 'conative' or 'directive' meaning in Arabic, whereas its much rarer pendant in Ethiopic does not exhibit any clearly identifiable semantic or functional profile of its own.[22] For Arabic, however, Henri Fleisch in his extensive study on the topic reclaimed the medieval grammarians' idea of 'participative' as the basic meaning, that is, as indicating an action done in connection with another person.[23] In the comparative part of his work, Fleisch, too, accepts most of the examples customarily subsumed under the idea of a Hebrew *poʿel* and distinguishes them, both formally

---

[19] Bauer and Leander, *Historische Grammatik*, § 38k, who explain the *polel* as resulting from secondary dissimilation of an original *piʿel* and the *poʿel* as an archaism unconnected with the *polel*; Rudolf Meyer, *Hebräische Grammatik* 2 (3rd ed.; Berlin, 1969), § 72.1b and § 79.4a.

[20] Gotthelf Bergsträsser, *Hebräische Grammatik* 2 (Leipzig, 1929), § 20b and d; Klaus Beyer, *Die aramäischen Texte vom Toten Meer* 2 (Göttingen, 2004), p. 69, revising the view expressed earlier in his *Althebräische Grammatik* (Göttingen, 1969), p. 56. For Beyer, as for Nöldeke, the Hebrew *polel* goes back to an original *pawlel.*

[21] Beyer, *Texte* 2, p. 332; *contra* Blau, 'Studies', p. 150.

[22] August Dillmann and Carl Bezold (transl. James A. Crichton), *Ethiopic Grammar* (London, 1903), §78.3; Wolf Leslau, 'Le type verbal qatälä en éthiopien méridional', *Mélanges de l'Université Saint Joseph* 31 / 2 (1954), pp. 15–95.

[23] Henri Fleisch, *Les verbes à allongement vocalique interne en sémitique* (Travaux et Mémoires de d'Institut d'Ethnologie 43; Paris, 1944), with a discussion of the evidence from Hebrew on pp. 6–22. The dissertation by Folkert Boonstra, *Nieuwere theorieën omtrent de verbaalstammen in de klassiek-semietische talen (oorsprong, relaties en funkties)*, Groningen 1982, pp. 137–157, adds nothing of significance.

and functionally, from the *polel*. Morphology speaks in favour of such a connection, since the 'imperfect' of this so-called 'third stem' in Arabic, *yuqātilu*, is obviously similar to Tiberian Hebrew *yqōṭẹl*: the 'Canaanite shift' */ā/>/ō/, the disappearance of the short vowel in the first, open, syllable, and the realization of */i/ as [ẹ] in the last, stressed, syllable once again all correspond to well-established sound laws in Hebrew and allow to derive the one from the other,[24] whereas the Arabic 'perfect' *qātala* as opposed to Hebrew *qōṭẹl* may reflect the original Semitic form whose */a/ between the second and third radical has been replaced by /ẹ/ in analogy with the 'imperfect' (the change */ā/>/ō/ in the first syllable is once more a result of the Canaanite shift) following the ever so common 'paradigmatic levelling'. From a purely morphological perspective, then, there seem to be no major obstacles to relating those Hebrew forms pointed as *poʿel* to the Arabic third stem.[25]

This fact is of course highly relevant for historical-comparative purposes: Semitists of preceding generations like Carl Brockelmann believed that Hebrew preserved some remainders (or 'shared retentions', as one would say nowadays) of what was once a much more common by-form of the D-stem.[26] The latter position was previously also held by Heinrich Zimmern[27] and others, in contradistinction to a yet earlier hypothesis which considered the *Zielstamm*-function primary and thus subsumed to it the *polel* of the 'hollow roots' and the *mediae geminatae*.[28] Accordingly, Brockelmann's classification would group together Arabic and Ethiopic as 'South Semitic', but such a branch is more difficult to accommodate with the current state of research which rather incorporates Arabic, together with Canaanite, Aramaic, and Sabaic, into 'Central Semitic'.[29] There can be no doubt that the theory put forward by these

---

[24] Klaus Beyer, 'Das biblische Hebräisch im Wandel', in Ronen Reichman (ed.), *'Der Odem des Menschen ist eine Leuchte des Herrn.' Aharon Agus zum Gedenken* (Heidelberg, 2006), pp. 159–180.

[25] A comparison along such lines would of course prove more difficult for the *polel*, since both hollow roots and *mediae geminatae* regularly inflect like sounds verbs in the Arabic D-stem, that is, the 'second stem'.

[26] Brockelmann, *Grundriß*, p. 513, and *idem*, *Semitische Sprachwissenschaft* (2nd ed.; Berlin, 1916), § 194.

[27] Heinrich Zimmern, *Vergleichende Grammatik der Semitischen Sprachen. Elemente der Laut- und Formenlehre* (Berlin, 1898), § 36 f.

[28] Martin Hartmann, *Die Pluriliteralbildungen in den semitischen Sprachen* 1 (PhD diss., Leipzig; Halle an der Saale, 1875), pp. 2–3.

[29] See now John Huehnergard, 'Features of Central Semitic', in Agustinus Gianto (ed.), *Biblical and Oriental Essays in Memory of William L. Moran* (Rome, 2005), pp. 155–203.

scholars was a methodical endeavour to integrate an already widespread view into a more rigorous historical framework, since the argument from history had by then long played a decisive role in almost all attempts to determine the function of the very few Hebrew examples. (Later on, Burkhart Kienast broke with this tradition firmly established in Comparative Semitics and subscribed to Bergsträsser's scepticism concerning the existence of a Hebrew L-stem).[30] While Brockelmann was cautious enough to view the specific use of the cognate pattern of this stem in Arabic and Ethiopic as a new semantic development,[31] Hebrew grammarians, at least those who showed themselves aware of the problem, generally explained the meaning of the *poʿel* in line with the Arabic third stem.

An evaluation of past opinions shows how a functional description based on this guiding idea gradually took shape until it was accepted as common knowledge and corroborated by historical considerations. At first, Wilhelm Gesenius in his brief remarks about its origin and function did not yet distinguish between the *poʿel* and the much more frequent *polel* as a by-form to the D-stem, with the effect that he considered the basic meaning of this category as a whole to be especially close to the *piʿel* of the sound verb.[32] But soon afterwards, Heinrich Ewald in his complex discussion of the same phenomenon saw in most alleged examples still a mere variant of the *hiphʿil* or the *piʿel*, but interpreted a few others in accordance with the, according to the traditional view, conative meaning, or 'conjugation of attack', typically associated with the Arabic *qātala* form.[33] The latter aspect has been integrated into Emil Kautzsch's widely-used edition of Gesenius's standard work[34] and is even more prominent in Bernhard Stade's paragraph about remnants of the *Zielstamm* in Hebrew (here the technical term itself has been transferred from Arabic to Hebrew grammar!)[35] as well as in Shlomo Morag's

---

[30] Burkhart Kienast, *Historische Semitische Sprachwissenschaft* (Wiesbaden, 2001), §198.5.

[31] Brockelmann, *Grundriß*, p. 511.

[32] Wilhelm Gesenius, *Ausführliches grammatisch-kritisches Lehrgebäude der hebräischen Sprache* 1 (Leipzig, 1817), §72.

[33] Ewald, *Lehrbuch*, §125a.

[34] Wilhelm Gesenius and Emil Kautzsch, *Hebräische Grammatik* (28th ed.; Leipzig, 1909), §55b–c. Contrary to Gesenius' old *Lehrgebäude*, *polel* and *poʿel* are plainly set apart here.

[35] Stade, *Lehrbuch*, §158. Justus Olshausen's comment that the Tiberian /ō/ in this form goes back to an original /ā/ seems to presuppose a similar connection, although it is not made explicit by the author: *Lehrbuch der hebräischen Sprache* (Braunschweig, 1861), §254.

remarks.[36] Takamitsu Muraoka took the same path in his revision of Paul Joüon's grammar,[37] whereas the original French edition was less specific in this respect and only referred to 'une certaine nuance d'intensité'.[38] Both versions, however, recognize the genuine *poʿel* for sound roots and the *polel* as two different forms. At least indirectly this idea also seems to determine Mayer Lambert's attempt to distinguish for the 'hollow roots' and the *mediae geminatae* between a genuine *piʿel* on the one hand and a *poʿel* or *polel* on the other, with the latter indicating 'l'effort pour exécuter l'acte',[39] as well as Arthur Ungnad's brief mention of a Hebrew *Zielstamm* as if it rested on secure evidence.[40] Of the prominent older grammarians (excluding Friedrich Böttcher, who does not explicitly comment on the possibility of such a parallel),[41] only Eduard König raised a dissenting voice and, while acknowledging the phenomenon of *poʿel* forms for sound roots itself, rejected the parallelism with the third stem in Arabic on morphological no less than on semantic grounds.[42] He thought that the formal identity of *poʿel* and *polel* was unlikely to be due to coincidence, especially since the *polel* could be explained as a natural substitute for the *piʿel* because of phonetic reasons (see above), and that none of the commonly assumed cases required a meaning similar to the Arabic *Zielstamm* or, perhaps better, 'participative stem'. Instead, König operated with by-forms modelled according to the irregular verb. In doing so, he avoided that historical considerations alone dominated the effort to establish a meaning of these forms and could, as in many other studies, override a synchronic functional analysis. One should not underestimate the methodological advance inherent in his argument, as will become clear from an examination of the evidence.

---

[36] Shlomo Morag, 'The Tiberian Tradition of Biblical Hebrew: Homogeneity and Heterogeneity', *The Annual of the Schocken Institute for Jewish Studies* 2 (1969–1974), pp. 105–144, esp. 120–125 (in Hebrew).

[37] Paul Joüon and Takamitsu Muraoka, *A Grammar of Biblical Hebrew* (SubBi 27; Rome, 2006), § 59a.

[38] Paul Joüon, *Grammaire de l'hébreu biblique* (2nd ed.; Rome, 1947), § 59a.

[39] Mayer Lambert, *Traité de grammaire hébraïque* (Paris, 1931), § 1007. According to § 839, Lambert also accepts the *poʿel* for the sound verb for Ps 101:5 and Job 9:15, but does not comment on the meaning. From a passing reference to Arabic *qātala* in note 3, however, a connection with the 'third stem' becomes apparent.

[40] Arthur Ungnad, *Hebräische Grammatik* (2nd ed.; Tübingen, 1926), § 282.5.

[41] Friedrich Böttcher, *Ausführliches Lehrbuch der hebräischen Sprache* 1–2 (Leipzig, 1866–1868), § 1016.

[42] Eduard König, *Historisch-kritisches Lehrgebäude der Hebräischen Sprache* 1 (Leipzig, 1881), § 26.1.

3. *A Review of the Hebrew Examples*

The standard grammars, dictionaries, and commentaries in general subsume a fairly consistent list of examples under the label *poʿel*. Admittedly, many authors voice doubts about individual passages, but the existence of the respective category as such is hardly ever contested. Returning to the sources themselves, however, and leaving out those instances which are exclusively derived from conjecture,[43] a fresh look confirms the impression that König's scepticism might not be entirely out of place. Whereas his objections based on morphology by necessity remain inconclusive, since identical surface forms in languages do derive from different historical ancestors, the argument from semantics proves valid and indeed crucial. Bergsträsser's razor, it is true, eliminated most of the possible examples, and even though not all of them can be explained away as easily as he wants his readers to believe, problems of text and vocalization bear heavily on the correct interpretation. This becomes obvious in two cases which could just as well be analysed as *puʿal*-forms, because they have a second radical which cannot be geminated in Tiberian Hebrew and hence lack the characteristic consonantal lengthening:

(1) זֹרְמוּ מַיִם עָבוֹת

The clouds poured out water (Ps 77:18)

(2) יִהְיוּ (...) כְּמֹץ יְסֹעֵר מִגֹּרֶן

They will be (...) like chaff that swirls from the threshing-floor (Hos 13:3)

In Ps 77:18, זֹרְמוּ could be a *puʿal* without any further modification of the transmitted text. The [o]-vowel would then not go back to an original */ā/, but result from compensatory lengthening of the /u/ which is typical for the *puʿal* (since etymological short */u/ was pronounced like short [o] in Hebrew, its *Dehnstufe* for tonic or compensatory lengthening is naturally /ō/), just as with ברך, another verb II-r.[44] If this is true, the form would have a passive or middle meaning ('the clouds are wrung out

---

[43] Like 1 Sam 18:9 (which is presumably a *qal* participle both in the Ketiv and the Qere) according to Gesenius and Kautzsch, *Hebräische Grammatik*, § 55c; similarly Ewald, *Lehrbuch*, § 125a, and Stade, *Lehrbuch*, § 229. Further, תְּרָצְּחוּ in Ps 62:4 has been proposed by Joüon and Muraoka, *Grammar*, § 59a (not in Joüon's original), but the text is doubtful and the long middle radical would at any rate point to a *piʿel*. See in any case Gesenius and Kautzsch, *Hebräische Grammatik*, § 52q.

[44] Stade, *Lehrbuch*, § 158; Bergsträsser, *Grammatik* 2, § 20b.

of water'), and such constructions are amply attested also with effected or affected objects.[45] Either explanation can thus be accommodated with the context.[46]

Likewise, יְסֹעֵר in Hos 13:3 has been thought to be an erroneous vocalization for the *pu'al* 'imperfect' יְסֹעַר by many commentators (so, too, in the apparatus of the BHS).[47] According to common methodology, a modification of the pointing is the slightest possible change. There is certainly much to say in favour of such an amendment, since the medio-passive nuance clearly appears from the context and the ancient versions, notably the Septuagint (ὥσπερ χνοῦς ἀποφυσώμενος ἀφ' ἅλωνος) and the Vulgate (*sicut pulvis turbine raptus ex area*). On the other hand, it is not evident how the *po'el* of an otherwise transitive verb like סער (or its variant form שׂער II) could be medio-passive in meaning, especially when one follows the mainstream opinion and credits the *po'el* with a passive as well as a reflexive counterpart![48] However, the semantics of both roots in other verbal stems, especially the *pu'al* of סער, where most possible examples actually derive from conjecture, is not known well enough to warrant a final decision. For the same reason, neither example can contribute positively to determining the meaning of the so-called *po'el*, even if it formally belongs to this pattern.

Another passage which often features as evidence for the *po'el* in grammars and older commentaries can now be safely classified as a corruption of the consonantal writing. The Masoretic Text reads:

(3) וְאֶת־הַנְּעָרִים יוֹדַעְתִּי אֶל־מְקוֹם פְּלֹנִי אַלְמוֹנִי

And I have appointed the lads to such and such a place (1 Sam 21:3)

---

[45] Carl Brockelmann, *Hebräische Syntax* (Neukirchen, 1956), § 98a–b.

[46] Compare Godfrey R. Driver, 'Some Hebrew Medical Expressions', *ZAW* 65 (1953), pp. 255–262, esp. 259, *pace* König, *Lehrgebäude*, § 26, who considers the parallelism with an active verb in the following expression an obstacle to this view. Unfortunately, the ancient versions are of little use here, since they all interpret this passage in an entirely different way.

[47] Friedrich Delitzsch, *Die Lese- und Schreibfehler im Alten Testament* (Berlin–Leipzig, 1920), § 75a; Bergsträsser, *Grammatik* 2, § 20b, who also entertains the possibility that this word is a *niph'al*; Hans-Walter Wolff, *Hosea* (BK 14; 4th ed.; Neukirchen–Vluyn, 1990), p. 286. Francis I. Andersen and David N. Freedman, *Hosea* (AncBi 24; New York, 1980), p. 633, want to keep the pointing as *po'el*, but do not say how this squares with the required passive meaning.

[48] *Pace* Andrew A. Macintosh, *A Critical and Exegetical Commentary on the Book of Hosea* (ICC; Edinburgh, 1997), pp. 525–526.

It has already been noted long ago that understanding the verb יוֹדַעְתִּי as a *po'el* of ידע leaves form, meaning, and evidence from the ancient versions unexplained.[49] If someone with such a feel for the language as Samuel Rolles Driver is not quite at ease with the received text and its conventional interpretation, this may be taken to say something about the problem at hand.[50] The discovery of a first-rate textual witness from Qumran (4QSam^b^), however, eventually confirmed that the old conjecture יעדתי, a *qal*-stem form derived from the root יעד, is correct. A *Vorlage* which has יעדתי also explains the reading of Septuagint (διαμεμαρτύρημαι, presumably meant to represent the *hiph'il* of עוד) and Vulgate (*condixi*) satisfactorily. Such excellent support justifies a slight modification of the Masoretes' consonantal text and delivers a *coup de grâce* to its interpretation as a putative *po'el*.[51]

The remaining examples, by contrast, are less easily assigned to another grammatical category. Hence, the derivational pattern underlying the alleged *po'el*-stem, whatever its possible function may be, has to be reckoned with as a morphological entity. It is no doubt significant that they all occur in poetry, since this register allows for more creative means of word formation and a less straightforward relation between form and meaning, as will be seen from the subsequent discussion. Especially in one case, König's theory of a by-form transferred from 'hollow roots' or *mediae geminatae* to another paradigm seems to work very well:

(4) בְּכֹחַ יָדִי עָשִׂיתִי וּבְחָכְמָתִי כִּי נְבֻנוֹתִי
וְאָסִיר גְּבוּלֹת עַמִּים וַעֲתִידֹתֵיהֶם (Q: וַעֲתוּדוֹתֵיהֶם) שׁוֹשֵׂתִי

By the strength of my hand I have done it and by my wisdom, for I have understanding.
And I have removed the boundaries of peoples and plundered their treasures. (Isa 10:13)

Although Stade and others doubt the integrity of the text,[52] שׁוֹשֵׂתִי is accepted as a *po'el* by most grammarians, including even Bergsträsser

[49] Delitzsch, *Schreibfehler*, § 33c, even calls it an 'Unform'!

[50] See his perceptive note in: Samuel R. Driver, *Notes on the Hebrew Text and the Topography of the Books of Samuel* (2nd ed.; Oxford, 1913), p. 173. Bergsträsser has the same reservations, but is much more laconic when he states: 'Textfehler.' (*Grammatik* 2, § 20b).

[51] Frank M. Cross, Donald W. Parry, and Richard J. Saley, '4QSam^b^', in Frank M. Cross *et.al.* (eds.), *Qumran Cave* 4.XII *1–2 Samuel* (DJD 17; Oxford, 2005), p. 235.

[52] Stade, *Lehrbuch*, § 158. See also Delitzsch, *Schreibfehler*, § 60b.

(who, together with Ps 101:5, counts it among the remaining two 'ganz unsicheren Formen'),[53] lexicographers, and commentators until today. Most probably, שׁ in the spelling of the Masoretic Text represents the phoneme /s/ normally written ס,[54] hence the root in question must be the well-attested verb שׁסה 'to plunder'. As the apparatus of the BHK duly notes, many manuscripts do indeed have שׁוסיתי, which might be seen as a secondary correction. Elsewhere, this root is always used in the *qal*. However, no meaning similar to the third stem in Arabic, as the traditional approach to the *poʿel* would require, can be detected. The fact that Arabic appears to lack this root altogether makes such a connection even more difficult to prove. On the other hand, there is hardly any difference in meaning as opposed to similar passages using the *qal*. Hence, it appears to be the easiest solution to view the *poʿel* of שׁסה here simply as a by-form with no specific nuance at all. In theory, this pattern might have been chosen on rhetorical grounds in order to assimilate the form in question to the two preceding verbs נְבֻנוֹתִי and אָסִיר, since they are both derived from 'hollow roots'.[55] Another slightly different, and perhaps somewhat less idiosyncratic, approach would simply identify שׁוֹשֵׂתִי as a hybrid form which combines the consonantal skeleton of the root שׁסה with the vowel melody of the—otherwise unattested—*polel*, that is, the D-stem, of its less frequent variant שׁסס which also means 'to plunder'.[56] If this reasoning is correct, then the *poʿel* here would be a mere device for creating a by-form on the spot. It seems quite feasible that the author of a piece as rhetorically forceful as the oracle against Assyria (Isa 10:5–19), not too preoccupied with the grammatical categories of later generations of interpreters, exploits such a possibility when it is part of the language.

Another passage which also seems to contain two *poʿel* forms of a verb *ultimae infirmae* could conceivably be explained in similar terms: the use of the absolute infinitives הֹרוֹ וְהֹגוֹ 'conceiving and uttering' (Isa 59:13), in effect subsumed under the *poʿel* by various grammarians,[57] has also

[53] Bergsträsser, *Grammatik* 2, § 20b.

[54] Such confusions occur quite often in various forms of Hebrew and Aramaic, see Beyer, *Texte* 1, p. 421, and Vol. 2, p. 320.

[55] See Gesenius, *Lehrgebäude* 1, p. 374, n. r, for supposedly comparable phenomena.

[56] Ewald, *Lehrbuch*, § 125a, comes close to such a view when he explicitly relates the *mediae geminatae* שׁסס to the *ultimae infirmae* שׁסה / שׁשׂה. Franz Delitzsch, *Das Buch Jesaja* (3rd ed.; Leipzig, 1879), p. 156, explicitly mentions the idea of a conflated form along these lines, but restricts it to the writing alone and classifies the verb as a genuine *poʿel*.

[57] So, for example, Olshausen, *Lehrbuch*, § 254; Delitzsch, *Jesaja*, p. 604.

been attributed to consonance.[58] However, the textual difficulties are such as to render this example unsuitable for wider-ranging interpretations. Not only has the Masoretic vocalization been doubted,[59] but one of the best witnesses, the great Isaiah Scroll from Qumran, omits הֹרוֹ altogether (the text of the passage in 1QIsa[a] reads והגוא מלב דברי שקר) and thereby makes it feasible that the word has entered the textual tradition due to dittography.[60] Despite its support from the Septuagint, the Vulgate, and the Syriac, the reading of the Masoretic Text on its own thus cannot carry the weight required for supporting the hypothesis just mentioned.

All remaining serious instances seem to further corroborate the idea that the *poʿel*-pattern was a largely unproductive device for creating by-forms, perhaps even on the spot, which could eventually acquire special meanings in a given context. It may therefore not be a coincidence that two of them concern nominal derivations otherwise attested in different stems only:

(5) אַף בַּל־שֹׁרֵשׁ בָּאָרֶץ גִּזְעָם וְגַם־נָשַׁף בָּהֶם

scarcely has their stem taken root in the earth when [the wind] blows over them (Isa 40:24)

(6) מְלוֹשְׁנִי (Q: מְלָשְׁנִי) בַסֵּתֶר רֵעֵהוּ אוֹתוֹ אַצְמִית

one who secretly slanders his neighbour, him I will destroy (Ps 101:5)

Admittedly, Bergsträsser considered שֹׁרֵשׁ in Isa 40:24 to be simply a *qal* participle.[61] This could theoretically be the case, but since comparative evidence suggests that the noun (*/šurš-/) is primary and not the verbal root, one would, generally speaking, not expect the latter to occur in the otherwise unattested *qal*, but in the *piʿel* (to which the present form has been corrected by some scholars)[62] or in the *hiphʿil*. Both are indeed attested elsewhere in the Hebrew Bible. Hence, it seems fair to assume that the verb שרשׁ is a denominal root and that the vowel melody [o]-[e] therefore points to a *poʿel*-pattern comparable to שׁוֹשֵׂתִי in Isa 10:13. The incontestable meaning 'to grow roots' here, as opposed to the one of the *piʿel*, which in all surviving instances expresses the exact opposite, namely 'to eradicate', requires some comment. Again, it is not obviously related

---

[58] Wilhelm Gesenius, *Philologisch-kritischer und historischer Commentar über den Jesaia* 2 (Leipzig, 1821), p. 235.

[59] Delitzsch, *Schreibfehler*, § 23 and 145.

[60] See Donald W. Parry and Elisha Qimron, *The Great Isaiah Scroll (1QIsa[a]). A New Edition* (StTDJ 32; Leiden, 1999), p. 97.

[61] Bergsträsser, *Grammatik* 2, § 20b.

[62] See, for example, Delitzsch, *Schreibfehler*, § 75a.

to the semantic spectrum of the third stem in Arabic,[63] especially since Arabic would use the second stem (that is, the counterpart of the Hebrew *piʿel*) both for 'to grow roots' and 'to eradicate'.[64] For the same reason, the specific difference in meaning in this verse would not be a constitutive feature of the *poʿel* vis-à-vis the *piʿel*; instead, it would be a mere corollary of the fact that a by-form is generated ad hoc on the basis of a variant pattern. In short, then, the most plausible solution is that with שֹׁרֵשׁ a new word is used or perhaps even coined precisely in order to distinguish 'to take roots' from the more usual 'to uproot' of the *piʿel* in the given context.[65] Nonetheless, the meaning expressed here does not depend in any direct way on the derivational category applied. Interestingly, even Brockelmann, although he does acknowledge the *poʿel* as the Hebrew equal to the Arabic third stem, treats שֹׁרֵשׁ as a 'secondary denominative' whose formal similarity to the *poʿel* is exclusively due to coincidence.[66] An explanation along these lines evidently requires the least amount of special pleading and thus deserves preference. With שֹׁרָשׁוּ 'they are rooted' in Jer 12:2, the same verb also provides the only alleged example of the passive counterpart of the *poʿel*, that is, the *poʿal*.[67] But since שֹׁרָשׁוּ could equally well be a pausal form of the *puʿal* (compare יְשֹׁרָשׁוּ in Job 31:8, although here meaning 'let it be rooted out'),[68] the passive equivalent of the expected verbal stem, there is no sufficient unambiguous evidence for positing a *poʿal* at all.

On the basis of similar reasoning, מְלָשְׁנִי (Qere) or מְלוֹשְׁנִי (Ketiv) 'someone who slanders me' in Ps 101:5 must be a derived form, too, since the

---

63 It seems unclear whether Ewald, *Lehrbuch*, § 125a, thinks that there is such a connection when he remarks: 'mehr mit absicht'. A nuance of intentionality according to Ewald's suggestion would of course be impossible to pinpoint. So John Goldingay and David Payne, *A Critical and Exegetical Commentary on Isaiah 40–55* 1 (ICC; London–New York, 2006), p. 122, are rightly sceptical about the alleged notion of aggressiveness or effort.

64 Hans Wehr, *Arabisches Wörterbuch für die Schriftsprache der Gegenwart* (5th ed.; Wiesbaden, 1985), s.v. *šrš* (p. 645). Theodor Nöldeke, *Neue Beiträge zur semitischen Sprachwissenschaft* (Straßburg, 1910), p. 101, explains this phenomenon by means of the time-honoured theory of 'Gegensinn' and consequently corrects the Tiberian שֹׁרֵשׁ in Isa 40:24 to a *puʿal* form. This change is unnecessary, since the semantic range of the D-stem of this verb in Arabic does not have to be identical with its Hebrew cognate in every respect.

65 Tentatively also suggested by Goldingay and Payne, *Isaiah 40–55* 1, p. 122.

66 Brockelmann, *Grundriß*, p. 513. Actually, Brockelmann refers to Jer 12:2, but this does not affect the point he makes.

67 Olshausen, *Lehrbuch*, § 254; König, *Lehrgebäude*, p. 201; Bauer and Leander, *Historische Grammatik*, § 38e; Meyer, *Hebräische Grammatik* 2, § 72.1b.

68 Bergsträsser, *Grammatik* 2, § 20b.

underlying noun, */lišān/ 'tongue', can also be reconstructed as primary.[69] For Bergsträsser it is, together with שׁוֹשֵׂתִי in Isa 10:13 (see above), one of the two doubtful cases which even he does not interpret otherwise.[70] It should furthermore be noted that the Babylonian pointing confirms the characteristic [o]-sound in the first syllable.[71] Lastly, the variation between Qere and Ketiv comes down to one between an open [å] as opposed to a closed [ọ] there, regardless of the quantity. Although the motivation for this divergence remains inexplicable at the moment,[72] the presence of the [o]-sound so well attested by various traditions virtually excludes the possibility of assigning the form in question to another stem. All evidence thus points to an underlying participle belonging to the *poʿel*-pattern and bearing the literal meaning 'someone who does something with his tongue'. Clearly, such a meaning does not have to be connected with the *Zielstamm* semantics as established for Arabic, since אַל־תַּלְשֵׁן in Prov 30:10 attests the identical nuance 'to slander' for the *hiphʿil*, and together with the *piʿel*, the *hiphʿil* would be a more natural choice for a denominal verb. Here, too, the available evidence suggests that the *poʿel* is employed for an ad hoc derivation without any sharply identifiable semantic implications.

Also the last member of the almost 'canonical' list of forms commonly believed in the Hebrew grammatical tradition to represent a *poʿel*-stem can best be explained as a secondary derivation. This time, however, it is based on a common verbal root instead of a nominal one:

(7) לִמְשֹׁפְטִי אֶתְחַנָּן

to my accuser (or: *my judge?*) *I must appeal for mercy* (Job 9:15b)

Because of the palpable difficulty caused by the word מְשֹׁפְטִי, many commentators correct the text to לְמִשְׁפָּטִי 'to my right' or לְמִשְׁפָּטוֹ 'to his right'.[73] This reading, it is true, would exactly corresponding to τοῦ κρίματος αὐτοῦ δεηθήσομαι in the Greek (contrary to Jerome's *meum iudicem deprecabor*). Since, however, מִשְׁפָּט is never used metonymically for a person, the context militates against such a conjecture, apart from the fact that it is not strictly necessary anyway.[74] Consequently, this form, too,

[69] Fox, *Noun Patterns*, p. 85.

[70] Bergsträsser, *Grammatik* 2, § 20b.

[71] See the passage in the manuscript printed by Paul Kahle, *Der masoretische Text des Alten Testaments. Nach der Überlieferung der babylonischen Juden* (Leipzig, 1902), p. 97.

[72] Despite the heroic effort by König, *Lehrgebäude* 1, § 26.

[73] See, for example, Delitzsch, *Schreibfehler*, § 74 (p. 71).

[74] So rightly Friedrich Horst, *Hiob 1–19* (BK 16 / 1; 5th ed.; Neukirchen–Vluyn, 1992),

has been adduced as decisive evidence for the existence of a *poʿel*-stem. Many years ago, Rudolf Meyer even made an attempt to relate מְשֹׁפְטִי as an analogous formation to the ancient present tense conjugation surviving in Hebrew,[75] but the historical foundations of his theory have been disproved several times and cannot be upheld anymore.[76] The supposed parallels from Qumran Hebrew, to which Meyer refers, rather have to be explained as non-standard variant forms of the normal 'imperfect' with an anaptyctic short vowel[77] and are thus completely unconnected to מְשֹׁפְטִי in Job 9:15b.

While the Masoretic vocalization therefore must be taken seriously, a semantic relationship with Arabic *qātala* remains just as opaque as for the other examples: nothing whatsoever in the text points to any notion of conation or reciprocity.[78] All one can say is that the underlying pattern creates a derivational by-form of an otherwise well-attested root. The reason might be that a different nuance than the straightforward *qal* participle שֹׁפֵט 'judge' was required. Hence, the translation 'accuser' might not miss the mark entirely,[79] although the exact connotations cannot be determined with certainty and, perhaps, never will be. Speculating about possible reasons, one could perhaps imagine that the presence of a verb *mediae geminatae*, the predicate חנן, which is also attested in the *polel* (Prov 14:21; Ps 102:15), prompted the use of a derivational pattern closely associated with the *polel*, much the same way another unexpected *poʿel* in Isa 10:13 (see above) occurs next to 'hollow roots' whose D-stem

p. 140; see also Samuel R. Driver and George B. Gray, *A Critical and Exegetical Commentary on the Book of Job* (ICC; Edinburgh, 1921), p. 57.

[75] Rudolf Meyer, 'Spuren eines westsemitischen Präsens-Futur in den Texten von Chirbet Qumran', in Johannes Hempel and Leonhard Rost (eds.), *Von Ugarit nach Qumran* (Berlin, 1958), pp. 118–128, reprinted in Rudolf Meyer, *Beiträge zur Geschichte von Text und Sprache des Alten Testaments* (BZAW 209; Berlin, 1993), pp. 93–103.

[76] See Holger Gzella, 'Unusual Verbal Forms in the Book of Proverbs and Semantic Disambiguation', in Martin F.J. Baasten and Reinier Munk (eds.), *Studies in Hebrew Language and Jewish Culture* (Dordrecht, 2007), pp. 151–168, esp. 153–154.

[77] Elisha Qimron, *The Hebrew of the Dead Sea Scrolls* (HSS 29; Atlanta, 1986), § 311.13g; G. Wilhelm Nebe, 'Zu Stand und Aufgaben der philologischen Arbeit an den hebräischen Handschriften vom Toten Meer', in Armenuhi Drost-Abgarjan and Jürgen Tubach (eds.), *Sprache, Mythen, Mythizismen. Festschrift für Walter Beltz zum 65. Geburtstag am 25. April 2000* (Hallesche Beiträge zur Orientwissenschaft 32, Institut für Orientalistik; Halle an der Saale, 2004), pp. 519–582, esp. 563–564.

[78] *Pace* Marvin H. Pope, *Job* (AncB 15; 2nd ed.; New York, 1973), p. 72.

[79] So, too, Franz Delitzsch, *Das Buch Iob* (2nd ed.; Leipzig, 1876), p. 129: 'Verkläger und Richter in Einer Person', although he derives this interpretation, unnecessarily, from an alleged *poʿel*-meaning 'richterlich bekämpfen' of שפט.

would also be a *polel*. But until such assimilatory phenomena underlying the choice of particular verbal stems are better researched, no sweeping conclusions should be drawn from observations like these.

4. *Conclusion: Po‘el-Forms and Isaian Poetics*

A survey of the evidence thus indicates that there is no reason to postulate a productive *po‘el*-pattern with a distinctive meaning in harmony with the Arabic third stem. Potential examples are extremely few, affected by textual difficulties, confined to poetic compositions, and in no case indicative of the 'participative' or 'conative' nuance characteristic for the respective pattern in Arabic. This applies even more to the supposed passive and reflexive variants: there is but one, problematic, instance of a passive *po‘al* (Jer 12:2), and since the two possible *hitpo‘el* forms in Jeremiah (25:16; 46:8),[80] if the vocalization is to be trusted,[81] are both derived from the same root, that is, געשׁ 'to waver' (or, with Godfrey R. Driver, 'to retch'),[82] they hardly point to a full-fledged pattern either; instead, they seem to be similarly instantaneous creations triggered by poetic licence.[83] Presumably, then, the so-called *po‘el* was nothing more than a readily available by-form to more regular derivational patterns and could be employed in order to create new words on the spot, either for a slightly different nuance or for a certain poetic or rhetorical effect. Arabic poetic license has often led to comparable results.[84] Morphologically, the *po‘el* corresponds to the D-stem series for 'hollow roots' or *mediae geminatae* and may have been extended from there by means of analogy to sound roots as well as to the verbs *ultimae infirmae* or III-ī (a process which can still be observed in Rabbinic Hebrew).[85] The idea of a Hebrew *Zielstamm* must therefore be abandoned, and this is all the present paper argues. It would be interesting to see in a subsequent step how much the

[80] Gesenius and Kautzsch, *Hebräische Grammatik*, § 55b; Bauer and Leander, *Historische Grammatik*, § 38t.

[81] Bergsträsser, *Grammatik* 2, § 20b, corrects them to *hitpa‘el* forms which are indeed better attested for this root.

[82] Godfrey R. Driver, 'Hebrew Roots and Words', *Welt des Orients* 1 (1947–1952), pp. 406–415, esp. 406.

[83] Another form, מְנֹאָץ in Isa 52:5, is highly controversial and perhaps corrupt, see Bauer and Leander, *Historische Grammatik*, § 15g, and Meyer, *Hebräische Grammatik* 2, § 72.1b, for some diverging opinions.

[84] Fox, *Noun Patterns*, pp. 102–105.

[85] Segal, *Grammar*, § 141.

idea of ad hoc by-forms can contribute to the understanding of pairs in other verbal stems, such as possible semantic overlaps between the *piʿel* and the *hiphʿil* for some verbs without any obvious difference in meaning.

The fact that two of the four possible instances occur in the Book of Isaiah may be particularly relevant in this context. Commentators have long drawn attention to the extent to which this book exploits the rhetorical possibilities of the Hebrew language through its various strata. Whatever its explanation in terms of specific social institutions (such as the older concept of a 'school' of Isaiah) may be, the surprising continuity of similar rhetorical means points to a remarkably consistent 'Isaian literary tradition'.[86] Existing work, however, focuses on syntax and style[87] or, more recently, on word play and sound patterning.[88] While it has been duly observed that a characteristic feature of this tradition is the 'coining of new words, whose meaning is transparent because based on familiar roots',[89] especially the morphological side of the same technique badly needs a systematic investigation. The use of *poʿel*-forms in Isaiah can therefore be seen as a contribution to a still largely unknown aspect of Isaian style no less than to Hebrew grammar.

These results immediately bear on issues of historical linguistics, too. First of all, they highlight the limits of comparative considerations when it comes to determining the finer shades of meaning within a specific language. Moreover, they dispel the idea so prominent in the previous discussion that the Hebrew forms reviewed here are remnants of a once productive pattern which is still fully functioning in Arabic and Ethiopic. As the *qātala* stem defies straightforward reconstruction, the most obvious modification of this view would be to classify it as a characteristic feature of 'South Semitic'.[90] But since the concept of a 'South Semitic' branch within the genealogical model finds much less sympathy among scholars nowadays than it used to do, this option has problems of its own. The differences in function and degree of productivity between Arabic

---

86 Cf. Joseph Blenkinsopp, *Isaiah 1–39* (AncB 19; New York, 2000), p. 80.

87 So in the early study by Ludwig Koehler, *Deuterojesaja (Jesaja 40–55) stilkritisch untersucht* (BZAW 37; Gießen, 1923), pp. 56–78 (the chapter title 'Grammatikalisches' is slightly misleading).

88 See especially Hugh G.M. Williamson, 'Sound, Sense and Language in Isaiah 24–27', *JJS* 46 (1995), pp. 1–9, and Klaus Seybold, *Die Sprache der Propheten. Studien zur Literaturgeschichte der Prophetie* (Zürich, 1999), pp. 200–210. On wordplays cf. also Koehler, *Deuterojesaja*, p. 101, and Blenkinsopp, *Isaiah*, pp. 80–81.

89 Williamson, 'Sound', p. 1.

90 Sabatino Moscati (ed.), *An Introduction to the Comparative Grammar of the Semitic Languages. Phonology and Morphology* (PLO 6; 3rd ed.; Wiesbaden, 1980), § 16.7.

and Ethiopic in this respect, as pointed out by Fleisch, do certainly not increase the plausibility of such an opinion. Therefore it seems wiser to assume that the *qātala* or *poʿel* form was a derivational pattern available in various Semitic languages, be it as a variant of the D-stem for certain classes of verbs or as something else, but without any sharply defined meaning. In some of the individual languages, it had been transferred with varying degrees of productivity and markedness to sound roots. This last process would be easiest to account for the evidence as it results from synchronic functional description. *Mutatis mutandis*, the same presumably applies to the other rare verbal stems as well, since they pose similar problems for historical reconstruction.

A WINDOW ON THE ISAIAH TRADITION IN THE ASSYRIAN PERIOD: ISAIAH 10:24–27

Matthijs J. de Jong

1. *Introduction*

Interpreting the prophetic books is a hazardous affair. This certainly holds true for the Book of Isaiah. Although no one would deny that the Book of Isaiah originated over the course of several centuries, it is extremely difficult especially within Isaiah 1–39 convincingly to distinguish between the different textual layers. At the same time however it is impossible to come to a full understanding of the book and its meaning without exploring the history of its development. Therefore, a reconstruction of the origins of the Isaiah tradition, its earliest developments and its gradual growth into the book, must remain part of the exegetical agenda.

The way this has been done in the past, however, is open to question. Diachronic reconstructions of the Isaiah tradition too often have been based on a preconceived image of the historical prophet—his life, words, deeds, views, and vocabulary. Those parts of chapters 1–39 that tallied with a preconception of the historical prophet and his words were then labelled 'Isaianic'. Such preconceptions of the historical prophet however are not based on fact but the product of traditional views on the biblical prophets and the prophetic books. This circular reasoning has been shown to be a house of cards and should be abandoned altogether.[1] The objective has been formulated thus: '(t)he current situation demands the adoption of a whole new agenda'.[2]

---

[1] See in particular Uwe Becker, 'Die Wiederentdeckung des Prophetenbuches. Tendenzen und Aufgaben der gegenwärtigen Prophetenforschung', *BTZ* 21 (2004), pp. 30–60; idem, *Jesaja. Von der Botschaft zum Buch* (FRLANT 178; Göttingen, 1997); Terence Collins, *The Mantle of Elijah. The Redaction Criticism of the Prophetical Books* (The Biblical Seminar 20; Sheffield, 1993); Matthijs J. de Jong, *Isaiah among the Ancient Near Eastern Prophets. A Comparative Study of the Earliest Stages of the Isaiah Tradition and the Neo-Assyrian Prophecies* (VT.S 117; Leiden, 2007), pp. 5–24, 36–38.

[2] Hugh G.M. Williamson, 'In Search of the Pre-exilic Isaiah', in John Day (ed.), *In*

A different approach would be to search for historical points of contact within the Book of Isaiah with the different periods of Judah's history. By this procedure, various parts of the book could be anchored in history, and different profiles of the Isaiah tradition during its course of development could be drafted. A much more historical approach is preferable to the traditional theological method. This involves searching for connections between the various profiles within the Book of Isaiah and respective episodes of Judah's history and providing reasoned explanations for the development of the Isaiah tradition through its successive stages until the final version evolved. Within this new approach, the image of the historical prophet—his words, deeds and views—is the outcome of the exegetical analysis rather than its starting-point. Furthermore, instead of deciding whether isolated passages are 'Isaianic' or not, each passage is to be connected with a particular profile or layer based on a coherent and comprehensive view of the development of the Isaiah tradition as a whole.[3]

It is my contention that within Isaiah 1–39 three different layers can be discerned that represent three different stages of the Isaiah tradition prior to the basic literary layer of Deutero-Isaiah. Whereas the latter may be dated in the late Babylonian or early Persian period,[4] the three preceding stages are to be connected with the eighth, the seventh, and the sixth century BCE respectively. The earliest of them consists of prophetic material that can be related to the circumstances of the late eighth century, circa 735–700 BCE. This material can be connected with three episodes in particular: (i) the Syro-Ephraimitic crisis and the campaigns of Tiglath-pileser to Philistia, Palestine and Syria in 734–732 BCE; (ii) Sargon's campaign against the West in 720 BCE; (iii) the controversy as to whether or not to rebel against Assyria, which reached a climax in 705–701 and resulted in the campaign of Sennacherib in 701 BCE.[5] The second layer consists of passages dealing with Assyria's destruction and

Search of Pre-exilic Israel. Proceedings of the Oxford Old Testament Seminar (JSOT.S 406; London, 2004), p. 183. For a similar view, see Odil H. Steck, *Die Prophetenbücher und ihr theologisches Zeugnis. Wege der Nachfrage und Fährten zur Antwort* (Tübingen, 1996), pp. 69–70.

[3] For an elaboration of this approach with regard to First Isaiah, see De Jong, *Isaiah among the Ancient Near Eastern Prophets*, pp. 38–170.

[4] See on this Reinhard G. Kratz, *Kyros im Deuterojesaja-Buch. Redaktionsgeschichtliche Untersuchungen zu Entstehung und Theologie von Jes 40–55* (FAT 1; Tübingen, 1991).

[5] For an overview of this prophetic material and a discussion of the texts within their historical setting, see De Jong, *Isaiah among the Ancient Near Eastern Prophets*, pp. 161 and 191–249.

Judah's restoration; these texts in all likelihood stem from the late seventh century BCE. They represent a seventh-century revision of the Isaiah tradition, elucidated by the decline of the Assyrian empire.[6] Finally, the third layer reflects the disastrous events of the early sixth century: the fall of Jerusalem, the end of the monarchy and the political state, and the exile of part of the population. The exilic reworking, characterised by the view that the disasters that befell Judah are to be seen as Yahweh's punishment of the people's disobedience, has been of a decisive influence on the character of First Isaiah and the image of the prophet as being a prophet of judgement.[7]

The Isaiah tradition in the Assyrian period consisted of two main stages. The first consists of the prophetic material relating to the circumstances of the eighth century BCE, the second is a literary revision of this prophetic material, to be dated to the late seventh century BCE and to be connected with the decline of Assyrian power. This article aims to open a window on these two stages of the Isaiah tradition in the Assyrian period by focussing on Isa 10:24–27.

2. *Discussion of Isaiah 10:24–27*

The new approach to the Book of Isaiah means that the traditional assessment of the individual passages is to be reconsidered. Isa 10:24–27 may serve as an illustration of this. With regard to this passage, scholars in the past have come to the agreement that it is 'certainly late'.[8] This prophecy, it is held, cannot stem from the mouth of the prophet Isaiah, but contains features typical of the post-exilic period.[9] Some commentators have gone as far in time as to connect this passage with the Maccabean era and read it as a pseudo-prophecy supporting the Jews in their fight against the Seleucid rulers.[10] In any case, most commentators agree that Isa 10:24–27

[6] For the seventh-century revision of the Isaiah tradition, see De Jong, *Isaiah among the Ancient Near Eastern Prophets*, pp. 357–394.

[7] For the exilic reworking of the Isaiah tradition, see De Jong, *Isaiah among the Ancient Near Eastern Prophets*, pp. 54–57, 80–89, 158–160, 327–333, 393–394.

[8] Eckart Otto, 'צִיּוֹן', in G. Johannes Botterweck, Helmer Ringgren, Heinz-Josef Fabry (eds.), *Theologisches Wörterbuch zum Alten Testament* 6 (Stuttgart, 1988), col. 1012: 'Unumstritten nachjesajanisch sind die von der Zionstheologie beeinflußten Heilsankündigungen', among which 10:24–27 is mentioned.

[9] Hans Wildberger, *Jesaja 1–12* (BK 10.1; 2nd ed.; Neukirchen–Vluyn, 1980), pp. 419–420.

[10] Bernhard Duhm, *Das Buch Jesaja* (4th ed.; HK 1; Göttingen, 1922), p. 102.

is the product of *Nachdichtung*. Consequently, 'Assyria' to which the passage refers must be understood as a *chiffre* for a later empire, be it Babylonian, Persian, or Greek. The following discussion aims to show that this interpretation does not hold. It will be argued that Isa 10:24–27 consists of material that is best interpreted against the background of the Assyrian period. Properly understood, the passage opens a window on the Isaiah tradition in the Assyrian period.

2.1. *Isaiah 10:24–25 as an Oracle of Encouragement*

Isa 10:24–25 is an oracle of encouragement for the people in Jerusalem. They are threatened and oppressed by Assyria's imperialistic aggression. The oracle condemns Assyria for beating the Judeans with a rod and lifting up its staff against them:

> Therefore thus says the Lord Yahweh of Hosts: "O my people, who live in Zion, do not be afraid of Assyria when it beats you with a rod and lifts up its staff against you on the way to Egypt. For in a very little time the limit will be reached, and then my anger will be directed at their destruction."[11]

The oracle is often misunderstood, because of two erroneous convictions. First, it is held that verse 24 contains an analogy between Assyria and Egypt. The words בְּדֶרֶךְ מִצְרָיִם are taken to mean 'as the Egyptians did'. Such a comparison with Egypt is considered to be illustrative of the late, post-exilic character of this text.[12] Second, verse 25 is commonly understood as containing the thought that Yahweh's anger is currently directed against his own people, whereas it will soon be re-directed against Assyria. Neither of these convictions holds true, as will be argued below.

The passage opens with לָכֵן, which functions on the compositional level as a connection word between the subsequent prophecy and the preceding text.[13] Since a causal connection with the immediately preceding verses can be ruled out—verses 22–23 state the opposite of verses 24–25—the prophecy of 10:24–25 is to be associated with 10:5–15 and 10:16–19. Isa 10:5–15 describes the aggression displayed by Assyria and 10:16–19 confronts Assyria with Yahweh's punishment. The same holds true for 10:24–25 and its continuation in 10:26–27, which is therefore

---

[11] The word תַּבְלִיתָם can be interpreted as a noun deriving from בלה (not further attested), meaning 'end, destruction', with suffix.

[12] Cf. for instance the late passages Isa 11:16 and 52:4.

[13] Wildberger, *Jesaja 1–12*, pp. 417–418.

to be connected with 10:5–19. With the words 'thus says the Lord Yahweh of Hosts' a prophetic oracle seems to begin: a word, delivered by a prophet who functions as the mouthpiece of the god who speaks in the first person. 10:24–25 applies to the characteristics of a prophetic oracle: a short word, in which the deity speaks in the first person, containing an announcement relating to the immediate future. The passage may either go back to a prophetic word, or represent an imitation of a prophetic oracle.

The addressee of the oracle is 'my (that is, Yahweh's) people, who live in Zion'. It has been claimed that the reference to the 'people who live in Zion' shows that this text cannot stem from the prophet Isaiah, because for him Zion was a name far too positive to be associated with the sinful people of his time.[14] This claim is to be rejected. First of all, the conviction that the historical Isaiah was first and foremost a 'prophet of judgement' needs to be reconsidered.[15] Furthermore, the two earliest layers of the Isaiah tradition, that is, the words that go back to the eighth-century prophet and their earliest literary development in the seventh century, contain elements clearly reminiscent of the Zion tradition. The earliest traceable Zion tradition, dating from the monarchic period and found in Psalms such as Psalms 46–48, 76, 93, and 96–99, presents Zion as a safe haven for Yahweh's people. Yahweh protects Zion against the threat of her enemies. Zion, in this tradition, is not only Yahweh's dwelling place, but also—being used as a synonym for Jerusalem—the protected place of Yahweh's people (cf. Ps 48; 69:36; 72:2–8; 76:2–4; 87:1, 5). Elements of this tradition are present in the Isaiah tradition of the Assyrian period (Isa 14:32; 28:12*, 16; 31:4–5, 8–9). Zion is portrayed as the place of safety for the people of Yahweh and the enemy threat posed to Zion is criticised as being unlawful. The prophecies of the historical Isaiah thus may very well have contained positive references to the people of Zion. In fact, they most probably did.[16]

---

[14] Wildberger, *Jesaja 1–12*, p. 418.

[15] See, for example, De Jong, *Isaiah among the Ancient Near Eastern Prophets*, p. 463: 'The earliest layer of the Isaiah tradition, the eighth-century prophetic material, does not resemble the characteristics of prophecy of judgement; and the prophetic figure behind these prophecies and sayings cannot be described as a "classical prophet"'.

[16] For references to the Zion tradition in the eighth-century prophecies of Isaiah and for a discussion of the Zion tradition in connection with the seventh-century revision of the Isaiah tradition, see De Jong, *Isaiah among the Ancient Near Eastern Prophets*, pp. 105–106, 110–111, 347 and pp. 385–390, respectively.

The people living in Zion are encouraged not to be afraid of the Assyrians. The words אַל תִּירָא are a typical characteristic of prophecy of encouragement; they occur also in Isa 7:4, in an oracle of encouragement to king Ahaz.[17] This same phrase, 'fear not', prominently occurs in the Assyrian prophecies.[18] It functions as encouragement in the face of the enemy and is connected with divine promises of future support.[19] Within oracles, the phrase 'fear not' in fact means 'trust me': the addressee is encouraged to trust in the power and promise of the deity, and not to fear any unauthorised power. The phrase is therefore appropriately called an 'encouraging formula'.[20]

Assyria's actions are described as 'he beats you with a rod and lifts up his staff against you'. This is a characterisation of the imperialistic aggression as displayed by the Assyrians. This element will be worked out below, after the discussion of the words בְּדֶרֶךְ מִצְרָיִם and the meaning of verse 25.

2.2. *The Road to Egypt*

The words בְּדֶרֶךְ מִצְרָיִם are commonly regarded as making a comparison: the aggressive acts of Assyria are compared to what the Egyptians had done to Israel in the past. The words are normally translated as 'as the Egyptians did'.[21] This reading is adopted in most commentaries and bible translations.[22] There are however three objections to be raised against this interpretation.

First, the way in which Assyria's aggression is described—beating with a rod and lifting up its staff—is in no way reminiscent of the Egyptian oppression of Israel as described in Exodus or in any other part of the Hebrew Bible. As far as the rod (מַטֶּה) plays a role in that context, it is Moses' rod used *against* the Egyptians (cf. Isa 10:26b, on which see below). The second objection is, that the metaphorical reading of בְּדֶרֶךְ

---

[17] The phrase also occurs in other oracles of encouragement, such as 2 Kgs 19:6 (Isa 37:6) and Hag 2:5.

[18] Martti Nissinen, 'Fear Not. A Study of an Ancient Near Eastern Phrase', in Ehud Ben Zvi and Marvin A. Sweeney (eds.), *The Changing Face of Form Criticism for the Twenty-First Century* (Grand Rapids, 2003), pp. 148–158.

[19] Nissinen, 'Fear Not', p. 149.

[20] Nissinen, 'Fear Not', pp. 131–132.

[21] Or similarly 'in the way of Egypt', 'after the manner of Egypt', 'as it was in Egypt'.

[22] Exceptions are John D.W. Watts, *Isaiah 1–33* (WBC 24; Waco, 1985), pp. 157–158; and Stuart A. Irvine, *Isaiah, Ahaz, and the Syro-Ephraimitic Crisis* (SBL.DS 123; Atlanta, 1990), pp. 268–269.

מִצְרַיִם as 'as the Egyptians did' poses difficulties. Although דֶּרֶךְ is often used metaphorically—'in the way of', 'in the manner of'—the Hebrew Bible does not provide clear parallels for this way of expression.[23] A third point to mention relates to the comment of 10:26a, which renders it even more unlikely that בְּדֶרֶךְ מִצְרַיִם in 10:24 is designed to compare Assyria's behaviour to that of Egypt. Isa 10:26a compares Assyria to Midian, both with regard to its behaviour and to its fate. This suggests that at least the commentator of 10:26a did not understand בְּדֶרֶךְ מִצְרַיִם metaphorically (see further on this below).

Whereas the metaphorical understanding poses difficulties, a plain and factual understanding of בְּדֶרֶךְ מִצְרַיִם is an obvious alternative. In fact, a number of arguments support the interpretation 'on the road to Egypt'. The first argument relates to the way roads were designated in ancient Israel. The Hebrew Bible contains many examples of the practice of naming roads according to their destination, such as דֶּרֶךְ תִּמְנָתָה, 'the Timnah Road' or 'the road to Timnah' (Gen 38:14).[24] This reflects the common ancient near eastern practice of naming roads after their destination.[25] In the light of this common practice, דֶּרֶךְ מִצְרַיִם looks like a normal road designation: 'the road to Egypt' or perhaps 'the Egypt Road'.[26]

---

[23] Metaphorical use of דֶּרֶךְ includes the following examples: 'to instruct the right way' (Ps 25:8, 12) or 'the way of wisdom' (Prov 4:11), but exact parallels for 'as Egypt did' are not found. Gen 19:31 and Ezek 20:30 are rather close, but not as elliptic as the supposed metaphorical reading of בְּדֶרֶךְ מִצְרַיִם would be. Moreover, 'the way of all the world' in Gen 19:31, and 'the way of your ancestors' in Ezek 20:30, have a clear proverbial connotation that is missing in the phrase 'the way of Egypt'. The closest parallel would be Amos 4:10, 'I sent among you a pestilence after the manner of Egypt' (דֶּבֶר בְּדֶרֶךְ מִצְרַיִם). However, בְּדֶרֶךְ מִצְרַיִם probably is a corruption of כְּדֶבֶר מִצְרַיִם 'like the pestilence of Egypt', referring to one of the ten plagues (see Exod 9:3, 15; cf. Ps 78:50). Even if the emendation is rejected, the expressions בְּדֶרֶךְ מִצְרַיִם in Amos 4:10 and Isa 10:24 mean different things: Amos 4:10, 'I will treat you the way Egypt was treated' (genitive objective); Isa 10:24, 'Assyria acts as Egypt acted' (genitive subjective). Markus P. Zehnder, *Wegmetaphorik im Alten Testament. Eine semantische Untersuchung der alttestamentlichen und altorientalischen Weg-Lexemen mit besonderer Berücksichtigung ihrer metaphorischen Verwendung* (BZAW 268; Berlin, 1999), p. 324, rejects the geographical interpretation in 10:24 in favour of a metaphoric understanding, but without good arguments.

[24] Further examples include דֶּרֶךְ אֶפְרָתָה, 'the Ephratah Road' or 'the road to Ephratah' (Gen 35:19; 48:7), דֶּרֶךְ הַר־שֵׂעִיר, 'the Mount Seir Road' or 'the road to Mount Seir'. For these and many other examples, see David A. Dorsey, *The Roads and Highways of Ancient Israel* (Baltimore, 1991), p. 49.

[25] See Dorsey, *The Roads and Highways of Ancient Israel*, pp. 47–49.

[26] According to Dorsey, *The Roads and Highways of Ancient Israel*, p. 49, most of the examples represent actual proper names of specific roads. He explains דֶּרֶךְ אֶפְרָתָה as 'the Ephratah Road' rather than 'the road to Ephratah'. Yet he admits some of the examples could be descriptive names.

The combination of דֶּרֶךְ and בְּ often means 'on the road', and followed by a topographical name it always has a locative meaning. Examples of this are found in Gen 16:7; 35:19; 48:7, and in 1 Sam 17:52. In Gen 16:7 the angel of Yahweh finds Hagar by a spring of water, that is 'the spring on the road to Shur (בְּדֶרֶךְ שׁוּר)'. In Gen 35:19 and 48:7 Rachel is buried 'on the road to Ephrath (בְּדֶרֶךְ אֶפְרָתָה)'. Finally, 1 Sam 17:52 relates that many wounded Philistines fell 'on the road to Shaaraim (בְּדֶרֶךְ שַׁעֲרַיִם)'.[27]

Furthermore, the reference to the road to Egypt in 10:24 makes sense from a historical point of view as well. The word דֶּרֶךְ is used as a designation for all kinds of roads, from short and local roads to international highways.[28] Here it refers to a highway: דֶּרֶךְ מִצְרַיִם refers to the international coastal highway, later known as *Via Maris*. Dorsey describes this road as '[t]he most important thoroughfare in ancient Israel … which passed through the coast of Canaan to connect Egypt in the south with Mesopotamia, Syria, Phoenicia, and the land of the Hittites in the north. … This highway was the main artery to and from Egypt. … Along it moved the ancient world's armies, caravans, messengers, and travelers.'[29] As to the name of this road, he remarks: 'The highway is referred to by modern scholars as the "Way of the Sea", the "Via Maris", the "Great Trunk Route", the "Coastal Highway", and similar designations. Its ancient name is not known.'[30] In the light of the normal practice of naming roads after their destination, the Judean name for this road, or better, for the part of this road running from Phoenicia and Philistia to Egypt, would be דֶּרֶךְ מִצְרַיִם, 'the road to Egypt' or 'the Egypt Road'. In fact, this road is elsewhere referred to in the Hebrew Bible as well,[31] and a similar route description is found in the Assyrian royal inscriptions. In his annals, Ashurbanipal claims that when he heard that the

---

[27] See also Dorsey, *The Roads and Highways of Ancient Israel*, p. 218.

[28] Dorsey, *The Roads and Highways of Ancient Israel*, p. 213.

[29] Dorsey, *The Roads and Highways of Ancient Israel*, p. 57. See pp. 57–92 for an extensive geographical description of this road.

[30] Dorsey, *The Roads and Highways of Ancient Israel*, p. 57. The suggestion that דֶּרֶךְ הַיָּם in Isa 8:23 refers to the coastal highway (*Via Maris*) is convincingly rejected by Dorsey, *The Roads and Highways of Ancient Israel*, pp. 49 and 248. Roads were not named after the region through which they ran. The name דֶּרֶךְ הַיָּם according to Dorsey is to be understood as a road that led to the sea, probably leading through Galilee to the Mediterranean.

[31] This road is referred to in Jer 2:18 and probably also in Deut 17:16 and 28:68. In Exod 13:17, this road is referred to as well, but from the opposite direction, as the 'road to the land of the Philistines' (דֶּרֶךְ אֶרֶץ פְּלִשְׁתִּים). According to Dorsey, *The Roads and Highways of Ancient Israel*, p. 248, this refers to the section of the coastal highway running from Egypt to Gaza.

Cushite king Taharqa had launched a campaign against the part of Egypt under Assyria's dominance, he quickly reacted by sending an army to Egypt. With regard to these military forces, he states: *ḫarrān māt Muṣur ušaškina šēpēšunu*, 'I had them take the road to Egypt'.[32] What happened then had happened before: the Assyrian army marched southward along the coastal highway. They took, according to the Judean perspective, the road to Egypt.

By taking דֶּרֶךְ מִצְרַיִם as 'the road to Egypt' the following picture emerges. The Assyrians, marching south along the coastal highway, displayed aggression and a threat to the people in Jerusalem. This does not mean of course that the people of Jerusalem themselves were present on this very road.[33] It means that Judah and Jerusalem got involved in Assyria's imperialistic actions. The 'beating with the rod and lifting up its staff' stands for Assyria's display of power aimed at bringing Judah and Jerusalem to submission. It will be argued that this in all likelihood refers to the circumstances of Sargon's campaign of 720 BCE (see section 2 below).

To conclude, the most natural and likely reading of דֶּרֶךְ מִצְרַיִם in Isa 10:24 is 'the road to Egypt'. This is also how the Septuagint translator understood it, interpreting this verse in the light of Deut 28:68, and formulating τοῦ ἰδεῖν ὁδὸν Αἰγύπτου.[34]

2.3. *Yahweh's Anger directed to Assyria*

The announcement in verse 25 deals with Yahweh's punishment of Assyria. Yahweh states that he will soon direct his anger against Assyria. Many commentators hold that the announcement implies that Yahweh's anger is at present directed against his own people. The words וְכָלָה זַעַם are usually interpreted in this way. This phrase is taken to mean 'the (that is, Yahweh's) indignation shall cease' or 'shall come to an end'.[35] In other words, Yahweh's indignation is directed against his own people; yet it will

[32] Large Egyptian Tablets, line 17, Hans-Ulrich Onasch, *Die Assyrischen Eroberungen Ägyptens* 1. *Kommentare und Anmerkungen* (Wiesbaden, 1994), pp. 104–105: 'Den Weg nach Ägypten ließ ich ihre Füße einschlagen.'; cf. also Prism E, line 53, Onasch, *Die Assyrischen Eroberungen Ägyptens* 1, pp. 96–97.

[33] Contra Zehnder, *Wegmetaphorik im Alten Testament*, p. 324.

[34] Arie van der Kooij, *Die Alten Textzeugen des Jesajabuches. Ein Beitrag zur Textgeschichte des Alten Testaments* (OBO 35; Freiburg–Göttingen, 1981), p. 39.

[35] The emendation of BHS app. crit. זַעְמִי 'my indignation' has been influential. Apart from being unsupported, this emendation is unnecessary since זַעַם can, without textual change, be interpreted as reflecting Yahweh's indignation.

soon come to an end. This understanding of וְכָלָה זַעַם is unlikely. First of all, it is illogical to say that Yahweh's indignation soon will be over and in the same breath to claim that his anger will be directed against Assyria.

The attraction of the common understanding of וְכָלָה זַעַם lies in the alleged parallel with 10:5–6. There, Assyria is presented as the rod of Yahweh's anger, sent to punish the people of Yahweh's anger. In the light of 10:5–6, Assyria's display of aggression in 10:24 is understood as being according to Yahweh's will: Yahweh uses Assyria to punish his own people, but, as 10:25 announces, soon his anger will cease and his wrath will be redirected against Assyria itself. This interpretation is however unconvincing, since the people of Yahweh's anger as referred to in 10:6 are not the same as Yahweh's people who live in Zion (10:24). According to 10:5–6, Yahweh ordered the 'rod of his anger', Assyria, to punish the 'people of his anger'. The second part of 10:6 specifies Assyria's task as the complete looting of the godless nation so that its land is left devastated and trampled down.[36] The godless nation against which Assyria is sent is to be identified as Ephraim, the Northern Kingdom. A parallel depiction of Ephraim is found in 28:1–4, in particular רמס in 28:3 and מִרְמָס in 10:6. Furthermore, Ephraim is included in the announcements of 8:1–4, where similar verbs are used to those in 10:6, שלל and בזז. The identification of the nation in 10:6 as Ephraim is confirmed by the enumeration of cities in 10:9, which has its climax with Samaria, the capital of the nation against which Assyria is sent.[37]

Whereas according to 10:5–6 Assyria's actions against Ephraim are ordered by Yahweh, Assyria's display of aggression against the people of Zion, in 10:24, is not at all part of Yahweh's command. The phrase וְכָלָה זַעַם does not mean 'the indignation will cease', but 'the indignation will be complete'. The meaning of וְכָלָה in this context, 'to become complete', 'to be accomplished', is found elsewhere,[38] and refers to the completion of Yahweh's anger.[39] Isa 10:25a is to be understood as follows: 'for yet a very

[36] Siegfried Mittmann, '"Wehe! Assur, Stab meines Zorns" (Jes 10,5–9.13aβ–15)', in Volkmar Fritz, Karl-Friedrich Pohlmann, and Hans-Christoph Schmitt (eds.), *Prophet und Prophetenbuch. Festschrift für Otto Kaiser* (BZAW 185; Berlin, 1989), pp. 115–116.

[37] Mittmann, "Wehe! Assur, Stab meines Zorns", pp. 118–119.

[38] Used in *qal*, 1 Sam 20:7, 9; 25:17; Est 7:7; in *pi'el* ('God makes his anger full / brings his anger to completion'), Lam 4:11; Ezek 5:13; 6:12; 7:8; 13:15; 20:8, 21.

[39] See Franz J. Helfmeyer, 'כלה', in G. Johannes Botterweck, Helmer Ringgren, Heinz-Josef Fabry (eds.), *Theologisches Wörterbuch zum Alten Testament* 4 (Stuttgart, 1982), pp. 172–173: 'das Ans-Ziel-kommen' of God's anger, or the 'Vollendung des göttlichen Zornes'.

little while and the indignation—that is, Yahweh's indignation provoked by Assyria's wicked behaviour—will be complete'.[40] As soon as the limit is reached, Yahweh's anger will be directed at Assyria's destruction.

This interpretation is preferable for various reasons. It results in a straightforward oracle of encouragement: although at present, Assyria behaves aggressively to Jerusalem, the limit will soon be reached and then Yahweh will punish them harshly. The view that the present aggression is according to Yahweh's will does not only destroy the clarity of the oracle, but is also at odds with the encouragement in 10:24 not to fear Assyria's acts of aggression. Besides, the words 'for yet a very little while' function to indicate that Yahweh soon will intervene. A similar aspect of imminence with regard to Yahweh's intervention is found in other oracles, such as 7:16, 8:4, and 28:4. In all these cases, Yahweh announces his imminent intervention: he will take action soon. In this light, it is unlikely that 10:25 announces that Yahweh soon will stop one action (punishing his own people) and then start another (punishing Assyria).

It may be concluded that 10:25 contains the announcement that within a short while the measure of Assyria's sins will be full; soon Yahweh's anger will be complete and then he will take harsh actions against Assyria.[41]

2.4. *The Meaning of the Oracle of 10:24–25*

With the terms 'rod' and 'staff' 10:24 is clearly related to 10:5. It is however important to point out the difference in formulation between 10:5 and 10:24. Assyria's actions against Ephraim are according to Yahweh's orders, but the actions against the people of Zion are perceived as an act of aggression. With regard to Judah and Jerusalem, Assyria is not

---

[40] The combination of זַעַם and כלה occurs in Dan 11:36 as well, in a description of the outrageous behaviour of the foreign king: 'He shall prosper till the wrath is complete (עַד־כָּלָה זַעַם), for what is determined shall be done'. This means that the king is free to act until the limit of God's indignation is reached. See further also Dan 8:19, אַחֲרִית הַזָּעַם 'the last end of the indignation', and 8:23, כְּהָתֵם הַפֹּשְׁעִים, 'when the transgressions have reached their full measure'. A similar view is expressed in 2 Macc 6:14, 'For in the case of the other nations the Lord waits patiently to punish them until they have reached the full measure of their sins' (NRSV). This view occurs often in the Old Testament (for example, Gen 15:16) and can also be taken as a background for Isa 10:25.

[41] The Dutch New Bible Translation (*De Nieuwe Bijbelvertaling*, 2004), in my view gives an excellent rendering of this verse: 'Want nog een korte tijd, dan is de maat van mijn toorn vol en richt mij woede zich op zijn ondergang.'

Yahweh's stick but an evil aggressor which will be punished itself. Yahweh announces that his wrath against Assyria will soon be complete, and that they will be destroyed.

Assyria's imperialism is described as being legitimate as long as it is directed against Judah's enemies, such as Aram and Ephraim (7:4–9a*; 7:14b.16; 8:1–4; 28:1–4; 10:5–6). In these oracles, Assyria is described as the agent of Yahweh's punishment of Judah's enemies. In the prophecies of Isaiah 10 however Assyria is accused of unbridled expansionism and brutal actions against Judah and Jerusalem (10:7–15; 10:24–25; 10:28–32). This is not according to Yahweh's will. On the contrary, this is unlawful aggression that will be punished. Isa 10:24–25 is a straightforward oracle of encouragement: although at present Assyria deals aggressively with Judah, Yahweh encourages the people of Zion not to fear, for in a little while the limit of his anger will be reached and then he will severely punish Assyria.

2.5. *Isa 10:26–27* as a Commentary to the Oracle*

Isa 10:26–27 closely relates to 10:24–25. Isa 10:26 further explains the actions Yahweh takes against Assyria and verse 27 relates the destruction of Assyria to Judah's freedom: the Assyrian yoke will be broken. The various parts of 10:26–27 however are not on one and the same level. Verse 26a is to be understood as a comment to 10:24–25. It is not part of the oracle, since Yahweh is referred to in the third person. It can be seen as an explanatory comment added to the oracle: 'Yahweh of Hosts will wield a whip against them, as when he struck Midian at the rock of Oreb.' This announces the destruction of Assyria by borrowing a term from another early prophecy, שׁוֹט, taken from Isa 28:15, 18. Verse 26a compares the destruction of Assyria to the destruction of Midian. This is the same line of thought as found in 9:3. The comment of v. 26a is on the same level as 9:1–6.

Isa 10:26b however is not on the same level as 26a. It is a later relecture that takes up the words בְּדֶרֶךְ מִצְרָיִם and מַטֶּה with נשׂא from 10:24. According to this relecture, Yahweh will raise his stick against the sea, as he did before against Egypt.[42] Although the meaning is difficult to grasp, it seems unlikely to belong originally to v. 26a, since v. 26a compares Assyria's fate with that of Midian, not with that of Egypt.

---

[42] Wildberger, *Jesaja 1–12*, pp. 418, 421.

Isa 10:27a provides a second comment, which continues that of 26a: 'On that day his burden will be removed from your shoulder, and his yoke will be destroyed from your neck.'[43] The words 'on that day' are often used as a formula introducing additions and it is difficult to say whether v. 27a originated with v. 26a or was added at a later stage. In any case, it closely resembles 9:3, as does v. 26a. Isa 10:26a and 27a can be seen as representing two sides of the same coin: Yahweh's punishment of Assyria on the one hand and the liberation of Judah on the other.

Isa 10:24–27* deals with the liberation of the people of Zion from Assyria. The unit consists first of a divine oracle, comprising 10:24–25. This is followed by a commentary (10:26–27) of which 10:26a and perhaps 27a constituted the earliest form. The oracle of 10:24–25 deals with Assyria as the current superpower; it reflects the military power of Assyria as a reality. The oracle is therefore best dated to the Assyrian period, to a particular episode of the eighth century (see below). The earliest comment on the oracle deals with Assyria's loss of power; the background is in all likelihood the decline of the Assyrian power in the late seventh century.

3. *Isaiah 10:5–11:5 and the Isaiah Tradition in Assyrian Period*

Isa 10:24–27 is part of a larger textual unit dealing with Assyria's imperialism. The unit of 10:5–34 contains three prophecies, 10:5–15*, 10:24–25, and 10:27b–32, each of which is followed by a commentary: 10:16–19, 10:26a.27a, and 10:33–34.[44] Directly connected with the final comment, 10:33–34, is a description of a new ideal king in 11:1–5. Since Isaiah 10 deals with Assyria as a current superpower,[45] it is mostly agreed that the earliest version of this chapter consists of material from the Assyrian period. The three prophecies, 10:5–15*, 10:24–25, and 10:27b–32, all stem from the eighth century. They condemn Assyria's expansion as a self-willed, arrogant, and godless enterprise. The three oracles belong together. They are likely to relate to one and the same historical situation and to reflect the same circumstances. It is probable that they once

[43] Read יְחֻבַּל; MT וְחֻבַּל and 10:27b are corrupted; see Wildberger, *Jesaja 1–12*, p. 417.

[44] The passage 10:20–23 has a different theme; it received its place within this unit at a later stage. On 10:20–23 as a later expansion, see Wildberger, *Jesaja 1–12*, pp. 412–416.

[45] The term אַשּׁוּר in 10:5 refers to Assyria as to a political-military power, which is personified in the oracle and represented by the king.

belonged to a collection of prophetic oracles dealing with a particular episode of Judah's history, and that, at a later stage, they were edited into a new, literary version. At that time, the commentaries were added to the oracles, and the critical depiction of Assyria was continued by a positive description of the new Judean king, resulting in the composition of 10:5–11:5*.

3.1. *Three Oracles dealing with Assyria's Imperialism*

The text of 10:5–15 contains two accusations against Assyria. On the one hand, Assyria is condemned for its aim to conquer the world. Whereas Yahweh ordered Assyria to punish a particular nation (10:6), Assyria planned to conquer the entire world. Assyria is condemned for its unbridled expansion. The other accusation is formulated in 10:11: Assyria aimed to conquer Jerusalem. These two different accusations represent two stages in the oracle's development: the earliest passage consists of 10:5–9.13–15, whereas 10:11 represents a revision of it.[46] Here, the prophecy in its earliest form is discussed first (for the discussion of 10:11, see below).

Assyria did not act according to Yahweh's commission. Although it conquered the nation specified by Yahweh (Ephraim), it also adopted a policy of wide-scale conquest. Assyria's dissent has two aspects: instead of spoiling and trampling down (10:6), Assyria aims at annihilation (10:7), and instead of taking actions against one nation, Assyria aims to cut off many nations (10:7). The aspect of the many nations is continued in the enumeration of 10:9, and in 10:14, 'I have gathered the whole earth'. The aspect of complete annihilation of nations and lands is continued in 10:13, 'I have removed their boundaries', and in the statement of the Assyrian king: 'Are my officials not all kings?' This related to the eradication of national identities due to Assyria's politics of deportation and provincialisation. The removal of boundaries, that is, the abolition of the territorial status quo by provincialisation and dispossession of land, implies a violation of the divine distribution of the lands from of

---

[46] This has been observed by various scholars, among them Wildberger, *Jesaja 1–12*, p. 392; Mittmann, "Wehe! Assur, Stab meines Zorns", p. 112; and Otto Kaiser, *Das Buch des Propheten Jesaja. Kapitel 1–12* (ATD 17; 5th ed.; Göttingen, 1981), pp. 219–222. Verse 11 is part of a first revision (discussed below); verse 10 is an addition based on 2 Kgs 18:33–35 // Isa 36:18–20; verse 12 forms a secondary explanation of 10:11: the work that is to be done is the abolition of idolatry in Jerusalem.

old.[47] According to the oracle, Yahweh ordered specific actions against Ephraim, but not against the whole world, and his order involved plunder and devastation, but not deportation and abolition of territorial boundaries.[48] This prophecy condemns Assyria's imperialism, which was a reality during the second half of the eighth century. The fictitious speech of the Assyrian king mirrors various political measures that were a reality in the Assyrian period, such as the exile of populations and the change of territorial borders.[49]

The focus of 10:5–15* is the discrepancy between Yahweh's order and Assyria's political agenda. Assyria's aim to conquer 'all the earth' (10:14) is condemned. 10:5–15* criticises Assyria for its unbridled expansion. Why would a Judean prophecy so vehemently criticise Assyria's imperialistic ambitions? The most likely answer is: because Judah too got involved. Judah, although not explicitly mentioned, is implied in the phrases 'nations not few' (10:7) and 'all the earth' (10:14). It was Judah's involvement in Assyria's expansion that elicited the prophecy of 10:5–15*.

Isa 10:24–25 further specifies Assyria's aggression against Judah: Assyria beats the Judeans with a rod and lifts up its staff against them on the road to Egypt. The oracle depicts the inhabitants of Jerusalem as suffering from Assyria's expansion as Assyria marches from Phoenicia, through Philistia, along the *Via Maris*, to the border of Egypt. Assyria no longer is presented as Yahweh's agent sent to destroy Judah's enemies, but as an evil aggressor, whose aggression unlawfully affected Judah and Jerusalem. The people of Jerusalem are encouraged with the typical phrase 'do not fear'. As in 10:5–15*, Assyria is condemned for its behaviour toward Judah and Jerusalem in the context of its wider expansion. The emphasis on the imminence of the outcome of the announcement (10:25; cf. 7:16; 8:4; 28:4) functions as encouragement of the addressees.

Isa 10:27b–32, the third prophetic word within Isaiah 10, refers to the approach of an Assyrian delegation coming to Jerusalem. Although not all sites mentioned have been securely identified, it is usually agreed that the list of names indicates a military operation approaching Jerusalem from the north.[50] This supports the restoration of the probably corrupted

---

[47] Mittmann, "Wehe! Assur, Stab meines Zorns", pp. 117–120; cf. Deut 32:8; Ps 74:17.

[48] Mittmann, "Wehe! Assur, Stab meines Zorns", p. 131.

[49] Wildberger, *Jesaja 1–12*, pp. 399–400. For the motif of the removal of boundaries, see Peter Machinist, 'Assyria and Its Image in the First Isaiah', *JAOS* 103 (1983), p. 725.

[50] Marvin A. Sweeney, 'Sargon's Threat against Jerusalem in Isaiah 10,27–32', *Bib.* 75 (1994), p. 464.

phrase of MT 10:27b, עַל מִפְּנֵי־שָׁמֶן, 'yoke in front of oil', into עלה מפני שמרון, 'He has marched from Samaria'.[51] Apparently, an Assyrian delegation came from the territory of Northern Israel to Jerusalem. The places mentioned indicate that the delegation left the main road from Beth-El to Jerusalem in order to bypass fortified Mizpah, and approached Jerusalem along the central ridge.[52] The delegation's aim was not to conquer Judah's fortified cities, but to march quickly to Jerusalem. At Nob (Mount Scopus) they halted and, as the prophetic word indicates, intimidated the people of Jerusalem.[53] Isa 10:32 forms a clear parallel to 10:24: the Assyrians threatened and intimidated Jerusalem. Whereas 10:24 in general terms describes the Assyrian army as marching along the *Via Maris*, 10:27b–32 refers to a specific expedition. The passage does not describe a huge army preparing for a siege of Jerusalem nor an actual fight, but probably refers to a specific military delegation, whose aim it was to intimidate and quickly subjugate Jerusalem, and by extension the land of Judah, to Assyria.[54]

3.2. *Historical Circumstances*

Judah's main concern during the latter part of the eighth century was the question of whether to accept or to resist Assyria's dominion. In the years 734–732, 723–720, and 713–711, various neighbouring states of Judah rejected Assyria's hegemony, and in 705–701 Judah attempted to liberate itself from Assyrian rule. Various major Assyrian campaigns close to, or in, the land of Judah, took place during the years 734–732, 720 and 701. First Isaiah contains prophetic material that can be connected with these historical circumstances. The circumstances of 734–732 are reflected, for example, by the oracles included within Isaiah 7–8 (namely 7:4–9a*; 7:14b.16; 7:20; 8:1–4).[55] Furthermore, the situation of 705–701 is reflected, for example, by oracles included in Isaiah 28–31 (namely 28:7b–10; 28:14–18*; 29:15; 30:1–5*; 30:6b–8; 31:1–3*).[56] The oracles included in 10:5–34 reflect a distinct historical situation. Whereas the

---

[51] Wildberger, *Jesaja 1–12*, p. 424.

[52] Joseph Blenkinsopp, *Isaiah 1–39. A New Translation with Introduction and Commentary* (AncB 19; New York etc., 2000), p. 261; Sweeney, 'Sargon's Threat against Jerusalem', p. 464; Wildberger, *Jesaja 1–12*, p. 431.

[53] Sweeney, 'Sargon's Threat against Jerusalem', p. 464.

[54] Sweeney, 'Sargon's Threat against Jerusalem', pp. 464–465.

[55] De Jong, *Isaiah among the Ancient Near Eastern Prophets*, pp. 202–210.

[56] De Jong, *Isaiah among the Ancient Near Eastern Prophets*, pp. 233–249.

oracles related to 734–732 describe Assyria as Yahweh's instrument to punish Judah's enemies, Israel and Aram, and the oracles related to 705–701 discredit Judah's political leaders advocating rebellion against Assyria as being godless and wicked leaders, in the oracles within 10:5–34 Assyria itself is cast in the role of the enemy. This in all likelihood reflects the situation of 720 BCE. In that period, Judah had not joined the rebellion against Assyria, unlike for example Samaria. Nevertheless, Judah suffered from Assyria's imperialistic measures. Assyria subjugated Judah with a display of aggression and this, according to the view presented in the prophecies, was an unlawful action that would not go unpunished. The most likely background of the prophecies of 10:5–15*, 10:24–25, and 10:27b–32, is Sargon's campaign against the West in 720 BCE.

When Shalmaneser died in 722 BCE, Sargon seized power. During the turbulent years that followed various countries and kingdoms tried to liberate themselves from Assyrian rule. Several Syro-Palestine kingdoms and provinces rebelled against Assyria. In his third year Sargon was able to deal with this rebellion in the West.[57] First, he defeated at Qarqar a coalition of revolting provinces, including Arpad, Ṣimirra, Damascus, and Samaria. This coalition was headed by Yau-biʾdi (Ilu-biʾdi) of Hamath.[58] Subsequently, Sargon captured the city of Samaria. After that, he invaded Philistia.[59] He marched south along the *Via Maris* to Gaza and there he defeated an Egyptian army, which had come to the aid of Hanunu of Gaza. The Egyptian army stood under the command of Reʾe, the commander-in-chief (*tartānu*) of Egypt.[60] According to the Assyrian

[57] Stephanie Dalley, 'Foreign Chariotry and Cavalry in the Armies of Tiglath-Pileser III and Sargon II', *Iraq* 47 (1985), pp. 33–34.

[58] K. Lawsom Younger Jr., 'Recent Study on Sargon II, King of Assyria. Implications for Biblical Studies', in Mark W. Chavalas and K. Lawsom Younger Jr. (eds.), *Mesopotamia and the Bible. Comparative Explorations* (Grand Rapids, 2002), p. 292; John D. Hawkins, 'The New Sargon Stele from Hama', in Grant Frame (ed.), *From the Upper Sea to the Lower Sea. Studies on the History of Assyria and Babylonia in Honour of A.K. Grayson* (Leiden, 2004), pp. 151–164.

[59] Part of the campaign of 720 BCE was the conquest of the cities Gibbethon and Ekron, depicted on a relief in Sargon's palace; Christoph Uehlinger, '"... und wo sind die Götter von Samarien?" Die Wegführung syrisch-palästinischer Kultstatuen auf einem Relief Sargons II in Ḫorṣābād/Dūr-Šarrukīn', in Manfried Dietrich and Ingo Kottsieper (eds.), *"Und Mose schrieb dieses Lied auf": Studien zum Alten Testament und zum alten Orient. Festschrift für Oswald Loretz* (AOAT 250; Münster, 1998), pp. 755, 766; K. Lawsom Younger Jr., 'Assyrian Involvement in the southern Levant at the End of the Eighth Century BCE', in Andrew G. Vaughn and Ann E. Killebrew (eds.), *Jerusalem in Bible and Archaeology. The First Temple Period* (SBL.SS 18; Atlanta, 2003), pp. 242–243.

[60] This Reʾe probably was the *tartānu* of Shabaka, the Cushite king who had come to the throne in 722/721 and had conquered Egypt in 720; see Danʾel Kahn, 'The Inscription

account, the Egyptian army was defeated, Gaza was conquered, Hanunu was deported to Assyria, and the city of Raphia on the Egyptian border was captured.[61]

These are probably the events reflected by the prophecies of Isaiah 10. Evidently, the campaign was directed against 'many nations' (Isa 10:7), and of the cities mentioned in 10:9, Hamath, Arpad, Damascus and Samaria, all were involved in the revolt against Assyria.[62] Assyria took actions against Ephraim, as referred to in 10:5–6: the capital Samaria was captured and part of the population was taken into exile. Then, the Assyrian army marched along the *Via Maris* to the border of Egypt. From the Judean perspective, they took the road to Egypt.[63] Judah itself had not taken part in the rebellion of 722–720 BCE. Yet there are indications that Judah in the course of the campaign against the West nevertheless became involved. Sargon's campaign probably involved actions against Judah. The Nimrud inscription describes Sargon as 'the subduer of (the land of) Judah, which lies far away' (*mušakniš māt Yaudu ša ašaršu rūqu*).[64] The term *mušakniš* (from the verb *kanāšu*) denotes the imposition of Assyria's authority. The term in itself does not reveal whether this was achieved by peaceful means or by military action.[65] Since the Nimrud inscription presumably dates from 717/716, the claim of the submission

of Sargon II at Tang-I Var and the Chronology of Dynasty 25', *Or.* 70 (2001), pp. 1–18, esp. 11–13. That Re'e was the *tartānu* of the Cushite ruler of Egypt is confirmed by reliefs from Sargon's palace at Khorsabad concerning the campaign of 720 BCE on which Cushite soldiers are depicted; see N. Franklin, 'The Room V Reliefs at Dur-Sharrukin and Sargon II's Western Campaigns', *TA* 21 (1994), pp. 264–267, with figures 3, 4, and 5; Uehlinger, "... und wo sind die Götter von Samarien?" pp. 749–750, 766.

[61] Younger, 'Recent Study on Sargon II', p. 293; Younger, 'Assyrian Involvement in the southern Levant', p. 237.

[62] Andreas Fuchs, *Die Inschriften Sargons II. aus Khorsabad* (Göttingen, 1994), pp. 89, 200–201, and see furthermore Sweeney, 'Sargon's Threat against Jerusalem', pp. 466–467, who argues that the series of six cities in 10:9 is to be connected with Sargon's campaign of 720.

[63] This was the quickest and most direct route to Philistia. The same road was taken by Tiglath-pileser in 734 and by Sennacherib in 701. Sweeney's objection ('Sargon's Threat against Jerusalem', pp. 465) that this route would have been too risky in a situation of Western revolt is unconvincing since Sargon had already defeated the coalition at Qarqar when he marched to Philistia.

[64] Nimrud inscription l. 8; Hugo Winckler, *Die Keilschrifttexte Sargons* 1 (Leipzig, 1889), pp. 168–173.

[65] Stephanie Dalley, 'Yabâ, Atalyā and the Foreign Policy of Late Assyrian Kings', *SAAB* 12 (1998), p. 85. Bob Becking, *The Fall of Samaria. A Historical and Archaeological Study* (SHANE 2; Leiden, 1992), p. 55.

of Judah has to refer to the campaign of 720 BCE.[66] After the battle of Qarqar and the conquest of Samaria, the Assyrian army moved further on to Philistia, where it conquered Gibbethon, Ekron, Gaza and Raphia. It is likely that sometime during this stage of the campaign Judah became involved. The most likely moment is after the conquest of Samaria, when the main army marched south along the *Via Maris*. The actions taken against Judah, forced Judah to submit to Assyria.[67]

Judah's involvement in the campaign of 720 BCE is reflected in the prophecies of Isa 10:5–15*, 10:24–25, and 10:27b–32. Although Judah had not joined the rebellion, it became nevertheless involved in Assyria's measures, probably after the conquest of Samaria. Isa 10:24 in general terms refers to Judah's involvement. The terms 'beat with a rod' and 'lift up the staff' are a general characterisation of imperialistic acting. The oracle of 10:24–25 suggests that the people of Jerusalem suffered from Assyria's imperialistic activity, while the latter marched south towards the border with Egypt. Generally, this fits in with Sargon's claim to be 'the subduer of Judah'. How Sargon subjugated Judah is not revealed in Assyrian sources. It has been suggested that this is exactly what is being described in Isa 10:27b–32.[68] This prophetic word may describe the scene which made Sargon 'the subduer of Judah'. After the capture of Samaria, when the Assyrian army headed for Philistia, Judah became involved. An Assyrian delegation quickly marched from Samaria to Jerusalem, not to lay siege to it, but to put pressure on it to renew its submissive stance towards Assyria, to enforce the payment of tribute, and to remind its king and its leaders of Assyria's hegemony.

Judah's subjugation in 720 BCE was not the first confrontation with Assyria's imperialism. In 734 BCE, also during an campaign against Philistia, king Ahaz of Judah was one of the Levantine rules who peacefully

---

[66] Nadav Na'aman, 'The Historical Portion of Sargon II's Nimrud Inscription', *SAAB* 8 (1994), pp. 17–20; Eckart Frahm, *Einleitung in die Sanherib-Inschriften* (AfOB 26; Vienna, 1997), pp. 231–232.

[67] Judah's submission to Assyria in 720 is confirmed by one of the Nimrud letters, mentioning Judean emissaries coming to Assyria (ND 2765, l. 34–39): 'the emissaries of Egypt, of Gaza, of Judah, of Moab, of the Ammonites, entered Calah on the twelfth (with) their tribute in their hands', see Henry W.F. Saggs, *The Nimrud Letters, 1952* (Cuneiform Texts from Nimrud 5; London, 2001), pp. 219–221 (Saggs's translation). The text is dated between 720 and 715, and reflects Sargon's successful campaign of 720; see J. Nicholas Postgate, *Taxation and Conscription in the Assyrian Empire* (Rome, 1974), p. 118.

[68] Sweeney, 'Sargon's Threat against Jerusalem', pp. 457–470; see also Younger 'Recent Study on Sargon II', p. 292, and 'Assyrian Involvement in the southern Levant', p. 238.

submitted to Assyria and paid tribute. At that time, no Assyrian military delegation needed to invade Judean territory. This was apparently different in 720 BCE. Although Judah was not one of the main targets of the Assyrian campaign, it nevertheless received a reminder of its submissive stance towards Assyria. It may have been the first time in Judean history that an Assyrian military delegation had invaded its territory. With the Assyrian army close by, Judah could not but accept the imperialistic terms offered by the Assyrian delegation.

The prophecies of Isaiah relating to the period of 734–732 BCE do not criticise Assyria's imperialism, nor Ahaz's peaceful submission to Assyria, but instead focus on Judah's enemies, Israel and Aram, who would according to the prophecies be destroyed through the actions of Assyria. The prophecies of Isaiah 10, to be related to the campaign of 720 BCE on the other hand, do criticise Assyria's imperialism. The Assyrian pressure on Judah is regarded as unlawful. Whereas Assyria's actions against Judah's enemy Samaria are depicted as in accordance with Yahweh's will, the overall campaign and especially Judah's involvement are condemned as being against Yahweh's will. The Assyrian pressure on Judah to submit, is described as a display of aggression and intimidation, for which Assyria will be punished. The prophecies of Isa 10:5–15*, 10:24–25, and 10:27b–32, in all likelihood relate to Sargon's campaign of 720 BCE.

The criticism directed against Assyria can be understood by looking at the earlier prophecies relating to 734–732. These prophecies describe Assyria as Yahweh's agent for taking action against Judah's enemies. This however provoked the question: if Assyria is Yahweh's agent, why then did Judah also suffer from Assyria's imperialism? The three prophetic words of Isaiah 10 attempt to answer this question. 10:5–15* distinguishes between the conquest ordered by Yahweh and the programme of expansion set up by Assyria itself. The point of 10:5–15* is that Sargon's conquest of Ephraim and Samaria was justified, whereas his submission of Judah was unlawful and against the will of Yahweh. 10:24–25 and 10:27b–32 furthermore criticise Assyria's display of aggression against Judah, and 10:25 makes explicit what was already implied in the *woe* of 10:5–15*: Yahweh is going to punish Assyria. Although one could argue that this announcement did not come true during the lifetime of the prophet, the violent death of Sargon in 705 BCE undoubtedly added to the credibility of the prophet. It seems likely that his prophecies were preserved, and later were revised, reedited and elaborated.

3.3. *Commentary to the Prophecies*

The literary afterlife of the prophetic prophecies of Isaiah was a long and complex process that ultimately resulted in the Book of Isaiah. Analysis of Isa 10:5–11:5 may shed some light on the earliest stages of this development of the prophecies. Isaiah's prophetic words were probably preserved in collections of prophecies relating to particular historical circumstances. The prophecies of Isa 10:5–15*, 10:24–25, and 10:27b–32, were preserved, perhaps as part of a collection of prophecies dealing with the events of 720 BCE. At a certain point, the prophecies underwent a literary revision. Each of the three prophecies within Isaiah 10 is followed by a commentary: 10:5–15* is followed by the commentary of 10:16–19, 10:24–25 is followed by the commentary of 10:26a.27a, and 10:27b–32 is followed by the commentary of 10:33–34. Furthermore 10:33–34 is directly continued by 11:1–5, which forms a conclusion to 10:5–11:5* as a whole. In other words, the unit of 10:5–11:5* represents a literary revision of three earlier prophetic words. In the following, the literary revision of the three oracles in 10:5–11:5* will be analysed. It will be argued that 10:5–11:5* was part of a literary revision of the Isaianic prophecies. This revision is dated to the late seventh century BCE, during the reign of king Josiah of Judah, when the Assyrian dominion of Judah had come to an end.[69]

As part of the seventh-century literary revision, the prophecies of 10:5–15*, 10:24–25, and 10:27b–32 received additional commentary. 10:5–15* received commentary in the form of 10:11, which adds a new perspective to the accusation against Assyria, and in the form of 10:16–19, which digresses on Yahweh's punishment of Assyria. Isa 10:11 can be regarded as a relecture of 10:5–15* which turns the focus to Jerusalem: 'Shall I not do to Jerusalem and her idols what I have done to Samaria and her images?' This relecture refers to Assyria's attempt to capture Jerusalem, thereby reflecting the circumstances of 701 BCE, when Sennacherib campaigned against Judah. In its elaborated form, 10:5–15 condemns Assyria for threatening Jerusalem and especially for regarding Yahweh as 'just another god'. The revised oracle was further extended by a depiction of the disasters to befall Assyria (10:16–19). The commentary of 10:16–19 digresses on Assyria's destruction. Whereas in the

[69] For the hypothesis of a seventh-century revision of the Isaianic material, related to the reign of king Josiah, see De Jong, *Isaiah among the Ancient Near Eastern Prophets*, pp. 358–394.

original prophecy of 10:5–15* the punishment of Assyria remains implicit, in the commentary of 10:16–19 this has become explicit, as the main theme. Assyria is described as wood that will be burned down by Yahweh. The intensity of destruction as expressed in 10:16–19 far exceeds that of the punishment implied in 10:5–15*. The oracle of 10:24–25 received a commentary in the form of 10:26a.27a. This commentary also elaborates on the destruction of Assyria. The same holds true for the commentary added to the word of 10:27b–32: 10:33–34. In all three cases, Yahweh's destruction of Assyria is the main theme. The passages 10:16–19, 10:26a.27a, and 10:33–34, can be compared to Isa 14:24–27, 30:27–33, and 31:8–9, which similarly are passages that belong to the seventh-century revision of the earlier prophetic oracles, in which Yahweh's violent punishment of Assyria is the main theme.

This new perspective—Yahweh destroys Assyria, thereby liberating his people from the Assyrian yoke—is best understood against the background of the events of the late seventh century. By that time, the power of Assyria had deteriorated and Assyria had had to give up its supremacy over the West. From the Judean perspective this meant that the yoke of Assyrian had been broken, that Yahweh had punished Assyria for its aggressive imperialism, and that Judah had been freed from oppression. Although even after Assyria's withdrawal from the West, Judah's space to manoeuvre remained fairly limited, from a nationalistic-ideological point of view a new and glorious time had begun. This is expressed in Isa 11:1–5.[70] The passage gives a portrayal of the ideal Judean king. First, it may be noticed that the characterisation of the ideal king that begins in 11:1 directly continues the preceding description of Yahweh's punishment of Assyria, by the use of a consecutive perfect. The two aspects belong together as two sides of a coin: the destruction of Assyria and the

[70] Although some scholars have argued that Isaiah 11 as a whole belongs to a seventh-century revision of the Isaianic material (see for example, Marvin A. Sweeney, 'Jesse's New Shoot in Isaiah 11: A Josianic Reading of the Prophet Isaiah', in Richard D. Weis and David M. Carr (eds.), *A Gift of God in Due Season. Essays on Scripture and Community in Honor of James A. Sanders* [JSOT.S 225; Sheffield, 1998], pp. 103–118) in my view only 11:1–5 can be plausibly situated in the seventh century. Isa 11:6–9 is a relecture that no longer focuses on the king, but presents a vision of salvation in general terms (see Thomas Wagner, *Gottes Herrschaft. Eine Analyse der Denkschrift (Jes 6,1–9,6)* [VT.S 108; Leiden, 2006], pp. 235–237). The issue of whether 11:11–16 goes back to an earlier passage is debated. Most scholars hold that 11:11–16 belongs to a late stage within the development of the Book of Isaiah, see for example Hugh G.M. Williamson, *The Book Called Isaiah. Deutero-Isaiah's Role in Composition and Redaction* (Oxford, 1994), p. 127; differently Sweeney, 'Jesse's New Shoot', p. 110.

reign of a new Judean king are tightly connected. Assyria's destruction means the liberation of Judah, and makes room for a new Judean king. Both aspects are the result of Yahweh's intervention: Yahweh destroys Assyria and the new Judean king is the king of his choice: the ideal king. The king portrayed in 11:1–5 can be identified as Josiah.[71]

3.4. *The Composition of 10:5–11:5**

The composition of 10:5–11:5* can be characterised as a literary revision of earlier, eighth-century, prophecies, produced in the late seventh century. The new historical circumstances—Assyria's loss of grip on the West resulting in a certain amount of political freedom and room to manoeuvre for Judah—seen from a Judean nationalistic-ideological perspective as a new and glorious time, induced this literary revision of the earlier Isaianic prophecies.

The composition of 10:5–11:5* deals with Assyria's imperialism and expansion; the climax is found in 11:1–5. The way in which the ideal king is characterised in 11:1–5 forms a clear and purposeful contrast to the brutal actions of Assyria as described in Isaiah 10*. In contrast to the pride, self-satisfaction, and godlessness of the Assyrian king, expressed in 10:5–15*, is the wisdom and piety of the ideal king. The Assyrian king boasts, 'by the strength of my hand I have done it, and by my wisdom, for I have understanding' (10:13a). The ideal king, by contrast, is endowed with the spirit of Yahweh, a 'spirit of wisdom and understanding, a spirit of counsel and might, a spirit of knowledge and fear of Yahweh' (11:2). In contrast to the brutal power of Assyria, 'the stick' (שֵׁבֶט, 10:5, 15), the ideal king rules with authority, 'the stick of his mouth' (שֵׁבֶט פִּיו, 11:4). Assyria rules with a brutal hand (יָד, 10:5, 10, 13, 14, 32), the Judean king rules with his mouth (11:4).[72]

The theme of the early prophecies included in the composition of 10:5–11:5* was that Assyria as Yahweh's instrument was ordered to take action against Ephraim (10:5–6), but went astray by following its own agenda of worldwide destruction, which included Judah. To this theme of the prophecies, the revision added a new theme: Assyria's severe punishment. The compositor of 10:5–11:5* was not interested in presenting

---

[71] Sweeney, 'Jesse's New Shoot', pp. 103–118; De Jong, *Isaiah among the Ancient Near Eastern Prophets*, pp. 389–392.

[72] See De Jong, *Isaiah among the Ancient Near Eastern Prophets*, pp. 162–169, esp. 166–167.

an accurate historical portrayal of Assyria and its imperialism. Whereas the prophetic words originally referred to Sargon and his campaign of 720 BCE, in the literary revision they became the basis of a typological presentation of the Assyrian oppression in general. What counted for the compositor of 10:5–11:5* was the conviction that the prophet Isaiah had rightly foretold the collapse of Assyrian rule.[73]

3.5. *The seventh-century Revision of the Isaiah Tradition*

Isa 10:5–11:5* is not the only example of the seventh-century literary revision of the Isaianic prophecies. The double picture of Yahweh's destruction of Assyria and the reign of a new king of Judah which characterises the revision of the prophecies in 10:5–11:5* is also found in Isa 9:1–6 and 31:4–5, 8–9, 32:1–2. In 9:1–6, both themes are tightly interconnected: the destruction of Assyria (9:2–4) is directly followed by a portrayal of the ideal king (9:5–6). Furthermore, in 31:4–5, 8–9, the destruction of Assyria is described in terms that match with the portrayal of the ideal king and his princes of 32:1–2 (סֶלַע, 'rock', 31:9, 32:2). As in 10:33–34 and 11:1–5, the two themes of 9:1–6 and 31:4–5, 8–9 and 32:1–2 belong together as two sides of a coin. Just as 11:1–5 forms the climax to a seventh-century revision of a series of earlier prophetic oracles, so do the portrayals of the ideal king of 9:5–6 and 32:1–2. The portrayal of the ideal king in 9:5–6 concludes the composition of 6:1–9:6*, which included and revised Isaianic prophecies dealing with the events of 734–732 BCE. The portrayal of the ideal king in 32:1–2 forms the climax to the composition of Isaiah 28–32*, which includes and revises Isaianic oracles that related to the circumstances of 705–701 BCE.[74]

4. *Conclusion*

The 'Assyrian profile' of material within First Isaiah is much more pronounced than is mostly realised. Concentrating on Isa 10:24–27 two layers can be discerned. The first is a prophetic oracle consisting of 10:24–25.

[73] Sweeney, 'Jesse's New Shoot', p. 116.

[74] The hypothesis that the seventh-century revision of the Isaianic material consisted of various compositions that concluded with a portrayal of the ideal king (Josiah) is expanded in De Jong, *Isaiah among the Ancient Near Eastern Prophets*, pp. 162–169 and 357–394.

It is an oracle of encouragement, which refers to Assyria as the current superpower. On closer scrutiny, it appears to be an oracle that must be dated to the eighth century BCE. Together with 10:5–15* and 10:27b–32, it can be related to the circumstances of Sargon's campaign against the West of 720 BCE. The second layer of 10:24–27 represents a commentary to this oracle, that first consisted of 10:26a and perhaps 10:27a. It is likely that this comment was added to the oracle at a later stage, together with the comments added to the other oracles within Isaiah 10. I have argued that these comments added to the prophecies were part of a seventh-century literary revision of the Isaianic material.

The findings in Isa 10:24–27 can be taken as a model for the texts of First Isaiah in general. Within this large textual corpus, various different layers can be identified and connected with particular periods of Judah's history. The two earliest layers stem from the pre-exilic time, the first consisting of prophetic words relating to the second half of the eighth century BCE, the second comprising various compositions from the late seventh century BCE in which the earlier prophecies were inserted and revised.

The Isaiah tradition during the Assyrian period was heavily marked by the 'Assyrian question': how to explain Assyria's role in Judah's history. The earliest prophecies of Isaiah, relating to the period 734–732 BCE, describe Assyria as Yahweh's instrument to punish Judah's enemies. Later prophecies, relating to 720 BCE, condemn Assyria for involving Judah in its imperialistic aggression. The prophecies relating to 705–701 BCE, condemn the revolt against Assyria as being opposed to Yahweh's will; in these prophecies, Assyria is described as a raging flood that will destroy the rebelling leaders of Judah. The seventh-century revision of the prophecies focuses on Yahweh's destruction of Assyria, Judah's liberation, and the reign of a new Judean king. The Isaiah tradition in the Assyrian period, both the prophecies of Isaiah and their earliest seventh-century revision, is much more coloured by political issues of that time than is often realised. Isaiah's prophecies can be characterised as representatives of ancient near eastern prophecy, and their literary afterlife in the seventh century has a profound nationalistic-ideological character. Of course, Isaiah has evolved into one of the great classical prophets of Israel's past. This development however occurred after the Assyrian period in response to the disasters that befell Judah in the sixth century. Behind the veil of the great biblical prophet hides, at least in the case of Isaiah, an ancient near eastern prophet.

ON THE IDENTITY OF THE ANONYMOUS RULER IN ISAIAH 14:4B–21

Percy van Keulen

1. *Introduction*

The identity of the anonymous ruler that is addressed in Isa 14:4b–21 has puzzled generations of biblical scholars. Various attempts have been made to link this ruler with a historical king, known from written, biblical or extra-biblical, sources. It seems that the majority of scholars who have recently expressed themselves on the issue assume that the ruler hinted at in the poem is the Assyrian king Sargon II. In this contribution in honour of Arie van der Kooij I will re-open the question of the tyrant's identity and put forward a new proposal.

The subject of the poem is the miserable fate of a tyrant following his demise. All the earth rejoices at his death, even the trees of the Lebanon are relieved (vv. 7–8); when he enters the netherworld, he is mocked by the shades of kings who reside there (vv. 9–11). 'He who aspired to ascend above the gods is thrust down to the depths of Sheol' (vv. 12–15).[1] The tyrant is not spared the ultimate humiliation of being cast out from his grave (vv. 18–20a). His memory will not be honoured since he ruined his own country, and his dynasty is likely to be eradicated (vv. 20b–21). The man who suffers this fate is depicted as the one-time ruler of a worldwide empire. In his lifetime, he cut down cypresses and cedars of the Lebanon to provide himself with timber for his building projects (v. 8). He ruthlessly oppressed other nations (vv. 4b–6), destroyed their cities (v. 17a), did not release captives (v. 17b; possibly an allusion to mass deportations), and even killed his own people (v. 20b).

This description fits more than one king of the Neo-Assyrian and Neo-Babylonian empires, which terrified the people of Judah from the late eighth to the sixth century BCE. Before trying to shed light on the tyrant's identity, we must deal with two issues of crucial importance for the

[1] Edward J. Kissane, *The Book of Isaiah. Vol. 1* (Dublin, 1960), p. 158.

interpretation of the poem, that is, the meaning of v. 19a in the Masoretic text, and the literary genre of the text.

2. *The interpretation of v. 19a*

In particular the interpretation of v. 19a has important implications for the question of the tyrant's identity. In translation vv. 18–19 read as follows:

18 All the kings of the nations, all of them lie in glory, each in his house,
19a But you are cast out from your grave, like an abhorrent plant,
19b Clothed with the slain, those who were pierced with the sword,
19c Who go down to the stones of the pit like a trampled corpse.[2]

The clause at v. 19a, ואתה השלכת מקברך, is often rendered as 'But you are cast out, *away from your grave*'[3] or even '*without a grave*'.[4] These translations represent different notions of separation expressed by the preposition מן:[5] remoteness and exclusion (so-called מן *privativum*), respectively. If מקברך is understood in the sense of separation from the grave, v. 19 seems to say that the body of the ruler who is addressed, is left unburied on the battlefield, lying amidst those killed in battle (v. 19b), carelessly thrown away as something disgusting. It has lately been argued, however, that this understanding of מקברך cannot be right,[6] because the preposi-

[2] Translation taken from R. Mark Shipp, *Of Dead Kings and Dirges. Myth and Meaning in Isaiah 12:4b–21* (Academia Biblica 11; Atlanta, 2002), pp. 132–133.

[3] See Klaas Spronk, *Beatific Afterlife in Ancient Israel and the Ancient Near East* (AOAT 219; Neukirchen–Vluyn, 1986), p. 216; Hermann Barth, *Die Jesaja-Worte in der Josiazeit. Israel und Assur als Thema einer produktiven Neuinterpretation der Jesajaüberlieferung* (WMANT 48; Neukirchen–Vluyn, 1977), pp. 121, 122–123; Christoph Uehlinger, *Weltreich und «eine Rede». Eine neue Deutung der sogenannten Turmbauerzählung (Gen 11,1–9)* (OBO 101; Freiburg–Göttingen, 1990), p. 539.

[4] Herbert C. Brichto, 'Kin, Cult and Afterlife—a Biblical Complex', *HUCA* 44 (1973), pp. 1–54, esp. 25; Otto Kaiser, *Der Prophet Jesaja. Kapitel 13–39* (ATD 18; Göttingen, 1973), p. 27; Hans Wildberger, *Jesaja 13–27* (BK 10.2; Neukirchen–Vluyn, 1978), pp. 533, 535. This interpretation requires that the second masculine singular suffix in מקברך is deleted as a dittography: מקברך כנצר (Thus Hedwig Jahnow, *Das Hebräische Leichenlied im Rahmen der Völkerdichtung* [BZAW 36; Giessen, 1923], p. 240; Arnold B. Ehrlich, *Randglossen zur hebräischen Bibel. 4. Jesaja, Jeremia* [Leipzig 1912], p. 56). The emendation is syntactically as well as semantically unwarranted.

[5] Wilhelm Gesenius and Emil Kautzsch, *Hebräische Grammatik* (28th ed.; Leipzig, 1909), English edition Arthur E. Cowley, *Gesenius' Hebrew Grammar*, (2nd ed.; Oxford, 1910), § 119 *v*, *w*.

[6] Saul M. Olyan, 'Was the "King of Babylon" Buried Before His Corpse Was Exposed? Some Thoughts On Isa 14,19', *ZAW* 118 (2006), pp. 423–426.

tion מן should not be detached from the verb by which it is preceded. Elsewhere in the Masoretic text, the idiom שלך followed by מן + noun occurs with the unambiguous meaning 'to cast/be cast from locus A (to locus B)'.[7] ואתה השלכת מקברך is clearly an example of this idiom, 'since a passive form of the verb שלך is used to describe the act, and the preposition מן indicates the locus from which the corpse is taken, in this case the king's tomb.'[8] Exhuming buried human remains as an act of hostility to the dead is a practice attested in the Hebrew Bible in 2 Kgs 23:16 and Jer 8:1–2.[9] Among extra-biblical ancient near-eastern texts describing this practice, one passage in the inscriptions of Ashurbanipal is especially noteworthy: 'The sepulchers of their earlier and later kings (...) I destroyed, I devastated, I exposed to the sun. Their bones I carried off to Assyria. I laid restlessness upon their shades. I deprived them of food-offerings and libations of water.'[10]

Against the background of these texts, Olyan's interpretation of v. 19a as a reference to exhumation as a *post mortem* punishment is tempting.[11] Due to the desecration of the ruler's remains, his spirit would not find rest in the underworld.[12] However, I do not exclude the possibility that v. 19 merely describes the looting of the royal tomb. The wording of v. 19a suggests that the ruler's remains are simply dumped as waste; there is no hint that his body is subjected to ritual punishment or that his bones

[7] See Olyan, 'King of Babylon', p. 425. Olyan mentions the following instances: Judg 15:17; Ps 51:13; Lam 2:1; Neh 13:8.

[8] Olyan, 'King of Babylon', p. 425.

[9] It is conceivable that Jer 22:19 and 36:36b also hint at this practice. Although it is reported in 2 Kgs 24:6 that Jehoiakim 'slept with his fathers', Nebuchadnezzar might have desecrated the grave of the king who escaped punishment during his lifetime (see Wilhelm Rudolph, *Jeremia* [HAT 12; Tübingen, 1947], p. 122).

[10] Prisms A, vi 70–76; F v 49–54. Translation from Daniel D. Luckenbill, *Ancient Records of Assyria and Babylonia. Volume 2* (Chicago, 1926), p. 310. The most recent edition of the prisms, including a translation in German, is Rykle Borger, *Beiträge zum Inschriftenwerk Assurbanipals: die Prismenklassen A, B, C, = K, D, E, F, G, H, J und T sowie andere Inschriften* (Wiesbaden, 1996). The Neo-Assyrian text under consideration appears on p. 55, the German translation on p. 241. Another interesting passage is Prism B, vi 97–vii 2: 'die Gebeine des ... die man aus Gambulu nach Assyrien mitgenommen hatte, selbige Gebeine liess ich von seinen Söhnen gegenüber dem Tor des Stadtzentrums von Ninive zermalmen' (text in Borger, *Beiträge*, p. 108; translation p. 228).

[11] It should be noted that Olyan is not the first scholar who interpreted v. 19 in this way. For instance, see William L. Holladay, 'Text, Structure, and Irony in the Poem on the Fall of the Tyrant, Isaiah 14', *CBQ* 61 (1999), pp. 633–643, esp. 638, 642; Karin Schöpflin, 'Ein Blick in die Unterwelt (Jesaja 14)', *ThZ* 58 (2002), pp. 299–314, esp. 310.

[12] According to Holladay, v. 19a 'on one level refers to the disinterment of the tyrant's corpse, but on a deeper level to the tyrant's ejection from Sheol' ('Text, Structure, and Irony', p. 642).

are collected and burned. Unfortunately, a full understanding of the text is hampered by the difficult phrase כנצר נתעב.[13] A further difficulty is posed by v. 20a, 'you will not be joined with them in burial'. This passage implies that the ruler, unlike those killed in battle, will not be buried. It could be taken to mean that the ruler's remains, once exhumed, would not be interred again, but this interpretation seems forced. On the whole, however, the view that v. 19a describes the disinterment of the corpse carries conviction.

---

[13] The originality of נצר, 'branch', to be taken in the metaphorical sense of 'scion', is defended by Shipp who argues that נצר in all three occurrences in the Hebrew bible has to do with a king (in fact, the term occurs four times: Isa 11:1; 14:19; 60:21; Dan 11:7), and that Isaiah is replete with botanical imagery which describe kings as trees (Shipp, *Dead Kings*, p. 132, note 11; also Ehrlich, *Randglossen*, p. 56; Kirsten Nielsen, *There is Hope for a Tree. The Tree as Metaphor in Isaiah* [JSOT.S 65; Sheffield, 1989], p. 163). These observations do not alter the fact that the simile 'like an abhorrent branch' does not make sense in the context of v. 19: a branch or scion is not abhorrent and one does not bury it (thus Holladay, 'Text, Structure, and Irony', pp. 633–643, esp. 638). Among the ancient versions, V stands alone in supporting נצר (*stirps*). If נצר is secondary, what did the original reading look like? Several proposals have been put forward: 1. יֵצֶר, 'Gebilde' (Jahnow, *Leichenlied*, p. 240); נוצר, 'what is formed', written defectively (Spronk, *Beatific Afterlife*, p. 216, note 1). Semantically, the parallelism with פגר, 'corpse', in v. 19c in unconvincing, and the conjecture lacks support from the ancient versions; 2. נֶשֶׁר, 'eagle, vulture', (Ludwig Koehler and Walter Baumgartner, *Lexicon in Veteris Testamenti Libros* [Leiden; 1958], col. 631). The reading does not make sense in the context (thus Wildberger, *Jesaja 13–27*, p. 536) and is not supported by the versions; 3. נֵפֶל, 'miscarriage' (Friedrich Schwally, 'Miscellen' [ZAW 11], 1891, pp. 257–258; Kaiser, *Jesaja*, p. 27; Wildberger, *Jesaja 13–27*, p. 536), might be presupposed by ἔκτρωμα, 'abortion', in Symmachus, and יחט, 'abortion', in Targum Jonathan (Marcus Jastrow, *A Dictionary of the Targumim, the Talmud Babli and Yerushalmi, and the Midrashic Literature* [reprint; New York, 1971], p. 574a; Gustaf H. Dalman, *Aramäisch-Neuhebräisches Handwörterbuch* [Göttingen 1938], p. 182a). According to Wildberger, נֵפֶל fits the context of v. 19 'weil man glaubt dass bei ihr böse Mächte im Spiele sind' (*Jesaja 13–27*, p. 536). Shipp, on the other hand (*Dead Kings*, p. 132, note 11), points out that aborted fetuses seem to be buried immediately in the Old Testament (see Job 3:16; Eccl 6:3). Nevertheless, the *tertium comparationis* in v. 19a could be that the ruler's dead body is considered as abhorrent as an abortion (thus Barth, *Jesaja-Worte*, p. 131); 4. נֶצֶל, 'decayed matter' (Jastrow, *Dictionary*, p. 929b; Dalman, *Handwörterbuch*, p. 276a), may be suggested by ἰχώρ in Aquila (Eberhard Nestle, Miscellen [ZAW 24], 1904, pp. 127–129; Holladay, 'Text, Structure, and Irony', p. 638). Though נֶצֶל is not attested in the Hebrew Bible, the reading is attractive because it makes good sense in v. 19a. Nestle assumed that νεκρός, 'corpse', of the LXX likewise reflects נֶצֶל. Seeligmann, on the other hand, believed νεκρός had developed from a Greek transcription of נצר as νεσρ (Isac L. Seeligmann, *The Septuagint Version of Isaiah. A Discussion of its Problems* [Mededelingen en Verhandelingen 9; Leiden, 1948], p. 30), whereas Auvray suggested that νεκρός reflects נבלה, 'corpse' (Paul Auvray, *Isaïe 1–39* [SBi; Paris, 1972], p. 162). In my view, the translator may have been inspired by פגר, which is not rendered at the end of v. 19 (thus also Dominique Barthélemy, *Critique textuelle de l'Ancien Testament. 2. Isaïe, Jéremie, Lamentations* [OBO 50.2; Göttingen, 1986], p. 104).

3. *Prophecy or Retrospective*

A further question to be discussed is whether the poem refers to an event which has already taken place or to an event in the future. If the poem is intended to announce doom to a contemporaneous, living person, the statements in v. 19, however literally they are meant to be understood, do not refer to an event in the past. In that event, only the retrospective references to the ruler's deeds and intentions, like those in vv. 6–7, 13–14, 20a, can be used to find out whom the author of the poem had in mind. If, on the other hand, the entire poem looks back on events of the (recent) past, the information in v. 19 may provide an important key to the ruler's identity.[14]

The poem has been characterized as a parody of the royal dirge.[15] Dirges used to be sung after a death had occurred. In prophetic literature, however, living persons and existing entities may also be the subject of a dirge. In those instances, the judgement speech is cast in the form of a dirge in order to envisage the judgement as a present reality. Examples of this are the laments concerning Pharaoh and Egypt in Ezek 32:1–16 and 17–32, respectively, and the lament concerning Israel in Amos 5:2–3. It is especially with the parody in Ezek 32:17–32 that Isa 14:4b–21 shares striking features, such as the description of the descent into the netherworld (Ezek 32:18b–21), the association with those slain or pierced by the sword (Ezek 32:20a, 21b, 31, 32) and the comment of mighty leaders already present in Sheol (Ezek 32:21). At least on the level of presentation, Ezek 32:17–32 is a prophecy: the doom announced to Egypt was yet to materialize. In view of the similarities with Ezekiel, one could argue that Isa 14:4b–21, too, is a prophecy concerning a living

---

[14] Scholarly opinion is divided on this issue. The problem and the implications of the choices made are clearly stated in George B. Gray and Arthur S. Peake, *The Book of Isaiah I-XXXIX* (2nd ed.; ICC; Edinburgh, 1928), pp. 250–251; Kissane, *Isaiah*, pp. 158–159; Wildberger, *Jesaja 13–27*, pp. 539–540; Shipp, *Dead Kings*, pp. 158–159. Those scholars who consider the poem a prophecy or an expression of hope are either reticent to suggest a candidate, or accept the claim in the introduction that the poem is a *mashal* about a Babylonian king: thus Bernhard Duhm, *Das Buch Jesaja* (5th ed.; Göttingen, 1968), p. 117; Karl Marti, *Das Buch Jesaja* (KHC 10; Tübingen, 1900), p. 123; Jahnow, *Leichenlied*, p. 242; Otto Procksch, *Jesaja I* (KAT 9; 1930, Tübingen), pp. 194–195; Kissane, *Isaiah*, pp. 158–159; Kaiser, *Jesaja*, p. 28; Wildberger, *Jesaja 13–27*, p. 543; Nielsen, *Hope for a Tree*, pp. 160–161; Matthijs J. de Jong, *Isaiah among the Ancient Near Eastern Prophets. A Comparative Study of the Earliest Stages of the Isaiah Tradition and the Neo-Assyrian Prophecies* (VT.S; Leiden etc., 2007), p. 142.

[15] Shipp, *Dead Kings*, pp. 33–66.

ruler. Second, scholars have seen in the designation of the poem as a *mashal* (v. 4a) an indication that the ruler who is addressed is alive. The term משל in v. 4a is often translated as a 'taunt song', but actually *mashal* does not refer to a particular literary genre but merely indicates that a formal comparison is to be made about a subject.[16] In Isa14:4b–21 the formal comparison takes the form of a lament for the dead. Since the referent is a much detested ruler, the lament is clearly a parody, intended to taunt him. It has been argued that for a dirge to function as a taunt, it is axiomatic that the addressee is still alive.[17] As Wildberger puts it: 'Ein spöttisches Leichenklagelied nach dem Tode des betreffenden anzustimmen ist sinnloss, wenn der Zweck einer solchen Leichenklage der Kamp gegen der politischen Gegner ist.'[18]

In my view, neither the similarities with Ezekiel 32 nor the aspect of taunt can be considered evidence that the poem refers to a living person. Since the ruler was evidently feared and detested in his lifetime, the taunt may be 'the ancient equivalent of spitting on his grave'.[19] Nothing in the poem itself suggests that it was meant to be understood as a prediction concerning the ignominious end of the ruler. This constitutes an important difference from Ezek 32:17–32, which, while being a parody on the lament for the dead, is also a prophecy concerning an existing entity. It is moreover assumed that Ezek 32:17–32 borrowed motives and phraseology from Isa 14:4b–21, so that the latter text would provide their original setting.[20]

While the poem does not contain any clear indications that it refers to a future event, it does not either contain unambiguous indications to the contrary. As we have seen, the retrospective character of the dirge, with its predominant use of the perfect, does not imply that the events referred to have already taken place, because we are dealing with a parody. Even so, a description of the royal body cast out from the grave, lying amidst those killed in battle might not be expected in a prophecy concerning a living ruler. Neither does it fit in with traditional conceptions of the fate of the wicked which are manifest in the poem.[21] In prophecies about kings,

[16] Shipp, *Dead Kings*, pp. 42–43.

[17] Thus Nielsen, *Hope for a Tree*, p. 159; Shipp, *Dead Kings*, pp. 158–159.

[18] Wildberger, *Jesaja 13–27*, p. 540.

[19] Shipp, *Dead Kings*, p. 43.

[20] Walther Zimmerli, *Ezechiel 2* (BK 13.2; Neukirchen-Vluyn, 1969), pp. 781–782, 784–785.

[21] Contra Kissane, *Isaiah*, p. 158. Barth rightly notes that 'sich die Aussagen V18–20a nicht so sehr in den Bahnen der gelaüfigen Topik bewegen (…), vielmehr relativ

announcements concerning the fate of the body after the king's demise are not uncommon (1 Kgs 14:11, cf. 13; 21:23–24; 2 Kgs 22:20; Jer 22:19; 36:30), but these refer to the body not being buried. In fact, vv. 19–21 refer to a extraordinary political and military situation: the city where the ruler is buried has apparently been captured by enemies, but his sons have not yet been taken prisoner. What is being described is the end of an empire, or at least a major crisis in its existence. These verses are best explained as a response to factual events in the recent past.

4. *Who is the Tyrant?*

I now return to the initial question: who is the mighty ruler addressed in the poem? The introduction tells that this ruler was King of Babylon (v. 4a). Undoubtedly, the most powerful king of the Neo-Babylonian empire was Nebuchadnezzar. During his long reign (605–562 BCE) many nations were subjected to his dominion. He is known to have recovered cedar timber from the Lebanon (cf. v. 8).[22] Nebuchadnezzar put an end to the kingdom of Judah, deported the upper social and economical classes of the population to Babylon (597 and 586 BCE), and burned large parts of Jerusalem and its temple. He fits the profile of an arrogant ruler that is sketched in the poem (cf. his portrayal in Daniel) and certainly was sufficiently detested among Judeans to be the subject of a taunt song.[23] Moreover, of all occurrences of the title 'King of Babylon' in the Hebrew Bible, the overwhelming majority involve references to Nebuchadnezzar.[24] However, he was succeeded by his son Amel-marduk, and there is no indication that his body was ever cast out from his grave.[25] Amel-marduk and his successors Nergal-shar-usur and Labashi-marduk are shadowy figures who reigned only for a short time. Nabonidus, who

konkrete, individuelle Kontur haben' (*Jesaja-Worte*, p. 137, note 135). See also Uehlinger: 'bei aller Stereotypie ist das Todesschicksal des "Beklagten" doch recht individuell gezeichnet' (*Weltreich*, p. 542).

[22] Wildberger, *Jesaja 13–27*, p. 546.

[23] Nebuchadnezzar is considered a plausible candidate by Procksch, *Jesaja 1*, pp. 194–195; Wildberger, *Jesaja 13–27*, p. 543; De Jong, *Isaiah*, p. 142 (with caution). For further references, see Wildberger, *Jesaja 13–27*, p. 543.

[24] According to Vanderhooft, 118 out of 132 occurrences refer to Nebuchadnezzar (David Stephen Vanderhooft, *The Neo-Babylonian Empire and Babylon in the Latter Prophets* [HSM 59; Atlanta, 1999], p. 129).

[25] Thus Marvin A. Sweeney, *Isaiah 1–39* (FOTL 16; Grand Rapids, 1996), p. 232.

succeeded to the throne in 555 BCE, is a more probable candidate.[26] His reign lasted sixteen years and marked the end of the Neo-Babylonian empire. In Babylonian texts written after his fall he is accused of social injustice, even of killing the weak (cf. v. 20). His portrayal in later Jewish literature is more ambiguous: arrogant but repentant.[27] Two days before the Persian army entered Babylon without a battle (539 BCE), Nabonidus fled. According to Xenophon he was later captured and killed in Babylon. The description in vv. 19–21, in particular 'covered with the slain', does not quite tally with his ignominious death. Nabonidus is not mentioned in the Hebrew Bible, and there are no indications that among the Jews in Babylonia he ever aroused the intense hatred to which Isaiah 14 bears witness.

In sum, identification of the tyrant in vv. 4b–21 with a historical Neo-Babylonian king proves problematic if the poem is interpreted as retrospective rather than as prophecy.[28] A few scholars have surmised that 'king of Babylon' is actually a reference to one of the Neo-Assyrian kings who, from Tiglath-pileser III onward, were crowned King of Babylon.[29] These scholars ascribe the poem to Isaiah himself because it shows terminological affinities with other Isaianic oracles (for instance, Isa 10:5–34; 14:28–32). It is difficult to explain, however, why the author of the poem would designate an Assyrian king as 'King of Babylon'.[30]

The problems caused by 'the king of Babylon' in v. 4a raise the question of whether the designation originates with the author of the poem. As has frequently been noted, within the poem 'Babel' is mentioned nowhere. The name appears in the framework of the poem, in its introduction in vv. 3–4a, and in vv. 22–23. Possibly, these verses are later than the poem itself. The connection in terminology between the introduction

---

[26] Among those who identify the anonymous ruler as Nabonidus are Duhm, *Das Buch Jesaja*, p. 117; Marti, *Jesaja*, p. 128; Jahnow, *Leichenlied*, pp. 239–240, 242; Adolphe Lods, *Les prophètes d'Israël et les débuts du judaïsme* (Paris, 1935), pp. 266–267; J.M. Wilkie, 'Nabonidus and the later Jewish Exiles', *JThS* 2 (1951), pp. 36–44, esp. 40–41.

[27] In the Aramaic 'Prayer of Nabonidus' (4Q242). Cf. Dan 4:28–37.

[28] Duhm (*Jesaja*, p. 117) and Jahnow (*Leichenlied*, p. 242) concluded that the poem must be prediction, since Nabonidus did not die in the manner described in v. 19.

[29] Thus William H. Cobb, 'The Ode in Isaiah xiv', *JBL* 15 (1896), pp. 18–35, esp. 31; Seth Erlandsson, *The Burden of Babylon. A Study of Isaiah 13:2–14:23* (CB.OT 4; Lund, 1970), p. 164; Shipp, *Dead Kings*, p. 160.

[30] Erlandsson notes that in 2 Kgs 15:19 Tiglath-pileser is mentioned by his name as king of Babylon, that is, Pul (Akkadian Pulu) (*Burden of Babylon*, p. 164). Still, Pul is called 'king of Assyria' (2 Kgs 15:19–20). In the Hebrew Bible there are no examples of an Assyrian king being referred to as 'King of Babylon'. It is also worth noting that according to 2 Chr 33:11 Manasseh is taken to Babylon (sic) by commanders of the *King of Assyria*.

and the poem is weak (root רגז, vv. 3, 16; root משל, vv. 4a, 10) and does not compel us to assume unity of authorship.[31] Within the complex of oracles against the nations in Isaiah 13–23, the references to Babylon have, as Begg puts it, 'a somewhat loose connection with the present contexts which, taken for themselves, do not (or do not necessarily) treat of Babylon at all.'[32] Moreover, the references are concentrated at the beginning and end of the complex. Probably, then, they 'have been introduced at a particular stage in the formation of Isaiah 13–23 with the intention of (...) "Babylonizing" its individual components (...).'[33] It is tempting to assume that the introduction in Isa 14:3–4a was designed to re-interpret the poem in vv. 4b–21 as a *mashal* concerning the King of Babylon.[34] The most suitable candidate for the ruler intended in the introduction is Nebuchadnezzar, the typical King of Babylon.[35] The term נצר in v. 19a could be a pun on his name,[36] although it is doubtful whether this pun dates back to the sixth century BCE.[37]

If Nebuchadnezzar is the ruler that is hinted at in the introduction to the poem, the ruler that was originally intended must predate him. It has been argued that this ruler was not a historical king, but a leading character in an ancient Canaanite Epic which in Hebrew translation was cited as a taunt song on the king of Babylon.[38] However, Isa 14:4b–21 does not present a continuous myth but the parody of

[31] Moreover, the terminological affinities with other passages in Isaiah 1–66 (for this, see the lists in Erlandsson, *Burden of Babylon*, pp. 129–238) by no means support Shipp's claim that vv. 3–4a are attributable to Isaiah himself (*Dead Kings*, p. 159).

[32] Christopher T. Begg, 'Babylon in the Book of Isaiah', in Jacques Vermeylen (ed.), *The Book of Isaiah/ le livre de'Isaïe. Les oracles et leurs relectures unité et complexité d'ouvrage* (BEThL 81; Leuven, 1989), pp. 121–125, esp. 121–122.

[33] Begg, 'Babylon', p. 122. The 'Babylon'-framework in Isaiah 13–23 rules out the possibility that the poem hints at a post-exilic, Persian ruler or even at Alexander the Great, unless 'Babylon' is considered a cipher for a later empire (cf. Kaiser, *Jesaja*, p. 28; Uehlinger, *Weltreich*, p. 542). In my opinion, there are no sound arguments in favour of the latter view.

[34] According to vv. 3–4a, the *mashal* in vv. 4b–21 will be taken up in the future when YHWH has given relief from suffering and bondage (v. 3). Hence it is meant to be understood as a retrospective also within its present context.

[35] Vanderhooft, *Neo-Babylonian Empire*, pp. 128–129; see also note 24 above.

[36] Thus, among others, Bernard Gosse, *Isaïe 13,1–14,23 dans la tradition littéraire du livre d'Isaïe et dans la tradition des oracles contre les nations* (OBO 78; Fribourg–Göttingen, 1988), p. 239; Holladay, 'Text, Structure, and Irony', p. 638.

[37] If the original reading is only, albeit indirectly, attested by Aquila, it is quite unlikely that its substitution with נצר would go back as far as the sixth century BCE.

[38] Thus Gottfried Quell ('Jesaja 14, 1–23', in *Festschrift Friedrich Baumgärtel zum 70. Geburtstag 14. Januar 1958* [ErF A.10; Erlangen, 1959], pp. 131–157, esp. 156–157), following William F. Albright (references in Quell, 'Jesaja 14', p. 157).

a royal dirge utilizing various mythological images and motifs.[39] The genre implies a historical setting. Within the context of the First Isaiah, the natural *terminus a quo* for the ruler hinted at in the poem is Isaiah's own lifetime. As a consequence, the poem probably addresses an Assyrian ruler. The first to be considered are the kings of Isaiah's time, Tiglath-pileser III, Shalmaneser V, Sargon II and Sennacherib. Of these, the first two can be quickly dismissed. The earliest prophecies of Isaiah depict Assyria and its kings Tiglath-pileser III and Shalmaneser V as YHWH's agents.[40] This runs counter to the image evoked by the poem.

In the Book of Isaiah, Sargon and Sennacherib, on the other hand, are each severely condemned for acting against YHWH's will. There is no doubt that both of them could have served as a model for the arrogant tyrant portrayed in the poem. Since the beginning of the 20th century, Sargon in particular has been favoured among scholars as a suitable candidate.[41] The reason for this is the—as it seems—striking concord between the description in vv. 18–19 and information from Assyrian sources on the circumstances of Sargon's death. In the entry for year 705 BCE of one version of the Assyrian Eponym Chronicle (B6 = K4446), it is stated that Sargon fell on a campaign against a rebellious vassal.[42] Another text, K4730, dating from Esarhaddon's time, reports that Sennacherib sought to reconcile 'sins' of Sargon on account of which he 'was not buried in his house'.[43] From these data it is inferred that Sargon's body could not be recovered on the battlefield and never received a proper royal burial.[44] It is exactly this situation to which vv. 19–20a seem

[39] Shipp, *Dead Kings*, pp. 129, 165–166.

[40] See De Jong, *Isaiah*, pp. 193–214. Tiglath-pileser III is suggested as a candidate by John H. Hayes and Stuart A. Irvine, *Isaiah the Eight-Century Prophet. His Times and His Preaching* (Nashville, 1987), pp. 226–228.

[41] Thus, among others, Hugo Winckler, *Altorientalische Forschungen* V. (Leipzig, 1897), p. 414; É. Paul Dhorme, 'Les pays bibliques et l'Assyrie', *RB* 7 (1910), pp. 368–390, esp. 389; H. Louis Ginsberg, 'Reflexes of Sargon in Isaiah after 715 BCE', *JAOS* 88 (1968), pp. 47–53; Brichto, 'Kin, Cult, Land', pp. 7, 25; Barth, *Jesaja-Worte*, pp. 136–138; Ronald E. Clements, *Isaiah 1–39* (NCBC; Grand Rapids–London, 1980), p. 140, with caution; Spronk, *Beatific Afterlife*, p. 220; Nielsen, *Hope for a Tree*, p. 160, with caution; Uehlinger, *Weltreich*, pp. 542–544; Sweeney, *Isaiah 1–39*, pp. 232–233; Brevard S. Childs, *Isaiah* (OTL; Louisville, 2001), p. 127; Shipp, *Dead Kings*, pp. 160–162.

[42] Alan Millard, *The Eponyms of the Assyrian Empire 910–612 BC* (SAAS 2; Helsinki, 1994), p. 48 (text), p. 60 (translation).

[43] Hayim Tadmor, Benno Landsberger, Simo Parpola, 'The Sin of Sargon and Sennacherib's Last Will', *SAAB* 3.1 (1989), pp. 3–51, esp. 11.

[44] See De Jong, *Isaiah*, pp. 224–225.

to allude, that is to say, if מן is taken in a privative sense: 'you are cast out, away from your grave (…), clothed with the slain, etc.'[45] However, a privative interpretation of מן in the grammatical context of v. 19 is quite unlikely, as we expounded above. Some scholars seem to assume that 'you are cast out from your grave' is not to be taken literally, and so it could still be a reference to Sargon who was left unburied on the battlefield, but such an understanding considerably weakens the case for Sargon.[46] It has also been argued that vv. 20b–21 do not fit the circumstances immediately following Sargon's death, since he was rapidly succeeded by his son Sennacherib,[47] but this objection can be easily met by considering these verses a later expansion.[48] A more pressing problem involves the attitude towards Assyria that is manifest in the poem. Whereas Isaiah's prophetic words after 705 BCE (Isa 28:15–18; 30:1–5; 31:1–3) may imply that Judah should remain loyal to Assyria, vv. 4b–20 'can hardly be read otherwise than (…) as a justification for Judah's rebellion against Assyria'.[49] Thus it is improbable that the poem hints at events of 705 BCE.[50] On the whole, then, the hypothesis that Sargon is the tyrant referred to in the poem is untenable.

[45] Thus Shipp, *Dead Kings*, p. 160.

[46] For instance, Shipp, who, while believing that v. 19a refers to Sargon's death on the battlefield, still renders v. 19a as 'cast out from his grave' (*Dead Kings*, pp. 132, 160).

[47] Gray–Peake, *Isaiah*, p. 251.

[48] In fact, the view that vv. 20b–21 (or v. 21 alone) are a later expansion of the original poem is taken by several scholars, for instance: Winckler, *Altorientalische Forschungen* V, p. 414; Wildberger, *Jesaja 13–27*, p. 537; Barth, *Jesaja-Worte*, pp. 127–129; Holladay, 'Text, Structure, and Irony', pp. 635–636.

[49] Matthijs J. de Jong, *Isaiah among the Ancient Near Eastern Prophets. A Comparative Study of the Earliest Stages of the Isaiah Tradition and the Neo-Assyrian Prophecies* (PhD diss.; Leiden, 2006) p. 109, note 444; also pp. 179–188 (= pp. 233–245 in De Jong, *Isaiah*, 2007).

[50] Various scholars have recognized connections between the poem and Gen 11:1–9 (Robert H. O'Connell, 'Isaiah XIV 4B–23: Ironical Reversal Through Concentric Structure and Mythic Allusion', *VT* 38 [1988], pp. 407–418, esp. 412–413; Uehlinger, *Weltreich*, p. 537, note 108). Common to both texts are the universal focus and the theme of world dominion, hybris and fall (Uehlinger, *Weltreich*, p. 545). Uehlinger considers the basic layer of Gen 11:1–9 a reflection on the fact that the city that was to be the new capital of Assyria, Dur-Sharrukin, which remained uncompleted due to Sargon's sudden death (see also Arie van der Kooij, 'The City of Babel and Assyrian Imperialism. Genesis 11:1–9 Interpreted in the Light of Mesopotamian Sources', in André Lemaire [ed.], *Congress Volume Leiden 2004* [VT.S 109; Leiden, 2006], pp. 1–17). However attractive this interpretation may be, the thematic affiliation between Gen 11 and Isa 14:4b–20 does not imply (nor is this claimed by Uehlinger) that the latter text, too, is a reflection on Sargon's death. In more general terms, however, the connection with Gen 11:1–9 supports the view that Isa 14:4b–20 is a reflection on the end of Assyrian imperialism.

In the Hebrew Bible, Sennacherib stands out as the typical boastful, arrogant Assyrian king, due to his presumptuous words recorded in Isa 36:4–10, 14–21; 37:10–13, 23–29 (cf. 2 Kings 18–19). Seen against the background of these texts, Sennacherib, more than any other king, seems to have sat model for the ruler described in the poem.[51] He destroyed many cities, including Babylon (cf. Isa 14:17).[52] The fact that Sennacherib received a proper royal burial poses no serious problem in itself, as I explained above.[53] Nevertheless, it is improbable that the poem hints at Sennacherib. Allusions to his death at the hands of assassins and of the subsequent struggle for the throne are notably lacking, whereas these events are recorded in Isa 37:38 (// 2 Kgs 19:37). One would have expected some reference to these humiliating circumstances if Sennacherib were the object of the taunt. Conversely, the situation to which vv. 19 and 21 do make reference does not seem to have occurred (soon) after Sennacherib's death.

For various reasons, the remaining Assyrian kings do not qualify to be the tyrant portrayed in the poem: either there are no indications for a period of disorder in Assyria itself soon after their demise (Esarhaddon, Ashurbanipal, with caution),[54] or the kings do not fit the image of the ruler of a world empire any more because their kingdom is in total decline (Shin-shar-ishkun, Ashur-uballit II).[55]

So far, we have tried to find out the tyrant's identity by comparing notes in vv. 4b–21 with historical data about individual kings of the Neo-Babylonian and the Neo-Assyrian empires. This approach has proved fruitless, however. On the one hand, we found that the description of an imperialistic conqueror fits most Assyrian kings from Tiglath-pileser III until Ashurbanipal. Within the literary framework of the Hebrew Bible,

[51] Sennacherib is advocated as a candidate by Hugo Winckler, *Altorientalische Forschungen* I. (Leipzig, 1893), pp. 193–194; Cobb, 'Ode', pp. 27–28; W. Staerk, *Das assyrische Weltreich im Urteil der Propheten* (Göttingen, 1908), pp. 144–145; Jean Steinmann, *Le prophète Isaïe. Sa vie, son oeuvre et son temps* (LeDiv 5; Paris, 1950), pp. 318–319.

[52] Joseph Blenkinsopp, *Isaiah 1–39* (AncB; New York, 2000), p. 287.

[53] Contra Uehlinger, *Weltreich*, p. 541, note 129; Blenkinsopp, *Isaiah 1–39*, p. 287.

[54] See Henry W.F. Saggs, *The Might That Was Assyria* (London, 1984), pp. 117–118.

[55] Uehlinger, *Weltreich*, p. 541, note 130. Rost thinks that the final verses vv. 18–21 hint at Ashur-uballit's death on the battlefield (P. Rost, 'Miszellen', in *Bruno Meissner zum sechzigsten Geburtstag am 25, April 1928 gewidmet* [MAOG 4; Leipzig, 1928–1929], pp. 175–179, esp. 176). Other scholars who identify the tyrant as Ashur-uballit are Auvray (*Isaïe 1–39*, p. 163) and Hubert Bost ('Le chant sur la chute d' un tyran en Esaïe 14', *ETR* 59 [1984], pp. 3–14, esp. 8).

the closest parallel to the tyrant is Sennacherib as he presents himself in direct speech in Isaiah 36–37.[56] On the other hand, since none of the aforementioned imperialistic rulers were cast out from the grave shortly after their demise, the situation described in vv. 18–21 cannot be satisfactorily linked to a particular king.

To overcome this deadlock, let us approach the question from a different angle and take as our point of departure the events hinted at in vv. 18–21. If we succeed in finding a plausible historical setting for these events, we may also gain a clear understanding of the ruler's identity. Vv. 19–20 as I understand them intimate that enemy forces forced their way into the palace or the mausoleum where the king was buried. The implication is that the city where the king's tomb was located—probably the capital or an important religious centre—had been conquered. This event does not indicate a momentary crisis in the history of the empire, but its very end. The historical dimensions of the situation are clearly indicated in the poem: all the earth rejoices because an era of ruthless oppression has come to an end (vv. 5–7; vv. 16–17). Since the merciless tyrant prompted nations to rise against him, he is to be held accountable for the destruction of his land and people (v. 20).

It is my conviction that the historical setting for the revolutionary events hinted at in the poem can be none other than the downfall of the Assyrian empire in 614–612 BCE. In 614 the city of Assur was captured and looted by the Medes. Nineveh followed in 612. In Assur, a venerable religious centre, several Neo-Assyrian kings were buried.[57] It is

[56] Several scholars have drawn attention to the parallels between Isaiah 36–37 and Isa 14:4b–21, like Nielsen (*Hope for a Tree*, p. 161), and in particular Gosse (*Isaïe 13,1–14,23*, pp. 240–242). This parallelism may account for 'das durch und durch assyrische Image des von Jes 14 anvisierten Königs' (Uehlinger, *Weltreich*, p. 542, note 131).

[57] In Assur six underground vaulted chambers, associated with the Old Palace, were excavated. The sarcophagi in three chambers could be identified as those of Ashur-bel-kala, Ashur-nasir-pal II and Shamshi-Adad V on the basis of inscriptions. The sarcophagi were smashed to pieces and ransacked (see Walter E. Andrae, *Das wiedererstandene Assur* [Leipzig 1938], pp. 136–140; Arndt Haller, *Die Gräber und Grüfte von Assur* [WVDOG 65; Berlin 1954], pp. 170–181; Nadav Na'aman, 'Death Formulae and the Burial Place of the Kings of the House of David', *Bib.* 85 [2004], pp. 245–254). Lately, chamber IV has been identified as Esarhaddon's (see Friedhelm Pedde and Steven Lundström, *Der alte Palast in Assur. Architektur und Baugeschichte* [Baudenkmäler aus assyrischer Zeit 11; WVDOG 120; Wiesbaden 2008], p. 59). So far, it is not known who was buried in chambers I and VI. Two inscriptions on brick discovered in Assur indicate that Sennacherib was buried in the Old Palace, but his tomb has not been found. Furthermore, Ashurbanipal is reported to have built a mausoleum in Assur, and Esarhaddon's wife is said to have been buried in her mausoleum in the same city (Ernst F. Weidner, 'Assurbânipal in Assur', *AfO* 13 [1939–1941], pp. 213–216, esp. 215–216). In 1989, two

reasonable to assume that, once the city had been taken, the invaders opened the tombs of these kings. Beside plunder, their motif could have been to punish the hated kings by exhuming their remains. It is by no means impossible that v. 19 reflects actual knowledge about what happened in Assyria. The prophet Nahum seems to have been acquainted with the circumstances of Nineveh's siege and fall (see especially Nahum 2).[58] More likely, however, v. 19 only conveys the author's impression of what happened after the important cities of Assyria had been taken.

The tyrant of the poem is not an individual Assyrian monarch, but the Assyrian king as a *typus*.[59] He is the archetypal cruel and arrogant ruler who manifested himself in Judah's history in the shape of Tiglath-pileser III, Sargon II, Sennacherib, and Ashurbanipal. The tyrant is nameless because the poem does not refer to one king in particular.[60] The downfall of the Assyrian empire marked the end of Assyrian kingship as an institution. This explains why in the poem references to concrete events relating to the fall of the empire are connected with a suprapersonal characterization of the ruler.[61]

---

partly undamaged tombs containing the remains of several Neo-Assyrian queens were discovered in the city of Calah. Inscriptions on various objects mention the names of wives of Ashur-nasir-pal II, Tiglath-pileser III, Shalmaneser V, and Sargon II (for literature see Klaas R. Veenhof, 'Assyrische Koninginnengraven te Kalach', *Phoen.* 38,1 [1992] pp. 14–23).

[58] Thus Peter Machinist, 'Assyria and its Image in the First Isaiah', *JAOS* 103 (1983), pp. 719–738, esp. 735–737.

[59] Cf. also Nah 3:18, where 'the king of Assur' transcends the person of Shin-shar-ishkun.

[60] It has been suggested that the ruler is nameless because the author meant to depict him as a representative of the 'Weltmacht überhaupt' (Wildberger, *Jesaja 13–27*, pp. 542–543; also Kaiser, *Jesaja*, p. 28), or as a personification of one of the great empires, 'soit l'ensemble du monde païen ou des forces opposées á Yahvé' (Jacques Vermeylen, *Du prophète Isaïe à l'apocalyptique. Isaïe, I–XXXV, miroir d'un demi-millénaire d'expérience religieuse en Israël. Tome I* [Paris, 1977], p. 293). These views ignore the textual indications that the poem was composed in response to concrete historical events.

[61] It has been noted that the poem does not only refer to the ruler, but also to the group of which he forms part (v. 5, 'the staff of the wicked, the rod of rulers'; v. 20b, 'the offspring who do evil'; v. 21 'the iniquity of their fathers'; see Barth, *Jesaja-Worte*, pp. 128–129). In my view, this fluctuation between singular and plural merely confirms that the poem does not indicate a particular ruler, but a collective; the singular refers to the typical Assyrian king, the plural to the individual representatives of Assyrian kingship. The fluctuation in number does not justify literary-critical differentiation (contra Barth, [*Jesaja-Worte*, pp. 140–141] and Uehlinger [*Weltreich*, p. 544], who hold that in the time of Josiah vv. 20b–21 were added in order to re-interpret the dirge about Sargon as a dirge about the fall of the Assyrian empire).

In all likelihood, the poem dates from shortly after 612 BCE. The summons in v. 21 to prepare a slaughtering-place for the tyrant's sons lest they rise again suggests that Assyrian troops had not been entirely defeated as yet.[62] In fact, one member of the royal family, one Ashur-uballit, was proclaimed king in Harran.[63] Though soon forced to withdraw from that city, he was able to maintain himself with Egyptian aid for some years. The poem's *terminus ante quem* may be 608 BCE, when king Josiah was killed at Megiddo. This event is likely to have eclipsed the joy about Assyria's downfall.

The fall of the hated empire had a tremendous impact in the ancient Near East.[64] In the Hebrew Bible literary echoes of this historical event can be detected in the Book of Nahum, Zeph 2:13–15, Ezek 31:3–17; 32:22–23, and, in my opinion, in Isa 14:4b–21 as well. It is with the reflection on Assyria's fall in Ezek 31:3–17 in particular that Isa 14:4b–21 shares motifs and terminology: the tree imagery, the motif of hybris (Ezek 31:10), and the topos 'descent into Sheol' (vv. 16–17), including references to 'those going down to the pit' (v. 16) and 'those pierced by the sword' (v. 17). This affinity with Ezek 31:3–17 is another indication that Isa 14:4b–21 looks back on Assyria's collapse.

Due the ruler's anonymity, in exilic times the poem could easily be re-interpreted as a prophecy against the king of Babylon. A subsequent contemporization is observable in the Septuagint: Arie van der Kooij has convincingly argued that the Greek version of the poem alludes to the end of the Seleucid king Antioch IV.[65]

---

[62] Thus Barth, *Jesaja-Worte*, p. 141. The summons in v. 21b, 'let them not arise and possess the earth, and fill the face of the world with cities', may be viewed in connection with Gen 10:8–12, where Nimrod is presented as the builder of the great cities of Babylonia and Assyria (Uehlinger, *Weltreich*, p. 545). The 'cities' in v. 21b could be seen as an allusion to the enormous building projects of the Assyrian kings (Uehlinger, *Weltreich*, p. 545, note 156).

[63] See Saggs, *Might*, pp. 120–121.

[64] Peter Machinist, 'The Fall of Assyria in Comparative Ancient Perspective', in Simo Parpola and Robert M. Whiting (eds.), *Assyria 1995. Proceedings of the 10th Anniversary Symposium of the Neo-Assyrian Text Corpus Project. Helsinki, September 7–11, 1995* (Helsinki, 1997), pp. 179–195, esp. 195.

[65] Arie van der Kooij, *Die alten Textzeugen des Jesajabuches. Ein Beitrag zur Textgeschichte des Alten Testaments* (OBO 35; Freiburg–Göttingen, 1981), pp. 39–42.

YHWH ṢEBA'OT DANS ISAÏE À LA LUMIÈRE DE L'ÉPIGRAPHIE HÉBRAÏQUE ET ARAMÉENNE

André Lemaire*

Le syntagme *Yhwh ṣ^e^bā'ôt*[1] est bien connu comme étant une des caractéristiques du livre d'Isaïe :[2] il apparaît 56 fois dans les chapitres 1 à 39[3] et 6 fois dans le Deutéro-Isaïe. La fréquence de cette appellation dans le premier Isaïe a été rapprochée de l'importance de Jérusalem et de son temple dans la prédication d'Isaïe à la fin du VIIIe s. av. J.-C. Plus précisément, ce syntagme semble avoir été lié, au moins en partie, à la proclamation que c'est Yhwh lui-même qui défend sa ville, Sion/Jérusalem, contre ses ennemis, qu'il s'agisse de Rezin, roi de Damas, et de Peqah, roi d'Israël (vers 734) ou encore, et surtout, de Sennachérib, roi d'Assyrie (en 701).

L'association de cette appellation avec le temple de Jérusalem apparaît clairement dès le récit de vocation d'Isaïe en Isa 6:3, 5, ainsi que dans 8:13–14, où elle est liée à la notion de sainteté (8:13; cf. aussi 5:16, 24). En effet, *Yhwh ṣ^e^bā'ôt* est ‹ celui qui habite sur la montagne de Sion › (8:18) et il ne peut pas défendre son peuple ‹ qui habite Sion › (10:24). C'est lui qui ‹ descend pour guerroyer sur la montagne de Sion › et ‹ protéger Jérusalem › (31:4–5; cf. 24:23; 29:6), éventuellement contre Damas (17:3)

---

* C'est avec plaisir que nous dédions cette modeste contribution à Arie van der Kooij qui a tant travaillé sur le livre d'Isaïe et sa traduction grecque avec le souci de les replacer dans leur contexte. C'est aussi une manière de le remercier pour assumer avec doigté et efficacité le secrétariat de l'I.O.S.O.T. et de l'*Editorial Board* de *Vetus Testamentum*.

[1] Nous ne discuterons ici ni de l'origine, ni de la signification primitive de ce syntagme. Cependant nous restons réservé devant l'hypothèse d'une origine égyptienne proposée par Manfred Görg, ‹ *Ṣb'wt*—Ein Gottestitel ›, *BN* 30 (1985), pp. 15–18 (= *Aegyptiaca—Biblica* [ÄAT 11; Wiesbaden, 1991], pp. 207–210) et Siegfried Kreuzer, ‹ Zebaoth-Der Thronende ›, *VT* 56 (2006), pp. 347–361. Cf. déjà Tryggve N.D. Mettinger, ‹ Yahweh Zebaoth ›, dans Karel van der Toorn *et al.* (éds), *Dictionary of Deities and Demons in the Bible* (2e éd. ; Leiden, 1999), pp. 920–924, spéc. 920.

[2] Cf., par exemple, Stefan Paas, *Creation and Judgement : Creation Texts in Some Eighth Century Prophets* (OTS 47; Leiden, 2003), p. 240: ‹ Among the pre-exilic prophets, the epithet occurs with a relatively higher frequency only in Isaiah 1–39 › ; Hans-Jürgen Zobel, ‹ *Ṣ^e^ bā'ôt* ›, dans G. Johannes Botterweck *et al.* (éds), *Theological Dictionary of the Old Testament* 12 (Grand Rapids, 2003), pp. 215–323, spéc. 229–230, 232.

[3] Isa 1:9, 24; 2:12; 3:1, 15; 5:7, 9, 16, 24; 6:3, 5; 8:13, 18; 9:6, 12, 18; 10:16, 23, 24, 26, 33; 13:4, 13; 14:22, 23, 24, 27; 17:3, 22, 25; 18:7(bis); 19:4, 12, 16, 17, 18, 20, 25; 21:10; 22:5, 12, 14(bis), 15; 23:9; 24:23; 25:6; 28:5, 22, 29; 29:6; 31:4, 5; 37:16, 32; 39:5.

ou contre l'Assyrie (10:16, 26; 14:24, 27). Mais c'est lui aussi qui se met en colère contre son peuple (1:9; 5:7, 9), qu'il s'agisse de Samarie (9:12, 18; 10:23; 28:5, 22) ou de Jérusalem (1:24; 3:1, 15; 22:5, 12, 14, 15). C'est encore lui qui interviendra lors de son jour (2:12; 18:7; 19:16; 22:12, 14; 24:21, 23; 25:6; cf. 13:4, 13).

Cependant l'emploi du syntagme *Yhwh ṣ^e^bā'ôt* ne paraît pas réservé aux oracles du prophète Isaïe de la fin du VIIIe s., comme cela semble indiqué par quelques oracles probablement plus tardifs (cf. en particulier les oracles contre Babylone: 14:22, 23; 21:10 ou les oracles liés à une affirmation monothéiste: 37:16) et confirmé par l'emploi de ce syntagme dans le Deutéro-Isaïe (44:6; 45:13; 47:4; 48:2; 51:15; 54:5).

On sait que, dans le livre de Jérémie, ce syntagme est rare dans la recension courte attestée par la Septante. Ce phénomène est alors expliqué soit par des ajouts du TM, soit par une tendance à supprimer *ṣ^e^bā'ôt* de la part de la recension représentée par la Septante, soit encore par ces deux raisons à la fois.[4] Dans ces conditions, on pourrait se demander si les fréquentes attestations de *Yhwh ṣ^e^bā'ôt* dans Isaïe 1 à 39 ne seraient pas aussi à attribuer à des ajouts assez tardifs du TM[5] et si ce syntagme était vraiment utilisé vers la fin du VIIIe siècle avant notre ère.

Par ailleurs, vers 140 avant notre ère,[6] la Septante d'Isaïe présente un phénomène original et bien connu: au lieu de traduire le terme *ṣ^e^bā'ôt*, elle se contente de le transcrire en grec: *sabaôth*,[7] la traduction *tôn dynameôn* ne semblant apparaître que dans des passages corrigés ultérieurement, apparemment par la recension *kaige*.[8] C'est à dire que, pour

[4] Cf. J. Gerald Janzen, *Studies in the Text of Jeremiah* (HSM 6; Cambridge, 1973), pp. 78–80; Staffan Olofsson, *God is my Rock. A Study of Translation Technique and Theological Exegesis in the Septuagint* (CB.OT 31; Uppsala, 1990), pp. 123–124; Alexander Rofé, ‹The Name YHWH ṢEBĀ'ÔT and the Shorter Recension of Jeremiah›, dans Rüdiger Liwak et Siegfried Wagner (éds), *Prophetie und geschichtliche Wirklichkeit im alten Israel. Festschrift für Siegfried Herrmann* (Stuttgart, 1991), pp. 307–316.

[5] Cette interprétation pourrait s'appuyer sur l'exemple d'Isa 37:16 et 39:5 où *ṣ^e^ bā'ôt* n'a pas de correspondant dans le TM de 2 Rois 19:15 et 20:16.

[6] Cf. Arie van der Kooij, *Die alten Textzeugen des Jesajabuches. Ein Beitrag zur Textgeschichte des Alten Testaments* (OBO 35; Freiburg–Göttingen, 1981), pp. 71–73.

[7] Isa 1:9 (cf. aussi Rom 9:29), 24; 2:12; 3:1; 5:7, 9, 16, 24, 25; 6:3, 5; 7:7; 8:18; 9:7(6); 10:16, 24, 33; 13:4, 13; 14:22, 24; 18:7; 19:4, 12, 16, 17, 18, 25; 21:10; 22:5, 12, 14, 15, 17, 25; 23:9, 11; 25:6; 28:5, 22, 29; 29:5(6); 31:4, 5; 37:16, 32; 39:5; 44:6; 45:13, 14; 47:4; 48:2; 51:15; 54:5.

[8] Cf. déjà les remarques de B. Nestor Wambacq, *L'épithète divine Jahvé Ṣ^e^ba'ôt* (Rome, 1947), pp. 77–83; Otto Eissfeldt, ‹Jahwe Zebaoth›, dans *Kleine Schriften* 3 (Tübingen, 1966), pp. 103–123; Olofsson, *God is my Rock*, pp. 121–122. Cf. surtout Dominique Barthélemy, *Les devanciers d'Aquila* (VT.S 10; Leiden, 1963), pp. 82–83; Van der Kooij, *Die alten Textzeugen*, p. 126.

le probable unique traducteur du livre d'Isaïe,[9] *ṣ*^{e}*bā'ôt* est devenu une sorte de nom propre de Yhwh alors que, ailleurs, il est généralement traduit *ad sensum pantokratôr* ou, plus occasionnellement, *tôn dynameôn*.

Ces deux aspects de la tradition textuelle du livre d'Isaïe peuvent être confrontées aux données épigraphiques.

En 2001, Joseph Naveh a publié une dizaine de graffiti apparus sur le marché des antiquités quelques années auparavant et conservés au Bible Lands Museum.[10] L'inscription nº 1 comporte deux lignes assez bien incisée :

1 'RR ḤG/*R*P BN ḤGB
2 LYHWH ṢB'T

1 Maudit soit *Ḥarif* / *Ḥagaf* fils de Ḥagab
2 Par *Yhwh ṣ*^{e}*bā'ôt*

Le seul problème de lecture concerne la deuxième lettre du premier nom propre de la ligne 1 où on peut hésiter entre un G et un R. La lecture LYHWH ṢB'T est assurée et parallèle à la bénédiction LYHWH dans l'inscription nº 4, ligne 2.

Bien que leur origine reste mal assurée car elles sont apparues sur le marché des antiquités, ces inscriptions sont probablement à rattacher au cimetière de Khirbet el-Qôm,[11] à l'ouest d'Hébron. En effet, les fouilles de William G. Dever ont permis d'y rattacher des graffiti du même type et le nom de l'inscription nº 2 publiée par Naveh, ‹ 'Uphai fils de Netan[yahu] ›, désigne probablement la même personne que celle des inscriptions 1 et 2 de la tombe 1 publiées par Dever.[12] Enfin, vers la

---

9 Cf. Van der Kooij, *Die alten Textzeugen*, p. 32.

10 Joseph Naveh, ‹ Hebrew Graffiti from the First Temple Period ›, *IEJ* 51 (2001), pp. 194–207, spéc. 198–207; Shemuel Aḥituv, *HaKetav VeHaMiktav. Handbook of Ancient Inscriptions from the Land of Israel and the Kingdoms beyond the Jordan from the Period of the First Commonwealth* (The Biblical Encyclopaedia Library 21; Jérusalem, 2005), pp. 203–207; André Lemaire, ‹ Khirbet el-Qôm and Hebrew and Aramaic Epigraphy ›, dans Seymour Gitin *et al.* (éds), *Confronting the Past. Archaeological and Historical Essays on Ancient Israel in Honor of William G. Dever* (Winona Lake, 2006), pp. 231–238, spéc. 233–234.

11 Cf. déjà Aḥituv, *HaKetav*, pp. 196–208; Lemaire, ‹ Khirbet el-Qôm ›, pp. 233–234.

12 William G. Dever, ‹ Iron Age Epigraphic Material from the Area of Khirbet el-Kôm ›, *Hebrew Union College Annual* 40–41 (1969–1970), pp. 139–204, spéc. 151–158; André Lemaire, ‹ Les inscriptions de Khirbet el-Qôm et l'ashérah de YHWH ›, *RB* 84 (1977), pp. 595–608, spéc. 595–597; Johannes Renz, *Die althebräischen Inschriften* (Handbuch der althebräischen Epigraphik 1.1; Darmstadt, 1995), pp. 200–202; Aḥituv, *HaKetav*, pp. 200–202.

même époque, sont apparus aussi sur le marché deux autres graffiti provenant très probablement de Khirbet el-Qôm.[13] Du point de vue de la paléographie, la forme des lettres de l'inscription comportant le syntagme LYHWH ṢB'T, spécialement la longueur des hampes, semble indiquer une date dans la seconde moitié du VIIIe siècle avant notre ère,[14] cette datation approximative correspondant probablement aussi à celle des trois premiers graffiti publiés par Dever.[15]

Malheureusement il nous est impossible de préciser le contexte archéologique et historique de cette attestation épigraphique. On ne peut donc savoir si cette malédiction a été écrite avant—ou après—la réforme religieuse d'Ézéchias supprimant les *bāmôt* et donc s'il s'agit d'une appellation probablement en lien avec le temple de Jérusalem. Il semble aussi impossible de préciser si cette inscription est—ou non—contemporaine des graffiti de Khirbet Beit Lei mentionnant le ‹ dieu de Jérusalem › (inscription 1, ligne 2) et très probablement à dater de la campagne de Sennachérib en 701 avant notre ère.[16] On peut seulement souligner que cette mention du syntagme YHWH ṢB'T semble à peu près contemporaine de l'activité du prophète Isaïe et révèle qu'un tel syntagme pouvait alors être aussi utilisé dans des malédictions populaires.

Plus de deux siècles plus tard, la documentation épigraphique de la communauté d'origine judéenne vivant à Éléphantine, en Haute Égypte, révèle aussi l'emploi populaire d'une autre forme de ce syntagme. Il s'agit d'une documentation araméenne et non plus hébraïque et, de façon peut-être caractéristique, le syntagme n'est pas attesté dans les nombreux et importants papyri de cette communauté mais seulement dans trois ostraca de la collection Clermont-Ganneau.[17] Il s'y présente sous la forme YHH ṢB'T. Dans deux des ostraca, il apparaît dans la formule de saluta-

[13] Robert Deutsch et Michael Heltzer, *Forty New Ancient West Semitic Inscriptions* (Tel Aviv etc., 1994), pp. 27–29; Aḥituv, *HaKetav*, pp. 207–208; Lemaire, ‹ Khirbet el-Qôm ›, p. 233.

[14] Contre Naveh, ‹ Hebrew Graffiti ›, pp. 206–207.

[15] Lemaire, ‹ Khirbet el-Qôm ›, pp. 597, 603; Renz, *Die althebräischen Inschriften*, pp. 200–211.

[16] Cf. André Lemaire, ‹ Prières en temps de crise : les inscriptions de Khirbet Beit Lei ›, *RB* 83 (1976), pp. 558–568; Renz, *Die althebräischen Inschriften*, p. 243, note 1. La datation au sixième siècle, proposée encore récemment par Naveh, ‹ Hebrew Graffiti ›, pp. 194 et 207, et par Aḥituv, *HaKetav*, p. 208, semble paléographiquement trop tardive.

[17] Cf. André Dupont-Sommer, ‹ « Yahô » et « Yahô-ṣeba'ôt » sur des ostraca araméens inédits d'Éléphantine ›, *CRAI* 224 (1947), pp. 175–191, spéc. 180–185; Bezalel Porten, *Archives from Elephantine* (Berkeley, 1968), p. 109.

tion en partie restituée: ‹Que Yhwh Sabaôt demande/veille sur (YŠʾL) la santé (ŠLM) de mon frère en tout temps› (CG 167,[18] concave 1; cf. 186,[19] concave 1–2 avec la variante ‹ta santé› et la restitution très probable du mot ṢBʾT), tandis que le troisième présente le syntagme complet, YHH ṢBʾT (CG J8=175 + 185, concave 9), dans un contexte malheureusement fragmentaire mais où il est probablement question d'avoir ‹passé la nuit›, de ‹femme›, de ‹pardon/expiation (KPR)›, de ‹jour où je mourrai›.

Il est difficile de tirer des conclusions assurées de ces trois attestations de ṢBʾT, dont une restituée. Cependant on doit noter que ce mot pose un problème linguistique dans les ostraca araméens d'Éléphantine. En effet, même si Bezalel Porten et Ada Yardeni ont traduit YHH [ṢBʾT], ‹YHH of [*Hosts*]›,[20] on cherche en vain le mot ṢBʾ dans le glossaire araméen et, d'une manière générale, dans les dictionnaires d'araméen. En fait, il ne s'agit pas d'un mot araméen mais hébreu: en araméen, l'armée est généralement désignée par ḤYL, mot bien attesté à Éléphantine.[21] Il vaut donc mieux, avec Hélène Lozachmeur, voir dans ṢBʾT un nom de divinité,[22] même si on peut supposer que l'emploi de cette appellation, apparemment guerrière, par des mercenaires d'origine judéenne au service de l'armée achéménide paraît avoir été assez naturel.[23]

En ne traduisant pas le terme hébreu ṢBʾT en araméen, les judéo-araméens d'Éléphantine en ont fait assez clairement un nom propre comme, plus tard, le traducteur de la Septante du livre d'Isaïe qui transcrira simplement le mot hébreu en grec: *sabaôth*,[24] et on sait que

[18] Dupont-Sommer, ‹Yahô›, pp. 179–181; Hélène Lozachmeur, *La collection Clermont-Ganneau. Ostraca, épigraphes sur jarre, étiquettes sur bois* 1 (Mémoires de l'Académie des Inscriptions et Belles-Lettres; Paris, 2006), pp. 316–318.

[19] André Dupont-Sommer, ‹Un ostracon araméen inédit d'Éléphantine (Collection Clermont-Ganneau nº 186)›, *Rivista degli studi orientali* 32 (*Scritti in onore di Giuseppe Furlani*; 1957), pp. 403–409; Bezalel Porten et Ada Yardeni, *Textbook of Aramaic Documents from Ancient Egypt* 4. *Ostraca and Assorted Inscriptions* (Jerusalem, 1999), p. 180: D7.35; Lozachmeur, *La collection Clermont-Ganneau*, pp. 335–337.

[20] Porten et Yardeni, *Textbook* 4 (1999), p. 180.

[21] Cf. Porten, *Archives from Elephantine*, p. 29; Bezalel Porten et Jeremy A. Lund, *Aramaic Documents from Egypt: A Key-Word-in-Context Concordance* (Winona Lake, 2002), pp. 133–134.

[22] Lozachmeur, *La collection Clermont-Ganneau*, p. 536.

[23] Cf. déjà Porten, *Archives from Elephantine*, p. 109: ‹To the Elephantine Jews, the «Lord of hosts,» no doubt heavenly hosts as well as military, was the «God of Heaven» who «dwelt in Elephantine»›.

[24] Outre Rom 9:29, citant Isa 1:9, Jacques 5:4 emploie aussi *sabaoth*, peut-être en référence au TM de Mal 3:7 (LXX: *pantokratôr*).

ce nom propre de divinité sera repris dans de nombreuses inscriptions magiques et dans les textes gnostiques.[25]

Ainsi, les attestations épigraphiques de ṢB'T en hébreu (Khirbet el-Qôm) et en araméen d'empire (Éléphantine), éclairent-elles quelque peu celles des oracles du prophète Isaïe dans la deuxième moitié du VIIIe siècle avant notre ère ainsi que sa simple transcription dans la Septante d'Isaïe.

[25] Cf., par exemple, F.T. Fallon, *The Enthronment of Sabaoth. Jewish Elements in Gnostic Creation Myths* (Nag Hammadi Studies 10; Leiden, 1978).

THE DIVINE TITLES
האדון AND אדני IN PROTO-ISAIAH AND EZEKIEL

Johan Lust

It is not without some hesitation that I present this paper to my colleague and friend Arie van der Kooij. As an eminent specialist in the Book of Isaiah and its text-critical problems, he undoubtedly knows more than I do about *Adōnay* in that prophetic book. Moreover, it is difficult to add to the information and insights on this divine title or Name after the publication of Martin Rösel's excellent monograph on the topic.[1] Nevertheless it may be worthwhile to have a fresh look at the data from a special angle: the comparison between Isaiah and Ezekiel.

1. *'Adōnay' (אדני) and 'Adōnay* YHWH*' (אדני יהוה): The Data*

The title or name אדני *Adōnay* occurs much more frequently in Ezekiel (222 times) than in Isaiah (48 times). The bulk of the attestations in Ezekiel are to be found in the typically prophetic framing formulas using the double name (217 times): the messenger formula כה אמר אדני יהוה 'thus says *Adōnay* YHWH' (Ezek 122 times; Isa 8 times), and the oracular formula נאם אדני יהוה 'oracle of *Adōnay* YHWH' (Ezek 81 times; Isa 2 times), in the introduction to a prophetic prayer or exclamation אהה אדני יהוה 'Ah *Adōnay* YHWH' (Ezek 4 times; Isa 0 times), and exceptionally in the frequently recurring recognition formula ידע כי אני אדני יהוה 'know that I am *Adōnay* YHWH' (Ezek 5 times; Isa 0 times).

In Isaiah, the distribution of the double name is completely different. Most of the attestations are found outside the formulaic contexts: 15 times (out of a total of 25), in sharp contrast to Ezekiel (two times out of a total of 217). The formulaic occurrences are almost exclusively limited to the messenger formula (8 times: 7:7; 10:24; 22:15; 28:16; 30:15; 49:22; 52:4; 65:13). Much more frequently, and without any obvious pattern, the same formula is used with יהוה alone (30 times), and once

[1] Martin Rösel, *'Adonaj'–Warum Gott 'Herr' genannt wird* (FAT 29, Tübingen, 2000).

with אדני alone (21:16). The oracular formula (נאם ...) is attested twice only with the double name (3:15; 56:8), and never with אדני alone. Moreover, Proto-Isaiah appears to have a predilection for the expanded form אדני יהוה צבאות '*Adōnay* YHWH Sabaoth' (Isa 8 times, exclusively in Proto-Isaiah; Ezek 0 times). The distribution of אדני on its own is also remarkably different. Proto-Isaiah uses it 22 times (and Deutero-Isaiah once),[2] whereas Ezekiel has it 5 times only. Meanwhile it should have become clear that Proto- and Deutero-Isaiah also differ from each other. Proto-Isaiah's favourite phrase אדני יהוה צבאות is absent from Deutero-Isaiah, and אדני alone, found 22 times in Proto-Isaiah, occurs once only in Deutero-Isaiah.

1.1. *'Ha-Adôn'* האדון*: Form and Meaning*

One of the distinctive characteristics of Isaiah is his use of האדון '*ha-Adôn*', 'the Lord'. He selects this form of the title five times, always in proto-Isaiah, and always followed by יהוה צבאות 'YHWH Sabaoth': Isa 1:24; 3:1; 10:16, 33; 19:4.[3] Ezekiel does not use האדון or צבאות. Indeed, the use of האדון is very rare in the Bible. In the other prophetic books one finds it only in Mal 3:1, without any further attributes or formulaic context. The Pentateuch contains two occurrences, in texts that are almost perfect doublets: Exod 23:1 and 34:23.

One wonders why the Book of Isaiah alternates the use of האדון, the form determined by the article, with אדני, a form without the article, in an exclusive combination with יהוה צבאות. Modern translations barely distinguish between the two. For examples we may refer to the RSV and NBV, where both phrases are most often translated alike. The RSV usually reads: 'the Lord, the LORD of hosts.' The new Dutch translation NBV[4] usually has: 'God, de HEER van de hemelse machten.' Some older versions, sticking closely to the Masoretic text, do note a difference. The Authorized Version systematically renders האדון יהוה צבאות 'the Lord, the LORD of hosts', and אדני יהוה צבאות 'the Lord GOD of hosts'. Indeed, this translation does not distinguish between האדון and אדני, since it

---

[2] Isa 3:17, 18, 4:4; 6;1,8, 11; 7;14, 20; 8;7; 9;7, 16; 10:12; 11:11; 21:6, 8, 16; 28:2; 29:13; 30:20; 37:24; 38:14, 16; 49:14. Note that the occurrences of אדני alone are particularly numerous in the so—called Immanuel book (Is 6:1–8:18, 6 times), whereas that section has the double name only once (7:7).

[3] Rösel, *Adonaj*, pp. 84–86.

[4] NBV = *Nieuwe Bijbelvertaling*, published in 2004. Arie van der Kooij is a member of the steering committee.

uses 'the Lord' in both cases. Rather, it notes the difference in syntax signalled by the Masoretic punctuation, as well as the fact that the *Qere* for YHWH in the second phrase is אלהים *Elōhîm* 'God' rather than אדני. In the first phrase it separates 'the LORD of hosts' (יהוה צבאות) from 'the Lord' האדון, whereas in the second, it joins 'GOD of hosts' (יהוה צבאות) to 'the Lord' (אדני). In both cases, small capitals indicate that 'GOD' and 'LORD' are substitutes for the *tetragrammaton*. The more recent NRSV re-adopts those differences, and adds a subtle distinction between האדון and אדני, rendering the first 'the Sovereign', and the second 'the Lord'.

We have already listed the occurrences of the phrase האדון יהוה צבאות Isa 1:24; 3:1; 10:16, 33; 19:4. For the alternative אדני יהוה צבאות, the instances are 3:15; 10:23, 24; 22:5, 12, 14, 15; 28:22. Note that both forms of the phrase occur in proto-Isaiah only. Remarkably, in 3:15 one finds the oracular formula נאם אדני יהוה צבאות, whereas in 1:24; 19:4 the same formula is used, but then with האדון instead of אדני.

In all these cases, the Masoretes neatly distinguish between the two phrases. The punctuation always connects האדון with the preceding word, such as נאם: 'oracle of the Lord'; the following expression functions as an apposition, explaining who this Lord is: יהוה צבאות 'YHWH of hosts'. When אדני is used in combination with יהוה צבאות, the three words function as one group giving name and titles of the Lord. When connected to נאם, the four words constitute one group: 'Oracle of *Adōnay* YHWH of hosts'.

Interestingly, the Septuagint does not note a syntactical difference between the two phrases, but clearly distinguishes between האדון and אדני. Its standard translation of the first phrase is ὁ δεσπότης κύριος σαβαωθ,[5] in which δεσπότης renders האדון, and κύριος יהוה. In the second phrase the Old Greek seems to omit אדני, because the translators considered it to be a substitute for the *Tetragrammaton*. Some copyists inserted a second κύριος or added ὁ θεός.[6] Nowhere in LXX-Isaiah is δεσπότης used as an equivalent of אדני or of any form of אדון without the article. There are no occurrences of the term in LXX Ezekiel.

As far as the preserved evidence allows us to see, the translations of Aquila, Symmachus, and Theodotion do not signal a difference in syntax between the two phrases. Moreover, the Three do not seem to correct the Septuagint when it renders האדון ὁ δεσπότης. But Aquila does insert

---

[5] In 1:24 some Greek manuscripts have a transposition; κύριος ὁ δεσπότης (26–106, B *L*—36 534 Bo). V reads *Dominus exercituum*, and thus seems to omit האדון.

[6] See, for example, 22:12, 15.

κύριος, rendering אדני, and obtaining κύριος κύριος. In 3:15 manuscript Q observes that Aquila reads πιπι πιπι, which probably stands for the repeated divine name in Hebrew characters.

1.2. *'Adōnay' (אדני) and 'Adōnay* YHWH*' (אדני יהוה): Form and Meaning*[7]

In Ezekiel, the stereotypical and systematic use of אדני in the framing formulas strongly suggests that the י- in אדני in these contexts originally was a pronominal suffix, and not a nominal afformative. The suffixed title 'my Lord' expresses the prophet's special relationship to 'his' Master.[8] He is the messenger of his heavenly King, and is thus entitled to use the formulas typical of a royal messenger, speaking with the authority of his master. When he begins his message with the words 'thus says my Lord', and ends with 'word of my Lord', he states that the one, speaking in the first person in the message, is the heavenly king speaking through his mouth. In Ezekiel's visionary account of his call this is emphatically confirmed by the thrice-repeated command 'you shall say to them "Thus says my Lord".' (2:4; 3:11, 27). The absolute use of the messenger formula emphasizes the prophet's mission as an ambassador of his Lord.

The characteristic prophetic messenger and oracle formulas are less prominently present in Isaiah. Moreover, when they occur, they do not systematically contain the term אדני. The messenger formula is attested 40 times, but only 8 times with אדני. The oracular formula is employed 23 times, but only twice with אדני and twice with האדון. Nevertheless, Isaiah shares some features with Ezekiel, which suggests that the suffixed י- in אדני has the same function and meaning in both books.

The title אדני is repeatedly used in the accounts of the call of both prophets. Like Ezekiel, Isaiah describes his assignment as a mission given to him by his heavenly king. He begins the description of his vision saying, 'I saw אדני sitting on a high and lofty throne.' (6:1). He then introduces the dialogue with his Lord as follows: 'I heard the voice of אדני saying, "Whom shall I send"?' (6:8). When he has received his commission, the prophet asks: 'How long, אדני?' In this context, אדני most likely means 'my Lord'. As in Ezekiel, the word indicates the personal

---

[7] Rösel, *Adonaj*, pp. 91–107.

[8] See, for example, Johan Lust, 'The Ezekiel Text', in Yohanan A.P. Goldman, Arie van der Kooij, and Richard D. Weis (eds.), *'Sôfer Mahîr'. Essays in Honor of Adrian Schenker. Offered by the Editors of 'Biblia Hebraica Quinta'* (VT.S 110; Leiden etc., 2006), pp. 153–168, esp. 165–167. In the section on textual criticism, we will return to this topic.

relationship between the prophet and his Lord. In the ensuing dialogue with Israel's king Ahaz, Isaiah adds weight to his message introducing it by the messenger formula in which he calls his commissioner אדני יהוה 'my Lord' (7:7). In the following oracle (7:10–16), he does the king a favour saying, 'Ask a sign of YHWH your God (יהוה אלהיך)' (7:11). Note that the prophet carefully avoids using the phrasing 'YHWH your Lord (יהוה אדניך)'. Obviously Ahaz is not allowed to call God 'my Lord', though he may call Him 'my God'. In his reaction to the king's refusal, the prophet announces, 'My Lord (אדני) will give you a sign'. In sharp contrast to Ahaz, Isaiah is permitted to refer to God as אדני. This confirms the impression that this title here indicates a special relationship between the prophet and his heavenly king.

Ezekiel repeatedly calls his Lord אדני when he addresses him directly in prayer or in other forms of speech (4:14; 9:8; 11:13; 21:5). Here again personal relationship is marked by the use of that title. In Isaiah such addresses are rare. We already noted his prayer in 6:8. Another address is to be found in his vision concerning a threatening invasion (21:1–10). The prophet is designated as a watcher (2:6), and reports: 'Upon a watchtower I stand, my Lord (אדני)' (21:8). In 22:14, a special revelation is given to Isaiah: 'YHWH of hosts has revealed himself in my ears.' The revelation ends with the formula 'says my Lord (אדני) YHWH of hosts.'[9] In the prayer, inserted in Isa 38:9–20, the speaker twice addresses God as אדני (38:14, 16). Originally this prayer or Psalm may have been attributed to a prophet. In its present context of Proto-Isaiah's historical appendix, however, Hezekiah is the one praying.

In Ezekiel, only the prophet is entitled to address God as אדני. In Proto-Isaiah, more people might seem to be allowed to do so. But the rare instances in which this happens, occur in the historical appendix, in 38:9–20 (Hezekiah), and in 37:24 (Zion).

By way of a conclusion to this section we may say that, like Ezekiel, Isaiah seems to have used אדני as a suffixed form of אדון. Addressing God as 'my Lord', these prophets expressed their personal relationship to the Lord.

---

[9] Rösel, *Adonaj*, p. 103, rightly notes that the formula אמר (אדני) יהוה does not normally function as a concluding formula in proto-Isaiah (39:6 is an exception, belonging to the historical appendix in 38–39). It may have been inserted in 22:14 as a correction of באזני, suggesting that באדני should be read: see Arnold B. Ehrlich, *Randglossen zur hebräischen Bibel. Textkritisches, Sprachliches und Sachliches* 4. *Jesaja, Jeremia* (Leipzig, 1914), pp. 78–79.

1.3. *Back to 'ha-Adôn' האדון, and its Relation to* אדני

The hypothesis which states that אדני means 'my Lord' and expresses a personal relationship, may be of some help when one tries to understand why the prophet alternates its use with the use of האדון, within the same section, and in combination with the same phrase יהוה צבאות. Let us have a closer look at the sections in question.

1.3.1. Isaiah 3:1–15

Isa 3:1–15 is most often taken as a unit.[10] The passage opens with the announcement that 'the Lord, YHWH of hosts' (האדון יהוה צבאות) takes away the leaders of his people (3:1), and it concludes with the stereotypical formula 'says my Lord YHWH of hosts' (נאם אדני יהוה צבאות 3:15).[11] The two phrases form an *inclusio*. The divine title of the first (האדון יהוה צבאות 3:1) expresses the majesty and universal might of the Lord, and fits the context well, forming a link with the preceding passage. The second is the usual concluding formula of an oracle (נאם אדני יהוה צבאות 3:15). In contrast to the phrase in verse 1, it belongs to the framework of the oracle rather than to the oracle proper, and legitimizes Isaiah as an ambassador of his Lord. According to Kaiser, אדני was added as a subsequent assimilation to verse 1, since the text-critical data show that 1QIsa[a] adds אדני, and that the word is absent from LXX.[12] This suggestion is questionable. If אדני in verse 15 had been an insert, intended as an assimilation to verse 1, why then was preference not given to האדון? It is more likely that אדני belongs to the original text, and was dropped by some scribe and/or translator, because of its adoption as a substitute for the Divine Name. If one fails to notice the fact that the two forms have different functions, it may seem strange that the form with the article האדון was used at the beginning of the section (3:1), and the form without the article אדני at the end (3:15). Once the respective functions are recognized, the tension disappears.

---

[10] See e.g. Marvin A. Sweeney, *Isaiah 1–39* (FOTL 16; Grand Rapids, 1996), p. 106; Willem A.M. Beuken, *Jesaja 1–12* (HThKAT; Freiburg im Breisgau, 2003), p. 109.

[11] Beuken, *Jesaja 1–12*, p. 109 '… literarisch durch die Klammer, "der Herr, JHWH Zebaot" (V 1 und V 15) eine Einheit'; Sweeney, *Isaiah 1–39*, p. 110.

[12] Otto Kaiser, *Der Prophet Jesaja Kapitel 1–12* (ATD 17; Göttingen, 1981), p. 83; see also Hans Wildberger, *Jesaja 1–12* (BK 10.1; Neukirchen, 1972), p. 131. BHS recommends the deletion of the phrase as a whole because of its absence in LXX. Compare, however, 22:14: in both cases the next verse begins with a similar formula. Most likely, the translator abbreviated the text, trying to avoid redundancies. See also 14:22–23, and our notes on textual criticism.

The tension may further diminish when one notes that verses 1–15 are not in origin a unit. The first section (3:1–7) is authentic according to most scholars.[13] It presupposes the deportation of leading figures as part of Sennacherib's sanctions in the aftermath of Hezekiah's revolt in 701 (3:1–3). The ensuing anarchy would bring about a government of incapable rulers (3:4–7). Verses 8–9 are probably an exilic addition referring to the fulfilment of this prophecy. With Williamson I am attracted to the view that these verses refer to the fall of Jerusalem.[14] Verses 10–11 are an addition in the tradition of wisdom.[15] Verse 12 quotes the Lord's lament over his people, misled and oppressed by their own leaders. In the final section (3:13–15), there is again a clear change of person as the prophet himself here is the speaker. These verses return to the themes dealt with in the first part. They are formulated as a judgement scene announcing the Lord's intervention against the oppression of the poor. The phrasing and contents have a connection with the vineyard passage in 5:1–7, and are a reapplication of this metaphor. The section is probably Isaianic, and may have come immediately after 5:1–7. At a later exilic stage it was moved to its present position, along with 3:1–7.[16] The divine titles in the concluding formula נאם אדני יהוה צבאות in verse 15 obviously echo the occurrence of the alternative form of the title האדון יהוה צבאות in verse 1.

1.3.2. Isaiah 10:5–34

Chapter 10 is also a composite unit in which the phrase האדון יהוה צבאות (10:16, 33) alternates with אדני יהוה צבאות (10:23, 24). The section is the result of a complex editorial history. It can be subdivided into three parts: 5–19; 20–26, and 27–34.[17] Following upon a woe cry over Assyria (10:5–

[13] See, for example, Hugh G.M. Williamson, *Isaiah 1–5* (ICC; Edinburgh, 2006), pp. 240–242, esp. 204; Beuken, *Jesaja 1–12*, p. 110; compare Sweeney, *Isaiah 1–39*, pp. 106–111; see also Wildberger, *Jesaja 1–12*, p. 120; Jacques Vermeylen, *Du prophète Isaïe à l'Apocalyptique. Isaïe I–XXXV* 1 (EtB; Paris, 1977), p. 144; Ronald E. Clements, *Isaiah 1–39* (NCBC; Eerdmans, 1980), pp. 46–47; Uwe Becker, *Jesaja. Vom Botschaft zum Buch* (FRLANT 178: Göttingen, 1997), pp. 162–169; Ulrich Berges, *Das Buch Jesaja. Komposition und Endgestalt* (HBS 16; Freiburg, 1998), pp. 81–82.

[14] *Isaiah 1–5*, pp. 240–242; compare Kaiser, *Jesaja 1–12*, pp. 77, 79; contrast Beuken, *Jesaja 1–12*, p. 110.

[15] Beuken, *Jesaja 1–39*, p. 110.

[16] Williamson, *Isaiah 1–5*, p. 268.

[17] Beuken, *Jesaja 1–39*, pp. 279–281: Isa 10:5–34 consists of 3 sections, each of which has an authentic Isaianic core, and a complex editorial history; compare Sweeney, *Isaiah 1–39*, p. 209, and Kaiser, *Jesaja 1–12*, pp. 218–238, who subdivides the section into five parts: 5–15; 16–19; 20–23; 24–27; 28–34.

15), verses 16–19 announce the Lord's punitive judgement on Assyria. The final verses 27–34 offer a description of the unstoppable march of the Assyrian army against Israel. The imagery of wood and forest, and the theme of pride brought low, connect this concluding section with verses 5–19. Many authors accept the Isaianic origin of these anti-Assyrian passages.[18] The exclusive Isaianic divine title האדון יהוה צבאות is used in both sections (10:16 and 33). The alternative form of the title אדני יהוה צבאות does occur in verses 23 and 24. These verses belong to the editorial section 10:20–26, with its post-exilic 'remnant theology'.[19] It interrupts the original oracle against Assur in 10:5–19 and 27–34. Obviously, the titles האדון יהוה צבאות and אדני יהוה צבאות belong to two different layers in the redaction of Isaiah. The האדון phrases are found in the original sections dealing with the arrogance of Assur. The title האדון again expresses the Lord's majesty and power as a ruler of the world. In the inserted section (10:20–26) He is depicted as the defender of the surviving remnant of Israel, more than as the dominator of the world. His intervention is focused on justice. The end of the first part of the insertion includes the phrase אדני יהוה צבאות in a sentence designed to show that there can be hope for no more than a remnant. LXX reduces the phrase to ὁ θεός. This probably implies that the translator did not find the full phrase in his *Vorlage*. Most often, when the LXX has ὁ θεός without any further added title, the MT also has one word only. The second part opens with the messenger formula, including the full title אדני יהוה צבאות. Here again the prophet is presented as a special envoy entitled to call God his Lord.

The two samples dealt with above suggest that the phrases in question do not only have a different meaning; they also seem to belong to different layers when used in one and the same section. This observation invites us to try to give a survey of the stages of literary growth of the Book of Isaiah, and to see how the titles אדני and האדון are used in the respective stages.

---

[18] See Beuken, *Jesaja 1–39*, pp. 279–281; Antoon Schoors, *Jesaja I* (BOT 9.A; Roermond, 1972), p. 87; compare Sweeney, *Isaiah 1–39*, p. 209, and Kaiser, *Jesaja 1–12*, pp. 218–238. According to Vermeylen (*Isaïe* 1, pp. 260, 267) 10:16–19 as well as 10:33–34 are later editorial compositions; similarly Becker, *Jesaja*, p. 206, Berges, *Jesaja*, pp. 125–126, and Clements, *Isaiah 1–39*, p. 113 and pp. 120–121, reject the Isaianic character of 10:16–19 and 10:33–34; Wildberger, *Jesaja 1–12*, pp. 407–408, 428–429 also denies the authenticity of 10:16–19, but not of 10:33–34.

[19] Beuken, *Jesaja 1–39*, pp. 279–280.

2. *Literary Criticism and the Meaning of* אדני *in Isaiah*

Although it is nowadays usual to consider Isaiah, or at least Proto-Isaiah, as a unified literary composition, most commentators agree that the preserved text is the result of a long literary growth. We will take Marvin Sweeney as our guide, comparing his position with that of some other scholars. He identifies four major steps in the history of the composition: (1) the final form of the book, produced in the mid- to late fifth-century BCE in relation to the reforms of Ezra and Nehemiah; (2) a late sixth-century BCE edition of the book in chapters 2–32*; 33–55; and chapters 60–62, an edition related to the return from the exile; (3) a late seventh-century BCE edition comprising chapters 5–23*; 27–32; and 36–37, written to support Josiah's reform; and (4) various texts in 1–32* that stem from the eighth-century BCE prophet.[20]

In Sweeney's view, the five passages in which האדון is used, all belong to the earliest stages of the composition. Isa 1:24 introduces the second part of an announcement of Zion's rehabilitation (1:21–26). Its metaphorical language is characteristic of Isaiah and indicates that the prophet is the author.[21] Isa 3:1 is part of a complex unity (2:22–24:6). It opens a first subunit (3:1–15) containing Isaiah's explanation of the punishment befalling Jerusalem and Judah, formulated as an accusation speech against the male leaders. We have already dealt with this passage. Isa 10:16, 33 also belongs to a composite unit (10:5–34). Although the basic setting of the unit is the period of Josiah's reform, 10:5–19 and 27–34 derive from the prophet and reflect Sargon II's campaign of 720.[22] The section as a whole (10:5–34) has also received our special attention earlier in this paper. Isa 19:4 belongs to an authentic Isaianic oracle that announces the Lord's impending judgement of Egypt (19:1–15).[23]

The dating of the more numerous אדני sections is rather different and much more diverse. אדני standing alone occurs frequently in Isaiah, especially in his vision (6:1.8.11) and in the so-called Immanuel Book

[20] Sweeney, *Isaiah 1–39*, pp. 51–60.

[21] Sweeney, *Isaiah 1–39*, p. 85. Compare Wildberger, *Jesaja 1–12*, p. 58; Clements, *Isaiah 1–39*, pp. 35–36; Berges, *Jesaja*, pp. 68–69; Beuken, *Jesaja 1–12*, p. 69; Williamson, *Isaiah 1–5*, pp. 128 and 140; contrast Vermeylen, *Isaïe* 1, pp. 76–105; Becker, *Jesaja*, p. 194.

[22] Sweeney, *Isaiah 1–39*, pp. 204–208.

[23] Sweeney, *Isaiah 1–39*, pp. 268–269; Wildberger (*Jesaja 1–12*, pp. 705–707) accepts the authenticity of 19:1–4 and 19:11–14; according to Vermeylen (*Isaïe* 1, p. 322), verse 4 belongs to a deuteronomistic editorial layer; according to Becker (*Jesaja*, p; 270), the section is definitely not written by the prophet; Clements (*Isaiah 1–39*, p. 167) seems to remain undecided; compare Beuken, *Jesaja 1–12*, pp. 179–180.

(7:7, 14, 20; 8:7; 9:7, 16). The core of the visionary account of a call (6:1–11) is most often considered to be Isaianic.[24] Apart from some modifications in verses 1, 3–4, 10, 17–19, 21–25, chapter 7 is said to date to the times of Hezekiah's reign.[25] The same applies to 8:1–17.[26] Isa 9:7–20 dates to the period following upon the Syro-Ephraimite war.[27] Rösel draws attention to the connections between the visions of Amos and Isaiah. He rightly suggests that the first-person context in these passages implies that אדני here means 'my Lord'.[28]

The following selection of instances of אדני alone is limited to the passages including the phrase אדני יהוה צבאות,[29] because of their similarity to the האדון יהוה צבאות cases. Sweeney and many authors accept the Isaianic origin of 3:15,[30] but this has been criticized by Becker and others.[31] In the wake of Williamson's analysis, one may hold that verses 13–15 have an Isaianic origin, but were not originally composed as part of chapter 3. Probably in an exilic stage, the verses were moved to their present position.[32] Most commentators agree that Isa 10:23 and 24 are postexilic additions (10:20–23, 24–26) introduced by the formula והיה ביום ההוא.[33] According to Sweeney the cases in 22:5, 12, 14, 15 all belong to two separate oracles pertaining to Sennacherib's invasion of Judah in 701 (22:1–14 and 15–25).[34] He admits that there is a general agreement that both oracles have been subjected to later editorial expansion. An original Isaianic oracle in verses 1–4 and 12–14 has been expanded by later additions in verses 5–11.[35] Sweeney does not agree with this. In his opinion, there is no cogent reason to deny the Isaianic authorship and integrity of the two oracles. What about Isa 28:22? This verse belongs to a chapter that

---

[24] Sweeney, *Isaiah 1–39*, pp. 136–140.
[25] Sweeney, *Isaiah 1–39*, p. 169.
[26] Sweeney, *Isaiah 1–39*, p. 182.
[27] Sweeney, *Isaiah 1–39*, p. 195.
[28] Rösel, *Adonaj*, pp. 91–92.
[29] Isa 3:15; 10:23, 24; 22:5, 12, 14, 15; 28:22.
[30] Sweeney, *Isaiah 1–39*, p. 110; Wildberger, *Jesaja 1–12*, p. 132; Williamson, *Isaiah 1–5*, pp. 128–129.
[31] Becker, *Jesaja*, pp. 167–169; Beuken, *Jesaja 1–12*, p. 110.
[32] See Williamson, *Isaiah 1–5*, pp. 268–289, and our note 23.
[33] Sweeney, *Isaiah 1–39*, p. 207; Wildberger, *Jesaja 1–12*, pp. 413, 418–419; Becker, *Jesaja*, p. 206; Beuken, *Jesaja 1–12*, pp. 279–280.
[34] Sweeney, *Isaiah 1–39*, pp. 294–298; compare Wildberger, *Jesaja 1–12*, pp. 835–836.
[35] See, for example, George B. Gray, *The Book of Isaiah I–XXXIX* (ICC; Edinburgh, 1912), pp. 363–365; Otto Kaiser, *Der Prophet Jesaja Kapitel 13–39* (ATD 18; Göttingen, 1973), pp. 113–114; Clements, *Isaiah 1–39*, pp. 182–183. In Becker's view, however, no part of Isa 22:1–14 is Isaianic (*Jesaja*, pp. 278–279).

stands at the beginning of a major block of material (chapters 28–33.) The chapter presents the punishment of Jerusalem as an analogy to that of the northern kingdom. According to Sweeney, the present form of the chapter stems from the late eighth century.[36] According to most recent authors, however, verse 22 belongs to an editorial addition.[37]

This brief survey gives the following results. According to Sweeney, the five occurrences of the האדון phrase belong to the original sections ascribed to the prophet. Some of the אדני expressions are found in later editorial inserts (10:23, 24). The large majority, however, may be attributed directly to the prophet. It is not difficult to find other authors who are of a different opinion, qualifying all the אדני phrases as belonging to later editorial compositions. But then the same authors also situate the האדון phrases, or at least some of them, in late editorial layers.[38] In any case, the two phrases do not seem to occur together in the same original prophetic word.

In passing, we noted that text-critical data further complicate the issue. These phenomena need to be compared with the text of Ezekiel.

3. *Textual Criticism in Isaiah and in Ezekiel*

The available sources differ largely. A series of Qumran Isaiah texts are preserved, one of which is complete: 1QIsa^{a}.[39] The remaining nineteen are very fragmentary, and only a few of them contain passages relevant to our topic: 1QIsa^{b}, 4QIsa^{a}, 4QIsa^{b}, 4QIsa^{c} 4QIsa^{f}.[40] The scribe of 4QIsa^{c} regularly writes יהוה in Palaeo-Hebrew letters. Similarly, he renders אדוני in Palaeo-Hebrew script in 22:12; 30:11.[41] In 1QIsa^{a} the divergences from MT are rather numerous, especially in as far as אדני alone is concerned.

---

36 Sweeney, *Isaiah 1–39*, p. 367.

37 Wildberger (*Jesaja 28–39*, p. 1071) accepts the authenticity of the core of 28:14–21, but definitely detects the hand of several editors in verse 22. See also Vermeylen, *Isaïe* 1, pp. 396–399; Becker, *Jesaja*, p. 233.

38 See, e.g. 1:24 and Vermeylen, *Isaïe* 1, pp. 76–105, followed by Becker, *Jesaja*, p. 194.

39 Millar Burrows (ed.), *The Dead Sea Scrolls of St Mark's Monastery*, 1 (New Haven, 1950).

40 Parts of 1QIsa^{b} have been published in Eleazar L. Sukenik (ed.), *The Dead Sea Scrolls of the Hebrew University* (Jerusalem, 1955), and in Dominique Barthélemy *et al.* (eds.), *Qumran Cave 1* (DJD 1; Oxford, 1955) pp. 66–68. The fragments 4QIsa^{a-r} are published in Eugene Ulrich *et al.* (eds.), *Qumran Cave 4. 10. The Prophets* (DJD 15; Oxford, 1997).

41 He uses square characters in 24:1 where MT gives the *Tetragrammaton*.

The rare Ezekiel Qumran materials are limited to a few scraps that are hardly relevant to our topic.[42] The fragments from Masada are more significant.[43] They largely confirm the data of MT in as far as the double name is concerned. None of the rare instances are preserved in which MT Ezekiel has the single name, אדני.

The Septuagint sources are also different. Codex B, the Vaticanus, is a witness to the pre-Hexaplaric text of Ezekiel, but not of Isaiah.

3.1. *Textual Criticism and the Meaning of* אדני יהוה *in Ezekiel*

Elsewhere, we repeatedly dealt with this topic.[44] A summary suffices here. According to several critical editions and commentators, אדני, in Ezekiel's favourite expression אדני יהוה, is a substitute of the tetragrammaton, and, with the exception of the instances in which it is used as a vocative, it does not belong to the original text.[45]

The evidence provided by the Septuagint is inconclusive. Especially in Ezekiel, the earliest pre-Hexaplaric manuscripts, as well as the Old Latin, demonstrate that the single κύριος was the original reading of LXX, at least in Ezek 1–39.[46] Theoretically, this may suggest that אדני יהוה may have replaced an earlier reading, יהוה. More probably, however, the Greek scribes assumed that אדני יהוה in their parent text was the result of a *Ketiv* and a *Qere* written together, and so have retained κύριος only,[47] or they

---

[42] The fragments are published in DJD: 1QEzek in Barthélemy, *Qumran Cave* 1, pp. 68–69; 3QEzek in Maurice Baillet *et al.* (eds.), *Les "petites grottes" de Qumrân. Explorations de la falaise, les grottes 2Q, 3Q, 5Q, 6Q, 7Q à 10Q, le rouleau de cuivre* (DJD 3; Oxford, 1962), p. 94; 4QEzek[a,b,c] in Ulrich, *Qumran Cave 4*, pp. 209–220; 11QEzek in Florentino García Martínez, Eibert J.C. Tigchelaar, and Adam S. van der Woude (eds.), *Qumran Cave 11* (DJD 23; Oxford, 1998), pp. 15–28.

[43] Shemaryahu Talmon, 'Fragments of an Ezekiel Scroll from Masada (Ezek 35:11–38,14) 1043–2220 MAS ID', *OLoP* 27 (1996), pp. 29–49.

[44] See Lust, '*Ezekiel Text*', pp. 165–167.

[45] The main propagator of this view is Wolf W. Baudissin, *Kyrios als Gottesname im Judentum und seine Stelle in der Religionsgeschichte* (Giessen, 1929). For a discussion of his thesis, see Lucien Cerfaux, *Le nom divin 'Kyrios' dans la Bible Grecque*, in *RSPhTh* 20 (1931), pp. 27–51 = Lucien Cerfaux, *Recueil Lucien Cerfaux. Études d'exégèse et d'histoire religieuse* (BEThL 6–7; Leuven, 1954), pp. 113–136; Otto Eissfeldt, 'אָדוֹן אֲדֹנָי', in G. Johannes Botterweck and Helmer Ringgren (eds.), *Theologisches Wörterbuch zum Alten Testament* 1 (Stuttgart, 1970), col. 62–77.

[46] Edmund H. Kase, 'The *Nomen Sacrum* in Ezekiel', in Allan C. Johnson, Henry S. Gehman, Edmund H. Kase (eds.), *The John H. Scheide Biblical Papyri* 1. *Ezekiel* (Princeton, 1938), p. 50.

[47] Lesley J. McGregor, *The Greek Text of Ezekiel. An Examination of Its Homogeneity* (SCSt 18; Atlanta, 1985), p. 90.

may have wished to avoid the redundancy of a repeated divine name. At a later stage of the development of the Greek text there was a tendency to adapt the Greek text to the Hebrew. Scribes had several options for rendering the double name: αδωναι κύριος, κύριος κύριος, κύριος ὁ θεός.

The Masada fragments of Ezekiel, dated to the second half of the first century BCE, preserved the double name, or traces thereof (Ezek 35:12, 15; 36:2, 3, 4, 7, 22, 23; 37:3, 5, 9, 12). All these instances exhibit full agreement with MT, thus offering support to the view that אדני was already present in the proto-Masoretic text of Ezekiel.

Supplementary reasons for the authenticity of the double name can be found in the contexts in which it is used. We noted that in Ezekiel, the double name occurs almost exclusively in the 'framing-formulae' at the beginning and at the end of the oracles and in the prophetic formulaic prayer 'Oh my Lord YHWH'.

In all these cases, אדני was most likely originally vocalized אֲדֹנִי 'my Lord'. Indeed, when the double name is used, it is never attributed to the enemy, or to the Israelites, but only to the prophet, when addressing his public in the name of his Lord. The same vocalisation explains why the title was hardly ever attributed to the Lord. Put in a more positive way, one may state that the double name expresses the privileged relationship between the prophet and 'his' Lord.

The five exceptional cases in which the Lord says: 'they / you shall know that I am אדני יהוה' in verses 13:9;[48] 23:49; 24:24; 28:24; 29:16, contrast with the 50 occurrences of this formula in which the double name is not attested. We can assume that these exceptions are due to the work of late glossators or copyists who no longer understood the system.

There are three special cases in which MT unexpectedly uses יהוה without the preceding אדני. LXX indirectly supports the view that these cases belong to later editorial inserts or re-workings. In two of them (21:8; 30:6) the pre-Hexaplaric witnesses codex Vaticanus and papyrus 967 do not have the said formula. The third instance (11:5) occurs in a section of the papyrus that is still missing. The insertion of λεγε in Codex Vaticanus demonstrates that the passage is influenced by recensional activity.[49] These data strongly suggest that the slightly anomalous

[48] אדני is absent in *Codex Petropolitanus* Heb B 3.

[49] Joseph Ziegler, *Ezechiel* (Septuaginta. Vetus Testamentum Graecum Auctoritate Societatis Litterarum Gottingensis editum 16.1; Göttingen, 1952), p. 41.

single name in the messenger formula in the Masoretic text of 11:5; 21:8; 30:6 was not present in the pre-Masoretic parent text of LXX.

None of the data listed above, call for a deletion of אדני in the double name in the Masoretic text of Ezekiel. Let us now briefly survey the relevant passages in Isaiah.

3.2. *Textual Criticism in Isaiah*

3.2.1. The Title האדון

The five cases featuring האדון יהוה צבאות do not raise real text-critical problems. In 1:24; 3:1; 10:33, the Qumran Hebrew scrolls as well as the early translations largely support MT. LXX reads ὁ δεσπότης κύριος σαβαωϑ,[50] clearly distinguishing between the title האדון and the name יהוה.[51] In 1:24 and 3:1 BHS and most commentators do not doubt the authenticity of האדון. Without much of a discussion, and in disagreement with BHS and his fellow commentators, Wildberger proposes to delete האדון in 10:33.[52]

In 10:16 and 19:4 the situation is somewhat different. 1QIsa[a] supports MT, but LXX reads κύριος σαβαωϑ, suggesting that the translator did not find האדון in his *Vorlage*. BHS deletes האדון because of its omission in LXX, in some MT manuscripts of 10:16, and in the Syriac version of 19:4, as does Wildberger also.[53]

The main conclusions of this section are that (1) in general, the textual witnesses do not raise many questions about the authenticity of האדון, (2) LXX clearly distinguishes between the title האדון, rendering it ὁ δεσπότης, and the divine name יהוה, rendering it κύριος. Let us now turn to the instances that have אדני. We first list the 12 cases in Proto-Isaiah (out of 25 in Isaiah as a whole) in which MT has the double name, and then the 22 cases (out of 23 in Isaiah) in which MT has אדני alone.

---

[50] In 1:24 some Greek manuscripts have a transposition; κύριος ὁ δεσπότης (26–106, B *L*—36 534 Bo). V reads *Dominus exercituum*, and thus seems to omit האדון.

[51] As also in Gen 15:8.

[52] Wildberger, *Jesaja 1–12*, p. 425.

[53] Wildberger, *Jesaja*, pp. 405 and 700, with reference to Marti and Driver.

3.2.2. The Title אדני יהוה

- In 3:15, 1QIsa[a] has יהוה with a supralinear אדוני. The pre-Hexaplaric manuscripts of LXX have no counterpart for נאם אדני יהוה צבאות. Many Hexaplaric and Lucianic manuscripts insert φησὶ(ν) κύριος κύριος στρατιῶν (V-*oI' L*) adapting the text to MT. Because the line as a whole is missing in LXX, BHS proposes to delete the phrase.[54] Wildberger sees no reason for this correction, but deletes אדני, referring to its later supralinear insertion in 1QIsa[a].[55] Kaiser also deletes אדני, for similar reasons.
- In 7:7, 1QIsa[a] supports MT; LXX reads κύριος σαβαωθ. The editions and commentaries do not propose any corrections.
- In 10:23, 1QIsa[a] supports MT. The pre-Hexaplaric, as well as the majority of the other Greek manuscripts, render the אדני יהוה צבאות in the MT by one word: ὁ θεός. Adding κύριος κύριος δυνάμεων, some Hexaplaric manuscripts adapt the text to MT. Rather hesitantly, BHS proposes to delete יהוה צבאות. Because of the omission of this phrase in two Hebrew manuscripts and in LXX, Wildberger simply deletes אדני, saying that, here and elsewhere in Isaiah, it functioned as a replacement for the Tetragrammaton.[56]
- In 10:24, 1QIsa[a] again supports MT. Pre-Hexaplaric LXX has κύριος σαβαωθ for MT אדני יהוה צבאות. S* and some Lucianic manuscripts insert ὁ θεός. Referring to LXX and to his observations on האדון in 10:16, Wildberger also omits אדני here.[57] BHS does not see any reason for this procedure.
- In 22:5, all LXX manuscripts have παρὰ κυρίου σαβαωθ for LXX לאדני יהוה צבאות supported by 1QIsa[a]. BHS and Wildberger do not question the authenticity of אדני.
- In 22:12 both 4QIsa[a] and 4QIsa[c] support MT, but pre-Hexaplaric LXX has κύριος σαβαωθ. Some Hexaplaric and Lucianic manuscripts insert κύριος before σαβαωθ. BHS and Wildberger delete אדני because it is missing in LXX and the Ethiopic version.[58]

[54] Here Moshe H. Goshen-Gottstein, *The Book of Isaiah* (Jerusalem, 1975), p. 12, characterizes LXX as a 'condensation', and compares the passage with Isa 14:22–23.
[55] Wildberger, *Jesaja*, p. 131.
[56] Wildberger, *Jesaja*, p. 412.
[57] Wildberger, *Jesaja*, p. 427.
[58] Wildberger, *Jesaja*, p. 808.

- In 22:14, LXX has no counterpart for the concluding line אמר אדני יהוה צבאות in MT and 1QIsa[a]. BHS, Wildberger, and many others delete the line, because of its omission in LXX.[59]
- In 22:15, 1QIsa[a] again supports MT. Pre-Hexaplaric LXX reads κύριος σαβαωθ. Some Hexaplaric manuscripts insert κύριος whereas some Lucianic manuscripts insert ὁ θεός and replace σαβαωθ by τῶν δυνάμεων. BHS as well as many commentators delete it, whereas Wildberger preserves it, saying that the Old Greek probably dropped it because κύριος was already used for the Tetragrammaton.[60]
- In 25:8, 1QIsa[a] again supports MT. The Old Greek[61] exceptionally has ὁ θεός. The Hexaplaric manucripts insert κύριος, in agreement with MT. BHS accepts MT. Wildberger and Kaiser have no text critical objections against MT.
- In 28:16, 1QIsa[a] has יהוה with supralinearly אדוני. The Old Greek reads κύριος alone. The Hexaplaric manuscripts insert κύριος, in agreement with MT. BHS accepts MT. Wildberger and Kaiser have no text critical objections against MT.
- In 28:22, MT reads אדני יהוה צבאות whereas 1QIsa[a] has יהוה צבאות, and is supported by LXX κυρίου σαβαωθ. BHS recommends the deletion of אדני. Kaiser follows.[62] Wildberger accepts MT.
- In 30:15, 1QIsa[a] has יהוה with supralinearly אדוני. The Old Greek[63] reads κύριος alone. The Hexaplaric manuscripts insert κύριος, in agreement with MT. BHS accepts MT. Wildberger and Kaiser have no text-critical objections to MT.

3.2.3. Summary of the Comments

In as far as the Qumran evidence for Isaiah as a whole is concerned, the conclusions may be summarized as follows: In four instances 1QIsa[a] reads יהוה for MT אדני, but adds אדוני above the line (3:15; 28:16; 30:15; 65:13). Once it adds אדוני where MT has יהוה alone (49:7). In four instances 1QIsa[a] reads יהוה, and simply omits אדני (28:22; 49:22; 52:4; 61:1).

---

[59] Wildberger, *Jesaja*, p. 809.
[60] Wildberger, *Jesaja*, p. 832.
[61] With the exception of manuscript S.
[62] Kaiser, *Jesaja 13–39*, p. 195.
[63] With the exception of manuscript Q 106.

Twice it construes the double name with אלוהים: (50:5 אדוני אלהים; 61:11 יהוה אלוהים). Once it seems to delete אדוני with supralinear dots (56:8).

In the days of the Qumran scribes, אדני and יהוה could be used indiscriminately, at least in the biblical texts. The variants in the large Isaiah scroll provide ample proof of this phenomenon. The origin of the practice is most likely to be found in the pronunciation of יהוה as אדני.

Whereas LXX usually renders האדון ὁ δεσπότης, it omits אדני. LXX most often renders אדני יהוה by κύριος alone. LXX's omission of אדני is no sufficient reason for its deletion.

Twice LXX has no counterpart for אדני because the whole speech formula in which it occurs is missing (3:15 and 22:14). The omission may be due to the fact that the translator did not find the line in his *Vorlage*. More likely, it is simply due to abbreviation. Williamson rightly observes that, in both instances, the next verse also begins with a divine speech formula. Each time LXX represents only one formula, at the start of the second verse.

In 10:23 LXX does not only omit אדני, but it also omits צבאות. The translator probably did not find the phrase in his *Vorlage*. This is confirmed by the fact that, according to BHS, the phrase אדני צבאות is also missing in two Kennicott Hebrew manuscripts.

3.2.4. אדני alone

1QIsa[a] as well as LXX (κύριος) support MT in 16 cases: 4:4; 6:1, 8; 7, 14, 20; 9:16; 10:12; 11:11; 21:6, 8; 29:13; 30:20; 37:24; 38:14, 16.

In 3:17, 1QIsa[a] has אדוני erased by dots, and supralinearly יהוה. Interestingly LXX, with the exception of the main group of *catenae* manuscripts, has ὁ θεός. The *catenae* often preserve the Hexaplaric reading. They may do so here: they read κύριος in conformity with the correction in 1QIsa[a] and with MT. In 3:18 1QIsa[a] has יהוה erased by dots, and supralinearly אדוני; LXX reads κύριος. In 6:11, 1QIsa[a] has יהוה. LXX (κύριε) supports MT. In 8:7, 1QIsa[a] has יהוה and supralinearly אדוני; the case can be compared with 3:18; due to scroll damage, it is no longer possible to see whether or not the original יהוה was erased by dots here as well. LXX reads κύριος. In 9:16, 1QIsa[a] supports MT; LXX reads ὁ θεός, which the Hexaplaric tradition changed into κύριος in agreement with MT. In 21:16, 1QIsa[a] has יהוה; 4QIsa[a] as well as LXX (κύριος) support MT. In 28:2, 1QIsa[a] has ליהוה where MT reads לאדני; LXX (κυρίου) supports MT.

3.3. *Text-critical Conclusions*

In 15 cases out of 22, 1QIsa[a] as well as LXX agree with MT. Five times 1QIsa[a] has יהוה for MT אדני (6,11; 7:14; 9:7; 21:16; 28:2). Twice it reads יהוה, but adds deleting dots underneath, and supralinearly אדוני (3:18; 8:7); in 3:17 1QIsa[a] reads אדוני, but adds deleting dots underneath, and supralinearly יהוה; in the parallel clause, however, it has ואדוני where MT reads ויהוה.[64] 4QIsa[c] has אדני in 24:1; MT and 1QIsa[a] read יהוה.

As a rule, LXX renders אדני κύριος, which implies that the translators did not distinguish between אדני and יהוה.

The main conclusion of the text-critical observations on Isaiah are, that scribes and translators scarcely distinguished between אדני and יהוה, whereas they clearly distinguished between האדון and יהוה.

4. *General Conclusions*

1. In as far as the use of אדני and האדון is concerned, Isaiah's exclusive use of האדון is the most distinctive feature of that book. Remarkably, the titles האדון and אדני seem to occur repeatedly and interchangeably in the phrases האדון יהוה צבאות and אדני יהוה צבאות. Within the same literary unit, the first phrase is employed in the opening verse (3:1), and the second in the final verse (3:15), forming an *inclusio*. The first occurs within the oracle, and qualifies the Lord as the ruler of the world. The second is part of a framing formula, and denotes the relationship between the Lord and his prophetic ambassador.
2. The history of the literary growth of Isaiah is complex. According to Sweeney, האדון always occurs in the more original sections, whereas אדני can be found in different editorial layers of the book. This view is disputable. Nevertheless, the data allow one to conclude that the two titles do not occur in the same original section.
3. Scribes and translators clearly distinguish between האדון and יהוה, but not between אדני and יהוה. A comparison between MT and 1QIsa[a] demonstrates that at the time of the Qumran community, אדני and יהוה were interchangeable, whereas האדון and יהוה were not. The Septuagint confirms this. The translator used δεσπότης as an equivalent for אדון, but never as an equivalent for אדני. Most often the Old Greek

[64] In 49:14 1QIsa[a] reads אדוני with supralinearly אלוהים accompanied by erasing dots.

rendered the double name κύριος. The Greek translators and scribes probably assumed that אדני יהוה in their parent text was the result of a *Ketiv* and a *Qere* written together, and so they retained κύριος only.

4. The stereotypical pattern in the application of אדני יהוה, found in Ezekiel, which argues in favour of the authenticity of the compound name, is completely missing in Isaiah. More often than not, Isaiah uses the messenger and oracular formulas without the double name. This does not necessarily mean that the personal relationship between the prophet and his Lord God, expressed in Ezekiel's exclusive use of the double name, is absent in Isaiah. Several factors argue in favour of the hypothesis that, in Isaiah, the title אדני also means 'my Lord'.
5. אדני alone occurs frequently in Proto-Isaiah, but only once in Deutero-Isaiah and twice in Ezekiel. Its frequent use in Isaiah's visionary account of his call suggests that it expresses the prophet's special relationship with his heavenly Lord.

'RUINS' IN TEXT AND ARCHAEOLOGY. A NOTE ON THE WORDING OF 'DESTRUCTION' IN THE LATTER PROPHETS

Karel Vriezen

1. *Introduction*

Studying the maps of Palestine as a student, I was amazed to find ancient ruins often indicated by 'Kh./Khirbeh' instead of by 'tell'. Modern Hebrew editions of these maps use the legend חָרְבָּה/ח׳ for these locations. The word חָרְבָּה is also known from the Hebrew Bible, especially from the books of the Latter Prophets, including Deutero- and Trito-Isaiah. There, the word occurs frequently, meaning 'ruin'. It is striking that in the books of the Hebrew Bible, in which the conquest of the Promised Land and the destruction of Canaanite cities is narrated, that is, the books of Joshua and Judges, the word חָרְבָּה and related vocabulary does not occur. This raises the question of whether the wording used by the authors/redactors of the books of the Latter Prophets reflects a material situation familiar to these writers. As my early encounters with the legends of 'Khirbeh'/'חָרְבָּה' happened in the mid-sixties, when I first met Arie van der Kooij, I would like to contribute a note on this topic to the volume in his honour.

2. *Archaeology: Theories of the Emergence of Ancient Israel in Palestine*

Since the 1920s and 30s the concept of 'destruction' has played a major role in the archaeology of Palestine, as at that time the search for the emergence of the people of ancient Israel had become a much debated topic. Following the narratives in the first half of the Book of Joshua, William Foxwell Albright developed the theory of the Hebrew Conquest of Palestine.[1] Excavations at sites such as Beitin/Bethel, Tell Beit

[1] William F. Albright, 'Observations on the Bethel Report', *BASOR* 57 (1935), pp. 27–30; idem, 'Archaeology and the Date of the Hebrew Conquest of Palestine', *BASOR*

Mirsim/Debir, Tell es-Sultan/Jericho and Tell ed-Duweir/Lachish had brought evidence of the devastation of the large Late Bronze Age (LBA) cities, and through investigations at sites such as Tell el-Ful/Gibea and et-Tell/Ai the material culture of the Early Iron Age (EIA) had become known. These archaeological results were seen as evidence of the uniform military campaign led by Joshua and the settlement of the Israelites, as described in the Book of Joshua. In the same period a different approach to the settlement process was developed by Albrecht Alt, the so-called Peaceful Infiltration theory.[2] According to this theory the settlement of the new population in the EIA had started as a slow process of infiltration by semi-nomads into the uninhabited areas of Palestine, where they became sedentary and from where they later spread over the country and came into conflict with the inhabitants of the LBA-cities.

In the sixties the scholarly debate on the Hebrew Conquest of Palestine was revived by the findings in the excavations on Tell el-Qedah/Hazor by Yigael Yadin[3] and on Tell es-Sultan/Jericho by Kathleen Kenyon.[4] The remains of a huge conflagration of the LBA-city excavated on the Tell el-Qedah seemed to substantiate the historical information about Joshua's conquests, but the absence of late-LBA finds on Tell es-Sultan seemed to put the historical information on the destruction of Jericho in doubt. In the same years scepticism was voiced about the evidence for a unified conquest, as the destruction of various LBA-cities was not dated to one period,[5] and questions on the principles of the Peaceful Infiltration theory led to a new, sociological approach postulating that the new settlement resulted from social and political upheavals in the LBA city states.[6] In recent decades the results of large-scale surveys on the West Bank have led to a widely accepted theory, that the new settlements

58 (1935), pp. 10–18; idem, 'Further Light on the History of Israel from Lachish and Megiddo', *BASOR* 68 (1937), pp. 22–26; idem, 'The Israelite Conquest of Canaan in the Light of Archaeology', *BASOR* 74 (1939), pp. 11–23.

[2] Albrecht Alt, 'Die Landnahme der Israeliten in Palästina', in *Reformationsprogramm der Universität Leipzig 1925* (Leipzig, 1925); idem, 'Erwägungen über die Landnahme der Israeliten in Palästina', *PJ* 35 (1939), pp. 8–63 (= idem, *Kleine Schriften zur Geschichte des Volkes Israel* 1 [München, 1953], pp. 89–125, 126–175).

[3] Yigael Yadin, *Hazor. The Schweich Lectures 1970* (London, 1972).

[4] Kathleen M. Kenyon, *Digging Up Jericho* (London, 1957).

[5] Hendricus J. Franken, *Van Aartsvaders tot Profeten* (Amsterdam, 1962), pp. 95–100, 135–143; Hendricus J. Franken and C.A. Franken–Battershill, *A Primer of Old Testament Archaeology* (Leiden, 1963), pp. 78–80.

[6] George E. Mendenhall, 'The Hebrew Conquest of Palestine', *BA* 25 (1962), pp. 66–87.

of the EIA did not result from an influx of people from outside, but had started as a sedentarization process of indigenous pastoralists in the marginal areas in the hill country due to its suitability for growing cereals and for pasturage.[7]

3. *Text: The Conquest of the Promised Land*

The biblical texts inspiring the theory of the Hebrew Conquest of Palestine occur in Joshua 1–12, to which texts from Deuteronomy and Judges may be added. Here, the narratives of the campaigns led by Joshua, waging war against the cities of Jericho, Ai, the Shephela and the southern and northern hill country are prominent. It should be stressed, however, that the dominant themes of these texts are indicated by the noun חֵרֶם and the verbs חרם, ירשׁ and נכה.

By their very nature, these narratives describe activities and events mainly directed against people and properties. An example of the phraseology exhibited by such texts is Josh 10:30b:

ויכה לפי חרב ואת כל הנפשׁ אשׁר בה
לא השׁאיר בה שׂריד

'He smote it (that is, Libnah) with the edge of the sword, namely
every person in it;
he left no one remaining in it'.

In this text the ו preceding את functions as a ו-explicativum[8] indicating which elements of the city were destroyed. Only in case of Jericho, Hazor and Ai is it stated that the cities themselves were destroyed.

Of the thematic roots חֵרֶם / חרם and ירשׁ, the first one is frequently used in the Book of Joshua.[9] As regards the occurrences of חֵרֶם / חרם, in Joshua 6 they seem to represent the ancient tradition of the

[7] Israel Finkelstein, *The Archaeology of the Israelite Settlement* (Jerusalem, 1988).

[8] Wilhelm Gesenius and Emil Kautzsch, *Hebräische Grammatik* (28th ed.; Leipzig, 1909), English edition Arthur E. Cowley, *Gesenius' Hebrew Grammar*, (2nd ed.; Oxford, 1910), § 154 *a*, note 1b.

[9] חרם *hiph'il*, 'put under a ban', 'devote to destruction', 'dedicate', (HALOT 353*a*–354*b*). The verb (V) חרם and its derivative (N) חֵרֶם occur in: Exodus (1 × V); Leviticus (3 × V; 4 × N); Numbers (2 × V; 1 × N); Deuteronomy (5 × V; 4 × N); Joshua (12 × V; 13 × N); Judges (2 × V); 1–2 Samuel (7 × V; 1 × N); 1–2 Kings (2 × V; 1 × N); Isaiah (3 × V; 2 × N); Jeremiah (4 × V); Ezekiel (1 × N); Micah (1 × V); Zechariah (1 × N); Malachi (1 × N); Daniel (1 × V); Ezra (1 × V); 1–2 Chronicles (3 × V; 1 × N).

war-חֵרֶם,[10] whereas in Joshua 10–11 they may be understood as a deuteronomistic element introduced into the text, recalling the חֵרֶם-laws of Deuteronomy 7 and 20:16–18.[11] However, in all these occurrences the root is usually translated as 'utterly destroy' (KJV and RSV). Nearly always, its objects involve persons and properties. In a few instances, cities are mentioned alongside persons. It is not clear whether this also implies the destruction of those cities (Josh 10:37; 11:21).[12]

Nor does the root ירשׁ,[13] which may be understood as a deuteronomistic element in our texts,[14] seem to indicate material destruction.[15] In the conquest narratives, the roots חֵרֶם / חרם and ירשׁ, together with the verb נכה, designate actions taken to capture the Promised Land and to eradicate from there non-Israelite people and their properties, who could seduce the Israelites to follow other gods than the Lord, and thus pose a threat to order and harmony in the community of Israel.

These narratives generally do not mention large-scale destruction by which cities are turned into ruins. This seems to be in harmony with the promise that the Israelites would inherit the Promised Land 'with great and good cities, which you did not build, houses full of all good things, which you did not fill …' (Deut 6:10–15; cf. Josh 24:13; Deut 19:1). Besides, one wonders how the prescriptions of the law of the *herem* may have been envisaged, since in deuteronomistic texts the theme of

---

[10] Christianus H.W. Brekelmans, *De Herem in het Oude Testament* (Nijmegen, 1959), pp. 153–163; Philip D. Stern, *The Biblical Herem. A Window on Israel's Religious Experience* (Atlanta, 1991), pp. 89–103.

[11] Brekelmans, *Herem*, pp. 101–103; for Josh 8:2, ibidem, pp. 98–101; Stern, *Biblical Herem*, pp. 157–160, 217.

[12] 'Jericho' and 'Ai' in Josh 10:1 refer to the destruction of those cities in Joshua 6 and 8. In the special case of a punishment-חֵרֶם, executed against an apostate Israelite city (Deut 13:12–18), the total destruction of the city itself is specified.

[13] The verb (V) ירשׁ and its derivatives (N) יְרֵשָׁה, יְרֻשָּׁה, מוֹרָשׁ, מוֹרָשָׁה and רֶשֶׁת occur in: Genesis (8×V); Exodus (2×V; 5×N); Leviticus (3×V); Numbers (15×V; 1×N); Deuteronomy (71×V; 6×N); Joshua (30×V; 3×N); Judges (27×V; 1×N); 1–2 Samuel (2×V); 1–2 Kings (8×V); Isaiah (10×V; 1×N); Jeremiah (7×V; 1×N); Ezekiel (6×V; 11×N); Hosea (2×N); Amos (2×V); Obadiah (3×V; 1×N); Micah (1×V); Habakkuk (1×V); Psalms (10×V; 9×N); Job (2×V; 2×N); Proverbs (4×V; 2×N); Lamentations (1×N); Ezra (2×V); Nehemiah (5×V); 1–2 Chronicles (5×V; 1×N).

[14] Norbert Lohfink, 'Kerygmata des Deuteronomistischen Geschichtswerks', in Joachim Jeremias and Lothar Perlitt (eds.), *Die Botschaft und die Boten. Festschrift für Hans Walter Wolff zum 70. Geburtstag* (Neukirchen–Vluyn, 1981), pp. 86–100; idem, 'Die Bedeutungen von hebr. *jrš qal* und *hif*', *BZ NF* 27 (1983), pp. 14–33.

[15] Lohfink, 'Bedeutungen', pp. 14–33.

remnants of the pre-Israelite population still left in the land amidst the Israelites seems to be an important one (cf. Josh 23:7, 12–13; Judg 2:23–3:4).

Therefore, from the idiom of these texts alone no evidence can be extracted in support of the theory that a unified Israelite conquest of Palestine brought about the destruction of the LBA-cities. Except for the record of the narratives of Jericho, Ai and Hazor, no destruction is mentioned, and the narratives concerning the first two cities may be interpreted as aetiological legends.[16] Only in Josh 8:28 do we find a Hebrew term indicating a waste place resulting from destruction: שְׁמָמָה (referring to Ai).

4. *Text: The Wording of Destruction and the Latter Prophets*

In contrast to the texts mentioned above, which played an important role in the archaeological discussion on conquest and destruction, another major group of texts in the Old Testament, that is, the Latter Prophets from Deutero-Isaiah onwards, do contain the idiom for 'ruins' and 'destruction'.

Words related to the root חרב II[17] occur 69× in Tanakh, frequently in the shape of the noun חָרְבָּה noted in the first lines of this contribution.[18] The vast majority of these occurrences are in the books of the Latter Prophets, mainly Deutero- and Trito-Isaiah, Jeremiah and Ezekiel. There, words related to this root are used in prophecies of doom describing the desolation which would come for the people of Judah/Israel[19] and the nations,[20] in prophecies of salvation announcing restoration for the people of Judah/Israel,[21] in descriptions of actual situations,[22] and in other

[16] Martin Noth, 'Grundsätzliches zur geschichtlichen Deutung archäologischer Befunde auf dem Boden Palästinas', *PJ* 34 (1938), pp. 7–22 (= idem, *Aufsätze zur biblischen Landes- und Altertumskunde* I [Neukirchen–Vluyn, 1971], pp. 3–16).

[17] חרב II = 'massacre' (HALOT 349*b*). According to DCH 3, 306*b*, חרב II = 'destroy'.

[18] The substantives (S) חָרְבָּה (41×) and (S1) חֹרֶב II (3×), the verb (V) חרב II (17×), and the adjective (A) חָרֵב II (8×).

[19] 9×(S): Isa 5:17; Jer 7:3; 22:5; 25:9, 11, 18; 27:17; Ezek 5:14; 35:4. 5×(V): Jer 26:9; Ezek 6:6 (2×); 12:20; Amos 7:9.

[20] 7×(S): Jer 49:13; Ezek 25:13; 26:20; 29:9, 10; 38:12; Mal 1:4. 2×(S1): Ezek 29:10; Zeph 2:14. 7×(V): Isa 60:12; Jer 50:21, 27; Ezek 26:2, 19; 29:12; 30:7.

[21] 9×(S): Isa 44:26; 49:19; 51:3; 52:9; 58:12; 61:4; Ezek 36:10, 33; 38:8. 1×(S1): Isa 61:4. 1×(V): Isa 49:17. 2×(A): Ezek 36:35, 38.

[22] 7×(S): Isa 64:10; Jer 44:2, 6, 22; Ezek 33:24, 27; 36:4. 2×(A): Jer 33:10, 12.

contexts.[23] In Haggai, Ezra, and Nehemiah these words occur in descriptions of the deplorable situation of Jerusalem.[24] Other occurrences are sparse and occur in various contexts.[25]

Other roots of the word-family indicating 'destroy' and 'destruction' have a similar distribution in Tanakh. Of the root שׁמם and its derivatives[26] (189 ×), most instances occur in the Latter Prophets and quite a number in the Writings, while the number of occurrences in the Torah and the Former Prophets is modest.[27] The vast majority of cases of the root שׁדד (78 ×)[28] are in the Latter Prophets (mainly in Jeremiah, Isaiah, Hosea and Amos) and the rest are in the Writings and, once, in Judges.[29] Words related to the root הרס and derivatives (41 ×)[30] are mainly used in the Latter Prophets, while the rest are distributed equally over Exodus, Judges/Samuel/Kings/Chronicles, and the Writings.[31]

These verbs generally have inanimate objects, and seldom animate ones. Their derivatives indicate the results of destructive actions: ruins.[32]

---

[23] 1 × (S): Ezek 13:4. 2 × (V): Jer 2:12; Zeph 3:6.

[24] 1 × (S): Ezra 9:9. 1 × (V[Aramaic]): Ezra 4:15. 4 × (A): Hag 1:4, 9; Neh 2:3, 17. Cf. Dan 9:2(S).

[25] 6 × (S): Lev 26:31, 33; Job 3:4; Ps 9:7; 102:7; 109:10. 1 × (V): 2 Kgs 3:23.

[26] שׁמם *qal*, 'be uninhabited/deserted', 'be removed from contact', 'shudder' (HALOT 1563*a*–1564*b*). The verb (V) שׁמם (80 ×) and its derivatives (N) שְׁמָמָה (59 ×), שַׁמָּה (45 ×), שְׁמֵם (3 ×), and שִׁמָּמוֹן (2 ×).

[27] Isaiah (10 × V; 10 × N); Jeremiah (11 × V; 41 × N); Ezekiel (26 × V; 32 × N); Hosea (1 × N); Joel (1 × V; 5 × N); Amos (2 × V); Micah (1 × V; 3 × N); Zephaniah (1 × V; 5 × N); Zechariah (1 × V; 1 × N); Malachi (1 × N); Genesis (1 × V); Exodus (1 × N); Leviticus (4 × V; 1 × N); Numbers (1 × V); Deuteronomy (1 × N); Joshua (1 × N); 1–2 Samuel (2 × V); 1–2 Kings (1 × V; 1 × N); Psalms (4 × V; 1 × N); Job (4 × V); Ecclesiastes (1 × V); Lamentations (5 × V; 1 × N); Ezra (2 × V); Daniel (1 × N); 1–2 Chronicles (2 × V; 2 × N).

[28] שׁדד 'devastate' (HALOT 1418*b*–1420*a*). The verb (V) שׁדד (53 ×) and its derivative (N) שֹׁד (25 ×).

[29] Isaiah (10 × V; 6 × N); Jeremiah (23 × V; 3 × N); Ezekiel (1 × V; 1 × N); Hosea (2 × V; 4 × N); Joel (1 × V; 1 × N); Amos (3 × N); Obadiah (1 × V); Micah (2 × V); Nahum (1 × V); Habakkuk (2 × N); Zechariah (3 × V); Judges (1 × V); Psalms (3 × V; 1 × N); Job (2 × V; 2 × N); Proverbs (3 × V; 2 × N).

[30] הרס 'tear down' (HALOT 256*a*–257*a*). The verb (V) הרס (40 ×) and derivatives (N) הֲרִסֻת / הֲרִיסָה (2 ×).

[31] Isaiah (3 × V; 1 × N); Jeremiah (7 × V); Ezekiel (8 × V); Joel (1 × V); Amos (1 × V; 1 × N); Micah (1 × V); Malachi (1 × V); Exodus (5 × V); Judges (1 × V); 1–2 Samuel (1 × V); 1–2 Kings (3 × V); 1–2 Chronicles (1 × V); Psalms (2 × V); Job (1 × V); Lamentations (2 × V); Proverbs (2 × V).

[32] As it seems, in general the root שׁבר (189 ×), which occurs frequently in the books of Isaiah, Jeremiah, and Ezekiel as the verb (V) שׁבר or its derivative (N) שֶׁבֶר, does not indicate material destruction. One exception is the Book of Lamentations, where it indicates the destruction of Jerusalem. Occurrences: Genesis (1 × V); Exodus (9 × V); Leviticus (6 × V; 2 × N); Numbers (1 × V); Deuteronomy (4 × V); Joshua (1 × N); Judges

Other verbs belonging to the word-family indicating 'destroy' and 'destruction', which have no nominal derivatives, occur more equally distributed over Tanakh.

Thus, of the verb נתץ (40+×), the majority of cases are equally distributed over the books of Judges, 2 Kings, Jeremiah, and 2 Chronicles.[33] In Jeremiah the verb is occasionally used together with הרס (see above), נתש, and אבד. The latter two verbs may have the meaning 'destroy', depending on the context in which they occur. As a rule, both are used with men or nations as the object. Occurrences of the verb נתש (20×) are concentrated in the Book of Jeremiah.[34] The verb אבד (171×) mainly occurs in the Latter Prophets and the Writings.[35] Its derivatives (14×), which have a general meaning of 'destruction' or 'lost property', are found in the Pentateuch and in the Writings only.[36] שמד (86×) is much used in Deuteronomy, while for the rest it is equally represented in the books of the Former and the Latter Prophets and the Writings.[37] This verb, even more than the latter two verbs, has persons or nations as an object.

This review leads to the conclusion that roots meaning 'destroy' with generally inanimate objects and noun-derivatives indicating the result of the destructive activity are mainly found in the Latter Prophets and seldom in the Former Prophets. Other roots, which, depending on the context in which they occur, may have the meaning 'destroy', often have

(1×V; 1×N); 1–2 Samuel (1×V); 1–2 Kings (9×V); Isaiah (14×V; 9×N); Jeremiah (28×V; 14×N); Ezekiel (21×V; 1×N); Hosea (2×V); Amos (1×V; 1×N); Jona (1×V); Nahum (1×V; 1×N); Zephaniah (1×N); Zechariah (1×V); Psalms (21×V; 1×N); Job (5×V; 1×N); Proverbs (2×V; 4×N); Ecclesiastes (1×V); Lamentations (3×V; 5×N); Daniel (8×V); 1–2 Chronicles (6×V).

[33] נתץ = 'tear down' (HALOT 736*ab*): Exodus 1×; Leviticus 2×; Deuteronomy 2×; Judges 8×; 1–2 Kings 6×; Isaiah 1×; Jeremiah 7×; Ezekiel 3×; Nahum 1×; Psalms 2×; Job 1×; 2 Chronicles 6×.

[34] נתש = 'remove' (HALOT 737*b*): Deuteronomy 1×; 1 Kings 1×; Jeremiah 13×; Ezekiel 1×; Amos 1×; Psalms 1×; Daniel 1×; 2 Chronicles 1×.

[35] אבד = 'become lost', 'go astray', 'perish', 'be destroyed' (HALOT 2*a*–3*a*): Exodus 1×; Leviticus 2×; Numbers 9×; Deuteronomy 22×; Joshua 3×; Judges 1×; 1–2 Samuel 3×; 1–2 Kings 7×; Isaiah 7×; Jeremiah 27×; Ezekiel 14×; Joel 1×; Amos 3×; Obadiah 2×; Jonah 3×; Micah 3×; Zephaniah 2×; Zechariah 1×; Psalms 25×; Job 15×; Proverbs 10×; Ecclesiastes 6×; Lamentations 2×; Esther 12×.

[36] אֹבֵד, אֲבֵדָה, אֲבַדֹּה, אֲבַדּוֹן, and אַבְדָן: Exodus 1×; Leviticus 2×; Numbers 2×; Deuteronomy 1×; Psalms 1×; Job 3×; Proverbs 2×; Esther 2×.

[37] שמד *hiph'il* = 'exterminate' (HALOT 1553*ab*): Genesis 1×; Leviticus 1×; Numbers 1×; Deuteronomy 30×; Joshua 6×; Judges 1×; 1–2 Samuel 6×; 1–2 Kings 6×; Isaiah 6×; Jeremiah 2×; Ezekiel 3×; Hosea 1×; Amos 4×; Micah 1×; Haggai 1×; Psalms 6×; Proverbs 1×; Esther 5×; 1–2 Chronicles 4×.

men or nations as an object and do not feature predominantly in the Latter Prophets; only some of them have noun-derivatives. This situation may reflect the world view of the Latter Prophets. The authors and redactors of these books were active in the period of the Neo-Assyrian campaigns in Palestine, during the Babylonian Exile, and in early post-exilic times. Apparently, they were not unfamiliar with the phenomenon of ruin and destruction.

5. *Archaeology of the Neo-Assyrian and the Neo-Babylonian Period and the Wording of Destruction in the Latter Prophets*

The Assyrian campaigns of Tiglath-Pileser III and his successors against areas and cities in Palestine may be viewed as the start of the Neo-Assyrian period in this region. They resulted in the devastation of large cities, such as Hazor, Samaria and Lachish, some of which remained waste places or were partly resettled, whereas others were rebuilt and flourished during the seventh century BCE and the beginning of the sixth.[38]

As for the sixth century BCE, the assumption that 'scores of large and small Jewish towns ... were destroyed by the Chaldeans in 597 and 587 BCE, after which the land lay fallow, with little or no sedentary population'[39] has been modified thanks to archaeological data recovered in recent decades. New insights into the continuity of habitation in Judah make it clear that after the Neo-Babylonian campaigns there were significant changes in settlement patterns, with a major decrease in settlements in the areas around and south of Jerusalem, and an increase in the area north of Jerusalem.[40] However, large cities had been destroyed and remained in ruins until the Persian period, such as the ones on Tell ed-

[38] Ephraim Stern, *The Archaeology of the Land of the Bible II: The Assyrian, Babylonian and Persian Periods (732–332 BCE)* (New York, 2001), pp. 46–51.

[39] William F. Albright, *The Archaeology of Palestine* (5th ed.; Harmondworth, 1960), pp. 130, 141–142.

[40] Cf. in Oded Lipschits and Joseph Blenkinsopp (eds.), *Judah and the Judeans in the Neo-Babylonian Period* (Winona Lake, 2003), for example, Hans M. Barstad, 'After the "Myth of the Empty Land": Major Challenges in the Study of Neo-Babylonian Judah', pp. 3–20; Joseph Blenkinsopp, 'Bethel in the Neo-Babylonian Period', pp. 93–107; C.E. Carter, 'Ideology and Archaeology in the Neo-Babylonian Period: Excavating Text and Tell', pp. 301–322; J.R. Zorn, 'Tell en-Nasbeh and the Problem of the Material Culture of the Sixth Century', pp. 413–447.

Duweir, Tell Beʾer Sheva, Tell Beit Mirsim, Ramat Rahel and Jerusalem.[41] The authors/redactors of the books of the Latter Prophets knew, probably from their own observation, of the destruction of major towns in Judah. This circumstance may have coloured the vocabulary of the Latter Prophets with nouns indicating ruin and destruction such as חָרְבָּה and שְׁמָמָה, nouns which were less frequently used or non-existent in the Books of Joshua and Judges in the vocabulary of conquest narratives about events long ago.

[41] Stern, *Archaeology*, pp. 323–325.

PATTERNS OF MUTUAL INFLUENCE IN THE TEXTUAL TRANSMISSION OF THE ORACLES CONCERNING MOAB IN ISAIAH AND JEREMIAH

Richard D. Weis*

1. *Introduction*

It has long been remarked that the oracles concerning Moab in the books of Isaiah and Jeremiah have a substantial amount of text in common, especially in Jer 48:29–38 and Isa 15:2–7 and 16:6–11. The oracle in Jeremiah also shares substantial text with verses from two passages related to Moab in Numbers (Num 21:27–28 and 24:17 with Jer 48:45–46) and with Isa 24:17–18 (Jer 48:43–44). The similarities between Jeremiah 48 and Isaiah 15–16 have often been interpreted quite reasonably as evidence that an earlier form of the Jeremiah oracle was expanded through the importation of text from the Isaiah oracle.[1] While much effort has been expended on tracing the influence of the Isaiah oracle on the Jeremian one in the course of the *literary* development of the Book of Jeremiah, rather less effort has been expended on considering whether there was influence between the two speeches during the *textual transmission* of the completed books.[2] This study will consider systematically

---

* I am delighted to offer this study in honour of Professor Arie van der Kooij, who through a long career has contributed so much to the study of the Book of Isaiah, especially its text and reception history. I offer it with deep appreciation for his friendship and colleagueship in our common work on *Biblia Hebraica Quinta*, in which—in addition to our duties as general editors—he is responsible for the Book of Isaiah and I for the Book of Jeremiah.

[1] For a relatively recent discussion, including citation of earlier literature, see Beat Huwyler, *Jeremia und die Völker* (FAT 20; Tübingen, 1997), pp. 150–193, especially pp. 180–191. See also William L. Holladay, *Jeremiah: A Commentary on the Book of the Prophet Jeremiah 2. Chapters 26–52* (Hermeneia; Minneapolis, 1989), pp. 347–348; and Jack R. Lundbom, *Jeremiah 37–52* (AncB 21C; New York etc., 2004), pp. 287–297. From the side of Isaiah note especially the discussion (also citing older literature) in Hans Wildberger, *Jesaja 2. Jesaja 13–27* (BK 10.2; Neukirchen, 1978), pp. 604–611.

[2] Of course, the possibility of such influence has been remarked in individual textual studies and in commentaries on the two oracles. However, it has not received systematic study as a phenomenon in itself except for a study by Emanuel Tov ('The Nature and

the possibility of such influence. Moreover, the focus will be on patterns of influence with the aim of discerning what that tells us about the way ancient readers saw the relations between these texts. In essence, by attending to the text of the Book of Jeremiah, we hope to be able to learn something about the reception history of the Book of Isaiah.

As we consider the possibilities for influence of one text on another in the transmission of the oracles concerning Moab, we may hope to find answers to several questions. First, are there signs of influence between the Isaiah and Jeremiah texts? Second, in which direction(s) does the influence flow—from Isaiah to Jeremiah, vice-versa, or in both directions? Third, is the influence between the Isaiah and Jeremiah texts part of a larger picture of mutual influence among all the Moab oracles/texts, simply because they refer to Moab, or is it particular to the Isaiah and Jeremiah speeches, or only to specific verses? Fourth, does the influence appear in particular witnesses, and if so, which ones?

This essay seeks to answer these questions through consideration of cases in Isaiah 15–16 and Jeremiah 48 of assimilation of these texts to other specific verses in the Bible, including those in these two passages. The total picture of assimilation between Jeremiah 48 and Isaiah 15–16 will be covered case by case. Likewise, all cases of assimilation between one of these passages and other Moab texts will be considered. Finally, cases of assimilation in Jeremiah 48 to 'non-Moab' texts will be considered as well.[3] At the end we will draw the conclusions the evidence suggests in relation to our questions, and consider what this says more broadly about the phenomenon of assimilation in the transmission of the biblical text, the reception of the text, and modern understandings of these phenomena.

Before examining the textual evidence an important methodological point needs clarification. The portions of Isaiah 15–16 and Jeremiah

Background of Harmonizations in Biblical Manuscripts', *JSOT* 31 [1985], pp. 3–29), which treats the phenomenon generally, without reference to Isaiah 15–16 and Jeremiah 48. Nevertheless, if one takes seriously Karel van der Toorn's point about the centrality of Deuteronomy, Isaiah, and Psalms to the scribal curriculum under the Second Temple (Karel van der Toorn, *Scribal Culture and the Making of the Hebrew Bible* [Cambridge, Mass., 2007], p. 102), the possibility merits investigation.

[3] The definition of assimilation used in this discussion is that of the *Biblia Hebraica Quinta* project: 'This characterization suggests that a particular force in generating the reading of a witness in the case has been an impulse to create or increase a degree of similarity with a text or contextual element with which a certain degree of similarity may already exist'. See Adrian Schenker *et al.*, *Biblia Hebraica Quinta* 18. *General Introduction and Megilloth* (Stuttgart, 2004), p. lxxxix.

48 that share common language are sometimes treated as parallel texts. Moreover, when this approach is taken and the Isaiah text is regarded as the source of that language in Jeremiah, the Isaiah text is then seen as a resource for 'correcting' the text of Jeremiah. In this study we will proceed from the position that Isaiah 15–16 and Jeremiah 48 are not true parallel texts, even in the verses where they have substantial verbiage in common. This may be seen from the fact that the verses that contain parallels do not occur in the same order in both texts, and also contain significant amounts of material that is not paralleled in the other oracle. This is rather different than the case of classic parallel texts such as Psalm 18 and 2 Samuel 22, Jeremiah 52 and 2 Kings 25 and the like.

2. *Assimilation to Jeremiah 48 in the Transmission of the Text of Isaiah 15–16*

An examination of the extant textual evidence for Isaiah 15–16 reveals seventeen cases where the reading of one or more witnesses is most effectively explained as assimilation to a portion of a verse in Jeremiah 48. Although a couple of the readings are those of 1QIsa[a], most come from the versions. In no cases does it seem that the reading of the Masoretic Text is to be explained as an instance of assimilation.

> Isa 15:2—הַבַּיִת וְדִיבֹן M V | ἀπολεῖται γὰρ Λεβηδών, G | ܠܒܝܬܐ ܕܝܒܘܢ S T (assim-Jer 48:18)[4]

Goshen-Gottstein, in the Hebrew University Bible volume on Isaiah, suggests that the readings of the Peshitta and Targum arise from assimilation to Jer 48:18, בַּת־דִּיבוֹן.[5] This seems the most reasonable explanation of

[4] The sigla, symbols, and abbreviations used in the entries for textual cases are these: M = Masoretic Text; G = Septuagint; S = Peshitta; V = Vulgate; T = Targum; α′ = Aquila; σ′ = Symmachus; θ′ = Theodotion; ιω′ = Iosippos; > = a minus; ⟨⟩ around a Hexaplaric siglum = retroverted reading; ( ) around a witness siglum = the witness departs from the given reading in some small detail(s); ampl = amplification; assim = assimilation to; confl = conflation; ctext = context; elus = elusive motivation; exeg = exegesis; explic = make explicit; facil = facilitation; indet = indeterminate in relation to the lemma; lib = liberty. For full definitions of the terms used to characterize readings, see Schenker *et al.*, *Biblia Hebraica Quinta*, pp. lxxxviii–xciv.

[5] Moshe H. Goshen-Gottstein, *The Book of Isaiah: Part One, Part Two* (HUB; Jerusalem, 1975), p. 59.

their deviation from the reading of the Masoretic Text, which has a pair of place names, rather than a construct chain.[6] However, it also entails the assumption that they vocalized בַּת as בֵּת.[7]

Isa 15:2—בְּכָל־רֹאשָׁיו M V S (T) | בכול ראושו 1QIsa[a] (confl) | ἐπὶ πάσης κεφαλῆς G (assim-Jer 48:37)

As will be seen from the following case, and from a number of cases from Jer 48:37, there are strong similarities between Isa 15:2bβγ and Jer 48:37a. Here the Septuagint reading in Isaiah most likely arises from assimilation to the corresponding text in Jer 48:37 (כָּל־רֹאשׁ), which lacks the pronominal suffix.[8]

Isa 15:2—כָּל־ M G σ′ θ′ V T | וכל 1QIsa[a] S (assim-Jer 48:37)

In Isa 15:2bβγ the parallelism of the poetic line serves well enough to structure the relation between the two clauses. In Jer 48:37a, however, they are explicitly coordinated with a conjunction (וְכָל־), to which text 1QIsa[a] and Peshitta seem to assimilate.

Isa 15:3—שָׂק M 1QIsa[a] V S T | σάκκους καὶ κόπτεσθε G (assim-Jer 48:38?)

Goshen-Gottstein suggests that the Septuagint reading κόπτεσθε implies a form from the root ספד.[9] The use of both שַׂק and a form from ספד in the sequence in the Isaian verse is found in Jer 48:37–38, which otherwise has many similarities to the Isaian context (note in particular וְעַל־מָתְנַיִם שָׂק: עַל כָּל־גַּגּוֹת מוֹאָב וּבִרְחֹבֹתֶיהָ כֻּלֹּה מִסְפֵּד, 'and on the loins sackcloth. On all the housetops of Moab and in the squares there is nothing but lamentation' [NRSV]).[10]

---

[6] Barthélemy suggests instead that the reading of Peshitta and Targum is a syntactic facilitation. See Dominique Barthélemy, *Critique textuelle de l'Ancien Testament 2. Isaïe, Jérémie, Lamentations* (OBO 50.2; Fribourg–Göttingen, 1986), p. 110.

[7] Wildberger emends to read with the text of Jer 48:18 (Wildberger, *Jesaja*, pp. 588, 590), arguably a modern assimilation to the Jeremiah text. Similarly, BHS emends on the basis of the reading of Peshitta and Targum and of Jer 48:18.

[8] Again Wildberger prefers a text that, following a few medieval manuscripts and the Septuagint, assimilates to Jer 48:37 (Wildberger, *Jesaja*, pp. 588, 590). Both BHK[3] and BHS cite Jer 48:37 as support for reading רֹאשׁ rather than the form in the Masoretic Text.

[9] Goshen-Gottstein, *Isaiah*, p. 59.

[10] Barthélemy, however, regards the Septuagint reading as assimilation, but to a usual pattern of expression, rather than a particular verse (Barthélemy, *Critique textuelle*, p. 112). BHS, on the other hand, instructs the reader to insert סִפְדוּ or נָהוּ on the basis of the Septuagint reading and Jer 48:38.

Isa 15:3—גַּגּוֹתֶיהָ M 1QIsa^a G V T | ܐܓܪܐ S (assim-Jer 48:38)

All of the witnesses to Isa 15:3 that preserve a reading for גַּגּוֹתֶיהָ render the suffix except for the Peshitta. This matches the corresponding text in Jer 48:38, עַל כָּל־גַּגּוֹת.

Isa 15:5—דֶּרֶךְ M 1QIsa^a G α′ V S | במחותית T (assim-Jer 48:5)

The extant witnesses for Isa 15:5 attest the reading דֶּרֶךְ except for the Targum which appears to render something like בְּמוֹרַד. That reading is found in the corresponding expression in the corresponding verse, Jer 48:5, בְּמוֹרַד חוֹרֹנַיִם, to which Targum assimilates its reading here.[11] Note that among the witnesses for Jer 48:5 the Septuagint assimilates to Isa 15:5 at exactly this point.

Isa 15:6—מְשַׁמּוֹת M 1QIsa^a G α′ σ′ θ′ V (S) | לצדו T (assim-Jer 48:34)

Isa 15:6a reads כִּי־מֵי נִמְרִים מְשַׁמּוֹת יִהְיוּ ('[for] the waters of Nimrim are a desolation' [NRSV]). Jer 48:34b reads כִּי גַם־מֵי נִמְרִים לִמְשַׁמּוֹת יִהְיוּ ('For even the waters of Nimrim have become desolate' [NRSV]). We will note later that the Peshitta for the Jeremiah verse assimilates to Isaiah in omitting the גַּם. Here we observe that the Targum for Isaiah assimilates to the Jeremiah verse by adding לְ before מְשַׁמּוֹת.

Isa 15:7—יִתְרָה עָשָׂה M (G) (V) S | שאר נכסיהון דקנו יתבזזון T (assim-Jer 48:36)

Whereas Isa 15:7a reads only עַל־כֵּן יִתְרָה עָשָׂה, Jer 48:36b adds the verb אָבָדוּ at the end (עַל־כֵּן יִתְרַת עָשָׂה אָבָדוּ׃). Accordingly, assimilation to Jer 48:36 is the best way to account for the additional verb (יתבזזון) at the end of the half verse in the Targum to Isaiah.

Isa 16:6—גֵּא M | גאה 1QIsa^a (assim-Jer 48:29) | G σ′ V S T (indet)

Admittedly, the form in the Masoretic Text, גֵּא, occurs only here in the entire Bible, so the form in 1QIsa^a, גֵּאֶה, could simply be the result of assimilation to the usual form. It may equally well, or additionally, be assimilation to Jer 48:29 where the expression גְּאוֹן־מוֹאָב גֵּא מְאֹד in Isa 16:6 has the corresponding expression גְּאוֹן־מוֹאָב גֵּאֶה מְאֹד.[12]

---

[11] So also Goshen-Gottstein, *Isaiah*, p. 60.

[12] Wildberger notes that the form in the Masoretic Text is a *hapax legomenon*, and then reads with the more usual form, following 1QIsa^a and Jer 48:29 (Wildberger, *Jesaja*, p. 593), another arguable case of modern-day assimilation. BHK^3 prefers the form with ה, and cites Jer 48:29 as the reason for this. BHS cites 1QIsa^a as well.

Isa 16:6—וְעֶבְרָתוֹ M 1QIsa[a] σ′ ϑ′ V S | > G | וגיותנותהון T (assim-Jer 48:29)

A number of commentators have observed that the noun in Isa 16:6 seems out of place in the context, but it seems most probable that the Targum reading simply arises from the assimilation of גַּאֲוָתוֹ וּגְאוֹנוֹ וְעֶבְרָתוֹ to Jer 48:29, גָּבְהוֹ וּגְאוֹנוֹ וְגַאֲוָתוֹ.

Isa 16:7—לָכֵן M σ′ V S T | οὐχ οὕτως G (assim-Jer 48:30) | ולכן לוא 1QIsa[a]

The reading of G could be simply an assimilation to the לֹא־כֵן of the preceding verse, but the sequence of terms in the corresponding text in Jer 48:30, וְלֹא־כֵן בַּדָּיו לֹא־כֵן, is a clear assimilatory context. It must at least have been a contributing influence. It may also have affected what looks a bit like a partial conflation in 1QIsa[a] ולכן לוא.

Isa 16:7—לְמוֹאָב M 1QIsa[a] 1QIsa[b] V | καὶ περὶ τῆς μωάβ σ′ S (assim-Jer 48:31) | ἐν γὰρ τῇ Μωαβίτιδι G (assim-Jer 48:31?) | ומואבאי T (assim-Jer 48:31?)

The conjunction in the readings in Symmachus and the Peshitta (and perhaps the Septuagint and Targum as well) probably reflects the expression וּלְמוֹאָב in the corresponding passage in Jer 48:31 although the idea of a simple facilitation of the clause structure in the Isaiah verse cannot be entirely ruled out.

Isa 16:7—לַאֲשִׁישֵׁי M 1QIsa[a] | τοῖς κατοικοῦσιν G (assim-Jer 48:31) | τοῖς πολυχρονίοις μου α′ S (via יָשִׁישׁ) | τοῖς εὐφραινομένοις σ′ V (via √שׂושׂ) | τοῖς αὐχμώδεσιν ϑ′ (elus)[13] | על אנש T (assim-Jer 48:31)

The reading of the Targum is surely a result of assimilation to the expression אֶל־אַנְשֵׁי קִיר־חֶרֶשׂ in Jer 48:31.[14] In the Hebrew University Bible Goshen-Gottstein likewise proposes that the reading of the Septuagint is assimilation to Jer 48:31.[15]

Isa 16:7—תֶּהְגּוּ M 1QIsa[a] α′ ϑ′ S V | μελετήσεις G (assim-Jer 48:31?) | יימרון T (assim-Jer 48:31?)

The verb in Isa 16:7 is a second person plural. The form in the Septuagint is a second person singular, and that in the Targum is a third person plural. Although neither form represents a complete assimilation to the

[13] For a possible explanation of the reading of ϑ′, see Arie van der Kooij, *Die alten Textzeugen des Jesajabuches* (OBO 35; Fribourg–Göttingen, 1981), p. 159. I otherwise agree with his explanations of the readings in α′ and σ′.

[14] So also van der Kooij, *Die alten Textzeugen*, p. 177; Wildberger, *Jesaja*, p. 594; and BHK³.

[15] Goshen-Gottstein, *Isaiah*, p. 62.

corresponding expression in Jer 48:31 (יֶהְגֶּה), their variation against the Masoretic Text probably represents assimilation to the Jeremiah text.[16]

Isa 16:9—קֵיצֵךְ M 1QIsa^a (G) σ′ S T | *vindemiam tuam* V (assim-Jer 48:32)

Isa 16:9—קְצִירֵךְ M 1QIsa^a σ′ V | τῷ τρυγήτῳ σου G S T (assim-Jer 48:32)

Isa 16:9b reads כִּי עַל־קֵיצֵךְ וְעַל־קְצִירֵךְ הֵידָד נָפָל: ('for over your fruit harvest and your grain harvest a shout has fallen' [NRSV]). Jer 48:32b reads עַל־קֵיצֵךְ וְעַל־בְּצִירֵךְ שֹׁדֵד נָפָל: ('upon your fruit harvest and your vintage a destroyer has fallen'). By far the most probable explanation of the Vulgate's reading for קֵיצֵךְ and the readings of the Septuagint, Peshitta and Targum for קְצִירֵךְ is assimilation to בְּצִירֵךְ in Jer 48:32.[17]

Isa 16:11—וְקִרְבִּי לְקִיר M 1QIsa^a G σ′ V S | וליבהון על אנש כרך T (assim-Jer 48:36)

Here the reading of the Targum surely reflects the text found at Jer 48:36, וְלִבִּי אֶל־אַנְשֵׁי קִיר־.

In two cases 1QIsa^a assimilates the Isaiah text to Jeremiah 48. The Vulgate and Symmachus each assimilate in one case. In five cases each the Peshitta and Septuagint assimilate. By far the predominance of cases of assimilation to Jeremiah 48 found in Isaiah 15–16 occur in the Targum (ten times).

3. *Assimilation to Other Texts in the Transmission of the Text of Isaiah 15–16*

There are at least two occasions where the transmission of the text of Isaiah 15–16 shows the influence of other texts concerning Moab.

Isa 15:1—עָר M ϑ′ V | עיר 1QIsa^a α′ σ′ S (assim-Num 22:36) | > G | T (indet)

Although there is not otherwise any similarity between Isa 15:1 and Num 22:36, the reading עִיר for עָר in multiple witnesses to Isa 15:1 may arise from assimilation to the expression אֶל־עִיר מוֹאָב at Num 22:36. It

[16] Barthélemy, on the other hand, proposes that both witnesses assimilate to their renderings in neighbouring verses of Isaiah 16 (Barthélemy, *Critique textuelle*, pp. 123–125).

[17] Wildberger, although he notes the corresponding reading in Jer 48:32, neither reports nor comments on the versional readings here for Isaiah (Wildberger, *Jesaja*, p. 594).

should also be noted, however, that the reading may also simply represent assimilation to the context since the parallel colon in Isa 15:1bβ contains קִיר, which can be read not as a proper name, but as a common noun synonymous with עִיר.

Isa 16:8—בַּעֲלֵי M 1QIsa[b] σ′ V S T | καταπίνοντες G (assim-Num 21:28, G)

Goshen-Gottstein has noted that the same equivalence as is found in the Septuagint here is also found at Num 21:28.[18] Since these are not products of the same translator, this may reflect the influence of the Numbers locus on the rendition in Septuagint Isaiah at this point.

When added to the textual cases concerning assimilation to the text of Jeremiah 48, the overall pattern in Isaiah 15–16 remains the same. The Targum, Septuagint, and Peshitta are the witnesses most likely to assimilate the Isaiah text to another. Given accepted views of these witnesses, this is not surprising.[19]

4. *Assimilation to Isaiah 15–16 in the Transmission of the Text of Jeremiah 48*

In Jeremiah 48 we find twenty-two cases where the reading of one or more witnesses is most effectively explained as assimilation to a portion of a verse in Isaiah 15–16. In distinction to what was found in the Isaiah text, in the case of Jeremiah 48, the Masoretic Text contains some of these cases even though the majority comes from the versions. The following list conveys the basic data for all of these cases. Some of the more interesting or difficult ones will be discussed in detail in a later section.

Jer 48:1—אֶל M G S T | *super* V (assim-Isa 15:2)

Although translation of prepositions is a point where one expects to find renderings that are governed more by context or by the demands of the receptor language, the Vulgate for Jeremiah is remarkably consistent in

[18] Goshen-Gottstein, *Isaiah*, p. 63.

[19] See, for example, Van der Kooij, *Die alten Textzeugen*, pp. 66–71, 175–181, 284–289; Philip S. Alexander, 'Jewish Aramaic Translations of Hebrew Scriptures', in Martin Jan Mulder (ed.), *Mikra* (CRINT 2.1; Assen/Maastricht–Philadelphia, 1988), pp. 227–228; and Gillian Greenberg, *Translation Technique in the Peshitta to Jeremiah* (MPIL 13; Leiden etc., 2002), pp. 57–60.

its rendering of אֶל.[20] In 511 occurrences of אל in Jeremiah the Vulgate has *ad* opposite it 322 times, a simple accusative 37 times, a simple dative 31 times, *in* 33 times, and *super* 30 times (48 times opposite a variety of other prepositions and 10 times with no equivalent). On the other hand, the Vulgate uses *super* massively for עַל. This matches Isa 15:2 where the expression is עַל־נְבוֹ rather than אֶל־נְבוֹ.

> Jer 48:5—מַעֲלֵה M (σ′) (V) (S) T (assim-Isa 15:5) | ἐπλήσθη G—Read with G.

In the Septuagint the opening of Jer 48(31):5 reads ὅτι ἐπλήσθη Ἁλαὼθ ἐν κλαυθμῷ ('Because Halaoth was filled by weeping').[21] It stands alone among the witnesses. Symmachus, the Vulgate, and Peshitta all add a preposition, but they together with the Targum follow the Masoretic Text. However, their support of the Masoretic Text is to be expected as proto-Masoretic witnesses, and there is no apparent motivation through which the Septuagint reading might arise from the Masoretic Text. Instead it is more likely that the Masoretic Text arises from assimilating the Jeremiah passage (proposing to read כִּי מָלֵא הַלֻּחוֹת בִּבְכִי) to Isa 15:5 כִּי מַעֲלֵה הַלּוּחִית בִּבְכִי.

> Jer 48:5—הַלֻּחוֹת בִּבְכִי יַעֲלֶה־בֶּכִי M ⟨σ′⟩ V (S) (T) (assim-Isa 15:5) | Ἁλαὼθ ἐν κλαυθμῷ, ἀναβήσεται κλαίων G—Read with G.

This case is related to the preceding and following case, also instances of the Masoretic Text assimilating Jer 48:5 to Isa 15:5b. The Septuagint for Jer 48(31):5 from the first כִּי through חוֹרֹנַיִם reads two clauses, 'Because Halaoth was filled by weeping, he will go up weeping by way of Horonaim'. In other words, the Septuagint puts the clause break after בִּבְכִי. The Masoretic Text also has two clauses, but it puts the break after בֶּכִי. This is the same clause structure as in Isa 15:5b. Both clause structures are coherent and meaningful. The motivations by which the Septuagint reading might have arisen from the M reading are obscure. On the other hand,

---

[20] This is not necessarily what one expects from V, whose translation technique is governed more by a norm of semantic and syntactic consistency with frequent formal adaptation as necessary to meet that norm, rather than by a norm of formal lexical consistency; see Richard D. Weis, 'The Textual Situation in the Book of Jeremiah', in Yohanan A.P. Goldman, Arie van der Kooij, and Richard D. Weis (eds.), *Sôfer Mahîr: Essays in Honour of Adrian Schenker Offered by Editors of Biblia Hebraica Quinta* (VT.S 110; Leiden etc., 2006), pp. 284–287.

[21] Translations from G in this essay are taken from Albert Pietersma and Benjamin G. Wright (eds.), *A New English Translation of the Septuagint* (Oxford, 2007).

the process that might derive the reading of the Masoretic Text from that behind the Septuagint is simple and clear—assimilation to the Isaiah passage.

Jer 48:5—כִּי[2] M V T (assim-Isa 15:5) | > G | ܘ S (lib, M)—Read with G.

Given Septuagint translation technique in Jeremiah, the Septuagint minus opposite כִּי in the Masoretic Text should be taken seriously as indicative of a variant *Vorlage*.[22] Given the parallelism of the verse, and the tight parallel with Isa 15:5b, it is hard to find a plausible motivation for the Septuagint minus, whereas the reading of the Masoretic Text is easily explained as assimilation to the parallel locus in Isa 15:5b. Given the structuring effect of the conjunction, it is not impossible that the difference between the Septuagint and the Masoretic Text actually belongs to the redactional work that created Edition 2 of the Book of Jeremiah (reflected in the Masoretic Text). In that case, the Isaianic parallel does not affect the textual transmission of the Jeremianic oracle, but rather is a factor in the work of the editor who produced Edition 2.

Jer 48:5—בְּמוֹרַד M V S T | ἐν ὁδῷ G (assim-Isa 15:5)

For the expression בְּמוֹרַד חוֹרֹנַיִם in the Masoretic Text, the Septuagint has ἐν ὁδῷ Ὡρωνάιμ. The Septuagint reading is self-evidently an assimilation to the close parallel in Isa 15:5b.[23] Interestingly, this is the reverse direction of the assimilation in the Targum which assimilates the same locus in Isa 15:5b to the one in Jer 48:5.

Jer 48:5—צָרֵי M ⟨σʹ⟩ V T | > G (assim-Isa 15:5) | κίδυνον θʹ S (via צר[I])

In Jer 48:5 the expression in the Masoretic Text, צָרֵי צַעֲקַת־שֶׁבֶר שָׁמֵעוּ, is matched in the Septuagint with the expression κραυγὴν συντρίμματος ἠκούσατε, matching the corresponding expression in Isa 15:5b, which lacks the צָרֵי (i.e., זַעֲקַת־שֶׁבֶר יְעֹעֵרוּ).[24]

---

[22] On G translation technique, see Weis, 'Textual Situation', pp. 281–283.

[23] So also C. Rabin, S. Talmon, and E. Tov (eds.), *The Book of Jeremiah* (HUB; Jerusalem, 1997), p. 256.

[24] A number of modern scholars similarly suggest that the preferred reading for the Jeremiah text here should match that in Isaiah. These include BHK[2,3]; BHS; Holladay, *Jeremiah*, p. 341; Wilhelm Rudolph, *Jeremia* (HAT 12; Tübingen, 1968), p. 274; John A. Thompson, *The Book of Jeremiah* (NICOT; Grand Rapids, 1980), p. 699; Gerald L. Keown, Pamela J. Scalise, and Thomas G. Smothers, *Jeremiah 26–52* (WBC 27; Dallas, 1995), p. 306. Arguably their position represents a modern assimilation of the text of Jeremiah to that of Isaiah. McKane and Volz prefer the Septuagint reading, but without appealing to the Isaiah text; William McKane, *A Critical and Exegetical Commentary on*

Jer 48:5—שָׁמֵעוּ M ⟨σ′⟩ V S (assim-Isa 15:5) | ἠκούσατε G | יבסרון T (assim-Isa 15:5, T)—Read with G.

While it is conceivable that the second plural verb of the Septuagint is assimilating to the following context, the form actually is unexpected in the context of what precedes and thus is a somewhat more difficult reading than that of the Masoretic Text. The reading of the Masoretic Text, however, can be explained as assimilation to the third plural form of the verb in Isa 15:5b, if not to its exact lexical form.[25] Indeed, the Masoretic Text has been observed to assimilate strongly to the Isaian verse at earlier points in the verse. The Targum's reading reflects assimilation to the Targum's own rendering at Isa 15:5b, rather than to the Hebrew of the Masoretic Text there.

Jer 48:29—שָׁמַעְנוּ M ⟨α′⟩ σ′ V S T (assim-Isa 16:6) | שמעו נא 2QJer | ἤκουσα G (assim-ctext)—Read with 2QJer.

Although the preceding verse contains plural imperatives, there is little reason that such a form as that in 2QJer should arise here since the audience is different. The imperatives in verse 28 are addressed to the Moabites, whereas the imperative here in 2QJer is necessarily addressed to the audience. On the other hand, the first plural perfect of the Masoretic Text is easily explained as arising from assimilation to שָׁמַעְנוּ גְאוֹן־מוֹאָב in Isa 16:6.[26]

Jer 48:29—גֵּאֶה M ⟨α′⟩ σ′ V (S) (T) (assim-Isa 16:6) | ὕβρισε G—Read with G.

The verb ὑβρίζω occurs only four times in the entire Septuagint, and only once in Ieremias, so conclusions about a *Vorlage* for the Septuagint reading are tentative at best. Nevertheless, in rendering with a verb the Septuagint implies a verb form in its *Vorlage*, perhaps גָּאָה. The Masoretic Text tradition then vocalized those consonants in light of the corresponding verse in Isaiah (גֵּא → גֵּאֶה).

Jeremiah 2. Commentary on Jeremiah XXVI–LII (ICC; Edinburgh, 1996), p. 1160; Paul Volz, *Studien zum Text des Jeremia* (BWAT 25; Leipzig, 1920), p. 307. Barthélemy, *Critique textuelle*, pp. 777–778, prefers the reading of the Masoretic Text, but regards the motivation for the Septuagint's reading as elusive (similarly Lundbom, *Jeremiah 37–52*, p. 254).

[25] BHK[2] calls attention to the parallel, and Holladay (*Jeremiah*, p. 341) seems to assume that the Jeremiah text must once have contained the same reading as in Isa 15:5, i.e., יְעֹעֵרוּ, for which the current text was substituted.

[26] By contrast Lundbom (*Jeremiah 37–52*, p. 288) argues for preferring the Masoretic Text reading precisely because it is found in Isa 16:6.

Jer 48:30—עֶבְרָתוֹ M α′ (assim-Isa 16:6) | ἔργα αὐτοῦ G (S) (T) | *iactantiam eius* V (assim-ctext)—Read with G (S) (T).[27]

While one obviously cannot exclude the possibility of a graphic error as the cause of the Septuagint reading,[28] the fact that it is supported by two proto-Masoretic witnesses, Peshitta and Targum, makes this less likely. This is especially the case since the Hebrew *Vorlage* of the Septuagint is not a proto-Masoretic text. Thus it appears more likely that this reading should be regarded as the earlier, and that of the Masoretic Text and Aquila arises by virtue of assimilation to the corresponding Isaiah verse.

Jer 48:30—וְלֹא־כֵן בַּדָּיו לֹא־ M S | וְלֹא־כֵן בַּדָּיו לֹא־ α′ (G) V T (assim-Isa 16:6) | ⟨σ′⟩ (indet)

Although there are also lexical variants in play here (e.g., in the Septuagint), the focal issue is the clause division, i.e., whether it comes before or after בַּדָּיו. Thus the reading of the Septuagint, Aquila, the Vulgate, and the Targum is represented for the sake of clarity as a Hebrew expression, rather than being given in the language of the witnesses. It is possible that a forgetting of the meaning of בַּד^{V}, 'oracle priest', is at work in this case. Even if that is the case, the difficulty posed by that loss of meaning, so that בַּדָּיו no longer made sense as the subject of עָשׂוּ, is solved by assimilating the clause structure of the verse to that of the corresponding verse in Isaiah.[29]

Jer 48:31—קִיר־חֶרֶשׂ M G α′-ιω′ V S T | חרשת [2QJer (assim-Isa 16:7)

Assimilation to the parallel expression in Isa 16:7, קִיר־חֲרֶשֶׂת, is the only possible explanation for the 2QJer reading.

Jer 48:32—מִבְּכִי M V S | ὡς κλαυθμόν G (assim-Isa 16:9 + err-graph) | בכין כמא דאיתיתי משרין T (exeg)

Given the nature of Septuagint translation technique in Jeremiah, the reading here surely implies an actual or imagined Hebrew text of כִּבְכִי.[30]

---

[27] So also BHS, and Robert Carroll, *Jeremiah: A Commentary* (OTL; Philadelphia, 1986), pp. 789–790.

[28] So Lundbom, *Jeremiah 37–52*, p. 288.

[29] Rudolph (*Jeremia*, p. 280) would divide the clauses as do Aquila *et al.* Other commentators would place the *atnah* on עֶבְרָתוֹ, appealing explicitly to the clause structure of Isa 16:6 (BHK³; BHS [!]; Lundbom, *Jeremiah 37–52*, p. 288; Volz, *Text des Jeremia*, p. 312).

[30] So also Keown, Scalise, and Smothers, *Jeremiah 26–52*, p. 308.

Such a reading easily arises from a *Vorlage* that has assimilated the Jeremiah text here to the corresponding expression in Isa 16:9, בִּבְכִי יַעְזֵר.[31]

Jer 48:32—הַגֶּפֶן M (S) | ג]פן 2QJer (assim-Isa 16:9) | ἄμπελος G (assim-Isa 16:9) | קטולין T (exeg) | V (indet)

The absence of the article in 2QJer and the Septuagint seems sufficiently secure to merit consideration. Assimilation to the corresponding expression in Isa 16:9 (גֶּפֶן), which lacks the article, seems the obvious explanation.[32]

Jer 48:33—מִכַּרְמֶל M V (S) T (assim-Isa 16:10) | > G—Read with G.[33]

Although it is certainly possible that the minus for מִכַּרְמֶל in the Septuagint is the result of homoioteleuton in its *Vorlage*, on the whole, I find the Septuagint in Jeremiah less haplographic than has been argued by some.[34] In light of the overall pattern of assimilation of Jeremiah 48 to Isaiah 15–16 in the Masoretic tradition that we have seen so far, it seems to me that assimilation in the Masoretic Text tradition (by adding מִכַּרְמֶל to match the corresponding Isaiah verse) is more probable in this instance than haplography in the Septuagint tradition.[35]

Jer 48:33—לֹא יִדְרֹךְ הֵידָד הֵידָד לֹא הֵידָד: M α′ σ′ ϑ′ | οὐκ ἐπάτησαν· αἴδεδ αἴδεδ, οὐκ ἐποίησαν αἴδεδ. G (lit) | οὐκέτι δὲ ληνοβατοῦντες λέγοντες ἴα ἴα συρ′ ⟨σ′⟩ V (assim-Isa 16:10 + facil) | ܠܐ ܢܕܘܫܘܢ ܕܪ̈ܘܟܐ ܘܠܐ ܢܗܘܘܢ ܘܠܐ ܢܐܡܪܘܢ ܗܝ ܗܝ S (T) (assim-Isa 16:10 + ampl + explic)

---

[31] BHK² assimilates the Jeremiah text to the Isaiah, but BHK³ and BHS are more restrained, merely noting the correspondence. Lundbom (*Jeremiah 37–52*, pp. 291–292), and Volz (*Text des Jeremia*, p. 312) prefer the Masoretic Text here. Indeed, Volz specifically rejects the option of following Isa 16:9.

[32] By contrast, BHK² and Holladay (*Jeremiah*, p. 343) cite the Septuagint reading and Isa 16:9 as the basis for deleting the article. Keown, Scalise, and Smothers (*Jeremiah 26–52*, p. 308) follow the Masoretic Text.

[33] So BHK³; Holladay, *Jeremiah*, p. 343; McKane, *Jeremiah*, p. 1186; Thompson, *Jeremiah*, p. 709; and Volz, *Text des Jeremia*, p. 312.

[34] For example, Jack R. Lundbom, 'Haplography in the Hebrew *Vorlage* of LXX Jeremiah', *Hebrew Studies* 46 (2005), pp. 301–320.

[35] By contrast, Lundbom (*Jeremiah 37–52*, p. 293) prefers the Masoretic Text precisely because its reading is found in Isa 16:10. Carroll (*Jeremiah*, p. 790) and Keown, Scalise, and Smothers (*Jeremiah 26–52*, p. 308) also prefer the reading of the Masoretic Text. Janzen, following older discussion (e.g., Volz, *Text des Jeremia*, p. 312) regards the expression missing in the Septuagint as having been added to the Masoretic Text from Isa 16:10; J. Gerald Janzen, *Studies in the Text of Jeremiah* (HSM 6; Cambridge, Mass., 1973), p. 59.

This portion of Jer 48:33 is difficult and fraught with intersecting textual cases. Only portions of some of the readings are probably due to assimilation, but they merit attention for our purposes. The variation between Septuagint and the Masoretic Text is probably due to redactional intervention, and so can be left aside. The other readings are each to some extent shaped by assimilation to the corresponding portion of Isa 16:10.[36] Thus the ληνοβατοῦντες of the reading from Syros, Symmachus, and Vulgate perhaps reflects the הַדֹּרֵךְ of Isa 16:10, and the ܢܕܘܫ ܕܘܫ ܕܘܪ̈ܐ of Peshitta, followed by Targum, probably reflects the יִדְרֹךְ הַדֹּרֵךְ of Isa 16:10.[37]

Jer 48:34—גַּם M G V T | > S (assim-Isa 15:6)

Isa 15:6 has כִּי־מֵי corresponding to the כִּי גַּם־מֵי of Jer 48:34. The ܡܛܠ ܕܡ̈ܝܐ of the Peshitta in Jer 48:34 clearly reflects the Isaian text.

Jer 48:34—לִמְשַׁמּוֹת יִהְיוּ׃ M ⟨α′-σ′⟩ T | εἰς κατάκαυμα ἔσται. G (elus) | *pessimae erunt* V S (assim-Isa 15:6)

The Septuagint reading here is difficult to explain. However, it is reasonably clear that the Vulgate and Peshitta do not reflect the preposition found in the Masoretic Text. In this they reflect the text at Isa 15:6, מְשַׁמּוֹת יִהְיוּ.

Jer 48:36—כַּחֲלִלִים M G V | ܐܝܟ ܟܢܪܐ S T (assim-Isa 16:11)

In Jer 48:36 the deity's 'heart moans for Moab like a flute' (NRSV) whereas in Isa 16:11 the divine heart 'throbs like a harp' (NRSV). The readings of the Peshitta and Targum reflect the Isaian musical instrument, not the Jeremianic.

Jer 48:37—כִּי M ⟨α′⟩ γ′ V T | > G S (assim-Isa 15:2)

There are strong similarities between Jer 48:37a and Isa 15:2bβ. There is no particular motivation in the Jeremian context for removing the כִּי. Indeed, several of the versions incorporate it into their renderings without strain. Homoioarcton is a possibility, but this seems less likely

---

[36] See also Barthélemy, *Critique textuelle*, pp. 789–790.

[37] A number of modern scholars also believe that at these points the text of Jeremiah should read as is found in Isaiah: BHK[2,3]; BHS; Holladay, *Jeremiah*, p. 344; Rudolph, *Jeremia*, p. 282; Thompson, *Jeremiah*, p. 709; and Volz, *Text des Jeremia*, p. 313. Others defend the Masoretic Text as the preferable reading: Barthélemy, *Critique textuelle*, pp. 789–790 (specifically attributing the Peshitta and Targum readings to assimilation to Isa 16:10); Carroll, *Jeremiah*, p. 791; Lundbom, *Jeremiah 37–52*, p. 294; McKane, *Jeremiah*, p. 1186.

since Peshitta, which is based on the proto-Masoretic text, aligns with the Septuagint, which is not. An explanation of the Septuagint and Peshitta readings as assimilation to Isa 15:2, which lacks the כִּי, seems the likeliest explanation.

> Jer 48:37—כָל ... וְכָל M G V | > συρ′ S (assim-Lev 21:5) | על כל ... וכל T (assim-Isa 15:2)

The addition of a preposition before the first כל in the Targum matches Isa 15:2bβ exactly, which has בְּכָל־ with ראשׁ and only כָּל־ with זָקָן. The minus for both occurrences of כָּל in Jer 48:37 in Syros and Peshitta probably reflects the wording of Lev 21:5, בְּרֹאשָׁם וּפְאַת זְקָנָם.

> Jer 48:37—גְּרֻעָה M (συρ′) (S) (T) (assim-Isa 15:2) | תגר[ע] 2QJer G σ′ V | κατατετμημένος α′ (via גדע, M)—Read with 2QJer G σ′ V.

The external support for a finite verb, rather than a participle is quite impressive, embracing a Qumran witness, the Septuagint tradition, and a pair of proto-Masoretic witnesses. Moreover, that would also be somewhat more difficult as a reading since the parallel stich for verse 37aβ contains no finite verb. On the other hand, the Masoretic Text is supported only by proto-Masoretic witnesses with known tendencies for assimilation, and Isa 15:2, כָּל־זָקָן גְּרוּעָה:, provides the context for that assimilation.[38]

The pattern of distribution of these cases among the various witnesses is quite interesting by comparison with the Isaiah text. In two instances each 2QJer and Syros show assimilation of the Jeremiah text to Isaiah 15–16. The Septuagint shows six such cases. Given the character of Septuagint translation technique in Jeremiah, these should probably be regarded as *Vorlage* variants.[39] Surprisingly, Aquila shows four instances of assimilation and Symmachus six. As might be expected, the Targum (thirteen times) and Peshitta (twelve times) have the highest number of cases where they assimilate the Jeremianic text to the Isaianic. However, in sharp contrast to the pattern of distribution of assimilation cases in Isaiah 15–16, in Jeremiah 48 the Masoretic Text, always followed by one or more proto-Masoretic witnesses, shows nine instances of assimilation

---

[38] Holladay (*Jeremiah*, p. 344) argues for the form in the Masoretic Text on the grounds that it is also in Isa 15:2. Keown, Scalise, and Smothers (*Jeremiah 26–52*, p. 308) as well as Lundbom (*Jeremiah 37–52*, p. 299) prefer the Masoretic Text, but without giving specific argumentation.

[39] On Septuagint translation technique in Jeremiah, see Weis, 'Textual Situation', pp. 281–283.

to the Isaiah text, and the Vulgate shows eleven instances. Almost all of the cases of assimilation in Aquila, Symmachus, and the Vulgate arise from their agreement with the Masoretic Text. This is true for many instances in the Targum and Peshitta as well. This pattern is rooted then, not so much in the tendencies of these individual witnesses as in their reliance on the proto-Masoretic text as their *Vorlage*.

Elsewhere I have noted the tendency of the Masoretic Text in Jeremiah to assimilate the text of Jeremiah.[40] This is further on display in these instances in Jeremiah 48, and is also visible in a number of likely cases of contextual assimilation or assimilation to usual patterns of expression.[41] In the case of Jeremiah 48, however, this may well be more than a reflection of this general tendency in the Masoretic Text in Jeremiah. It should probably also be seen as a reflection of the status of the Book of Isaiah in Judaism during the Second Temple period as the proto-Masoretic tradition was taking shape.[42]

5. *Assimilation to Other Texts in the Transmission of the Text of Jeremiah 48*

Isaiah 15–16 is not the only text to which witnesses assimilate in Jeremiah 48. Other oracles pertaining to Moab, other prophetic texts, and texts outside the prophetic corpus all exert their influence on the transmission of the Jeremiah text. First we turn to assimilation of the Jeremiah text to the text of other oracles pertaining to Moab.

> Jer 48:26—בְּקִיאוֹ M α′-ϑ′ V S | ἐν χειρὶ αὐτοῦ G (assim-Num 24:10) | > T (lib)

Jer 48:26 and Num 24:10 have little verbiage in common. However, the Jeremiah verse contains the expression וְסָפַק מוֹאָב בְּקִיאוֹ and the Numbers

---

[40] Weis, 'Textual Situation', pp. 290–291.

[41] Note: 48:2—לְכוּ: omit with G; M V (S) (T) assim-usu; 48:2—וְנַכְרִיתֶנָּה: read with G S: ἐκόψαμεν αὐτήν M ⟨α′-σ′⟩ V T assim-usu; 48:26—הִגְדִּיל: read with 2QJer: הגדילה; M V S T assim-ctext; 48:28—יֹשְׁבֵי: Read with 2QJer: יושבת; M G V S T assim-ctext.

[42] The high status of the Book of Isaiah in different Jewish communities during the Second Temple period can be seen in the large number of manuscripts devoted to the book at Qumran, and in the fact that it is the most cited biblical book in the New Testament (James A. Sanders, 'Isaiah in Luke', *Interpretation* 36 [1982], p. 144). Indeed, our results may corroborate Van der Toorn's contention of the centrality of Isaiah—along with Deuteronomy and Psalms—to the Second Temple scribal curriculum (van der Toorn, *Scribal Culture*, p. 102).

verse has the expression וַיִּסְפֹּק אֶת־כַּפָּיו. The latter is the only reasonable source of the reading in the Septuagint for the Jeremiah text.[43]

Jer 48:45—יָצָא M ϑ′ V T | ܢܦܩܬ S (assim-Num 21:28)

The expression כִּי־אֵשׁ יָצָא מֵחֶשְׁבּוֹן in Jer 48:45b has a corresponding expression in Num 21:28, which otherwise closely parallels Jer 48:45b. That expression, כִּי־אֵשׁ יָצְאָה מֵחֶשְׁבּוֹן, contains the feminine form יָצְאָה, which is presumably the source through assimilation of the Peshitta's reading in Jer 48:45.[44]

Jer 48:45—וְלֶהָבָה M ϑ′ V S | ועבדי קרבא כשלהביתא T (exeg, cf. Num 21:28, T)

The Targum's reading for וְלֶהָבָה in Jer 48:45 is certainly exegesis, but since the same exegetical rendering occurs in Targum Onqelos to Num 21:28 (עבדי קרבא כשלהביתא for לֶהָבָה), the Jeremiah reading appears to be assimilation to Num 21:28 at the level of the Targum.

Jer 48:45—מִבֵּין M V T | מ]קרית 2QJer ϑ′ S (assim-Num 21:28) | G (indet)

Among the substantial similarities between Num 21:28 and Jer 48:45b is the correspondence between the expression וְלֶהָבָה מִבֵּין סִיחֹן in Jeremiah and the expression לֶהָבָה מִקִּרְיַת סִיחֹן in Numbers. The simplest explanation by far for the reading encountered in 2QJer, Theodotion and the Peshitta at Jer 48:45 is assimilation to the corresponding form in Numbers.[45]

---

[43] So also Rabin, Talmon, and Tov, *Jeremiah*, p. 259. McKane (*Jeremiah*, pp. 1179–1180) argues for preferring the Masoretic Text, but does not interpret the Septuagint reading as assimilation to the verse in Numbers. Similarly, Volz (*Text des Jeremia*, pp. 310–311) defends the Masoretic Text, but without explaining the Septuagint reading as assimilation. Rudolph (*Jeremia*, p. 278; also BHS) proposes deleting the preposition as a dittography.

[44] The following modern scholars propose a feminine form as the text to be read here in Jeremiah on the basis of Num 21:28: BHK[2,3]; BHS; Holladay, *Jeremiah*, p. 345; Keown, Scalise, and Smothers, *Jeremiah 26–52*, p. 308. Rudolph (*Jeremiah*, p. 284) and Volz (*Text des Jeremia*, p. 315) both prefer a feminine form, but do not cite Num 21:28 in support. Lundbom (*Jeremiah 37–52*, p. 310) defends the Masoretic Text.

[45] So Barthélemy, *Critique textuelle*, pp. 793–794; and Lundbom, *Jeremiah 37–52*, p. 310. On the other hand, others essentially follow the ancient witnesses in assimilating to Num 21:28 by preferring to read מקרית, i.e., BHK[2,3]; Thompson, *Jeremiah*, p. 712. Others read מבית with a few medieval manuscripts: BHS; Carroll, *Jeremiah*, p. 794; Holladay, *Jeremiah*, p. 345; Keown, Scalise, and Smothers, *Jeremiah 26–52*, p. 308; Rudolph, *Jeremia*, p. 284.

Jer 48:45—פְּאַת M α′ V S | ἀρχήγους ϑ′ T (assim-Num 24:17, vrss) | πρόσωπον ⟨σ′⟩ (via פֶּה)

Jer 48:45bβγ shows notable similarities with Num 24:17bβγ. Among the correspondences are those between the expressions וַתֹּאכַל פְּאַת מוֹאָב in Jeremiah and וּמָחַץ פַּאֲתֵי מוֹאָב in Numbers. At the Numbers locus פַּאֲתֵי is rendered as τοὺς ἀρχήγους in the Septuagint, as *duces* in the Vulgate, and as רברבי in Targum Onqelos. Since the versions offering these common renditions are not the same in Numbers and Jeremiah (Septuagint, Vulgate, and Targum Onqelos versus Theodotion and Targum Jonathan), the likeliest explanation of the readings in the Jeremiah case is that they represent assimilation to the versions at Num 24:17, specifically to Septuagint and Targum Onqelos. This is more probable than that the assimilation goes in the other direction since the witnesses at Jeremiah are younger than those at Numbers. Since פֵּאָה is a relatively rare word in the Bible, perhaps we would not go far wrong if we imagined that Theodotion and Targum Jonathan, on meeting the word in the Jeremiah text, resorted consciously to the existing renditions at Num 24:17 to explain the rare word in their Jeremianic *Vorlage*.

Jer 48:45—וְקָדְקֹד M ⟨α′-σ′⟩ V | καὶ ἐξηρ. ϑ′ (assim-Num 24:17) | ܘܬܒܪܐ S T (assim-ctext)

If one assumes a form derived from ἐξαιρέω or ἐξαίρω for the reading in Theodotion, then that witness at Jer 48:45 seems to represent a *Vorlage* of וקרקר. This would represent assimilation to the corresponding form in Num 24:17bβγ (פַּאֲתֵי מוֹאָב וְקַרְקַר), which is much like the expression פְּאַת מוֹאָב וְקָדְקֹד in Jer 48:45bβγ.[46]

Jeremiah 48 also contains thirteen instances of assimilation to specific verses in the Bible apart from oracles against Moab. Seven of these are found in the Peshitta. Three assimilate expressions in Jer 48:37 to expressions in the corresponding legal text in Lev 21:5.[47] Two assimilate expressions in Jer 48:44 to expressions in the corresponding verse Isa 24:18.[48] In both of these cases there is a substantial content or verbal correspondence between the verse in Jeremiah and the assimilatory context in Leviticus

[46] So Barthélemy, *Critique textuelle*, pp. 794–795.

[47] 48:37 -וְכָל- ... כָל: ὁ συρ′ and S omit = assim-Lev 21:5 (בְּרֹאשָׁם וּפְאַת זְקָנָם); 48:37—רֹאשׁ: ὁ συρ′: κεφαλαὶ αὐτῶν and S: ܪ̈ܝܫܝܗܘܢ = assim-Lev 21:5 (בְּרֹאשָׁם); 48:37—זָקָן: ὁ συρ′: καὶ οἱ πώγωνες αὐτῶν and S: ܘܕܩܢܝܗܘܢ = assim-Lev 21:5 (זְקָנָם).

[48] 48:44—מִפְּנֵי: S: ܡܢ ܩܠܐ = assim-Isa 24:18 (מִקּוֹל); 48:44—מִן: S: ܡܢ ܓܘ and T: מגו = assim-Isa 24:18 (מִתּוֹךְ).

or Isaiah. The remaining two assimilating readings in the Peshitta are to other verses in Jeremiah.[49]

A pair of cases of assimilation in other witnesses is found in Jer 48:27, which refers to thieves, and reflects influence of Exod 22:1, a law on a thief taken in the act of breaking and entering.[50] Three cases of assimilation to non-OAN texts occur in the Septuagint, sometimes with other witnesses. In none of these cases is there any other substantive or verbal correspondence between the Jeremiah verses and those with the assimilatory context apart from the words involved in the assimilation.[51] All but two of these cases of assimilation to passages outside of Isaiah 15–16 involve the versions. The two exceptions are readings in 2QJer.

There remains, however, one case that involves assimilation on the part of the Masoretic Text and some allied witnesses.

> Jer 48:43—פחד ופחת ופח M V S T (assim-Isa 24:17) | παγὶς καὶ φόβος καὶ βόθυνος G—Read with G.

There are extensive verbal similarities between Jer 48:43–44a and Isa 24:17–18a. Jer 48:43–44a read: פחד ופחת ופח עליך יושב מואב נאם־יהוה: הניס מפני הפחד יפל אל־הפחת והעלה מן־הפחת ילכד בפח (‘Terror, and pit, and snare are upon you, O inhabitant of Moab! says the Lord. Whoever flees from the terror shall fall into the pit, and whoever climbs out of the pit shall be caught in the snare’). Isa 24:17–18a read: פחד ופחת ופח עליך יושב הארץ: והיה הנס מקול הפחד יפל אל־הפחת והעולה מתוך הפחת ילכד בפח (‘Terror, and pit, and snare are upon you, O inhabitant of the earth! Whoever flees at the sound of the terror shall fall into the pit; and whoever climbs out of the pit shall be caught in the snare’). Given these similarities one might expect assimilation between these two contexts, and indeed above we have remarked such cases in the Peshitta for the Jeremiah verses. Although the three words that begin 48:43 are not terribly common in Jeremiah, the Septuagint translates them consistently everywhere else in the book. The lexical equivalencies vary here only if one assumes that the Septuagint's *Vorlage* was the text we meet in the

---

[49] 48:39—סביביו: S: ܠܥܡ̈ܡܐ = assim-Jer 29:18 (הגוים); 48:40—ידאה: S: ܢܣܩ ܘܢܦܪܘܚ = assim-Jer 49:22 (יעלה וידאה).

[50] 48:27—בגנבים: possible influence of Exod 22:1 on reading of 2QJer and G: בגנבכ]ה; 48:27—K/Q נמצא/נמצאה: Iosippos: ἐν αὐτοφώρῳ λαβοῦσα = harm-Exod 22:1 (במחתרת ימצא).

[51] 48:12—ונבליהם: G: καὶ τὰ κεράσματα αὐτοῦ = assim-Ps 75(74):9 and assim-ctext for pronoun; 48:19—ערוער: G: ἐν Ἀροήρ and T: בערוער = assim-1 Chr 5:8 (בערער); 48:27—השחק: G V S: εἰς γελοιασμόν = assim-v 26 (לשחק).

Masoretic Text. If one accepts that the translation technique remains consistent here, then the order of the words in the Septuagint's *Vorlage* must have been פַּח וָפַחַת וָפַחַד. There is no clear reason why the Septuagint reading should arise from the Masoretic. The Masoretic Text, however, is easily explained by assimilation to the sequence of the words in Isa 24:17. That all the other witnesses agree with the Masoretic Text is of little weight since they are all proto-Masoretic in character and that agreement should be expected.

6. *Assimilation of the Text of Jeremiah 48 to Isaiah 15–16 in Modern Scholarship*

As can be seen from the references to previous discussion in the footnotes for the preceding cases, modern scholarship has often been as prone to assimilate the texts of Jeremiah 48 and Isaiah 15–16 to each other as ancient scribes were. This is illustrated nowhere more strikingly than in the following case from Jeremiah 48.

For the reading בְּבֶכִי in Jer 48:5 *all* extant witnesses support the reading of the Masoretic Text. From the point of view of the surviving evidence of the text's transmission, there is no text critical case here because there is no variation to be explained. However, modern scholars mostly propose to read here בוֹ, not בְּבֶכִי. Mostly, they do so on the grounds that Isa 15:5 reads בוֹ at the corresponding point in that verse.[52] Since there is no basis in the external evidence at Jer 48:5 for supposing any text other than בְּבֶכִי, the arguments to read the text according to Isa 15:5 only amount to assimilation of the text of Jeremiah to that of Isaiah. There appear to be a couple of assumptions behind the generalized tendency to modern-day assimilation. Both are on display in this specific case as well.

The first assumption has to do with what occasions a text critical case. Do we have a text critical case when the external evidence of the surviving witnesses for the text disagree, or do we have a text critical case when there is an exegetical or translational difficulty with the Masoretic Text. The second view that translational or exegetical difficulty is a sign

---

[52] So BHK[2,3]; BHS; Carroll, *Jeremiah*, p. 779; Holladay, *Jeremiah*, pp. 340–341; Keown, Scalise, and Smothers, *Jeremiah 26–52*, p. 306; Rudolph, *Jeremia*, p. 274; Thompson, *Jeremiah*, p. 699; Volz, *Text des Jeremia*, p. 306. McKane (*Jeremiah*, pp. 1155, 1159) opts to delete בבכי. Barthélemy (*Critique textuelle*, pp. 775–777) and Lundbom (*Jeremiah 37–52*, p. 254) defend the Masoretic Text. See Barthélemy, Lundbom, or McKane for a list of earlier commentators who emend the Jeremiah text on the basis of the text in Isaiah.

of 'corruption' of the text in its transmission has been a widespread view throughout the twentieth century. For example, Rudolph Kittel in the preface to the first edition of *Biblia Hebraica*, indicated that the text critical task is occasioned by a perceived exegetical difficulty in the MT regardless of the presence or absence of variation among the witnesses.[53] The text critic's task then is to consult what alternate readings might be available among the surviving witnesses, any conjectures that have already been proposed, or any new ones that the critic might develop, in search of an appropriate solution to the exegetical difficulty. From this perspective the awkwardness of בְּכִי signals a disturbance of the text, and the resort to the corresponding text in Isa 15:5 is the consultation of a sensible source for a presumed original. This entails a second assumption, namely, that the Bible is assumed to speak in a coherent, that is, homogeneous way, so that when two verses are identical in many respects, their differences should be regarded as arising through error in the transmission of the text.[54]

The situation is altered if text criticism proceeds from the first option for what constitutes a text critical case: disagreements among the surviving witnesses for a case. Then the aim of textual criticism is not to find a reading that smoothes the perceived difficulty in the text, but is rather to explain the genetic relations among the extant readings so that we may understand both how those readings arose and which one is the earliest of them.[55] From this perspective the assumption behind assimilation becomes not a criterion for a viable option for the text, but a frame of

[53] Rudolph Kittel, *Biblia Hebraica* (2 vols.; Leipzig, 1905), p. iii. See also Arie van der Kooij, 'The Textual Criticism of the Hebrew Bible before and after the Qumran Discoveries', in Edward D. Herbert and Emanuel Tov (eds.), *The Bible as Book: The Hebrew Bible and the Judaean Desert Discoveries* (London, 2002), pp. 167–177, especially p. 168; and Dominique Barthélemy, 'Problématique et tâches de la critique textuelle de l'Ancien Testament hébraïque', in *Études d'histoire du texte de l'Ancien Testament* (OBO 21; Fribourg–Göttingen, 1978), pp. 366–368.

[54] See Emanuel Tov, *Textual Criticism of the Hebrew Bible* (2nd ed.; Minneapolis–Assen, 2001), p. 307; and Dominique Barthélemy *et al.*, *Preliminary and Interim Report on the Hebrew Old Testament Text Project* 1 (2nd ed.; New York, 1976–1980), pp. xi, xxv (Factor 5).

[55] See Tov, *Textual Criticism*, pp. 287–291; and Arie van der Kooij, 'Textual Criticism of the Hebrew Bible: Its Aim and Method', in Shalom M. Paul *et al.* (eds.), *Emanuel: Studies in Hebrew Bible, Septuagint and Dead Sea Scrolls in Honor of Emanuel Tov* (VT.S 94; Leiden etc., 2003), pp. 729–739. This, of course, is the approach of *Biblia Hebraica Quinta*. See Schenker *et al.*, *Biblia Hebraica Quinta*, pp. xii–xvi. See also Richard D. Weis, '*Biblia Hebraica Quinta* and the Making of Critical Editions of the Hebrew Bible', *TC: A Journal of Biblical Textual Criticism* 7 (2002), §§ 10 and 22, accessible online at http://rosetta.reltech.org/TC/vol07/Weis2002.htm.

reference that can be seen to have been at work in the transmission of the text. In other words, it becomes a *descriptive* principle—texts that are similar tend over time to be made more like each other, rather than a *prescriptive* principle—texts that are similar really should not differ at all.

7. *Conclusions*

When considered as a total picture, these cases of assimilation in Isaiah 15–16 and Jeremiah 48 display patterns that point us to several conclusions.

First, the frequency of cases of assimilation is not markedly different between the two speeches. A case of assimilation occurs on average every 1.2 verses in the Isaian oracle, and on average every 1.15 verses in the Jeremianic.

Second, there is little evidence that all of the Moab oracles/texts in the Bible were read in relationship to each other. For instance, there seems to be no instance of assimilation in either Isaiah 15–16 or Jeremiah 48 to the Moab oracle in Amos. Moreover, there are only three cases of assimilation from one of these two speeches to another Moab text where there is not already substantial verbal similarity between the verses that are assimilated. Those three cases are: Isa 15:1 עָר, Isa 15:2 הַבַּיִת וְדִיבֹן, and Isa 16:8 בַּעֲלֵי. The first and last of these involve assimilation to Moab texts in Numbers, and the other to Jeremiah 48—all three without substantial verbal similarity between the verses in Isaiah and those in Numbers or Jeremiah. This might point to a context in which these texts are associated simply because they are about Moab. However, these are a very small proportion of the forty-five cases of assimilation among Isaiah 15–16 or Jeremiah 48 and the other passages about Moab.

Third, assimilation occurs in these two chapters in verses where there is already a substantial verbal or content similarity between the verse in Isaiah or Jeremiah and that to which it is assimilated. This is true for the remaining forty-two cases of assimilation between these two speeches and other Moab texts, whether in Isaiah, Jeremiah, or Numbers. It is also the case for another eight cases where the text of Jeremiah is assimilated to Isa 24:17–18, Lev 21:5, or Exod 22:1. In the case of Isaiah 24 there is substantial verbal identity between the verses in Jeremiah and Isaiah *apart from* the assimilation. In the cases of Lev 21:5 and Exod 22:1 there is a significant content connection that then carries into some verbal correspondence through assimilation.

Fourth, with one exception the influence in assimilation seems to flow fairly equally from Isaiah to Jeremiah and from Jeremiah to Isaiah. The Peshitta and Targum engage in assimilation most frequently, and the Septuagint at a lesser level. Allowing for the greater number of cases in Jeremiah 48 because of its greater length, the frequency of assimilation of Jeremiah 48 to Isaiah 15–16 and vice versa seems equivalent for these three witnesses.

Fifth, the exception to the previous conclusion is due to the Masoretic Text tradition in Jeremiah. The Masoretic Text, Aquila, Symmachus, and the Vulgate in Jeremiah all display notable levels of assimilation to Isaiah 15–16. There is no corresponding pattern of assimilation of Isaiah 15–16 to Jeremiah 48 for these witnesses. Moreover, most of the cases in Aquila, Symmachus, and the Vulgate occur when these witnesses agree with the Masoretic Text, which itself is assimilating. So we are dealing with a proto-Masoretic phenomenon. In Jeremiah 48 the proto-Masoretic tradition assimilates that text to Isaiah 15–16. This is surely a result of a tendency in this tradition that is specific to the Book of Jeremiah, as noted above. It may also reflect the level of importance of the Book of Isaiah for this tradition. The way that the first three cases of assimilation in Jer 48:5 (כִּי; הַלֻּחוֹת בִּבְכִי יַעֲלֶה־בֶּכִי; מַעֲלֵה) lead to a restructuring of the opening part of the verse in the proto-Masoretic text suggests that this may have been deliberate activity, rather than sub-conscious. Thus we are faced with the results of activity by scribes who consciously saw a link between Isaiah 15–16 and Jeremiah, and who made use of that link both to ameliorate textual difficulties in their Jeremiah *Vorlage* by recourse to the text of Isaiah 15–16, thus enhancing the pre-existing correspondence between the two texts. This activity must have been grounded in assumptions similar to those of many contemporary scholars: difficulty or infelicity in a text is a sign of disturbance; that disturbance can be ameliorated by using the readings of a similar text to improve the troublesome one.

Sixth, the nature of the process of assimilation means that, as Barthélemy *et al.*, have put it, 'Whenever it seems clear that an assimilation has occurred, the unassimilated form is presumably earlier'.[56] Thus modern scholars' tendency to use Isaiah 15–16 to 'correct' or otherwise improve difficult expressions in Jeremiah 48 and vice versa, making the two texts *more* alike in their details is actually not proper text critical procedure.

[56] Barthélemy *et al.*, *Preliminary and Interim Report*, p. xi.

Indeed, it continues the ancient tendencies in the transmission of the text, and substitutes a later reading for the earlier, thus moving away from the goal of textual criticism, the establishment of the earliest reading attested in the surviving witnesses.[57]

[57] For this definition of the text-critical task, see the works cited in note 56.

ISAIAH 30:1

H.G.M. Williamson

The received Hebrew text of Isaiah 30:1 reads as follows:

הוי בנים סוררים נאם־יהוה
לעשות עצה ולא מני ולנסך מסכה ולא רוחי
למען ספות חטאת על־חטאת

and this is rendered in the Revised Version as:

> Woe to the rebellious children, saith the Lord,
> that take counsel, but not of me;
> and that cover with a covering (*or* make a league), but not of my spirit,
> that they may add sin to sin.

In the immediate context which follows, as well as in the wider setting usually preferred for this part of the book of Isaiah in general, this appears to make good sense in terms of a condemnation of Judah's policy of seeking to make an alliance with Egypt as part of the preparation for rebellion against Assyria which led eventually to the campaign of Sennacherib against Judah in 701 BCE.

Closer examination of the text reveals, however, that there are several difficulties with this approach which, with only a few exceptions, have generally been glossed over by the commentators. Individually, they might not be thought overwhelming, but in combination they suggest that the search for an alternative interpretation should be attempted.

In the first place, the syntax following the opening 'Woe!' is unparalleled. We have first, as is regular, a reference to those over whom the woe is pronounced—'the rebellious children'.[1] Following that (if for the

[1] I am aware of the debate over whether this should be construed as vocative or impersonal, but this is not relevant to the present argument; for discussion, with references to older contributions, see Christof Hardmeier, *Texttheorie und biblische Exegese. Zur rhetorischen Funktion der Trauermetaphorik in der Prophetie* (BEvTh 79; Munich, 1978); Delbert R. Hillers, '*Hôy* and *Hôy*-Oracles: A Neglected Syntactic Aspect', in Carol L. Meyers and Michael O'Connor (eds.), *The Word of the Lord Shall Go Forth. Essays in Honor of David Noel Freedman in Celebration of His Sixtieth Birthday* (Winona Lake, 1983), pp. 185–188; H.-J. Zobel, 'הוי', in G. Johannes Botterweck, Helmer Ringgren, Heinz-Josef Fabry (eds.), *Theologisches Wörterbuch zum Alten Testament* 2 (Stuttgart, 1977), cols. 382–388 = *Theological Dictionary of the Old Testament* 3 (Grand Rapids, 1978), pp. 359–364.

moment we disregard the speech formula) we expect that if there is to be elaboration it will be either in the form of a participle in agreement with the subject, 'who do/es X', or of clauses that make use of a finite verb. For an example of the first, see, for instance, 5:18–19, 'Woe to those who drag iniquity (הוי משכי העון) ..., who say (האמרים) ...', and for the second, 5:8, 'Woe to those of you who add house to house, who join (יקריבו) field to field'. The rendering of the Revised Version of our verse has clearly assimilated its translation to this expectation, 'that take counsel', but this cannot strictly be justified as a rendering of the infinitive construct with ל, לעשות. To make sense of this, the best that can be done is to construe gerundially, 'by making';[2] as Oswalt explains, '[t]he verbs here are infinitives which are used to describe the nature of the rebellion (rebellion ... by doing ...)'.[3] It is far from certain whether this can be justified, however. Of the approximately fifty occurrences of הוי, there is a ל + infinitive construct in the following clauses on only five occasions. In four of these, the infinitive is clearly dependent on a preceding participle; for instance, at Isa 10:1–2 להטות, 'to turn aside', is dependent on החקקים and כתבו, 'who decree' and 'who write', so that there is no parallel with the supposed construction in 30:1; see similarly Isa 29:15; Ezek 13:18; Hab 2:9. Indeed, at Hab 2:15 this becomes completely clear in that there we have the use of למען,[4] something which obviously could not be substituted for the ל in Isa 30:1. The only possible analogy, so far as I can see, is Isa 5:22: הוי גבורים לשתות יין, 'Woe to those who are heroes at drinking wine'. On closer examination, however, even this does not exactly fit our passage, because the infinitive is governed by the noun, whereas in 30:1 it does not follow smoothly from the subject, 'sons'. It has to be understood as a qualification of 'rebellious', but that itself is not a separate clause, as if it were 'sons who have rebelled' (i.e. בנים הסוררים), which is what the continuation as usually understood would demand. I accept that the combined noun + adjective, 'rebellious sons', might be construed as a single element, parallel with גבורים in 5:22, but even so it is extremely rare and awkward and

[2] Cf. Emil Kautzsch, *Wilhelm Gesenius' hebräische Grammatik* (Leipzig, 1909), § 114o; Paul Joüon and Takamitsu Muraoka, *A Grammar of Biblical Hebrew* (2nd ed.; Subsidia Biblica 27; Rome, 2006), § 124o; Ilmari Soisalon-Soininen, 'Der Infinitivus constructus mit ל im Hebräischen', *VT* 22 (1972), pp. 82–90, who prefers to refer to the construction as 'epexegetical' (though without specific reference to this verse).

[3] John N. Oswalt, *The Book of Isaiah Chapters 1–39* (NICOT; Grand Rapids, 1986), p. 542.

[4] I am well aware of the textual uncertainties in the first line of this verse, but my point stands whichever of the various proposed solutions is adopted.

gives rise to suspicion. And without any doubt, in the light of this, we may certainly conclude that Gonçalves's analysis is incorrect. He claims that verses 1 and 2 are closely parallel: the people described followed by infinitives construct introduced with ל and then a negative qualifier.[5] But this formal similarity is misleading. The participles in verses 1 and 2 do not function in the same way at all. As already mentioned, סוררים is an adjective qualifying 'sons', whereas ההלכים is the introduction of a subordinate relative clause. Furthermore the infinitives in verse 2 are used in their regular sense to express the purpose of why the people are 'going', whereas in verse 1, as already explained, they have to be construed gerundially. The parallel which Gonçalves observes is more apparent than real. Our first problem, then, is a virtually unparalleled construction which as it stands makes only questionable good sense.

A second difficulty with our verse, though admittedly less serious, is the unusual use of the verb עשה with עצה. According to Ruppert, the only other example of this combination is at Isa 25:1.[6] It is uncertain how much weight can be put upon this parallel, however, given that there is a strong probability that it is itself derivative of earlier Isaianic usage. With the generally accepted repositioning of the *athnach*, the phrase reads כי עשית פלא עצות. This combination of פלא and derivatives of the root יעץ is characteristic of the Isaiah tradition (cf. 9:5; 28:29). In addition to this, however, Hibbard argues that there is particular dependence of 25:1–5 as a whole on 30:1–5.[7] That being the case, it is likely that the author of 25:1 was influenced by what he thought was the sense of 30:1, including the choice of the verb עשה. The singularity of this combination thus stands out all the more.

The third difficulty with our verse is again a serious one, in my opinion. Commentators have struggled to make sense in what they suppose to be the context of the expression לנסך מסכה. Since in their view the regular meaning of מסכה, '(molten) image', is meaningless, they usually try to link it with the noun נסך, 'drink-offering' and explain that the pouring

---

[5] Francolino J. Gonçalves, *L'Expédition de Sennachérib en Palestine dans la littérature hébraïque ancienne* (EBib NS 7; Paris, 1986), p. 152.

[6] Lothar Ruppert, 'יעץ', *ThWAT* 3, cols. 718–751 (730) = *TDOT* 6, pp. 156–185 (166); William H. Irwin, *Isaiah 28–33: Translation with Philological Notes* (Biblica et Orientalia 30; Rome, 1977), pp. 72–73, n. 5, adds 2 Sam 17:23, but there the verb is *niphʿal* (לא נעשתה עצתו) and has to mean 'his counsel was not followed/carried out', so that in any case it would not fit with the supposed active meaning of 'to make a plan' in Isa 30:1.

[7] J. Todd Hibbard, *Intertextuality in Isaiah 24–27: the reuse and evocation of earlier texts and traditions* (FAT 16; Tübingen, 2006), pp. 104–105.

out of a drink-offering was part of a treaty-making ceremony, so that the phrase as a whole might be paraphrased as 'make an alliance' (so NRSV, for example). The Septuagint συνθήκας is not surprisingly adduced in support.[8] I am not aware of any evidence for this suggestion, however; so far as I can see it is nothing more than an assumption based on the attempt to make sense of an apparently obscure expression. But everything speaks against it: if that is what the writer intended to convey, why did he not say so plainly (the language for sealing a treaty is hardly scarce),[9] and if he wanted to do it by referring to one (unattested) part of the ceremony, why did he use מסכה in a sense that it carries nowhere else instead of the regular נסך? The proposal is, frankly, desperate.

There is an alternative, also attested in antiquity (cf. Vulgate *telam*), and that is to link the word with a different root נסך (or סכך), 'to weave'.[10] In that case, the sense would be 'to weave a web', referring, presumably, to secret intrigue (cf. Kimhi). That at least furnishes a more plausible parallel for the first half of the line as usually understood. Once again, however, it seems probable that ingenuity has outstripped the available evidence. The noun מסכה from which this interpretation begins is found twice elsewhere, at 25:7 (cf. Ibn Ezra) and 28:20. In the latter, although there is some dispute about the qualifying verb, the meaning of מסכה is clear and uncontentious: '(bed-)covering'. The same meaning is also very suitable at 25:7, despite some minor uncertainties earlier in the verse. Following one reference to a covering that is wrapped over the peoples (לוט; cf. 1 Sam 21:10), the parallel מסכה seems clearly to have a closely similar meaning. There can thus be no doubt that there is a second noun מסכה, whose suitability for Isa 30:1 should certainly be considered. It is far from clear, however, that one can move from a covering made of fabric to that of weaving a web of intrigue. The connection, of course, would be that cloth is woven, and from this the related verb, לנסך, has

---

[8] See, for instance, Wilhelm Gesenius, *Commentar über den Jesaia* (Leipzig, 1821), p. 863; Bernhard Duhm, *Das Buch Jesaia* (4th ed.; HAT 3.1; Göttingen, 1922), p. 215; Otto Procksch, *Jesaia* 1 (KAT 9; Leipzig, 1930), pp. 384–385; Hans Wildberger, *Jesaja* 3. *Jesaja 28–39: Das Buch, der Prophet und seine Botschaft* (BK 10.3; Neukirchen, 1982), pp. 1147–1148; Willem A.M. Beuken, *Isaiah* 2. *Isaiah Chapters 28–39* (HCOT; Leuven, 2000), p. 134.

[9] See Paul Kalluveettil, *Declaration and Covenant: A Comprehensive Review of Covenant Formulae from the Old Testament and the Ancient Near East* (AnBib 88; Rome, 1982).

[10] See, for instance, Franz Delitzsch, *Commentar über das Buch Jesaia* (4th ed.; Leipzig, 1889), p. 329; Jesper Høgenhaven, *Gott und Volk bei Jesaja: Eine Untersuchung zur biblischen Theologie* (AThD 24; Leiden, 1988), p. 136; Oswalt, *Isaiah*, p. 545.

been thought to mean 'weave'.[11] But for this latter step in the argument there is no evidence; indeed, to the contrary, the passive form of נסך also occurs in 25:7, there clearly with the meaning 'covered/spread'. So far as I can see, the evidence for 'weaving' has been attributed to the verb only in 30:1 in order to try to make sense of the word in context, so that any appeal to the meaning to explain the verse is self-evidently circular.

A final approach has been to suggest that somehow our phrase should be associated with the noun מסך, which occurs relatively frequently, also with the meaning covering. In particular, attention is drawn to its metaphorical use at Isa 22:8, where it may be understood to refer to Judah's 'covering' in the sense of the protection that should be afforded by chariotry and cavalry.[12] The idea here, therefore, would be that Judah was seeking some form of protective covering from Egypt, hence 'seeking security', as Blenkinsopp renders it. The problem with this suggestion, however, is that מסך comes from the root סכך I, 'overshadow, screen' (not, of course, סכך II, 'weave together', whence סכה etc.!), and our author seems to be quite clear that this is not what he has in mind, as may be seen from his use of the verb לנסך in the *figura etymologica*. There is no evidence, however, that מסכה II, 'material covering', was ever used with the metaphorical sense of 'protection'.

In conclusion on this third point, it is difficult to escape the impression that commentators and translators have struggled to derive what they regard as a satisfactory sense from לנסך מסכה as a parallel for לעשות עצה understood as 'make/carry out a plan' but that they either all suffer from circular argument or import meanings which are unattested or face basic philological difficulties.[13] As we have seen, however, the starting point is itself questionable, since we do not normally expect עצה = 'counsel' to be governed by the verb עשה, and in any case the construction in this line as a whole is awkward following the הוי + noun construction in the previous line. It is thus difficult to avoid the impression that we have been approaching the understanding of this verse from the wrong angle.

---

[11] Dillmann also draws attention to מסכה, 'web' of unfinished material on the loom; August Dillmann, *Der Prophet Jesaia* (5th ed.; KHAT; Leipzig, 1890), p. 269.

[12] Jörg Barthel, *Prophetenwort und Geschichte. Die Jesajaüberlieferung in Jes 6–8 und 28–31* (FAT 19; Tübingen, 1997), p. 393; Joseph Blenkinsopp, *Isaiah 1–39: A New Translation with Introduction and Commentary* (AncB 19; New York, 2000), p. 411.

[13] These difficulties are well observed by Oswald Loretz and Ingo Kottsieper, *Colometry in Ugaritic and Biblical Poetry. Introduction, Illustrations and Topical Bibliography* (UBL 5; Altenberge, 1987), pp. 57–63.

In seeking a way forward, I should like to suggest that both aspects of the problems as outlined—the unusual construction and the philological difficulties—should be solved jointly. In the past, as we shall see, some have dealt with one aspect and others with the other. As a result it has not been difficult for the majority of commentators to reject the proposals. But when they are taken in combination, those objections are themselves emptied of much of their force.

So far as the philological problems are concerned, it seems natural as a starting point to allow מסכה to have its usual meaning of (molten) image, with the verb before it meaning 'to cast'. Taken in isolation, that is undoubtedly how anyone would construe it, and it seems logical to progress from what is more certain to what is less so. Inevitably, therefore, we shall then look with more favour than some others have done on the proposal that לעשות עצה has nothing to do with 'taking counsel', but rather with the making of another sort of image, namely a wooden one. Dahood was the first to suggest this,[14] and although he has attracted only minimal support,[15] there seems to be a good deal to be said in favour of his main idea. עץ is certainly used a number of times as the material from which images could be made (e.g. Deut 28:36, 64; 29:16; 2 Kgs 19:18; Isa 37:19; 40:20; 45:20), and sometimes, indeed, the word seems virtually to mean a wooden idol (e.g. Deut 4:28; Jer 2:27; 3:9; Ezek 20:32; Hos 4:12;[16] Hab 2:19). Dahood proposed that עצה was an accusative form of this, but apart from the issue of the propriety of such a definition, it would surely be simpler merely to regard this as a feminine form of the same word, used specifically for a wooden image. Whether such a form is attested elsewhere in Biblical Hebrew is disputed—a case can certainly be made for Hos 10:6, at the least,[17] and it would be attractive to

---

[14] Mitchell Dahood, 'Accusative *'ēṣah*, "Wood", in Isaiah 30,1b', *Bib* 50 (1969), pp. 57–58.

[15] See, for instance, Irwin, *Isaiah 28–33*, p. 72; Christoph Dohmen, 'מסכה', *ThWAT* 4, cols. 1009–1015 (1013–1014) = *TDOT* 8, pp. 431–437 (435), allows at least for the possibility of wordplay in the line.

[16] See the comments of Andrew A. Macintosh, *A Critical and Exegetical Commentary on Hosea* (ICC; Edinburgh, 1997), p. 151; Graham I. Davies, *Hosea* (NCBC; London and Grand Rapids, 1992), p. 124.

[17] Cf. Wilhelm Rudolph, *Hosea* (KAT 13.1; Gütersloh, 1966), pp. 196–197; Jörg Jeremias, *Der Prophet Hosea* (ATD 24.1; Göttingen, 1983), p. 127; Loretz and Kottsieper, *Colometry*, p. 61; Francis I. Andersen and David Noel Freedman, *Hosea. A New Translation with Introduction and Commentary* (AncB 24; Garden City, NY, 1980), p. 558; *HALAT* 3, p. 821. Suggestions have been made that elsewhere עצה was used generally for wood, but these remain doubtful; cf. Jer 6:6 (where most commentators take the final letter as the 3rd fem. sg. suffix) and Prov 27:9, as suggested by G.R. Driver, 'Hebrew Notes',

postulate it at Ps 106:43—but ultimately immaterial, given the transparency of the root and meaning in context.

The principal objection that has been offered to this suggestion is its apparent lack of suitability to the wider context in Isaiah 30.[18] While this is understandable, the objection falls away once it is realized that the second two lines of verse 1 are likely a later addition to the earlier context. As I have already observed, there is some syntactical difficulty in reading verse 1 as it stands, whereas the expected continuation of the first line of the verse comes at verse 2. Regardless of the meaning of the lines, we should already independently conclude that they are an addition.[19] And once we reach that conclusion, then we may join the result with a feature of the first part of Isaiah to which I have drawn attention elsewhere, namely that at several places the text has been unexpectedly glossed with short anti-idol additions.[20]

The starting point for the whole process was apparently a very slight error in the textual transmission of Isa 2:19 whereby a probable original imperative, 'Enter into the caves of the rocks' (as at verse 10), has become a continuation of the preceding verse with its reference to idols: 'and they

---

ZAW 52 (1934), pp. 51–56 (54), *idem* 'Suggestions and Objections', *ZAW* 55 (1937), pp. 68–71 (69); for discussion of the latter, see, for instance, William McKane, *Proverbs: A New Approach* (OTL; London, 1970), pp. 612–613; Bruce K. Waltke, *The Book of Proverbs. Chapters 15–31* (NICOT; Grand Rapids, 2005), p. 368.

[18] So, for example, Wolfgang Werner, *Studien zur alttestamentlichen Vorstellung vom Plan Jahwes* (BZAW 173; Berlin, 1988), p. 89; Blenkinsopp, *Isaiah 1–39*, p. 411.

[19] Scholastika Deck, *Die Gerichtsbotschaft Jesajas: Charakter und Begründung* (FzB 67; Würzburg, 1991), pp. 119–122, proposes that only the first word הוי in verse 1 is original and that it is continued immediately by ההלכים in verse 2. But, as Uwe Becker, *Jesaja—von der Botschaft zum Buch* (FRLANT 178; Göttingen, 1997), p. 247, observes, the only stated grounds are what is considered to fit with an eighth-century setting. The argument is couched in terms of a reply to Werner's late dating of the whole paragraph rather than an internal literary analysis. Most recently, a similar conclusion to that of Deck has been reached by Matthijs J. de Jong, *Isaiah among the Ancient Near Eastern Prophets: A Comparative Study of the Earliest Stages of the Isaiah Tradition and the Neo-Assyrian Prophecies* (VT.S 117; Leiden, 2007), pp. 92–94. His reason is different, however: he considers that two oracles have here been combined, a 'woe' oracle and a '*nĕʾum*-oracle', the former comprising *hoy* + verse 2, and the latter verse 1 (less the opening word) + 5*b*. While De Jong is right to draw attention to the unusual nature of a saying which combines both 'woe' and '*nĕʾum*' (though cf. Jer 23:1), an oracle beginning simply 'Rebellious sons—oracle of Yahweh—to carry out a plan, etc.' is not convincing. If two earlier oracles have been combined, it seems that they cannot now be disentangled.

[20] 'A Productive Textual Error in Isaiah 2:18–19', in Yairah Amit *et al.*(eds.), *Essays on Ancient Israel in Its Near Eastern Context: A Tribute to Nadav Na'aman* (Winona Lake, 2006), pp. 377–388.

will enter into the caves of the rocks'—a superficially curious notion![21] Indeed, it was sufficiently curious to have been felt to call for an explanation even in Antiquity, and this has given rise to the addition of the prose material in verses 20–21, two verses which set out just how it came about that the idols of silver and gold came to end up entering the caves: 'In that day a man shall cast away his idols of silver, and his idols of gold, which they made for him to worship, to the moles and to the bats; to go into the caverns of the rocks, and into the clefts of the ragged rocks, ...' The prose nature of these two verses, the manner in which their vocabulary is drawn almost entirely from the preceding poem and the introductory 'on that day' are only the most striking indications that these verses are a classic case of *Fortschreibung*. In the light of so much repetition, it is almost inevitable that we should regard the use of לבוא at the start of verse 21 as dependent upon the ובאו of verse 19. It might be considered unclear who is the subject of this infinitive. Most commentators treat it as האדם, and so imply that people will throw away their idols 'in order to enter' the caves, presumably more speedily because unencumbered. However, once it is realized that verses 20–21 are an explanation for the curious (corrupt) text in verses 18–19, it becomes clear that it is the idols who are the subject, picking up on ובאו in verse 19.[22] It is thus almost the equivalent of 'So that is how they will enter ...', a conclusion strengthened by the observation that the motivation in each case is presented in identical wording, as we have already seen.

The close similarity in vocabulary and phraseology shows beyond any doubt that the equally prosaic addition at Isa 31:7 must come from the same hand (or circle): 'For in that day they shall cast away every man his idols of silver, and his idols of gold, which your own hands have made unto you for a sin'. Furthermore, it becomes clear from the context in which it has been inserted that the writer regards the summons to repentance (see verse 6) as first and foremost the rejection, even the 'casting away', of idols. We should note too that idolatry is further described by the somewhat loosely attached addition of חטא, 'sin', at the end of the verse.

[21] The original text probably read יחלפו בוא, and this has become corrupted (though in two stages) to MT's יחלף ובאו; for the slightly more complex process that seems to have been involved than the mere mistaken division of words, see (in addition to the article cited in the previous note) my comments in Hugh G.M. Williamson, *A Critical and Exegetical Commentary on Isaiah 1–27*, 1. *Commentary on Isaiah 1–5* (ICC; London–New York, 2006), p. 201.

[22] So correctly Karl Marti, *Das Buch Jesaja* (KHAT 10; Tübingen, 1900), p. 33.

On the basis of these two integrally related additions concerning idols, I further argued previously that we should be inclined to ascribe another addition to the same hand or circle, even though the wording is not quite so close as in the first two examples, namely Isa 30:22: 'And ye shall defile the overlaying of thy graven images of silver, and the plating of thy molten images of gold: thou shalt cast them away as an unclean thing; thou shalt say unto it, Get thee hence'.[23] While there remain some close connections with the two verses previously mentioned, I suggested that some of the new vocabulary had been introduced under the influence of the story of the golden calf (Exodus 32). In this instance, it seems that the words were added to indicate that for this writer the removal of idols was the first step in 'walking in the way' of verse 21.

The relevance of this brief résumé of an argument set out more fully elsewhere is that it brings to bear on our major topic the independently established observation that a glossator or commentator has been at work specifically in chapters 30–31 and that he was concerned to interpret repentance and ethical conduct in terms of the abolition of idol worship. What is more, the phraseology of 30:22 suggests that the vocabulary used is not quite as rigid as might have been supposed on the basis of 2:20–21 and 31:7 alone. The way is thus clear for us to propose that the second two lines of 30:1 may be due to the self-same glossator. In particular we may note that the use of מסכה for idol occurs also at 30:22 and the categorization of idolatry as sin (חטא) is paralleled in 31:7. In addition, the loose use of ל + infinitive construct as found in 30:1b is not unlike the use of לבוא in 2:21. Finally, it is striking that at Isa 31:7 the addition follows a reference to the rebellious children of Israel (העמיקו סרה בני ישראל) while in 30:1 we also have a reference to 'rebellious children' (בנים סוררים) as the peg on which the addition in hung.

It will not have escaped notice that after the first intervention by the glossator in chapter 2, caused by an oddity in the form of text that he inherited in the same passage, the other two close parallels already referred to come precisely in Isaiah 30–31. These are the two chapters which record in particular Isaiah's bitter condemnation of Hezekiah's planned alliance with Egypt. The association of such alliances with idolatry has often been mooted in the past, partly as a matter of historical reality, in that it is supposed that such alliances may have involved a

[23] This is the rendering in the Revised Version. There are several textual and philological issues in this verse that cause difficulty, but they need not detain us here, as they do not affect the main line of the argument.

ceremony in which other gods besides Israel's were invoked, and partly because such alliances could be regarded by Isaiah as elevating human strength above that of God, a form of hubris to which he was always sharply opposed.[24] These views are probably reflected in Isa 2:7–8, verses from Isaiah which have contributed to the vocabulary used by our glossator, and thus it is not surprising to find that the latter should also have included comments in Isaiah 30–31 which deal with foreign alliances in order to heighten the focus on this particular line of interpretation.

It is possible that the passage has been further expanded under the same influence. Interestingly, Vermeylen took what he deemed to be two later additions to the text of 30:1–5 to be evidence that at some stage verse 1 had been understood as anti-idol polemic, even though Vermeylen himself did not consider this to be the original meaning of the verse.[25] First, in verse 5 it has long been suspected that the words ולא להועיל have been added secondarily; it is repetitious, metrically superfluous, and not represented in the Septuagint.[26] Although the *hiph'il* of יעל does have wider application (as the previous line of this very verse shows), it is certainly most familiar in the context of anti-idol polemic (for instance 1 Sam 12:21; Isa 44:9–10; 57:12; Jer 2:8, 11; 16:19; Hab 2:18),[27] so that one could well imagine that the motive for adding it here was to interpret the pointless trust in another 'people' for 'help' as a form

---

[24] See, for instance, John Barton, 'Natural Law and Poetic Justice in the Old Testament', *JThS.NS* 30 (1979), pp. 1–14, and *idem*, 'Ethics in Isaiah of Jerusalem', *JThS.NS* 32 (1981), pp. 1–18, both reprinted in John Barton, *Understanding Old Testament Ethics: Approaches and Explorations* (Louisville, 2003), pp. 32–44 and 130–144 respectively; Gonçalves, *L'Expédition de Sennachérib*, pp. 267–269.

[25] Jacques Vermeylen, *Du prophète Isaïe à l'apocalyptique. Isaïe, I–XXXV, miroir d'un demi-millénaire d'expérience religieuse en Israël* 1 (EtBib; Paris, 1977), pp. 409–410. Becker, *Jesaja*, p. 248, argues that the whole passage is an anti-idol polemic, and dates it much later than Isaiah in consequence. This seems to me to go further than is necessary; I should prefer to remain with his less radical conclusion that 'Das Wehewort 30,1–5* verfolgt also den Zweck, das Hilfeersuchen an Ägypten als frevlerischen Götzendienst … zu verurteilen', with the reservation that the element of 'Hilfeersuchen an Ägypten' may be best ascribed to the eighth-century prophet.

[26] See, for instance, Duhm, *Jesaia*, p. 216; Herbert Donner, *Israel unter den Völkern. Die Stellung der klassischen Propheten des 8. Jahrhunderts v. Chr. zur Aussenpolitik der Könige von Israel und Juda* (VT.S 11; Leiden, 1964), pp. 132–134; Wildberger. *Jesaja* 3, p. 1149.

[27] Cf. Horst Dietrich Preuß, *Verspottung fremder Religionen im Alten Testament* (BWANT 92; Stuttgart, 1971), pp. 209 and 239; *idem*, 'יעל', *ThWAT* 3, cols. 706–710 = *TDOT* 6, pp. 144–147.

of idolatry. Secondly, again following a number of other scholars,[28] Vermeylen also proposes that Isa 30:3 has also been added by the same redactor. The verse certainly has the appearance of being another example of *Fortschreibung*. At the formal level, its use of second person address in a surrounding context which is uniformly third person is disturbing, as, indeed, is its quite different poetic rhythm. More significantly, however, it repeats the main elements in the two halves of verse 2b, namely 'the strength of Pharaoh' and 'trust in the shadow of Egypt', and (in anticipation of verse 5) declares them to be 'shame' (בשת) and 'contempt' (כלמה, cf. verse 5, חרפה).[29] Once again, while not exclusively used of idols, such language is familiar from such contexts (for instance, Isa 1:29; cf. Mic 3:7) and may be thought to bring them especially to mind.

Whether Vermeylen is correct to see what he regards as two additions as evidence that 30:1b was later interpreted as a reference to idols may be questioned. Indeed, this issue of whether they should be regarded as additions at all is difficult to decide, and there have been some robust attempts to defend their originality.[30] The importance for our discussion, rather, is that the process might have been the very reverse of what Vermeylen thinks, namely that the steer which this material gave to a later reader to interpret the alliance with Egypt in terms of idolatry gave our glossator the excuse to state the matter firmly right at the start. Either that, or the same hand is responsible for all three additions.

Whatever may finally be decided on this delicate issue (and agreement is unlikely to be reached in the near future), it seems to me clear that there is sufficient evidence in the context as we have it to conclude that a reading of the second half of verse 1 as an anti-idol polemic is not isolated in the present context and moreover that it may be associated with the activity of a glossator who we know independently was concerned to interpret the substance of Isaiah 30–31 along such lines. The objections of those who have rejected this approach to verse 1 thus fall away, and

[28] See, for instance, Donner, *Israel*, p. 132; Otto Kaiser, *Der Prophet Jesaja. Kapitel 13–39* (ATD 18; Göttingen, 1973), p. 228; Werner, *Plan*, pp. 86 and 91; Deck, *Gerichtsbotschaft*, p. 121; Becker, *Jesaja*, p. 246; De Jong, *Isaiah*, p. 93.

[29] For a full study of these three words, see Martin A. Klopfenstein, *Scham und Schande nach dem Alten Testament: Eine begriffsgeschichtliche Untersuchung zu den hebräischen Wurzeln bôš, klm und ḥpr* (AThANT 62; Zürich, 1972), though his conclusions require some modification in the light of the further work of Johanna Stiebert, *The Construction of Shame in the Hebrew Bible: The Prophetic Contribution* (JSOT.S 346; London, 2002).

[30] See especially Barthel, *Prophetenwort*, pp. 400–403; for verse 3, see Wildberger, *Jesaja* 3, p. 1149; Gonçalves, *L'Expédition de Sennachérib*, p. 152.

it may be submitted that there is then no reason not to translate and interpret the line in the way that seems to make the most natural and readily comprehensible sense of the Hebrew text.

It gives me great pleasure to dedicate this brief study to a volume which fittingly honours one who has done so much to advance our understanding of the interpretation of the book of Isaiah both in antiquity and in the modern world, and one, moreover, whom it has been a privilege and a pleasure to support in his valuable editorial work on *Vetus Testamentum*.

PART TWO

ISAIAH IN THE CONTEXT OF SEPTUAGINT, PESHITTA, AND MODERN INTERPRETATIONS

THE RELATIONSHIP BETWEEN THE SEPTUAGINT VERSIONS OF ISAIAH AND PROVERBS

Johann Cook

1. *Introduction*

Arie van der Kooij has made a decisive contribution towards the study of the Septuagint. This applies especially to the Book of Isaiah, although he has dealt with other translated units from this corpus as well.[1] His main contribution lies in the field of methodology. He actively promoted the view that the ancient versions are relevant for more than just textual criticism.[2] He is particularly renowned for his clearly defined, well-considered and comprehensive methodological approach towards the Septuagint. As he recently demonstrated in his monograph on the oracle of Tyre, he distinguishes between specific methodological steps.[3] Hence he purposefully deals with each corpus individually before comparing them. In order to determine what the Septuagint of Isaiah has in store in the oracle of Tyre (Isaiah 23), he firstly approaches the Hebrew (Masoretic) text of this chapter as an individual text *an sich*. Then he does the same with the Septuagint version. Only after completing these steps independently does he address the question of the relationship between the Septuagint and its Hebrew *Vorlage*. It is indeed an honour to present this contribution as a gesture of appreciation to Arie, from whom I have learnt much. To mention just one aspect, drawing on his methodology,

---

[1] For instance, see his 'The Story of David and Goliath: The Early History of Its Text', *ETL* 68 (1992), pp. 118–131. He also dealt with Exodus, Ben Sira, the Psalms, Amos, Daniel, 1 Esdras, and 2 Maccabees.

[2] Cf. his contribution to the IOSOT congress of 1995 in Cambridge: 'Zum Verhältnis von Textkritik und Literarkritik: Überlegungen anhand einiger Beispiele', in John A. Emerton (ed.), *Congress Volume. Cambridge 1995* (VT.S 66; Leiden etc., 1997), pp. 200–216.

[3] *The Oracle of Tyre. The Septuagint of Isaiah 23 as Version and Vision* (VT.S 71; Leiden etc., 1998), pp. 8–19, see also Van der Kooij, 'Zum Verhältnis von Textkritik und Literarkritik' and my 'The Relationship Between Textual Criticism, Literary Criticism and Exegesis—An Interactive One?', *Textus* 24 (2009), pp. 119–132.

which he defines as a 'contextual'[4] one, I have developed a related method which I call 'a cultural-contextual' approach.[5]

In this contribution I intend to compare some aspects of the Septuagint of Isaiah and Proverbs only. In order to make an appropriate comparison I will therefore address correspondences as well as differences. The method I follow is a comparative one and I take seriously the concepts of *text* and *context*.[6] Whereas the Old Greek text of Isaiah has been determined by Ziegler,[7] the *Handausgabe* of Rahlfs[8] will be used as textual basis as far as the Septuagint version of Proverbs is concerned.[9]

2. *Correspondences between* LXX-*Isaiah and* LXX-*Proverbs*

Because of the difference in genre between these two translated units, one would not expect too many correspondences. After all, Isaiah belongs to the corpus of prophetic literature, whereas Proverbs is wisdom literature proper. However, the fact that we are dealing with translational literature and not compositional literature[10] affects the situation. This is of crucial importance since translational literature requires a different methodological approach.[11] Another crucial issue is the question of an acceptable paradigm for interpreting the Septuagint.[12] As is well-known

[4] Van der Kooij, *The Oracle of Tyre*, p. 17.

[5] Johann Cook, *The Septuagint of Proverbs—Jewish and/or Hellenistic Proverbs? Concerning the Hellenistic Colouring of LXX Proverbs* (VT.S 69; Leiden etc., 1997), p. 41.

[6] See footnote 5.

[7] Joseph Ziegler, *Isaias* (*Septuaginta Vetus Testamentum Graecum Auctoritate Societatis Litterarum Gottingensis editum* 14; Göttingen, 1967).

[8] Alfred Rahlfs, *Septuaginta Id est Vetus Testamentum Graece iuxta LXX interpretes* (Stuttgart, 1935).

[9] In my monograph *The Septuagint of Proverbs*, I reconstructed the Old Greek of some chapters.

[10] Cf. Cameron Boyd-Taylor, 'In a Mirror, Dimly—Reading the Septuagint as a Document of its Times', in Wolfgang Kraus and R. Glenn Wooden (eds.), *Septuagint Research. Issues and Challenges in the Study of the Greek Jewish Scriptures* (SBL.SCS 53; Atlanta, 2006), pp. 15–31.

[11] According to Cameron Boyd-Taylor, *Reading between the Lines—Towards an Assessment of the Interlinear Paradigm for Septuagint Studies* (unpublished doctoral dissertation; University of Toronto, 2005), p. 17: 'Translations deviate from the conventions governing well-formed texts and this fact has both linguistic and social cultural implications'.

[12] Cf. Albert Pietersma, 'A New Paradigm for Addressing Old Questions: The Relevance of the Interlinear Model for the Study of the Septuagint', in Johann Cook (ed.), *Computer and Bible. The Stellenbosch AIBI-6 Conference. Proceedings of the Association Internationale Bible et Informatique "From Alpha to Byte". University of Stellenbosch 17–21 July, 2000* (Leiden etc., 2002), pp. 337–364.

these two translated units show similarities as far as their translation technique is concerned.

2.1. *Translation Technique*

There is a broad consensus amongst scholars that both Isaiah and Proverbs in the Septuagint should be placed amongst the more freely rendered units.[13] Methodologically one would thus be inclined to expect differences between the translations and their supposed parent texts to derive from the individual translators. Needless to say, this supposition can act as a general guideline only. Freeness of approach is observed on both the micro and the macro level. For one thing, the individual translators add nuances to their translations by uniquely employing exegetical renderings. As far as the Septuagint of Proverbs is concerned, I defined this approach as one of *diversity* and *unity*.[14] This broad definition can be used in respect of Isaiah as well. One example is the application of the participle/noun οἰκουμένη. It is mostly used as an equivalent for ארץ, that is, in Isa 10:23; 13:5, 9; 14:26; 24:1; 37:16, 18, and according to Van der Kooij[15] it is mainly used as equivalent for תבל in the Psalms. In the Septuagint of Proverbs ארץ is rendered in 2:21 (οἰκήτωρ) and 22 (γῆ); 3:19 (γῆ); 8:23 (–), 26 (οἰκουμένη?), 29 (γῆ) and 31 (οἰκουμένη); 10:30 (γῆ); 11:31 (–); 17:24 (γῆ); 21:19 (γῆ); 25:3 (γῆ) and 25 (γῆ); 28:2 (–); 30:4 (γῆ), 14 (γῆ), 16 (γῆ) and 24 (γῆ); 29:4 (χώρα) and 31:23 (γῆ). The noun γῆ is the equivalent 13 out of 21 times, representing the unity side of the equation.[16] οἰκουμένη occurs only three times in LXX-Proverbs and in 8:26 it is apparently used to render תבל.[17] This Hebrew lexeme again occurs only twice in Proverbs, namely in 8:26 and 31, where it is seemingly rendered

[13] Emanuel Tov and Benjamin G. Wright, 'Computer-Assisted Study of the Criteria for Assessing the Literalness of Translation Units in the LXX', *Textus* 12 (1985), pp. 149–187, esp. 159.

[14] Johann Cook, 'Ideology and Translation Technique: Two Sides of the Same Coin?', in Raija Sollamo and Seppo Sipilä (eds.), *Helsinki Perspectives on the Translation Technique of the Septuagint* (Helsinki etc., 2001), pp. 195–210, esp. 197.

[15] Van der Kooij, *The Oracle of Tyre*, p. 79.

[16] Tyler F. Williams, 'Towards a Date for the Old Greek Psalter', in Robert J.V. Hiebert, Claude E. Cox, and Peter J. Gentry (eds.), *The Old Greek Psalter. Studies in Honour of Albert Pietersma* (JSOT.S 332; Sheffield, 2001), pp. 248–276, detected an interesting trait in the Psalms. He found a clear differentiation between singular and plural in the Psalms. According to him γῆ is used as equivalent when ארץ is in the singular and χώρα when the plural is intended.

[17] Cook, *The Septuagint of Proverbs*, p. 227.

by means of οἰκουμένη. In Isaiah it appears in 13:11 (οἰκουμένη); 14:17 (οἰκουμένη) and 21 (γῆ); 18:3 (κατοικουμένη); 24:4 (οἰκουμένη); 26:9 (γῆ); 27:6 (οἰκουμένη) and 34:1 (οἰκουμένη). It is of course difficult to make inferences on account of individual lexemes, however, there seem to be similarities in the way these translators approach their subject matter on a lexical level. This is markedly different from the more literally rendered translations where stereotyping is mostly the rule. I will return to the issue of the macro level in due course.

2.2. *Intertextual Relations*[18]

The intention of all translators is to explicate the original subject matter. They also seem to apply all sorts of internal and external traditions in order to bring this about. I have dealt with a multitude of *intertextual* relations that are created in LXX-Proverbs, on the one hand *intratextual* readings, on the other hand *intertextual* ones in respect of other books such as the Psalms.[19] It is natural to expect such relationships between the books of Proverbs and Isaiah.

Since the genres of these books differ, one would expect words to occur in each corpus that are typical of that genre. On the one hand, lexemes that would be expected in prophetic literature are used more often in Isaiah than in Proverbs. Ἀκούω, for example, occurs 87 times in LXX-Isaiah and 17 times in Proverbs. Ἀναγγέλλω appears 47 times in Isaiah and only three times in Proverbs. There are, on the other hand, typically sapiential words that appear more frequently in Proverbs. Ἀσεβής occurs 92 times in Proverbs but only 15 times in Isaiah. There are also 104 occurrences of δίκαιος in Proverbs and just 17 in Isaiah. However, as Ziegler[20] notes, one has to be careful in this regard.

Ziegler has found some possible links between LXX-Isaiah and LXX-Proverbs. One example is Isa 23:16 and Prov 7:12:[21]

---

[18] I thank the editors for suggestions made concerning this paragraph.

[19] See Johann Cook, 'Intertextual Relationships between the Septuagint of Psalms and Proverbs' in Hiebert, Cox, and Gentry (eds.), *The Old Greek Psalter*, pp. 218–228; id., 'Intertextual Readings in the Septuagint', in Cilliers Breytenbach, Johan C. Thom, and Jeremy Punt (eds.), *The New Testament Interpreted. Essays in Honour of Bernard C. Lategan* (Leiden etc., 2006), pp. 119–134.

[20] Joseph Ziegler, *Untersuchungen zur Septuaginta des Buches Isaias* (ATA 12.3; Münster i.W., 1934), p. 103.

[21] Ziegler, *Untersuchungen*, p. 113.

Isa 23:16

MT קחי כנור סבי עיר זונה נשכחה היטיבי נגן הרבי־שיר למען תזכרי׃

NRSV Take a harp, go about the city, you forgotten prostitute! Make sweet melody, sing many songs, that you may be remembered.

LXX Λαβὲ κιθάραν, ῥέμβευσον, πόλις, πόρνη ἐπιλελησμένη· καλῶς κιθάρισον, πολλὰ ᾆσον, ἵνα σου μνεία γένηται.

NETS Take a lyre, roam, you city, you forgotten prostitute! Play the lyre well: sing much that you may be remembered.[22]

Prov 7:12

MT פעם בחוץ פעם ברחבות ואצל כל־פנה תארב׃

NRSV Now in the street, now in the squares, and at every corner she lies in wait.

LXX χρόνον γάρ τινα ἔξω ῥέμβεται, χρόνον δὲ ἐν πλατείαις παρὰ πᾶσαν γωνίαν ἐνεδρεύει.

NETS For some time she roams outside, and at another time she lies in wait in the streets, at every corner.

In order to evaluate this passage appropriately it is necessary to read it within the context of the whole of the chapter. The verb ῥέμβομαι is a *hapax legomenon* and its use is widespread in classical Greek sources. On a lexical level the translation of this chapter again contains many *hapax legomena* and words not used abundantly in the Septuagint. The translator also again renders the text in a nuanced and stylistically appropriate way. For example, contrary to Prov 2:16 the אשה זרה is translated literally in v. 5, indicating that the sexual content was not an issue to the translator. This possible link between LXX-Isaiah and LXX-Proverbs has been picked up by Van der Kooij as well.[23] He mentions the fact that the verb ῥεμβεύω is used in Isaiah in connection with the city as a harlot. This is contrary to MT, which does not describe the city as a harlot. Van der Kooij mentions that in Prov 7:12 the cognate verb ῥέμβομαι is used in connection with a harlot. Whether this is evidence of direct or indirect intertextual connections is difficult to determine. As stated already, ῥέμβομαι is a *hapax legomenon*. Nevertheless the context of both passages agrees to some extent, and this could have led to intertextual activity.

[22] For the LXX I use the translation of NETS: Albert Pietersma and Benjamin G. Wright (eds.), *A New English Translation of the Septuagint and the Other Greek Translations Traditionally Included Under That Title* (Oxford, 2007).

[23] Van der Kooij, *The Oracle of Tyre*, p. 71.

D'Hamonville also recognises this link but offers no explanation.[24] It is nevertheless interesting that he deems chapter 7 in LXX-Proverbs one of the key passages of evidence that the translator indeed made use of platonic terminology.[25] This issue is not at stake in the verse under discussion but in the chapter as a whole. I have demonstrated my scepticism to this point of view.[26] Although I did not conduct an exhaustive study of the situation in LXX-Isaiah, I could not detect any evidence of such influence (see also below).

A second passage is Isa 58:11 and Prov 16:2 (15:30):

Isa 58:11

MT ונחך יהוה תמיד והשביע בצחצחות נפשך ועצמתיך יחליץ והיית כגן רוה וכמוצא מים אשר לא־יכזבו מימיו:

NRSV The Lord will guide you continually, and satisfy your needs in parched places, and make your bones strong; and you shall be like a watered garden, like a spring of water, whose waters never fail.

LXX καὶ ἔσται ὁ θεός σου μετὰ σοῦ διὰ παντός· καὶ ἐμπλησθήσῃ καθάπερ ἐπιθυμεῖ ἡ ψυχή σου, καὶ τὰ ὀστᾶ σου πιανθήσεται, καὶ ἔσῃ ὡς κῆπος μεθύων καὶ ὡς πηγὴ ἣν μὴ ἐξέλιπεν ὕδωρ.

NETS And your God will be with you continually, and you shall be satisfied exactly as your soul desires, and your bones shall be enriched, and they shall be like a soaked garden and like a spring whose water has never failed.

Prov 16:2 (15:30)

MT מאור־עינים ישמח־לב שמועה טובה תדשן־עצם:

NRSV The light of the eyes rejoices the heart, and good news refreshes the body.

LXX θεωρῶν ὀφθαλμὸς καλὰ εὐφραίνει καρδίαν, φήμη δὲ ἀγαθὴ πιαίνει ὀστᾶ.

NETS The eye that observes good things rejoices the heart, and good news refreshes the bones.

---

[24] David-Marc d'Hamonville, *Les Proverbes* (La Bible d'Alexandrie 17; Paris, 2000), p. 201.

[25] D'Hamonville, *Les Proverbes*, p. 106.

[26] Johann Cook, 'The Translator of the Septuagint of Proverbs. Is His Style the Result of Platonic and/or Stoic Influence?', in Martin Karrer and Wolfgang Kraus (eds.), *Die Septuaginta-Texte, Kontexte, Lebenswelten. Internationale Fachtagung veranstaltet von*

The translator added explicatively that the eye observes good things. Θεωρέω occurs in Prov 15:30 and 31:16. Πιαινέω is used only here in Proverbs, but also in Ps 19(20):3; 64(65):30; Sir 26:13; Isa 58:11 and in Ezek 17:8 and 10. This is the sole occurrence of φήμη in Proverbs (שמועה); in addition it appears in 2 Macc 4:39; 3 Macc 3:2 and 4 Macc 4:22.

Concerning these passages Ziegler expresses his view as follows: "Es kann sein, daß LXX nach diesen Parallelen (he refers to Eccl 26:13 (16) too) übersetzt hat".[27] It concerns the phrase καὶ τὰ ὀστᾶ σου ὡς βοτάνη ἀνατελεῖ καὶ πιανθήσεται. The problem is that the Hebrew could have been understood differently or perhaps a different reading could have been used in individual cases. Ziegler mentions that the verb חלף could have been used instead of חלץ as in Job 14:7. The only real correspondence therefore is the verb πιαινέω. This is surely no sound basis for finding deliberate intertextual activity.

A third example is Isa 45:23 and Prov 3:16:

Isa 45:23

MT בי נשבעתי יצא מפי צדקה דבר ולא ישוב כי־לי תכרע כל־ברך תשבע כל־לשון׃

NRSV By myself I have sworn, from my mouth has gone forth in righteousness a word that shall not return: "To me every knee shall bow, every tongue shall swear."

LXX κατ' ἐμαυτοῦ ὀμνύω Ἦ μὴν ἐξελεύσεται ἐκ τοῦ στόματός μου δικαιοσύνη, οἱ λόγοι μου οὐκ ἀποστραφήσονται ὅτι ἐμοὶ κάμψει πᾶν γόνυ καὶ ἐξομολογήσεται πᾶσα γλῶσσα τῷ θεῷ.

NETS By myself I swear, "Verily righteousness shall go forth from my mouth; my words shall not be turned back, because to me every knee shall bow and every tongue shall acknowledge God."

Prov 3:16

MT ארך ימים בימינה בשמאולה עשר וכבוד׃

NRSV Long life is in her right hand; in her left hand are riches and honor.

LXX μῆκος γὰρ βίου καὶ ἔτη ζωῆς ἐν τῇ δεξιᾷ αὐτῆς, ἐν δὲ τῇ ἀριστερᾷ αὐτῆς πλοῦτος καὶ δόξα· [16a] ἐκ τοῦ στόματος αὐτῆς ἐκπορεύεται δικαιοσύνη, νόμον δὲ καὶ ἔλεον ἐπὶ γλώσσης φορεῖ.

Septuaginta Deutsch (LXX.D), Wuppertal 20.–23. Juli 2006 (WUNT 219; Tübingen, 2008), pp. 544–559, esp. 558.

[27] Ziegler, *Untersuchungen*, p. 131.

NETS for longevity and years of life are in her right hand, and in her left hand are riches and repute; [16a] out of her mouth righteousness comes forth, and she carries law and mercy upon her tongue.

There is a relationship of sorts between the addition in Prov 3:16a and Isa 45:23a. Fox,[28] following Tov,[29] in fact thinks that the translator took account of this passage in Isaiah. However, there is also a relationship between Prov 31:25(26) and 28, witnessing to intratextual activity in the Greek. Moreover, 3:16 does not agree in detail with the Hebrew of the parallel passage in 31:26, which reads:

MT פיה פתחה בחכמה ותורת־חסד על־לשונה׃

NRSV She opens her mouth with wisdom, and the teaching of kindness is on her tongue.

The translator is clearly interpreting, hence the addition is not the result of a deviating parent text. He interprets wisdom as a religious category[30] and then he uses two further religious terms, law and mercy, which are taken from the Hebrew (ותורת־חסד). The interpretation of two categories occurs elsewhere in Proverbs. For instance, in 6:23, which I discuss below, the opposite process took place and the two Hebrew words מצוה ותורה are interpreted as a genitive construction (ἐντολὴ νόμου). This is in line with what the translator usually did, for example in 31:25, where wisdom is interpreted as προσεχόντως καὶ ἐννόμως (cautiously and legally), also based upon ותורת־חסד. The translator does the same in v. 28, where wisdom is rendered by means of σοφῶς καὶ νομοθέσμως (wisely and lawfully), which is based upon the same Hebrew phrase. The point to make is that this translator is interpreting in these cases. I therefore argue that the translator is responsible for these interpretations and that the differences do not reflect a different parent text. Whether intertextual activity took place between Isaiah 45 and Proverbs 3 is not immediately

---

[28] Michael V. Fox, *Proverbs 1–9. A New Translation with Introduction and Commentary* (AncB 18A; New York etc., 2000), p. 380.

[29] Emanuel Tov, 'Recensional Differences between the Masoretic Text and the Septuagint of Proverbs,' in Harold W. Attridge, John J. Collins, and Thomas H. Tobin (eds.), *Of Scribes and Scrolls. Studies on the Hebrew Bible, Intertestamental Judaism, and Christian Origins Presented to John Strugnell on this Sixtieth Birthday* (Lanham, 1990), pp. 43–56, esp. 49.

[30] See my discussion in Johann Cook, 'The Text-critical Value of the Septuagint of Proverbs', in Ronald L. Troxel, Kelvin G. Friebel, and Dennis R. Magary (eds.), *Seeking out the Wisdom of the Ancients. Essays Offered to Honor Michael V. Fox on the Occasion of his Sixty-fifth Birthday* (Winona Lake, Indiana, 2005), pp. 407–419, esp. 417.

evident. To me it seems more likely that the translator took account of these readings intratextually in the Book of Proverbs. A final example concerns Isa 26:9 and Prov 6:23:

Isa 26:9

MT נפשי אויתיך בלילה אף־רוחי בקרבי אשחרך כי כאשר משפטיך לארץ צדק למדו ישבי תבל:

NRSV My soul yearns for you in the night, my spirit within me earnestly seeks you. For when your judgments are in the earth, the inhabitants of the world learn righteousness.

LXX ᾗ ἐπιθυμεῖ ἡ ψυχὴ ἡμῶν. ἐκ νυκτὸς ὀρθρίζει τὸ πνεῦμά μου πρὸς σέ, ὁ θεός, διότι φῶς τὰ προστάγματά σου ἐπὶ τῆς γῆς, δικαιοσύνην μάθετε, οἱ ἐνοικοῦντες ἐπὶ τῆς γῆς.

NETS ... that our soul desires. In the night my spirit rises early toward you, O God, because your ordinances are a light upon the earth. Learn righteousness, you who dwell on the earth.

The translator is clearly interpreting. Firstly the plural form ἡμῶν is used in connection with 'soul' instead of the singular. A more interesting difference is the interpretation of 'ordinances as a light' on the earth. A similar concept is used in Prov 6:23:

Prov 6:23

MT כי נר מצוה ותורה אור ודרך חיים תוכחות מוסר:

NRSV For the commandment is a lamp and the teaching a light, and the reproofs of discipline are the way of life.

LXX ὅτι λύχνος ἐντολὴ νόμου καὶ φῶς, καὶ ὁδὸς ζωῆς ἔλεγχος καὶ παιδεία.

NETS for the law's commandment is a lamp and a light and a way of life, reproof and discipline.

In these verses the translator also interprets. As stated already the syndetic phrase מצוה ותורה is understood as a genitive construction in the Greek. The opposite is the case in the second stich. It is possible that this combination was brought about on account of the combination ὁδὸς ζωῆς in the second stich. These word combinations occur frequently in the Book of Proverbs. I think the translator actually combined these lexemes deliberately in order to underline that this passage concerns the law of Moses.[31] This becomes even more evident in the light of the next verse,

[31] Johann Cook, 'The Law of Moses in Septuagint Proverbs', *VT* 49 (1999), pp. 448–461, esp. 454.

which should be understood against the background of Prov 2:16 and 17. Hence it is the law of Moses that has to guard the young man against a married woman and from a foreign tongue.

The noun φῶς is used abundantly in the Septuagint. In Proverbs it occurs five times, but only this once in connection with the law. In Isaiah there are 28 occurrences of this noun, but the only passage that can perhaps be interpreted in a similar manner is Isa 51:4:

LXX ἀκούσατέ μου ἀκούσατε, λαός μου, καὶ οἱ βασιλεῖς, πρός με ἐνωτίσασθε· ὅτι νόμος παῤ ἐμοῦ ἐξελεύσεται καὶ ἡ κρίσις μου εἰς φῶς ἐθνῶν.

NETS Hear me; hear my people, and you kings, give ear to me, because a law will go out from me, and my judgement for a light to nations.

The Hebrew reads:

MT הקשיבו אלי עמי ולאומי אלי האזינו כי תורה מאתי תצא ומשפטי לאור עמים ארגיע:

NRSV Listen to me, my people, and give heed to me, my nation; for a teaching will go out from me, and my justice for a light to the peoples.

However, here the translator, as in the Hebrew text, actually identifies judgement with the light and not the law. One would expect to find parallels in the Psalms; however, the only verse that is vaguely comparable is Ps 118(119):195 where the word of God is called a light.

In the light of this discussion it seems as if there is some intertextual relationship between Isaiah and Proverbs. It remains difficult to determine the direction of this activity, but the fact that the Proverbs passage actually has the seminal reading in its *Vorlage* could tip the scale towards accepting that the translator of Isaiah did indeed make use of Proverbs in this regard.

In conclusion it may then be inferred that clear intratextual activity took place in the books under discussion. Ziegler has discussed a number of examples in LXX-Isaiah. However, none of the examples dealt with by me display clear-cut evidence that either of these translators indeed used the other. Much more research should be done on this issue.

2.3. *Isaiah and Proverbs as Actualized Units*

Seeligmann[32] has demonstrated convincingly that LXX-Isaiah has been translated as an actualizing unit. Van der Kooij developed this point further and argued 'that LXX Isaiah contains passages where the ancient

---

[32] Isac L. Seeligmann, *The Septuagint of Isaiah. A Discussion of its Problems* (MEOL 9; Leiden, 1948).

text of Isaiah has been actualized, not only in the sense of modernization (of names of places or countries, for instance), but more particularly in the sense of the updating of a prophecy or oracle of Isaiah, a phenomenon which is well-known in the Targumim'.[33] In the context of Isaiah 23 Van der Kooij interprets the prominent differences between MT and LXX hermeneutically as describing a vision, and more specifically as a fulfilment-interpretation of the oracular in the prophetic Hebrew text. His conclusions are far-reaching and consist of external references to (1) the complete destruction of Carthage by the Romans in 146 BCE; (2) the Parthian invasion of Babylonia, presumably understood as a sign of the imminent breakdown of the Seleucid Empire, and (3) the involvement of Tyre in the Hellenisation of the city and temple of Jerusalem. Van der Kooij offers a rather complex argument in support of his claim that LXX-Isaiah 23 is a fulfilment-interpretation of an ancient prophecy underlying the Hebrew text.[34]

I have demonstrated that the Greek version of Proverbs can also be regarded as a contextualized writing.[35] This text has been translated antithetically and more specifically anti-Hellenistically in order to assist the Jewish readers resist a society that was becoming progressively Hellenized. This is observed on various levels. This translator was undoubtedly steeped in Greek (and Jewish) culture. I do argue, however, that he directly applied the knowledge he obtained only as far as the external *form* goes.[36] He explicitly shies away from applying Hellenistic ideas. The prominent role of the Mosaic law in this unit attests to its Jewishness. Probably the most convincing example of this is the view of the law of Moses as a surrounding wall in Prov 28:4:

MT עזבי תורה יהללו רשע ושמרי תורה יתגרו בם:

NRSV Those who forsake the law praise the wicked, but those who keep the law struggle against them.

LXX οὕτως οἱ ἐγκαταλείποντες τὸν νόμον ἐγκωμιάζουσιν ἀσέβειαν, οἱ δὲ ἀγαπῶντες τὸν νόμον περιβάλλουσιν ἑαυτοῖς τεῖχος.

NETS Likewise those who forsake the law and praise impious deeds; However, those who love the law build a wall around themselves.

---

[33] Van der Kooij, *The Oracle of Tyre*, p. 11.
[34] Van der Kooij, *The Oracle of Tyre*, p. 187.
[35] See the discussion in my contribution to the IOSOT congress in Ljubljana, 2007: Johann Cook, 'Towards the Formulation of a Theology of the Septuagint', in André Lemaire (ed.), *Congress Volume. Ljubljana, 2007* (VT.S 133; Leiden etc., 2010), pp. 621–640.
[36] Cook, 'Platonic and/or Stoic Influence?', pp. 544–558.

This tradition is widespread in Judaism in earlier (LXX-Proverbs and the Book of Aristeas—surrounding the righteous) and later (the Damascus Document[37] and the Mishna—surrounding the Torah) contexts. It is the application of this tradition in LXX-Proverbs that makes it especially significant. The role of the law of Moses is actually underlined more explicitly than is the case in the Hebrew version of Proverbs. There is a reason for this. I have argued that this law was actually devalued in the Hellenistic environment in which these Proverbs came into being.[38] Another decisive example of this anti-Hellenistic inclination of the translator(s) is found in the addition in Prov 9:10 and 13:15 of the equivalent of the phrase 'For to know the law is the sign of a good mind'.

Prov 9:10

MT תחלת חכמה יראת יהוה ודעת קדשים בינה׃

NRSV The fear of the Lord is the beginning of wisdom, and the knowledge of the holy one is insight.

LXX ἀρχὴ σοφίας φόβος κυρίου, καὶ βουλὴ ἁγίων σύνεσις· [10a] τὸ γὰρ γνῶναι νόμον διανοίας ἐστὶν ἀγαθῆς·

NETS The beginning of wisdom is the fear of the Lord, And the counsels of saints is understanding, *for to know the law is the sign of a sound mind*;

I argued that the translator actually used the equivalent of this phrase twice, in two different contexts, in order to underline the relevance of the law for its readers. This Judaic interpretation must be read in conjunction with the interpretation of the two inclinations that occur in Prov 2:11 and 17. This is a well-known rabbinic tradition concerning the יצרים of mankind.[39]

Another characteristic is the moralizing or religionizing element present in LXX-Proverbs. I think this stems from a group of religiously conservative Jews, most probably at the time of translation. The person(s) responsible for this unit was anti-Hellenistically inclined and deliberately warned his readers of the dangers inherent in the surrounding Hellenism. This concept of anti-Hellenism is a difficult one, but I agree with Nickelsburg that an author can at the same time be Jewish, anti-Hellenistic and

[37] Johann Cook, 'Law and wisdom in the Dead Sea Scrolls with reference to Hellenistic Judaism', in Florentino García Martínez (ed.), *Wisdom and Apocalypticism in the Dead Sea Scrolls and the Biblical Tradition* (BEThL 168; Leuven, 2003), pp. 323–342, esp. 339.

[38] Cook, 'The Law of Moses', pp. 448–461.

[39] Johann Cook, 'The Origin of the Tradition of the יצר הטב and יצר הרע', *JSJ* 38 (2007), pp. 80–91.

Hellenistic.[40] This is especially true for a person as highly qualified as this translator. As demonstrated, he made use of well-known literary devices and creatively made up novel proverbs apparently without any basis in the Semitic parent text. He followed a rather free translation technique; he rearranged the order of some chapters towards the end of Proverbs on the basis of thematic and 'ideological' considerations.[41] He made use of contrasts to a greater extent than appears in the Hebrew. The religionizing terminology which I discussed in the *Festschrift* for Siegfried Mittmann[42] is decisive evidence of the ideological intention of this translator. In this regard Baumgartner has argued that the translator of Proverbs was deeply influenced by Jewish midrash.[43] Bertram also held the view that this unit represents Jewish legalism.[44] This position is contrary to that of Gerleman,[45] who thought that a Greek philosophical rather than a Jewish way of thinking is to be taken as the background to issues of religion and ethics in LXX-Proverbs.

It should therefore be clear that LXX-Proverbs could be defined as a contextualized unit, which is not exactly the same as being an actualized one. I think the difference is mainly found in the difference of genre. The point of correspondence is that in both units the immediate historical contexts are taken into account by the respective translators. However, there are also pertinent differences between these translators.

3. *Differences*

The differences concern firstly the question of the translation technique to which I referred to above. From the examples I analysed it is clear that these translators actually generally followed a free approach towards

---

[40] George W.E. Nickelsburg, *Ancient Judaism and Christian Origins. Diversity, Continuity and Transformation* (Minneapolis, 2003), p. 152.

[41] Johann Cook, 'The Greek of Proverbs—Evidence of a Recensionally Deviating Hebrew Text?' in Shalom M. Paul *et al.* (eds.), *Emanuel. Studies in the Hebrew Bible, Septuagint, and Dead Sea Scrolls in Honor of Emanuel Tov* (VT.S 94; Leiden etc., 2003), pp. 605–618.

[42] Johann Cook, 'Exegesis in the Septuagint', *JNSL* 30 (2004), pp. 1–19.

[43] Antoine J. Baumgartner, *Étude critique sur l'état du texte du livre des Proverbes d'après les principales traductions anciennes* (Leipzig, 1890), p. 253.

[44] Georg Bertram, 'Die religiöse Umdeutung altorientalischer Lebensweisheit in der griechischen Übersetzung des AT', *ZAW* 54 (1936), pp. 153–167.

[45] Gilles Gerleman, 'The Septuagint as a Hellenistic Document', *OTS* 8 (1950), pp. 15–27.

their parent texts, and had the freedom to interpret freely, hence the focus on contextualization. The translation of Isaiah, however, does not contain differences in the order of chapters to the same extent as does Proverbs. I have argued that this adapted order of chapters was brought about deliberately by the translator, on the basis of the considerations of the literary aspects, contrasts and even ideology.[46] Moreover, I could not detect the same prominent indications that the Isaiah version is indeed a Jewish oriented writing which I detected in LXX-Proverbs.[47] I did not make an exhaustive analysis, but I found no relevant evidence in this regard. In the exegetical commentary on LXX-Proverbs that is in progress,[48] I detected many Jewish, pre-rabbinical traditions that on the face of it seemed to derive from Greek philosophical traditions, more specifically Stoically minded writters (contrary to D'Hamonville).[49] The same issues do not seem to be at stake in LXX-Isaiah. These differences I think should be ascribed to differences in the historical contexts of these two units.

4. *Different Provenances?*

Scholars have made the methodological error of interpreting the Book of Aristeas in relation to the whole of the Old Greek text and not only to its initial intention, the Pentateuch. Hence there is some resistance to seeking for the provenance of Old Greek units outside of Alexandria. Van der Kooij, however, ventured into a novel direction by arguing that Egypt was indeed the place of provenance, however, not Alexandria, but rather the circles of the Oniad priests in Egypt in Leontopolis.[50] He also has definite ideas about the dating of this unit. On account of Isa 14:4—which he sees as a direct reference to Antiochus IV Epiphanes—he takes as *ter-*

---

[46] Cook, 'The Greek of Proverbs'.

[47] Cook, 'Platonic and/or Stoic Influence?'.

[48] Johann Cook, *Text and Tradition. An Exegetical Commentary on the Septuagint of Proverbs*. This monograph will be published by the Society of Biblical Literature as part of the Septuagint Commentary Series (in preparation).

[49] D'Hamonville, *Les Proverbes*. See my 'Semantic Considerations and the Provenance of Translated Units', in Melvin K.H. Peters (ed.), *XIII Congress of the International Organization for Septuagint and Cognate Studies. Ljubljana, 2007* (SBL.SCS 55; Atlanta, 2008), pp. 65–83.

[50] Arie van der Kooij, *Die alten Textzeugen des Jesajabuches. Ein Beitrag zur Textgeschichte des Alten Testaments* (OBO 35; Fribourg–Göttingen, 1981), pp. 61–65.

minus post quem for LXX-Isaiah 164 BCE.[51] According to his interpretation of Isa 23:10, the fall of Carthage was known to the translator, which means that LXX-Isaiah was translated between 146 and 132. This is substantiated by Isa 21:1–9 which, according to Van der Kooij, refers to the fall of Babylon. This difference in provenance, namely Leontopolis and not Alexandria, could therefore have been one of the reasons why the translator(s) had a different, freer approach towards his parent text.

I think the same could be argued for the Greek version of Proverbs. I have demonstrated that the person(s) who was responsible for this unit was a creative interpreter. As demonstrated above, he had an excellent knowledge of the Greek (and Jewish) culture and had a characteristic anti-Hellenistic inclination. The question is to identify a suitable context for such an approach. I would argue that there are two possibilities: Egypt and Palestine. If the Book of Aristeas is to be taken seriously, Alexandria is the place of origin of the Pentateuch, the original Septuagint. Whether this site should also be accepted as location for the other units in the Septuagint is unclear. Theoretically at least, Palestine should also be considered a possibility. Judaism was fundamentally influenced by Hellenism in all contexts to the extent that Hengel suggested that all Judaisms of the second century BCE onwards should be deemed Hellenistic Judaism in nature.[52]

Palestine was also subjected to extensive Hellenising, especially after the advent of Antiochus Epiphanes, even though the extent to which it was Hellenised is still being debated.[53] I think it is possible to argue that LXX-Proverbs came into being in the wake of the Hellenisation of Palestine, after the Antiochian crisis.[54] There is historical evidence of the systematic Hellenisation of Palestine during and after the Antiochian crisis. In this regard the first chapter of the First Book of Maccabees refers to the Jewish Hellenisers as a definite group that endeavoured to hide or remove evidence of their Jewishness.[55] Other primary sources also attest to this phenomenon. One example is the wisdom of Ben Sira. There is for exam-

[51] Van der Kooij, *Die alten Textzeugen*, p. 71.

[52] Martin Hengel, *Judentum und Hellenismus. Studien zu ihrer Begegnung unter besonderer Berücksichtigung Palästinas bis zur Mitte des 2. Jhs. V.Chr.* (Tübingen, 1973), p. 568.

[53] Cf. the apologetic position of Louis Feldman, 'How much Hellenism in the Land of Israel?', *JSJ* 33 (2002), pp. 290–313.

[54] Cf. the interesting interpretation of the reasons why Antiochus in fact repressed Jerusalem in Erich S. Gruen, 'Hellenism and Persecution: Antiochus IV and the Jews', in Peter Green (ed.), *Hellenistic History and Culture* (Berkeley etc., 1993), pp. 238–274.

[55] Cf. Jonathan A. Goldstein, *I Maccabees. A New Translation with Introduction and Commentary* (AncB 41; New York etc., 1976), p. 199.

ple a marked difference between LXX-Proverbs and the grandfather, Ben Sira's wisdom, which originally came to be in Palestine before the time of Epiphanes.[56] Ben Sira reveals a more relaxed attitude towards Greek philosophy. This is surely the result of contextual factors and more specifically because the wisdom of Ben Sira was composed before the advent of this Seleucid ruler. Aristobulus, a Jewish-Hellenistic scribe who wrote in Alexandria, also had a different attitude towards Greek philosophy than the person(s) responsible for the Greek Proverbs. Aristobulus endeavoured to apply Greek philosophical insights in order to understand the Pentateuch, an intention that is absent from the person(s) responsible for the Septuagint of Proverbs.[57] I have therefore argued that these differences are the result of contextual differences.

In the final analysis I therefore conclude that the Septuagint of Proverbs is an example of a biblical book that was translated by an educated, but conservative Jew,[58] who eagerly followed the literary conventions of the Greek language, but deliberately evaded the idea world of Greek thought. As a matter of fact he must be regarded as anti-Hellenistically inclined as far as the religious ideas of Hellenism are concerned. This stance is the result of the historical context in which he lived and worked, Jerusalem circa 150 BCE.

5. *Conclusion*

It should be clear that there are prominent correspondences and differences between the units under discussion. These phenomena are the result of contextual factors and hence each translated unit should be researched individually. In the final analysis I would therefore agree with Van der Kooij that a number of Septuagint units are to be regarded as actualized, in the sense of contextualized units. This applies at least to LXX-Isaiah and Proverbs.

---

[56] See Patrick W. Skehan and Alexander A. Di Lella, *The Wisdom of Ben Sira. Introduction and Commentary* (AncB 39; New York etc., 1987), p. 8.

[57] Cf. my contribution to the conference on Ptolemy Philadelphus: Johann Cook, 'Ptolemy Philadelphus and Jewish Writings. Aristobulus and Pseudo-Aristeas as examples of Alexandrian Jewish Approaches', in Paul MacKechnie and Philippe Guillaume (eds.), *Ptolemy Philadelphus and his World* (Mnemosyne 300; Leiden etc., 2008), pp. 196–206.

[58] In this regard Van der Kooij, *The Oracle of Tyre*, p. 189, refers to the translator being a scribe-translator who had the competence of a sage. This is another significant correspondence between these two units.

AN EXPLORATION OF THE WISDOM OF SOLOMON AS THE MISSING LINK BETWEEN ISAIAH AND MATTHEW

Kristin De Troyer

1. *Introduction*

In Matt 27:38–43 Jesus is derided on the cross. The episode appears in Mark, in Matthew, and in a short form in Luke. In the passage, some passers-by utter the following scoffing words: 'Aha, you who would destroy the temple and build it in three days, save yourself and come down from the cross' (Mark 15:29b–30 // Matt 27:40 with variants). Then, the chief priests, the scribes (and in Matthew, also the elders) mock Jesus saying: 'He saved others; he cannot save himself. Let the Christ, the King of Israel come down now from the cross, that we may see and believe' (Mark 15:31b–32 // Matt 27:42 with variants). After this sentence, Matthew adds yet another mocking word: 'He trusts in God; let God deliver him now, if he desires him; for he said, "I am the Son of God"' (Matt 27:43). This article will focus on the sentence added by Matthew to the Markan source.

In his 1997 article, 'Matthew's Use of the Old Testament', Donald Senior claims that in Matt 27:43, and more particularly in the words of mockery, Ps 22:9 is quoted and there is an allusion to the Wisdom of Solomon 2:13.[1] Next, under the heading of 'Elements of the narrative inspired in whole or part by reference to Old Testament passages', he states that 'the words used by the mockers in 27:43 are clearly drawn from Psalm 22:8 (also Wisdom 2:18)'.[2] 'Thus', he concludes, 'they could be considered a direct quotation'.[3] In this section, Senior explains his reason

[1] Donald Senior, 'The Lure of the Formula Quotations. Re-assessing Matthew's Use of the Old Testament with the Passion Narrative as Test Case', in Christopher M. Tuckett (ed.), *The Scriptures in the Gospels* (BETHL 131; Leuven, 1997), pp. 89–115. See also Kurt Aland, *Synopsis of the Four Gospels. Greek-English Edition of the Synopsis Quattuor Evangeliorum. On the Basis of the Greek Text of Nestle-Aland 26th edition and Greek New Testament 3rd edition* (Stuttgart, 1983), pp. 318–319.

[2] Senior, 'The Lure of the Formula Quotations', p. 111.

[3] Senior, 'The Lure of the Formula Quotations', p. 111.

for suspecting this connection. Some allusions have become 'a structural element of the story itself'.[4] Senior points to two clear inspirational narratives: Mark's mocking scene is 'inspired at least in part by the portrayal of the Suffering Servant of Isaiah 50–53'[5] and 'interaction with Psalm 22 has undoubtedly had a strong influence on the crucifixion scene in Mark and is also carried over into Matthew's account'.[6] Senior then continues to prove how typical it is of Matthew to make use of quotations and leading texts from the Hebrew Bible.[7] He mentions both Ps 22:9 and Wisd 2:18 in this regard. Indeed in the margins of Nestle-Aland 26, reference is also made to Ps 22:9 and the Wisdom of Solomon 2:13, 18–20.

Maarten Menken, in his 2004 volume,[8] elaborated on the idea that Matthew took the Ps 22:8 quotation from Mark 15:29 and that Matthew extended the use of other texts including Psalm 22: '... Matthew has not only borrowed but also expanded the Markan references to Psalms 22 and 69 in the context of our quotation'.[9] In his expansion, however, Matthew uses a revised Old Greek text.[10] In Menken's words: 'We have to conclude that the translation of Psalm 22:9 in Matthew 27:43 has the characteristics of a revised LXX: we see an obvious LXX basis, and corrections intended to render the Hebrew more adequately'.[11] The previous quotation was taken from a chapter on 'Old Testament Quotations Inserted in Markan Contexts'.[12] The chapter is part of Menken's analysis of Matthew's use of the Biblical text. His general argument is outlined below. In four places, Matthew refers to the Prophet Isaiah and sees the text of Isaiah being fulfilled: Matt 1:22–23 fulfils Isa 7:14; Matt 4:14–16 fulfils Isa 8:23–9:1;

---

[4] Senior, 'The Lure of the Formula Quotations', p. 111.
[5] Senior, 'The Lure of the Formula Quotations', p. 112.
[6] Senior, 'The Lure of the Formula Quotations', p. 112.
[7] Senior, 'The Lure of the Formula Quotations', pp. 112–114.
[8] Maarten J.J. Menken, *Matthew's Bible. The Old Testament Text of the Evangelist* (BEThL 173; Leuven, 2004).
[9] Menken, *Matthew's Bible*, p. 235. The quotation is in Matt 27:43.
[10] In his work, Menken uses the general term 'Septuagint'. In this contribution, I use the term Old Greek (OG) translation for the oldest Greek translation of a given book. The Septuagint is more a collection of books, as it is for instance found in Codex Vaticanus. It is however, precisely Codex Vaticanus that does not offer an Old Greek text for Isaiah, but a Hexaplaric text; see Joseph Ziegler, *Isaias* (Septuaginta Vetus Testamentum Graecum Auctoritate Academiae Scientiarum Gottingensis editum 14; 3rd ed.; Göttingen, 1983), pp. 38–40.
[11] Menken, *Matthew's Bible*, p. 237.
[12] Menken, *Matthew's Bible*, pp. 227–238.

Matt 8:17 fulfils Isa 53:4 and Matt 12:17–21 fulfils Isa 42:1–4.[13] Menken organizes the differences between the 'Septuagint'[14] text of Isaiah and the text quoted by Matthew into three categories:[15] corrections to the text so as to make the quotation agree better with the Hebrew text, improvements to the Greek; the third category is 'due to ancient biblical exegesis'. None of this is done by Matthew; these differences come from Matthew's source. Besides Mark and Q, there are what Menken calls 'pre-Matthean materials'.[16] Menken also explains that Matthew added other quotations to his text and that these quotations show the same textual character as the fulfilment quotations: 'that of a LXX revised for the sake of better agreement with the Hebrew text or of better Greek'.[17] In short, according to Menken, Matthew 'makes use of a revised LXX text'.[18]

With regard to the extra sentence in Matt 27:43, he writes: 'It is fairly obvious that Matthew as editor of Mark inserted the verse 27:43, and that it does not come from another source'.[19] Menken's main argument is that the use of 'son of God' is a theme that Matthew took from Mark, which he clarified and expanded.[20] Similarly, Menken argues that Matthew expanded Mark's reference to Psalms 22 and 69. There is for example an allusion to Ps 22:8 in Matt 27:29 and to Ps 69:22 in Matt 27:34.[21] He concludes that an 'existing revised LXX text' of Ps 22:9[22] lies behind Matt 27:43.[23]

In this contribution, I would like to explore further the idea advanced by Senior that Matt 27:43 is composed of material from (Ps 22:8 and) Wisd 2:18. Moreover, I will argue that Matthew found his inspiration for the additional line of mockery in the Book of Isaiah, as he did earlier, that is, not in a revised Old Greek text of Isaiah, but in the re-interpreted Isaiah text as found in Wisd 2:18.[24]

---

[13] Menken, *Matthew's Bible*, p. 279.

[14] Menken's use.

[15] Menken, *Matthew's Bible*, p. 280.

[16] Menken, *Matthew's Bible*, p. 280: 'Matthew's other OT quotations come for a large part from his main source, the Gospel of Mark; some have been borrowed from Q, and a few come from other pre-Matthean materials'.

[17] Menken, *Matthew's Bible*, p. 281.

[18] Menken, *Matthew's Bible*, p. 281.

[19] Menken, *Matthew's Bible*, pp. 234–235. Matt 27:43, however, is also studied by Menken as one of the cases where Matthew added another quote to his source text.

[20] Menken, *Matthew's Bible*, p. 235.

[21] Menken, *Matthew's Bible*, pp. 235–236.

[22] Reference should be made to Ps 22:9 in Hebrew or 21:9 in the Old Greek.

[23] Menken, *Matthew's Bible*, p. 238.

[24] This contribution is an attempt to go beyond the vague analysis of intertextual

2. *From the Hebrew text of Isaiah to the Greek of Matthew*

2.1. *From the Hebrew text of Isaiah 42:1 to the Old Greek of Isaiah 42:1*

The Hebrew text of the Isaiah runs as follows:

הן עבדי אתמך בו
בחירי רצתה נפשי
נתתי רוחי עליו
משפט לגוים יוציא

In translation (NRSV):

> Here is my servant whom I uphold
> My chosen, in whom my soul delights
> I have put my spirit upon him
> He will bring forth justice to the nations.

Menken offers the following translation:

> Behold, my servant, whom I uphold
> My chosen one, in whom my soul finds pleasure;
> I have given my Spirit upon him,
> He will bring forth justice to the Gentiles.[25]

As, however, the going up of the nations is a theme of Isaiah, I prefer to render גוים by nations.[26] Moreover, I prefer to render משפט by judgement.[27] Hence, the last phrase, I translate: He will bring forth judgement to the nations.

The four phrases are the first of a collection commonly called the Suffering Servant Poems, which appear in the second part of Isaiah: 42:1–9; 49:1–6; 50:4–9; 52:13–53:12.[28] In other words, these poems belong to what is often called Second Isaiah. In his form-critical work, Marvin Sweeney identifies Isaiah 40–54 as 'a prophetic instruction that YHWH

---

allusions to the Wisdom of Solomon 2:18 found in Matt 27:39–44 by Susan Lochrie Graham, 'A Strange Salvation. Intertextual Allusion in Matthew 27,39–44', in Tuckett, *The Scriptures in the Gospels*, pp. 501–511.

[25] Maarten J.J. Menken, 'The Quotation from Isaiah 42,1–4 in Matthew 12,18–21. Its Relation with the Matthean Context', in *Bijdragen* 59 (1998), pp. 251–266, republished in Menken, *Matthew's Bible*, pp. 51–65, esp. 51.

[26] See especially Norbert Lohfink and Erich Zenger, *The God of Israel and the Nations. Studies in Isaiah and the Psalms* (Collegeville, 2000), pp. 45–53.

[27] Against Menken; see Menken, 'The Quotation-Matthean Context', p. 261 = Menken, *Matthew's Bible*, pp. 60–61.

[28] John F.A. Sawyer, 'The Book of Isaiah', in Bruce M. Metzger and Michael D. Coogan (eds.), *The Oxford Companion to the Bible* (Oxford, 1993), pp. 325–329, esp. 328.

is maintaining the covenant and restoring Zion'.[29] He summarizes Isaiah 40–54 as follows:

> They [= the chapters, KDT] begin with a renewed prophetic commission in 40:1–11 to announce YHWH's restoration of Zion (...). The instruction proper in 40:12–54:17 includes five basic contentions: (1) that YHWH is the master of creation (40:12–31); (2) that YHWH is the master of human events (41:1–42:13); (3) that YHWH is the redeemer of Israel (42:14–44:23); (4) that YHWH will use the pagan king Cyrus for the restoration of Zion (44:24–48:22); and (5) that YHWH is restoring Zion (chs. 49–54).[30]

Sweeney adds: 'The structure of this unit is clearly designed to lead the reader to the conclusion that YHWH's restoration of Zion is now taking place'.[31] Moreover, Sweeney argues that the final edition of the Book of Isaiah and the later chapters of Isaiah presuppose the reign of Cyrus and not that of a Davidic monarch.[32] Cyrus is mentioned by name in Isa 44:28 and then again in 45:1. Before the identification of Cyrus with the anointed one of God, the text describes the anointed one as 'his arm': 'See, the Lord God comes with might and his arm rules for him' (40:10). In 41:2, the person is identified as 'a victor from the east'. Israel, Jacob, is reassured that this victor is going to help them (41:8–10, 14). Then come the famous words of 42:1a–b: 'Here is my servant whom I uphold, my chosen in whom my soul finds pleasure'. In these words, the servant is introduced, albeit without giving his name. Of this servant, God says: 'I have put my spirit upon him; he will bring forth judgement to the nations' (Isa 42:1c–d). Now, before any examination of the Greek translation of this text, it should be observed that the Suffering Servant is never as such identified within the four poems *stricto sensu*. 'There is no answer to the question of who the servant is ....'[33]

It is precisely the problem of the identification of the Suffering Servant that the translator of Isaiah was trying to solve in the first verse of the four Servant Poems. The translation into Greek of Isa 42:1 runs as follows:[34]

---

[29] Marvin A. Sweeney, *Isaiah 1–39 with an Introduction to Prophetic Literature* (FOTL 16; Grand Rapids, 1996), p. 48.

[30] Sweeney, *Isaiah 1–39*, p. 48.

[31] Sweeney, *Isaiah 1–39*, p. 48.

[32] Sweeney, *Isaiah 1–39*, p. 52.

[33] Sawyer, 'The Book of Isaiah', p. 328.

[34] Ziegler, *Isaias*; Alfred Rahlfs and Robert Hanhart, *Septuaginta. Id est Vetus Testamentum graece iuxta LXX interpretes, Editio altera* (Stuttgart, 2006).

Ιακωβ ὁ παῖς μου, ἀντιλήμψομαι αὐτοῦ·
Ισραηλ ὁ ἐκλεκτός μου, προσεδέξατο αὐτὸν ἡ ψυχή μου·
ἔδωκα τὸ πνεῦμα μου ἐπ' αὐτόν,
κρίσιν τοῖς ἔθνεσιν ἐξοίσει.

Brenton translates:[35]

Jacob is my servant, I will help him
Israel is my chosen, my soul has accepted him
I have put my spirit upon him
He shall bring forth judgment to the Gentiles.

Menken offers a slightly different translation:[36]

Jacob my servant, I shall uphold him,
Israel my chosen, my soul has accepted him;
I have given my Spirit upon him,
He will bring forth justice to the Gentiles.

The main change in the translation of Isa 42:1 is the identification of the servant.[37] Indeed, the Old Greek translator identifies the servant with Jacob/Israel.[38] God will uphold his servant Jacob, God's soul has accepted Israel, which is God's chosen one. It is this servant and chosen one that will bring justice to the Gentiles. In the Hebrew text, the servant brings justice to the nations. The servant, however, is certainly not Jacob/Israel, but another person,[39] possibly the pagan Cyrus who would later help Israel. In 42:1, at the beginning of the four poems, the Old Greek, however, identifies the servant as Jacob/Israel. It is Jacob/Israel that will bring justice to the Gentiles—the others. In other words, the direction

---

[35] Lancelot Charles Lee Brenton, *The Septuagint Version of the Old Testament and Apocrypha, with an English Translation, and with Various Readings and Critical Notes* (London, 1851; Grand Rapids, 1978).

[36] Menken, 'The Quotation from Isaiah 42,1–4 in Matthew 12,18–21. Its Textual Form,' *ETL* 75 (1999), pp. 32–52, esp. 34; republished in Menken, *Matthew's Bible*, pp. 67–88, esp. 69.

[37] Menken observes that 'The Book of Wisdom shows how easily the παῖς θεοῦ from Second Isaiah was interpreted as "son of God" among Greek-speaking Jews'; he refers to the Wisdom of Solomon 2:13, 16, and 18. See Menken, 'The Quotation-Textual Form,' pp. 37–38 = Menken, *Matthew's Bible*, p. 72. 'Besides,' he notes, 'in Greek the meaning "son" for παῖς was much more common then the meaning "servant"' (*ibidem*).

[38] For a detailed analysis, see Eugene R. Ekblad Jr., *Isaiah's Servant Poems according to the Septuagint. An Exegetical and Theological Study* (CBET 23; Leuven, 1999), pp. 56–65.

[39] There is also the possibility that the Hebrew text saw the Suffering Servant as referring 'to the experience of Israel rather than any individual,' see Sawyer, 'The Book of Isaiah,' p. 328.

of the text has changed: no longer is there a right hand of God that will help Israel/Jacob within the context of the nations, but there is Israel/Jacob who with the support of God will bring judgement[40] to the Gentiles.

With regard to the translation of the noun עבד which appears in the following verses of the four Servant Songs: 42:1, 49:5, 49:6, 52:13, and 53:11, in 42:1, the OG translator identifies the servant as Jacob/Israel. Aquila and Symmachus revise the OG into ὁ δοῦλος μου and Theodotion gives ὁ παῖς μου. In 49:5, the OG translator keeps the distinction between the servant and Jacob/Israel as found in the Hebrew text. God speaks to the servant (δοῦλος), who is supposed to bring back Jacob/Israel to God. In 49:6, the OG continues the distinction between the servant and Jacob/Israel. The OG however uses παῖδά μου (and the three Jewish revisers[41] change that into δοῦλόν μου). In 52:13, the OG renders עבדי by ὁ παῖς μου, corrected again by Aquila and Symmachus into δοῦλος μου. Finally, in 53:11, the servant is spoken about using the participle δουλεύοντα. In other words, in the OG rendering of the Servant Songs, the distinction between the Servant and Jacob/Israel is kept, except here in 42:1. Moreover, the OG seems to alternate between ὁ δοῦλος μου (49:5; compare δουλεύοντα in 53:11) and ὁ παῖς μου (49:6; 52:13). It is no surprise that Aquila consistently revises παῖς to δοῦλος; however, that Theodotion also uses παῖς might seem to point to the interchangeability of the two nouns.

Finally, the servant is identified in 53:11 as the just one. God will justify the just one who serves many well: δικαιῶσαι δίκαιον εὖ δουλεύοντα πολλοῖς—a theme to which I will return later.

2.2. *From the Old Greek of Isaiah 42:1 to the Wisdom of Solomon 2:18*

The Wisdom of Solomon 2:18 runs as follows:[42]

> εἰ γάρ ἐστιν ὁ δίκαιος υἱὸς θεοῦ,
> ἀντιλήμψεται αὐτοῦ·
> καὶ ῥύσεται αὐτὸν
> ἐκ χειρὸς ἀνθεστηκότων.

---

[40] For a discussion of the meaning of the word κρίσις, see Ekblad, *Isaiah's Servant Poems*, pp. 64–65.

[41] Or more vaguely, 'the rest' (of the Jewish revisers).

[42] Joseph Ziegler, *Sapientia Salomonis* (Septuaginta Vetus Testamentum Graecum Auctoritate Societatis Litterarum Gottingensis editum 12.1; Göttingen, 1962).

NRSV:

> For if the righteous man is God's child
> He will help him
> And will deliver him
> from the hand of his adversaries.

In his commentary on the Book of the Wisdom of Solomon, Winston states: 'The author's treatment of the suffering and vindication of the child of God is a homily based chiefly on the fourth Servant Song in 52:12 with some help from earlier and later passages in this book'.[43] In his comments on Wisd 2:18, besides acknowledging the influence of Ps 22:9, Winston refers to the Old Greek of Isa 42:1 and to Matt 27:43.[44]

If indeed the author of Wisdom uses the Old Greek text of Isaiah, in particular 42:1–4, then he/she did not read that the servant brings justice to the nations, but that Jacob/Israel brings justice to the Gentiles.

The Wisdom of Solomon, however, does not contain the names Jacob/Israel. The first large unit (1:1–6:21) argues that God helps the righteous. Indeed, Wisdom goes beyond the question of helping Israel among the nations or the Gentiles; the distinction made in the book is 'between the righteous (δίκαιοι) and the impious (ἀσεβεῖς)'.[45]

In 2:18, the text seems to make yet another claim: if a righteous (person) is a child of God, then 'God will assist him and rescue him from the clutches of his opponents'.[46] Now, the Greek text literally states: 'because, if the righteous one is a child of God'. The rescue promise is thus conditional: if the righteous one is God's child, then .... The question is now whether or not we can find out who the righteous one is and what it means to be a child of God.

With regard to 'child of God', Winston claims the following: 'Although the meaning "child" for *pais* is fixed here by verse 16d and 18a, this may be due to our author's misunderstanding of the Septuagint's oscillation between *pais* and *doulos*'.[47] Winston notes that in the Old Greek of Isa 49:1–6 δοῦλος is used twice and παῖς once. In 52:12 and 53:1 only παῖς is used, not δοῦλος.

---

[43] David Winston, *The Wisdom of Solomon. A New Translation with Introduction and Commentary* (AncB 43; New York, 1979), pp. 119–120.

[44] Winston, *Wisdom of Solomon*, p. 120.

[45] Frederic Raurell, 'From ΔΙΚΑΙΟΣΥΝΗ to ΑΘΑΝΑΣΙΑ', in Núria Calduch-Benages and Jacques Vermeylen (eds.), *Treasures of Wisdom. Studies in Ben Sira and the Book of Wisdom. Festschrift M. Gilbert* (BEThL 143; Leuven, 1999), pp. 331–349, esp. 331.

[46] Winston, *Wisdom of Solomon*, p. 112.

[47] Winston, *Wisdom of Solomon*, p. 120.

The issue, however, is not just the oscillation between παῖς and δοῦλος in the OG text of Isaiah, but how the author of Wisdom saw the function of the child of God. The Wisdom of Solomon uses the Old Greek text of Isaiah in a new context: from Wisd 1:16 onwards, the ungodly are reasoning among themselves and trying to set a trap for the just (2:12–20). Wisd 2:18 is part of this testing of the just person. As in Ps 22:9 the direction of the text has changed; it is no longer a description of the servant, and how God will help him and how the servant will help others (whether Israel among the nations or the Gentiles, in respectively MT and OG), but a description of the righteous put in the mouth of the ungodly mockers who are testing the righteous (Ps 22:9 and Wisd 2:18). Indeed, the theme of righteousness and/or the righteous is crucial for the Wisdom of Solomon. Raurell points to all its uses and aptly summarizes them: 'The use of the root δικα- in Wisdom is significant for its number as well as for the variety of forms employed'.[48] Compared with the OG of Isaiah, we notice indeed that δίκαιος is used 17 times in Isaiah, but only once in the Servant Poems (53:11, rendering צדיק); δίκαιοσύνη appears 52 times, but again only once in the Servant Poems (42:6, rendering צדק); finally δικαιοῦν appears 8 times in OG Isaiah, but only twice in the Servant Poems (50:8; 53:11 rendering צדק). Although present in the Hebrew text as well as the Old Greek translation of Isaiah, righteousness as a topic seems to occur less often in the Servant Poems than in the overall book. Moreover, the topic of righteousness is of utmost importance to the author of the Wisdom of Solomon. It should be also noted that it is particularly in 53:11 that the Isaiah connected the theme of servant with righteousness and the translator adopted that theme. The link between the servant and righteousness is then further developed by the author of the Wisdom of Solomon who reflects on the child of God as the righteous one—a child, who will be helped by God.

The Wisdom of Solomon however does not often use the root δοῦλος. In 9:5 Solomon identifies himself as a 'servant'; in 15:7, a reference is made to vessels that 'serve' clean uses; in 18:11, the noun 'slave' is used in opposition to 'master'; and finally, in 19:14 a reference is made to 'slaves' of guests. In other words, the concept 'servant' as attested in the Servant Poems is not found in the Wisdom of Solomon.

When the author of Wisdom of Solomon uses the word παῖς, he uses it in two meanings: in 8:19, 12:25, 18:10 (and maybe 18:9), it refers to real

[48] Raurell, 'From ΔΙΚΑΙΟΣΥΝΗ to ΑΘΑΝΑΣΙΑ', p. 335, n. 16.

children and in 9:4, 12:7, 12:20, and 19:6 to servants—plural—of God, people, who serve God. In 18:9, there is a reference to 'holy children' and in 19:6, the translation could be either children of God or servants of God. In other words, in the Wisdom of Solomon, the servants of God are called children of God, the emphasis being on children, not on (suffering) servants. In 2:13, is it used in connection with the righteous one—in the singular. When the Wisdom of Solomon uses the word υἱός it almost always has a 'religious' meaning, namely God's children (5:5, 9:7; 12:19, 12:21, 16:10, 16:26, 18:4, and 18:13), except in 9:5 where Solomon refers to himself as a son and 9:6 where he talks about the children being human beings. Moreover, in 5:5, the term 'son' is used in the context of the righteous ones, as in 2:18 although in the singular in the latter. From this survey it becomes clear that the terms 'son' and 'servant' (παῖς) are almost identical in the Wisdom of Solomon.[49]

2.3. *From the Wisdom of Solomon 2:18 to Matthew 27:43*

A comparison between the Greek texts of Wisd 2:18 and Matt 27:43 gives the following picture:[50]

εἰ γάρ ἐστιν ὁ δίκαιος υἱὸς θεοῦ,	πέποιθεν ἐπὶ τὸν θεόν,
ἀντιλήμψεται αὐτοῦ·	ῥυσάσθω νῦν
καὶ ῥύσεται αὐτὸν	εἰ θέλει αὐτόν·
ἐκ χειρὸς ἀνθεστηκότων.	Εἶπεν γὰρ ὅτι θεοῦ εἰμι υἱός.
For if the righteous man is God's child	He trusts in God
He will help him	let God deliver him now
And will deliver him	if he desires him;
From the hand of his adversaries	for he said, 'I am the Son of God'.

Menken claims that the extra mocking sentence in Matt 27:43 is, apart from the interest in the terminology concerning the Son of God and possibly three other words, not typical of Matthew and hence, that it is more likely that it is derived from a revised OG text of Psalms.[51] I think, however, that Matthew was aware of the re-interpretation of the

[49] We note that in Wisd 2:13, the Old Greek uses παῖδα, whereas in the Old Latin and the Syriac, *filium* / ܒܪ is used.

[50] Aland, *Synopsis of the Four Gospels*, pp. 318–319.

[51] Maarten J.J. Menken, 'The Quotation—Textual Form', pp. 32–52, esp. 52; republished in Menken, *Matthew's Bible*, pp. 67–88, esp. 88. Note that Menken discusses the readings of Aquila, Symmachus, and Theodotion; see Menken, 'The Quotation—Textual Form', pp. 32–52, esp. 36–40; republished in Menken, *Matthew's Bible*, pp. 67–88, esp. 71–75. If I, however, had been Menken, I would have elaborated more on

servant theme as the righteous one as offered by Wisdom and that he used the OG Isaiah text of the first Suffering Servant poem as retold by the Wisdom of Solomon. Moreover, Matthew turned to this text inspired by his quotation of Ps 22:9 (the text of Matt 27:43 is printed on the right):[52]

Ἤλπισεν ἐπὶ κύριον,	a2	πέποιθεν ἐπὶ τὸν θεόν,	(a2)
ῥυσάσθω αὐτόν·	b	ῥυσάσθω νῦν	(b)
σωσάτω αὐτόν,	c	εἰ θέλει αὐτόν·	(c)
ὅτι θέλει αὐτόν.	d	Εἶπεν γὰρ ὅτι θεοῦ εἰμι υἱός.	

He trusts in God	He hoped in the Lord
Let God deliver him now	let him deliver him
If he desires him;	let him save him
For he said, 'I am the son of God.'	because he wanted him.[53]

Matthew quotes the imperative ῥυσάσθω αὐτόν from Ps 22:9b. He also uses ὅτι θέλει but turns it into a condition (εἰ θέλει), which is appropriate for the context. With regard to the first phrase of 22:9, Matthew changes the first verb (from Ἤλπισεν to πέποιθεν). Menken explains how the OG translator read the Hebrew text of Psalm 22 and how she/he in analogy with verse 5, decided on ἤλπισεν. Menken writes: 'Both verbs are current translations of the Hebrew בטח, but πέποιθεν renders the basic meaning of this Hebrew verb slightly better than ἤλπισεν. … [T]he later Greek translator of the OT unmistakably prefers πεποιθέναι to ἐλπίζειν: they regularly use the former where the LXX translators chose the latter.'[54] Menken notes eighteen instances where one or more of the later translations have πεποιθέναι while the Septuagint has ἐλπίζειν.[55] Unfortunately there are no precise references attached in the footnote. In another article, however, Menken notes the following with regard to the verb ἐλπίζειν:[56] 'the use of ἐλπίζειν with the preposition ἐπί, εἰς, and ἐν is unusual or rare in Greek, which normally has the dative to indicate the basis of hope. On this point, the Greek of Matt 12:21 is better than that of the LXX.'[57]

the Theodotionic/kaige reading and see how these readings would have related to the text of Matthew.

[52] See Rahlfs and Hanhart, *Septuaginta*, for the Psalm text, and Aland, *Synopsis of the Four Gospels*, for the text of Matthew.

[53] Albert Pietersma, *The Psalms* (NETS; Oxford, 2000), p. 18.

[54] Menken, *Matthew's Bible*, p. 237.

[55] Menken, *Matthew's Bible*, p. 237, n. 50.

[56] Menken, 'The Quotation-Textual Form', pp. 44–45; republished in Menken, *Matthew's Bible*, p. 80.

[57] Menken, 'The Quotation—Textual Form', p. 44; republished in Menken, *Matthew's Bible*, p. 80.

I also noted that Matthew kept the verb ἐλπίζειν in his quotation of Isa 42:1–4 in Matt 12:18–21.[58] The question is therefore why Matthew did not adopt the verb from Ps 22:9. Menken can not come up with any reason as to why Matthew changed the verb, and hence he concludes that Matthew must have found it in his source, a revised Septuagint text: 'We have to assume then that πέποιθεν was already in the text used by Matthew'.[59] I note that there was already some debate about this in the time of Tertullian, for he and Cyprian read 'credent'.[60] Finally, Matthew changes ἐπὶ κύριον into ἐπὶ τὸν θεόν—a change that is typical of Matthew.[61]

Second, inspired by the words ῥυσάσθω αὐτόν from Ps 22:9b, Matthew turns to yet another passage that not only uses the same verb, but also deals with the idea of a child of God being delivered by God: Wisd 2:18. Matthew reorganizes the material that he found in Wisd 2:18 (left Wisdom, right Matthew):

εἰ γάρ ἐστιν ὁ δίκαιος υἱὸς θεοῦ,	πέποιθεν ἐπὶ τὸν θεόν,
ἀντιλήμψεται αὐτοῦ·	ῥυσάσθω νῦν
καὶ ῥύσεται αὐτὸν	εἰ θέλει αὐτόν·
ἐκ χειρὸς ἀνθεστηκότων.	Εἶπεν γὰρ ὅτι θεοῦ εἰμι υἱός.

The opening phrase from Wisd 2:18 with some alterations moves to the closing phrase of Matt 27:43. The third phrase of 2:18 becomes the second phrase in 27:43, again with some alterations, due to the incorporation of the quotation of Ps 22:9. The question then arises as to why Matthew omits the righteous one. The theme of righteousness and/or the righteous fits into his Gospel. The two nouns (righteousness and the righteous) as well as the verb (to act righteously) occur in 3:15; 5:6, 10, 20; 6:1, 33; 21:32; the righteous Jesus in 27:19, 24; and the righteous (believers) in 1:19; 5:45; 9:13; 10:41; 13:17, 43, 49; 23:28–29, 35; 25:37, 46. In all these instances, except for two, the word is spoken by Jesus. In Matt 27:19, however, Pilate's wife identifies Jesus as a righteous man. Similarly,

[58] In the context of his article on Matt 12:18–21, Menken argues that Matthew quotes from a revised Septuagint text, more specifically from the Greek Isa 42:1–4. He states: 'Matthew [12:18–21, KDT] took the quotation from a revised LXX text'; Menken, 'The Quotation—Textual Form', pp. 32–52, esp. 34–35; republished in Menken, *Matthew's Bible*, p. 70. The problem is thus twofold: why did Matthew keep the verb ἐλπίζειν in 12:18–21 and not in 27:43? See Menken's reflection on this issue: Menken, *Matthew's Bible*, p. 238.

[59] Menken, *Matthew's Bible*, p. 238.

[60] Ziegler, *Isaias*, p. 277, ad lemma ἐλπιοῦσιν.

[61] Menken, *Matthew's Bible*, p. 236.

when Joseph is introduced into the narrative, Matthew refers to him as being righteous (Matt 1:19). Again, all other occurrences of the noun are spoken by Jesus. Could it be that Matthew did not want to put the word δίκαιος into the mouths of the mockers of Jesus? Or was it because Pilate's wife used it? Could it however, also not be that the context of 27:43 does not allow for an allusion to the debate between the righteous and the ungodly? In Matthew, it is precisely the opponents of the righteous who utter the words. If they were using the concept of the righteous, they—that is the chief priests, the scribes, and the elders—would identify themselves with the ungodly. The same holds true for the last phrase: who else could the opponents be than those who uttered the scoffing words themselves?

3. *Conclusion*

In Matt 27:43, there is a sentence added by Matthew to his source text. It is not a fulfilment quotation *stricto sensu*. There is no direct reference to, for instance, Isaiah. The text of Matt 27:43, however, is clearly inspired by Ps 22:9. In the verse just before 27:43, in his Markan source text, Matthew found a reference to Ps 22:8. For his additional sentence, Matthew continued with Psalm 22 and used Ps 22:9. For his construction of the extra sentence in Matt 27:43, Matthew, however, also used Wisd 2:18, weaving the texts from Ps 22:9 and Wisd 2:18 into a new sentence, and adapting them slightly to his own vocabulary and theology. The phrases and words that Matthew did not copy from Ps 22:9 and Wisd 2:18 can be explained as deliberate omissions.

Where did Matthew get his idea of reworking the Wisdom of Solomon? In order to answer this question, further study needs to be done and this further study could start with the references noted in Nestle-Aland's list of 'loci citati vel allegati': besides Mark 4:11 (Wisd 2:22), there is Matt 4:4 (Wisd 16:26), 6:33 (Wisd 7:11), 16:18 (Wisd 16:13), 22:13 (Wisd 17:1), and of course 27:43 (Wisd 2:13 and 2:18–20).

L'INDÉPENDANCE DU TRADUCTEUR GREC D'ISAÏE PAR RAPPORT AU DODEKAPROPHETON

Cécile Dogniez*

La traduction grecque du livre d'Isaïe a un statut particulier parmi les livres de la Septante. Bien que sa *Vorlage* soit pour une large part identique au texte massorétique, le traducteur n'a aucunement le souci de traduire mot à mot le texte hébreu; il lui arrive d'omettre des mots ou des membres de phrases qui lui paraissent redondants ou, au contraire, de procéder à des ajouts pour expliquer ou paraphraser le sens de l'original. Outre le fait d'être écrite dans un bon grec de la *koinè*, avec un riche vocabulaire, et d'être dotée de nombreuses interprétations actualisantes, cette traduction parfois libre d'Isaïe a pour autre caractéristique de présenter des passages parallèles avec d'autres livres bibliques. Ce phénomène des influences scripturaires qu'a subies le texte grec d'Isaïe en de nombreux endroits a depuis longtemps été étudié, principalement, par Alfred Zillesen en 1902,[1] Richard Ottley en 1904,[2] Joseph Ziegler en 1934,[3] Isac Seeligmann en 1948[4] et, plus récemment, par Jean Koenig.[5] Ainsi ont été notés les liens avec d'autres passages d'Isaïe, avec le Pentateuque, les Psaumes, Ezéchiel et les Douze Petits Prophètes, sans qu'il soit toujours aisé de déterminer si le traducteur d'Isaïe utilisait, dans ces cas d'emprunts, le texte hébreu ou le texte grec.

---

* C'est un plaisir et un grand honneur pour moi de dédier cette contribution à Arie van der Kooij, chercheur qui a consacré l'essentiel de sa recherche à ce témoin biblique qu'est la traduction grecque du livre d'Isaïe.

[1] Alfred Zillesen, «Bemerkungen zur alexandrinischen Übersetzung des Jesaja (c. 40–46)», *ZAW* 22 (1902), pp. 238–263.

[2] Richard R. Ottley, *The Book of Isaiah According to the Septuagint (Codex Alexandrinus)* 1. *Introduction and Translation* (Cambridge, 1904); 2. *Text and Notes* (Cambridge, 1906).

[3] Joseph Ziegler, *Untersuchungen zur Septuaginta des Buches Isaias* (ATA 12.3; Münster i.W., 1934).

[4] Isac L. Seeligmann, *The Septuagint Version of Isaiah* (MEOL 9; Leiden, 1948), réédité par Robert Hanhart, Hermann Spieckermann, *The Septuagint Version of Isaiah and Cognate Studies* (FAT 40; Tübingen, 2004).

[5] Jean Koenig, *L'herméneutique analogique du judaïsme antique d'après les témoins textuels d'Isaïe* (VT.S 33, Leiden, 1982).

Concernant les Douze Prophètes, Armand Kaminka,[6] puis Joseph Ziegler[7] ont repéré les rapports existant entre la traduction grecque de ces livres et celle d'Isaïe mais ils n'ont pu établir aucune dépendance certaine entre les deux traductions. Seeligmann est revenu sur un certain nombre de passages de la Septante d'Isaïe faisant écho au Dodekapropheton et en a conclu : « our translator was acquainted with the Septuagint of the Dodekapropheton and ... this work shows traces of its influence. »[8]

Au terme d'une étude parue récemment,[9] qui reprend les trois exemples étudiés par Seeligmann (Is 45:13 // Am 9:4; Is 2:6b // Os 5:7 et Is 13:22 // Ha 2:3) et qui envisage d'autres parallèles, en particulier dans les chapitres 8 et 9 d'Isaïe (Is 8:2 // Za 1:7, 7; Is 9:1 // Ez 25:16 et Is 9:8 // Am 4:10), nous avons conclu, pour notre part, que l'on ne pouvait pas confirmer avec certitude la thèse selon laquelle le traducteur d'Isaïe était familier du Dodekapropheton. Certes, les rapprochements lexicaux existent entre les deux collections, mais la filiation entre les deux traductions grecques reste difficile à prouver.

Dans le présent article, nous aimerions poursuivre l'examen de cette éventuelle dépendance de la Septante d'Isaïe par rapport à celle du Dodekapropheton, en nous appuyant d'abord sur d'autres exemples d'accords lexicaux entre les deux traductions, puis en considérant les nombreux cas d'indépendance de la traduction d'Isaïe par rapport au corpus grec des Douze Prophètes, afin de voir s'il est possible de confirmer ou non l'existence d'un lien entre les deux livres de la Septante et, le cas échéant, d'en préciser la nature.

1. *Quelques exemples d'accords lexicaux entre la Septante d'Isaïe et celle du Dodekapropheton*

En Is 1:6 le traducteur grec emploie le verbe φλεγμαίνω, dans l'expression πληγὴ φλεγμαίνουσα, « blessure enflammée », correspondant au texte massorétique ומכה טריה, « plaie récente ». Très rare dans la Septante, le verbe grec φλεγμαίνω ne se lit à nouveau ailleurs qu'en Na 3:19: ἐφλέ-

[6] Armand Kaminka, « Studien zur Septuaginta an der Hand der zwölf kleinen Prophetenbücher », *MGWJ* 72 (1928), pp. 49–60; 242–273, édité séparément, Francfort-sur-le-Main, 1928, sp. pp. 56–59.

[7] Ziegler, *Untersuchungen*, pp. 31–46.

[8] Seeligmann, *The Septuagint Version of Isaiah*, p. 226.

[9] Cécile Dogniez, « Le traducteur d'Isaïe connaissait-il le texte grec du Dodekapropheton ? », *Adamantius* 13 (2007), pp. 29–37.

γμανεν ἡ πληγή σου, «ta blessure s'est enflammée», correspondant au texte massorétique נחלה מכתך, «ta plaie est incurable». L'analogie verbale entre les deux passages de la version grecque est en effet remarquable, mais les contextes sont très différents: en Isaïe, même si le verset grec est difficile à comprendre, c'est le peuple de Juda, fautif, qui est visé dans le procès de YHWH, tandis qu'en Nahum l'oracle est dirigé contre Ninive. Ainsi, on ne voit pas pourquoi le traducteur d'Isaïe se serait délibérément reporté à la traduction grecque de Na 3:19 pour traduire Is 1:6. Certes le mot hébreu מכה, «plaie, blessure», est commun aux deux textes bibliques, mais c'est un terme courant qui a pour équivalent majoritaire dans la Septante le mot grec πληγή de même sens. Quant à l'hébreu טרי, c'est en effet un mot très rare dont la seule autre occurrence se trouve en Jg 15:15 pour désigner une mâchoire d'âne fraîche et qui a été rendue en grec non de façon littérale, mais selon le contexte.[10] En Is 1:6, pour traduire ce mot hébreu de sens sans doute difficile, le traducteur a recours à l'expression attendue «plaie enflammée», bien adaptée au contexte. Dès lors, ne faut-il pas plutôt songer à une coïncidence verbale entre les passages d'Isaïe et de Nahum, compte tenu de l'emploi bien attesté en grec du verbe φλεγμαίνω dans des expressions relevant du vocabulaire médical?

En Is 1:8 et 24:20 le néologisme non attesté avant la Septante ὀπωροφυλάκιον, «cabane d'un gardien de jardin», est a priori une bonne traduction pour traduire le substantif hébreu מלונה, formé sur la racine לון, «loger, passer la nuit», et désignant un abri de gardien, de construction très légère, pour passer la nuit; ce mot hébreu n'apparaît nulle part ailleurs dans la Bible. Dans la Septante, ὀπωροφυλάκιον est un mot rare mais il est également utilisé pour traduire l'hébreu עי, qui signifie autre chose, «tas de pierres, ruine», en Mi 1:6 et 3:12, ainsi qu'en Ps 78(79):1, et en Jr 33(TM 26):18, dans la citation de Mi 3:12, selon la leçon de l'*Alexandrinus*—le *Vaticanus* et le *Sinaiticus* retenus par les éditeurs Alfred Rahlfs[11] et Joseph Ziegler[12] donnent ἄβατον à la place de ὀπωροφυλάκιον. Le lien lexical qui réunit ici la Septante d'Isaïe, des Douze Prophètes et des Psaumes a depuis longtemps été remarqué. Pour Martin Flashar ce serait le traducteur des Psaumes et celui des Douze

[10] Cf. Paul Harlé, *Les Juges* (La Bible d'Alexandrie 7; Paris, 1999), p. 214.

[11] Alfred Rahlfs, *Septuaginta, id est Vetus Testamentum Graece iuxta LXX interpretes* (Stuttgart, 1935).

[12] Joseph Ziegler, *Jeremias, Baruch, Threni, Epistula Jeremiae* (Septuaginta Vetus Testamentum Graecum Auctoritate Academiae Scientiarum Litterarum Gottingensis editum 15, Göttingen, 1957).

Prophètes qui auraient emprunté au traducteur d'Isaïe.[13] Seeligmann pense que le traducteur d'Isaïe était familier de la traduction des Douze Prophètes et des Psaumes mais ne peut décider qui du traducteur des Psaumes ou du traducteur des Douze Prophètes a eu recours, le premier, à ce néologisme.[14] Plus récemment, Anneli Aejmelaeus a pris position sur cet exemple particulier et estime que le texte grec d'Is 1:8 dépend du texte grec de Ps 78:1, tandis que le Psautier grec dépendrait de la traduction des Douze Prophètes.[15] On aurait ainsi la séquence : Mi 1:6; 3:12, puis les Psaumes, puis Isaïe.[16] Jennifer Dines a récemment formulé une autre hypothèse : en Mi 3:12 la leçon originale serait εἰς ἄβατον comme en Jr 33:18 mais, sous l'influence d'Isaïe, celle-ci aurait été retouchée en ὡς ὀπωροφυλάκιον.[17] Dans ce cas, le grec d'Is 1:8 ne peut absolument pas dépendre du grec de Mi 3:12 mais ce serait l'inverse. Quoi qu'il en soit, une totale indépendance du traducteur d'Isaïe à l'égard des traductions des Psaumes et des Douze Prophètes n'est cependant pas à exclure : ὀπωροφυλάκιον est certes un mot rare dont on ne possède aucune autre attestation en dehors de la Septante mais, de formation aisée sur ὀπωροφύλαξ,[18] « gardien de verger », ce néologisme, constitue une bonne appellation de l'abri sommaire du gardien d'un jardin ou d'un champ—c'est en ce sens que le traducteur d'Isaïe utilise le mot ; abandonnée, puis souvent démolie en raison de son peu de solidité, cette construction utilisée

[13] Martin Flashar, « Exegetische Studien zum Septuagintapsalter », *ZAW* 32 (1912), pp. 181–182.

[14] Seeligmann, *The Septuagint Version of Isaiah*, p. 227.

[15] Anneli Aejmelaeus, « ‹ Rejoice in the Lord ! › A Lexical and Syntactical Study of the Semantic Field of Joy in the Greek Psalter », in Martin F.J. Baasten, Wido Th. Van Peursen (eds.), *Hamlet on a Hill. Semitic and Greek Studies Presented to Professor T. Muraoka on the Occasion of his Sixty-Fifth Birthday* (OLA 118, Leuven, 2003), pp. 512–513.

[16] Concernant la difficile question de la chronologie des traductions des différents livres de la Septante, nous nous fondons, pour notre part, sur celle établie par Gilles Dorival (Psaumes, Douze Prophètes, Isaïe) dans Marguerite Harl, Gilles Dorival, Olivier Munnich, *La Bible grecque des Septante. Du Judaïsme hellénistique au christianisme ancien* (Paris, 1994²), pp. 110–111. Voir aussi l'article récent de Tyler F. Williams, « Towards a Date for the Old Greek Psalter », in Robert J.V. Hiebert, Claude E. Cox, Peter J. Gentry (eds.), *The Old Greek Psalter. Studies in Honour of Albert Pietersma* (JSOT.S 332; Sheffield, 2001), pp. 248–276.

[17] Jennifer Dines a traité des relations de dépendance entre Isaïe et les Douze dans ses Grinfield Lectures à Oxford, en mars 2007, et a bien voulu nous communiquer ses notes : qu'elle en soit ici remerciée.

[18] Ce substantif est attesté chez Aristote, *Pr.* 938a, chez Diodore de Sicile, 4.6.4, et dans plusieurs papyrus datant des deuxième et troisième siècles de notre ère, par exemple, P. Oxy. IV 729, P. Ryl. II 244, PSI VIII 890. Nous remercions ici Dries De Crom pour toutes ces informations.

pendant l'été formait rapidement un tas de pierres, d'où l'emploi imagé de ce nouveau mot ὀπωροφυλάκιον pour signifier également la ruine ou la dévastation d'une ville ou d'un pays dans des textes comme Ps 78:1[19] et Mi 1:6. Ce mot de la Septante correspondrait assez bien à une réalité agricole propre aux pays de l'Orient et de la Méditerranée où l'on voit dans les jardins ou dans les champs, de loin en loin, des tas de pierres, vestiges d'abris de gardien en ruine.

En Is 2:2 l'expression grecque ἐμφανὲς τὸ ὄρος κυρίου, « visible la montagne du Seigneur », se trouve à l'identique dans le grec de Mi 4:1. Le traducteur d'Isaïe dépendrait-il ici du texte grec de Michée? Selon Takamitsu Muraoka, « il est plus plausible de supposer que la Septante d'Isaïe avait rendu נכון יהיה par ἐμφανές qui aurait ensuite été adopté par l'autre traducteur, plutôt que d'imaginer que ce dernier a rendu יהיה par ἐμφανές. »[20] Jennifer Dines précise davantage cette hypothèse: selon elle, « ἐμφανές appartient en propre à Is 2:2 et aurait été importé par un scribe ou par un réviseur à un stade ancien de la tradition manuscrite afin d'aligner davantage Michée sur Isaïe. »[21] Ceci se remarque, poursuit-elle, au fait que « le mot a été ajouté à une place que le traducteur des Douze Prophètes n'aurait sûrement pas choisie. » Dans le texte massorétique ces deux passages bibliques sont en effet très proches, mais hormis cet accord verbal avec le mot ἐμφανές, les deux textes grecs, comme Kaminka le remarquait déjà, diffèrent beaucoup l'un de l'autre.[22]

En Is 24:23, pour traduire l'hébreu וחפרה הלבנה, « et la lune sera confondue », le traducteur grec donne καὶ τακήσεται ἡ πλίνθος, « et la brique fondra » : Kaminka signale le lien lexical avec l'expression de Mi 7:11 ἡμέρας ἀλοιφῆς πλίνθου, « le jour de l'enduit (?) de la brique », là où le texte massorétique dit: יום לבנות גדריך, « le jour de rebâtir tes murs ». Il voyait là une allusion à une utilisation cultuelle de la brique.[23] De prime abord, bien que l'hébreu ne soit pas difficile, il semble que les deux traducteurs grecs aient commis une erreur de vocalisation: en Is 24:23 לְבָנָה, « la lune », aurait été lu לְבֵנָה, « la brique », et en Mi

[19] Sur cette image, bien appropriée au contexte de Ps 78(79):1, voir par exemple Ariane Cordes, *Die Asafpsalmen in der Septuaginta. Der griechische Psalter als Übersetzung und theologisches Zeugnis* (Herders Biblische Studien 41; Freiburg, 2004), pp. 163–165.

[20] Cf. l'Introduction au volume de Eberhard Bons, Jan Joosten, Stephan Kessler (eds.), *Osée* (La Bible d'Alexandrie 23.1; Paris, 2002), p. xi.

[21] Voir note 17.

[22] Kaminka, « Studien zur Septuaginta », p. 57.

[23] Kaminka, « Studien zur Septuaginta », p. 56.

7:11 לְבֵנוֹת aurait été vocalisé également לְבֵנָה. Entre nos deux passages, certes, la coïncidence verbale existe, mais rien ne nous indique que le traducteur d'Isaïe se soit ici inspiré de Mi 7:11, ou l'inverse. On peut tout au plus imaginer que la modification, de part et d'autre, n'est peut-être pas une erreur mais constitue un changement délibéré reposant sur un jeu d'assonance entre les différents termes hébreux formés avec les mêmes consonnes: l'un et l'autre traducteur, mais de façon tout à fait indépendante, a pu avoir la même volonté de faire référence à l'emploi, sacré ou non, de la brique; en Is 24:23, on peut penser avec David Baer[24] que le traducteur a voulu éviter une personnification des corps célestes, la lune et le soleil, au profit d'une métaphore avec la brique et le mur évoquant la ruine de la ville, tandis qu'en Mi 7:11 la mention de l'enduit de la brique évoque tout aussi bien que dans le texte massorétique la reconstruction des murs de Jérusalem. Plus vraisemblablement, encore, le traducteur d'Isaïe, en 24:23, a pu être influencé par un autre passage d'Isaïe, 65:3, où le contexte de jugement futur est identique et où il est explicitement question des sacrifices[25] que l'on fait sur des briques (καὶ θυμιῶσιν ἐπὶ ταῖς πλίνθοις), le terme πλίνθος traduisant l'hébreu לְבֵנָה. Il est toutefois difficile de préciser si le rapprochement des textes bibliques s'est fait à partir du texte hébreu ou du texte grec.

En Is 25:2 l'étrange[26] traduction de θεμέλια, « fondations », pour rendre l'hébreu ארמון, « citadelle, palais », alors que le même mot hébreu est plusieurs fois rendu autrement ailleurs en Isaïe, ne se retrouve qu'en Os 8:14, en Am 1:4, 7, 10, 12, 14; 2:5 et en Jr 6:5. Or, même si cette équivalence se rencontre « fréquemment dans la version de la première moitié du Dodekapropheton »,[27] étant donné la difficulté qu'avaient sans doute l'ensemble des traducteurs alexandrins à comprendre le sens du

---

[24] David A. Baer, *When We All Go Home. Translation and Theology in LXX Isaiah 56–66* (JSOT.S 318; Sheffield, 2001), pp. 164–170. Selon l'auteur, p. 168, la divergence serait intentionnelle puisqu'en Is 30:26 les mêmes substantifs sont rendus littéralement par σελήνη et par ἥλιος.

[25] Sur ces sacrifices idolâtres au cours desquels on fait brûler des parfums sur des briques—autels à encens ou simples plaques de terre cuite—en l'honneur des faux dieux, voir par exemple Pierre E. Bonnard, *Le Second Isaïe. Son disciple et leurs éditeurs. Isaïe 40–66* (EtB; Paris, 1972), p. 466 et n. 4.

[26] Cf. Arie van der Kooij, « The Cities of Isaiah 24–27 According to the Vulgate, Targum and Septuagint », in Hendrik J. Bosman *et al.* (eds.), *Studies in Isaiah 24–27. The Isaiah Workshop* (OTS 43; Leiden etc., 2000), pp. 183–198, sp. 192; article repris dans *SBL.SP* 40 (Atlanta, 2001), pp. 224–239.

[27] Cf. J. Coste, « Le texte grec d'Isaïe, XXV, 1–5 », *RB* 61 (1954), pp. 36–66, sp. 40.

mot hébreu ארמון,[28] au point de lui attribuer différentes significations selon les contextes, on ne peut absolument pas affirmer que la Septante d'Is 25:2, pour ce terme, dépend du grec des Douze Prophètes. Ce peut être une simple coïncidence ou tout au plus le résultat non concerté d'un même rattachement à la racine plus connue רמה signifiant «jeter, déposer», pouvant être employée par exemple pour parler de fondations.[29]

En Is 26:11 l'expression λαὸς ἀπαίδευτος, «peuple qui n'a pas été éduqué», dans laquelle ἀπαίδευτος est sans équivalent dans le texte massorétique rappelle étrangement les mots grecs de So 2:1, ἔθνος τὸ ἀπαίδευτον correspondant à l'hébreu הגוי לא נכסף, «peuple sans désir» ou «sans honte». Ziegler avait déjà perçu cette ressemblance en grec sans pour autant l'expliquer,[30] tandis que, selon Baer,[31] le traducteur d'Isaïe dépendrait ici du grec, et non de l'hébreu, de So 2:1; et cette dépendance serait confirmée par plusieurs accords contextuels entre les deux passages: le thème du jour (Is 26:1 et So 1:7), les destinataires, Juda et Jérusalem (Is 26:1; So 1:4, 12), ainsi que ses habitants (Is 26:5, 9, 18, 21 et So 1:4, 11, 18), la punition du Seigneur (Is 26:14, 21 et So 1:8, 9, 12) et surtout son amour jaloux (Is 26:11 et So 1:18). En réalité, tous ces motifs, bien que très prégnants en Sophonie, ne sont pas propres à ce livret et se retrouvent abondamment ici ou là dans le corpus des Douze Prophètes. Par ailleurs, comme Baer le remarque, mais uniquement à propos du verbe hébreu אכל, «manger, dévorer, consumer», rendu par ἐσθίω en Is 26:11 et non par καταναλίσκω comme en So 1:18, le lexique grec d'Isaïe se différencie le plus souvent de celui de la Septante de Sophonie: par exemple la main, יד, de Dieu se nomme χείρ en So 1:4 et βραχίων en Is 26:11; le verbe פקד, «punir», est rendu par ἐπάγω plusieurs fois en Isaïe et par ἐκδικέω en So 1:8; 3:7. Il est vrai que l'ajout de ἀπαίδευτος en Is 26:11 peut surprendre; dans la Septante le mot est rare et apparaît essentiellement dans les livres sapientiaux. Mais sa présence au v. 11 du chapitre 26 d'Isaïe, qui est un chant à la fois «psalmique et sapientiel»,[32] ne peut-elle s'expliquer que par une allusion

---

[28] Cf. Seeligmann, *The Septuagint Version of Isaiah*, pp. 197–198; Emanuel Tov, «The Septuagint», in Martin J. Mulder (ed.), *Mikra. Text, Translation, Reading and Interpretation of the Hebrew Bible in Ancient Judaism and Early Christianity* (CRI 2.1; Assen etc., 1988), p. 170.

[29] Cf. Seeligmann, *The Septuagint Version of Isaiah*, p. 198, n. 23.

[30] Ziegler, *Untersuchungen*, p. 67.

[31] Baer, *When We All Go Home*, pp. 206–212.

[32] Samuel Amsler, «Des visions de Zacharie à l'apocalypse d'Isaïe 24–72», in Jacques

à So 2:1? Ne peut-on pas penser à un ajout motivé par le souci d'éclairer, au sein de cette prière de salut pour Juda, les deux versets portant sur ceux qui ne sont pas concernés par cette libération, l'impie et le peuple: pour faire pendant à l'impie, le traducteur d'Isaïe comprend le peuple en mauvaise part—on ne sait s'il s'agit d'Israël ou d'une nation ennemie—et le qualifie de ἀπαίδευτος, «non éduqué, inculte», c'est-à-dire qui n'a pas reçu l'éducation, l'enseignement, au sens de la correction par le châtiment. S'il n'est pas rare, en effet, que ce motif de la παιδεία apparaisse dans la Septante alors qu'il est absent du texte massorétique, ainsi en Ha 1:12 ou en Am 3:7, la correction éducative du Seigneur, מוסר en hébreu, παιδεία en grec, est en tout cas explicite, quelques versets plus loin, en Is 26:16:[33] ainsi l'ajout du qualificatif ἀπαίδευτος en Is 26:11 est-il tout à fait cohérent dans le contexte immédiat du passage et, selon nous, ne nécessite nullement une référence à So 2:1.

En Is 42:13 l'expression grecque bien connue συντρίψει πόλεμον, «il brisera la guerre», qui serait une traduction libre, voire inverse, du texte hébreu qui compare YHWH à «un homme de guerre» (כגבור), a souvent été considérée comme un emprunt au texte grec d'Ex 15:3 (κύριος συντρίβων πολέμους) qui rejetterait pareillement cet anthropomorphisme appliqué à YHWH (יהוה איש מלחמה).[34] Souvent aussi ont été mentionnés les passages de Ps 75(76):4 (συνέτριψεν τὰ κράτη τῶν τόξων ...) et d'Os 2:20 (πόλεμον συντρίψω) qui évoquent cette même idée d'un dieu pacifique qui brise les armes de guerre. Selon Baer, il est fort probable que le traducteur d'Isaïe dépende aussi en 42:13 de la traduction grecque d'Osée.[35] Or cette relation entre le grec d'Isaïe et le grec d'Osée n'est qu'une probabilité. On peut même suggérer qu'en Is 42:13 et en Ex 15:3 il n'est nullement question d'éviter cette idée de Dieu comme homme de guerre pour reprendre ce thème de l'alliance pacifique, mais plutôt d'employer le verbe συντρίβω à partir du sens de «briser, moudre, broyer» (le grain au pilon), pour dire «bien préparer» (par exemple la nourriture).[36] Dans la Septante d'Isaïe et d'Exode, l'expression «broyer la guerre» ne contredirait pas l'hébreu mais signifierait «bien préparer la

---

Vermeylen (ed.), *The Book of Isaiah. Le Livre d'Isaïe. Les oracles et leurs relectures. Unité et complexité de l'ouvrage* (BEThL 81; Leuven, 1989), pp. 263–273 sp. 271.

[33] TM: «YHWH, dans la détresse ils ont eu recours à toi; ils ont été angoissés, ton châtiment étaient sur eux»; LXX: «... ta παιδεία était sur nous».

[34] Cf. par exemple Koenig, *L'herméneutique analogique*, pp. 59–63.

[35] Baer, *When We All Go Home*, pp. 87–98.

[36] Une telle hypothèse est suggérée dans Cécile Dogniez, Marguerite Harl (eds.), *La Bible d'Alexandrie. Le Pentateuque* (Paris, 2001), pp. 364–365.

guerre», la «mener», au sens où l'un des Targums d'Ex 15:3 dit «Yahvé est un vaillant, menant nos combats».[37] Dès lors, il n'y aurait dans le grec d'Is 42:13 aucune influence d'Os 2:18, fût-ce même en hébreu.

Il faudrait encore examiner d'autres accords lexicaux entre la Septante d'Isaïe et celle du Dodekapropheton: par exemple l'emploi de χειροπέδη,[38] «menottes», en Is 45:14 et en Na 3:10 pour traduire le terme hébreu זק, «chaînes», mais, il faut en convenir, ce mot grec bien attesté dans les inscriptions et chez les auteurs hellénistiques est courant dans la version grecque et constitue la traduction quasi systématique de l'hébreu sauf en Ps 149:8 où l'on a πέδη, «entraves». L'emploi en Is 49:19 du participe substantivé τὰ πεπτωκότα, «ruines», est aussi présent en Am 9:11; toutefois cette expression est usuelle en ce sens en grec et se rencontre du reste ailleurs dans la Septante, en Dn-LXX 11:14. Le recours dans le grec d'Is 64:1–2 au thème de la cire (absent du texte massorétique en Is 63:19–64:1), avec l'emploi du mot κηρός, se remarque également en Mi 1:4 et en Ps 68(67):3 et Ps 97(96):5;[39] l'emprunt, cependant, a tout aussi bien pu se faire à partir du texte hébreu de Michée et des Psaumes.

Il existe donc bien de nombreux passages dans la Septante d'Isaïe qui présentent des analogies avec le texte grec des Douze Prophètes, mais peut-on pour autant en conclure sans autre forme de procès qu'il s'agit bien d'emprunts au Dodekapropheton?

2. *Quelques exemples de divergences ponctuelles entre les deux traducteurs*

Venons-en maintenant aux divergences de traduction entre les deux traducteurs. Kaminka avait déjà remarqué qu'en de nombreux endroits le grec des Douze Prophètes ne présente aucun rapport avec la Septante d'Isaïe.[40] Rappelons certains de ces passages et examinons-en d'autres, non mentionnés par ailleurs, où le traducteur d'Isaïe offre une indépendance totale par rapport à la traduction grecque des Douze Prophètes, alors qu'il eût été possible de s'y référer, soit en raison d'un contexte identique, soit pour le même emploi d'un mot hébreu rare.

[37] Cf. Roger Le Déaut (ed.), *Targum du Pentateuque 2. Exode et Lévitique* (SC 256; Paris, 1979), *ad loc.*

[38] Cet exemple est déjà mentionné par Kaminka, «Studien zur Septuaginta», p. 56.

[39] Cf. Koenig, *L'herméneutique analogique*, p. 66 et Ziegler, *Untersuchungen*, p. 100.

[40] Kaminka, «Studien zur Septuaginta», pp. 57–59.

En Is 1:13, dans ce contexte fameux de la condamnation du culte extérieur s'il n'est pas accompagné d'une pratique juste, le traducteur d'Isaïe rend le mot hébreu עצרה, qui désigne « l'assemblée » solennelle correspondant au dernier jour d'une fête, par le terme ἀργία, signifiant « l'oisiveté, la paresse, le repos ». Le mot hébreu rare עצרה, probablement difficile à rendre par les traducteurs de la Septante qui le traduisent de diverses façons,[41] se trouve plusieurs fois dans le corpus des Douze Prophètes: en Jl 1:14 et 2:15 il est traduit en grec par θεραπεία, au sens de « culte »—à l'opposé d'Is 1:13, le contexte est celui d'une injonction divine à pratiquer le jeûne et à convoquer une assemblée festive—et en Am 5:21 le mot est rendu en grec par πανήγυρις, « fête générale, assemblée solennelle ». Le traducteur d'Isaïe, en 1:13, aurait pu reprendre la terminologie d'Am 5:21 et employer le mot πανήγυρις, étant donné que les contextes de condamnation du culte par YHWH sont absolument identiques dans les deux livres bibliques. Or il n'en est rien. Comme Ziegler le souligne, le choix de ἀργία en Is 1:13 est intentionnel et fait référence aux différents textes de la Torah qui mentionnent cette assemblée comme fête chômée, c'est-à-dire comme un jour sans travail, d'inactivité.[42] Le traducteur utiliserait par conséquent ἀργία avec sa connotation péjorative de « paresse » pour mieux justifier le rejet du culte par le Seigneur. Ici, le traducteur d'Isaïe se démarque donc nettement du Dodekapropheton.

En Is 3:12 le traducteur emploie l'hapax πράκτωρ, « exacteur », qui est un mot technique appartenant au vocabulaire financier du grec hellénistique et utilisé en milieu alexandrin pour désigner celui qui collecte les taxes.[43] Ce mot grec traduit le participe hébreu substantivé נגש, nommant « celui qui exige », le chef, le tyran, l'oppresseur, souvent dans un contexte de guerre. En Ex 3:7 et plusieurs fois au chapitre 5, ce mot est rendu en grec par le terme ἐργοδιώκτης attesté dans les papyrus au sens de « contremaître ». Dans le Dodekapropheton, ce participe hébreu figure deux fois, en Za 9:8 et en Za 10:4, et à chaque fois il est traduit par le participe substantivé ὁ ἐξελαύνων, « l'homme qui attaque ». On constate donc que pour traduire en grec ce mot hébreu assez rare dans toute la Bible, qui connote toujours l'asservissement, l'oppression, et qui est rendu de façons variées, le traducteur d'Isaïe, ici en Is 3:12, mais également en 9:3 et en 14:2, 4 où figurent d'autres traductions exprimant cette même idée

[41] Cf. Cécile Dogniez, « Les noms de fêtes dans le Pentateuque grec », *JSJ* 37 (2006), pp. 344–366, sp. n. 47.

[42] Ziegler, *Untersuchungen*, pp. 106–107.

[43] Voir Ziegler, *Untersuchungen*, pp. 200.

d'oppression, ne s'inspire nullement de la traduction des Douze Prophètes.

En Is 3:22, pour traduire le mot hébreu très rare מחלצות désignant probablement un vêtement d'apparat en linge fin que portent les femmes de Jérusalem, le traducteur emploie l'hapax τὰ περιπόρφυρα, nommant des vêtements brodés de pourpre.[44] La seule autre occurrence de ce mot hébreu se trouve en Za 3:4, traduite avec un mot grec déjà utilisé dans le Pentateuque, en Ex 25:7; 28:4 et 29:5, pour nommer la robe « talaire » des prêtres qui descend jusqu'aux talons, ποδήρης, « la tunique longue ». Comme Kaminka le faisait remarquer,[45] ici le grec du Dodekapropheton s'écarte du grec d'Isaïe. Et cette même indépendance entre les deux textes grecs se retrouve en Is 62:3 qui emploie le terme διάδημα, « couronne », et non κίδαρις, « tiare », comme en Za 3:5, pour traduire le mot hébreu rare צניף désignant un turban.

En Is 4:5 l'une des trois seules occurrences du mot hébreu rare חפה désignant la chambre nuptiale, l'abri, le dais des nouveaux époux, n'est pas rendue par le mot παστός nommant dans le grec hellénistique un voile, un dais déployé au-dessus de la mariée, comme c'est le cas en Jl 2:16[46] mais aussi en Ps 18(19):6. Non influencé par la traduction du Dodekapropheton ou des Psaumes, le traducteur d'Isaïe, comme l'indique Dominique Barthélemy,[47] a pris חפה non pour le substantif mais pour un parfait pual et l'a rendu par σκεπασθήσεται (« pour toute gloire il y aura protection »).

De la même façon, en Is 10:4 et 14:17, le traducteur traduit en toute indépendance le mot hébreu אסיר signifiant « prisonnier » à l'aide du substantif ἐπαγωγή, « détresse, captivité », sans reprendre l'adjectif substantivé δέσμιος qu'utilise le traducteur des Douze Prophètes en Za 9:11, 12 pour ce même terme hébreu assez rare et poétique.

En Is 13:6 et en Jl 1:15,[48] alors qu'il s'agit d'un même contexte d'annonce de la venue proche du jour du Seigneur, la même expression hébraïque שד משדי, « dévastation de Shaddai », reçoit deux traductions

[44] Sur l'ensemble de ce passage, Is 3:18–23, qui traite des femmes de Jérusalem, voir par exemple Arie van der Kooij, « La Septante d'Isaïe et la critique textuelle de l'Ancien Testament », in Adrian Schenker, Philippe Hugo (eds.), *L'enfance de la Bible hébraïque. L'histoire du texte de l'Ancien Testament à la lumière des recherches récentes* (MoBi 52; Paris, 2005), pp. 185–198.

[45] Kaminka, « Studien zur Septuaginta », p. 58.

[46] Cf. Marguerite Harl, Cécile Dogniez *et al.*, *Les Douze Prophètes. Joël, Abdiou, Jonas, Naoum, Ambakoum, Sophonie* (La Bible d'Alexandrie 23.4–9; Paris, 1999), *ad. loc.*

[47] Dominique Barthélemy, *Critique textuelle de l'Ancien Testament 2. Isaïe, Jérémie, Lamentations* (OBO 50.2; Fribourg—Göttingen, 1986), pp. 29–30.

[48] Kaminka, « Studien zur Septuaginta », p. 57, signale cette divergence de traduction.

différentes : en Is 13:6 le traducteur traduit fidèlement l'hébreu par συντριβὴ παρὰ τοῦ θεοῦ, « l'écrasement venant de Dieu », et se différencie de la traduction plus libre de Jl 1:15, ταλαιπωρία ἐκ ταλαιπωρίας, « misère de misère ». D'une façon générale, on peut même dire que le traducteur d'Isaïe, pour cette racine hébraïque שד, est totalement indépendant de la traduction des Douze Prophètes qui offre systématiquement pour équivalent de l'hébreu שדד le grec δείλαιος ou des mots de la famille de ταλαιπωρ- qui ne sont pour ainsi dire jamais employés par le traducteur d'Isaïe.[49]

En Is 13:16, dans l'évocation des malheurs qui attendent Babylone, « la perle des royaumes » (v. 19), figure le massacre des nouveaux-nés : « et leurs jeunes enfants seront écrasés sous leur yeux » ; le texte hébreu ועלליהם ירטשו est ainsi traduit en grec : καὶ τὰ τέκνα αὐτῶν ἐνώπιον αὐτῶν ῥάξουσιν, « et leurs enfants, ils les bousculeront devant eux ». Or un tel acte de cruauté barbare consistant à piétiner les nourissons se lit à plusieurs reprises dans les Douze Prophètes mais ces passages n'ont nullement influencé le traducteur d'Isaïe qui procède à ses propres choix lexicaux. En Os 14:1, à propos de Samarie, rebelle contre son Dieu, il est dit « et leurs petits enfants seront écrasés », traduit en grec καὶ τὰ ὑποτίτθια ἐδαφισθήσονται. En Na 3:10, dans ce même contexte de malheur réservé cette fois à la ville de Thèbes, on lit dans le grec « et ses petits, ils les écraseront », καὶ τὰ νήπια αὐτῆς ἐδαφιοῦσιν. L'hébreu est identique en Is 13:16 et dans les Douze Prophètes, avec ce même emploi du verbe רטש, toujours traduit dans les Douze Prophètes par ἐδαφίζω,[50] signifiant en grec « faire un sol pavé », « paver », mais employé dans la Septante au sens spécifique de « mettre au niveau du sol », « écraser par terre », « fracasser ».[51] Le traducteur d'Isaïe, alors qu'il connaît l'emploi de ἐδαφίζω en ce sens puisqu'il l'utilise en Is 3:26 pour une autre racine hébraïque, ne reprend pas ce verbe grec, mais utilise ῥάσσω, qui veut dire, non pas « écraser » mais « heurter, bousculer ».

Dans ce même passage, en Is 13:16, le traducteur emploie le verbe ἕξουσιν, « ils posséderont », au sens sexuel, comme en Dt 28:30, là où le texte massorétique parle de femmes « violées » ; le choix du verbe ἔχω se distingue du verbe μολύνω, « souiller », que l'on trouve employé au passif en Za 14:2 (« les femmes seront souillées ») pour traduire le même

---

[49] Cf. Bons, Joosten, Kessler, *Osée*, note sur Os 7:13. En Is 33:1, uniquement, on trouve l'équivalence שדד / ταλαιπωρέω.

[50] Voir aussi en Os 10:14.

[51] Cf. Harl, Dogniez *et al.*, *Joël, Abdiou, Jonas, Naoum, Ambakoum, Sophonie*, p. 226.

hébreu שגל et dans ce même contexte de ville assiégée, Babylone en Isaïe, Jérusalem en Zacharie avec, de part et d'autre, la même mention des maisons saccagées. Il apparaît donc clairement que le traducteur d'Isaïe, en 13:16, ne s'inspire nullement du grec de Za 14:2.[52]

En Is 30:26, dans un passage poétique sur le pardon divin, le texte massorétique utilise la double expression métaphorique « panser » (חבש) la blessure et « guérir » (רפא) le coup porté, pour dire le réconfort de YHWH à l'égard de son peuple. Le traducteur d'Isaïe ne distingue pas les deux verbes hébreux qu'il rend avec le seul verbe ἰάσομαι, « guérir », contrairement au traducteur des Douze Prophètes qui, confronté à cette même parole de réconfort à deux termes en Os 6:1, emploie tour à tour ἰάσομαι, puis l'hapax tout à fait approprié à l'hébreu חבש, μοτόω, « panser avec du tissu ». Pour le même hébreu et dans un contexte identique, entre le grec d'Is 30:26 et celui d'Os 6:1, il n'y a de fait aucune relation lexicale.[53]

En Is 49:26, avec la traduction οἶνος νέος, « vin nouveau », comme traduction du mot hébreu rare עסיס, « jus », le traducteur se démarque de celui des Douze Prophètes qui, en Jl 3(4):18 et en Am 9:13, rend ce même mot hébreu par γλυκασμός, « crème ».

En Is 51:13 et en Za 12:1, et seulement dans ces deux lieux bibliques,[54] le texte massorétique offre un hébreu absolument identique pour décrire le créateur YHWH comme « le déployeur du ciel (et le fondateur de la terre) », נוטה שמים ויסד ארץ. Mais le traducteur d'Isaïe a sa propre terminologie—τὸν ποιήσαντα τὸν οὐρανόν (καὶ θεμελιώσαντα τὴν γῆν)—différente de celle du traducteur des Douze Prophètes—ἐκτείνων οὐρανόν (καὶ θεμελιῶν γῆν), « qui étend le ciel (et fonde la terre) ».

En Is 55:1 la particule exclamative הוי du texte massorétique qui ouvre un appel adressé au peuple à participer aux biens de la nouvelle alliance n'est pas rendue dans le grec de la Septante (Οἱ διψῶντες ...);[55] or ce passage peut être compris comme une invitation par le prophète à revenir dans la nouvelle Jérusalem et peut donc être rapproché de Za 2:6 (TM 2:10) qui est un appel à quitter Babylone pour revenir à Sion où YHWH

[52] Cf. Kaminka, « Studien zur Septuaginta », p. 58.

[53] Partout ailleurs dans le grec d'Isaïe, à l'exception d'Is 61:1 où l'on trouve le verbe ἰάσομαι, cette racine hébraïque חבש n'est pas rendue littéralement : en Is 1:6, le verbe חבש n'est pas traduit ; en 3:7 le « guérisseur », avec le participe de חבש, devient en grec le « dirigeant », ἀρχηγός.

[54] Voir d'autres formulations très proches, typiques du Deutéro-Isaïe, en 42:5 et 44:24, qui reçoivent en grec diverses traductions.

[55] Voir une même omission dans la LXX, en Is 45:9, 10.

régnera à nouveau;[56] mais en grec le traducteur des Douze Prophètes traduit bien la double exclamation הוי הוי (ὦ ὦ φεύγετε ...). Ainsi, bien que très proches par le contenu, Is 55:1 et Za 2:6 reçoivent en grec deux formes littéraires indépendantes.

En Is 58:14 l'expression du texte massorétique במתי ארץ, « les hauteurs du pays », qui ne se rencontre que quatre fois dans l'Ancien Testament est traduite par τὰ ἀγαθὰ τῆς γῆς, « les bienfaits du pays ». En ce passage, le traducteur d'Isaïe n'a fait aucun emprunt au grec de Dt 32:13 où la même expression hébraïque est rendue par ἡ ἰσχὺς τῆς γῆς, « la vigueur de la terre »; il ne s'est pas non plus inspiré du traducteur des Douze Prophètes qui rend à deux reprises, en Am 4:13 et en Mi 1:3, cette même expression symbolique de la toute-puissance de YHWH qui marche sur les hauteurs du pays, par la même traduction τὰ ὕψη τῆς γῆς, « les hauteurs de la terre ».

Outre ces divergences ponctuelles que nous venons d'examiner entre la traduction d'Isaïe et celle du Dodekapropheton, alors qu'il s'agit de passages au contexte identique ou bien dans lesquels figure un même mot hébreu rare, de sens incertain ou difficile à traduire en grec, revenons pour finir sur quelques écarts notables de traduction entre la Septante d'Isaïe et celle des Douze Prophètes.

3. *Des divergences notables entre la Septante d'Isaïe et celle des Douze Prophètes*

חרב

Muraoka a rappelé que le traducteur d'Isaïe ne traduit jamais, à une exception près, en Is 66:16,[57] le terme hébreu חרב par le terme grec courant ῥομφαία, « épée », comme le fait systématiquement le traducteur du Dodekapropheton, mais qu'il emploie le mot plus rare μάχαιρα, « coutelas », présent une seule fois en Za 11:17.[58]

[56] Sur ce rapprochement littéraire entre Is 55:1 et Za 2:10, voir Hendrik C. Spykerboer, « Isaiah 55:1–5: The Climax of Deutero-Isaiah. An Invitation to come to the New Jerusalem », in Vermeylen (ed.), *The Book of Isaiah*, p. 358.

[57] Sur cette exception, voir déjà Ziegler, *Untersuchungen*, p. 43; Joseph Ziegler, « Die Einheit der Septuaginta zum Zwölfprophetenbuch », *Sylloge. Gesammelte Aufsätze zur Septuaginta* (MSU 10; Göttingen, 1971), pp. 29–42, sp. 42.

[58] Takamitsu Muraoka, Introduction à Bons, Joosten, Kessler, *Osée*, p. xi.

משא

Dans son étude sur le sens et l'histoire du mot λῆμμα désignant l'oracle, Marguerite Harl a souligné que, contrairement à l'équivalence λῆμμα / משא que l'on trouve de façon constante dans le grec des Douze Prophètes et de Jérémie, le traducteur d'Isaïe n'utilise jamais λῆμμα pour rendre le mot משא au sens d'annonce prophétique qui figure dans son substrat hébreu;[59] il emploie ὅρασις, « vision » (en Is 13:1; 19:1 et 30:6), ὅραμα (en Is 15:1; 21:1, 11; 22:1 et 23:1),[60] de même sens, et ῥῆμα, « parole » (en Is 14:28; 15:1; 17:1). Qu'il y ait ignorance ou même rejet de cette traduction de λῆμμα jugée « mauvaise ou inopportune », le traducteur d'Isaïe fait preuve d'indépendance par rapport au grec des Douze Prophètes lorsqu'il traduit משא.

פקד

Pour traduire le verbe hébreu פקד, en son sens négatif de « visiter pour punir », ou « châtier », le traducteur d'Isaïe n'utilise jamais le verbe ἐκδικέω, « tirer vengeance », un mot favori qu'emploie toujours le traducteur des Douze Prophètes pour rendre ce même verbe hébreu,[61] mais il use le plus souvent du verbe ἐπάγω, « amener », en Is 10:12; 24:21; 26:14, 21; 27:1 ou des expressions comme ἐπισκοπὴ εἶναι en Is 24:22 et 29:6 ou ἐπισκοπὴν ποιεῖν, « rendre visite » en 23:17. Au contraire, le texte grec des Douze Prophètes n'offre aucune occurrence de ἐπισκοπή et les cinq emplois du verbe ἐπισκέπτομαι, « inspecter », se trouvent dans des contextes de faveur et non de punition.[62] Ainsi, qu'il ait connu ou non la traduction du Dodekapropheton, le traducteur d'Isaïe n'a pas repris ce verbe ἐκδικέω apparu tardivement dans la langue grecque mais bien attesté dans la documentation papyrologique et qui certes a fini par disparaître chez certains écrivains chrétiens lorsqu'il s'agit de décrire la venue eschatologique du Seigneur.

---

[59] Cf. Harl, Dogniez *et al.*, *Joël, Abdiou, Jonas, Naoum, Ambakoum, Sophonie*, pp. 302–310.

[60] Sur cette équivalence propre au traducteur d'Isaïe, voir par exemple Arie van der Kooij, « A Short Commentary on Some Verses of the Old Greek of Isaiah 23 », *BIOSCS* 15 (1982), p. 37; Arie van der Kooij, *The Oracle of Tyre. The Septuagint of Isaiah XXIII as Version and Vision* (VT.S 71; Leiden etc., 1998), pp. 48, 107.

[61] Signalons, par exemple, un autre mot favori du traducteur des Douze Prophètes, ἀσέβεια, « impiété », jamais utilisé comme équivalent de l'hébreu חמס, « violence », par le traducteur d'Isaïe.

[62] Sur l'emploi de ce verbe ἐκδικέω dans la Septante, voir Harl, Dogniez *et al.*, *Joël, Abdiou, Jonas, Naoum, Ambakoum, Sophonie*, note sur Na 1:2, p. 197.

תרשיש

D'une façon générale,[63] lorsqu'il rencontre le nom propre תרשיש dans sa *Vorlage*, le traducteur d'Isaïe ne reprend pas la transcription Θαρσις que donne le traducteur des Douze Prophètes en Jon 1:3 et 4:2 comme lieu vers lequel Jonas prend la fuite au lieu d'obéir à Dieu. En effet pour nommer le port maritime de localisation incertaine, en Is 23:1, 6, 10, 14, le traducteur emploie Καρχηδών, Carthage.[64] Que ce soit une traduction non littérale mais tout à fait adaptée au contexte[65]—Carthage ayant été une colonie de Tyr, ville contre laquelle est dirigé l'oracle d'Isaïe 23—ou que ce soit une actualisation à un événement contemporain[66]—par exemple une allusion à la destruction de Carthage par les Romains en 146 avant notre ère[67]—, la mention de Carthage dans le grec d'Isaïe 23 est une démarcation de la traduction des Douze Prophètes.

צמח

En Is 4:2, dans un passage à valeur messianique très forte (« En ce jour-là, le germe de YHWH sera beau et glorieux »), le traducteur d'Isaïe offre une traduction très libre et rend l'hébreu צמח, « germe », par le verbe ἐπιλάμπω, « briller » (« Or, en ce jour-là, Dieu brillera en son conseil avec gloire sur la terre »). En introduisant ici le motif de la lumière à la place de l'image de la végétation, il est possible que le traducteur s'appuie sur un des sens du verbe צמח signifiant « lever », « jaillir » en parlant d'un astre.[68] En Za 3:6 et 6:12, dans ce même contexte de promesse messianique, le

---

[63] A deux exceptions près : en Is 60:9 et 66:19 תרשיש est transcrit Θαρσις en grec ; en Is 2:16 la LXX donne θάλασσα.

[64] Cette équivalence se trouve également dans la LXX d'Ez 27:12, 25; 38:13. Sur Carthage et Tarshish, voir Edward Lipiński, « Carthage et Tarshish », *BiOr* 45 (1988), col. 60–81, sp. 60.

[65] Cf. Peter W. Flint, « The Septuagint Version of Isaiah 23:1–14 and the Massoretic Text », *BIOSCS* 21 (1988), pp. 35–54, sp. 45–54; Peter W. Flint, « From Tarshish to Carthage : The Septuagint Translation of « Tarshish » in Isaiah 23 », *Proceedings. Eastern Great Lakes and Midwest Biblical Societies* 8 (1988), pp. 127–133.

[66] Cf. Seeligmann, *The Septuagint Version of Isaiah*, pp. 235, 251.

[67] Cf. van der Kooij, « A Short Commentary », pp. 38–47; *The Oracle of Tyre*, pp. 49, 96–98.

[68] On peut également faire l'hypothèse d'une lecture du verbe צחח, « briller », rendu par le verbe λάμπω de même sens en Lam 4:7: voir ainsi Olivier Munnich, « Le messianisme à la lumière des livres prophétiques de la Bible », in Michael A. Knibb (ed.), *The Septuagint and Messianism* (BEThL 195; Leuven, 2006), pp. 329-330. Voir déjà Ziegler, *Untersuchungen*, p. 107.

traducteur grec traduit ce même mot צמח par Ἀνατολή,[69] attesté en grec au sens astral de ce qui se lève, le soleil levant, le Levant, mais aussi au sens végétal de ce qui pousse. Il paraît donc évident qu'ici, en Is 4:2, le traducteur d'Isaïe ne s'inspire nullement du grec de Zacharie, alors qu'il s'agit d'une même annonce du messie, portant le même titre en hébreu.[70]

צבאות

Enfin, phénomène bien connu, le traducteur d'Isaïe n'utilise jamais le titre divin παντοκράτωρ, « tout-puissant », majoritairement employé dans le Dodekapropheton pour désigner יהוה צבאות, « YHWH des armées », mais la simple transcription σαβαώθ.[71] S'agit-il d'un rejet délibéré de la traduction bien connue ? C'est pour le moins une marque incontestable d'indépendance, voulue ou non.

4. *Conclusion*

Le réexamen de certains accords depuis longtemps relevés entre la Septante d'Isaïe et celle des Douze Prophètes ainsi que l'étude d'autres passages du grec d'Isaïe présentant des liens avec les Douze Prophètes nous ont montré, semble-t-il, qu'il était impossible de confirmer avec certitude la thèse d'une dépendance entre le grec d'Isaïe et celui des Douze. Face aux analogies verbales entre les deux corpus, nous avons en revanche suggéré des explications d'une autre nature : il peut s'agir d'une coïncidence verbale dans des contextes très différents (Is 1:6 // Na 3:19), d'un accord dû à une retouche scribale postérieure ou de l'emploi d'un néologisme de formation aisée pour traduire une même réalité agricole (Is 1:8 et 24:20 //Mi 1:6; 3:12), d'un alignement dans la tradition textuelle (Is 2:2 //Mi 4:1), du recours, sans doute indépendant, à une même tradition exégétique (Is 24:23 // Mi 7:11; Is 25:2 // Os 8:14 et Am 1:4), d'une même

---

[69] Sur ce nom comme titre messianique, voir Marguerite Harl, Michel Casevitz, Cécile Dogniez, *Aggée—Zacharie* (La Bible d'Alexandrie 23.10–11; Paris, 2007), pp. 181–187.

[70] Si l'on se reporte au deuxième apparat de l'édition d'Isaïe de Joseph Ziegler (Göttingen), on constate que les autres traducteurs grecs donnent une leçon où figure le mot ἀνατολή.

[71] Cf. Dominique Barthélemy, *Les Devanciers d'Aquila* (VT.S 10; Leiden, 1963), pp. 82–83. Cécile Dogniez, « Le Dieu des armées dans le Dodekapropheton : quelques remarques sur une initiative de traduction », in Bernard A. Taylor (ed.), *IX Congress of the IOSCS. Cambridge, 1995* (SCSt 45; Atlanta, 1997), pp. 19–36.

référence thématique, mais en relation étroite avec le contexte (Is 26:11 // So 2:1), ou d'une même formulation en un sens différent (Is 42:13 // Os 2:20).

Ainsi, l'idée selon laquelle le traducteur d'Isaïe aurait fait des emprunts au Dodekapropheton mérite donc d'être, sinon revue, du moins avancée avec beaucoup de prudence. Et cela d'autant plus que l'examen de plusieurs passages montre de grandes divergences entre la Septante d'Isaïe et celle du Dodekapropheton—alors que l'on aurait pu s'attendre à une influence du texte grec des Douze Prophètes sur la Septante d'Isaïe si le traducteur d'Isaïe était réellement familier de la version grecque des Douze, étant donné le même emploi d'un mot hébreu rare (Is 1:13; 3:12; 3:22; 4:5; 10:4; 14:17; 49:26; 58:14) ou bien la très grande proximité des contextes (Is 13:6; 13:16; 30:26; 51:13; 55:1). Enfin, nous avons vu que le traducteur d'Isaïe ne reprend pas, d'une façon générale, certains des choix lexicaux caractéristiques du traducteur des Douze, comme ῥομφαία, λῆμμα, ἐκδικέω, Θαρσις, ἀναθολή et παντοκράτωρ; il a sa propre terminologie, élaborée en toute indépendance par rapport à celle des Douze Prophètes. A supposer même que le traducteur d'Isaïe connaissait le texte grec du Dodekapropheton, la présente étude semble montrer qu'il ne l'utilise pas. Bien entendu, seules d'autres recherches menées plus avant dans cette direction pourront confirmer ou infirmer une telle hypothèse.

IS THERE AN ANTIOCHENE READING OF ISAIAH?

Natalio Fernández Marcos*

1. *Introduction*

Much has been written on Antioch, the city founded by Seleucus on the river Orontes, second only to Alexandria in importance for the Jewish community in the Hellenistic and Roman period, the first place where the followers of Jesus were called 'Christians' (Acts 11:26).[1] The glory of this city, first as a focus of Hellenism and later as a pole of expansion of early Christianity is paramount. However, in the framework of the history of the biblical text, when asking for the Antiochene or Lucianic reading, we do not refer only to the city, but to the district of the διοίκησις with an ecclesiastical jurisdiction which includes the whole school of the Antiochene Fathers: Eusebius of Emesa, Diodore of Tarsus, Eustathius, Theodore of Mopsuestia, Theodoret of Cyrrhus, and John Chrysostom.

It is my purpose in this contribution to focus on the reading of Isaiah in this geographical area which produced some of the most brilliant and original commentators and exegetes of the Septuagint. After some remarks on the Scriptures as read by the Antiochene Fathers, I will concentrate on the analysis of the Antiochene text commonly used in the public reading of the Bible to conclude with the kind of exegesis and hermeneutics carried out by the authors living in this district, the subject of some relevant monographs written over the last decades.

---

* May these notes contribute to honour Arie van der Kooij, an excellent and appreciated scholar, and a loyal friend since our first meeting, many years ago, when we both were young and postgraduate students.

[1] See the recent monograph of Robert C. Hill, *Reading the Old Testament in Antioch* (Bible in Ancient Christianity 5; Leiden, 2005); Wayne A. Meeks and Robert L. Wilken, *Jews and Christians in Antioch in the First Four Centuries of the Common Era* (SBL.SBibSt 13; Missoula, 1978), and especially André-Jean Festugière, *Antioche païenne et chrétienne. Libanius, Chrysostome et les moines de Syrie* (Paris, 1959).

2. *An Antiochene Canon*

At the level of the biblical canon it is worth emphasizing the priority given by the Antiochene Fathers to the Old Testament as a Christian collection of Jewish Books, Christianized mainly through the new hermeneutics. As John Chrysostom states: 'While the books are from them, the treasure of the books now belongs to us; if the text is from them, both text and meaning belong to us'.[2] The priority of the Old Testament is one of the characteristics of the exegesis of Theodoret, who dedicates the largest part of his commentaries to the books of the Hebrew Scriptures in Greek, those inspired if obscure Scriptures, as stated in Isa 29:11: 'and all these things shall be to you as the words of this sealed book'. Another feature of the Antiochene reading is the primacy of the literal, historical sense, while emphasizing the coherence and συμφωνία in the interpretation of the whole Scripture, the Old and New Testament.

It can be deduced from the biblical books quoted in their commentaries, that the local canon of Antioch included 4 Esdras according to the Vulgate, whose chapters 3–14 contain the Apocalypse of Ezra, a Jewish writing of the first or second century CE. It is generally recognized that there was a Semitic original of this Apocalypse lying behind the lost Greek text. The seventh vision (Chapter 14) gives an extra-biblical account of the loss of the Jewish Scriptures under Manasseh and their recomposition by Ezra. Diodore quotes the story to support his view that the Psalms had to be collected anew and that their titles were not original. Theodoret cites it to defend the inclusion in the canon of the Song of Songs. Besides the Apocalypse of Ezra, the Antiochene canon includes some of the deuterocanonical and apocryphal/pseudepigraphic books such as Ben Sira and the Wisdom of Solomon, Baruch (but not the Epistle of Jeremiah) and 1 and 2 Maccabees, Tobit, and Judith, while any form of the Book of Esther was, apparently, missing.[3] Theodoret refers also, although with less frequency, to 1 and 2 Esdras and to 3 Maccabees. His text of Daniel (in the version of Theodotion) comprises chapters 1–12 plus verse 1 of Bel and the Dragon, but not Susanna, although the story is widely known to the Antiochenes.

The Antiochene Fathers rely on the local form of the Septuagint and do not know the Hebrew, though they are the first Christians to recognize

---

[2] Sermon 2 to Genesis (SC 433.188.1).

[3] Hill, *Reading the Old Testament*, pp. 23–25.

its importance, even before Jerome.[4] They fail to recognize cases where the translators of the Septuagint have misread the tense of the Hebrew verbs or vocalized the Hebrew in a different way.[5] This Greek text of the Old Testament, in common use in the Church of Antioch, differed significantly from the Greek text used in other churches. It was the *textus receptus* for the Gentile Church of Antioch, quoted in their questions and commentaries as τὸ κείμενον, but never mentioned by the geographical name or under the name of Lucian, due perhaps to the connection of the latter with the Arian heresy. It was recognized as such by Jerome. It was a text which was widespread and which can be seen in the verse-by-verse reading of the commentaries of the Antiochene Fathers. Although the book-by-book identification of the characteristics of such a distinctive text is still in progress, it can be confidently said that it has been identified in the historical books and in the Prophetical and Wisdom books which have appeared until now in the Göttingen major critical edition.

3. *A Different Greek Text*

First of all it should be taken into account that the Antiochene text or recension did not extend to, or at least has not been detected, in all the books of the Old Testament. It has not been found in the Pentateuch nor in the Book of Esther. In the Psalms it should be referred to as a Byzantine text rather than as an Antiochene recension. The absence of this recension in corpora such as the Pentateuch or the Psalms is probably due to the constant use of these books in the liturgy and the frequent copying which transformed this text into a kind of standardized Byzantine text. In other books some common characteristics and distinctive features are shared by all the witnesses of the Antiochene text, but it should be stressed that a great fluidity is frequently manifest. The Antiochene

[4] Bas ter Haar Romeny, *A Syrian in Greek Dress: The Use of Greek, Hebrew, and Syriac Biblical Texts in Eusebius of Emesa's Commentary on Genesis* (TEG 6; Leuven, 1997), pp. 100–139.

[5] Hill, *Reading the Old Testament*, pp. 54–61, and Natalio Fernández Marcos, 'Teodoreto de Ciro y la lengua hebrea', *Henoch* 9 (1987), pp. 39–54. For the Book of Isaiah, Seeligmann supplies sufficient examples proving that the Lucianic revisor corrected the Old Greek without consultation of the Masoretic text, cf. Isac L. Seeligmann, *The Septuagint Version of Isaiah. A Discussion of its Problems* (MEOL 9; Leiden, 1948), pp. 17–20.

text of Samuel-Kings-Chronicles with its homogeneous set of textual and literary features can hardly be compared with the Antiochene text of Psalms. And throughout the Prophetic books, the main characteristics of this recension fall into two categories: certain changes toward the Hebrew text, and a large number of stylistic variants.[6]

Turning to the Antiochene text of Isaiah; besides the critical edition by Joseph Ziegler,[7] two monographs by Ziegler and Seeligmann are particularly relevant.[8] With regard to the changes of the first category, these authors insist on stressing the fact that for the Antiochene recension, unlike the Hexaplaric, the Hebrew was not the ultimate criterion for the change. In all probability, the Antiochene recension did not use the Hebrew text but the Hexaplaric tradition as a source for the corrections towards the Masoretic text. Although the Antiochene text of Isaiah is closer to the Masoretic text than the Old Greek, the aim of this recension was not an exact accommodation to the Hebrew at all. Moreover, the common opinion that Lucian had before him complete editions of Aquila, Symmachus, and Theodotion, and that in the Prophets he exploited especially the readings of Symmachus, has to be duly nuanced.[9] Undoubtedly Lucian had access to a larger body of Hexaplaric material than that transmitted by our extant manuscripts. He may have been inspired by all these readings in his search for the exact meaning of the Hebrew text, but, with all this material at hand, he created his own text. Lucian reshaped the text even in disagreement with and against the Hebrew. To get a correct view of the Antiochene recension one has to evaluate not only the Hexaplaric loans but also the rejections of the Hexaplaric material. As Munnich states:

---

[6] Natalio Fernández Marcos, 'Some Reflections on the Antiochian Text of the Septuagint', in Detlef Fraenkel, Udo Quast, and John W. Wevers (eds.), *Studien zur Septuaginta-Robert Hanhart zu Ehren* (MSU 20; Göttingen, 1990), pp. 219–229; *idem*, 'Einführung in den antiochenischen Text der griechischen Bibel in den Samuel- und Königsbüchern (1–4 Kön LXX)', in Siegfried Kreuzer and Jürgen-Peter Lesch (eds.), *Im Brennpunkt: Die Septuaginta. Studien zur Entstehung und Bedeutung der Griechischen Bibel* 2 (BWANT 161; Stuttgart, 2004), pp. 177–213.

[7] Joseph Ziegler, *Septuaginta. Vetus Testamentum Graecum. Isaias* (2nd ed.; Göttingen, 1967), pp. 83–92.

[8] Joseph Ziegler, *Untersuchungen zur Septuaginta des Buches Isaias* (ATA 12.3; Münster i.W., 1934), and Seeligmann, *The Septuagint Version*, pp. 16–22.

[9] Natalio Fernández Marcos, 'On Symmachus and Lucian in Ezekiel', in Florentino García Martínez and Marc Vervenne (eds.), *Interpreting Translation. Studies on the LXX and Ezekiel in Honour of Johan Lust* (BEThL 192; Leuven, 2005), pp. 151–161.

> Au contraire, lorsque l'on considère à la fois les emprunts du recenseur à la recension hexaplaire mais aussi ses refus, on saisit la perspective qui est la sienne: l'établissement d'un texte clair, propre à nourrir la recherche exégètique sur le seul texte grec.[10]

The rules of classical Greek grammar seem to be of more concern to him. This trend can be perceived in the stylistic changes; in his aim to make clear the text by general additions taken from the context, by parallel passages or familiar expressions; in the frequent addition of pronouns, articles, or particles that make explicit the meaning of the phrase, as well as in some Atticizing corrections. It results in an explicit, clear text probably intended for public reading. Some of the frequent exchanges of synonyms are drawn from the three younger translators, but most of them are due to stylistic motivations.

The double readings are another characteristic of this recension. Probably in respect for tradition, Lucian did not erase the old readings, but placed them side by side with the new ones reflecting a more accurate translation from the Hebrew, and coming from the younger revisions or the new translations of Aquila, Symmachus, and Theodotion. In many cases the double readings witness a vocalization different from that of the Masoretic text. In Isaiah the Lucianic readings, far from being purely stylistic improvements, frequently transmit exegetical alterations and additions which supply valuable evidence concerning the ancient interpretation of the Septuagint. From this procedure emerges the paradoxical result that Lucian witnesses a revised, corrected text, and, at the same time, brings a wealth of ancient readings very close to the Old Greek. As Seeligmann states:

> the data available ... would seem to indicate the possibility that the Antiochenic manuscripts which form the foundation of the material qualified as Lucianic, contained certain ancient components that have disappeared from the remainder of the transmitted material.[11]

It is difficult to represent this process of heterogeneous, sometimes contradictory corrections as the work of a single author. Moreover, it is from the agreement of these readings with Josephus and the Old Latin that the question of Proto-Lucian has come up, one of the most vexed

---

[10] Olivier Munnich, 'Le texte lucianique d'Isaïe-Septante', in García Martínez and Vervenne, *Interpreting Translation*, pp. 269–299, esp. 299. 'Chez le recenseur lucianique, l'établissement du text nous a paru intimement lié à un établissement du sens' (*Ibid*., p. 297).

[11] Seeligmann, *The Septuagint Version*, p. 22.

problems in Septuagint research.[12] But leaving aside those uncertainties concerning the historical Lucian and his participation in the production of the Antiochene text as well as the present debate on Proto-Lucian, some plausible conclusions can be drawn from the analysis and evaluation of the text itself. Therefore, I turn now to an analysis of the two last chapters of Isaiah[13] in order to test the main characteristics of this recension described by the above mentioned authors with reference to the *corpus* of the Prophets or to the whole Book of Isaiah.

3.1. *Small Additions*

In the Antiochene recension, a series of small additions according to the Masoretic text complete the translation of the Old Greek. Some of these additions are registered in the Hexaplaric apparat of Ziegler's edition as material from the 'Three', and are reproduced in the first apparatus as variants of some Septuagint manuscripts with the indication of their provenance = M (Masoretic Text).[14]

65:1 Ἰδού εἰμι] + ἰδού εἰμι, which reproduces the repetition of the Hebrew: הנני הנני. The addition is attested by Theodotion and the Syrohexapla under asterisk.

65:2 οἱ οὐκ ἐπορεύθησαν ὁδῷ ἀληθινῇ] τοῖς πορευομένοις ὁδῷ οὐ καλῇ, which is a more literal translation of the Hebrew *Vorlage*.

65:4 κρέα ὕεια] κρέας ὕειον, in agreement with the singular of M.

65:7 αὐτῶν 2°] + ἐπὶ τὸ αὐτό, taken from Theodotion in accordance with M: יחדו.

65:14 ἐν εὐφροσύνῃ] + καρδίας, attested by the three younger translators and M: לב.

65:15 κύριος] + ὁ θεός, corresponding to M: יהוה in the formula אדני יהוה.

65:18 ἐν αὐτῇ] + ὅσα ἐγὼ κτίζω attested by Theodotion following M: אשר אני בורא.

65:20 ἄωρος] + ἡμέραις attested by Theodotion and the Syrohexapla according to M.
ἑκατόν 1°] prec υἱός, attested by Aquila and Theodotion in accordance with M.

[12] John W. Wevers, 'Proto-Septuagint Studies', in William S. McCullough (ed.), *The Seed of Wisdom: Essays in Honour of Th.J. Meek* (Toronto, 1964), pp. 58–77, esp. 69.

[13] On the role of these chapters as conclusion of the Book of Isaiah, see Marvin A. Sweeney, 'Prophetic Exegesis in Isaiah 65–66', in Craig C. Broyles and Craig A. Evans (eds.), *Writing and Reading the Scroll of Isaiah. Studies of an Interpretive Tradition* (VT.S 70.1; Leiden, 1997), pp. 455–474.

[14] The reading after the bracket corresponds to a good deal of the Antiochene manuscripts. For more precise information the critical apparatus of Ziegler's edition, mentioned in note 7, should be consulted.

Other small interventions to conform the Old Greek to M can be detected also in verses 19, 23, and 25.

66:3 μόσχον] + ὡς ὁ τύπτων ἄνδρα θυσιάζων πρόβατον, attested (with variants) by Symmachus and Theodotion in conformity with M: מכה איש זובח השה.
66:9 ταύτην] + καὶ ἐγὼ οὐ γεννήσω in conformity with M: ולא אוליד, which is not supported by the Hexaplaric recension.
66:10 εὐφράνθητι] εὐφράνθητε, with Aquila, Symmachus = M.
χάρητε] + ἅμα αὐτῇ attested by Theodotion and Syrohexapla = M.
66:15 ἀποσκορακισμόν] + αὐτοῦ with the rest of the interpreters and M.
66:19 σημεῖα] σημεῖον in conformity with the singular of M: אות.

The agreement of the Antiochene recension with the 'Three' is difficult to evaluate, since one has to rely on fragmentary evidence which has been transmitted in connection with the text of the Septuagint. But in the light of the above comparison the common opinion of Lucian's preference for Symmachus is not confirmed. Moreover, the results of this comparison should be complemented with other interventions which tend to improve the Greek version quite independently of the Masoretic text. The following examples in the next section supply sufficient proof of this tendency.

3.2. *Stylistic Improvements*

The reshaping of the text in the Lucianic recension often ignores the Masoretic Hebrew and contains a set of stylistic improvements of different kinds, not always followed systematically. Many of them tend to complete the text or make it more explicit by adding a proper name, the article, the pronoun, an exchange of preposition, an exchange of singular and plural or a simple and composite verb, the juxtaposition of double translations, or the exchange of synonyms, a different distribution of the words in order to improve the Greek hyperbaton, etc.

65:2 πρός] ἐπί
65:3 θυσιάζουσιν] θυμιάζουσιν
65:4 ἔσθοντες] ἐσθίοντες. The same correction in 66:17.
ζωμόν] ζωμούς
65:6 Οὐ] + μή
65:7 τὰς ἁμαρτίας] pr πάσας
65:8 εὐλογία] + κυρίου
65:12 ἐν σφαγῇ] om ἐν
65:14 κεκράξεσθε] κεκράξετε
65:15 αὐτῷ] μοι
65:21 καταφυτεύσουσιν] φυτεύσουσιν

65:25 οὐδὲ μὴ] om μή
τῷ ἁγίῳ μου] tr
66:1 καταπαύσεως] κατοικήσεως
66:2 τοὺς λόγους μου] tr
66:4 οὐκ ἤκουσαν] + μου
66:8 ἐτέχθη] ἔτεκεν
καὶ ἔτεκε Σιων] tr
66:9 ἐγὼ 2°] post στεῖραν tr, following a better hyperbaton in Greek
66:10 πενθεῖτε] ἐπενθεῖτε
ἐπ' αὐτῆς] ἐπ' αὐτῇ
66:14 σεβομένοις] φοβουμένοις[15]
66:18 τὰ ἔργα et τὸν λογισμόν] tr
ἔρχομαι συναγαγεῖν] tr and pr καὶ ἀνταποδώσω αὐτοῖς ἰδού
66:19 οἵ] αἵ a better construction in agreement with the feminine antecedent τὰς νήσους.
τὴν δόξαν μου] tr

These corrections represent small additions of a possessive pronoun or a noun, the exchange of words, and transpositions which taken together improve the style of the Greek and make it more readable for a Hellenistic audience.

3.3. *Preference for Attic Forms*

Another characteristic of Antiochene is the preference for Attic forms over the Hellenistic. All the Lucianic manuscripts for Isaiah usually read the second aorist εἶπον instead of εἶπα, εἶδον instead of εἴδοσαν, καθεῖλον instead of καθείλοσαν, ἦλθον instead of ἤλθοσαν. The feeling for the language constitutes the key for these corrections as for other Atticisms found in chapters 65 and 66.

65:1 εἶπα] εἶπον
65:8 ὁ ῥώξ] (ἡ) ῥάξ
65:12 ἀρθήσονται] ἀρθήσεται
παρακληθήσονται] παρακληθήσεται. Both verbs in the singular with a neuter subject in the plural, τὰ παιδία.
66:20 ἐνέγκαισαν] ἐνέγκοιεν, second aorist optative instead of the first aorist.

[15] Φοβέω is extensively represented in the Antiochene text of the historical books, while σέβομαι is absent, see Natalio Fernández Marcos, Maria Victoria Spottorno Díaz-Caro, and José Manuel Cañas Reíllo, *Índice griego-hebreo del texto antioqueno en los libros históricos* 1. *Índice general* (TECC 75; Madrid, 2005).

The correction of 65:8 is well documented in the Atticistic Lexica. Photius comments: ῥάξ θηλυκῶς· ὁ δὲ ῥὼξ καὶ βαρβαρισμὸς καὶ σολοικισμός ('ῥάξ is feminine. ὁ ῥώξ is a barbarism and a solecism').[16] And Phrynichus remarks: ἡ ῥὰξ ἐρεῖς· ὁ γὰρ ῥὼξ δύο ἔχει ἁμαρτήματα ('you should say ῥάξ; since ῥώξ has two mistakes'), that is, solecism in gender and barbarism in form.[17] The forms that the Atticists condemned were the forms current at the time, or becoming current, while the forms they recommended were the forms that were falling into disuse. Caragounis has reacted against considering the Atticistic movement as a hindrance to the natural development of Greek, emphasizing the beneficial influence of Atticism for the history of the Greek language. It condemned forms and syntax not witnessed in the best classical authors and preserved the language intact throughout Byzantine and into modern Greek times.[18] This word can be traced up to the modern Greek. As Shipp states:

> 'Ράξ is the Attic form on all evidence. 'Ρώξ was perhaps the Ionic form, as used by Archilochus. It is the LXX form. That it was usual later is shown by Hsch. ῥᾶγα· ἣν ἡμεῖς ῥῶγα. It is also Pontic, which supports Ionic.
>
> The survival of the two forms in Mod. is one of Hatzidakis' remarkable examples. He states that ῥῶγα is the form in the Pelop. and islands, ῥᾶγα in some districts of the mainland, e.g. Amphissa, Aetolia, Acarnania, Doris, Epirus.[19]

Through this Atticistic correction one can realize that the reviser(s) of the Antiochene recension shared the concern of the literary authors of their time for the purity of the Greek language, also that of the Septuagint, and that they left sporadic traces of this stylistic fashion in the manuscripts. This part of the verse (Isa 65:8a) in Greek, 'as a grape-stone shall be found in the cluster', differs from M which states 'as the wine is found in the cluster'.

As with other small revisions it tends to improve the Greek making it more acceptable for public reading.

---

[16] S.A. Naber (ed.), *Photii Patriarchae Lexicon. Volumen Alterum* (Amsterdam, 1965; reprint of Leiden, 1864–1865), p. 128.

[17] William Gunion Rutherford (ed.), *The New Phrynichus, Being a Revised Text of the Ecloga of the Grammarian Phrynichus with Introduction and Commentary* (Hildesheim, 1968; reprint of London, 1881), pp. 148–149.

[18] Chrys C. Caragounis, *The Development of Greek and the New Testament: Morphology, Syntax, Phonology, and Textual Transmission* (WUNT 167; Tübingen, 2004), pp. 122–123.

[19] George P. Shipp, *Modern Greek Evidence for Ancient Greek Vocabulary* (Sydney, 1979), p. 481, and Georgios N. Hatzidakis, *Einleitung in die neugriechische Grammatik* (Bibliothek indogermanischer Grammatiken 5; Leipzig, 1892), p. 29.

3.4. *Ancient Readings*

As is well known, the Antiochene text, which separated from the rest of the Septuagint tradition at an early time, probably in the first century CE,[20] preserves a great number of ancient, genuine readings which may represent the Old Greek. In the chapters we have examined there may well be a good example of this. In Isa 65:3 the Septuagint reads: 'This is the people that provokes me continually in my presence; they offer sacrifices in gardens, and burn incense on bricks *to devils, which exist not* (τοῖς δαιμονίοις, ἃ οὐκ ἔστι)'. In this verse the translation of the Old Greek is extremely literal except for the last two words, which are lacking in the Masoretic text, although they may quite well reflect the translation of the first word of verse 4 הישבים, which is omitted in the Old Greek of verse 4. But the Greek of verse 3, as it stands, can hardly be a translation of הישבים. However, instead of the Greek ἃ οὐκ ἔστι, the Antiochene tradition transmits a double variant: one part of the manuscripts reads καὶ τοῖς οἰκοῦσιν and another part καὶ τοῖς οὐκ οὖσιν. *Pace* Ziegler, it is quite plausible that τοῖς οἰκοῦσιν, a literal rendering of הישבים, be the original translation, which was corrupted into the secondary variant τοῖς οὐκ οὖσιν, and later transformed into the Midrashic paraphrase printed by Ziegler, τοῖς δαιμονίοις, ἃ οὐκ ἔστιν.[21] Ziegler's discussion focuses on which of the two readings is authentic Lucianic.[22] However, he does not doubt that they are secondary readings 'die den alten Sept.-Text ἃ οὐκ ἔστιν verdrängt haben'. In my opinion the reverse is true: the rest of the variants can best be explained from the original Old Greek τοῖς οἰκοῦσιν, transmitted by part of the Antiochene recension.

In 65:11 two gods are mentioned in the Hebrew text, גד and מני, the first a Syrian or Nabatean god of good fortune, and the second probably a goddess or personification of Destiny: 'who set a table for Fortune and fill cups of mixed wine for Destiny'. The Old Greek translates the first one by τῷ δαίμονι, and the second one by τῇ τύχῃ, 'they prepare a table for the devil, and fill up a mixture to Fortune'. The Antiochene text alternates both translations and uses τῇ τύχῃ for גד, following the younger

[20] Cf. Sebastian P. Brock, 'A Doublet and its Ramifications', *Bib.* 56 (1975), pp. 550–553.

[21] Seeligmann, *The Septuagint version*, pp. 21 and 30–31.

[22] Ziegler, *Isaias*, p. 90: 'Es kann sein, dass και τοις οικουσιν bereits auf Lukian selbst zurückgeht; και τοις ουκ ουσιν kann auch sekundäre innergriechisch verderbte Lesart sein.'

translators and τῷ δαίμονι for מני, probably with a better knowledge of these divinities[23] or taking advantage of the homophonic similarity between מני and δαίμονι.

4. *A Different Exegesis*

Seeligmann dedicated chapter four of his excellent monograph to the Greek translation of Isaiah as a document of Jewish-Alexandrian theology. As a matter of fact, he is dealing with the Old Greek as a witness of this Alexandrian theology. Is it possible to go a step further and ask whether the Antiochene text generated in the Antiochene Fathers an exegesis of its own? I have tried to outline the profile of the Antiochene text, different from the Old Greek and closer to the Masoretic text, because it has benefited from Origen's Hexaplaric recension and the philological corrections made in Caesarea by Eusebius and Pamphilus, as well as from the readings of the three younger translators. The text has also been adapted for public reading with small additions of names and pronouns, changes of verbs and synonyms, and other stylistic improvements which include slight Atticisms. It is the ecclesiastical, common text, of the διοίκησις of Antiochia. From the point of view of the exegesis, can we also speak of a common Antiochene reading of this text, a shared exegesis?

The question cannot be answered without nuances. The Antiochene Fathers share several common features in their hermeneutics and exegeses, as has been pointed out by Schäublin's monograph,[24] and by Simonetti's, Viciano's, and Amirav's studies.[25] However, there is not one reading but various readings and exegetical perceptions of the same text. One is the reading of Diodore or Theodore and another, that of

---

[23] On the Hellenistic cults to (Ἀγαθὸς) Δαίμων and Τύχη as arbiters of fate, see Seeligmann, *The Septuagint Version*, p. 99.

[24] Christoph Schäublin, *Untersuchungen zu Methode und Herkunft der antiochenischen Exegese* (Theoph. 23; Köln–Bonn, 1974), and Hill, *Reading the Old Testament*, pp. 135–165.

[25] Manlio Simonetti, *Lettera e/o Allegoria: Un contributo alla storia dell'esegesi patristica* (SEAug 23; Rome, 1985); Alberto Viciano, 'Das formale Verfahren der antiochenischen Schriftauslegung. Ein Forschungsüberblick', in Georg Schöllgen and Clemens Scholten (eds.), *Stimuli. Exegese und ihre Hermeneutik in Antike und Christentum. Festchrift für Ernst Dassmann* (JAC.E 23; Münster, 1996), pp. 370–405; Hagit Amirav, *Rhetoric and Tradition: John Chrysostom on Noah and the Flood* (TEG 12; Leuven, 2003).

Theodoret. Concretely, the exegesis of Theodoret as representative of the Antiochene School has been analysed by Ashby, Guinot, Childs, and Hill.[26]

The Antiochene School is characterized by its criticism of the Alexandrian allegories and its defence of the θεωρία, the genesis of the spiritual sense from the literal and historical sense. As Schäublin has demonstrated, the hermeneutic technique of the school fully relies on the technique used by the ancient grammarians for the interpretation of the classical texts. They received the main impulse to interpret the sacred texts from Greek philology and rhetoric, and they tried to implement the Aristarchian maxim Ὅμηρον ἐξ Ὁμήρου σαφηνίζειν, applied to the Scriptures. The Antiochene Fathers were not trained in Hebrew, nor in the Rabbinic tradition and culture, but in the Greek and Christian tradition. The genre of ζητήματα καὶ λύσεις, *quaestiones* and *responsiones*, was developed in the Hellenistic period and goes back to the exegesis of Homer.[27] These trends of the school are best represented in Theodore of Mopsuestia's commentary to the Psalms, where he avoids explaining the prophecies as directed to Christ and prefers to interpret them within the framework of the Old Testament. But it can be stated that there is a plural reading of the Old Testament among the Antiochene authors. In recent research, Theodoret is no longer considered a compilator, but an original exegete, faithful to the principles of the school which chooses a middle way against the extreme literalism of Theodore. Theodoret is more open to the figurative and typological exegesis than his predecessors Diodore and Theodore; he accepts the historical scope of the prophecy and states that a prophet is quite capable of predicting future events, including the advent of Christ. The distinction between the literal and the figurative interpretation becomes a dynamic one in Theodoret; the figurative or metaphorical (τροπικῶς) sense extends rather than denies the significance of the literal. He rejects the Jewish, carnal interpretation as well as Theodore's exegesis which is radically literal and is not open to the spiritual sense. As Ashby observes:

[26] Godfrey W. Ashby, *Theodoret of Cyrrhus as Exegete of the Old Testament: A Modern Fifth Century Commentary on Scripture* (Grahamstown, 1972); Jean-Noel Guinot, *L'exégèse de Theodoret de Cyr* (ThH 100; Paris, 1995); Brevard S. Childs, *The Struggle to Understand Isaiah as Christian Scripture* (Grand Rapids, Mich—Cambridge, 2004), pp. 130–148; Hill, *Reading the Old Testament*, pp. 135–165.

[27] On this subject, see now also Annelie Volgers and Claudio Zamagni (eds.), *Erotapokriseis: Early Christian Question-and-Answer Literature in Context* (Contributions to Biblical Exegesis and Theology 37; Leuven, 2004).

> There is a double assumption that events in Hebrew history have a meaning not only within Hebrew annals, but within God's action of revelation, and secondly that events in Hebrew history are set within God's being God, and also within God's being about to be in Christ. This, in Theodoret's terms is *historia* and *theoria*.[28]

According to Vaccari, the Antiochene θεωρία presupposes the historical reality of the events described by the biblical author; it embraces simultaneously a second future reality linked to the first, and the relation of the first historical event to the second is that of the sketch to the finished work. The first and less significant event is the vehicle used by the prophet to describe a greater future event in human history.[29] Theodore of Mopsuestia would also agree with this concept of θεωρία; the main difference between him and Theodoret is perhaps the fact that the latter is more open to Christological references.

Theodoret's exegesis, as heir of the tradition of Eusebius of Emesa, Diodore, Theodore, and John Chrysostom, is characterized by his balance. He mediates between the extremes of the Alexandrian allegorical interpreters and the overly literal, historicist interpretation of Theodore of Mopsuestia. For Theodoret, the biblical text rests on a historical basis that can be verified by the facts. He underlines the harmony (συμφονία) and coherence (ἀκολουθία) of the Scriptures and, especially, between the Old and New Testaments, emphasizing the unity of the two Testaments; its intent (σκοπός), and especially its end (τέλος). Sometimes the sense of Scripture is hidden, sealed (cf. Isa 29:11–12), and one has to search for the meaning beyond the appearance of the letter. But he stands in the patristic tradition that Jesus Christ is the key to the understanding of the Old Testament.

His exegesis is fully based on the Antiochene text, τὸ κείμενον, different from the Hexaplaric and the text of other copies or ἀντίγραφα. He recognizes the plural transmission of the Septuagint and frequently quotes, without prejudice, the three younger translators as other forms of translating the original Hebrew. His intention is not to produce a text-critical work but to look after the clarity and intelligibility of the biblical text. It is important to realize that Theodoret does not content himself with the Antiochene text, but tries to clarify or control it in different ways. As Guinot remarks:

[28] Ashby, *Theodoret of Cyrrhus*, p. 157.

[29] Alberto Vaccari, 'La θεωρία nella scuola esegetica di Antiochia', *Bib.* 1 (1920), pp. 3–36.

> Malgré ses insuffisances et ses limites, l'exemplaire biblique de Théodoret devait être, dans une certaine mesure, un exemplaire critique, une manière de Bible glosée, contenant dans ses marges un certain nombre de variantes empruntées aux versions et que ne signalaient pas toujours le commentaire d'Eusèbe.[30]

5. *Conclusions*

In spite of the multiple nuances applicable to each particular author, we can truly talk of an Antiochene reading of Isaiah. Through the biblical quotations of the Antiochene Fathers it had become clear that they used their own canon in this geographical area. They also read the Greek Bible in their own text, a text that should no longer be called Lucianic but Antiochene. The Antiochene authors were aware of the plural transmission of the Septuagint and were able to compare their ecclesiastical text (τὸ κεί-μενον) with that of the Hexapla and other manuscripts. They were especially influenced by Origen and Eusebius but they followed their own text which had been created with different recensional criteria. Finally, they shared a set of common exegetical principles, based on the hermeneutics of the Greek grammarians and Homer's exegetes rather than on the Hebrew and the Jewish and Rabbinic traditions.

It should, however, be emphasized that within this common framework there are different degrees in the implementation of these principles. All authors defend the literal, historical exegesis of the Old Testament, but Theodoret is less radical than Diodor and Theodore in the application of the literal sense. He is more open to apply the figurative or metaphorical sense to the same biblical texts.

Childs detects a certain similarity between Theodoret's exegesis and the Reformers' hermeneutical theory concerning *scriptura sui interpres*; and between Theodoret's and Von Rad's use of typology as an attempt to overcome an impasse between two competing positions: the allegory of the Alexandrians and the historicism of Theodore, and the problem arising from the Enlightenment between faith and history.[31] These simple facts are indicators of the strong impact of the Antiochene reading in the history of exegesis. In this sense the reading of Isaiah may be paradigmatic.

---

[30] Guinot, *L'exégèse*, p. 230.
[31] Childs, *The Struggle*, pp. 139 and 145.

ZWEI NIEDERLÄNDER DES 19. JAHRHUNDERTS ÜBER DIE WAHRHEIT VON JESAJAS PROPHETIEN[1]

Cornelis Houtman

In diesem Artikel kommen zwei Niederländer des 19. Jahrhunderts über die Wahrheit der Prophetien im Buch Jesaja zu Wort. Der eine war ein bekannter Theologe und ein berühmter Kanzelredner, der andere ein Freidenker, der die Anonymität suchte. Es soll ein Eindruck ihrer Standpunkte vermittelt werden. Auf die Darstellung ihrer Auffassungen folgen ein Kommentar und eine Verortung. Den Abschluss bildet ein kurzer Rückblick.

1. *Abraham des Amorie van der Hoeven*

1.1. *Van der Hoeven als Führer durch die Welt der Bibel*

Ab 1937 war bei dem Verleger G.J.A. Beijerinck in Amsterdam in Lieferungen ein biblischer Bildband erschienen, der 1838 und 1839 in zwei Bände unter dem Titel *Bijbelsche landschappen naar afbeeldingen, op de plaats zelve vervaardigd, met bijgevoegde tafereelen*[2] erhältlich war. Es beinhaltete sechsundneunzig Stahlgravuren nach englischer Art mit Abbildungen aus dem Vorderen Orient und Palästina. Der Begleittext wurde von Abraham des Amorie van der Hoeven verfasst, Professor am Seminar der Remonstranten in Amsterdam, der wegen seiner Rhetorik nationale Bekanntheit genoss.[3] Van der Hoeven verfügte über keine besondere Kenntnis der Welt des Vorderen Orients und konnte sich keiner eigenen Reiseerfahrungen rühmen. Ebenso wenig war er auf dem Gebiet der Bibelwissenschaften ein Spezialist. Der Verlag Beijerinck hatte

---

[1] Aus dem Niederländischen übersetzt von Walter Hilbrands.

[2] *Biblische Landschaften nach Abbildungen, vor Ort selbst angefertigt, mit hinzugefügten Beschreibungen.*

[3] S. zu ihm Eric Henri Cossee, *Abraham des Amorie van der Hoeven (1798–1855): Een Remonstrants theoloog in de Biedermeiertijd* (Kampen, 1988); Simon Vuyk, *Uitdovende Verlichting: Remonstranten als deftige vaderlanders (1800–1860)* (Amsterdam, 1998), S. 233–247.

ungezweifelt ein Auge auf ihn geworfen, um die textlichen Beschreibungen für die Drucke zu verfassen, weil er ihn für geeignet hielt, einen Text zu erstellen, der dem Geschmack des zahlungskräftigen Teils der an der Bibel interessierten Kirchenmitglieder entsprechen und einen guten Verkauf garantieren würde.

Van der Hoeven trat aus seinem Studierzimmer als Führer auf und leitete seine Leser anhand der Bilder durch die Welt der Bibel. Nicht nur das Heilige Land und Jerusalem wurden ‚besucht', sondern auch u. a. Ägypten, Syrien, und Kleinasien. Für die Erklärung vertiefte er sich in Reiseberichte. Informationen unterschiedlicher Art über den jeweils abgebildeten Ort wurden präsentiert, über ihre Rolle in der Bibel, die eventuell um Informationen aus den Werken von Flavius Josephus und anderer antiker Autoren ergänzt wurden, über ihre Position in der nachbiblischen Zeit, über die Existenz von Kirchen und Klöstern auf ihrem Gebiet und über ihr Schicksal in ‚der heutigen Zeit'.[4] Die Welt der Bibel war für Van der Hoeven—und wie er voraussetzt auch für seine Leser—kein neutrales Gebiet. Er setzte sich zum Ziel, ‚den Leser durch getreue Abbildungen und Beschreibungen durch die heiligen Stätten zu führen, die Schauplätze der göttlichen Offenbarung des grauen Altertums waren, oder durch die Fußtritte von Gottes eigenem Sohn und die Arbeit seiner ersten Gesandten verherrlicht sind'. Aber er beließ es nicht dabei. So nahm er sich die Rolle eines Interpreten heraus mit dem Ziel, ‚um im gegenwärtigen Zustand dieser Landschaften wie mit dem Finger auf die Wahrheit der biblischen Geschichte und Vorhersagen zu weisen'.[5] Auf seine Rolle als Interpret gehen wir hier näher ein.

1.2. *Die Erfüllung der Prophetie als Beweis der Wahrheit*

Wer in den ersten Jahrzehnten des 19. Jahrhunderts nach den Stätten, die in der Bibel genannt werden, auf die Suche ging, landete häufig wie von selbst mitten in Ruinen oder—das Osmanische Reich war ernsthaft in Verfall geraten—in armseligen Orten. So überrascht es nicht, dass Abbildungen derartiger Stätten in *Biblische Landschaften* dominieren. Wo einst imposante Bauwerke standen, blieben nur die Überbleib-

---

[4] Zu einer ausführlichen Beschreibung seines Werks s. Cornelis Houtman, ‚God regeert! Bijbelse plaatsen als bewijsplaatsen in de *Bijbelsche landschappen* van Abraham des Amorie van der Hoeven', in *Jaarboek voor de geschiedenis van het Nederlandse protestantisme na 1800* (Zoetermeer, 2008).

[5] So Van der Hoeven in der Widmung an Anna Paulowna, der Ehefrau des späteren Königs Willem II.

sel einer vergangenen Pracht zurück. Wo einst das volle Leben pulsierte, fristete man ein kümmerliches Dasein. Van der Hoeven beließ es nicht dabei, den Untergang festzustellen. Er unterschied darin die Hand Gottes und die Erfüllung des in der Bibel über die betreffenden Stätte angekündigten Gerichts. Häufig weist er auf die Erfüllung alttestamentlicher Unheilsankündigungen hin. Von seinen Ausführungen über Stätten, die in den Prophetien Jesajas genannt werden, vermitteln wir einen Eindruck.

Eine Abbildung des Ortes, wo einst Babylon gelegen war, führt Van der Hoeven, nachdem er die historische Größe des Ortes skizziert hat, zu der Bemerkung:

> Und von all dieser Größe ist kaum mehr eine Spur übrig! Dies ist zwar in der Geschichte der Welt keine ungewöhnliche Erscheinung. Aber was den völligen Untergang des stolzen und mächtigen Babylon höchst bemerkenswert macht und einen unwiderlegbaren Beweis für den göttlichen Ursprung der biblischen Offenbarung liefert, ist die punktgenaue Übereinstimmung aller Besonderheiten dieser Verwüstung, so wie sie von den glaubwürdigen Geschichtsschreibern übereinstimmend erwähnt werden, mit den Vorhersagen in den Orakelrollen des Alten Bundes. Zu einem Zeitpunkt, als Babel in voller Pracht und Blüte stand und nichts unglaublicher schien als der Fall dieser unbesiegbaren Mauern, hundertsechzig Jahre, bevor der Fuß eines Feindes seinen Boden betreten hatte, sprach Gott durch den Mund seiner Propheten: ‚So stehe ich gegen sie auf ...‘ (Jes 14:22 f.). Alle merkwürdigen Umstände der Belagerung und der Eroberung dieser Stadt durch Kyros werden von Jesaja und Jeremia genauso *vorausgesagt*, wie sie von Herodot und Xenophon *erzählt* werden.[6] (I, S. 13)

Van der Hoeven beschließt seine Erklärung über Babylon mit der Bemerkung: ‚Gott regiert! Er ist groß von Rat und mächtig von Tat. Er hat das Wort erfüllt, das Jahrhunderte zuvor durch seinen Propheten gesprochen wurde: „Und Babel, das Kleinod unter den Königreichen (...), wird wie Sodom und Gomorra werden ...“ (Jes 13:19–22).‘ (I, S. 14).

Abbildungen des alten Petra, des alttestamentlichen Sela, an dem Ort, wo einst die Hauptstadt Edoms (2 Kön 14:7; Jes 16:1) gestanden sein soll, die 1812 von Johann Ludwig Burckhardt entdeckt wurde, eine hoch in die Felsen ausgehauene ‚stolze Stadt‘ (I, S. 28; vgl. Obad 3–4) mit ‚prächtigen Ruinen‘, die ‚ein fremdes und unvergleichliches Schauspiel liefern (...), von der Natur selbst mit verschiedenen Farben gezeichnet und von Menschen in Grabhöhlen und Wohnungen ausgehöhlt!‘ (II, S. 89), geben Van

[6] S. Jes 13–14; 21:9; 44:27 f.; 45:1; 46:1; 47:1, 5, 7–11; Jer 50–51.

der Hoeven ebenfalls Anlass, über die Erfüllung prophetischer Worte zu reden. Sie zeigen die Stadt in ihrem desolaten, verwüsteten Zustand ‚als einen Zeugen, aus den Toten auferstanden', um ‚mit ihren verlassenen Wohnungen und schweigenden Ruinen' den Beweis für die Wahrheit der Orakelsprache der Propheten zu liefern (I, S. 59 f.; II, S. 75 f., 89 f.).[7] ‚Diese Orakelsprache wird von den Berichten aller Reisenden bestätigt, die dieses Gebiet besucht und ihre Empfindungen beim Besichtigen desselben umschrieben haben, sogar ohne an die Gottesrede zu denken. Alle stimmen darin überein, dass sie beim Betrachten einer derart vollständigen Verheerung und Vernichtung erschüttert waren' (I, S. 59 f.).

Abbildungen von ägyptischen Ruinen werden von Van der Hoeven als Monumente bezeichnet, die ‚für den Christen Gedenkzeichen für die Erfüllung von Gottes Androhungen sind' (I, S. 50)[8] und entlocken ihm—im Falle des alten Theben—die Bemerkung:

> Tausende von Jahren sind über diese Gedenkzeichen hinweggeeilt und noch immer versinkt der Reisende unter den kolossalen Gebäuden—aber sie stehen allein und verlassen; keine Priester verehren mehr die Götter in ihren prächtigen Heiligtümern; keine Scharen von Anbetern beugen sich mehr vor ihren Standbildern nieder: Ägyptens Götzen ...
>
> (Jes 19:1) (II, S. 51)

1.3. *Traditionelle Theologie, die eine neue Argumentation erhält*

Für Van der Hoeven genießt die Bibel in jeder Hinsicht Autorität. Von irgendeinem Einfluss der zumindest außerhalb der Niederlande in der ersten Hälfte des 19. Jahrhunderts aufkommenden literar-historischen Bibelkritik[9] ist in seinen Darstellungen nichts erkennbar. Traditionelle Ansichten bezüglich der Entstehung und Verfasserschaft der biblischen Schriften stehen nicht zur Diskussion. Mit der vorherrschenden Theologie seiner Zeit ist Van der Hoeven der Auffassung, dass das Jesajabuch als Ganzes Jesaja von Jerusalem zugeschrieben werden kann, der im Zeitraum 740–690 v. Chr. wirkte und in die ferne Zukunft zu

---

[7] S. Jes 34:5–17; Jer 49:16 f.; Ez 35:3 f.; Mal 1:4 f.

[8] S. Jes 19:1; Ez 29:10; 30:13.

[9] S. z. B. Henning Graf Reventlow, *Epochen der Bibelauslegung 4. Von der Aufklärung bis zum 20. Jahrhundert* (München, 2001), S. 227–278. J. Döderlein und J.G. Eichhorn werden in der Literatur stets als diejenigen angeführt, die am Ende des 18. Jahrhunderts den exilischen Ursprung von Jesaja 40 und den folgenden Kapiteln verteidigt haben. S. z. B. J.F.A. Sawyer in J.H. Hayes (Hg.), *Dictionary of Biblical Interpretation* 1 (Nashville, 1999), S. 550, 552. Zweifel an der jesajanischen Verfasserschaft waren bereits zuvor von Reimarus geäußert worden (s. u.).

schauen vermochte. Die Meinung wird treffend zum Ausdruck gebracht, *in Bild* auf einer Gravur von Gerard Hoet (1648–1733) (Abb. 1) vor der Dichtung des Verlegers und Poeten François Halma (1653–1722) mit dem Titel ‚De Messias in zyn lyden, ofte uitbreidinge van het LIII hooftdeel van Jesias voorzegginge,'[10] und *in Reim* in der ersten Strophe eines Jesaja gewidmeten Gedichts von Johan Frederik Schimsheimer (1805–1878):[11]

> Jesaja, Gottes Gesandter und rechter Trostprophet!
> Der das Unwetter vorhergesehen hat und auch die Segensströme,
> Die mit dem lang Verheißenen auf die Erde kommen sollten,
> Nachdem er am Kreuz das Recht Gottes vollbringt.[12]

Viele Jahrhunderte können zwischen dem Gotteswort und seiner Erfüllung liegen. Wie deutlich geworden ist, vertritt auch Van der Hoeven diese Auffassung. Eine Stadt kann eine wechselvolle Geschichte von Untergang und Blüte erfahren haben, bis in die christliche Zeit hinein, bevor die Prophetie in Erfüllung gegangen ist. Neu in seinen Ausführungen ist die Tatsache, dass die Situation vor Ort, wie es in neueren Reiseberichten beschrieben wird, ein entscheidendes Kriterium für die Feststellung der Erfüllung ist. Van der Hoeven stützt sich in dieser Hinsicht ganz auf Alexander Keith (1792–1880), Pastor der Free Church of Scotland und Verfasser einer Studie mit dem Titel *Evidence of the Truth of the Christian Religion Derived from the Literal Fulfilment of Prophecy; Particularly as Illustrated by the History of the Jews, and by the Discoveries of Recent Travellers*, was von ihm als ein ‚bedeutendes Werk' (I, S. 13) bezeichnet wird.[13] Keiths Buch erschien in Übersetzung in verschiedenen modernen Sprachen, auch auf Niederländisch, mit dem noch umfassenderen Titel: *Die stipte en letterlijke vervulling der bijbelsche profetiën, opgehelderd door de geschiedenis der Joden en de ontdekkingen van nieuwere reizigers, en aangevoerd als een bewijs van de waarheid der christelijke godsdienst*.[14]

---

[10] Jegliches Verständnis für das Urteil der Vertreter der Aufklärung über die Bibel und traditionelle Auffassung fehlt. Vgl. Vuyk, *Verlichting*, S. 237 f., 247, 272 f., 292 f. Seine Auffassung von der Bibel als Quelle eines nicht-dogmatischen ‚biblischen Christentums', wie beschrieben von Cossee, *Van der Hoeven*, S. 78, 83, 117, 123 f., 146, 154 f., mutet naiv an.

[11] S. zu ihn F.L. van 't Hooft in *BLGNP* 1, S. 318 f.

[12] *Bijbelsche gedichten* (Amsterdam, 1876), S. 110.

[13] Van der Hoeven verwendete die 14. Aufl. (Edinburgh, 1836). Das Buch wurde seitdem viele Male nachgedruckt. Hier wird die 37. Aufl. von 1859 konsultiert. Keith ist ebenfalls der Verfasser einer ausschließlich Jesaja gewidmeten Studie: *Isaiah as It Is: Or, Judah and Jerusalem the Subjects of Isaiah's Prophesying* (Edinburgh, 1850).

[14] *Die präzise und wörtliche Erfüllung der biblischen Prophetien, erklärt durch die jüdische Geschichte und die Entdeckungen neuerer Reisenden und dargelegt als Beweis für die Wahrheit der christlichen Religion*. In Amsterdam erschienen bei J.F. Schleijer (erste Aufl. 1836, nach der 13. engl. Aufl.; gekürzte Aufl. 1841 und 1855) und H. Höveker (zweite, erweiterte Aufl. 1854). Keith selbst hat 1839 mit drei schottischen Kollegen Palästina

Keith verteidigte die Auffassung, dass die Analyse der Prophetien des Alten Testaments[15] deutlich macht, dass ihre Erfüllung als ein Wunder betrachtet werden muss. Denn durch die Propheten werden häufig Ereignisse Hunderte oder sogar Tausende von Jahren vor ihrer Verwirklichung angekündigt:

> they ventured to raise, from the succeeding ages of the world, that veil which no uninspired mortal could touch. They spoke of a deliverer of the human race; they described the desolation of cities and of nations, whose greatness was then unshaken, and whose splendour has ever since been unrivalled; and their predictions were of such a character, that time would infallibly refute or realize them. (S. 11)

Die wunderbare Erfüllung der Prophetien liefert den Beweis dafür, dass Gott die Geschichte lenkt. Denn:

> The foreknowledge of the actions of intelligent and moral agents is one of the incomprehensible attributes of the Deity (...). The past, the present, and the future, are alike open to his view, and to his alone; and there can be no stronger proof of the interposition of the Most High, than that which prophecy affords. (S. 7)

Die wörtliche und unzweideutige Erfüllung zahlloser biblischer Prophetien wird nach Auffassung von Keith vor allem durch das Zeugnis der Reisenden in den Vorderen Orient bewiesen, aber nicht im geringsten durch das der Ungläubigen unter ihnen und derjenigen, denen nicht daran gelegen war, eine Bestätigung der biblischen Wahrheit zu erhalten. Keith ist der Meinung, dass die Erfüllung der Prophetie einen teilweisen Beweis der Wahrheit des Christentums liefert (S. 11). Sein Buch ist gemeint als ‚a general and concise sketch of such of the prophecies as have been distinctly foretold and clearly fulfilled, and as may be deemed sufficient to illustrate the trutch of Christianity' (S. 13). Seine Studie, die auf traditionellen Ansichten im Hinblick auf die Verfasserschaft der bib-

besucht im Rahmen einer Reise mit der Absicht, ‚die verlorenen Schafe des Hauses Israels' zu besuchen und zu untersuchen, wo Missionssposten eingerichtet werden könnten. Der Reisebericht, der mir nur in niederländischer Übersetzung zur Verfügung stand, wimmelt von Bibelzitaten. Die Erlebnisse werden in verschiedener Hinsicht als Beweise für die biblische Wahrheit betrachtet. Siehe *De Joden in Europa en in Palestina, voorgesteld in eene reisbeschijving van de HH. Keith, Black, Bonar en Mac Cheijne door de Schotse kerk afgevaardigd* (Dordrecht, o. J. [1851]). Die Übersetzung stammt von Pastor D. Serrurier. Keith selbst veröffentlichte nach der Reise ein Buch über Palästina: *Land of Israel According to the Covenant with Abraham, Isaac and Jacob* (London, 1843).

[15] So wie übrigens auch die des Neuen Testaments. Er widmet u.a. auch ein Kapitel den Sendschreiben an die sieben Gemeinden in der Offenbarung des Johannes (S. 518–532).

lischen Bücher beruht,[16] betrachtet er als eine adäquate Reaktion an die Adresse derjenigen (z. B. David Hume), die meinen, dass das Christentum mit der Wirklichkeit der Wunder steht oder fällt (S. 539 f.).

Bevor er sich den Prophetien gegen Städte, Länder und Völker widmet, geht Keith auf die klassischen Beweistexte im Hinblick auf die Christuserwartung des Alten Testaments ein[17] und schlussfolgert, dass derjenige, der sorgfältig die Schriften untersucht, nur zu der Schlussfolgerung kommen kann, dass sie von Christus zeugen (S. 48): ‚The doctrine of the gospel is in complete accordance with the predictions respecting it' (S. 37). Anschließend lässt er vor allem Unheilsprophetien Revue passieren. In sehr breiten Ausführungen—z. B. Babylon werden ca. 85 Seiten gewidmet, Edom ca. 65 und Ägypten 13 Seiten—wird anhand klassischer Geschichtsbeschreibungen, Reiseberichte und anderer zeitgenössischer Information dargelegt, wie die Prophetien bis in die Details hinein in Erfüllung gegangen sind. So wird z. B. der Umstand, dass die Araber die Ruinen von Babylon meiden und sie nicht wie anderswo gebrauchen, um ihr Vieh unterzubringen, als eine Erfüllung von Jes 13:20 betrachtet (S. 465).

Das Buch Jesaja beinhaltet auch eine Prophetie gegen Damaskus und Aram (Syrien) (Jes 17:1, 3). Der Untergang von Damaskus, einer Stadt, die sich durch die Jahrhunderte hindurch zu behaupten wusste, wird angekündigt. Keith lässt Jes 17:1 unkommentiert; Jes 17:3 bezieht er auf die wenig gedeihliche Position der 40er Jahre des 19. Jahrhunderts (S. 237–239). Van der Hoeven scheint davon auszugehen, dass die Unheilsankündigung noch nicht in Erfüllung gegangen ist. Seine Erklärung einer Abbildung von Damaskus beschließt er mit folgenden Worten: ‚Noch steht Damaskus da, ein Paradies der Erde, eine der wenigen Städte Asiens, die ihren alten Ruhm bewahrten (. . .). Mit gespannter Erwartung harrt sie der Zukunft, die dunkel und drohend über dem Reich der Ottomanen schwebt.' (II, S. 82; vgl. Jes 17:1–3; Jer 49:23–27; Amos 1:5).

1.4. *Auswertung*

Ein sauberes wissenschaftliches Interesse an Palästina und der Welt der Bibel war Van der Hoeven fremd. Wie deutlich geworden ist, war er

---

[16] So geht er z. B. freimütig davon aus, dass die Weissagungen über Kyros (Jes 44:28; 45:1) von Jesaja von Jerusalem stammen (S. 423).

[17] Z. B. Gen 49:10; Deut 18:15, 18; 2 Sam 7:16; Jes 7:14; 9:1–6; 11:1–5; 35:4; 40:11; 42:2 f.; 50:4, 7; 53; 59:20; 62:11; Jer 23:5 f.; Dan 9:24 f.; Mi 5:1; Sach 9:9; Mal 3:1.

weit davon entfernt, die ‚biblischen Landschaften' neutral zu beurteilen. Für ihn hatten sie eine Stimme und eine deutliche Botschaft. Für Van der Hoeven waren Katheder und Kanzel nicht geschieden. Der Professor war Pastor, auch in seiner Rolle als Führer durch Palästina und die Welt der Bibel. Letztendlich ging es ihm darum, ‚die Wahrheit der biblischen Offenbarung in ein helles Licht zu stellen', wobei er sich insbesondere auf ‚die höheren Stände' konzentrierte (Vorwort 1837). Bei Gleichgesinnten in diesen Kreisen wird er für seine Ausführungen ein offenes Ohr gefunden haben.[18] Auf Skeptiker werden seine Erklärungen keinen Eindruck gemacht haben. Die Position eines von ihnen werden wir nun kennenlernen.

2. *Ferdinand Alexander de Mey van Alkemade*

2.1. *Die Prophetien sind großer Unsinn*

Ferdinand Alexander de Mey van Alkemade (1828–1864)[19] ist der Verfasser eines dreibändigen Werks *De Bijbel beschouwd in zijne eigenlijke waarde* (Amsterdam, 1859),[20] das unter dem verkürzten Namen Alexander de M. erschien. Er qualifiziert das Buch mit dem Namen des Propheten Jesaja als ‚sehr beeindruckend' wegen ‚seines bündigen Stils und seiner furchtbaren Voraussagen' (S. 183). Seine Charakterisierung bedeutet jedoch nicht, dass der Stil und der Inhalt des Buches positiv beurteilt werden. Das Gegenteil ist nämlich der Fall. Hinsichtlich des Stils unterscheidet er zwischen dem Stil von Kap. 36 bis Kap. 54, der ‚viel geordneter ist und man wird sagen können: durch eine weit geschicktere Hand als die übrigen Kapitel geschrieben wurde' (vgl. auch S. 161 f.), und dem Stil der anderen Kapitel, ‚die alle so verworren sind und voller weitreichender extremer Vorstellungen, dass man sie unverkennbar für das Produkt eines Geistesgestörten halten muss' (S. 184). De Mey scheint wenig Gefühl für den metaphorischen Sprachgebrauch zu haben, was zur Folge

[18] Die Vorlesung über ‚Weissagungen über Völker und Weltstädte' von Isaac da Costa (1798–1860) in *Voorlezingen over de waarheid en waardij der schriften van het Oude Testament* 2 (Leiden, 1845), S. 74–94 (vgl. auch Teil II, zweites Stück [Leiden, 1848], S. 386f.), hat denselben Tenor wie Van der Hoevens Ausführungen. Zu Da Costa s. P.L. Schram in *BLGNP* 3, S. 85–88.

[19] Bis jetzt ist es nicht möglich gewesen, biografische Details über ihn ausfindig zu machen.

[20] *Die Bibel in ihrem eigentlichen Wert betrachtet.* Wir vermitteln einen Eindruck der Überlegungen zum Buch Jesaja in Band 2, S. 130–184.

hat, dass die Beschreibungen seiner Meinung nach, die in z. B. Jesaja 24 (S. 148–151), 30 (S. 152), 34 (S. 153) und 60 (S. 181) präsentiert werden, in einem ‚Anfall von Wahnsinn' (S. 153) im Gehirn eines ‚Irren' zustande gekommen sein müssen, von dem Jesaja 20 handelt (S. 146). Alle können sie unter den Nenner ‚dummes Geschwätz' (S. 153, 181), ‚Gerede eines Trunkenboldes' (S. 151), ‚Nonsens' (S. 152) gebracht werden. So entlockt z. B. Jes 60:19 f. ihm die Bemerkung: Man muss ‚einige seiner fünf Sinne verloren haben, um sich vorzustellen, dass tatsächlich zu einer bestimmten Zeit Sonne und Mond aufhören werden zu scheinen und an ihre Stelle ein glänzender Manngott über Jerusalem scheinen werde.' (S. 181).

Die Charakterisierung des Propheten als ‚geistesgestört' geht wie von selbst mit der Auffassung einher, dass das Buch Jesaja kaum von einem hohen Gottesbild ausgehe. Denn die Tatsache, dass der Prophet der Wortführer des Herrn ist, impliziert, ‚dass das höhere Wesen keine vernünftige Sprache als die eines begeisterten Dummkopfs sprechen kann' (S. 146). Aus dem, was über sein Tun und Lassen gesagt wird, schlussfolgert De Mey, dass er ‚für einen solch vornehmen Herrn, wie es der Gott Israels war', doch wohl ‚kindisch' und ‚außergewöhnlich borniert' handelt (zu Jes 2:10–18 [S. 132]), er ‚sein Auf und Ab von gutem und schlechtem Humor' hat (zu Jes 4:5 f. [S. 133]), er ‚zuweilen Dinge für heilig hält, die Menschen mit gewöhnlicher Einstellung nicht heilig erscheinen' (zu Jes 23:18 [S. 147]), er seine Meinung ändern konnte und einsehen konnte, ‚dass er früher ein ungerechtes Gebot gegeben hatte' und ‚es nie zu spät sein konnte, einen Fehler wieder gutzumachen'. (zu Jes 56:3–7 neben Deut 23:1–8 [S. 178]; vgl. auch z. B. S. 131 [zu Jes 1:11–15]). So, wie er im Jesajabuch beschrieben wird, kann Gott De Mey zufolge nicht sein. Jes 34:2–10 verleitet ihn zu der Bemerkung: ‚Es ist wahrlich traurig zu bedenken, dass so viele Menschen diesen Unsinn als göttliche Rede betrachten, denn es beweist, welche unglücklichen Vorstellungen sie hinsichtlich des höheren Wesens hegen' (S. 153).

2.2. *Die Prophetien sind nicht erfüllt*

Ein für De Mey sehr anstößiger Punkt ist, dass die Prophetien des Jesajabuches nicht in Erfüllung gegangen sind. Sie beruhen nicht auf übernatürlicher Eingebung. Wenn ein prophetisches Wort sich als wahr erweist, verdankt sich dies der Kenntnis und der Einsicht in die historische Situation des Propheten (zu Jes 5:1–7 [S. 133]). Tatsächlich ist die Beschreibung über das Auftreten von Kores (Jes 44:24–45:8), auf das in den Abschnitten Bezug genommen wird, die hinsichtlich des Stils zu den

Kapiteln gehören, die von einer anderen Hand als der Rest des Buches stammen (s. o.), der einzige Fall erfüllter ‚Prophetie'. De Mey schreibt die betreffenden Textabschnitte einem Zeitgenossen des Kores zu, ‚der eine oder andere Prophet oder Schriftgelehrte', der das Jesajabuch um Kores mit der Absicht erweitert haben soll, dass der König dem Volk Gottes erlauben werde, nach Jerusalem zurückzukehren, um die Stadt und den Tempel wieder aufzubauen. Nach Esra 1 ist ihm dies gelungen (S. 184; vgl. S. 160–162). Die Zeit hat jedoch gelehrt, dass alle anderen Prophetien Jesajas ‚nichts anderes als großartig klingender Unsinn sind.' (S. 184). De Mey weist u. a. auf das Folgende hin:

- Die Prophetie von Jesaja 13 über Babel ist nicht erfüllt. Die Stadt wurde nicht ‚von den Heerscharen des Herrn' verwüstet, sondern ihr widerfuhr dasselbe Schicksal wie vielen Städten der Antike. Nach der großen Blütezeit verfiel sie (S. 143 f.; vgl. auch S. 162 f. [zu Jesaja 47]);
- Die Prophetie von Jes 17:1–3 über Damaskus ist nicht erfüllt. Die Stadt ist keine Ruine geworden, sondern ‚noch stets eine der angesehensten Städte Asiens.' (S. 145);
- Der Fluch über Arabien in Jes 21:13–17 verwirklichte sich nicht. Im Gegenteil, Arabien ist ‚ein mächtiges Reich geworden' und ist ‚noch bis zum heutigen Tag in besserem Zustand als das vom Herrn gesegnete Land.' (S. 147);
- Jerusalem, das in Jesaja 54 Gegenstand beeindruckender Heilszusagen ist, hat in der Geschichte wenig Frieden gekannt. Die Stadt ist Schauplatz blutiger Kämpfe und erbitterten Streits gewesen und wurde ‚schließlich zu einer Wohnung der Kinder Mohammeds, nicht der Kinder des Herrn.' (S. 177; vgl. auch S. 182 [zu Jesaja 62]). Die Spannung zwischen Prophetie und Wirklichkeit führt De Mey anlässlich von Jesaja 61 zu der ironischen Bemerkung: ‚Trauere lieber über die [die Juden], dass der Herr später vergessen hat, seine Verheißung zu erfüllen.' (S. 181).

Die Prophetien sind nicht erfüllt. Auch nicht auf die von Christen angenommene Weise. Ein wiederkehrender Refrain in den Darlegungen von De Mey ist, dass die jesajanischen Texte, die in christlicher Auslegung auf Jesus Christus[21] bezogen werden, zu Unrecht mit ihm in Verbindung gebracht werden, weil die Berührungspunkte gänzlich fehlen (z. B.

[21] Für Anspielungen in Jesaja auf die christliche Heilsgeschichte s. z. B. S. 154, 156.

S. 144f., 152, 164f., 178–183 und s.u.). Die christliche Auslegung bezeichnet er als ‚mutwilligen Betrug' (S. 138). Bekannte messianische Texte wie Jes 7:14; 8:23–9:6; 11:1–10 bezieht er auf den Sohn von König Ahas (S. 136–140), wobei er u.a. anmerkt, dass Jesus kein Friedefürst war, sondern ‚viel Unruhe auf Erden gestiftet hat' (S. 141) und die christliche Lehre bestimmt nicht geleitet hat zur Erfüllung der Erde ‚mit der Erkenntnis des Herrn' (S. 141). Die Knechtsgestalt von Jes 41:8; 42:1; 44:1; 49:6; 50:10; 52:13–53:12 betrachtet er als eine Personifikation des Volkes Israel (S. 157–160, 163–175). Der strenge Monotheismus dieser Abschnitte (z.B. Jes 44:6–8; 45:5f., 18, 21f.) hält er mit der christlichen Theologie für unvereinbar, die neben Gott noch von einem ‚Substitut-Gott', dem Sohn, ausgeht (S. 159–162). Zudem stimme die Beschreibung des Knechtes im Ganzen nicht mit dem Jesus der Evangelien überein. Jesus hatte keine unansehnliche Gestalt und war kein verachteter und kranker Mensch (Jes 53:2f.); sein Grab war nicht bei den Gottlosen und er war in seinem Tod nicht bei den Reichen (Jes 53:9) usw. (S. 166–176). Dass in seinem Mund kein Betrug war (Jes 53:9), ist vollkommen unwahr. Er hatte versprochen, bald auf den Wolken des Himmels zurückzukommen (Mat 24:30; 26:64; Mar 14:62; Luk 21:27 [S. 171f.; vgl. S. 142]), aber sein Wort hat er nicht gehalten. Es gibt dann auch keinen einzigen Grund für die christliche Auffassung, dass die Erfüllung bestimmter Prophetien noch in der Zukunft liegt (S. 146). Eine Untersuchung der Prophetien wird die Christen nicht zu der Schlussfolgerung führen müssen, dass ‚die Offenbarung' wahr ist, sondern zu der Auffassung, ‚dass die Schreiber von Prophetien [auch die des Neuen Testaments] die Worte voneinander übernommen haben und diese, jeder auf seine Weise, mit neuen Vorstellungen bereichert haben.' (S. 151; vgl. z.B. S. 142).

2.3. *Die mit der Stimme der Vernunft beurteilte Schrift*

Triebfeder für die Veröffentlichung seines Kommentars zur Bibel war für De Mey das Bedürfnis aufzuzeigen, dass der Schrift der Christenheit das Attribut ‚heilig' wegen des verwerflichen Gottesbildes und ihrer Legitimierung von Gewalt und Betrug keineswegs zusteht.[22] Die Vorstellung, dass die Bibel von Menschen geschrieben wurde, die vom Geist Gottes inspiriert waren, hält er angesichts des Inhalts für einen geisteskranken

[22] S. die Vorrede zu Teil 1, v–xv.

Gedanken. Eine Untersuchung der Bibel erweist, dass es ein Buch von Menschen ist und von leichtem Gehalt. De Meys Ausführungen beruhen auf einer eigenen Analyse der Bibel anhand der Staten-Bibel, die niederländische ‚nationale' Bibel, und einer jüdischen Übersetzung ‚auf Englisch von Dr. Leeser in Philadelphia' (S. xiii).[23] Niemals, so teilt er mit, las er ‚irgendein Buch, das gegen die Bibel geschrieben war' (S. xiii). Die Schlussfolgerung kann jedoch gezogen werden, dass bereits vorher von anderen vergleichbare Ansichten verteidigt wurden. Zwei von ihnen lassen wir zu Wort kommen, einen Franzosen und einen Deutschen.

2.4. *Jean Meslier*

Jean Meslier (1664–1729) war von 1689 bis zu seinem Tod Pastor in Etrépigny in der Gegend des nordfranzösischen Charleville-Mézières. Als er starb, hinterließ er ein umfangreiches Manuskript in dreifacher Ausfertigung, das an seine Parochianer gerichtet war, dessen Titel mit den Worten beginnt ‚Mémoires des pensées et des sentimens de J.M. … Prêtre, Curé d'Estrep$^{y.}$ et de But'. In dem als ‚Le Testament' bekannt gewordenen Werk erweist sich Meslier, der zeitlebens als Dorfpastor treu seinen Pflichten nachgekommen war, als ein Atheist und philosophischer Materialist und als ein radikaler Kritiker der Religion und der Bibel im Allgemeinen und der christlichen Religion in Gestalt der römisch-katholischen Kirche im Besonderen. Auch äußert er scharfe Kritik an den gesellschaftlichen Verhältnissen und Institutionen seiner Zeit und entpuppt sich als werdender Kommunist.[24] Vollständig wurde ‚Le Testament' mit einer Einleitung des Verlegers zuerst 1860–1864 in Amsterdam von Rudolf Carel Meijer (1826–1904) veröffentlicht, der auch unter dem Namen R.C. d'Ablaing van Giessenburg bekannt war, ein Vertreter niederländischer Freidenker.[25]

---

[23] Gemeint ist die Übersetzung von Isaac Leeser (1806–1868): *Twenty-Four Books of the Holy Scriptures Transl. After the Best Jewish Authorities*, erschienen 1845.

[24] S. zu ihm H.R. Schlette in Karl-Heinz Weger (Hg.), *Religionskritik von der Aufklärung bis zur Gegenwart: Autoren-Lexikon von Adorno bis Wittgenstein* (Herder-Bücherei 716; Freiburg im Breisgau, 1979), S. 233–235. In *RGG*[4] und *TRE* findet sich kein Artikel über ihn, wohl aber in *Wikipedia*. Auch in Magne Sæbø (Hg.), *Hebrew Bible/Old Testament: The History of Its Interpretation 2. From the Renaissance to the Enlightenment* (Göttingen, 2008), wird er nicht genannt.

[25] S. zu ihm T. Haan und J.M. Welcker in P.J. Meerten *et al.* (Hg.), *Biografisch woordenboek van het socialisme en de arbeidersbeweging in Nederland* 3 (Amsterdam, 1988), S. 143–147. Die erste Ausgabe umfasste drei Bände mit insgesamt über 1160 Seiten. In diesem Artikel wird der 1974 beim Georg Olms Verlag, Hildesheim/New York, erschie-

Nach dem Urteil von Meslier gibt es keine wahre Religion. Alle Religionen erweisen sich, wenn sie der Vernunft unterworfen werden, als menschliche Schöpfungen. Auf Wahn und Betrug basiert, werden sie von Machthabern zur Bestätigung und Legitimation ihrer Macht verwendet. Seinem Urteil zufolge kann die Bibel unmöglich als Zeugnis für einen allmächtigen, unendlich guten und weisen Gott betrachtet werden. Eine Untersuchung ihres Inhalts kann nur zu der Schlussfolgerung führen, dass die christliche Religion eine Religion wie andere Religionen ist und in jedem Fall nicht ein höheres Niveau aufweist (z B. I, S. 314; II, S. 38). Sollte das Christentum die wahre Religion und die Bibel das Zeugnis für den allmächtigen, unendlich guten und weisen Gott sein, dann sollte der Beweis hierfür mit soviel Evidenz geliefert werden, dass eine Diskussion unmöglich ist. Dieser Beweis kann jedoch nicht geliefert werden. Die biblischen Schriften können im Hinblick auf den Inhalt unmöglich das Resultat göttlicher Inspiration und ebenso wenig menschlicher Weisheit sein. Infolgedessen steht ihnen nicht zu, dass man ihnen irgendeinen Glauben schenkt (I, S. 134; vgl. auch z.B. I, S. 231).

Für seinen Standpunkt führt Meslier in Band 1 eine Anzahl Beweise an. U.a. behauptet er, dass die Propheten hinsichtlich des Inhalts ihrer sogenannten Offenbarungen keine Vertreter Gottes sein können (S. 231–276). Was in 2 Petr 1:19, 21 von dem prophetischen Wort gesagt wird, dass es wie eine Lampe ist, die in der Finsternis scheint, bis dass der Tag anbricht, und es durch den Heiligen Geist inspiriert ist, hat im Licht der Tatsachen keinen Bestand. Die Auffassung, dass die Propheten Ereignisse lange Zeit, bevor sie eintrafen, ankündigten, stimmt nicht. Sie werden nicht vom Geist Gottes getrieben, sondern vom Geist der Lüge und des Betrugs. Phantasten und Fanatiker sind es, Betrüger und Schwindler, die auf der Suche nach Dummköpfen sind, um sie hinters Licht zu führen, boshafte Leute, die vorsätzlich den Namen und die Autorität Gottes mit der Absicht gebrauchen, die Menschen irrezuführen und dieses oder jenes persönliche Ziel zu erreichen (S. 232–234). Meslier weist darauf hin, dass die Bibel selbst, Altes und Neues Testament, mit dem Phänomen falscher Propheten vertraut ist und stellt sie aufgrund der biblischen Angaben dar (S. 234–243). Die Propheten, die von den Christen für wahre Propheten gehalten werden, sind jedoch ebenfalls falsche Propheten. Sie können dem Prüfstein von Deut 18:20–22 und Jer 28:9 nicht standhalten. Ihre Worte erweisen sich nicht als wahr (S. 243 f.).

---

nene Nachdruck verwendet. In Paris ist 1970–1972 eine kritische Ausgabe von Mesliers gesamtem bekannten schriftlichen Werk erschienen, herausgegeben von J. Deprun *et al.*

Als Beweis hierfür zitiert Meslier ausführlich aus den Heilsprophetien des Alten Testaments (S. 245–276). Abschnitte aus dem Buch Jesaja nehmen unter den zitierten Texten einen bedeutenden Platz ein.[26] Diese werden vom Refrain unterbrochen ‚Alle diese schönen und großartigen Verheißungen erwiesen sich offensichtlich als falsch.' (S. 250, 255, 269). Meslier illustriert diese Aussage im Hinblick auf Prophetien über die Stadt Jerusalem, zu denen er auch Jes 46:13 zählt, mit der Bemerkung: Sollten sie wahr sein, ‚dann wäre Jerusalem lange Zeit und nun noch und für immer die glorreichste, die schönste, die größte, die reichste, die erfreulichste, die herrlichste, die triumphierendste und die glücklichste und die heiligste aller Städte der Welt, weil Gott selbst sie erwählt haben soll, um dort den Thron seiner Herrlichkeit zu gründen (...).' (S. 275). Auch verweist er auf Aussagen von Jesus über das Mitleid erregende Schicksal der Christen (Mat 10:17; Luk 21:16 f.; Joh 16:20), die zu ‚all diesen schönen Verheißungen' (S. 255) im Widerspruch stehen.

Seine Erörterungen führen Meslier zu der Schlussfolgerung, ‚dass es sicher und deutlich ist, dass diese Verheißungen und diese sogenannten Prophetien niemals erfüllt wurden und dass es keine einzige Sicherheit gibt, dass sie sich jemals erfüllen werden; ebenso sicher und deutlich ist, dass sie falsch sind und dass diejenigen, die sie ersonnen und erdacht haben, nichts anderes waren (...) als Phantasten und Fanatiker, die bei ihrem Reden nur ihrer Leidenschaft folgen, oder Betrüger, die dadurch den Menschen gefallen und imponieren wollen, sie am Ende aber betrügen und irreführen' (S. 275 f.).

Historische Kritik ist bei Meslier nicht auszumachen. Er führt Jesaja ein als ‚Jesaja, der Sohn des Amos' (Jes 1:1 [S. 249]). Prophetien aus Jesaja 40–66 leitet er als Worte ‚desselben Propheten' ein (S. 250, 254).

2.5. *Herrmann Samuel Reimarus*

Bekannter unter den Vertretern der Bibelwissenschaft als Meslier ist Herrmann Samuel Reimarus (1694–1768), ein vielseitiger Gelehrter[27] und ebenfalls Verfasser eines ‚Testaments', *Apologie oder Schutzschrift für die vernünftigen Verehrer Gottes*,[28] das vollständig erst 1972 veröffentlicht

---

[26] Jes 2:1–4, 17 f.; 9:5 f.; 11:1 f.; 35:4–10; 40:1, 10 f.; 43:25; 45:17; 46:13; 52:1; 54; 60; 62; 65:13 f.; 66:11, 16.

[27] S. zu ihm z. B. Christoph Bultmann, ‚Early Rationalism and Biblical Criticism', in Sæbø (Hg.), *Hebrew Bible/Old Testament*, S. 875–901.

[28] In zwei Bände (1 über das AT; 2 über das NT) herausgegeben von G. Alexander (Frankfurt am Main, 1972).

wurde. Von seinen in Band 1 dem Jesajabuch gewidmeten Ausführungen vermitteln wir hier einen Eindruck.

Reimarus stellt fest, dass prophetische Bücher drei Arten von Stoff beinhalten: (1) Kritik gegenüber dem Verhalten, das sich gegen das Gesetz richtet, Abgötterei, unmoralische Handlungsweisen und Verachtung des levitischen Kultus; (2) gegen das Volk gerichtete Unheilsprophetien; (3) Verheißungen, Heilsprophetien über die zukünftige Erlösung, Wiederherstellung, Wachstum und Herrlichkeit des jüdischen Volkes (S. 896). Er konkludiert, dass die prophetischen Bücher wegen der mangelhaften chronologischen Ordnung des Stoffes auf einer Sammeltätigkeit beruhen und die Worte der Propheten auf losen Blättern, Abschriften von Privatpersonen, überliefert wurden (S. 898–900, 903 f.). Bei der Sammeltätigkeit ist z. B. zu bedenken, dass Dubletten in der prophetischen Literatur begegnen (Jes 2:2–4; Mi 4:1–3)—und wir infolgedessen von einer Prophetie auch unter dem Namen eines Propheten hören, von dem sie nicht stammt (S. 899)—und ferner z. B., dass wir im Jesajabuch drei Kapiteln begegnen, die wörtlich aus 2. Könige entnommen sind (2 Kön 18–20; Jes 36–39 [S. 899]).

Reimarus stellt fest, dass die Prophetien Jesajas sehr spät seinem Namen zugeschrieben wurden und nicht alle vom ihm stammen müssen. Die unzulängliche und nicht-offizielle Überlieferung der Prophetenworte bietet für die Annahme genügend Anlass, dass heimliche, spätere, falsche und nach den Tatsachen konstruierte Texte, die als Prophetien dieses oder jenes alten Propheten ausgegeben wurden, zusammengeschmiedet wurden, um dem Volk Vertrauen, Hoffnung, und Mut zu geben. Vielleicht, so äußert Reimarus, wird mit derartigen Erdichtungen auch versucht, die Gunst des fremden Herrschers zu gewinnen. Angesichts des Charakters der prophetischen Bücher und der Wirren der Zeiten braucht es nicht zu verwundern, dass die Menschen sich davon überzeugen ließen, dass ‚dasjenige vor den Factis schon geweissaget sey, was erst nach den Factis als eine Weissagung kund gemacht worden'. Für den Urteilenden gilt: ‚Und je genauer es in den besondern Umständen bestimmt ist, desto grösseren Verdacht des Betruges erweckt es, wenn es nachher als eine alte Weissagung unter die Leute gebracht ward' (S. 903). Denn: ‚Dunkele Bilder und unverständliche Sprüche kann die Phantasey eines Menschen wohl zum voraus entwerffen, daraus die Nachwelt machen kann was sie will' (S. 904). Mit bloßen Fakten gelingt dies nicht. Sie bedürfen eines notariellen Aktes und Zeugen. Aufs Ganze gesehen, gibt es, wenn man die Regeln der gesunden Kritik beachtet, allen Grund, an dem jesajanischen Ursprung der Prophetien über Kyros (Jes 44:28;

45:1–4), zu zweifeln—Jesaja soll bereits 200 Jahre zuvor sein Auftreten mit Namen und Zunamen angekündigt haben!—und zu vermuten, dass ‚der nach der Befreyung lebende Sammler entweder selbst aus dem, was schon geschehen war, ein prophetisches Gesichte getichtet, oder auch eine von andern schon dem Jesaia angetichtete Weissagung unbedachtsam in seine Sammlung aufgenommen habe' (S. 899; vgl. S. 903 f.). Die Abschnitte über Kores gehören also zu den vielen Texten, die unter den Nenner *piae fraudes* gehören (S. 904).

Ironisch äußert sich Reimarus zu der Erfüllung der Prophetien. Die Dublette Jes 2:2–4; Mi 4:1–3 veranlasst ihn zu der Bemerkung: ‚Und ungeachtet der einstimmigen Versicherung durch Mund und Feder zweyer Propheten, haben wir doch in 2000 Jahren nachher die Zeit noch nicht gelebt, da alle Völker ihre Schwerter in Pflugschaaren und ihre Spiesse in Sicheln verwandelt hätten' (S. 899).

Besondere Aufmerksamkeit widmet Reimarus der Frage, ob der Heiland und Erlöser im Alten Testament angekündigt wird (S. 725–755). Er ist der Meinung, dass nicht nur die Christen, sondern auch die Juden die messianischen Texte missverstanden haben: ‚Es ist fast keine Stelle des A.T. von den Evangelisten und Aposteln auf Jesum gedeutet worden, welche nicht von den Rabbinen überhaupt auf den künftigen Messias gleichfalls wäre gezogen worden' (S. 726). Die Verwendung des Alten Testaments im Neuen muss jedoch als ‚Missbrauch' bezeichnet werden (S. 740). Um dies zu demonstrieren, lässt Reimarus viele Texte, die als Beweis angeführt werden, dass im Alten Testament ‚die Lehre, von einem geistlichen leydenden Erlöser der gantzen Welt von ihren Sünden' (S. 729) bekannt war, Revue passieren. Texte aus dem Jesajabuch nehmen dabei eine bedeutenden Rolle ein (S. 735–749).

Reimarus stellt fest, dass die messianischen Texte nicht auf Jesus Christus bezogen werden können. Er verweist u.a. darauf, dass Jes 9:5 f. (S. 722, 737 f.) und ebenso Jesaja 7 (zitiert in Mat 1:22 f.), wo in V. 14 übersetzt werden muss: ‚sie (die junge Frau) *ist* schwanger' (S. 736), auf Prinz Hiskia bezogen werden muss. Zu Jesaja 7 bemerkt er: ‚Hier ist ja wohl klar genug, daß keine Geburt eines Knaben kann gemeynt seyn, der erst 700 Jahr nachher zur Welt kommen sollte.' (S. 735). Jes 40:3 redet nicht über jemanden, der in der Wüste ruft (Mat 3:3), sondern über jemanden, der ruft, dass in der Wüste ein Weg bereitet werden muss (S. 739). Der Knecht von Jesaja 53 ist auf das Volk Israel zu beziehen (S. 742–747), ‚und ein jeder, der nur gesunde Vernunft hat, kann daran [an einer adäquaten Übersetzung] erkennen, daß dieses Capittel des Jesaiä kein christliches System von Jesu Leyden enthalte' (S. 746).

Jesaja, der für den größten Evangelisten des Alten Testaments gehalten wird, scheint der Erlöser unbekannt zu sein, so wird es auch aus dem, was über sein Leben berichtet wird deutlich. Wenn König Hiskia todkrank ist und Jesaja ihn auf den Tod vorbereitet, richtet Hiskia sein Vertrauen nur auf die eigene Frömmigkeit (2 Kön 20:3). Reimarus bemerkt hierzu: ‚Wenn das einer jetzt in Gegenwart seines Herrn Beichtvaters sagte, und seine Zuflucht nicht zur Genugthuung Jesu nähme:

so würde er als ein Werkheiliger oder Pelagianer bestraft werden. Aber Jesaias schweigt davon.' (S. 749). So ist nach Reimarus sonnenklar, dass ,die Heils-Ordung des N.T. weder nach dem Verstande der Worte, noch nach dem Gebrauche, im A.T. zu finden sei' (S. 749). Und weil Christus sich dort nun nicht ,im Lichte' offenbart, muss er gewiss nicht ,im Schatten', d.h. durch allegorische und typologische Auslegung gesucht werden. Reimarus geht auf eine derartige Art der Auslegung ein (S. 749–755), eine Form der Exegese, die bereits zuvor von Meslier umständlich verurteilt wurde (I, S. 327–352; II, S. 1–24).

2.6. *Auswertung*

Der Gebrauch ,der Stimme der Vernunft' (S. xi) bei der Beurteilung der Bibel erklärt die Übereinstimmungen der Auffassungen zwischen De Mey und seinen illustren Vorgängern. Mit Meslier und Reimarus behauptet er, dass die Prophetien die Qualifizierung ,Wahrheit' nicht verdienen, was sehr stark von Meslier unterstrichen wird, der im Gegensatz zu Reimarus keinen Versuch unternimmt, die Prophetien als *vaticinia ex eventu* zu entlarven. Die Prophetien Jesajas sind Unsinn. In seiner *La Bible amusante* (1882),[29] einer fortlaufenden Entsakralisierung des Alten Testaments, verliert Léo Taxil, Pseudonym von Marie Joseph Gabriel Antoine Jogand-Pagès (1854–1907), Atheist und Verfasser antiklerikaler Publikationen,[30] deshalb keine Worte darüber (S. 761). Die Karikatur von Frid' Rick auf S. 718 (Abb. 2), die durch die Beschreibung von Jesajas Lebensende im Martyrium des Jesaja (Kap. 5; vgl. Heb 11:37) inspiriert ist, wird für angemessen gehalten, ein adäquates Bild des Propheten darzustellen.

3. *Rückblick*

Wir haben die Positionen von zwei Niederländern aus dem 19. Jahrhundert hinsichtlich der Wahrheit der Prophetien des Jesaja kennengelernt. Ihre Auffassungen unterscheiden sich himmelweit. Die Ursache hierfür liegt in der Tatsache begründet, dass sie die Bibel mit unterschiedlichen

---

[29] Verwendet wird ein Nachdruck der niederl. Übersetzung aus dem Jahr 1907: *De amusante Bijbel* (Zandvoort o.J. [ca. 1920]).

[30] Zu Taxil findet sich kein Eintrag in *RGG*^{4} und *TRE*, jedoch in *RGG*^{2} 5, Sp. 1029f., und *LThK*^{2} 9, Sp. 1305, und in *Wikepedia*.

Augen gelesen haben, was eine unterschiedliche Schriftauffassung, ein unterschiedliches Gottesbild und ein unterschiedliches Ergebnis in der Prüfung biblischer Prophetien anhand des in der Bibel selbst gebotenen Kriteriums für die Wahrheit der Prophetie zur Folge hatte: die Erfüllung (vgl. Deut 18:20–22; Jer. 28,9). Für Van der Hoeven war der Gott der Bibel der Gott, der die Geschichte nach einem Programm ablaufen ließ, das in der Schrift festgelegt war. Für De Mey war der Gott der Bibel eine ‚launische und eitle Gestalt', die nichts mit seinem Gott, ‚der Vorsehung' zu tun hat, die in der Natur durch die Vernunft zu erkennen ist (I, x), ‚das unendliche Wesen (...), das man gewöhnlich Gott nennt' (II, v).

Die von Reimarus bereits in der ersten Hälfte des 18. Jahrhunderts geäußerte und von De Mey im 19. Jahrhundert wiederholte Auffassung, dass die Prophetien über Kyros nicht von Jesaja von Jerusalem stammen können, wurde in der zweiten Hälfte des 19. Jahrhunderts an der Leidener Akademie von Abraham Kuenen (1828–1891)[31] doziert und wurde trotz ihrer Bestreitung durch dessen Leidener Kollegen Antonie Rutgers (1805–1884)[32] allmählich tonangebend. Die Vernunft siegte. Die Position der Freidenker wurde in die akademische theologische Wissenschaft integriert.

---

[31] In seinem *Historisch-kritisch onderzoek naar het ontstaan en de verzameling van de boeken des Ouden Verbonds* 2 (Leiden, 1863), S. 98–143, liefert Kuenen Argumente für die Existenz ‚des zweiten Jesaja'. In der zweiten Auflage *Historisch-critisch onderzoek* 2 (Leiden, 1889), S. 99–150, präsentiert er eine überarbeitet Fassung seiner Argumentation. Zu Kuenen s. Cornelis Houtman in *BLGNP* 4, S. 270–274.

[32] Rutgers war von 1837–1875 Professor an der literarischen Fakultät für Hebräisch und die Auslegung des Alten Testaments. In seinem *De echtheid van het tweede gedeelte van Jesaja aangetoond* (Leiden, 1866), bestreitet er die u.a. von Kuenen akzeptierte Auffassung, ohne dessen Namen zu nennen.

VISIONS FROM MEMPHIS AND LEONTOPOLIS: THE PHENOMENON OF THE VISION REPORTS IN THE GREEK ISAIAH IN THE LIGHT OF CONTEMPORARY ACCOUNTS FROM HELLENISTIC EGYPT

Michaël N. van der Meer*

1. *Search for a suitable setting for the Septuagint*

Over the last century the question of the *Sitz im Leben* has played an important role in Septuagint research. The approach to this corpus of Greek translations of the books of the Hebrew Bible depends to a considerable extent on presuppositions about Septuagint origins, provenance, and purpose. No modern scholar will adopt uncritically the claim made in the Letter of Aristeas that the Greek Pentateuch owes its existence exclusively to King Ptolemy II Philadelphus's awe for Jewish theology and philosophy, even though there are other, more pragmatic reasons why this king may have had an interest in a Greek translation of the constitution of an important ethnic group within his empire.[1]

* It is my pleasure to thank Dr. Brian P. Muhs of the Leiden Papyrological Institute for his stimulating remarks and helpful suggestions, corrections of the Demotic documents, and my English text.

[1] See Bruno H. Stricker, *De brief van Aristeas. De Helleense Codificaties der praehelleense godsdiensten* (VNAW.L NR 62.4; Amsterdam, 1956); Leonhard Rost, 'Vermutungen über den Anlass zur griechischen Übersetzung der Tora', in Hans-Joachim Stoebe (ed.), *Wort, Gebot, Glaube. Beiträge zur Theologie des Alten Testaments, Walther Eichrodt zum 80. Geburtstag* (AThANT 59; Zürich, 1970), pp. 39–44; Dominique Barthélemy, 'Pourquoi la Torah a-t-elle été traduite en grec?', in *On Language, Culture and Religion. In Honor of E.A. Nida* (The Hague, 1974), pp. 23–41; reprinted in Dominique Barthélemy, *Études d'histoire du texte de l'Ancien Testament* (OBO 21; Fribourg–Göttingen, 1977), pp. 322–340; Elias Bickerman, 'The Septuagint as a Translation', in *PAAJR* 28 (1959), reprinted in Elias Bickerman, *Studies in Jewish and Christian History* 1 (AGJU 9.1; Leiden, 1976), pp. 167–200; Nina L. Collins, *The Library in Alexandria and the Bible in Greek* (VT.S 82; Leiden etc., 2000); Wolfgang Orth, 'Ptolemaios II. und die Septuaginta-Übersetzung', in Heinz-Josef Fabry and Ulrich Offerhaus (eds.), *Im Brennpunkt: Die Septuaginta. Studien zur Entstehung und Bedeutung der griechischen Bibel* 1 (BWANT 153; Stuttgart etc., 2001), pp. 97–114; Arie van der Kooij, 'The Septuagint of the Pentateuch and Ptolemaic Rule', in Gary N. Knoppers and Bernard M. Levinson (eds.), *The Pentateuch as Torah. New Models for Understanding Its Promulgation and Acceptance* (Winona

Instead of the Ptolemaic court as the original *Sitz im Leben* for the Septuagint, scholars have proposed the synagogue,[2] the office of the professional dragoman in the law court,[3] the statutes of self-administration of the Jewish *politeuma*,[4] the prestigious library of the Mousaion,[5] or the school benches of the primary education in Hebrew[6] as the Septuagint's crib.

What makes the search for a suitable setting for the Septuagintal books so special is the fact that the various theories draw upon the wealth of contemporary texts from the Greco-Roman world. Ptolemaic Egypt in particular has provided a large amount of documents that provide parallels for the alleged principal and pristine functions of the Jewish-Greek translations. The fact that early in the Hellenistic period priests like Manetho and Berossus produced Greek versions of Egyptian and Babylonian history respectively at the request of Ptolemy I Soter (332–282 BCE) and Antiochus I (285–261 BCE), has often been adduced as a parallel to royal involvement in the production of the Greek Pentateuch.[7] Yet, these works are not literal translations of canonical works, but rather free

---

Lake, Ind., 2007), pp. 289–300.

[2] Henry St.J. Thackeray, *The Septuagint and Jewish Worship. A Study in Origins. The Schweich Lectures 1920* (London, 1921).

[3] Chaim Rabin, 'The Translation Process and the Character of the Septuagint', *Textus* 6 (1968), pp. 1–26.

[4] Joseph Mélèze Modrzejweski, *The Jews of Egypt. From Rameses II to Emperor Hadrian* (Princeton, 1997), pp. 99–112.

[5] Sylvie Honigman, *The Septuagint and Homeric Scholarship in Alexandria. A Study in the Narrative of the Letter of Aristeas* (London, 2003); Erich S. Gruen, 'The Letter of Aristeas and the Cultural Context of the Septuagint', in Martin Karrer, Wolfgang Kraus, and Martin Meiser (eds.), *Die Septuaginta-Texte, Kontexte, Lebenswelten. Internationale Fachtagung veranstaltet von Septuaginta Deutsch (LXX.D), Wuppertal 20. -23. Juli 2006* (WUNT 219; Tübingen, 2008), pp. 134–156.

[6] Sebastian P. Brock, 'The Phenomenon of the Septuagint', in M.A. Beek *et al.*, *The Witness of Tradition. Papers Read at the Joint British–Dutch Old Testament Conference Held at Woudschoten, 1970* (OTS 17; Leiden, 1972), pp. 11–36; Brock's thesis has been adopted and modified by Albert Pietersma, 'A New Paradigm for Addressing Old Questions: The Relevance of the Interlinear Model for the Study of the Septuagint', in Johan Cook (ed.), *Bible and Computer. The Stellenbosch AIBI–6 Conference. Proceedings of the Association Internationale Bible et Informatique "From Alpha to Byte". University of Stellenbosch 17–21 July, 2000* (Leiden etc., 2002), pp. 337–364; see also Cameron Boyd-Taylor, 'A Place in the Sun: The Interpretative Significance of LXX-Psalm 18:5c', *BIOSCS* 31 (1998), pp. 71–105. It should, however, be noted that the primary aim of Pietersma's interlinear model is not to offer a theory about Septuagint origins, but rather to offer a heuristic model that accounts for the very literal, 'translationese' character of the majority of Septuagintal books.

[7] Stricker, *De brief van Aristeas*; Bickerman, 'The Septuagint as a Translation', pp. 174–175.

compositions based on indigenous sources. Bilingual texts, such as the Aramaic–Greek edicts of King Asoka (257–256 BCE) and the Ptolemaic edicts of Canopus (238 BCE), Raphia (217 BCE), and Rosetta (196 BCE), are closer to the Septuagint when it comes to the aspect of translation, but are much shorter and bound to a particular historical situation than Greek translations of Jewish Scripture. Other scholars, in particular Joseph Méléze Modrzejewski, have pointed to Aramaic and Greek translations of native Egyptian law codes as a parallel for the Greek translation of the Jewish law, that is, the Pentateuch.[8] Although recently published papyri from the archive of a Jewish *politeuma* from ancient Herakleopolis attests to the existence of such a Jewish self-regulating juridical body already at the second century BCE and their application of Jewish family law with respect to divorce,[9] there is little evidence that the Septuagint had a juridical function in Ptolemaic law courts. Moreover, even the Pentateuch consists only to a limited extent of legal material.[10] Advocates of a school setting of the Septuagint have pointed to interlinear Homeric texts with both the ancient Greek and *koine* Greek translation[11] and bilingual

[8] Méléze Modrzejewski, *The Jews of Egypt*, pp. 99–112. Diodore of Sicily 1.95.4 mentions the involvement of King Darius I in the compilation of Egyptian laws. A Demotic law code was discovered in 1938–1939 at ancient Hermopolis and published by Girgis Mattha and George R. Hughes (eds.), *The Demotic Legal Code of Hermopolis West* (Cairo, 1975). That edition is now superseded by Koenraad Donker van Heel (ed.), *The Legal Manual of Hermopolis (P.Mattha). Text and Translation* (Uitgaven vanwege de stichting 'Het Leids Papyrologisch Instituut' 11; Leiden, 1990). UPZ II 162 (court records of the lawsuit of Hermias against choachytes in Thebes, 117 BCE), col. ix, line 13, makes reference of the sale of a house κατ' Αἰγυπτίας συγγραφάς, 'according to Egyptian contracts'. A Greek translation of the Demotic law code (or a version closely related to P.Mattha) was found among the Oxyrhynchus papyri and published as P.Oxy. XLVI 3285 by John R. Rea (ed.), *The Oxyrhynchus Papyri* 46 (PEES.GR 65; London, 1978), pp. 30–38. For a list of abbreviations for documentary papyri, see John F. Oates *et al.*, 'Checklist of Greek, Latin, Demotic and Coptic Papyri, Ostraca and Tablets'. Cited 12 September 2008. Online: http://scriptorium.lib.duke.edu/papyrus/texts/clist_papyri.html.

[9] James M.S. Cowey and Klaus Maresch (eds.), *Urkunden des Politeuma der Juden von Herakleopolis (144/3–133/2 v.Chr.) (P.Polit.Iud.)* (Pap.Colon. XXIX; Wiesbaden, 2001). P.Polit.Iud. 4 (134 BCE), lines 22–24 refers to the practice of handing over ṭọ̀ εἰθισμένον τοῦ ἀποστασίου βυβλίọν, 'the usual bill of divorce', known only from Jewish sources, in particular LXX-Deut 24:1–24.

[10] P.Ent.23 (= CPJ I 128; 218 BCE), line 2 seems to refer to a practice [κατὰ τὸν νομόν π]ọλιτικὸν τῶν ['Ιου-]δαίων. In this case too, we are dealing with Jewish matrimonial customs.

[11] PSI XII 1276 (= LDAB 2270 = TM 61131) dating from the first century BCE with the text of Illiad 2.617–638, 639–670, interspersed with lines with colloquial Greek counterparts to the ancient Greek Homeric hexameters. The abbreviations LDAB and TM refer to digital databases for ancient literary compositions found in Egypt: the Leuven Database

Latin–Greek versions of Virgil,[12] as parallels to the word-for-word translation style found in many of the books of the Septuagint.[13]

This short overview of possible parallels to Greek translations of Jewish Scripture makes clear, at least to my mind, that it is worthwhile to study the Septuagint within its cultural context. Documents from the *Umwelt* of the Septuagint can be helpful to assess the profile, provenance, and purpose of the Greek translations of the biblical books.[14] At the same time, the variety in genres of the documents just mentioned (law codes and legal documents, school texts, monumental inscriptions, presentation and promotion of cultural traditions) makes it highly unlikely that a single setting can be found that suits the entire corpus of Greek writings now included under the general title 'Septuagint'. Septuagint research has made it increasingly clear that the Septuagint is by no means the result of a unified Bible translation project. We should rather think of a process of different translations of individual books or group of books. These Greek translations were produced over a long span of time: almost half a millennium from the Greek translation of the Pentateuch (early third century BCE) to the Greek version of Ecclesiastes (early second century CE). Furthermore, the character and style of translations ranges from very free (Greek Job, Greek Proverbs, and the Greek versions of Esther) to very literal (*kaige*-like translations in Judges, Reigns, Canticles, Psalms, Ecclesiastes, Jeremiah, Lamentations, and 2 Esdras).[15] Each version and each translation unit should be studied in its own right and within its own literary, historical, and cultural context.

---

of Ancient Books. Cited 3 August 2009. Online: http://www.trismegistos.org/ldab/index.php; and the Trismegistus database for ancient literary texts from Egypt in Hieratic, Demotic, Aramaic, Greek, Latin, Coptic, and Arabic from *c.* 800 BCE to *c.* 800 CE. Cited 3 August 2009. Online: http://www.trismegistos.org/index.html.

[12] P.Oxy. VIII 1099 (= LDAB 4162 = TM 62970).

[13] Brock, 'The Phenomenon', pp. 29–31; Pietersma, 'A New Paradigm', pp. 346–349.

[14] For the parallels between Ben Sira and Demotic wisdom texts, see Jack T. Sanders, *Ben Sira and Demotic Wisdom* (SBL.MS 28; Chico, 1983). For an Aramaic parallel to Psalm 20 written in Demotic script, see Sven P. Vleeming and Jan-Wim Wesselius, *Studies in Papyrus Amherst 63. Essays on the Aramaic/Demotic Papyrus Amherst 63* (Amsterdam, 1985).

[15] See the helpful categorization in Henry St.J. Thackeray, *A Grammar of the Old Testament in Greek According to the Septuagint* 1. *Introduction, Orthography and Accidence* (Cambridge, 1909), p. 13.

2. *The context of the Greek Isaiah*

This brings me automatically to the question of the cultural context of the Old Greek version of the Book of Isaiah, a topic to which our honouree has devoted many distinctive contributions.[16] Based upon the works of Ziegler and Seeligmann,[17] Van der Kooij has argued that the Greek version of Isaiah presents a document in its own right reflecting the particular interests and interpretation of a Jewish group around the exiled High Priest Onias IV in Leontopolis around 140 BCE.[18] According to Van der Kooij, the Greek version of Isaiah is not only a fairly free translation of the Hebrew original, but also an actualization of the ancient prophecies. In his view, the Greek translator understood the prophecies in the Book of Isaiah as predictions that found their fulfilment in his own times. Thus the major events in the middle of the second century BCE can be discerned in actualizing renderings in the Greek Isaiah,

---

[16] See, for instance, Arie van der Kooij, 'Die Septuaginta Jesajas als Dokument jüdischer Exegese—Einige Notizen zu LXX-Jes. 7', in *Übersetzung und Deutung. Studien zu dem Alten Testament und seiner Umwelt Alexander Reinard Hulst gewidmet von Freunden und Kollegen* (Nijkerk, 1977), pp. 91–102; Arie van der Kooij, *Die alten Textzeugen des Jesajabuches. Ein Beitrag zur Textgeschichte des Alten Testaments* (OBO 35; Freiburg–Göttingen, 1981); Arie van der Kooij, '"The Servant of the Lord": A Particular Group of Jews in Egypt according to the Old Greek of Isaiah. Some Comments on LXX Isa 49,1–6 and Related Passages', in Jacques van Ruiten and Marc Vervenne (eds.), *Studies in the Book of Isaiah. Festschrift Willem A.M. Beuken* (BETL 132; Leuven, 1997), pp. 383–396; Arie van der Kooij, 'Isaiah in the Septuagint', in Craig C. Broyles and Craig A. Evans (eds.), *Writing and Reading the Scroll of Isaiah* (VT.S 70.2; Leiden etc., 1997), pp. 513–529; Arie van der Kooij, *The Oracle of Tyre. The Septuagint of Isaiah 23 as Version and Vision* (VT.S 71; Leiden etc., 1998); Arie van der Kooij, 'The City of Alexandria and the Ancient Versions of the Hebrew Bible', *JNSL* 25 (1999), pp. 137–149; Arie van der Kooij, 'Wie heißt der Messias? Zu Jes 9,5 in den alten griechischen Versionen', in Christoph Bultmann, Walter Dietrich, and Christoph Levin (eds.), *Vergegenwärtigung des Alten Testaments. Beiträge zur biblischen Hermeneutik für Rudolf Smend zum 70. Geburtstag* (Göttingen, 2002), pp. 156–169; Arie van der Kooij, 'LXX-Isaiah 8–9 and the Issue of Fulfilment-Interpretation', *Adamantius* 13 (2007), pp. 20–28; Arie van der Kooij, 'The Septuagint of Isaiah and the Mode of Reading Prophecies in Early Judaism. Some Comments on LXX Isaiah 8–9', in Karrer and Kraus, *Die Septuaginta*, pp. 597–611.

[17] Joseph Ziegler, *Untersuchungen zur Septuaginta des Buches Isaias* (ATA 12.3; Münster i.W., 1934); Isac Leo Seeligmann, *The Septuagint Version of Isaiah. A Discussion of Its Problems* (MEOL 9; Leiden, 1948).

[18] Van der Kooij, *Die alten Textzeugen*, pp. 60–65; see already Wilhelm Gesenius, *Philologisch-kritischer und historischer Commentar über den Jesaja* 1 (Leipig, 1821), p. 62; Zacharias Frankel, *Historisch-kritische Studien zu der Septuaginta* 1.1 (Leipzig, 1841), p. 40, n. f; Seeligmann, *Septuagint Version*, pp. 86, 91–94, considers this temple, which he locates at Heliopolis, to be an intermediary station between the Palestinian tradition and 'the Alexandrian translation of Isaiah'.

particularly allusions to the Seleucid Empire where the Hebrew text refers to Aram (LXX-Isa 9:21[20] and 17:13) or the Assyrian-Babylonian Empire (LXX-Isa 10:5), the invasion in Egypt and the plundering of the Jerusalem Temple by Antiochus IV Epiphanes (170–167 BCE as reflected in LXX-Isa 22:1–14), the Hellenizing policy of High Priest Menelaus (172–162 BCE as reflected in LXX-Isa 22:15–25), the move of Onias IV to Egypt (reflected in LXX-Isa 8–9), the death of Antiochus IV in Persia (164 BCE as reflected in LXX-Isa 14:4–21), the fall of Carthage (146 BCE as reflected in LXX-Isa 23:1), and the Parthian raid of Babylon (140 BCE as reflected in LXX-Isa 14:22–27).

In order to contextualize the notion of fulfilment interpretation in Bible translation, Van der Kooij points to contemporaneous Jewish texts that also express the same idea of fulfilment.[19] Examples for this strong interest into actualization of the ancient prophecies, particularly from the Book of Isaiah, do not come only from eschatological writings such as the Books of Daniel (11–12), 1 Henoch (83–90), and the third Book of Sybiline Oracles from the second century BCE, the Qumran pesharim (e.g. 1QpHab, 3QpIsa, 4QpIsa[a–e]) from the first century BCE and the citations in early Christian literature from the first century CE and later translations of the Book of Isaiah such as the Targum and Vulgate. Also less eschatological writings from the second century BCE, such as the Books of Ben Sira (36:13–21), Tobit (14:4), and 1 Maccabees (7:40–41) reflect the same tendency to read the ancient text in the light of contemporaneous events.

Van der Kooij's approach has recently been challenged in a monograph on the Septuagint of Isaiah written by Ron Troxel, culminating into a major critique of contemporization.[20] He adopts a 'minimalist approach' which he defines as follows:[21]

> Only if the translator can be shown to refer deliberately to people, countries, ethnic groups, circumstances, or events by deviating from his *Vorlage* is it legitimate to entertain the possibility that he sought to identify such entities as the 'true' referents of his Hebrew exemplar. More stringently, it must be shown that the translator did not arrive at a rendering from the

[19] Van der Kooij, *Die alten Textzeugen*; *The Oracle of Tyre*, pp. 88–94; *idem*, 'Issue of Fulfilment-Interpretation'; *idem*, 'Mode of Reading Prophecies'.

[20] Ronald L. Troxel, *LXX-Isaiah as Translation and Interpretation. The Strategies of the Translator of the Septuagint of Isaiah* (JSJ.S 124; Leiden etc., 2008).

[21] Troxel, *LXX-Isaiah*, p. 164, see further pp. 173–199: 'A Critique of Contemporization'.

literary or broader *literary* contexts, but that he fashioned it with an eye to circumstances or events in his day.

Literal rendering is default, free the deviation. As a general rule, this principle may seem sound, but one wonders whether it is applicable to the Greek Isaiah. Troxel himself falls prey to a more maximalist approach when he tries to detect a reference in LXX-Isa 33:18 to the expulsion of scholars (γραμματικοί) from the Mousaion in Alexandria under Ptolemy VII Euergetes II in 145 BCE.[22] Although Troxel considers this Mousaion to be the cultural setting for the Greek translation of Isaiah, the literary activities that took place there, e.g. the preservation of the Greek epics and the collection of all available knowledge, failed to affect the Greek translator of Isaiah, since there are hardly any traces of this Alexandrian body of literature.

3. *LXX-Isaiah 7:14–17 as a Case in Point*

Troxel refers repeatedly to LXX-Isa 7:14–17 as example for his approach.[23] The text contains the famous Emmanuel prophecy, which in Christian tradition has become the proof-text for the virginity of the mother of the Messiah, based on the Greek rendering παρθένος for Hebrew עלמה.[24] This passage serves as a good test for the search for an appropriate context for the Greek Isaiah:[25]

MT לכן יתן אדני הוא לכם אות הנה העלמה הרה וילדת בן וקראת שמו עמנו אל: חמאה ודבש יאכל לדעתו מאוס ברע ובחור בטוב: כי בטרם ידע הנער מאס ברע ובחר בטוב תעזב האדמה אשר אתה קץ מפני שני מלכיה: יביא יהוה עליך ועל עמך ועל בית אביך ימים אשר לא באו למיום סור אפרים מעל יהודה את מלך אשור:

NRSV Therefore the Lord himself will give you a sign. Look, the young woman is with child and shall bear a son, and shall name him Immanuel. He

---

[22] Troxel, *LXX-Isaiah*, pp. 20–35. I follow the revised numbering of Ptolemaic kings as offered by Werner Huß, *Ägypten in hellenistischer Zeit, 332–30 v. Chr.* (München, 2001).

[23] Troxel, *LXX-Isaiah*, pp. 87–88, 98–99, 139–145. The material is drawn from an earlier article: Ronald L. Troxel, 'Isaiah 7,14–16 through the Eyes of the Septuagint', *EThL* 79 (2003), pp. 1–22.

[24] Matt 1:21; Luke 1:31. See also the polemic against Greek mythology by Justin Martyr, 1 *Apol.* 33.

[25] The Hebrew text is based upon HUB: Moshe H. Goshen-Gottstein, *The Book of Isaiah* (The Hebrew University Bible; Jerusalem, 1997). This text is supported by 1QIsa[a] and the fragmentary remains of 4QIsa[e], 4QIsa[f], and 4QIsa[l]. The Greek text is based upon the Göttingen edition: Joseph Ziegler, *Isaias* (Septuaginta Vetus Testamentum Graecum Auctoritate Societatis Litterarum Gottingensis editum 14; Göttingen, 1939).

shall eat curds and honey by the time he knows how to refuse the evil and choose the good. For before the child knows how to refuse the evil and choose the good, the land before whose two kings you are in dread will be deserted. The Lord will bring on you and on your people and on your ancestral house such days as have not come since the day that Ephraim departed from Judah—the king of Assyria.

LXX διὰ τοῦτο δώσει κύριος αὐτὸς ὑμῖν σημεῖον· ἰδοὺ ἡ παρθένος ἐν γαστρὶ ἕξει καὶ τέξεται υἱόν, καὶ καλέσεις τὸ ὄνομα αὐτοῦ Εμμανουηλ· βούτυρον καὶ μέλι φάγεται· πρὶν ἢ γνῶναι αὐτὸν ἢ προελέσθαι πονηρὰ ἐκλέξεται τὸ ἀγαθόν· διότι πρὶν ἢ γνῶναι τὸ παιδίον ἀγαθὸν ἢ κακὸν ἀπειθεῖ πονηρίᾳ τοῦ ἐκλέξασθαι τὸ ἀγαθόν, καὶ καταλειφθήσεται ἡ γῆ, ἣν σὺ φοβῇ ἀπὸ προσώπου τῶν δύο βασιλέων. ἀλλὰ ἐπάξει ὁ θεὸς ἐπὶ σὲ καὶ ἐπὶ τὸν λαόν σου καὶ ἐπὶ τὸν οἶκον τοῦ πατρός σου ἡμέρας, αἳ οὔπω ἥκασιν ἀφ᾽ ἧς ἡμέρας ἀφεῖλεν Εφραιμ ἀπὸ Ιουδα, τὸν βασιλέα τῶν Ἀσσυρίων.

NETS Therefore the Lord himself will give you a sign. Look, the virgin shall be with child and bear a son, and you shall name him Emmanouel. He shall eat butter and honey; before he knows or prefers evil things, he shall choose what is good. For before the child knows good or bad, he defies evil to choose what is good, and the land that you fear from before the two kings will be abandoned. But God will bring on you and on your people and on your ancestral house such days as have not yet come since the day that he took Ephraim away from Ioudas—the king of the Assyrians.

Since both Hebrew עלמה and Greek παρθένος mean 'young woman' rather than 'virgin', the Greek translator did not introduce a novel concept, thus Troxel. The real departure from the Hebrew text can be found, according to Troxel, in the plus ἀγαθὸν ἢ κακὸν in verse 16. This plus, Troxel continues, is taken from Deut 1:39 and was added in other Pentateuchal passages as well (LXX-Num 14:23; 32:11). The Greek translator of Isaiah only wanted to emphasize the character of the young boy, rather than the character of his mother. In order to achieve his goal, the translator drew upon Hebrew Scripture, rather than contemporary concepts. Although Troxel is certainly right about the corresponding Hebrew and Greek meanings for עלמה and παρθένος, he does not explain why the Greek translator employed a rendering which he consistently employed for the Hebrew word בתולה,[26] whereas the rendering of עלמה by Greek νεᾶνις would have been more in line with both the translation options attested in the Greek Pentateuch and elsewhere.[27] Further-

[26] Thus Isa 23:4; 37:22; 17:1; 62:5.

[27] Thus LXX-Exod 2:8; LXX-Ps 67(68):28; LXX-Cant 1:3; 6:8; cf. the versions of Theodo-

more, it remains unclear why the Greek translator would have wanted to apply the qualification of a specific Israelite generation of the past to the child Emmanuel. The changes detected by Troxel in the Pentateuch are not restricted only to the Septuagint, but other ancient versions as well, such as the Samaritan Pentateuch, the Peshitta, and the Greek Joshua, and require a study of their own.[28]

Troxel's interpretation of LXX-Isa 7:14–17 is a reaction to earlier studies of this passage that allowed for a considerable amount of interpretation, theology, contemporization, and even eschatologizing on the part of the Greek translator of Isaiah. In a much neglected article from 1972, the Portugese scholar Joaquim Carreira das Neves had argued that the Greek translator of Isaiah had transformed the passage from an ambivalent oracle into an oracle of salvation for a specific Jewish community. According to Das Neves, the translator applied the theme of 'the remainder of Israel', present in the first symbolic name of Isaiah 7, שאר ישוב, 'a remnant will return', to the second symbolic name.[29] Both mother and son signify the Jewish community in the translator's lifetime, just as the new name in Isa 65:15 refers to a new future for this community. Throughout LXX-Isaiah 7 similar changes can be found that strengthen the positive transformation of an oracle of doom. In 7:17, the Greek translator contrasted the positive future for the new Israel with the judgment over Achaz by means of the insertion of the adversative ἀλλά,[30] and in verses 4–5 by means of the promise πάλιν ἰάσομαι as free rendering of the names of Achaz's enemies רצין וארם.[31]

---

tion, Aquila, and Symmachus of Isa 7:14, and Targum Jonathan: עולימתא, 'young girl'. Christian translations in Syriac and Latin (Peshitta and Vulgate) render the Hebrew word in the sense of 'virgin': ܒܬܘܠܬܐ and *virgo*.

[28] See Michaël N. van der Meer, 'The Next Generation. Textual Moves in Numbers 14,23 and Related Passages', in Thomas Römer (ed.), *The Books of Leviticus and Numbers* (BEThL 215; Leuven etc., 2008), pp. 399–416.

[29] Joaquim Carreira des Neves, 'Isaías 7,14 no Texto Massorético e no Texto Greco–A obra de Joachim Becker', *Did(L)* 2 (1972), pp. 79–112.

[30] Also acknowledged by Troxel, 'Isaiah 7,14–16', p. 19.

[31] Troxel, 'Isaiah 7,14–16', pp. 13–14, n. 63, argues that πάλιν ἰάσομαι reflects a Hebrew reading רצון rather than the reading attested by MT and 1QIsa[a]. Although this Hebrew word has usually been rendered with Greek δεκτός, 'acceptable' (Isa 49:8; 56:7; 58:5; 60:7; 61:2), it has once been rendered with ἔλεος, 'mercy'. Richard R. Ottley, *The Book of Isaiah according to the LXX (Codex Alexandrinus) 2. Text and Notes* (Cambridge, 1906), p. 140, suggested that the translator read ארפא, 'I will heal', which is the Hebrew text underlying καὶ ἰάσομαι αὐτούς in Isa 6:10, thus Ziegler, *Untersuchungen*, p. 62; Seeligmann, *Septuagint Version*, p. 56. Although these reconstructions may perhaps help to understand *how* the Greek translator arrived at his unusual Greek rendering in Isa 7:4,

Whereas Das Neves speaks only in rather general terms about the Greek translator's audience, Van der Kooij in one of his earliest articles—in a *Festschrift* for his *Doktervater*—finds evidence for fulfilment interpretation in the Greek translation.[32] Van der Kooij finds a striking parallel to the use of παρθένος in LXX-Isa 7:14 in the narrative of Sanherib in Isa 37:25, where the besieged city of Jerusalem is called παρθένος θυγάτηρ Σιων. That chapter shares with Isa 7 the imagery of birth giving and oppression, thus Isa 37:3b in a free rendering of the Hebrew text:[33]

LXX Ἡμέρα θλίψεως καὶ ὀνειδισμοῦ καὶ ὀργῆς ἡ σήμερον ἡμέρα, ὅτι ἥκει ἡ ὠδὶν τῇ τικτούσῃ, ἰσχὺν δὲ οὐκ ἔχει τοῦ τεκεῖν.

NETS Today is a day of affliction and reproach and of rebuke and of anger, because the pangs have come to the woman giving birth, but she has no strength to give birth.

MT יום צרה ותוכחה ונאצה היום הזה כי באו בנים עד משבר וכח אין ללדה

NRSV This day is a day of distress, of rebuke, and of disgrace; children have come to the birth, and there is no strength to bring them forth.

The purpose of the free rendering in 37:3 can be explained on the basis of another passage from Isaiah, where the Greek and Hebrew versions do not differ, i.e. Isa 66:8b:

LXX ὅτι ὤδινεν καὶ ἔτεκεν Σιων τὰ παιδία αὐτῆς.

NETS Because Sion was in labour and she gave birth to her children.

MT כי חלה גם ילדה ציון את בניה

NRSV Yet as soon as Sion was in labour she delivered her children.

In the light of these parallels from within the Greek Isaiah, Van der Kooij finds it plausible to interpret LXX-Isaiah 7 as a fulfilment interpretation of the Hebrew Isaiah in which the παρθένος stands for mother Zion and her son as metaphor for the remnant of Israel. After all, the phrase 'he shall eat butter and honey' occurs twice in this chapter, the first time in 7:15 and the second in 7:22 with 'everyone that is left in the land' as subject:

---

it does by no means explain *why* he did so. If he was merely translating as literal as possible a corrupt Hebrew text, he would have chosen his default rendering δεκτός. Furthermore, he would not have added the adverb πάλιν, a word that has no direct counterpart in Classical Hebrew. If, however, the relatively free character of the translation technique is duly recognized, one wonders why the translator had not simply harmonized the alleged corrupt Hebrew reading to the most logical Hebrew reading, i.e. the text attested in MT.

[32] Van der Kooij, 'Die Septuaginta als Dokument jüdischer Exegese', pp. 91–102.

[33] Van der Kooij, 'Notizen zu LXX-Jes 7', pp. 97–98.

LXX καὶ ἔσται ἀπὸ τοῦ πλεῖστον ποιεῖν γάλα βούτυρον καὶ μέλι φάγεται πᾶς ὁ καταλειφθεὶς ἐπὶ τῆς γῆς.

NETS And it shall be, because of the abundance of milk that they (i.e. a young cow and two sheep) give, everyone that is left on the land will eat butter and honey.

According to Van der Kooij, the parallel with Isa 37:25 makes clear that LXX-Isaiah 7 alludes to the threat posed by the Assyrian army, which is then easily deciphered as the Syrian-Seleucid Empire. As a consequence, the remnant-son would stand for the exiled Jews in Egypt who hoped to return to the restored Jerusalem.[34] For Van der Kooij, the proper context for interpreting the Greek Isaiah is thus twofold: the Greek Isaiah as a whole (both the passages where the Greek differs from and corresponds with the Hebrew text)[35] and the historical context of the second century BCE.

Whereas the literary and cultural horizon for the Greek translator of Isaiah in Troxel's view seems to be restricted to the Protestant canon of the Old Testament and broadened in the view of Das Neves and Van der Kooij to the concepts and literature of second century BCE Judaism, such limits in time and space are transcended in yet another interpretation of LXX-Isa 7:14–17. Following a suggestion made by Eduard Norden and Rudolf Kittel,[36] and adopted even by Seeligmann,[37] Martin Rösel has argued that the unusual rendering of עלמה by παρθένος should be understood against the background of Hellenistic mystery cults.[38] According to this explanation the Greek version of Isaiah echoes the proclamation of the birth of Aion at the winter solstice (the night from December, the 25th to the 26th) as transmitted by Hippolytus, *Refutatio omnium haeresium* 5.8.45: ἡ παρθένος ἡ ἐν γαστρὶ ἔχουσα καὶ συλλαμβάνουσα καὶ τίκτουσα υἱόν.

[34] Van der Kooij, 'Notizen zu LXX-Jes 7', pp. 99–100. Van der Kooij (pp. 94–95) also points to the unusual Greek rendering πάλιν ἰάσομαι as free rendering of the names of Achaz's enemies רצין וארם, already noted by Das Neves.

[35] Van der Kooij, 'Notizen zu LXX-Jes 7', p. 93.

[36] Eduard Norden, *Die Geburt des Kindes. Geschichte einer religiösen Idee* (SBW 3; Leipzig etc., 1924); Rudolf Kittel, *Die hellenistische Mysterien-religion und das Alte Testament* (BWAT 32; Stuttgart, 1924). See further Hugo Gressmann, *Der Messias* (FRLANT.NF 26; Göttingen 1929).

[37] Seeligmann, *Septuagint Version*, pp. 119–120.

[38] Martin Rösel, 'Die Jungfrauengeburt des endzeitlichen Immanuel. Jesaja 7 in der Übersetzung der Septuaginta', *JBTh* 6 (1991), pp. 135–151.

Although the reference comes from a third-century Christian source,[39] it has its roots, according to Norden, Kittel, and Rösel, in the ancient Egyptian Isis cult.[40] The implication of this interpretation is that both mother and child become transcendental, metaphysical figures, detached from a particular historical setting.[41] In order to support his renewal of the ancient thesis, Rösel not only points to the other variants in LXX-Isaiah 7—the phrase πάλιν ἰάσομαι (7:4), the use of the verb συνίημι (7:9) which has an apocalyptic connotation in the Greek Daniel, and the use of the noun ἀγών (7:13) as signal word for 'religious polemic'[42]—but also to other pagan elements in the Septuagint of Isaiah, such as the morning star Ἑωσφόρος (הֵילֵל בֶּן־שָׁחַר) in Isa 14:12,[43] and the Hellenistic deities for Fortune (Τύχη) and Luck (Δαίμων) in Isa 65:11:[44]

MT	ואתם עזבי יהוה השכחים את הר קדשי הערכים לגד שלחן והממלאים למני ממסך:
NRSV	but you who forsake the Lord, who forget my holy mountain, who set a table for Fortune and fill cups of mixed wine for Destiny.
LXX	ὑμεῖς δὲ οἱ ἐγκαταλιπόντες με καὶ ἐπιλανθανόμενοι τὸ ὄρος τὸ ἅγιόν μου καὶ ἑτοιμάζοντες τῷ δαίμονι τράπεζαν καὶ πληροῦντες τῇ τύχῃ κέρασμα,

---

[39] The work was written between 222 and 235 CE, see Johannes Quasten, *Patrology* 2. *The Ante-Nicene Literature after Irenaeus* (Utrecht etc., 1953), pp. 163–168.

[40] According to Epiphanius, *Panarion* 51.52.5 (GCS vol. 2, p. 284) the winter solstice festival was called Κικέλλια by the Alexandrians, a name that already occurs in the Greek version of the Canopus decree of 238 BCE, line 64. Norden, *Geburt des Kindes*, p. 25, Kittel, *Mysterienreligion*, pp. 21–24, and Rösel, 'Jungfauengeburt', p. 146, conclude that the festival must have been known in Egypt already in the third century BCE.

[41] Rösel, 'Jungfrauengeburt', p. 149.

[42] Rösel, 'Jungfrauengeburt', pp. 136–144.

[43] Rösel, 'Jungfrauengeburt', p. 149, with a reference to Seeligmann, *Septuagint Version*, p. 100. According to Rösel, Ἑωσφόρος was worshiped in Alexandria as protecting deity, but apparently Rösel confuses Ἑωσφόρος with Ἀγαθὸς Δαίμων; see further Cornelia E. Visser, *Götter und Kulte im ptolemäischen Alexandrien* (Amsterdam, 1938), pp. 5–7. As a matter of fact, there is no evidence that there was a cult of the morning star in Alexandria. Only in Hesiodus, *Theogonia* 381, do we find a personification (or: deification) of the morning star. In Callixenus's description of the festival procession in honour of Alexander as transmitted by Athenaeus, *Deipnosophistae* 5.197d, we find the division of the morning star at the opening of the procession, but that in itself does not mean that the morning star was worshiped. It would rather seem, therefore, that the Greek Isaiah demythologizes the ancient Semitic deity. See further Simon B. Parker, 'Shahar', in Karel van der Toorn, Bob Becking, and Pieter W. van der Horst (eds.), *Dictionary of Deities and Demons in the Bible* (2nd ed.; Leiden etc., 1999), cols. 754a–755b.

[44] Martin P. Nilsson, *Geschichte der griechische Religion* 2. *Die hellenistische und römische Zeit* (HAW 5.2; München, 1988), pp. 200–218.

NETS But as for you who forsake me and forget my holy mountain and prepare a table for the demon and fill a mixed drink for Fortune.

The implication of this interpretation of LXX-Isa 7:14–17 is that the Greek translator was influenced by pagan Hellenistic concepts, or, alternatively, that he sought to demythologize such ideas, as argued by Henri Cazelles in another much neglected study of our passage.[45]

4. *Greek Isaiah and the Egyptian-Greek 'prophetical' texts*

On the basis of this small example we have seen that the Greek Isaiah can be studied not only as a document with its own consistent theological agenda (Das Neves, Van der Kooij), but also in the light of the Hebrew and Greek Pentateuch (Troxel), contemporary Jewish texts (Van der Kooij), and contemporary pagan Hellenistic texts. Yet, there is a corpus of texts that is closer in time and space than either the writings of the early church fathers (third century CE) or the Ptolemaic decrees (third century BCE), the Greek Pentateuch (third century BCE), or the Qumran pesharim (first century BCE).

This concerns Egyptian texts written on papyri or ostraca, such as the Oracle of the Potter, the Oracle of the Lamb of Bokchoris, the oracles of Ḥor, and the Dream of Nectanebo.[46] Several of these texts reflect the upheaval caused by the Sixth Syrian war.[47] In 170 BCE Antiochus IV Epiphanes defeated the Ptolemaic army of the young King Ptolemy VI Philometor, and occupied Egypt for two years until Roman pressure forced him to retreat (168 BCE). In the years following these events, not only the temple of Jerusalem was defiled (167 BCE), but Egypt witnessed several years of political instability caused by Egyptian revolts in the *chora* and dynastic rivalry between Ptolemy VI, his sister and wife Cleopatra II, and his brother and successor Ptolemy VII Euergetes II.

[45] Henri Cazelles, 'La Septante d'Is 7,14', in Achille M. Triacca and Alessandro Pistoia (eds.), *La mère de Jésus-Christ et la communion des Saints dans la liturgie. Conférences Saint-Serge XXXIIe semaine d'études liturgiques, Paris, 25–28 juin 1985* (BEL.S 37; Rome, 1986), pp. 45–54.

[46] See the collection of transliterations, translations, and recent scholarly opinions gathered by Andreas Blasius and Bernd U. Schipper (eds.), *Apokalyptik und Ägypten. Eine kritische Analyse der relevanten Texte aus dem griechisch-römischen Ägypten* (OLA 107; Leuven etc., 2002).

[47] Günter Hölbl, *Geschichte des Ptolemäerreiches. Politik, Ideologie und religiöse Kultur von Alexander der Großen bis zur römischen Eroberung* (Darmstadt, 1994), pp. 128–134, and Huß, *Ägypten*, pp. 544–567.

The Egyptian oracles from Hellenistic times have largely been ignored in biblical scholarship. When they are studied, it is usually in the context of the search for the roots of the phenomenon of apocalypticism.[48] However, these texts also have a bearing on our research into the cultural context of the Greek translation of Isaiah. Most of these texts existed both in an Egyptian–Demotic form and a Greek translation. Common to these Egyptian texts is the theme of the expectation of a righteous native leader. These Egyptian Hellenistic texts are furthermore all related to the religious centre of Lower Egypt, the ancient capital city Memphis, and reflect to some extent the political interests of the Memphite priesthood.[49] In a few cases these texts share vocabulary and imagery also attested in the Greek Isaiah, more particularly the passage under discussion, Isa 7:14–17.

4.1. *The Dream of Nectanebo*

The clearest example of a Greek translation of Egyptian prophetical-political literature from the early Hellenistic period comes from the Serapeum archive near Memphis, now housed at the Leiden Museum of Antiquities, and known as UPZ I 81.[50] The Greek text has been

[48] See e.g. J. Gwyn Griffiths, 'Apocalyptic in the Hellenistic Era', in David Hellholm (ed.), *Apocalypticism in the Mediterranean World and the Near East. Proceedings of the International Colloquium on Apocalypticism Uppsala, August 12–17, 1979* (Tübingen, 1983), pp. 273–293; John J. Collins, 'The Sibyl and the Potter: Political Propaganda in Ptolemaic Egypt', in John J. Collins, *Seers, Sybils and Sages in Hellenistic-Roman Judaism* (JSJ.S 54; Leiden etc., 1997), pp. 199–210, and the volume mentioned in the previous footnote as well as the literature mentioned there, pp. 303–306. The theme of the relation between these Greco-Egyptian prophecies and the Greek Isaiah has also been discussed by our honoree—although with a different outlook and scope—in a still unpublished paper: Arie van der Kooij, 'The Old Greek of Isaiah and Other Prophecies Published in Ptolemaic Egypt', in Martin Karrer and Wolfgang Kraus (eds.), *Die Septuaginta-Texte, Theologien, Einflüsse, Projekt Septuaginta Deutsch, Kirchliche Hochschule Wuppertal, 23–27 Juli 2008* (WUNT; Tübingen, forthcoming).

[49] See Dorothy J. Thompson, *Memphis under the Ptolemies* (Princeton, 1988). The author kindly put at my disposal an unpublished lecture from her hand on 'Dreams and Prophecy in Hellenistic Memphis', and drew my attention to the publication of a study dealing with the socio-juridical background of the dream reports from the Serapeum papyri and ostraca: Bernard Lagras, 'Droit et culture dans le Sarapieion de Memphis. Les rêves d'Apollionios fils de Glaukias', in Robert W. Wallace and Michael Gagarin (eds.), *Symposium 2001. Vorträge zur griechischen und hellenistischen Rechtsgeschichte (Evanston, Illinois, 5.–8. september 2001). Papers on Greek and Hellenistic Legal History* (Vienna, 2005), pp. 223–236.

[50] UPZ I 81 = LDAB 6863 = TM 65612. See Ulrich Wilcken, *Urkunden der Ptolemäerzeit (ältere Funde) 1. Papyri aus Unterägypten* (Berlin etc., 1927), pp. 369–374, and Ludwig

identified as a scribal exercise by Apollonius, the younger brother of a Macedonian soldier called Ptolemaeus who had been called by the deity to remain in custody (κατοχή) in the temple devoted to Serapis at Saqqara–Memphis.[51] The copy was made between 160–150 BCE.

The Greek text describes the dream that Pharaoh Nectanebo II had some weeks before the Persian invasion that was to put a definitive end to Pharaonic Egypt. The dream relates the vision of a heavenly court around Isis with the patron deity of Sebbenytos, the home town of Nectanebo II, complaining before Isis the lack of respect paid by the pharaoh to his sanctuary.[52] The pharaoh hastens to fulfil his religious obligations but is unable to avert disaster, since the hieroglyph cutter Petisis spends his money on wine and women instead of providing a suitable sanctuary for the deity.[53] The remainder of the narrative is not preserved, since Apollonius broke off his scribal narrative and produced a scribble.

Due to the Egypticims in this relatively short text,[54] it is clear that the text is in fact a Greek translation of an Egyptian–Demotic original. Thanks to the preliminary publication of several Demotic documents from the Danish Carlsberg collection, it is now beyond doubt that there once existed a Demotic counterpart of the Greek text.[55] The recently discovered texts are four small fragments texts dating from the first or second century CE: P.Carlsberg 562, 424, 499, and 599, the latter three being scribal exercises. Where the Greek and Demotic texts overlap,[56] it is clear that the Demotic text underwent some revision between the original composition and the extant Demotic text. It is likely that the Greek version of the Demotic text is related to the Nectanebo-narrative in the

---

Koenen, 'The Dream of Nektanebos', *BASPap* 22 (1985), pp. 171–194. See further the bibliography in Blasius and Schipper, *Apokalyptik und Ägypten*, pp. 313–314, and the contribution in the same volume by Jörg-Dieter Gauger, 'Der "Traum des Nektanebos"—Die griechische Fassung', pp. 189–219.

[51] See Wilcken, *Urkunden* 1, pp. 1–95, for a detailed and instructive introduction to the Serapeum, its gods, people, and papyri.

[52] UPZ I 81, column ii, line 1–column iii, line 11.

[53] UPZ I 81, column iii, line 11–column v, line 4.

[54] UPZ I 81, col. ii, lines 7–8: πλοῖον παπύρινον, ὃ καλεῖται [l. 8]ἀγυπιστεὶ ῥώψ; col. ii, lines 18–19: ἐν τῷ ἀδύτωι τῶι καλουμένοι Φέρσωι. For the rare word ῥώψ, related to Demotic *rms*, see Steve Vinson, *The Nile Boatman at Work* (Münchener Ägyptologische Studien 48; Mainz, 1998), p. 18, n. 28. See further Koenen, 'Dream of Nektanebos', p. 172, n. 5.

[55] Kim Ryholt, 'Nectanebo's Dream or The Prophecy of Petesis', in Blasius and Schipper, *Apokalyptik und Ägypten*, pp. 221–241.

[56] UPZ I 81, column ii, line 1–column iii, line 11, and P.Carlsberg 562, lines 1–10.

Alexander romance attributed to Callisthenes.[57] In this story Nectanebo becomes a sorcerer-king who flees from Egypt to Macedonia, enchants Olympias and becomes father of Alexander the Great. Due to the fragmentary state of the Greek and Demotic papyri it is unclear whether this story formed part of the Dream of Nectanebo. If so, it would have formed a counterpart to Isaiah's narrative of the birth of the marvellous child Immanuel (Isa 7:14–17).

The extant fragments provide a parallel to another part of the Book of Isaiah, i.e. the opening vision in Isaiah 6, where Isaiah sees the God of Israel seated on the throne and encircled by seraphs. Like the narrative of Nectanebo's dream, as well as many other literary compositions from the ancient Near East, such as the Akkadian Enuma Elish, the Aramaic visions of Bileʿam from Deir ʿAlla,[58] the Hebrew Book of Job, the Aramaic visions of Ḥor, son of Punesh,[59] and the Demotic stories of the high priests of Memphis,[60] such a vision functions as the ominous opening of a tragic story. Although the details of the elevated divine throne, the circle of heavenly beings at the right-hand and left-hand side of that throne, and the messenger of that council all belong to the stock vocabulary of that genre, it is nevertheless striking to see the collocation of terms attested both in the Dream of Nectanebo and the Greek Isaiah, Isa 6:1–4:

MT בשנת מות המלך עזיהו ואראה את אדני ישב על כסא רם ונשא ושוליו מלאים את ההיכל: שרפים עמדים ממעל לו ... וינעו אמות הספים מקול הקורא והבית ימלא עשן:

NRSV [1]In the year that King Uzziah died, I saw the Lord sitting on a throne, high and lofty; and the hem of his robe filled the temple. [2]Seraphs were in attendance above him ....[4] The pivots of the threshold shook at the voices of those who called, and the house was filled with smoke.

[57] See e.g. Wilhelm Kroll (ed.), *Pseudo-Callisthenes. Historia Alexandri Magni* 1. *Recensio vetusta* (Berlin, 1926); Leif Bergson, *Der griechische Alexanderroman. Rezension β* (SGS 3; Stockholm, 1965). See further Koenen, 'Dream of Nektanebos', pp. 172–173, 192–193.

[58] Jaap Hoftijzer and Gerrit van der Kooij, *Aramaic Texts from Deir ʿAlla* (DMOA 19; Leiden, 1976).

[59] Bezalel Porten and Ada Yardeni, *Textbook of Aramaic Documents from Ancient Egypt Newly Copied, Edited and Translated into Hebrew and English* 3. *Literature, Accounts, Lists* (Textbook of Aramaic Documents from Ancient Egypt; Winona Lake, Ind., 1993), number C1.2, pp. 54–57.

[60] Francis L. Griffith, *Stories of the High Priests of Memphis. The Sethon of Herodotus and the Demotic Tales of Khamuas* (Oxford, 1900), pp. 150–157.

LXX [1]Καὶ ἐγένετο τοῦ ἐνιαυτοῦ, οὗ ἀπέθανεν Οζιας ὁ βασιλεύς, εἶδον τὸν κύριον καθήμενον ἐπὶ θρόνου ὑψηλοῦ καὶ ἐπηρμένου, καὶ πλήρης ὁ οἶκος τῆς δόξης αὐτοῦ. [2]καὶ σεραφιν εἱστήκεισαν κύκλῳ αὐτοῦ, … [4]καὶ ἐπήρθη τὸ ὑπέρθυρον ἀπὸ τῆς φωνῆς, ἧς ἐκέκραγον, καὶ ὁ οἶκος ἐπλήσθη καπνοῦ.

NETS [1]And it happened in the year that King Ozias died that I saw the Lord sitting on a throne, lofty and raised up, and the house was full of his glory. [2]And seraphim stood around him; … [4]And the lintel was raised at the voice with which they cried out, and the house was filled with smoke.

In the Dream of Nectanebo we find a similar overture with the elements of date, temple, throne (θρόνος), seating (κάθημαι), glory (δόξα), and divine entourage standing around ([παρ-]ίστημι κύκλῳ) the (major) Deity:

COL. II [l. 1]Ἔτους ιϛ Φαρμοῦθι κᾱ εἰς τὴν κβ̄ [l. 2]κατὰ θεὸν διὰ δεχομενιαν. Νεκτοναβὼς [l. 3]τοῦ βασιλέως καταγινομένου ἐΜέμφει καὶ θυσίαν [l. 4]ποτὲ συβτελεσμένου καὶ ἀξιώσαντος τοῦς [l. 5]θεοὺς δηλῶσαι αὐτῶι τὰ ἐνεστηκότα ἔδοξεν [l. 6]κατ’ ἐνύπνον πλοῖον παπύρινον, ὃ καλεῖται [l. 7]ἀγυπτιστεὶ ῥώψ, προσορμῆσαι εἰς Μέμφιν, [l. 8]ἐφ’ οὗ ἦν θρόνος μέγας, ἐπὶ τε τούτου καθῆσαι [l. 9]τὴν μεγαλώδοξον εὐεργέτειαν καρπῶν [l. 10]εὐεργέτιαν καὶ θεῶν ἄνασον Ἶσιν καὶ τοὺς [l. 11]ἐν Ἀγύπτῳ θεοὺς πάντας παραστάναι αὐτῇ [l. 12]ἐγ δεξιῶν καὶ εὐωμένων αὐτῆς, ἕνα δὲ [l. 13]προελθόντα εἰς τὸ μέσον, οὗ ὑπολάμβανον εἶναι [l. 14]τὸ μέγεθος πηχῶν εἴκοσι ἑνὸς τὸν ποσαγορευ-[l. 15]όμενον ἀγυπτιστεὶ Ὀνοῦρει, ἑλληνιστεὶ δὲ [l. 16]Ἄρης πεσόντα ἐπὶ κοιλίαν λέγιν τάδε· …

[l. 1]In the 16th (regal) year on the 21th to the 22nd (day) of the (month) Pharmouthi (i.e. on July 5–6, 343 BCE) [l. 2]after the Deity in the full month (the Demotic text is considerably longer here). After Nectanebo [l. 3]the king had gone to Memphis and had brought a [l. 4]sacrifice and had prayed to the [l. 6]gods to reveal the future, there appeared to him [l. 6]in a dream a papyrus boat (P.Carlsberg 562, line 3: *i.ir=f p[r-r=f n rswy)* called [l. 7]in Egyptian *roops*, coming to anchor at Memphis, [l. 8]on which (P.Carlsberg 562, line 4: *ḥr-ꜣtꜣ[=f)*was a great throne; on it was seated [l. 9]the greatly honored, [l. 10]benefactress of fruits and commandress of gods, Isis, while [l. 11]all the gods of Egypt were standing around her [l. 12]at the right-hand and left-hand side of her. One of them [l. 13]came forward to the middle (P.Carlsberg 562, line 5: *ḫꜣʿ wʿ ntr ʿꜣ [rdwy.ṯ=f r tꜣ mrty)*, with the estimated [l. 14]size of 21 feet tall, called [l. 15]in Egyptian Onouris, in Greek however [l. 16]Ares, he fell on his belly and said: …

Perhaps a relation exists between the stress on the vertical dimensions in the Egyptian text (a high throne, a huge figure),[61] and the fact that the

[61] See Koenen, ‘Dream of Nektanebos’, p. 185, n. 99.

Greek translator of Isaiah substituted the horizontal dimension in Isa 6:4 with the heavy doors of the Temple shaking open (וינעו אמות הספים) for a vertical one (ἐπήρθη τὸ ὑπέρθυρον).

Although the preserved fragments of the Dream of Nectanebo in Demotic and Greek do not contain the fulfilment part of this prophetical introduction, there can be no doubt that the narrative continued to describe the evils that were to fall upon Egypt in 343 BCE and probably also the liberation of Egypt from the Persians by Alexander the Great. Unlike the Hebrew and Greek versions of the Book of Isaiah the Egyptian and Greek versions of this narrative were probably produced not long after one another. It is further noteworthy to see the emphasis on priestly elements in both the Book of Isaiah and the Dream of Nectanebo, as the latter explains the loss of Egyptian autonomy as the result of neglect of the ritual duties. The religious capital of (Lower) Egypt, Memphis, is mentioned explicitly in this text.

4.2. *The Oracle of the Lamb of Bokchoris and the Oracle of the Potter*

The element of fulfilment prophecy can be detected in two Egyptian prophetical texts called the Oracle of the Lamb and the Oracle of the Potter.

The title 'Oracle of the Lamb of Bokchoris' refers to a composition now consisting of four fragments found in Soknopaiou Nesos (present-day Dime) in the Fayum oasis and at present preserved in the Austrian national library under inventory number Pap.Vindob. D 10000.[62] The text was copied in year 4 CE by a scribe called *Ḫtbꜣ*. It tells the story of a learned scribe called Psinyris (*Pꜣ-sꜣ-n-ḥr*) who finds a book with prophecies of doom over Egypt (column 1). In a part of the story that has not been preserved a speaking lamb is introduced (perhaps in a vision or dream in a temple?). The lamb gives further predictions of doom (column 2) and mentions the rule of 2 years by 'someone who is not ours' over against 'someone who is ours' who rules for fifty-five years (column 2, line 5). The text further bemoans the children and women

---

[62] The most recent transliteration of the Demotic text is offered by Karl-Theodor Zauzich, 'Das Lamm des Bokchoris', in *Papyrus Erzherzog Rainer (P.Rainer Cent.). Festschrift zum 100-jährigen Bestehen der Papyrussammlung der Österreichischen Nationalbibliothek* (Wien, 1983), pp. 165–174, hence the abbreviation P.Rainer Cent. 3 (= TM 4888). A German translation with survey of scholarly opinions is offered by Heinz-Josef Thissen, 'Das Lamm des Bokchoris', in Blasius and Schipper, *Apokalyptik und Ägypten*, pp. 113–138.

that are taken captive to Syria (column 2, lines 12–14) and mentions seven Egyptian cities that will weep (column 2, lines 15–18: Heliopolis, Bubastis, Nilupolis, Abydos,[63] Memphis, Thebes, Letopolis). After the list of curses the lamb promises that after a period of 900 years fortune will return to Egypt: the 'Mede' (*pꜣ Mty*) will turn back from Egypt (column 2, line 21) and the stolen statues of the Egyptian gods will return from 'Nineveh in the nome of the Assyrians' (*Nnywꜣ pꜣ tš pꜣ Išʿr*, column 2, line 23–column 3, line 1) and the Egyptians that have survived the catastrophes will rejoice. After these predictions the lamb dies. Psinyris reports all these predictions to Pharaoh Bokchoris, who reads the book with curses. Finally, the lamb receives a royal burial (column 3, lines 5–10) and the text closes with a colophon indicating title, scribe, and the year of copying.

Biblical scholars will find parallels between this story and that of the discovery of the scroll in the time of King Josiah (2 Kgs 22) and will be reminded of the story of a speaking ass in the Balaam narrative (Num 22). For our research it is noteworthy that the predictions of the lamb seem to employ an image known only from the Book of Isaiah (1:8), i.e. the comparison of a city razed to the ground like a cucumber field (מקשה), which in column 2, line 17 of the Oracle of the lamb is called 'a bundle of cucumbers and gourds' (*be bnṯy špy*).[64]

More important for the present search for contemporary Egyptian Hellenistic parallels for the Greek Isaiah is the fact that the Demotic Oracle of the Lamb has a counterpart in another Egyptian composition called 'The Oracle of the Potter'.[65] This composition is extant in five fragmentary papyri. Although all of these papyri are written in Greek, there is no doubt

---

[63] According to Jaroslav Černý, *Coptic Etymological Dictionary* (Cambridge, 1976), p. 356, the word *Wpky*, Coptic ΟΥΠΩΚΕ, literally 'district of the *pḳr* tree', refers to the 'sacred district at Abydos in which lay the tomb of Osiris'. For the sake of convenience I therefore adopted the translation 'Abydos'.

[64] Thissen, 'Das Lamm des Bokchoris', p. 118: 'ein Gebüsch von Gurken und Kürbissen', following a reading by Joachim F. Quack, 'Korrekturvorschläge zu einigen demotischen literarischen Texten', *Enchoria* 21 (1994), pp. 63–72, esp. p. 72.

[65] The main publication is still that by Ludwig Koenen, 'Die Prophezeiungen des Töpfers', *ZPE* 2 (1968), pp. 178–209, in which Koenen offers a new reading of the Greek papyri. In the years following this publication, Koenen and others have proposed several corrections to this edition, see now Ludwig Koenen, 'Die Apologie des Töpfers an König Amenophis oder das Töpferorakel', in Blasius and Schipper, *Apokalyptik und Ägypten*, pp. 139–187, and the bibliography in *ibid.*, pp. 312–313. A helpful English translation based upon Koenen, 'Prophezeiungen', with several emendations is offered by Allen Kerkeslager, 'The Apology of the Potter: A Translation of the Potter's Oracle', in Irene

that the composition is a translation of a Demotic original.[66] Perhaps the unpublished Demotic Papyrus EA 10660 from the British Museum contains fragments of this Demotic *Vorlage*.[67] The five papyri are: P_1: a papyrus dating from the last third of the second century CE now preserved in Vienna (P.Graf G. 29787) containing the beginning of the framing narrative and the prophecies,[68] P_2: another Vienna papyrus dating from the third century CE (P.Rainer G. 19813),[69] containing the end of the prophecies and the framing narrative; P_3: a late-third century CE Oxyrhynchus papyrus (P.Oxy. XXII 2332),[70] with a section of prophecies that correspond considerably with the prophecy section of P_2; P_4: a short fragment dating from the third or second century BCE with a very anti-Jewish tone;[71] and P_5: another, still unpublished, Oxyrhynchus papyrus.[72] Although these texts form part of the same composition, they reveal several variants reflecting a process of reinterpretation.

The composition relates the prophecies of a potter who became possessed by the god Hermes in the time of King Amenophis.[73] When the

---

Shirun-Grumach (ed.), *Jerusalem Studies in Egyptology* (Wiesbaden, 1998), pp. 67–79. A new edition of all available material incorporating all the new readings still remains a *desideratum*.

66 Koenen, 'Prophezeiungen', p. 178; Kerkeslager, 'Apology of the Potter', p. 68. See the 'colophon' at the end of P_2, col. ii: [l. 54]Ἀπολογία κεραμέως {μεθηρμενευμέ̣ν̣η} [l. 55]πρὸ̣[ς] Ἀμενῶπιν τ̣ὸ̣ν βασιλέα, ⟨μεθηρμενευμένη⟩ κατ̣ὰ̣ τ̣ὸ [l. 56]δ̣υν[α]τ̣ό[ν] περὶ τῶν τῇ Α̣ἰ̣γύπ-τῳ̣ [με]λ̣λ̣ό̣ν̣-[l. 57]τ̣ων. '[l. 54]The Potter's Defense [l. 55]made to Amenophis the king, translated as best as possible. Concerning the things that will happen in [l. 57]Egypt'.

67 Carol A.R. Andrews, 'Unpublished Demotic Papyri in the British Museum', *EVO* 17 (1994), pp. 29–37, esp. pp. 29–31 = TM 55544.

68 Editio princeps: Carl Wessely, *Neue griechische Zauberpapyrus* (DAWW.PH 42; Vienna, 1893), pp. 3–6; Re-editions: Ulrich Wilcken, 'Zur aegyptischen Prophetie', *Hermes* 40 (1905), pp. 544–560; Robert Reitzenstein and H.H. Schaeder, *Studien zum antiken Synkretismus aus Iran und Griechenland* (SBW 7; Leipzig etc., 1926), pp. 38–68; Georgius Manteuffel, *De opusculis graecis aegypti e papyris, ostracis lapidibusque collectis* (Prace Towarzystwa Naukowego Warszawskiego 12; Warsaw, 1930), pp. 29–34, 99–106; and Koenen, 'Apologie des Töpfers'. See further LDAB 9911 and TM 68639.

69 Wessely, *Neue griechische Zauberpapyri*; Manteuffel, *De opusculis*; Koenen, 'Prophezeiungen'. LDAB 5142 = TM 63927.

70 Colin H. Robertson, 'The Oracle of the Potter', in E. Lobel and Colin H. Roberts, *The Oxyrhynchus Papyri* 22 (PEES.GR 31; London, 1954), pp. 89–99.

71 PSI VIII 982 = CPJ III 520 = LDAB 5250 = TM 64035.

72 See Koenen, 'Apologie des Töpfers', p. 140, note 4; pp. 162–163, n. 88.

73 P_1 line 17. It remains unclear which of the four pharaoh's of the eighteenth dynasty (New Kingdom) is meant: Amenophis I Djeserkare (according to the low chronology 1525–1504 BCE), Amenophis II Aacheperoere (1425–1398 BCE), Amenophis III Nebma'atre (1390–1352 BCE), or his son Amenophis IV Nefercheperoere (1352–1336 BCE) better known as Echnaton. Koenen, 'Prophezeiungen', p. 182, pleads for the first king, Amenophis, who legitimized his rise to power on the basis of the much older Prophecy

potter is brought before the pharaoh at his visit of the temple of Isis and Osiris on the island of Helios, he announces a long list of oracles of doom: Egypt will be subdued by foreigners who carry the code-names 'Typhonians' (Τυφώνιοι) and 'belt-wearers' (ζωνοφόροι). Among these oracles are the predictions of the defeat of the Egyptian king, the introduction of new gods, loss of temple revenues, drought, embarrassment of the sun, bad harvests, fratricide, migration, revolt in the chora, murder, and infanticide. Once the social hierarchy is completely disrupted,[74] the tides turn and the belt-wearers start to slay themselves,[75] after which the Good Fortune (Ἀγαθὸς Δαίμων) returns to Memphis, while the city of the belt-wearers remains abandoned like a drying place for fisherman. The stolen cult images will return to Egypt, the divinely appointed king will rule for fifty-five years and the harmony in nature will be restored. Having uttered his prophecies of doom and salvation, the potter dies, just as the Lamb died immediately after delivering his oracles.

The Greek wording of these oracles show some striking similarities with the Greek text of Isaiah, particularly the oracle over Egypt (Isaiah 19), where we find the same prediction of the drying up of the Nile and the disharmony between land and sowing (Isa 19:5–7):

MT ונשתו מים מהים ונהר יחרב ויבש: והאזניחו נהרות דללו וחרבו יארי מצור קנה וסוף קמלו: ערות על יאור על פי יאור וכל מזרע יאור ייבש ואיננו:

NRSV The waters of the Nile will be dried up, and the river will be parched and dry; its canals will become foul, and the branches of Egypt's Nile will diminish and dry up, reeds and rushes will rot away. There will be bare places by the Nile, on the brink of the Nile; and all that is sown.

LXX καὶ πίονται οἱ Αἰγύπτιοι ὕδωρ τὸ παρὰ θάλασσαν, ὁ δὲ ποταμὸς ἐκλείψει καὶ ξηρανθήσεται· καὶ ἐκλείψουσιν οἱ ποταμοὶ καὶ αἱ διώρυγες τοῦ ποταμοῦ, καὶ ξηρανθήσεται πᾶσα συναγωγὴ ὕδατος καὶ ἐν παντὶ ἕλει καλάμου καὶ παπύρου· καὶ τὸ ἄχι τὸ χλωρὸν πᾶν τὸ κύκλῳ τοῦ ποταμοῦ καὶ πᾶν τὸ σπειρόμενον διὰ τοῦ ποταμοῦ ξηρανθήσεται ἀνεμόφθορον.

NETS And the Egyptians will drink water that is by the sea, but the river will fail and be dried up, and the rivers and the canals of the river will fail, and every gathering of water, even in every marsh of reed and papyrus, will be dried up. And the green marsh, all that is around the river and all that is sown by the river, will be dried up, blasted by the wind.

---

of Neferty, a text with a similar structure and context as the Oracle of the Potter, see Hans Goedicke, *The Protocol of Neferyt (The Prophecy of Neferti)* (John Hopkins Near Eastern Studies; Baltimore, 1977).

[74] P_3 column 2, lines 45–46.

[75] P_2 column 1, lines 27–28 = P_3 column 2, ll. 49–50.

It has long been noted that the Greek version of Isaiah not only differs in several aspects from the Hebrew text, but also that the Greek Isaiah reflects typically Egyptian terms and words, known from the documentary and magical papyri from Egypt.[76] It has not been noted, however, that this image has a striking parallel in the Oracle of the Potter:

P3 COL. I διὰ τὴν τοῦ Νείλου ἔνδειαν ἡ ἄτοκος [l. 14][γ]ῆ̣ ἐκ̣φ̣θ̣α̣ρ̣εῖ̣σ̣α̣ ἔ̣σ̣ται ἀ̣π̣ο̣τ̣ὲ τόκυῖα. ... [(l. 18)]ἡ̣ γῆ οὐ συμ-[l. 19]φ⌊ωνήσει τοῖς⌋ σ⌊πέρμ⌋ασιν· ἔσται τὰ πλεῖστα ταύτης ἀνεμό-[l. 20]φ̣⟨θ⟩ο̣ρ̣α̣.

On account of the insufficiency of the Nile the barren [l. 14]land will utterly be ruined after it has given birth ⟨i.e. to seedling plants⟩. ... The land will not [l. 19]harmonize with the seeds. The majority of its things[77] will be destroyed by the [l. 20]wind.

P2 COL. I [l. 1]ὁ δὲ π̣[ο]τ̣αμὸς [l. 2][ἐλεύσεται οὐκ ἔχων ἱκα]νὸν ὑδάτιον, ἀλλ' ὀλίγον, ὥ[σ]τε πυ̣[ρ]ε̣ύ̣εσθαι [l. 3][τὴν γῆν ὑπὸ τοῦ ἡλίου], ἀλλὰ παρὰ φύσιν. ...[(l. 7)] ἡ̣ γῆ οὐ συμφων⌋ή̣σει τοῖς σπόρ̣οις· ἔσται τὰ π̣[λεῖ]στα τ̣α̣ύ̣τ̣⌊ῆ⌋ς [l. 8]⌊ἀνεμόφθορα⌋.

And the [ri]ver [l. 2][will come not having adequ]ate water, but a little, s[o] that [the land] will be scorched [l. 3][...] but unnaturally. ...[(l. 7)] The land will not harmonize with the seeds. The majority of its things will be destroyed by the [l. 8]wind.

Likewise, the Greek version of the prediction that the Egyptians will rise against another is (Isa 19:2) differs somewhat from the Hebrew text, but introduces the typically Egyptian administrative concept of the νομός, 'district':[78]

MT וסכסכתי מצרים במצרים ונלחמו איש באחיו ואיש ברעהו עיר בעיר ממלכה בממלכה:

NRSV I will stir up Egyptians against Egyptians, and they will fight, one against the other, neighbor against neighbor, city against city, kingdom against kingdom;

LXX καὶ ἐπεγερθήσονται Αἰγύπτιοι ἐπ' Αἰγυπτίους καὶ πολεμήσει ἄνθρωπος τὸν ἀδελφὸν αὐτοῦ καὶ ἄνθρωπος τὸν πλησίον αὐτοῦ πόλις ἐπὶ πόλιν καὶ νομὸς ἐπὶ νομόν.

NETS And Egyptians will be stirred up against the Egyptians, and a man will war against his brother, and a man against his neighbour, city against city and *nomos* against *nomos*.

---

[76] See Ziegler, *Untersuchungen*, pp. 189–191 (ἕλος, κάλαμος, πάπυρος, ἄχι, συναγωγὴ ὕδατος, διῶρυξ) and Louis Robert, 'Ἀνεμοφθορία', *Hell(P)* 9 (1950), p. 63 (n. 1).

[77] See Koenen, 'Die Apologie des Topfers', p. 154, n. 38, for the new reading of this line.

[78] Ziegler, *Untersuchungen*, 192.

Again, there is a striking counterpart in the Oracle of the Potter:

P3 COL. I τ⸤ο⸥ύ̣τ̣ο̣υ̣ τοῦ γέν̣[ο]υ̣ς [l. 24][πόλεμος καὶ φόνος ἀσεβ]ὴ̣ς ἔ̣σ̣τ̣αι τῶν ἀδελφῶν [l. 25][καὶ τῶν γαμετῶν· ἐπεὶ ὁ] Κμῆφις[79] ἐβουλ̣ήθη εἰς τὴν [l. 26][πόλιν ἀνελθ]⸤εῖν καὶ ἑαυτο⸥ὺ̣ς οἱ ζωνοφόροι ἀνελοῦσι⟨ν⟩ ὄν-[l. 27] [τες Τυφώνιοι.

During this genera[ti]on [l. 24]there will be [war and im[1]pi]ous murder of brothers [l. 25][and of wives. For] Kmephis has decided to [l. 26][return] to the city. And the belt-wearers, be[ing Typhonians], will slay themselves.

Whereas these images for doom over Egypt are rather general, the Oracle of the Potter and the Greek Bible (Ezek 26:4–5, 14, Ezekiel's dirge over Tyre) also share a unique image, viz. that of the deserted city turned into a drying place for fishermen (ψυγμὸς ἁλιέων):[80]

P2 COL. II ἥ τε παραθαλάσσιος πόλις ψυγμ[ὸς] ἁλιέων ἔσται διὰ [l. 36]τ[ὸ] τὸν Ἀγαθὸν Δαίμονα καὶ Κνῆφιν εἰς [Μ]έμφιν πεπορεῦσθαι, [l. 37]ὥ̣σ̣τε τινας διερχομένους λέγειν· «αὕτη π̣[ό]λις ἦν παντοτρόφος, [l. 38]εἰς ἣν κατοικίσθη πᾶν γένος ἀνδρῶν.»

And the city by the sea will be a drying pl[ace] for fishermen because [l. 36]the Agathos Daimon and Knephis will have gone away to [M]emphis, [l. 37]so that some passing will say, 'This ci[t]y was nourisher of all, [l. 38]into which was settled every nationality of men'.

EZEK 26 [4]καὶ καταβαλοῦσιν τὰ τείχη Σορ καὶ καταβαλοῦσι τοὺς πύργους σου, καὶ λικμήσω τὸν χοῦν αὐτῆς ἀπ' αὐτῆς καὶ δώσω αὐτὴν εἰς λεωπετρίαν [5]ψυγμὸς σαγηνῶν ἔσται ἐν μέσῳ θαλάσσης, … [14]καὶ δώσω σε εἰς λεωπετρίαν, ψυγμὸς σαγηνῶν ἔσῃ· οὐ μὴ οἰκοδομηθῇς ἔτι, ὅτι ἐγὼ ἐλάλησα, λέγει κύριος.

And they shall overthrow the walls of Sor and cast down its towers, and I will winnow its soil from it and render it as a bare rock, and it shall be a drying-place for dragnets in the midst of the sea (משטח הרמים תהיה בתוך

[79] In his 1968 edition, 'Die Prophezeiungen', Koenen reconstructed καὶ τῶν γαμετῶν· ὁ γὰρ] Μ̣ῆφις. He changed it in his 2002 re-edition into the present text. The text of P_2 differs somewhat from P_3: τούτο⸤υ τοῦ⸥ γ⸤ένο⸥υς [l. 11][πόλεμός τε καὶ φόνος] ἔσται, ὃς καὶ τοὺς ἀδελφοὺ[ς] καὶ̣ [τοὺς γα]μετὰ⟨ς⟩ [l. 12][ἀνελεῖ· ταῦτα ἔσται γ]άρ, ἐπεὶ ὁ μέγας θεὸς Ἥφα[ισ]τ̣ος ἐ̣⸤β⸥ο̣⸤υ⸥λήθη [l. 13]⸤εἰς τὴν⸥ [πόλιν ἀνελθ]εῖν καὶ ἑαυτοὺς οἱ ζωνοφόροι ἀνε̣λ̣ο̣ῦσι⟨ν⟩ ὄν-[l. 14][τες Τυφώνιοι. 'During this generation [l. 11]there will be [both war and murder] which [will slay] even brothers and [wi]ves. [l. 12]Fo[r these things will happen] when the great god Hepha[es]tos has decided [l. 13][to return] to the [city]. And the belt-wearers, be[ing Typhonians], will slay themselves'.

[80] Kerkeslager, 'Apologie of the Potter', p. 77, n. 69. The word ψυγμός occurs almost exclusively in Greek documentary papyri, see Friedrich Preisigke, *Wörterbuch der griechischen Papyrusurkunden mit Einschluß der griechischen Inschriften, Aufschriften, Ostraka, Mumienschilder usw. aus Ägypten* 2 (Berlin, 1927), col. 773.

הים) ... And I will give you as bare rock; you shall be a drying-place for dragnets. You shall never again be built, for I have spoken, says the Lord.

Even where the Oracle of the Potter and the Greek version of Isaiah 19 differ, i.e. in the appreciation of cult-images, they share the same terminology. Unlike the other Greek words employed by the Septuagint translators for foreign cult image, such as εἴδωλον, εἰκών, γλυπτός, βδέλυγμα, χώνευμα, we find the common Greek word for cult image, ἄγαλμα, a word that seems to be avoided by the Greek translators of Hebrew Scripture,[81] both in the Oracle of the Potter and LXX-Isa 19:3:

P2 COL. II l. 34τ˪ὰ ἀγά˩[λμ]ατα ἐκεῖ μετενεχθέντα πάλιν ἐ[πα]νήξει ἐπὶ τὴν l. 35 Αἴγυπ̣τ̣ον.

l. 34The cu[lt imag]es that have been transferred there[82] will come back to l. 35Egypt again.

ISA 19:3 καὶ ταραχθήσεται τὸ πνεῦμα τῶν Αἰγυπτίων ἐν αὐτοῖς, καὶ τὴν βουλὴν αὐτῶν διασκεδάσω, καὶ ἐπερωτήσουσιν τοὺς θεοὺς αὐτῶν καὶ τὰ ἀγάλματα αὐτῶν καὶ τοὺς ἐκ τῆς γῆς φωνοῦντας καὶ τοὺς ἐγγαστριμύθους.

and the spirit of the Egyptians will be troubled within them, and I will scatter their council, and they will consult their gods and images (ודרשו אל האלילים ואל האטים) and those who speak out of the earth and the ventriloquists.

Even more important than these agreements in wording is the fact that both the Greek Isaiah, the Oracle of the Potter, and the Oracle of the Lamb share a common enemy: the Syrian king. In the middle of these prophecies[83] we find a contrast between the Syrian king who will be hateful to all men and will rule for two years and the autochthonous king who will rule for fifty-five years, as predicted by the lamb in the time of King Bokchoris:

---

[81] The word ἄγαλμα occurs in the Greek Bible only in LXX-Isa 19:3, 21:9; EpBar 4:34; 2 Macc 2:2.

[82] There, that is: to Alexandria, the city of the foreigners. The statues will return home to Memphis. Koenen 'Die Apologie des Topfers', p. 159, n. 60, shows how the phrase transforms the ancient royal ideology of the king bringing back the stolen gold images to an inner-Egyptian perspective.

[83] P2 column 1, ll. 16–20 = P3 column 1, ll. 30–33.

P3 COL. I καὶ κ]⸤αθήξει δ' ἐ⸥κ̣ Σ̣υρί̣α̣ς [ὁ] βασιλεύς, ὃς l. 31[ἔσται] ⸤μισητὸς πᾶ⸥ιν ἀνθρώποις. ὁ δὲ δύο[84] (col. ii) l. 32οὐκ ἦν ἡμέτερος· ὁ δὲ τὰ πεντήκοντα πέντε ἔτη l. 33{κοντα πέντη ἔτη} ἡμέτερος ὑπάρχων τοῖς Ἕλλησ⟨ι τελ⟩εῖ l. 34τὰ κακά, ἃ̣ Β̣αχάρι ἀ̣π̣ή̣γ̣γ̣ε̣ι̣λ̣εν ὁ ἀμ{μ}νός.}

l. 30[And] a king will [co]me down out of Syria who l. 31[will be] hateful to all men. And [the one (ruling) for two years] l. 32was not ours. But the one (ruling) for fifty-five years l. 33{ }, because he is ours, will bring to the Greeks l. 34the evils which the lam{m}b announced to [B]acharis.

P2 COL. I καὶ κ]α̣θήξει δὲ ἐκ Συρίας, ὃ⟨ς⟩ μισ̣ητὸ̣ς ἔ̣σ̣τ̣α̣ι πᾶσι(ν) l. 17⸤ἀνθρ⸥ώ⸤ποις⸥ [καὶ..]. ολης ὑπάρχων καὶ ἀπὸ Αἰθ̣[ι]ο̣π̣ί̣α̣ς τε̣ l. 18[καθή]ξ[ει ....] αὐτὸς ἐκ τῶ̣ν̣ ἀνοσίων εἰς Αἴγυπτον κ̣αὶ κ̣α̣θ̣-l. 19[εσθή]σ̣εται̣ [ἐν πόλει, ἣ] ὕ̣στερον ἐρημωθήσεται. {ὁ δὲ τὰ δύο οὐκ ἦ⟨ν ἡ⟩μέ-l. 20⸤τερο⸥ς̣ τοῖ[ς Ἕλλησι τε]λῶν ⟨τὰ⟩ κ̣ε̣χ̣ρ̣η̣μένα̣, ἀμ{μ}νός τ̣ε̣ἔφη καλῶς.}[85]

And the one who will be hateful to all men [and abominable] [will c]ome down out of Syria. l. 17And also from Eth[i]opia l. 18[another one who is] himself from the unholy ones will [come d]o[wn ...] to Egypt. And he l. 19will set[tle in the city which] later will be made desolate. And the one (ruling) for two (years) l. 20was [not o]urs, who brought to the Greeks prophecies (into fulfilment), as ⟨the⟩ la{}mb spoke well.

The two versions of this prophecy agree with respect to the domination of the hateful king of the Syrians over Egypt for the period of two years and the reference to the oracle of the lamb. As a matter of fact, the preserved text of this older Demotic text does contain this prediction:

COL. II l. 5[.....] ... [*ḥry*] ... [*pa-tꜣ-2.t nty bn iw*] *pꜣy=n in pꜣy pa-tꜣ-55 pꜣ nty iw pꜣy=n* [*pa-tꜣ-sḥny.t*]

... The one of 2 (years?), who is not ours. The one of 55 years is ours (?) ...

It is important to note that the P_2 version of the Oracle of the Potter only mentions the prophecy of the two-year rule of the Syrian king and omits the period of the fifty-five years rule of the autochthonous ruler, whereas it adds the element of another unholy figure from Ethiopia. Although it is difficult to establish the literary priority of the versions of the Oracle of the Potter, it is clear that we find re-interpretations of an older oracle, i.e. the Oracle of the Lamb. Scholars have been divided regarding the application of these two references.[86] The combination of the prophecy as we find it in the Oracle of the Lamb and the application

[84] Koenen, 'Prophezeiungen', p. 203, originally read: {[ἐ]κ̣ε̣ῖ̣[νο]ς δ̣ὲ̣.

[85] Koenen, 'Prophezeiungen', p. 202, originally read: {ὁ δὲ τὰ δύο ἔ̣[τ]η̣ ἡμέ-l. 20⸤τερο⸥ς̣ τοι[..... κα]λ̣ῶ̣ς̣.[.].....μ̣ένα ⟨ὁ⟩ ἀμ{ω}νός τε ἔφη καλῶς.}

[86] Koenen, 'Prophezeiungen', pp. 187–193, considered the reference to the Syrian to

to the hateful one coming from Syria in P_2 makes it very likely, to my mind, that the author of the Oracle of the Potter had the figure of Antiochus IV Epiphanes in mind who occupied Egypt for two years (170–168 BCE).[87] The fact that the reference to the fifty-five years rule of an autochthonous ruler as found in the Oracle of the Lamb and in P_2 gave way to a polemic against an Egyptian impious ruler, may perhaps reflect a polemic against the unpopular King Ptolemy VII Euergetes II, who ruled for fifty-four years (170–116 BCE).[88] If this is true, we have an interesting parallel between the Greek Isaiah and the contemporary Egyptian–Greek prophetical text in as far as they both apply oracles of doom to the figure of Antiochus IV Epiphanes. We would then have an interesting parallel to the phenomenon of fulfilment interpretation in a non-Jewish document from a relatively early Hellenistic period.

The comparison can perhaps be extended to the Assyrian period for the original non-Greek compositions as well. The Demotic text of the Oracle of the Lamb may very well have been composed before the Hellenistic period. A clue that this composition goes back to an earlier, probably Persian period, comes from a reference in the historical work *Aigyptiaka* of the Egyptian High Priest Manetho (*c.* 280 BCE), who mentioned the speaking lamb during the reign of King Bokchoris: Βόχχωρις Σαΐτης, ἔτη ϛ', ἐφ' οὗ ἀρνίον ἀφθέγξατο.[89] This Pharaoh Bokchoris (*c.* 717–

be an allusion to the Sixth Syrian War, the reference to the Ethiopian ruler to be an allusion to the rule of the Egyptian pharaoh Harsiesis (131–130 BCE) and the reference to the rule of fifty-five years to be a symbolical figure derived from the ideal number of 110 years. Likewise Hölbl, *Geschichte des Ptolemäerreiches*, pp. 176–177, and Werner Huß, *Der makedonische König und die ägyptischen Priester: Studien zur Geschichte des ptolemaiischen Ägypten* (Hist. Einzelschriften 85; Stuttgart, 1994).

[87] Huß, *Ägypten*, p. 562; Andreas Blasius, 'Zur Frage des geistigen Widerstands im griechisch-römischen Ägyptens: die historische Situation', in Blasius and Schipper, *Apokalyptik und Ägypten*, pp. 41–62, esp. 55.

[88] There is a long discussion about the question whether the Oracle of the Potter also reflects anti-Ptolemaic tendencies when it designates the enemies of Egypt as 'beltwearers' and 'Typhonians' and predicts the desolation of the city at the sea (= Alexandria?), extant only in version P_3 col. ii, lines 143–144: καὶ ⟨ἡ⟩ τῶν ζωνοφόρων πόλι⟨ς⟩ ἐρη-[l. 44]μωθήσεται ὃν τρόπον ⟨ἡ⟩ ἐμὴ{ν} κάμινο⟨ς⟩, 'And ⟨the⟩ cit[y] of the beltwearers will [l. 44]be made desolate in the same way my kiln was'. To my mind, the opposition between Egyptians and Greeks, presupposed by this interpretation does not fit the political reality of early second century BCE Egypt where both Greek dynasties (Seleucid versus Ptolemaic) and Egyptian priestly houses (Memphis versus Thebes) were divided.

[89] Felix Jacoby, *Die Fragmente der griechischen Historiker* 3.C (Leiden, 1958), No. 609 F2, F3a, 3b, 3c. Similar references to this miraculous lamb are found in the works of Aelian, *On Animals* 12.3 (second century CE), and pseudo-Plutarch, *De proverbiis Alexandrinorum*, No. 21: τὸ ἀρνίον σοι λελάξκεν. Αἰγύπτιοι τοῦτο ἀνέγραψαν ὡς

712 BCE) ruled over Egypt in the time of the great Western expansion of the Assyrian empire, and was more or less a contemporary of King Hezekiah of Judah and the prophet Isaiah. A few decades after his reign an Assyrian king, Esarhaddon, conquered Egypt (671 BCE), captured the ancient capital Memphis, and ruled over the country for two years (671–669 BCE). His sudden death in Egypt (669 BCE) may have been interpreted as a divine punishment, just as the violent deaths of his father Sennacherib (2 Kgs 19:37) and grandfather, Sargon II (Isa 14:16–20), were interpreted as divine punishments.

The period of two years Assyrian occupation of Egypt period was followed by a period of instability after which Pharaoh Psammetich I gained control over the country and ruled it for fifty-five years (664–610 BCE, i.e. around the time King Josiah ruled over Judah, 640–609 BCE).[90] In the light of these data, it seems likely that the Demotic Oracle of the Lamb looks back at the two years of Assyrian rule by King Esarhaddon, followed by the fifty-five years rule of Pharaoh Psammetich I. The reference to this Demotic prophecy in the Oracle of the Potter then implies a kind of fulfilment interpretation of this oracle to the period of the new Syrian, i.e. Seleucid invasion under Antiochus IV Epiphanes.[91] As a result, the point of comparison would be that both in Egyptian literature (Oracle of the Lamb) and Jewish literature (Oracles of Isaiah) we find an older oracle that originally referred to the Assyrian period,[92] was later applied in Greek re-interpretations of these oracles (Oracle of the Potter and the

ἀνθρωπείᾳ φωνῇ λαλῆσαν. εὑρέθη δὲ ἔχον βασίλειον δράκοντα ἐπὶ τῆς κεφαλῆς αὐτοῦ πτερωτόν, καὶ τῶν βασιλέων τινὶ λελάληκε τὰ μέλλοντα, 'The lamb has spoken to you. Egyptians have recorded a lamb speaking with a human voice. It was found to have upon its head a royal winged serpent; and it foretold the future to one of the kings'.

[90] See Zauzich, 'Das Lamm des Bokchoris', p. 170.

[91] In this respect I agree with Robert Meyer, 'Die eschatologische Wende des politischen Messianismus im Ägypten der Spätzeit. Historisch-kritische Bemerkungen zu einer spätägyptischen Prophetie', *Seac* 48 (1997), pp. 177–212. Meyer also finds a parallel between the Oracle of the Lamb and the Book of Isaiah, but concludes on the basis of this parallel that the formation of the Demotic composition must likewise have known three stages: a Proto-Lamb from the Assyrian period, a Deutero-Lamb from the Persian period and a Trito-Lamb from the Hellenistic period. The fragments of the Demotic text are too scant to support such a far-reaching thesis, see the vehement criticism by Thissen, 'Das Lamm des Bokchoris', p. 121: 'ein Ausfluß ungebändigter Phantasie'. The designation of the foreign king as 'Mede' (*pꜣ Mty*) in the Oracle of the Lamb does not necessarily imply that an older composition was edited during the Persian period, but may very well indicate the time of the original composition, in which the authors looked back at the time of independence after the first Assyrian invasion and before the Persian rule over Egypt (525–404 BCE and 342–332 BCE).

[92] That is: the rule of Esarhaddon over Egypt in 671–669 BCE followed by the rule of

Greek Isaiah) to the period of Antiochus IV Epiphanes who also occupied Egypt for two years (170–168 BCE) and formed a threat to the existence of the Jewish religion. The oracles of doom both in the Egyptian and Hebrew prophecies thus found their fulfilment in the figure of Antiochus IV Epiphanes.

4.3. *The Oracles of Ḥor*

But what about the birth of the innocent child as sign for a better future (Isa 7:14–17)? Neither the Oracle of the Lamb, nor the Oracle of the Potter make mention of such a child born from a young woman. Yet we do have reports of a prophecy, or rather predicatory dream, from the archive of Ḥor of Sebennytos, who worked in the administration of the Ibis cult at the Serapeum of Saqqara–Memphis during the years 163–150 BCE, and had gained a considerable reputation as a seer by means of an oracle of salvation to the Ptolemaic king during the Seleucid occupation.[93]

The author of these ostraca texts was an Egyptian priest who came from Sebennytos in the Egyptian delta, who was born around 200 BCE.[94] In one of the 58 Demotic documents Ḥor describes his calling by the God Thoth, who ordered him to spend the rest of his life in Memphis. In this dream-vision the Deity claims exclusive veneration in a way similar to several statements found in Deuteronomistic literature and Deutero-Isaiah:

> Text 8, recto, line 5: *ỉnk pꜣy=k ṯs Ḏḥwty wꜣḥ=ỉ ḏd-s n=k (n) tꜣ ḥꜣt tm-ỉr šms ntr ẖr-bl=ỉ.*
>
> I am your officer, Thoth. I have told you before, 'Do not worship any god except me'.

In Memphis Ḥor became entangled in a dispute about the proper execution of the Ibis cult, which in Ḥor's opinion had not been preformed correctly during the reign of Ptolemy V Epiphanes (205–180 BCE).[95] Ḥor

---

Pharaoh Psammetich I in 664–610 BCE in Egypt and the Syro-Ephraimite War followed by the Assyrian retreat from Jerusalem in 701 BCE in Judah.

[93] John D. Ray, *The Archive of Ḥor* (Texts from Excavations 2; London, 1976). The text is corrected after the corrections published in A.A, den Brinker, Brian P. Muhs, and Sven P. Vleeming, *A Berichtigungsliste of Demotic Documents* B. *Ostrakon Editions and Various Publications* (Studia demotica 7.B; Leuven etc., 2005), pp. 414–416.

[94] Ray, *Archive*, pp. 117–124: 'The career of Ḥor'.

[95] Ray, *Archive*, pp. 136–146: 'The administration of the ibis-cult'.

wrote petitions to the court of his successor, Ptolemy VI Philometor (180–145 BCE) in order to plead for the restoration of this cult. Within the context of these pleas, Ḥor appealed to a prophecy he had made about the Ptolemaic house during the Sixth Syrian War. The Demotic ostraca contain several drafts of this dream report, dating from 163–158 BCE. It is fascinating to see several changes in these drafts, before they were put on papyrus and translated into Greek. The drafts come from a decade after the prophecy was delivered and attest not only to a *vaticinium ex eventu*, but also to the redaction of that *vaticinium*. Although we do not have the official version of the text written on papyrus, nor its Greek translation, there is no doubt that these versions must have existed in order to function properly.[96]

Ḥor claims to have had a vision during the Seleucid occupation predicting the retreat of the Syrian by sea. He writes that he had reported this dream to the *strategos Hrynys* (Eirenaios), who after a period of neglect, bureaucracy, and scepticism, passed the report on to the Ptolemaic court and granted Ḥor an audience during the visit of Ptolemy VI Philometor and his brother Ptolemy VII Euergetes II, to the Serapeum on 29 August 168 BCE. The drafts of the report of these events are retrospective and date from some ten years later. One of them, O.dem.Ḥor 1 dates from 159 BCE and predicts not only the retreat of the Syrian, but also offers proof (*ʿḥʿ-rd*)[97] for the veracity of his prophecy: 'the Queen will bear a male child':[98]

> [l. 1]A memorandum before the priests from Ḥor, the scribe, a man of Pi-Thoth in the nome of [Sebennytos. I observed the habit of spending] (my) days at the sanctuary of [l. 2]Osormnevis at Heliopolis, and likewise the sanctuary of Osorapis at Memphis. It happened in year 21, Pakhons, day 2 (= 31 May 160 BCE), that I was in Heliopolis. [My heart said, [l. 3] 'Journey ....].' (I) abandoned my papyrus-roll and my palette from my hand in Memphis [to receive instruction from] [l. 4] [......] *mnḥ* (?) (the) priest of the chapel of Imḥōtep which is within Heliopolis, to cause it to be told to me in person. (For) I said this to myself, namely, [l. 5]'When I came to Heliopolis in Khoiak [day ...?], (within) the sanctuary of Osormnevis I was told (in) a dream to put this (in) writing before the great men.' [l. 6][I went before (?)] *Tryn* the prophet of Khons, the scribe of Pharaoh at Memphis, (in) [Year] 23, Hathyr (= December 159 BCE); that which was verified [l. 7](at) the time (when) *ȝtyks* (= Antiochus) was to the north of *Pr-ʿ-ȝwrys* (and) Egypt

[96] Ray, *Archive*, pp. 120–123.

[97] See Janet H. Johnson, *The Demotic Dictionary of the Oriental Institute of the University of Chicago* 3. ʿ, p. 120 (*sub* ʿḥʿ [r] rṯ=f). Cited 13 October 2009. Online: http://oi.uchicago.edu/pdf/CDD_c.pdf.

[98] Text and translation: Ray, *Archive*, pp. 7–14.

> divorced itself. l. 8I stood with *Hryns* who was the head of the army [and who acted as] the agent (of) Pharaoh l. 9Ptolemy our Lord. I caused him to discover the matters [....] which had come before me, l. 10the fortune of Pharaoh. The lady of the two lands, Isis, was the one who ordained them, the great god Thoth the one who l. 11recorded in connection with them. I was told a dream [as follows]: l. 12Isis, the great goddess of this portion of Egypt and the land of Syria, is walking upon the face (of) l. 13the water of the Syrian sea. Thoth stands before her (and) takes her hand, (and) she reached the harbour l. 14(at) Alexandria. She said, 'Alexandria is secure [against the] enemy. Pharaoh records within it l. 15together with his brethren. The eldest son of Pharaoh wears the diadem. His son wears the diadem after him. The son of this son l. 16wears the diadem after him. The son of the son of the son of this son wears the diadem after him, for very l. 17many lengthy days. The confirmation of this (*pꜣ ʿḥʿ-rd nꜣy*): l. 18the Queen bears a male child'. (*tꜣ Pr-ʿꜣt ms šr ḥwty*)

Ḥor refers in this memorandum to the vision he had reported before the royal scribe in December 159 BCE at the time when Antiochus was stationed in the north-eastern part of the country, Ptolemy VI held the country, while his brother Ptolemy VII held Alexandria, i.e. the state of affairs after November 170 BCE.[99] The dream describes the Divine intervention of Isis against Syria and the welfare of the Ptolemaic brothers and the prolongation of the Ptolemaic dynasty for at least five generations. Other drafts of this vision mention explicitly the retreat from Egypt to Syria that Antiochus IV Epiphanes had to make under Roman pressure. The second ostracon of the Ḥor archive, O.dem.Ḥor 2, recto, dating from the period between 168–163 BCE, refers to this dream as follows:

> l. 1From Ḥor the scribe l. 2a man from the town of Isis, lady of the caverns, l. 3the great goddess, in the nome (of) Sebennytos. l. 4The dream which was told to me of the safety of Alexandria l. 5(and) the journeyings of *ꜣtyks*, namely that he would go l. 6[[that he would go]] by sail from Egypt by l. 7Year 2, Paoni, final day. ...

In these and other ostraca Ḥor deals at length with the long procedure to have his dream reported to the kings. Therefore he adds a proof for the reliability of his prediction, namely the prediction that the queen shall bear and deliver a male heir to the Ptolemaic throne. The reference to the Queen (*tꜣ Pr-ʿꜣt*) is undoubtedly to Cleopatra II, the sister of the two kings and wife of Ptolemy VI. The reference to the male son may be to her son Ptolemy Eupator who ruled along with his father in 152 BCE, but died in the same year.[100] Interestingly, Cleopatra must have been a

[99] Ray, *Archive*, p. 13, n. p; Huß, *Ägypten*, pp. 544–567.
[100] Huß, *Ägypten*, pp. 576–578.

teenager (παρθένος) when she gave birth to this child, since she was born probably around 185 BCE. Here we have a striking parallel with Isa 7:14, where we also find the mention of the birth of a male heir to the throne by a Queen who was still in her teen ages within the context of the threat of a Syrian invasion as a confirmation (אות–σημεῖον–*ḥʿ-rd*) for the veracity of the prophecy.

It is further interesting to see the process of contemporization attested by a later draft of the same dream report, dating from *c.* 150 BCE, in which mention to Ptolemy VII has been omitted and in which the death of the promised son (Ptolemy Eupator) is 'predicted':

> O.dem.Ḥor 4: [l. 1]Account of the letter which was written by *Hrynys*, who was *strategos* [l. 2]before me to Pharaoh and the Queen, when he was in command (?) over me, because of the matters [l. 3](which) I reported to him in Year 13, Epeiph [..... up to Year .... at the time] [l. 4]when [Egypt divorced itself from] Alexandria: behold (?) the journeyings (in) every detail [l. 5][................]. That which concerns the eldest son (of) Pharaoh means (that) he shall be born [l. 6](and) cause to endure another province of his supreme inheritance. That which concerns the salvation of Alexandria [l. 7]means (that) it is secure upon its [....] authority (?) [.....] every [.......]. That which concerns [l. 8]the journeyings (of) *ʒtyks* means (that) it is from Egypt (?) [l. 9]that he went [.....]. That which concerns the voyages (of) Pharaoh means (that) he shall go [l. 10](to) the isle (of) the sea, embarking at Alexandria, his heart being happy. [l. 11]That which concerns the month (?) of groaning (?) means (that) the son shall not [.....] from him again. (lines 12–20).

Perhaps we have another prophecy related to the birth of this untimely deceased crown prince from the same sanctuary at Memphis written down at almost the same time (2 June 158) by Ptolemaios, the older brother of Apollonius, scribe of the Greek version of the Dream of Nectanebo. He kept a record of his dreams (UPZ I 77) and one of them deals with the procreation of a bull, which may apply to Queen Cleopatra II:

> UPZ I 77, col. ii: [l. 22](Ἔτους) κγ̄ Παχὼν δ̄. Ὤμην [l. 23]ἐν τῷ ὕπνῳ ἐπει-καλεῖν με τὸν [l. 24]μέγιστον Ἄμμωνα ἔρχεσθαι ἀ[πὸ] [l. 25]βορρᾶ μου τρί-τος ὤν, ἥως παραγ[ί]νηται. [l. 26]Ὤμην με βοῦν ἐν τῷ τόπῳ εἶναι κα[ὶ] [l. 27]οὐδείνουσα⟨ν⟩. Ἐπειλαμβάνεται τῆς [l. 28]βοὼς καὶ καταστροννύσει αὐτήν. [l. 29]Ἐμβάλλει αὐτοῦ τὴν χεῖρα εἶς [l. 30]τὸ οἶδην καὶ ἐκσπᾶι ταῦρον. [l. 31]Ἃ εἶδον ἐν τῷ ὕπνῳ, εὖ εἴη μοι. [l. 32]Παχὼν κγ̄ γενεσίος. [docket]Ἃ εἶδον περεὶ τῆς βα‘/ (= βασιλίσσης?).
>
> [l. 22]Year 23, Pachon 4 (= 2 June 158 BCE). I imagined [l. 23]in a dream to call upon the [l. 24]great Ammon, who came from the [l. 25]North to me as Triad, until he reached me. [l. 26]I imagined (to see) a cow on the spot [l. 27]while being

> in labor. He took the [l. 28]cow and laid her down. [l. 29]He put his hand into her [l. 30]private parts and pulled out a bull. [l. 31]What I saw in my dream, may be well for me. [l. 32]Pachon 23 on the birthday. [docket]The things I saw concerning the (Queen?).

Ulrich Wilcken has argued that the enigmatic letters περεὶ τῆς βα'/ refer to the Queen. Ptolemaios, deeply immerged into Egyptian religion, probably saw the birth of a son to Queen Cleopatra II in terms of the cow goddess Hathor giving birth to a bull while being aided by the god Ammon.[101] In that case, we would be would have another dream prophecy *ex eventu* referring to the delivery of a Crown prince by a maiden Queen.

Needless to say, the theme of the birth of a male heir to the throne is by no means exceptional within the vast range of ancient Egyptian and ancient near eastern literature, see e.g. the birth narratives of Sargon, Greek heroes, Remus and Romulus, the stories of Setne Khamwas si-Osire, and others.[102] What makes the parallel between O.dem.Ḥor 1–4, UPZ I 77, and LXX-Isa 7:10–17 so unique is their shared historical-political setting in the decades following the Sixth Syrian war (170–168 BCE) and the fact that the birth of a son serves as a valid proof for the reliability of the oracle both in O.dem.Ḥor 1 and LXX-Isa 7:14.

5. *Conclusions*

In the preceding section several Egyptian–Greek 'prophetical' texts have been presented, viz. the Demotic and Greek versions of the Dream of Nectanebo, the Demotic Oracle of the Lamb, the Greek Oracle of the Potter, the Demotic dream report of Ḥor and the Greek dream report of Ptolemaios. In a number of cases some striking parallels can be drawn between these writings and the Greek version of Isaiah, particularly Isa 6:1–4, 7:14–17; and 19:1–10.

On a more general level, there is a parallel between these texts and the Greek version of Isaiah in as far as both groups reflect a strong anti-Syrian bias roused by the campaigns of Antiochus IV Epiphanes in Egypt and Palestine. The Greek version of the Dream of Nectanebo, the Oracle of the Potter, the Oracles of Ḥor, and the dreams of the κάτοχος Ptolemaios

[101] Wilcken, *Urkunden* 1, p. 357.

[102] Griffith, *Stories*, pp. 142–207; Miriam Lichtheim, *Ancient Egyptian Literature* 3. *The Late Period* (Berkeley etc., 1980), pp. 138–151.

all share the same provenance: Memphis in the sixties and fifties of the second century BCE. If the Greek version of Isaiah was produced around 140 BCE at Leontopolis, it could hardly have escaped the influence of the nearby religious capital of Egypt, Memphis. Perhaps that is why we find a striking variant in the Greek Isaiah (19:13), promoting the prominence of Memphis over other Egyptian cities:[103]

MT נואלו שרי צען נשאו שרי נף התעו את מצרים פנת שבטיה:

NRSV The princes of Zoan have become fools, and the princes of Memphis are deluded; those who are the cornerstones of its tribes have led Egypt astray.

LXX ἐξέλιπον οἱ ἄρχοντες Τάνεως, καὶ ὑψώθησαν οἱ ἄρχοντες Μέμφεως, καὶ πλανήσουσιν Αἴγυπτον κατὰ φυλάς.

NETS The rulers of Tanis have failed, and the rulers of Memphis have been exalted, and they will lead Egypt astray tribe by tribe.

Do these parallels prove direct literary dependence? To my mind the texts can not carry the burden of such a far-fetched claim. The Greek version of Isaiah remains first and foremost a translation of the ancient Hebrew Book of Isaiah, rather than a completely new composition. Yet, the way the original text is rephrased in Greek reveals something of the cultural and religious background of its historical context, i.e., Egypt and Palestine after the Sixth Syrian war. The parallels presented by the Hellenistic Egyptian oracles do reflect a common cultural background and a similar understanding of past and present events. Apparently prophetical texts served political-propagandistic interests, rather than metaphysical perceptions or scholarly purposes. Often these texts were meant to legitimize the authority of an otherwise illegitimate new ruler (Pharaoh Amenemhet in the Prophecy of Neferty, Pharaoh Amenophis I, and Alexander in the Alexander-Romance) or the prevalence of one priestly group over another (the priesthood of Memphis over Alexandria in the Oracle of the Potter, the Priest Ḥor over his priestly rivals in Memphis). If the Greek version of Isaiah was intended to support the legitimacy of the Jewish circle in Leontopolis around the exiled High Priest Onias IV and was intended as polemic against the Hellenizing

[103] Cf. Pesh-Isa 19:13 ܐܬܬܪܝܡܘ ܪܘܪܒܢܐ ܕܡܦܝܣ. Ottley, *Isaiah* 2, p. 200, and others, e.g. Moshe H. Goshen-Gottstein, *The Book of Isaiah* (The Hebrew University Bible; Jerusalem, 1975), p. 72, suggest that the Greek translator read נִשְׂאוּ, 'they are lifted', rather than MT נִשְּׁאוּ, 'they are deceived'. Although this may very well have been the case, it does not explain why the Greek translator chose the equivalent ὑψόω rather than the default rendering αἴρω and composita for Hebrew נשׂא.

pro-Seleucid priesthood in Jerusalem, then we have an interesting parallel in the Ḥor ostraca, where we find a polemic between rival priestly parties about the proper execution of the ibis-cult.[104]

In the light of these general observations, it becomes unlikely to interpret the Greek Isaiah in terms of Hellenistic mystery cults as was done by Norden, Kittel, and Rösel, or solely in terms of a well-researched innerbiblical harmonizing rendering with the Greek Pentateuch as argued by Troxel. Rather, the Greek version of Isa 7:10–17 while remaining within the narrative world of the Prophet Isaiah and the Judean kings Uzziah, Achaz, and Hezekiah, envisages a typological correspondence between the events of the Assyrian period and his own times in which the new Syrian rulers, Antiochus IV Epiphanes and his successors, form the background against the hope for a new future is set. The quotation of the Oracle of the Lamb in the Oracle of the Potter provides a parallel for the phenomenon of fulfilment interpretation and re-contextualization in second century BCE Egypt.

The conclusion of this paper must be, then, that the Septuagint, particularly the Septuagint version of Isaiah, should not be detached from its historical and cultural background. Among the many things I have learnt from my mentor and *Doktervater*, Arie van der Kooij, it is precisely this insight and I take the opportunity here to thank him for this and so many other insights.[105]

---

[104] Meyer, 'Eschatologische Wende', p. 193, n. 52, points to another priestly polemic, viz. that between the priesthood of Thebes and Memphis as reflected in the Demotic Chronicle, column vi, ll. 10–11.

[105] See Arie van der Kooij, 'Review of Ronald L. Troxel, LXX-Isaiah as Translation and Interpretation', *BIOSCS* 42 (2009), pp. 147–152.

Appendix: Timechart

Date	Events	Texts
1991–1962	Rule of Pharaoh Amenemhet I, founder of the twelfth dynasty (= begin of the Middle Kingdom)	Prophecy of Neferty
1525–1504?	Rule of Pharaoh Amenophis I Djeserkare, son of Ahmose I, founder of the eighteenth dynasty (= begin of the New Kingdom)	
736–719?	Rule of Ahaz over Judah	
735–734	Syro-Ephraimite war	Immanuel prophecy in Isaiah 7?
729–687?	Rule of Hezekiah over Judah	
722–705	Rule of Sargon II	
717–712?	Rule of Pharaoh Bokchoris	
705–681	Rule of Sennacherib	
701	Siege of Jerusalem by Sennacherib	
689–664	Rule of Pharaoh Taharqa	
681–669	Rule of Esarhaddon	
672–664	Rule of Pharaoh Necho I	
671	Esarhaddon captures Memphis	
669	Esarhaddon dies in Egypt	
664–610	Rule of Pharaoh Psammetich I	
640–609?	Rule of Josia over Judah	
525–402	First Persian rule over Egypt	
379–363	Rule of Pharaoh Nectanebo I, founder of the thirtieth (and last native Egyptian) dynasty	
373	Nectanebo I withstands Persian attack on Egypt	
360–343	Rule of Pharaoh Nectanebo II	
343–332	Second Persian rule over Egypt	
c. 285–280		Berossus and Manetho
c. 280		Greek Pentateuch
257–256		Aramaic–Greek Asoka Edicts
238		Edict of Canopus
217		Edict of Raphia
196		Edict of Rosetta

Date	Events	Texts
175	Onias III murdered	
172–162	Menelaus High Priest of Jerusalem	
170–168	Antiochus IV Epiphanes occupies Egypt	
167	Antiochus IV Epiphanes defiles the temple of Jerusalem	O.dem.Ḥor 8
165	Revolt in Egypt by Dionysios Petosarapis	
164	Death of Antiochus IV in Persia	
		UPZ I 81 (dream of Nektanebo)
159		O.dem.Ḥor 1
158		UPZ I 77 (dreams of Ptolemaios)
150		O.dem.Ḥor 4
146	Fall of Carthage	
145	Conflict between Ptolemies in Egypt; death of Ptolemy VI; Ptolemy VII Euergetes II expels scholars from the Musaion	
140	Parthian raid of Babylon	
140		Greek translation of Isaiah?
144–132		P.Polit.Iud. (archive of Jewish politeuma)

ISAIAH 2 IN THE SEPTUAGINT

Takamitsu Muraoka

It is a great privilege and honour to be invited to contribute to this volume in honour of a longstanding colleague with whom I have had the pleasure of very stimulating scholarly exchanges. One of the most significant emphases in Arie's scholarly publications is a close reading of the ancient versions of the Old Testament as against an atomistic, too narrowly focused textual criticism. Results of a close study of a version can take the form of a running commentary on it, and that is what I have the pleasure of presenting here.

Isaiah 2:1[1]

LXX Ὁ λόγος ὁ γενόμενος παρὰ κυρίου πρὸς Ησαιαν υἱὸν Αμως περὶ τῆς Ιουδαίας καὶ περὶ Ιερουσαλημ.

ET The word that came from the Lord[2] to Isaiah son of Amoz concerning Judaea and concerning Jerusalem

MT הדבר אשר חזה ישעיהו בן אמוץ על יהודה וירושלם

Ὁ γενόμενος παρὰ κυρίου πρὸς Ησαιαν. That the translator has reworded his Hebrew *Vorlage* is almost certain. In other words, it is unlikely to have read: היה מאת יהוה לישעיהו or something like that.[3] The Hebrew verb חזה occurs two more times in the book in a caption introducing a pericope, and in each case it is translated with εἶδεν with Isaiah as the subject: 1:1; 13:1. The reason for this transformation of the *Vorlage* is probably the object of the prophetic vision. In the latter two cases it is חזון and משא respectively and rendered each time with ὅρασις. In other words

---

[1] We give first the Septuagint text as edited by Joseph Ziegler in his *Isaias* (Septuaginta. Vetus testamentum graecum auctoritate Academiae litterarum Gottingensis; Göttingen, 1967[2]), followed by our own translation of it and the Masoretic text as in BHS.

[2] Thus, *pace* Cazelles, there is no need to postulate the influence of Hos 1:1; Micah 1:1; Zeph 1:1; see Henri Cazelles, 'Texte massorétique et Septante en Is 2,1–5', in Pierre Casetti et al. (eds), *Mélanges Dominique Barthélemy* (OBO 38; Fribourg–Göttingen, 1981), pp. 51–59, esp. 53.

[3] Cf. Jer 11:1 הדבר אשר היה אל־ירמיהו מאת יהוה; LXX Ὁ λόγος ὁ γενόμενος παρὰ κυρίου πρὸς Ιερεμιαν.

our translator reasoned that a word can hardly be seen or envisioned. And yet the verbal, not visual, message was of divine origin, hence the addition 'from the Lord'.

The topic of the message is marked with the neutral preposition περί + gen. By contrast, at 1:1 we have a marked preposition: κατά + gen., κατὰ τῆς Ιουδαίας καὶ κατὰ Ιερουσαλημ 'against Judaea and against Jerusalem', reflecting the largely condemnatory nature of the message of the chapter as against that of our chapter. Note that, also at 13:1, the same Hebrew preposition is similarly rendered: κατὰ Βαβυλῶνος.

As against the Hebrew text, our translator repeats the preposition at both 1:1 and 2:1.[4]

Isaiah 2:2

LXX Ὅτι ἔσται ἐν ταῖς ἐσχάταις ἡμέραις ἐμφανὲς τὸ ὄρος τοῦ κυρίου καὶ ὁ οἶκος τοῦ θεοῦ ἐπ' ἄκρων τῶν ὀρέων καὶ ὑψωθήσεται ὑπεράνω τῶν βουνῶν· καὶ ἥξουσιν ἐπ' αὐτὸ πάντα τὰ ἔθνη,

ET That sometime in the future the mountain of the Lord will become visible and the house of God on the top of the mountains and it will be exalted above the hills. And all the nations will come onto it,

MT והיה באחרית הימים נכון יהיה הר בית יהוה בראש ההרים ונשא מגבעות ונהרו אליו כל הגוים

The initial conjunction is striking; there is nothing to justify it in the MT. It is hardly causal, but must be meant to introduce a message, following its caption announced at the start of the chapter.

The eschatological Hebrew temporal phrase does not occur elsewhere in our book, but appears already four times in the Pentateuch and is rendered there in the LXX differently: Gen 49:1 ἐπ' ἐσχάτων τῶν ἡμερῶν, Num 24:14 ἐπ' ἐσχάτου τῶν ἡμερῶν, Deut 4:30 ἐπ' ἐσχάτῳ τῶν ἡμερῶν, and 31:29 τὰ κατὰ ἔσχατον τῶν ἡμερῶν, here, in both cases, the translation reproduces the construct syntagm of Hebrew, the only difference being in the grammatical number, now plural and now singular. The rendering as in Gen 49:1 is followed in some other prophetic passages, such as Hos 3:5; Mic 4:1; Ezek 38:16.

More importantly, our translator is probably not thinking in eschatological terms. His ἐν ταῖς ἐσχάταις ἡμέραις may be translated: 'in future',

[4] On this question, see Raija Sollamo, 'Repetitions of Prepositions in the Septuagint of Genesis', in Florentino García Martínez and Marc Vervenne (eds), *Interpreting Translation. Studies on the LXX and Ezekiel in Honour of Johan Lust* (BEThL 192; Leuven, 2005), pp. 371–384.

whereas the substantivized use of the adjective, whether singular or plural, means 'end-point'.[5]

Comparison of our verse with Mic 4:1, which is almost identical, is instructive. The LXX there reads:

> Καὶ ἔσται ἐπ' ἐσχάτων τῶν ἡμερῶν ἐμφανὲς τὸ ὄρος τοῦ κυρίου, ἕτοιμον ἐπὶ τὰς κορυφὰς τῶν ὀρέων, καὶ μετεωρισθήσεται ὑπεράνω τῶν βουνῶν· καὶ σπεύσουσι πρὸς αὐτὸ λαοί,

Although the adjective, ἐμφανής, is a rare word in the LXX, occurring a total of merely seven times (twice in Isaiah), the choice to render נכון 'firmly established' is confined to Isa 2:2 and Mic 4:1. One would also note that the collocation of this *niph'al* verb with the temple mount occurs nowhere else in the Hebrew Bible. The influence of the one on the other is almost certain. The presence in the latter of a doublet, ἕτοιμον, suggests that the translator of the Twelve Prophets is drawing upon the Isaianic parallel.[6] The dependence of Micah, however, is seen to be confined to this particular detail, and for the rest of the text he has gone his own way as in the rendering ἐπ' ἐσχάτων τῶν ἡμερῶν, ἐπὶ τὰς κορυφὰς, μετεωρισθήσεται, σπεύσουσι, and the single subject for ἔσται.

The sense of ἐμφανής can be defined as 'physically visible', etymologically justifiable as derived from ἐμφαίνω 'to come into appearance'.[7] Note Wisd 14:17 ἐμφανῆ εἰκόνα τοῦ τιμωμένου βασιλέως ἐποίησαν, 'they made a visible image of the king being honoured'. Though the notions of 'being firmly established' and 'emergence' are not totally exclusive of each other this is nonetheless quite a departure from what the Hebrew *niph'al* participle is agreed to mean.

Another significant disparity between LXX and MT here is the splitting of a single construct phrase 'the mount of the house of the Lord' into 'the mount of the Lord' and 'the house of the God'. Note that the second component is not 'His house'. This appears to be a harmonization with

---

[5] Takamitsu Muraoka, *A Greek-English Lexicon of the Septuagint* (Leuven, 2009), s.v.

[6] See Takamitsu Muraoka, 'Introduction', in Eberhard Bons, Jan Joosten, and Stephan Kessler, *Les douze prophètes* 1. *Osée* (La Bible d' Alexandrie 23.1; Paris, 2002), pp. i–xxiii, esp. pp. xi–xii. Ziegler mentions some examples which he believes point to the reverse direction of influence: Joseph Ziegler, *Untersuchungen zur Septuaginta des Buches Isaias* (Münster i. W., 1934), pp. 104–105. See also Isac L. Seeligmann, *The Septuagint Version of Isaiah. A Discussion of Its Problems* (MEOL 9; Leiden, 1948), pp. 72–73, as well as the article by Cécile Dogniez in this volume.

[7] See Muraoka, *Lexicon*, s.v. 2.

verse 3, for the text of which see below. *Pace* NETS,[8] therefore, we should not translate the second clause as if it were a self-contained clause as 'and the house of God shall be on the tops of the mountains', but it is to be analysed as sharing ἔσται … ἐμφανές as its predicate, though its syntax is admittedly loose.

ἐπ' ἄκρων τῶν ὀρέων—בראש ההרים. The text is obviously not talking about multiple temples emerging on the top of each of the multiple mountains. The plural הרים must mean a mountainous, hilly area with one prominent elevation there, and the entire Hebrew construct phrase means then 'the highest spot of the mountainous area'. Thus the use of the singular ראש is most appropriate, and our case is distinct from Gen 8.5 נראו ראשי ההרים—ὤφθησαν αἱ κεφαλαὶ τῶν ὀρέων 'the summits of the mountains became visible'. By the same token, the Greek plural, ἄκρων, is not to be translated mechanically: 'on the tops of the mountains' (NETS). It denotes a wide expanse as distinct from, for instance, Gen 47:31 τὸ ἄκρον τῆς ῥάβδου αὐτῆς, 'the tip of his staff'. Cp. Exod 34:2 ἐπ' ἄκρου τοῦ ὄρους, 'on the summit of the mount', with 1 Reg 2:10 αὐτὸς κρινεῖ ἄκρα γῆς.

ὑψωθήσεται—נשא. Just as the Hebrew *niph'al*, the passive, especially in Hellenistic Greek,[9] has often merged with the classic middle voice. In this particular case, therefore, it is futile to attempt to determine the agent: Who did the lifting?

ἐπ' αὐτό—אליו. The *Vorlage* of the LXX most likely had עליו as in Mic 4:1. Cf. 1QIsa[a] עלוהי,[10] an Aramaic equivalent. On the other hand the LXX of Micah reads πρὸς αὐτό, which better reflects אליו! In any event, the Hebrew preposition על here indicates not only direction, 'towards', but upward direction, which can be marked by ἐπί + acc., as in Hag 1:8 ἀνάβητε ἐπὶ τὸ ὄρος 'Go up to the mountain'.

ἥξουσιν, a rather colourless choice for נהר *qal*. Cp. Mic 4:1 σπεύσουσιν, 'they will hasten'.[11] The Hebrew verb is attested four times in the sense of massive population movement. The other two attestations are:

[8] Albert Pietersma and Benjamin G. Wright (eds.), *A New English Translation of the Septuagint and the Other Greek Translations Traditionally Included under That Title* (New York–Oxford, 2007).

[9] Friedrich Blass and Albert Debrunner, trans. Robert W. Funk, *A Greek Grammar of the New Testament and Other Early Christian Literature* (Chicago–London, 1961), §§78–79, 307, 313.

[10] Donald W. Parry and Elisha Qimron, *The Great Isaiah Scroll (1QIsa[a]). A New Edition* (STDJ 32; Leiden etc., 1999).

[11] Cazelles, 'Texte', p. 54, rightly points out that the LXX better represents מהרו.

Jer 38:12 (MT 31:11) ἥξουσιν ἐπ’ ἀγαθὰ κυρίου; 28:44 (MT 51:44) οὐ μὴ συναχθῶσι πρὸς αὐτὴν ἔτι τὰ ἔθνη.[12]

ἔθνη—גוים. The MT uses a different substantive in the echoing part of the following verse: עמים, which, however, is rendered with the same Greek substantive. In the parallel passage in Micah, the sequence of the Hebrew substantives is reversed, and the LXX there uses the standard equivalents: λαοί, ἔθνη.

Isaiah 2:3

LXX καὶ πορεύσονται ἔθνη πολλὰ καὶ ἐροῦσι Δεῦτε καὶ ἀναβῶμεν εἰς τὸ ὄρος κυρίου καὶ εἰς τὸν οἶκον τοῦ θεοῦ Ιακωβ, καὶ ἀναγγελεῖ ἡμῖν τὴν ὁδὸν αὐτοῦ, καὶ πορευσόμεθα ἐν αὐτῇ· ἐκ γὰρ Σιων ἐξελεύσεται νόμος καὶ λόγος κυρίου ἐξ Ιερουσαλημ.

ET and many nations shall march and say, Come on, let's ascend (and enter) the mountain of the Lord and the house of God of Jacob, and he will let us know His way and we shall walk in it, for from Zion the law will issue forth and the word of the Lord from Jerusalem.

MT והלכו עמים רבים ואמרו לכו ונעלה אל הר יהוה אל בית אלהי יעקב וירנו מדרכיו ונלכה בארחתיו כי מציון תצא תורה ודבר יהוה מירושלם

πορεύσονται for הלכו echoes ἥξουσιν—נהרו of the preceding verse. The latter Greek verb underlines the end-point of a movement, arrival, and presence at a destination. By contrast, this verse is a description of the process of realization of a prophecy in vs. 2, for which the choice of πορεύομαι is felicitous: they are about to set out on the prophesied journey.

Δεῦτε ἀναβώμεν—לכו ונעלה. The idiomatic use of the imperative of הלך introducing an exhortation or inciting to an action has been nicely captured with δεῦτε.[13] Rahlfs prefers a syndetic structure with the conjunction καί, but both the LXX Greek and Hebrew allow both syndesis and asyndesis in a case like this.[14] Exactly the same phenomenon meets us at vs. 5.

[12] Another possible indication that a second translator worked from Jer 29 up to 50? See Henry St J. Thackeray, 'The Greek translators of Jeremiah', *JThS* 4 (1903), pp. 245–266.

[13] Cf. Paul Joüon and Takamitsu Muraoka, *A Grammar of Biblical Hebrew* (SubBi 27; Rome, 2006), § 105e.

[14] See Takamitsu Muraoka, 'Hosea 6 in the Septuagint', in Hans Ausloos, Bénédicte Lemmelijn, and Marc Vervenne (eds.), *Florilegium Lovaniense. Studies in Septuagint and Textual Criticism in Honour of Florentino García Martínez* (BEThL 224; Leuven, 2008), pp. 335–349, esp. 336.

With the choice of the hortative subjunctive instead of the future, ἀναβησόμεθα, our translator has identified the unmarked נעלה as cohortative, probably in view of ונלכה later in the verse, though translated with the future, πορευσόμεθα.[15]

εἰς τὸ ὄρος κυρίου καὶ εἰς τὸν οἶκον τοῦ θεοῦ Ιακωβ. The choice of the specific preposition εἰς now, instead of ἐπί in vs. 2 or πρός in the parallel passage in Micah, is probably meant to suggest that the crowd were going to enter the sacred precinct to take part in the liturgy there.

καὶ ἀναγγελεῖ ἡμῖν—וירנו. The Tiberian pointing וְיֹרֵנוּ indicates the form as volitive in line with נלכה later in the verse: 'May He instruct us'. Our translator, however, has analysed it as a plain indicative.[16]

τὴν ὁδὸν αὐτοῦ—מדרכיו. If the plural of the Hebrew noun were genuine, so would the preposition be. The Hebrew preposition may mean 'on the basis of' as in Ps 94:12 מתורתך תלמדנו, for which the LXX has ἐκ τοῦ νόμου σου διδάξῃς αὐτόν. This particular nuance of the Hebrew particle has then escaped our translator.

καὶ πορευσόμεθα ἐν αὐτῇ—ונלכה בארחתיו. It is not immediately apparent why our translator has not chosen a synonym to render בארחתיו, as he does, for instance, at 30:11 where the MT has the same two synonymous nouns as here, for which the LXX has chosen ὁδός and τρίβος, as is also done in the parallel passage in Micah.

Isaiah 2:4

LXX καὶ κρινεῖ ἀνὰ μέσον τῶν ἐθνῶν καὶ ἐλέγξει λαὸν πολύν, καὶ συγκόψουσι τὰς μαχαίρας αὐτῶν εἰς ἄροτρα καὶ τὰς ζιβύνας αὐτῶν εἰς δρέπανα, καὶ οὐ λήμψεται ἔτι ἔθνος ἐπ' ἔθνος μάχαιραν, καὶ οὐ μὴ μάθωσιν ἔτι πολεμεῖν.

ET and He will judge between the nations and will chastise a populous people, and they will shatter their swords into ploughs and their spears into sickles, and no nation will grasp a sword against a fellow nation any more, and they will not learn to wage wars any more.

MT ושפט בין הגוים והוכיח לעמים רבים וכתתו חרבותם לאתים וחניתותיהם למזמרות לא ישא גוי אל גוי חרב ולא ילמדו עוד מלחמה

[15] Note, however, a variant πορευσώμεθα attested by Codex Sinaiticus, among other witnesses.

[16] For the normally applicable rule concerned, see Joüon–Muraoka, *Grammar*, § 61 f. One must of course allow for a measure of flexibility in poetry, and much depends on the vocalization.

καὶ κρινεῖ ἀνὰ μέσον τῶν ἐθνῶν—ושפט בין הגוים. The collocation κρίνω ἀνὰ μέσον is already attested as a rendering of שפט בין in Gen 31:53. The compound preposition ἀνὰ μέσον + gen. appears to become common in late Classical Greek.[17]

λαὸν πολύν—עמים רבים. The use of the singular is intriguing, especially in view of the τῶν ἐθνῶν in parallelism. The parallel in Mic 4:3 reads καὶ κρινεῖ ἀνὰ μέσον λαῶν πολλῶν καὶ ἐξελέγξει ἔθνη ἰσχυρά. Has the translator a particular, populous people in mind? Then which?

The collocation of κρίνω ἀνὰ μέσον is most likely a Hebrew calque.[18]

καὶ συγκόψουσι τὰς μαχαίρας αὐτῶν εἰς ἄροτρα—וכתתו חרבותם לאתים. There is little difference in meaning between συγκόπτω and κατακόπτω, the latter chosen by the translator of Micah at Mic 4:3. On the other hand, the difference between μάχαιρα of Isaiah and ῥομφαία of Micah is striking. Given the nearly perfect distribution of the two translation equivalents between the two corpora in question, this can be fairly safely accounted for by assuming that we have here two different translators.[19]

ζιβύνη chosen to render חנית is a rather rare word in the LXX, occurring a mere three times, whereas the standard rendering of the Hebrew noun in question is δόρυ, 35 times out of a total of 47 occurrences of חנית. In the parallel Micah passage we find this standard equivalent. In Joel 3(4):10, which describes a reverse politico-military situation, we read: συγκόψατε ἄροτρα ὑμῶν εἰς ῥομφαίας καὶ τὰ δρέπανα ὑμῶν εἰς σειρομάστας, the last noun being another rare synonym occurring in the LXX six times, all in the prose, except in the Joel passage in question where the Hebrew word is different: רמח.

The first ἔτι has nothing to correspond to it in the Hebrew text; it is most likely a result of harmonization with the following clause. The parallel Micah passage also repeats οὐκέτι despite the fact that here, too, we find עוד only in the second clause.

---

[17] Cf. Martin Johannessohn, *Der Gebrauch der Präpositionen in der Septuaginta* (Berlin, 1926), pp. 170–173, esp. 170, n. 6; Edwin Mayser, *Grammatik der griechischen Papyri aus der Ptolemäerzeit mit Einschluß der gleichzeitigen Ostraka und der in Ägypten verfassten Inschriften* 2.2 (Berlin–Leipzig, 1934), p. 403; Walter Bauer, ed. by Frederick W. Danker, *A Greek-English Lexicon of the New Testament and other Early Christian Literature* (Chicago–London, 2000), s.v. ἀνά, 1.

[18] On this pseudo-preposition, see Raija Sollamo, *Renderings of Hebrew Semi-prepositions in the Septuagint* (AASF.DHL 19; Helsinki, 1979), pp. 347–350.

[19] Muraoka, 'Introduction', p. xi.

Isaiah 2:5

LXX Καὶ νῦν, ὁ οἶκος τοῦ Ιακωβ, δεῦτε πορευθῶμεν τῷ φωτὶ κυρίου.

ET And now, the house of Jacob, come on, let's march by the light of the Lord.

MT בית יעקב לכו ונלכה באור יהוה

Καὶ νῦν appears to be a free addition on the part of the translator designed to mark a new turn in the discourse.

δεῦτε πορευθῶμεν. On the structure, see above at vs. 3.

τῷ φωτὶ κυρίου—**באור יהוה**. The translator recognized here a *bet* of instrument, not local[20] in the sense of 'in an area lit up, not dark'. The dative here cannot be local in function. The translator could have mechanically rendered ἐν τῷ φωτὶ ... The preposition can mark an instrument[21] as in Ps 77:14 ὡδήγησεν αὐτοὺς ... ὅλην τὴν νύκτα ἐν φωτισμῷ πυρός, 'he guided them ... the whole night with a fire-like light (**באור אש**)'.

Isaiah 2:6

LXX ἀνῆκε γὰρ τὸν λαὸν αὐτοῦ τὸν οἶκον τοῦ Ισραηλ, ὅτι ἐνεπλήσθη ὡς τὸ ἀπ' ἀρχῆς ἡ χώρα αὐτῶν κληδονισμῶν ὡς ἡ τῶν ἀλλοφύλων, καὶ τέκνα πολλὰ ἀλλόφυλα ἐγενήθη αὐτοῖς.

ET For He abandoned His people, the house of Israel, since their country, as in former days, filled[22] with diviners' messages as the country of the Philistines, and there were born to them many alien children.

MT כי נטשתה עמך בית יעקב כי מלאו מקדם ועננים כפלשתים ובילדי נכרים ישפיקו

ἀνῆκε γὰρ τὸν λαὸν αὐτοῦ—**כי נטשתה עמך**. By changing the second person singular of the Hebrew text into the third person singular the translator makes the prophet adduce a theological argument for his call to the nation instead of turning to his God in despair: the nation had sunk so low that they were abandoned and left to their own lot by their God.

The choice of a rather rare verb, ἀνίημι in the sense of 'to leave uncared for',[23] is noteworthy. Another rendering could have been ἐγκαταλείπω,

---

[20] So Ernst Jenni, *Die hebräischen Präpositionen* 1. *Die Präposition Beth* (Stuttgart etc., 1992), p. 210.

[21] See Muraoka, *Lexicon*, s.v. **6**.

[22] On the pseudo-passive form, see above on ὑψωθήσεται (vs. 2).

[23] See Muraoka, *Lexicon*, s.v. **4**.

which actually occurs in parallelism with ἀνίημι in Deut 31:5 ὁ θεός σου … οὐ μή σε ἀνῇ οὔτε μή σε ἐγκαταλίπῃ, similarly 31:8, where also God is the subject and His people the object. This is one of only three cases where ἀνίημι is used to render נטש *qal*. In the remaining two cases (Exod 23:11; Neh 10:31) the Greek verb means 'to leave unused'.

ὡς τὸ ἀπ' ἀρχῆς—מקדם The Hebrew phrase is equivocal: it can be taken either temporally, 'since ancient times' or locally, 'from the east'. The former analysis has been applied at Isa 45:21 as well and rendered ἀπ' ἀρχῆς. The particle of comparison has apparently been added freely as a result of this interpretation. Cf. Zech 12:7 καθὼς ἀπ' ἀρχῆς—בראשנה. The neuter singular definite article is sometimes added to adverbials:[24] e.g., Josh 24:2 τὸ ἀπ' ἀρχῆς 'formerly'; Tob 7:11 G^{I} τὸ νῦν (G^{II} νῦν); Num 9:11 τὸ πρὸς ἑσπέραν (9:3 πρὸς ἑσπέραν). In Isa 63:19 we find the same rendering for מעולם.

ἡ χώρα αὐτῶν appears to be a free and sensible expansion, most likely an attempt to harmonize our verse with the following. The verb has accordingly been adjusted to the singular.

κληδονισμῶν—עננים. The only other occurrence of this rare Hebrew word in our book at 57:3 is rendered somewhat loosely: בני עננה—υἱοὶ ἄνομοι. Our translator's understanding of the Hebrew word is shared by the translator of Deuteronomy: Deut 18:10 κληδονιζόμενος alongside μαντευόμενος μαντείαν, οἰωνιζόμενος, and φαρμακός; 18:14 κληδών.

ὡς ἡ τῶν ἀλλοφύλων—כפלשתים. χώρα is to be supplied. The substantivizing, elliptical use of the definite article with a following genitive is fairly common,[25] especially so with proper nouns. By the time of translation of the Book of Isaiah οἱ ἀλλόφυλλοι had acquired the status of a proper noun. פלשתים or פלשתי is never phonetically transliterated in the Septuagint except in an Hexaplaric addition at 1 Reg 17:23 and a few places in the Three.[26]

καὶ τέκνα πολλὰ ἀλλόφυλα ἐγενήθη αὐτοῖς—ובילדי נכרים ישפיקו. The LXX translator has undoubtedly identified the verb as שפק 'to suffice, abound', not ספק 'to strike, clap'. The first is attested only here and in 1 Kgs 20:10,[27] though it is quite common in post-biblical Hebrew. See,

---

[24] See Muraoka, *Lexicon*, s. v. ὁ **3 f**, **g**.
[25] See Muraoka, *Lexicon*, s. v. ὁ **3 d**.
[26] For details, see Edwin Hatch and Henry A. Redpath, *A Concordance to the Septuagint* 3. *Supplement* (Oxford 1906), p. 155.
[27] Correctly rendered in the LXX (3 Reg 21:10) with ἐκποιέω.

for instance, Sir 15:18 ספקה חכמת יהוה—πολλὴ ἡ σοφία τοῦ κυρίου.[28] This understanding of the Hebrew text fits better in the three verses, in which the notion of plenitude of detestable objects and phenomena is highlighted through the verb מלא repeated as often as four times and translated each time with ἐνεπλήσθη, which notion is expressed in our verse (6c) differently with πολλά.

Our translator has at his disposal a number of discriminatory words to refer to ethnic groups, who follow religious beliefs and practices unacceptable to Israelites. When נכר or נכרי is used in a context of such a confrontation, three Greek adjectives are used, namely ἀλλόφυλος, ἀλλογενής, and ἀλλότριος. Five passages are interesting in this respect, and they all have sg. בן נכר or pl. בני נכר. 56:3, 6; 61:10 are concerned with an inviting, welcoming attitude towards a group called ἀλλογενής. At 61:5 we have בני נכר in parallelism with זרים, where the former is rendered with ἀλλόφυλοι and the latter with ἀλλογενεῖς. Finally at 62:8 we have a parallelistic expression indicating a hostile relationship: איבים ... בני נכר rendered ἐχθροὶ ... ἀλλότριοι, where both Greek adjectives have an unmistakably negative connotation.[29] On the scale of alienness and hostility we may arrange these terms in descending order as follows:

ἐχθρός > ἀλλότριος > ἀλλόφυλος > ἀλλογενής

Isaiah 2:7

LXX ἐνεπλήσθη γὰρ ἡ χώρα αὐτῶν ἀργυρίου καὶ χρυσίου, καὶ οὐκ ἦν ἀριθμὸς τῶν θησαυρῶν αὐτῶν· καὶ ἐνεπλήσθη ἡ γῆ ἵππων, καὶ οὐκ ἦν ἀριθμὸς τῶν ἁρμάτων αὐτῶν·

ET For their country filled with silver and gold, and there was no counting their treasures, and the land filled with horses and there was no counting their chariots.

MT ותמלא ארצו כסף וזהב ואין קצה לאצרתיו ותמלא ארצו סוסים ואין קצה למרכבתיו

οὐκ ἦν ἀριθμὸς τῶν θησαυρῶν αὐτῶν ... οὐκ ἦν ἀριθμὸς τῶν ἁρμάτων αὐτῶν—אין קצה לאצרתיו ... אין קצה למרכבתיו. The Hebrew collocation denoting unlimited quantity -אין קצה ל is attested only here and in three more passages in Nahum. In the latter it is consistently rendered with οὐκ ἦν πέρας or οὐκ ἔστιν πέρας + gen. This may be adduced as

---

[28] *Pace* Ottley, our translator is not guessing: Richard R. Ottley, *The Book of Isaiah according to the Septuagint (Codex Alexandrinus) 2. Text and Notes* (Cambridge, 1906), p. 112.

[29] On the latter in particular, see Muraoka, *Lexicon*, s. v., 2, 3.

another piece of evidence that Isaiah and the Twelve Prophets were translated by two different translators.[30] The Greek phrase chosen by our Isaiah translator is common for (ל)אין מספר as in Gen 41:49; Joel 1:6.

γῆ—ארצו. The change from χώρα to γῆ must be meant for stylistic variation, a change maintained in the next verse.

Isaiah 2:8

LXX καὶ ἐνεπλήσθη ἡ γῆ βδελυγμάτων τῶν ἔργων τῶν χειρῶν αὐτῶν, καὶ προσεκύνησαν οἷς ἐποίησαν οἱ δάκτυλοι αὐτῶν·

ET and their land filled with abominations, the works of their hands, and they prostrated themselves to what their fingers fashioned.

MT ותמלא ארצו אלילים למעשה ידיו ישתחוו לאשר עשו אצבעתיו

βδελυγμάτων—אלילים. This equivalence occurs only once more in the LXX, and that later in our chapter at vs. 20. On the other hand, the Hebrew noun in its plural form as here occurs eight more times in Isaiah, and each time it is rendered with χειροποίητα 'hand-made objects' except once:[31] 2:18, 20; 19:1; 31:7.[32] It appears thus that, for our translator, not only the abominable nature of the pagan objects of worship, but also the fact that they are human, manual products is to be stressed.

τῶν ἔργων τῶν χειρῶν αὐτῶν—למעשה ידיו. Either the translator's *Vorlage* did not have the preposition *lamed* or he decided to ignore it. If the latter were the case, his decision may have had to do with another textual aspect, namely his *Vorlage* may have had the conjunction *waw* prefixed to ישתחוו or he mentally inserted it there, as his translation with καί shows. This assumption gains in plausibility, given the aorist tense chosen. The Hebrew imperfect here, without *waw*, can be either an iterative, habitual past or a plain, poetic, simple preterite. The former analysis is more likely.

οἷς is an antecedentless relative pronoun, and its case is determined not by its syntactic value in the relative clause, but governed by the verb in the main clause, προσκυνέω, which requires a dative.[33]

---

30 See our remarks above at v. 4.

31 19:3 τοὺς θεούς, probably reading אלים or אלהים instead of אלילים.

32 At 2:20 and 31:7 the translation is elliptical with χειροποίητα not repeated.

33 See Muraoka, *Lexicon*, s.v. ὅς g.

Isaiah 2:9

LXX καὶ ἔκυψεν ἄνθρωπος, καὶ ἐταπεινώθη ἀνήρ, καὶ οὐ μὴ ἀνήσω αὐτούς.

ET and one bent forward, and one prostrated oneself, and I will never forgive them.

MT וישח אדם וישפל איש ואל תשא להם

ἔκυψεν—ישח. The Greek verb meaning 'to bend forward' is applied here to the posture taken by someone prostrating himself in deference as is manifest in Isa 46:6 κύψαντες προσκυνοῦσιν αὐτοῖς. In a similar context at Isa 51:23 κύψον it is used to render a related Hebrew root שחה. For the collocation of the Greek verb with προσκυνέω, see also Gen 43:28; Exod 4:31, 12:27, 34:8; Nu 22:31; Jdt 13:17. This must be implied in our passage here, too, following the description of pagan worship in the preceding verse.

καὶ ἐταπεινώθη ἀνήρ—וישפל איש. The Greek verb, which is rather frequent in the LXX, is used in Isaiah some 25 times, of which 11 times to render the Hebrew verb שפל *qal*[34] or *hiph'il*. In this passage the Greek verb, parallel with κύπτω, is most likely used as a synonym of it.[35] The passive is only so in form, but not in function.[36] Further, ἀνήρ is used here as a synonym of ἄνθρωπος in parallelism, with no emphasis on the maleness,[37] just as at 56:2: ἀνήρ (אנוש) || ἄνθρωπος (בן אדם). But cf. vss. 11 and 17 below. From this point up to the end of vs. 10 there is a major omission in 1QIsa[a].

καὶ οὐ μὴ ἀνήσω αὐτούς—ואל תשא להם. The Greek would represent ואל אשא להם (or: ולא). Here the translator makes the Lord speak instead of addressing Him, just as at the start of the pericope, vs. 6, he had decided to make 'He deserted' out of 'you deserted'. His *Vorlage* probably read the same as the MT, and he decided to take some liberty with the difficult text in order to make some sense out of it.

The sense of the Greek verb here, ἀνίημι, can be defined as 'to let go unpunished'.[38] This sense is attested already at Gen 18:24 οὐκ ἀνήσεις

[34] Including 3:17 with ושפח.

[35] Thus not as in NETS: 'a man was humbled,' in any case not *in sensu bono*. For the same reason a paraphrastic rendering of Ottley, 'a mean man boweth down, and a great man is humbled' is unjustifiable: Ottley, *Book of Isaiah* 1, p. 67.

[36] See above on ὑψωθήσεται (vs. 2) and ἐνεπλήσθη (vss. 6, 7, 8).

[37] See Muraoka, *Lexicon*, s. v., **2a**.

[38] See Muraoka, *Lexicon*, s. v., **2**. Ottley's 'I will not let them be' is too vague: Ottley, *Book of Isaiah* 1, p. 67.

πάντα τὸν τόπον . . . ; 'Surely you will forgive the whole place . . . ?', where it is paralleled by ἀφίημι at vs. 26.[39] The verb can take an accusative of inanimate object: Isa 1:14 οὐκέτι ἀνήσω τὰς ἁμαρτίας ὑμῶν 'I shall not forgive your sins yet again.'

Isaiah 2:10

LXX καὶ νῦν εἰσέλθετε εἰς τὰς πέτρας καὶ κρύπτεσθε εἰς τὴν γῆν ἀπὸ προσώπου τοῦ φόβου κυρίου καὶ ἀπὸ τῆς δόξης τῆς ἰσχύος αὐτοῦ, ὅταν ἀναστῇ θραῦσαι τὴν γῆν.

ET And now, enter the rock caves and hide in the ground from the terror of the Lord and from His mighty glory, when He rises to crush the earth.

MT בוא בצור והטמן בעפר מפני פחד יהוה ומהדר גאנו

καὶ νῦν. Just as at vs. 5, one need not postulate ועתה in the Hebrew *Vorlage*. The translator probably recognized here a new start, inserting this discourse marker. As vs. 5 started with an exhortation, here the verse begins with an imperative.

εἰσέλθετε εἰς τὰς πέτρας—בוא בצור. The switch from the singular of the Hebrew text to the plural conforms with αὐτούς at the end of the preceding verse. This is simpler than to assume that our translator shared the analysis of בוא and הטמן as the infinitives as suggested by Rashi and Ibn Ezra *ad loc*. Their analysis was probably triggered by the apparent singular number if they are to be understood as imperatives.[40] The grammatical number of the following noun has been adjusted accordingly: from 'rock' to 'rocks'.

ἀπὸ προσώπου τοῦ φόβου κυρίου—מפני פחד יהוה. The pseudo-preposition, ἀπὸ προσώπου, a Hebrew calque, is often used with verbs of moving away from a fearful or hostile person or object, so with Gen 16:6 ἀποδιδράσκω; Exod 14:25 φεύγω; Deut 3:8 κρύπτω; 31:6 φοβέομαι.

The analysis of the Greek genitive here is just as ambiguous as that of the Hebrew construct phrase: subjective 'terror awakened by the Lord' or objective 'terror and fear felt towards the Lord'. In any event, φόβος does not mean here pious fear, sense of awe as in Isa 26:18 διὰ τὸν φόβον σου, κύριε; Prov 1:7 ἀρχὴ σοφίας φόβος κυρίου, and that in spite of its juxtaposition with τῆς δόξης τῆς ἰσχύος αὐτου, for God's mighty glory

[39] Note Sym. here: και μη αφης αυτοις.

[40] One of the alternative analyses mentioned by Ibn Ezra. David Qimhi ad loc. takes the forms as imperatives, supplying 'then people would say to one another, . . .' See the discussion in Dominique Barthélemy, *Critique textuelle de l'ancient testament 2. Isaïe, Jérémie, Lamentations* (OBO 50.2; Fribourg–Göttingen, 1986), pp. 19–20.

or glorious might[41] could strike and instil fear and terror into the hearts of beholders.[42] The collocation with κρύπτεσθε … ἀπὸ προσώπου as at Gen 3:8 ἐκρύβησαν ἀπὸ προσώπου τοῦ κυρίου … ἐν μέσῳ τοῦ ξύλου renders further support to this analysis.

ἀπὸ τῆς δόξης τῆς ἰσχύος αὐτοῦ—מהדר גאנו. The Greek genitival collocation occurs only here and in the two parallel passages later in the chapter, vss. 19 and 21. Besides, the unusual choice of ἰσχύς as a rendering of גאן is confined to these three cases in the entire LXX. This Hebrew construct chain is equally unique to these three cases in the Hebrew Bible. One would only note a case of juxtaposition of the two Greek nouns, also applied to God as here: 1 Chr 16:28 δότε τῷ κυρίῳ δόξαν καὶ ἰσχύν, where the Greek noun concerned renders, however, עז.

ὅταν ἀναστῇ θραῦσαι τὴν γῆν. This plus has probably penetrated from the two parallel passages, vss. 19 and 21. No reason suggests itself to explain why the corresponding Hebrew clause should have fallen out here.[43]

Isaiah 2:11

LXX οἱ γὰρ ὀφθαλμοὶ κυρίου ὑψηλοί, ὁ δὲ ἄνθρωπος ταπεινός· καὶ ταπεινωθήσεται τὸ ὕψος τῶν ἀνθρώπων, καὶ ὑψωθήσεται κύριος μόνος ἐν τῇ ἡμέρᾳ ἐκείνῃ.

ET For the eyes of the Lord are lofty. Man, however, is lowly; the loftiness of men will be lowered, and the Lord alone will be exalted on that day.

MT עיני גבהות אדם שפל ושח רום אנשים ונשגב יהוה לבדו ביום ההוא

οἱ γὰρ ὀφθαλμοὶ κυρίου ὑψηλοί—עיני גבהות. The Hebrew text as it stands in the MT and the following clause seem to express similar thought in parallelism, namely a radical downward shift in the status of the people as a consequence of God's action. By contrast, in the MT, the contrast sets in only in the third clause. Thus, the Septuagint is, in a sense, more symmetrical with the insertion of ὁ δὲ ἄνθρωπος ταπεινός, which is most likely of secondary nature; as a result the LXX presents two sets of antithetical parallelism, and the two sets are in turn in the form of chiastic parallelism. This structure is evident in the repetition of identical roots:

---

41 On how to analyse this construct chain, cf. Joüon–Muraoka, *Grammar*, § 141m.

42 Clines argues for the basic unity of these two aspects: David J.A. Clines, '"The Fear of the Lord is Wisdom" (Job 28:28)', in Ellen van Wolde (ed.), *Job 28: Cognition in Context* (BINS 64; Leiden, 2003), pp. 57–92, esp. pp. 69–70.

43 See the discussion in Barthélemy, *Critique*, pp. 15–16.

a) Lord ὑψηλοί
b) man ταπεινός
c) man ταπεινωθήσεται
d) Lord ὑψωθήσεται

The first Greek clause of the verse, when retroverted into Hebrew, might read something like עיני יהוה גבוהות. One would never know what the prophet wrote, but one need not postulate that the LXX translator's *Vorlage* read as just retroverted.[44] Even that retroverted text would leave שפל incongruent.[45] Then the LXX form here was probably induced by our translator's view of the overall literary structure of the verse as presented above. This literary aspect, it seems, was to our translator such an overriding concern that it did not occur to him to ponder over the fact that, in the biblical language, the notion of raised, lofty eyes carries a negative connotation as in Prov 30:13 ἔκγονον κακὸν ὑψηλοὺς ὀφθαλμοὺς ἔχει 'wicked offspring has lofty eyes'; Isa 10:12 τὸ ὕψος τῆς δόξης τῶν ὀφθαλμῶν αὐτοῦ 'the arrogant look arising from his glory' and even in our own passage.

ταπεινωθήσεται τὸ ὕψος τῶν ἀνθρώπων—שח רום אנשים. Unlike at vs. 9, we have here a genuinely passive form. The decline of the status is going to be brought upon them, imposed on them. The grammatical subject is people no longer. In vs. 9 the parallelism of two synonymous nouns, אדם and איש, were reproduced in Greek with ἄνθρωπος and ἀνήρ. Here, however, the parallelism has been sacrificed in order to highlight the opposition between God and man, and for that reason the same noun, ἄνθρωπος, is used to represent the term opposed to God.

Isaiah 2:12

LXX ἡμέρα γὰρ κυρίου σαβαωθ ἐπὶ πάντα ὑβριστὴν καὶ ὑπερήφανον καὶ ἐπὶ πάντα ὑψηλὸν καὶ μετέωρον, καὶ ταπεινωθήσονται,

ET For the day of the Lord of Sabaoth is on every arrogant and haughty person and on every overweening and proud person, and they will be laid low,

MT כי יום ליהוה צבאות על כל גאה ורם ועל כל נשא ושפל

[44] The translator's *Vorlage* may have had an abbreviated Tetragrammaton, עיני י׳, as Seeligmann, *Septuagint Version*, p. 66, thinks, which does not affect our argument. See also Ziegler, *Untersuchungen*, p. 61.

[45] תשפלנה of 1QIsa^a is most likely an early attempt to improve on a Hebrew text such as the MT.

ἡμέρα γὰρ κυρίου σαβαωθ—כי יום ליהוה צבאות. True, the syntagm 'noun phrase—*lamed*—noun phrase' replaces sometimes a bound, construct phrase.[46] Here, however, the Hebrew phrase is best analysed as a self-contained nominal clause further supplemented by what follows: 'the Lord Sabaoth has (set) a day (to visit every ...)'. The LXX translator, by contrast, has analysed the first part as the subject and what follows as its predicate.

ὑβριστὴν—גאה. This rare noun, occurring only ten times in the LXX, meets us once again at 16:6 where its Hebrew equivalent is most likely a faulty spelling for גאה, which we find in 1QIsa[a].

ἐπὶ πάντα ὑψηλὸν καὶ μετέωρον, καὶ ταπεινωθήσονται—על כל נשא ושפל. Seeing that the preceding על כל is also followed by a pair of two substantivized, synonymous adjectives joined by the coordinating conjunction, one can reasonably anticipate the same here. Besides, the following three verses, 13–15, all consist of two prepositional phrases also introduced by על כל. Syntactically speaking, therefore, from 12b to the end of vs. 15 of the MT constitutes one long adjunct of the nominal clause יום ליהוה צבאות in 12a. Therefore, שפל standing at the very end of vs. 12 is highly suspect, though the *Vorlage* of the LXX did have it, as is evidenced by καὶ ταπεινωθήσονται.[47]

What Hebrew lexeme could be supplied then as a synonym of נשא? The Greek collocation ὑψηλὸς καὶ μετέωρος occurs in the next verse, but is one of the terms in the synonymous pair earlier in 12b, so that its repetition so soon after is unlikely. The same collocation is found also at Isa 57:7, where the MT has גבה ונשא. Though the sequence of the synonyms is reverse and the pair is used in its literal sense, applied to mountains, גבה emerges as a plausible candidate, as was suggested by Winton Thomas in his edition of BHS. Note also Isa 5:15 with the same Hebrew adjective used figuratively in related context: οἱ ὀφθαλμοὶ οἱ μετέωροι ταπεινωθήσονται—עיני גבהים תשפלנה.

Isaiah 2:13

LXX καὶ ἐπὶ πᾶσαν κέδρον τοῦ Λιβάνου τῶν ὑψηλῶν καὶ μετεώρων καὶ ἐπὶ πᾶν δένδρον βαλάνου Βασαν

ET and on every tall and lofty cedar of Lebanon and every oak-tree of Bashan

---

[46] See Joüon–Muraoka, *Grammar*, § 130.

[47] Cf. the discussion in Barthélemy, *Critique*, pp. 16–18.

MT ועל כל ארזי הלבנון הרמים והנשאים ועל כל אלוני הבשן

ἐπὶ πᾶσαν κέδρον τοῦ Λιβάνου τῶν ὑψηλῶν καὶ μετεώρων—**על כל ארזי הלבנון הרמים והנשאים**. The construct phrase, which occurs five times in the Bible, has the nomen regens invariably in the plural. That the same was true here is betrayed by the inadvertent use of the plural adjectives. The use of the singular κέδρον can best be explained as due to the fact that in the immediately preceding verse 12, each of the two **על כל** phrases was followed by a pair of two coordinated lexemes in the singular. This decision by the translator has been carried through up to vs. 14 where every plural form has been systematically converted to the singular.

ἐπὶ πᾶν δένδρον βαλάνου Βασαν—**על כל אלוני הבשן**. The noun βάλανος primarily means 'acorn', but also denotes a tree which bears such fruit as at Gen 35:8 ὑπὸ τὴν βάλανον, 'under the oak-tree'. Our translator sticks to its primary meaning, hence the addition of δένδρον.[48] See also Isa 6:13 ὡς βάλανος ὅταν ἐκπέσῃ ἀπὸ τῆς θήκης αὐτῆς, 'like an acorn when it falls out of its husk'.

Isaiah 2:14

LXX καὶ ἐπὶ πᾶν ὄρος καὶ ἐπὶ πάντα βουνὸν ὑψηλὸν

ET and on every mountain and on every high hill

MT ועל כל ההרים הרמים ועל כל הגבעות הנשאות

ἐπὶ πᾶν ὄρος—**על כל ההרים הרמים**. In view of the parallelism the first noun is expected to have an attributive adjective. We have here most likely a scribal error due to the graphic similarity between the two lexemes.

Isaiah 2:15

LXX καὶ ἐπὶ πάντα πύργον ὑψηλὸν καὶ ἐπὶ πᾶν τεῖχος ὑψηλὸν

ET and on every high tower and on every high wall

MT ועל כל מגדל גבה ועל כל חומה בצורה

τεῖχος ὑψηλὸν—**חומה בצורה**. The choice of ὑψηλός lacks precision. Walls are usually high, but fortification and height are two distinct notions. Cf.

[48] It is unnecessary to suppose, *pace* Goshen-Gottstein, that we have here a doublet under Aramaic influence אילני אלוני, which would make the phrase one word too long in comparison with the parallel phrase: Moshe H. Goshen-Gottstein (ed.), *The Book of Isaiah* (Jerusalem, 1995), *ad loc.*

Deut 28:52 τὰ τείχη σου τὰ ὑψηλὰ καὶ τὰ ὀχυρά, 'your high and fortified walls'. The use of ὑψηλός in our passage is probably due to the translator's desire to underline the opposition between ὑψηλός and ταπεινός, an important theme which runs through this pericope.

Isaiah 2:16

LXX καὶ ἐπὶ πᾶν πλοῖον θαλάσσης καὶ ἐπὶ πᾶσαν θέαν πλοίων κάλλους·

ET and on every sea-going boat and every beautiful-looking boat

MT ועל כל אניות תרשיש ועל כל שכיות החמדה

ἐπὶ πᾶν πλοῖον θαλάσσης—על כל אניות תרשיש. On the use of the singular, see above at vs. 13.

The standing phrase meaning 'the ships of Tarshish' occurs three more times in Isaiah, translated in two different manners: 23:1, 14 πλοῖα Καρχηδόνος;[49] 60:9 πλοῖα Θαρσις. In our passage the LXX witnesses are unanimous with not a single variant. To state under which flag the ships were sailing appears, in these latter cases, to provide important information, given the general message of the two chapters concerned, whereas in our chapter this was not vital information. This is the likely reason why our translator was content with a generic lexeme, θάλασσα.[50] Among the remaining biblical passages where this fleet is mentioned, note especially Ezek 27:25 πλοῖα, ἐν αὐτοῖς Καρχηδόνιοι.

πᾶσαν θέαν πλοίων κάλλους—כל שכיות החמדה. The Greek phrase, literally translated, would mean 'every sight of boats of beauty'. The Hebrew lexeme *שְׂכִיָּה / שְׁכִיָּה is a hapax. Its parallelism with אניות as well as the attestation of *ṯkt* in Ugaritic[51] (most likely denoting a kind of boat) give us some clue about the meaning of this Hebrew *hapax*. Whether our LXX translator arrived at his rendering with πλοῖον unaided by the parallelism

---

[49] On the identification of Tarshish with Carthage and its implications, see Arie van der Kooij, 'A Short Commentary on Some Verses of the Old Greek of Isaiah 23', *BIOSCS* 15 (1982), pp. 36–50, esp. 40–45.

[50] There is thus, *pace* Seeligmann (*Septuagint Version*, p. 30), no need to blame copyists for a careless error for Θαρσης. Mordechay Mishor shows that in Talmudic Hebrew the Hebrew lexeme is understood as meaning 'sea': 'תרשיש "sea", in Talmudic Sources', *Leš* 34 (1969–1970), pp. 318–319. We need, however, to take into account the LXX rendering of the lexeme in the two other Isaiah passages.

[51] Cf. Gregorio del Olmo Lete and Joaquín Sanmartín, tr. Wilfred Watson, *A Dictionary of the Ugaritic Language in the Alphabetic Tradition* (HO 67; Leiden, 2003), pp. 904–905. If this Ugaritic etymology were valid, the Hebrew noun would begin with שׁ, not שׂ.

is hard to tell.[52] On the other hand, the immediately preceding θέαν looks intrusive. It might be a secondary, doublet rendering based on an Aramaicizing analysis of the Hebrew word, namely √ שׂכה 'to gaze, look forward to'.[53]

This is the only case of the equation חמדה—κάλλος in the LXX. See also Isa 53:2 נחמדהו—κάλλος.

Isaiah 2:17

LXX καὶ ταπεινωθήσεται πᾶς ἄνθρωπος, καὶ πεσεῖται ὕψος ἀνθρώπων, καὶ ὑψωθήσεται κύριος μόνος ἐν τῇ ἡμέρᾳ ἐκείνῃ.

ET and every man shall be brought low, and the loftiness of people will drop, and the Lord alone will be exalted on that day.

MT ושח גבהות האדם ושפל רום אנשים ונשגב יהוה לבדו ביום ההוא

πᾶς ἄνθρωπος—גבהות האדם. In comparison with the parallel passage at vs. 11a the positions of the synonymous lexemes, שח and שפל, have been reversed here. The parallelism ensures the correctness of גבהות, which, however, is not represented in the LXX. In vs. 11 ὑψηλός was set in parallelism with ὕψος. The translator could have written πᾶς ἄνθρωπος ὑψηλός. A probable reason why he has not done so is that in the preceding series of entities to be visited by God the pattern 'πᾶς + singular noun' with no further expansion has been consistently used.

The Hebrew phrase here contrasts with its parallel in vs. 11 on account of the definite article, which cannot be justified as anaphoric, for then רום אנשים should equally have the article. In the edition of 1QIsa[a] its editors restore it, though a consideration of space in comparison with the line immediately above makes its restoration somewhat implausible.

πεσεῖται ὕψος ἀνθρώπων—שפל רום אנשים. The translator, who used, at vs. 11, two Greek lexemes derived from one root, ταπεινός and ταπεινόω, as he rendered two Hebrew synonyms of two distinct roots, שחח and שפל, here uses two Greek verbs derived from two distinct bases, ταπεινόω and πίπτω. A possible reason for this is that, whilst in vs. 11 he used an adjective and a verb of the same basis, here he uses two verbs, and was disinclined to use one and the same verb twice.

[52] Ziegler, *Untersuchungen*, p. 61, mentions Job 40:31 where שכה is rendered with πλωτόν 'floating vessel', parallel to πλοῖον.

[53] Goshen-Gottstein, *Isaiah*, *ad loc.*, would not accept a doublet or the Egyptian-Ugaritic-Aramaic etymology. But the parallelism of πλοῖον alone cannot account for the LXX text.

It is intriguing that both nouns are anarthrous, whilst they are both articular in the parallel passage at vs. 11, and that despite the complete identity in Hebrew between the two passages. See also vs. 20.

Isaiah 2:18

LXX καὶ τὰ χειροποίητα πάντα κατακρύψουσιν

ET and they will stack away the handmade objects altogether

MT והאלילים כליל יחלף

τὰ χειροποίητα—האלילים, on which see above at vs. 8.

πάντα κατακρύψουσιν—כליל יחלף. In its choice of κατακρύπτω the LXX departs considerably from the Hebrew original. In spite of the incongruence in the grammatical number,[54] the verb concerned should have occasioned no particular difficulty. Moreover, the *qal* verb is intransitive, whereas its Greek rendering is transitive. Even its transitive *hiph'il* transform, 'to cause to pass away', means something quite different from 'to hide away'. Our translator might be wanting to underline what the people are going to do, their reaction to God's visitation, rather than to say what is going to happen to them, their fate. This, he may have thought aloud, is in keeping with vs. 20a, which describes what the people are going to do to their pagan objects of worship fashioned by themselves, an equivalent of τὰ χειροποίητα of our verse. The choice of the verb meaning 'to conceal' for this purpose was probably influenced by an earlier parallel at vs. 10 with הטמן rendered with a simplex, κρύπτεσθε.

Isaiah 2:19

LXX εἰσενέγκαντες εἰς τὰ σπήλαια καὶ εἰς τὰς σχισμὰς τῶν πετρῶν καὶ εἰς τὰς τρώγλας τῆς γῆς ἀπὸ προσώπου τοῦ φόβου κυρίου καὶ ἀπὸ τῆς δόξης τῆς ἰσχύος αὐτοῦ, ὅταν ἀναστῇ θραῦσαι τὴν γῆν.

ET carrying (them) into the caves and into the clefts of rocks and into the crevices of the ground from the terror of the Lord and from His mighty glory, when He rises to crush the earth.

MT ובאו במערות צרים ובמחלות עפר מפני פחד יהוה ומהדר גאונו בקומו לערץ הארץ

εἰσενέγκαντες—ובאו. The transitivization process continues from the immediately preceding verse. This grammatical transformation, however, carries a theological implication. For the message thus conveyed implies that the people were stacking away their objects of profane wor-

[54] Note יחלופו in 1QIsa[a].

ship for possible future reuse. They did not hide themselves in caves, as the kings in Josh 10:16 did: 'And these five kings fled and hid themselves in the cave (κατεκρύβησαν εἰς τὸ σπήλαιον) in Makeda'.

The use of the conjunctive participle is stylistically more elegant than mechanically reproducing the Hebrew structure such as εἰσοίσουσιν (αὐτά).

εἰς τὰ σπήλαια καὶ εἰς τὰς σχισμὰς τῶν πετρῶν καὶ εἰς τὰς τρώγλας τῆς γῆς—במערות צרים ובמחלות עפר. The translation is rather expansive with three hiding-places as against two in the Hebrew text. In the Hebrew each of the two locations is in the form of a construct phrase, the nomen rectum of which specifies the substance of the location, rock as against soil. In the Greek version only the last two follow the Hebrew pattern, whilst the first consists of a single noun. The chart below displays how our translator has handled the three parallel passages:[55]

vs 10		צור	πέτρα
	+	עפר	γῆ
vs 19		מערות	σπήλαιον
	+	ø	σχισμή
		צור	πέτρας
	+	מחלה	τρώγλη
		עפר	γῆς
vs 21		נקרה	τρώγλη
		צור	στερεᾶς πέτρας
	+	סעיף	σχισμή
		סלע	πέτρας

Let us note first that each of the two nouns in vs. 10 appears in the other two verses in the genitive in Greek and as nomen rectum in Hebrew. Moreover, Hebrew uses seven different nouns, which correspond to as many Greek renderings. The correspondence, however, is not exactly one-to-one. צור is rendered in two different ways, apparently with a view to indicating a subtle distinction between צור and סלע. On the other hand τρώγλη renders two different Hebrew nouns. The increase in the number of hiding locations in our verse appears to derive from the translator's desire to harmonize vs. 19 with vs. 21 by introducing one of the two elements missing in vs. 19, σχισμή, but at the same time not deleting an element in vs. 19, though absent in vs. 21.

55 The definite article has been deleted, and what corresponds to the nomen regens is given in the nominative case, ignoring the preceding preposition. The plus (+) symbol marks the coordinating conjunction Waw or καί.

καὶ εἰς τὰς τρώγλας τῆς γῆς—ובמחלות עפר. τρώγλη occurs only eight times in the LXX, half of them in Isaiah, rendering four different Hebrew words. Note especially 7:19.

θραῦσαι—לערץ. The choice of θραύω 'to crush' to render ערץ 'to strike terror (into somebody's heart)' is unique to this passage in the entire LXX.[56] A comparison with the other passages in Isaiah where the verb root occurs not only in *qal*, but also in *hiph'il* and *niph'al* with an associated sense suggests that our translator was uncertain of the precise meaning of this verb. At 47:12 and 8:13 it is left untranslated, and in the latter passage despite its parallelism with מורא. At 8:12 it is rendered with the passive of ταράσσω 'to be troubled', despite its parallelism with ירא. Finally, at 29:23, ערץ *hiph'il* is rendered with φοβέομαι. However, it is parallel with קדש *hiph'il*, just as in a closely related passage, 8:12 where we see קדש *hiph'il*, ירא, and ערץ in parallelism, and one might suspect that at 29:23 our translator mentally replaced יעריצו with ייראו.

Isaiah 2:20

LXX τῇ γὰρ ἡμέρᾳ ἐκείνῃ ἐκβαλεῖ ἄνθρωπος τὰ βδελύγματα αὐτοῦ τὰ ἀργυρᾶ καὶ τὰ χρυσᾶ, ἃ ἐποίησαν προσκυνεῖν, τοῖς ματαίοις καὶ ταῖς νυκτερίσι

ET For on that day man will throw out his silver and golden abominations, which he made in order to worship (them), to the meaningless objects and the bats

MT ביום ההוא ישליך האדם את אלילי כספו ואת אלילי זהבו אשר עשו לו להשתחות לחפר פרות ולעטלפים

ἐκβαλεῖ—ישליך. Apparently the contradiction between carrying some objects of pagan worship into hiding-places in the preceding verse and throwing some out here has escaped the translator.

τὰ χρυσᾶ. The decision not mechanically to repeat τὰ βδελύγματα αὐτοῦ is stylistically elegant and commendable.

ἐποίησαν—עשו לו. The incongruence between the plural of the verb and the singular pronominal referent throughout the verse apparently did not bother our translator. It is quite likely that 1QIsa[a] with אצבעותיו (partly restored) has preserved the original form of the text. The absence in the LXX of a reflexive pronoun, restored in some witnesses, mainly Lucianic, in conformity with the MT, may also be secondary. A comparison between the two penultimate lines of Column II of 1QIsa[a] suggests

---

[56] David Qimhi follows the Targum here, which reads למתבר 'to break, crush'.

that, *pace* the editors of the scroll, לו should be deleted from their restoration. Then we obtain a text completely identical with the parallel passage, vs. 8.

τοῖς ματαίοις καὶ ταῖς νυκτερίσι—לחפר פרות ולעטלפים. The first half of the MT is admittedly in disorder, a wrong word-division. See 1QIsa[a] לחפרפרים. The singular of the noun could take a feminine morpheme: cf. יונים—יונה. The parallelism could have signalled to our translator that the first term probably refers to some living creature. Though he did correctly render the second term, perhaps aided by the tradition of exegesis going back to the Pentateuch (Lev 11:19 and Deut 14:18 where the LXX has νυκτερίς in both cases), the first term, a *hapax* in Biblical Hebrew, was a puzzler, and he solved the problem by offering a generic, colourless rendering, though an epithet often applied to objects of idol worship.

The question of whether לחפר פרות ולעטלפים should be construed with להשתחות or ישליך has been raised already by Rashi and David Qimhi. Bats, however, are not worshipped anywhere in the Bible. Though the syntax with the relative clause intervening is slightly awkward, there is no want of such examples in Biblical Hebrew.[57]

Isaiah 2:21

LXX τοῦ εἰσελθεῖν εἰς τὰς τρώγλας τῆς στερεᾶς πέτρας καὶ εἰς τὰς σχισμὰς τῶν πετρῶν ἀπὸ προσώπου τοῦ φόβου κυρίου καὶ ἀπὸ τῆς δόξης τῆς ἰσχύος αὐτοῦ, ὅταν ἀναστῇ θραῦσαι τὴν γῆν.

ET to enter the crevices of solid rock and the clefts of rocks from the terror of the Lord and from His mighty glory, when He rises to crush the earth.

MT לבוא בנקרות הצרים ובסעפי הסלעים מפני פחד יהוה ומהדר גאונו בקומו לערץ הארץ

τὰς τρώγλας τῆς στερεᾶς πέτρας καὶ εἰς τὰς σχισμὰς τῶν πετρῶν—בנקרות הצרים ובסעפי הסלעים. The Hebrew noun, נקרה, occurs only once more in the Bible: Exod 33:22בנקרת הצור—εἰς ὀπὴν τῆς πέτρας. In his interpretation of סעפי הסלעים the translator was probably aided by its preceding parallel phrase. At 57:5, where we have the same Hebrew phrase, his translation leaves something to be desired: ἀνὰ μέσον τῶν πετρῶν 'between the rocks' for MT תחת סעפי הסלעים.

[57] See Joüon–Muraoka, *Grammar*, § 158u.

The concluding verse, vs. 22, of the MT is missing from the mainline witnesses of the Septuagint, the reason for which is not clear.[58]

[58] For a possible reason for the omission, see A. van der Kooij, 'The Septuagint of Isaiah and the Hebrew Text of Isaiah 2:22 and 36:7', in Peter W. Flint, Emanuel Tov, and James C. VanderKam (eds.), *Studies in the Hebrew Bible, Qumran, and the Septuagint Presented to Eugene Ulrich* (VT.S 101; Leiden etc., 2006), pp. 377–386, esp. 377–382.

THE TEXT OF ISAIAH 26:9–19 IN THE SYRIAC ODES

Wido van Peursen

1. *Introduction*

Some passages of the Syriac version of Isaiah have the particularity that they have been transmitted in two different contexts: as part of the Book of Isaiah and as part of the Odes. This applies to Isa 26:9–19, 38:10–20, as well as the combination of 42:10–13 and 45:8.[1]

The Odes are a series of psalms and hymns from the Bible that were used in liturgy. In the first of a series of articles dealing with the Odes,[2] H. Schneider describes the development of the Odes in various steps, beginning with the use of some biblical passages in Jewish liturgy (such as the use of Exodus 15 in the night of Passover); the adaption of this usage by Christians, who included more Old Testament passages as well as some hymns from the New Testament; the appearance of Odes lists in the third and fourth century (including the lists of Origen and Ambrosius); the codification of these lists in the fifth century (attested, for example, in the list of Niceta of Remesiana); the practice of adding these Odes to the Psalter, both in Psalter manuscripts and in complete Bible manuscripts (as in the fifth-century Codex Alexandrinus); the spread of this Greek practice in Eastern Christianity, including the Coptic, Ethiopic, and Syriac Churches; and the development of various

[1] The investigations were supported by the Netherlands Organisation for Scientific Research (NWO).

[2] Heinrich Schneider, 'Die biblischen Oden im christlichen Altertum', *Bib.* 30 (1949), pp. 28–65; the other parts of the series appeared also in *Bib.* 30: 'Die biblischen Oden seit dem sechsten Jahrhundert' (pp. 239–272); 'Die biblischen Oden in Jerusalem und Konstantinopel' (pp. 433–452); and 'Die biblischen Oden im Mittelalter' (pp. 479–500). On the Syriac Odes see further Schneider, 'Wenig beachtete Rezensionen der Peschitta', *ZAW* 62 (1950), pp. 168–199; and the introduction to the Odes in the Leiden Peshitta edition: Heinrich Schneider, 'Canticles or Odes', in *The Old Testament in Syriac according to the Peshiṭta Version* 4.6 *Canticles or Odes, Prayer of Manasseh, Apocryphal Psalms, Psalms of Solomon, Tobith, I (3) Esdras* (Leiden, 1972). On the Greek Odes see Alfred Rahlfs, *Psalmi cum Odis* (Septuaginta Vetus Testamentum Graecum Auctoritate Academiae Litterarum Gottingensis editum 10; Göttingen, 1967), pp. 78–80.

competing Odes selections, especially the Fourteen Odes list (attested in the Codex Alexandrinus) and the Nine Odes list (which eventually became dominant).

I will not go into all details of Schneider's reconstruction. For my present purposes two elements of it are important. First, that the selection of Odes and the practice of treating them as an appendix to the Book of Psalms arose in the Greek tradition and from there entered the Syriac tradition; and second, that there were several series of Odes, before the Nine Odes list became the standard.

The three chapters from Isaiah mentioned above befell different fates in the Odes series. The use of Isa 26:9–19 as one of the Odes is well established and the text appears in almost all Odes lists and collections in Greek, Latin, Coptic, Ethiopic, Syriac, and Armenian.[3] It is included in both the Fourteen Odes series and the Nine Odes series. Isa 38:10–20, the Prayer of Hezekiah, was part of the Fourteen Odes list, and in the Codex Alexandrinus it is recognized as an Ode both by the superscription 'Ode' in Isaiah and by its inclusion in the Odes.[4] However, it was not included in the Nine Odes series and finally felt into disuse when the latter became dominant.[5] The appearance of the combination of Isa 42:10–13 and 45:8 among the Odes is restricted to the Syriac and, due to Syriac influence, the Armenian tradition.

Some other passages from Isaiah, which belonged neither to the Fourteen Odes series nor the Nine Odes series, occasionally functioned as Odes as well: Isa 25:1–12 and 26:1–8 (in the Isaiah text of the Codex Alexandrinus and in the Coptic tradition),[6] Isa 12:1–6 (in the Latin

---

[3] Schneider, 'Die biblischen Oden seit dem sechsten Jahrhundert', pp. 241, 243, 256.

[4] The superscriptions and the Odes section belong to two different scribes; cf. Schneider, 'Die biblischen Oden seit dem sechsten Jahrhundert', p. 241.

[5] Cf. Schneider, 'Die biblischen Oden seit dem sechsten Jahrhundert', p. 269: 'Die Oden des *Ezechias* und des *Manasse* wurden zu Blütezeit der Vierzehnodenreihe im Morgenofficium rezitiert. Durch die Neunodenreihe verloren sie jedoch diese Stellung. Das Gebet des *Ezechias* scheint seitdem aus dem byzantinischen Stundengebet völlig verschwunden zu sein.' The Prayer of Manasseh, however, began a new career as part of the Great Compline, a penitential office that is chanted on a number of special occasions; see section 1.5.3 of Ariel Gutman and Wido van Peursen, *The Two Syriac Versions of the Prayer of Manasseh*, forthcoming in the series Gorgias Eastern Christian Studies.

[6] In the Codex Alexandrinus we find the heading 'Ode' before Isa 25:1 and before Isa 26:1, even though in the Odes section in the same codex they are not included; see Schneider, 'Die biblischen Oden im christlichen Altertum', p. 56, and our remark above (note 4) on the two scribes of this codex. On the custom to treat Isa 25:1–12 and Isa 26:1–8 as Odes in the Coptic tradition, see Schneider, 'Die biblischen Oden seit dem sechsten Jahrhundert', p. 242; Walter Till and Peter Sanz, *Eine griechisch-koptische Odenhandschrift*

Church in Western Europe),[7] and Isa 5:1–7 (in some third- en fourth-century Odes lists,[8] in a sixth-century hand in the Codex Sinaiticus,[9] and in the Odes section in a sixth-century bilingual Greek-Latin Psalter).[10]

The practice to treat the Odes as an appendix to the Psalms, as attested in the Greek Codex Alexandrinus, also became common usage in the Syriac tradition. From the eight century onwards the Odes follow the Psalms in all liturgical Psalters and in a number of biblical manuscripts.[11] The selection of Odes differs in the various traditions. The first three Odes, which are common to both the Western and the Eastern traditions, are Exodus 15; Deuteronomy 32; and the combination of Isa 42:10–14 and 45:8. As indicated above, the third Ode is characteristic of the Syriac tradition. The East Syriac manuscripts 8a1 and 18<13dt1 and the Maronite manuscripts 14t1, 15t1, and 16t1 contain these three Odes plus the Song of the Three (Dan 3:57–90). The Melkite manuscripts 10t1, 12t2.5.7.8 contain the Greek series of Nine Odes, thus excluding the typically Syriac third Ode.[12] The West Syriac evidence includes the following manuscripts: 10t2.4.5, 10/7t1, 11t1, which contain Odes I–III (+ three Odes from the New Testament); 9a1, which contains the Fourteen Odes;[13] 9t1–3 and 12t3, which contain the Nine Odes; and 16t4.5, 17t5, which contain abbreviations of the Nine Odes.[14]

Since the selection of Odes and the common practice to include them in Psalters and biblical manuscripts arose in the Greek tradition, the question arises as to whether also a textual relationship with the Greek

---

(Papyrus Copt. Vindob. K. 8706) (Monumenta Biblica et Ecclesiastica 5; Rome, 1939), pp. 21–22.

[7] Schneider, 'Die biblischen Oden seit dem sechsten Jahrhundert', pp. 244–245.

[8] Those of Origen, Ambrosius, and Philo of Karpasia; see Schneider, 'Die biblischen Oden im christlichen Altertum', p. 51.

[9] This hand added the heading 'Ode' before Isa 5:1; see Schneider, 'Die biblischen Oden im christlichen Altertum', p. 41.

[10] In Rahlfs's edition of the Greek Odes marked by the siglum R; see Rahlfs, *Psalmi cum Odis*, p. 10 (description of the manuscript) and p. 80 (contents of the Odes section in this manuscript). In this manuscript Isa 5:1–7 replaces Isa 26:9–19.

[11] Schneider, 'Canticles or Odes', Introduction, p. ii.

[12] The Greek influence concerns not only the selection of the Odes, but also their text form. According to Schneider, 'Canticles or Odes', Introduction, iii, Odes IV–IX 'have been revised to bring their text even closer to that of the Septuagint than the versions in the Jacobite MSS'.

[13] On 9a1 as 'a lonely but interesting witness to the use of the Fourteen Odes series in the Syriac tradition' see Gutman and Van Peursen, *The Two Syriac Versions of the Prayer of Manasseh*, section 1.5.2.

[14] Schneider, 'Canticles or Odes', Introduction, pp. ii–iv; the omission of Isa 26:15 in 17t5 can regarded as part of the abridgment.

version can be established: Were the biblical passages that were selected as Odes according to the Greek model copied from the Peshitta, or were they translated from or influenced by the Greek translation?

In the present paper I will investigate the situation with regard to Isa 26:9–19. This section from Isaiah was particular apt for liturgical purposes and its characterization as an Ode is already attested in the Greek Codex Alexandrinus, both by the superscription 'Ode' in Isaiah and by its inclusion in the Odes section following the Psalms.[15] According to Schneider its liturgical use is already reflected in the New Testament, in Eph 5:14.[16] The references to Resurrection made this biblical passage appropriate for occasions such as the week after Easter and the commemoration of the deceased; the reference to the early morning in the beginning of the prayer gave it a place as a morning prayer,[17] and the opening with 'in the night' triggered an association with the night of Good Friday, an association that may have been reinforced by references to Resurrection later on in this Ode.

Sometimes other sections from Isaiah 26 were used in the liturgy that overlap only partly with the Ode under discussion. Thus according to manuscript called 'COMES', the oldest available Syriac index of scriptural readings, dating from the fifth or sixth century, Isa 26:16–27:13 was read on the Friday of the Week of Rest (i.e. the week after Easter).[18] The same usage is reflected in the section heading ܕܥܪܘܒܬܐ ܕܫܒܬܐ ܕܢܝܚܬܐ 'of the Friday of the Week of Rest' in manuscript 8a1.[19] 6h5 has the three titels: ܕܥܪܘܒܬܐ ܕܢܝܚܬܐ ܕܒܥܘܬܐ 'of the Friday of (the Week of) Rest and of Rogation' (26:12–27:11); ܕܘܟܪܢܐ ܕܥܢܝܕܐ 'in Memory of the Departed' (26:16–27:3); and [ܕܥܪܘ]ܒܬܐ [ܕܛܒ]ܬܐ ܒܠܠܝܐ 'of Good Friday in the Night' (26:16–?).[20] In the liturgy of the Upper

[15] Cf. above, note 4.

[16] Schneider, 'Die biblischen Oden im christlichen Altertum', p. 35. Eph 5:14 is often considered as a baptismal hymn, but according to Schneider, the introduction with 'This is why it says' (διὸ λέγει), which is also used in Eph 4:8 to introduce a quotation from Ps 68:18, suggests that Paul had the words of the Isaiah Ode in mind.

[17] Already John Chrysostom (ca. 347–407 CE) was acquainted with the use of this passage in the monastic morning service; cf. Schneider, 'Die biblischen Oden im christlichen Altertum', p. 47.

[18] F.C. Burkitt, 'The Early Syriac Lectionary System', *Proceedings of the British Academy* 10 (1923), pp. 301–338, esp. 311.

[19] Konrad D. Jenner, *De perikopentitels van de geïllustreerde Syrische kanselbijbel van Parijs (MS Paris, Bibliothèque Nationale, Syriaque 341): een vergelijkend onderzoek naar de oudste Syrische perikopenstelsels* (PhD diss., Leiden University, 1994), p. 54.

[20] Jenner, *Perikopentitels*, p. 403, numbers 59–61; cf. ibid. pp. 80 (especially note 3), 389.

Monastery Isa 26:1–19 was read on the Sunday of Elijah in the Summer, that is, the period after Pentecost.[21]

2. *Analysis*

If we compare the Hebrew Masoretic Text (= MT-Isaiah), the Greek text of the Septuagint of Isaiah (= LXX-Isaiah), the Greek text of the Odes (= LXX-Odes), the Syriac text of Isaiah (= Pesh-Isaiah) and the Syriac text of the Odes (= Pesh-Odes), we can make the following observations.

First, there are major differences between MT-Isaiah and LXX-Isaiah. These differences are mainly due to the difficult Hebrew text of this chapter and a proper evaluation of them would require a thorough exegetical and text-critical study, which is beyond the scope of the present article.[22] It is important to note, however, that any Syriac translator or scribe who was acquainted with both the Hebrew text or the Syriac translation based on it and the Greek text, will have noted the differences and will have had to decide whether he stayed with the Hebrew or Syriac text or followed the Greek text.

Second, between LXX-Isaiah and LXX-Odes there are only minor differences. This agrees with Schneider's observations, who comments:

> Wer die Geschichte der griechischen Oden überblickt, dem erscheinen die einzelnen Oden als wohlbehauene Bausteine; sie wurden einmal aus dem heiligen Berg der Septuaginta gebrochen; seitdem aber ist der Hammer und Meissel der Textbearbeiter anscheinend nicht mehr über sie gekommen (…) Die Entwicklung der griechischen Textgestalt der Oden war also im wesentlichen bereits abgeschlossen, als die Geschichte der Odenreihen begann.[23]

[21] Anton Baumstark, *Nichtevangelische syrische Perikopenordnungen des ersten Jahrtausends* (2nd ed.; LWQF 15; Münster, 1972), p. 25.

[22] Such a study will be part of Wilson de Angelo Cunha's PhD dissertation, *LXX Isaiah 24–27*, which is being written under the supervision of Professor Arie van der Kooij. Note that Van der Kooij himself has always rejected the view that the differences between the Hebrew and the Greek texts can be explained from the difficulties that the Greek translators had with the Hebrew text, a view that was common in the beginning of the twentieth century and represented by the works of R.R. Ottley and Johann Fischer. Following the studies by Joseph Ziegler and Isac L. Seeligmann in the middle of the twentieth century, Van der Kooij considered the translators' theology the main cause for differences between the Hebrew and the Greek.

[23] Schneider, 'Die biblischen Oden in Jerusalem und Konstantinopel', p. 433. Schneider makes an exception for the Song of the Three (Dan 3:57–90).

The differences are so small that in our discussion of possible influence from the Septuagint on the Syriac text, there is not need to differentiate between LXX-Isaiah and LXX-Odes.

Third, in general Pesh-Isaiah agrees with MT-Isaiah rather than with LXX-Isaiah. If we follow the model that 9a1 represents the earliest text type (see below), there is hardly any need to assume Greek influence on the original translation of this chapter.[24] There are a few cases in which the Peshitta agrees with the Septuagint vis-à-vis the Masoretic Text, but even in these cases the assumption of influence from the Greek on the Syriac is not compelling. See the examples given in table 1. In 26:14 the use of the causative in 14b in the Peshitta (as in the Greek) may be triggered by the causative in 26:14a, where the Greek does not have it. Moreover, in this verse there remain fundamental differences between the Greek and the Syriac in which the Syriac is closer to the Hebrew. In 26:18 the Peshitta and the Septuagint reflect the same understanding of יפלו as 'fall' rather than 'give birth', which seems to be the meaning of the Hebrew text,[25] but this too can easily be explained from polygenesis, since the alleged meaning of נפל in this verse, 'to give birth', is uncommon.[26] Polygenesis is also a likely explanation for 26:19, where the pronominal suffix pronoun 'my' attached to 'corpse' was probably as difficult to the ancient translators as it is to modern scholars.[27]

---

[24] The alleged influence of the Septuagint on the Peshitta translators is a debated issue. For bibliographical references to studies on this subject by Weitzman, Lund, and Dirksen, as well as a methodological discussion applied to the Book of Ben Sira, see W.Th. van Peursen, *Language and Interpretation in the Syriac Text of Ben Sira. A Comparative Linguistic and Literary* Study (MPIL 16; Leiden, 2006), pp. 23–32. See now also Ignacio Carbajosa, *The Character of the Syriac Version of Psalms. A Study of Psalms 90–150 in the Peshitta* (MPIL 17; Leiden, 2008), 187–272.

[25] Thus, e.g., NIV 'we have not given birth to people of the world', but contrast AV and RSV, which read '... have not fallen'; compare the pregnancy mentioned earlier in the verse.

[26] Cf. HALOT col. 710*a*; BDB col. 657*b*.

[27] See the discussion of this verse in De Angelo Cunha's forthcoming PhD dissertation.

Table 1: Agreements between the Peshitta and the Septuagint that can be explained from polygenesis

	MT	LXX-Isa (= Odes)	Pesh-Isaiah
14	מתים בל יחיו רפאים בל יקמו	οἱ δὲ νεκροὶ ζωὴν οὐ μὴ ἴδωσιν, οὐδὲ ἰατροὶ οὐ μὴ ἀναστήσωσιν	ܡܝ̈ܬܐ ܠܐ ܡܚܝܢ ܘܓܢܒܪ̈ܐ ܠܐ ܡܩܝܡܝܢ
	Dead ones will not come to live; departed spirits will not *rise*.	The dead will not see life, neither will physicians *raise*.	They do not bring the dead to life and they do not *raise* the mighty men.
18	ובל יפלו ישבי תבל	ἀλλὰ πεσοῦνται οἱ ἐνοικοῦντες ἐπὶ τῆς γῆς.	ܘܠܐ ܢܦܠܘܢ ܥܡܘ̈ܪܝܗ ܕܬܒܝܠ
	... but inhabitants of the earth were not *born*.	... but those who dwell on the earth will *fall*.	(lest) ... and the inhabitants of the earth *fall*.
19	יחיו מתיך נבלתי יקומון	ἀναστήσονται οἱ νεκροί, καὶ ἐγερθήσονται οἱ ἐν τοῖς μνημείοις,	ܢܚܘܢ ܡܝ̈ܬܝܟ ܘܫ̈ܠܕܝܗܘܢ ܢܩܘܡܘܢ
	Your dead will live, —(with) *my corpse*—they will rise.	The dead shall rise and *those who are in the tombs*[28] shall be raised.	Your dead shall rise and *their corpses* shall rise.

In some cases the Peshitta makes distinctions that agree with the Hebrew text, but are not visible in the Greek. Thus it has ܐܪܥܐ where the Hebrew has ארץ (26:9, 10, 15, 18) and ܬܒܝܠ where the Hebrew has תבל (26:9, 18), whereas the Septuagint renders both Hebrew words with γῆ. Sometimes the Peshitta goes its own way, differing from both the Hebrew and the Greek. This happens, for example, in 26:10, where it has ܐܬܪܚܩ ܥܘܠܐ 'the evildoer fled afar',[29] corresponding to Hebrew יחן רשע 'grace is shown to the wicked' and Greek πέπαυται γὰρ ὁ ἀσεβής 'the ungodly is put down'.[30]

[28] For the equivalence of 'corpses' and 'those who are in the tomb', see again De Angelo Cunha's discussion of this verse.

[29] Thus Jessie Payne Smith, *A Compendious Syriac Dictionary Founded upon the Thesaurus Syriacus by R. Payne Smith* (Oxford, 1903; reprint Winona Lake, 1998), col. 538*a*.

[30] This reading may be the result of an inner-Syriac corruption of ܐܬܪܚܡ into ܐܬܪܚܩ; cf. Ernst Liebmann, 'Der Text zu Jesaia 24–27', *ZAW* 24 (1904), pp. 51–104, esp. 66.

Table 2: Peshitta-Isaiah and Peshitta-Odes

	Peshitta-Isaiah	Peshitta-Odes[31]
		ܬܫܒܘܚܬܐ ܕܐܫܥܝܐ
9	ܢܦܫܝ ܐܬܬܐܘܒܬ ܠܟ ܒܠܠܝܐ	ܒܠܠܝܐ ܢܦܫܝ † ܐܬܬܐܘܒܬ † ܠܟ.
	ܘܐܦ ܪܘܚܝ ܒܓܘܝ ܡܩܕܡܐ ܠܘܬܟ	ܐܦ ܪܘܚܝ ܒܓܘܝ ܡܩܕܡܐ ܠܘܬܟ.
	ܡܛܠ ܕܐܝܟ ܕܝܢܝܟ ܥܠ ܐܪܥܐ	ܡܛܠ ܕܐܝܟ ܕܝܢܝܟ ܥܠ ܐܪܥܐ.
	ܙܕܝܩܘܬܐ ܝܠܦܘ ܥܡܘܪܝܗ ܕܬܒܝܠ	ܙܕܝܩܘܬܐ ܝܠܦܘ ܥܡܘܪܝܗ ܕܬܒܝܠ
10	ܐܬܪܚܡ ܥܘܠܐ	ܐܬܪܚܡ ܥܘܠܐ.
	ܕܠܐ ܢܐܠܦ ܙܕܝܩܘܬܐ	ܕܠܐ ܝܠܦ ܙܕܝܩܘܬܐ
	ܒܩܘܫܬܐ ܒܐܪܥܐ ܥܒܕܐ.	ܘܒܩܘܫܬܐ ܒܐܪܥܐ ܥܒܕܐ. ܢܬܛܠ ܪܫܝܥܐ
	ܘܠܐ ܢܚܙܘܢ ܒܫܘܒܚܗ ܕܡܪܝܐ	ܕܠܐ ܢܚܙܐ ܬܫܒܘܚܬܗ ܕܡܪܝܐ
11	ܡܪܝܐ ܒܪܡܬܐ ܕܐܕܪ̈ܥܝܟ	ܡܪܝܐ ܒܪܡܬܐ ܕܐܕܪ̈ܥܝܟ
	ܠܐ ܚܙܘ	ܠܐ ܚܙܘ.
	ܚܙܘ ܘܢܒܗܬܘܢ ܛܢܢܗ ܕܥܡܐ	ܚܙܘ ܘܢܒܗܬܘܢ ܛܢܢܗ ܕܥܡܟ.
	ܘܐܝܟ ܬܢܘܪܐ ܬܐܟܘܠ ܐܢܘܢ	ܘܐܝܟ ܬܢܘܪܐ ܬܐܟܘܠ ܐܢܘܢ
	ܠܒܥܠܕܒܒܝܟ	ܠܒܥܠܕܒܒܝܟ
12	ܡܪܝܐ ܬܬܠ ܠܢ ܫܠܡܐ	ܡܪܝܐ ܬܬܠ ܠܢ ܫܠܡܐ.
	ܡܛܠ ܕܐܝܟ ܟܠܗܘܢ ܥ̈ܒܕܝܢ ܥܒܕܬ ܠܢ	ܡܛܠ ܕܐܝܟ ܟܠܗܘܢ ܥܒܕܝܢ ܥܒܕܬ ܠܢ
13	ܡܪܝܐ ܐܠܗܢ	ܡܪܝܐ ܐܠܗܢ ܩܢܝ ܠܢ.
	ܗܘܘ ܒܠܥܕ ܡܪܝܐ ܠܒܪ ܡܢܟ	ܡܛܠ ܕܗܘܘ ܒܠܥܕ ܡܪܝܐ ܠܒܪ ܡܢܟ
	ܒܠܚܘܕ ܫܡܟ ܕܝܠܟ ܢܬܕܟܪ	ܒܠܚܘܕ ܫܡܟ ܕܝܠܟ ܢܬܕܟܪ
14	ܡܝܬܐ ܠܐ ܢܚܘܢ	ܡ̈ܝܬܐ ܠܐ ܢܚܘܢ.
	ܘܓܢܒܪܐ ܠܐ ܢܩܘܡܘܢ	ܘܓܢܒܪܐ ܠܐ ܢܩܘܡܘܢ
	ܡܛܠ ܗܢܐ ܦܩܕܬ ܘܐܘܒܕܬ ܐܢܘܢ	ܡܛܠܗܢܐ ܦܩܕܬ ܘܐܘܒܕܬ ܐܢܘܢ
	ܘܐܘܒܕܬ ܟܠܗ ܕܘܟܪܢܗܘܢ	ܘܐܘܒܕܬ ܟܠܗ ܕܘܟܪܢܗܘܢ
15	ܐܘܣܦܬ ܡܪܝܐ ܥܠ ܥܡܐ	ܐܘܣܦܬ ܥܠ ܥܡܟ ܡܪܝܐ
	ܐܘܣܦܬ ܥܠ ܥܡܐ	† ܐܘܣܦܬ ܥܠ ܥܡܟ. †
	ܐܬܝܩܪܬ ܘܪܚܩܬ ܠܟܠܗܘܢ ܣܘ̈ܦܝܗ ܕܐܪܥܐ	ܐܬܝܩܪܬ ܘܪܚܩܬ ܠܟܠܗܘܢ ܪ̈ܘܫܟܐ ܕܐܪܥܐ
16	ܡܪܝܐ ܒܐܘܠܨܢܐ ܦܩܕܢܟ	ܡܪܝܐ ܒܐܘܠܨܢܐ ܦܩܕܢܟ.
	ܘܒܡܫܟܢܐ ܠܚܫܐ ܡܪܕܘܬܟ	ܘܒܡܫܟܢܐ ܠܚܫܐ ܡܪܕܘܬܟ
17	ܐܝܟ ܒܛܢܬܐ ܕܩܪܒܐ ܠܡܝܠܕ ܘܡܚܒܠܐ	ܐܝܟ ܒܛܢܐ ܕܩܪܒܐ ܠܡܝܠܕ ܘܡܚܒܠܐ
	ܘܡܝܠܠܐ ܒܚܒܠܝܗ	ܘܡܝܠܠܐ ܒܚܒܠܝܗ.
	ܗܟܢܐ ܗܘܝܢ ܡܢ ܩܕܡܝܟ ܡܪܝܐ	ܗܟܢܐ ܗܘܝܢ ܡܢ ܩܕܡܝܟ ܡܪܝܐ
18	ܒܛܢܢ ܘܚܒܠܢ	† ܒܛܢܢ ܘܚܒܠܢ
	ܐܝܟ ܗܘܝܢ ܕܝܠܕܢ ܪܘܚܐ	ܐܝܟ ܗܘܝܢ ܕܝܠܕܢ ܪܘܚܐ. †
	ܦܘܪܩܢ ܕܠܐ ܢܥܒܕ ܒܐܪܥܐ	† ܦܘܪܩܢ † ܕܠܐ ܢܥܒܕ ܒܐܪܥܐ.
	ܘܠܐ ܢܦܠܘܢ ܥܡܘܪܝܗ ܕܬܒܝܠ	ܘܠܐ ܢܦܠܘܢ ܥܡܘܪܝܗ ܕܬܒܝܠ

[31] The symbols † … † are used in the Leiden Peshitta edition to indicate corrections of 'obvious clerical errors' in the basic text (in this case the manuscript 9t3).

	Peshitta-Isaiah	Peshitta-Odes
19	ܢܚܘܢ ܡ̈ܝܬܝܟ ܘܢܩܘܡܘܢ ܦܓܪ̈ܝܗܘܢ ܘܢܬܬܥܝܪܘܢ ܘܢܫܒܚܘܢ ܫ̈ܟܝܢܝ ܥܦܪܐ ܡܛܠ ܕܛܠܠܝܟ ܛܠܐ ܗܘ ܕܢܘܗܪܐ ܘܐܪܥܐ ܕܓܢ̈ܒܪܐ ܬܬܡܣܦ	ܢܐܚܘܢ ܡ̈ܝܬܐ ܘܢܩܘܡܘܢ ܦܓܪ̈ܝܗܘܢ ܢܬܬܥܝܪܘܢ ܘܢܫܒܚܘܢ ܫ̈ܟܢܝ ܥܦܪܐ ܡܛܠ ܕܛܠܠܝܟ ܛܠܐ ܗܘ ܕܢܘܗܪܐ ܘܐܪܥܐ ܕܥܘ̈ܠܐ ܬܡܣܦ

The two Syriac versions of Isa 26:9–19, in Pesh-Isaiah and in Pesh-Odes, are given in table 2. A comparison of the two versions shows that they basically offer the same text, which demonstrates that the text of the Ode was taken from the Peshitta and, consequently, generally agrees with MT-Isaiah rather than with the Septuagint.

Table 3: Differences between Isa 26:19–29 in Pesh-Isaiah and Pesh-Odes

9	ܢܦܫܝ] *pr* ܬܫܒܘܚܬܐ ܕܐܫܥܝܐ (cf. LXX Προσευχὴ Ησαιου)
	ܢܦܫܝ - ܠܟ \ ܒܠܠܝܐ] *tr* (cf. LXX Ἐκ νυκτὸς …)
	ܐܬܐܘܐܒܬ] ܐܬܐܝܒܬ (cf. I.O. 2.3.1.2)[32]
	ܘܐܦ] *om* ܘ
10	ܐܠܦ] ܠܦ (cf. I.O. 2.3.1.2)
	ܡܟܝܢܘܬܐ] *pr* ܘ
	ܥܘܠܐ] *add* ܢܫܬܩܠ ܪܫܝܥܐ (cf. LXX ἀρθήτω ὁ ἀσεβής)
	ܘܠܐ] ܕܠܐ (cf. LXX ἵνα μὴ)
	ܢܚܘܢ] ܢܚܐ (cf. LXX ἴδῃ)
	ܓܐܘܬܗ] ܬܫܒܘܚܬܗ
11	ܕܥܡܐ] ܕܥܡܟ (cf. LXX λαὸν ἀπαίδευτον)
13	ܐܠܗܢ] *add* ܩܢܝ ܠܢ (cf. LXX κτῆσαι ἡμᾶς)
	ܘܗܘ] *pr* ܡܛܠ ܕ
14	ܡܛܠ ܗܢܐ] ܡܛܠܗܢܐ (cf. I.O. 1.1)
15	ܡܪܝܐ ܥܠ ܥܡܐ] *tr* (cf. LXX πρόσθες αὐτοῖς κακά, κύριε)
	ܥܡܐ I°] ܥܡܟ
	ܥܡܐ II°] ܥܡܟ
	ܣܘ̈ܦܝܗ̇] ܕܐܪܥܐ (cf. LXX τοῖς ἐνδόξοις τῆς γῆς)
17	ܒܚܒܠܬܐ] ܒܚܒܠܐ
	ܘܡܝܠܠܐ] ܘܡܝܠܐ (cf. I.O. 2.4.4)
19	ܢܚܘܢ] ܢܐܚܘܢ
	ܡ̈ܝܬܝܟ] ܡ̈ܝܬܐ (cf. LXX οἱ νεκροί)
	ܘܢܬܬܥܝܪܘܢ] *om waw*
	ܕܓܢ̈ܒܪܐ] ܕܥܘ̈ܠܐ (cf. LXX τῶν ἀσεβῶν)
	ܬܬܡܣܦ] ܬܡܣܦ

[32] The abbreviation I.O. refers to the Index Orthographicus, which was included in the *General Preface* to the Leiden Peshitta edition by Piet A.H. de Boer and Willem Baars (Leiden, 1972) and which was republished in *The Old Testament in Syriac according to the Peshiṭta Version* 1.1 *Preface—Genesis Exodus* (Leiden, 1977).

In spite of the fundamental agreements, there are also a number of differences between Pesh-Isaiah and Pesh-Odes. In table 3 we present them in the form of a critical apparatus that presuposses Pesh-Isaiah as the basic text.[33] Sometimes Peshitta-Odes is closer to the Septuagint, even though in these cases Pesh-Odes most often does not give a precise rendering of the Greek.[34] An interesting case appears the opening lines of the Ode (table 4).

Table 4: Opening line of Isa 26:9–19

MT	LXX-Isaiah	LXX-Odes	Pesh-Isaiah	Pesh-Odes
	Ὠδή[35]	Προσευχὴ Ησαιου.		ܬܫܒܘܚܬܐ ܕܐܫܥܝܐ
נפשי אויתיך בלילה	Ἐκ νυκτὸς	Ἐκ νυκτὸς	ܢܦܫܝ ܐܬܪܓܪܓܬ ܠܟ ܒܠܠܝܐ	ܒܠܠܝܐ ܢܦܫܝ ܐܬܪܓܪܓܬ ܠܟ.
אף־רוחי בקרבי אשחרך	ὀρθρίζει τὸ πνεῦμά μου πρὸς σέ, ὁ θεός,	ὀρθρίζει τὸ πνεῦμά μου πρὸς σέ, ὁ θεός,	ܘܐܦ ܪܘܚܝ ܒܓܘܝ ܡܩܕܡܐ ܠܘܬܟ	ܐܦ ܪܘܚܝ ܒܓܘܝ ܡܩܕܡܐ ܠܘܬܟ.
	Ode	Prayer of Isaiah		Canticle of Isaiah
My soul yearns for You in the night;	From the night	From the night	My soul yearns for You in the night;	In the night my soul yearns for You;
Also my spirit inside me longs for You early.	my spirit longs for You early, O God.	my spirit longs for You early, O God.	and also my spirit inside me longs for You early.	also my spirit inside me longs for You early.

Here we see that the opening of the Ode with 'In the night' agrees with the Greek text, even though the Greek text differs in that Isa 26:9a does not belong to the Ode but is connected to the preceding section: ᾗ ἐπιθυμεῖ ἡ ψυχὴ ἡμῶν '(… the memory of You) which our soul yearns for', which in the Septuagint editions is given as 26:9a, is rather a translation of נפש תאות in 26:8, and MT נפשי אויתיך is not rendered in the Septuagint.[36] The position of 'In the night' right at the beginning of the Ode is also significant because it probably gave this section its place on various liturgical occasions (see above).

[33] This table is based on the main text of the Peshitta edition for both Isaiah and the Odes; variant readings will be discussed below. The Peshitta of Isaiah appeared in *The Old Testament in Syriac according to the Peshiṭta Version* 3.1 *Isaiah*, prepared by Sebastian P. Brock (Leiden, 1987); for the edition of the Odes, see above, note 2.

[34] Cf. Schneider, 'Wenig beachtete Rezensionen', p. 191.

[35] Thus Codex Alexandrinus. For other headings in Septuagint manuscripts, see Joseph Ziegler, *Isaias* (Septuaginta Vetus Testamentum Graecum auctoritate Academiae Litterarum Gottingensis editum 14; Göttingen, 1939), p. 210.

[36] See the discussion of this verse in De Angelo Cunha's forthcoming PhD dissertation.

In the case of Isa 26:9–19 the differences between Pesh-Isaiah and Pesh-Odes are larger than between LXX-Isaiah and LXX-Odes, and hence Schneider's description of the situation in the Septuagint quoted above does not apply to the situation in the Peshitta. The differences are also more significant than those between Pesh-Isaiah and Pesh-Odes for the two other Syriac Odes taken from Isaiah, 42:10–13 & 45:8 and 38:10–20. For Isa 42:10–13 & 45:8 (Ode III) this concurs with the general tendency that the textual form of Odes I–III agrees with the Peshitta text, whereas the other Odes, which were added to the series in a later stage, underwent various revisions, mainly to make the text accord with the Septuagint.[37] Isa 38:10–20 is a different case because it is only attested in 9a1, as part of the Fourteen Odes series (see above).

Finally it should be noted that sometimes Pesh-Odes goes its own way, differing from both Pesh-Isaiah and MT-Isaiah and LXX-Isaiah/Odes. Consequently, not all the differences between Pesh-Isaiah and Pesh-Odes can be explained from influence of the Septuagint. This happens, for example, in 26:15 where the Odes have twice 'your people' instead of 'the people' in the Hebrew text (the Septuagint has twice a different object, namely κακά 'evils').[38]

These observations can be refined if we take into account the variants to Pesh-Isaiah and Pesh-Odes recorded in the critical apparatuses of the Leiden Peshitta edition, which reflect the following tendencies:

1. Some minor variants to Pesh-Isaiah agree with the main text of Pesh-Odes. See table 5.[39]

---

[37] Cf. Schneider, 'Wenig beachtete Rezensionen', pp. 188–196; idem, 'Canticles or Odes', Introduction, pp. ii–iv (cf. above, note 12).

[38] Cf. Schneider, 'Wenig beachtete Rezensionen', p. 195: 'Besonders frappant ist die targumistische Paraphrase in 5 15c.' Targum Jonathan to Isaiah has indeed the same suffix pronoun, but the qualification of this variant as a 'Targumic paraphrase' is not convincing. The same applies to Schneider's interpretation of the reverse word order in 26:15 mentioned in table 3, and the addition of ܟܠ in 26:19, mentioned in table 9; cf. Schneider, 'Wenig beachtete Rezensionen', p. 195: 'Danach wird man auch in … 5 15a.c 19d den Einfluß des Targums als naheliegende Erklärung einräumen'.

[39] The sigla of the manuscripts and their notation follows the practice of the Leiden Peshitta edition. Hence 12d1.2 means: manuscripts 12d1 and 12d2. For an explanation of the sigla see [W. Baars and M.D. Koster,] *List of the Old Testament Peshiṭta Manuscripts* (Preliminary Issue, edited by the Peshiṭta Institute, Leiden University; Leiden, 1961).

Table 5: Variants to Pesh-Isaiah agreeing with Pesh-Odes

9	ܘܐܦ] *om waw* 9l6 10d1 11d1 12a1 12d1.2 →
10	ܡܫܒܚܘܬܐ] *pr waw* 9a1*fam* →
19	ܬܣܬܚܦ] ܬܣܚܦ 6h3 8a1 9a1*fam* 10d1 11d1 12a1 12d2 → (5ph1 = 7a1)

2. Some variants to Pesh-Isaiah agree with variants to Pesh-Odes. See table 6. A few times this concerns cases where Pesh-Isaiah 9a1 and Pesh-Odes 9a1 agree vis-à-vis 7a1 (the main text in the edition of Pesh-Isaiah) and 9t3 (chosen as the main text of Pesh-Odes).

Table 6: Variants to Pesh-Isaiah agreeing with variants to Pesh-Odes

	Pesh-Isaiah	Pesh-Odes
13	ܥܡܟ] ܥܡܐ 9l6	ܥܡܟ] ܥܡܐ 12t2.7 16t4.5 17t5
14	ܘܕܒܪܬ] ܘܕܒܪ̇ܬ 9a1*fam* → [uncertain]	ܘܕܒܪܬ] ܘܕܒܪ̇ܬ 9a1 10t1 12t7.8 16t4(?)
15	ܠܟܠܗܘܢ] ܟܠܗܘܢ 6h3.5 9a1*fam* 9l1 10d1 11d1 12a1 12d1.2 →	ܠܟܠܗܘܢ] ܟܠܗܘܢ 9a1 12t3
18	ܗ̈ܢܝܢ] ܗܠܝܢ 6h3.5 9l1	ܗ̈ܢܝܢ] ܗܠܝܢ 12t2.7.8
	ܦܘܪܩܢ] ܦܘܪܩܢ 9a1 →	† ܦܘܪܩܢ †] ܦܘܪܩܢ 9a1 9t3
19	ܡ̈ܝܬܝܟ] + ܡܪܝܐ 12d2mg (*vid*)	ܡ̈ܝܬܐ] + ܡܪܝܐ 16t4.5 17t5
	ܘܢܫܒܚܘܢ] ܘܢܫܒܚܘܢܟ 9a1*fam*	ܘܢܫܒܚܘܢ] ܘܢܫܒܚܘܢܟ 10t1 12t2
	ܥ̈ܦܪ] ܥܦ̈ܪ 12a1	ܥ̈ܦܪ] ܥܦ̈ܪ 12a1

3. Some variants to Pesh-Odes agree with Pesh-Isaiah. See table 7. Quite often these variants occur in 9a1 and 12t3. Sometimes they occur in 16t4.5 and 17t5. In other words, in these cases 9t3 differs from Pesh-Isaiah whereas the manuscripts mentioned in the apparatus do not; in some of these cases 9t3 agrees with LXX-Isaiah/Odes.

Table 7: Variants to Pesh-Odes agreeing with Pesh-Isaiah

9	ܒܠܠܝܐ \ ܢܦܫܝ - ܠܟ] *tr* 9a1
	ܐܦ] *pr* ܘ 9a1 12t2.8
10	ܘܡܫܒܚܘܬܐ] *om* ܘ I° 9a1 12t3
	ܢܬܝܠܦ ܪܫܝܥܐ] *om* 9a1 12t3 16t4.5 17t5
	ܕܠܐ] ܘܠܐ 9a1 12t3
	ܢܚܙܐ] ܢܚܙܘܢ 9a1 12t3 17t5: ܢܚ̈ܙܘܢ 16t4.5
	ܬܫܒܘܚܬܗ] ܒܐܝܩܪܗ 9a1 12t3 16t4.5 17t5
11	ܕܥܡܟ] ܕܥܡܐ omnes—10t1
13	ܡܢ ܠܟ.] *om* 9a1 12t3
	ܡܛܠ ܕ.] *om* 9a1 12t3
15	ܥܠ ܥܡܟ ܡܪܝܐ] *tr* 9a1 10t1 12t3
	ܥܡܟ I°] ܥܡܐ 9a1 12t3
	ܥܡܟ II°] ܥܡܐ 12t3
	ܪ̈ܚܝܩܐ (ܪ̈ܚܝܩܝܗ 12t2)] ܣܘܦܝܗ 9a1 12t3
17	ܟܠܐ] ܟܠܬܐ omnes

19 ܬ̈ܫܒܚܬܐ] ܬ̈ܫܒܚܬܝܢ omnes
ܢܬܬܚܝܢܘܢ] *pr* ܘ omnes—12t8
ܬܫܒܚܘܢ] ܬܫܬܒܚܘܢ 10t1 12t2.3.7.8

---

4. Some variants to Pesh-Odes agree with the Greek text, as against the Hebrew text and Pesh-Isaiah. See table 8. The variants occur often in clusters of manuscripts, such as the group 10t1, 12t7 and the group 16t4.5, 17t5.

Table 8: Variants to Pesh-Odes agreeing with the Septuagint

---

9 ܕܐܝܟ] ܕܥܒܕܬ 10t1 12t7 (cf. Vetus Latina[40] *fecisti*): ܕܦܘܩܕܢܐ ܢܘܗܪܬ ܐܢܘܢ 12t2 (cf. LXX διότι φῶς τὰ προστάγματά σου ἐπὶ τῆς γῆς)
11 ܕܐܝ̈ܕܝܟ] ܕܐܝܕܟ 12t2 (cf. sing. in both MT and LXX)
12 ܬܬܠ] ܬܠ 12t2 16t4.5 17t5 (for the imperative form cf. LXX δὸς)
ܡܪܝܐ] + ܐܠܗܐ 10t1 16t4.5 17t5 (cf. LXX κύριε ὁ θεὸς ἡμῶν)
13 ܕܗܘܘ] ܕܗܘܐ 16t5 and ܡܪ̈ܝܐ] *om sey* 12t2.7 16t5 17t5 (for use of singular cf. LXX ἄλλον οὐκ οἴδαμεν)
17 ܐܝܟ] *pr* ܘ 10t1 16t4.5 17t5 (cf. LXX καὶ ὡς)
18 ܩܕܡܝܟ] *pr* ܡܢ ܕܚܠܬܐ 12t7: *pr* ܡܢ ܕܚܠܬܟ ܡܪܝܐ 12t8 (cf. LXX διὰ τὸν φόβον σου, κύριε)
19 ܕܥ̈ܘܠܐ] ܕܓܢ̈ܒܪܐ 9a1 12t3.8 16t4.5 17t5: ܕܪ̈ܫܝܥܐ 12t2.7 (cf. LXX τῶν ἀσεβῶν)

---

5. Some other variants occur, most often in the same clusters of manuscripts mentioned above. See table 9.[41]

Table 9: Other variants to Pesh-Odes

	MS 9t3	MSS 9a1 12t3	MSS 10t1 12t2.7.8	MSS 16t4.5 17t5
–	ܕܐܫܥܝܐ	+ ܕܢܒܝܐ 12t3	+ ܕܢܒܝܐ 10t1 12t2	+ ܕܢܒܝܐ 16t4.5 17t5
9	ܒܗ,			ܒܗ ܠܗ 16t4.5 17t5
	ܙܕܝܩܘܬܐ		*pr* ܘ 10t1 12t7.8	*pr* ܘ 16t5 17t5
			ܘܙܕܝܩܘܬܟ 12t2	ܘܙܕܝܩܘܬܟ 16t4
10	ܐܬܪܥܝܢ		ܐܬܪܥܝܢܘ 12t2.7	ܐܬܪܥܝܢܘ 16t5[txt]
	ܚܙܐ	ܚܙܘܗ 9a1 12t3		ܚܙܘܗ 17t5
				ܚܙܝܘܗ 16t4.5
11	ܬܢܘܪܐ	+ ܕܢܘܪܐ 9a1	+ ܕܢܘܪܐ 12t2.7	+ ܕܢܘܪܐ 16t4.5 17t5
	ܚܙܘܗ I°			ܚܙܝܘܗ 16t4.5
12	ܠܟ I°			*om* 16t4.5 17t5
	ܕܐܝܟ		ܕܠܐ ܗܘܐ ܐܝܟ 12t7.8	

---

[40] The Vetus Latina may be regarded as an indirect witness to the Greek version; cf. Schneider, 'Wenig beachtete Rezensionen', p. 175: 'Manches, was die syrischen Rezensenten in ihren griechischen Handschriften lasen, scheint uns nur noch indirect durch altlateinische Zeugen überliefert zu sein.'

[41] Variants that occur in only one manuscript and that do not belong to one of the patterns of agreement described above have not been included.

	MS 9t3	MSS 9a1 12t3	MSS 10t1 12t2.7.8	MSS 16t4.5 17t5
13	ܐܠܗܝ	ܐܠܗܐ 9a1 12t3	ܐܠܗܐ ܕܠܝ 12t2.7.8	
	ܕܗܘܘ		ܕܠܐ ܗܘܘ 10t1 12t7 ܕܠܐ ܗܘܐ 12t8	
14	ܠܗ		ܡܢ ܐܪܥܐ 10t1 12t2.7.8	ܡܢ ܐܪܥܐ 16t4.5 17t5
15				*om* 16t4.5 17t5
17	ܗܟܢܐ		ܗܟܢ 12t2.7.8	
	ܗܘܝ		ܗܘܢ 12t2.7.8	*om* 17t5
19	ܢܦܩܝܢ		ܢܦܩܘܢ 12t7.8	ܢܦܩܘܢ 17t5
	ܥ̈ܒܕܝ		*pr* ܟܠ 10t1 12t2.7.8	

These observations give the impression that the Syriac translation of Pesh-Odes as represented in 9t3 was influenced by the Greek (because of those cases where 9t3 agrees with the Greek) and that in its textual transmission it has been modified on the one hand towards Pesh-Isaiah (cf. the variants in 9a1 and 12t3) and on the other hand towards the Septuagint (in the manuscript groups 10t1 12t7 and 16t4.5 17t5). However, this reasoning suggests that 9t3 reflects the earliest text type, which is not the case. The editors of the Odes in the Leiden Peshitta edition chose 9t3 as the basic text 'because it is the oldest MS that contains the complete series of Odes common to all Syriac churches', whereas 9a1 lacks Ode III (Isa 42:10–13 & 45:8).[42] The text of 9t3, however, is the product of a 'drastic revision'[43] towards the Septuagint,[44] and 9a1[45] (and 12t3) contain the earliest text type available.[46]

For this reason, the variation in the manuscripts is better accounted for in a model that assumes that 9a1 (and 12t3) reflects a more original text and that 9t3, as well as the manuscript clusters 10t1, 12t7 and 16t4.5, 17t5, reflect revisions towards the Septuagint. These clusters agree with the various recensions identified by H. Schneider and W. Baars, namely an early 'Jacobite' recension, attested in 9a1, 12t3, 9t3 (in this group a

[42] Schneider, 'Canticles or Odes', Introduction, p. xiv.

[43] Schneider, 'Canticles or Odes', Introduction, p. iii.

[44] Schneider, 'Canticles or Odes', Introduction, p. iii.

[45] It should be emphasized that this observation applies only to the Odes section of 9a1 and that the characterization of its text as the earliest text type available does not necessarily hold true for other biblical books. In other parts of the Bible the text in this manuscript has a much more mixed character.

[46] Nevertheless, the text form of 9t3 is put forward as an argument for the editors' preference for this manuscript over 9a1, because it is more representative of the text of the Odes in the Syriac tradition, which is characterized by revisions according to the Septuagint. 9a1, though reflecting an earlier text type that is much nearer to the Peshitta, 'would give a one-sided picture of the textual tradition'; see Schneider, 'Canticles or Odes', Introduction, p. xiv.

distinction can be made between 9a1 and 12t3 on the one hand and 9t3 on the other); a late 'Jacobite' recension, represented by 16t4.5, 17t5; and a Melkite recension, which can be found in 10t1, 12t2.7.8.[47]

Here, again, the influence from the Septuagint does not result in a precise translation from the Greek. In 26:14, for example, the use of the singular may be due to Greek influence, but other adjustments to the Greek text have not been made (see also below on the addition of the negation in this verse in the Melkite recension).

Influence from the Septuagint was not the only driving force behind these recensions. Especially in the late West Syriac recension there are some other signs of revision, as appears from table 9. Sometimes a variant can best be explained from influence of other biblical passages. Thus the addition of ܕܢܘܪܐ 'of fire' to 26:11 ܘܐܝܟ ܬܢܘܪܐ ܬܐܟܘܠ ܐܢܘܢ ܠܒܥܠܕ̈ܒܒܝܟ 'and like a furnace (*of fire*) it will devour your enemies'[48] may have been influenced by Ps 21:10 where we find both ܐܝܟ ܬܢܘܪܐ ܕܢܘܪܐ, and, later on in the same verse, ܬܐܟܘܠ ܐܢܘܢ ܢܘܪܐ, and perhaps also by the ܐܬܘܢܐ ܕܢܘܪܐ 'oven of fire' of Daniel 3. The addition ܡܢ ܐܪܥܐ 'from the earth' in 26:14 comes from Ps 34:17, where we also find ܕܘܟܪܢܗܘܢ 'their memory' and ܡܢ ܐܪܥܐ.[49] Other variants include the addition of the negation in 26:12 'because *not* like all our works You have prepared for us' in 12t7.8; the result is a completely different reading which, however, still makes sense in the context.[50] The same applies to the addition of the negation in 26:13 to '(an)other lord(s) beside You has/have *not* been over us' in 10t1, 12t7.8, which is one of the inner-Syriac peculiarities that have become characteristic for the Melkite recension.[51] The reading ܐܠܗܐ in 26:13 in 9a1, 12t3 is interesting, because in this case it is the reading of the other manuscripts, ܐܠܗܢ (cf. ܐܠܗܐ ܕܠܢ in the Melkite manuscripts) that agrees with Pesh-Isaiah, whereas it is usually the text of 9a1 and 12t3 that does so (compare the examples given above in table 7).

The various recensions mentioned above can be characterized more accurately if we look at the various patterns of agreement in the variant

[47] The East Syriac and the Maronite recensions of the Odes will not concern us here, because they do not include Isaiah 26:9–19; see above.

[48] But Schneider, 'Wenig beachtete Rezensionen', p. 196, seems to suggest that 9t3, which does not have this plus, reflects an adaptation to the Hebrew; cf. also ibid. p. 189.

[49] Schneider, 'Wenig beachtete Rezensionen', p. 183 (but Schneider has '33[32]:17').

[50] Note that 12t8 has 'your works' instead of 'our works', which results in still another sense of this verse.

[51] Thus Schneider, 'Wenig beachtete Rezensionen', p. 195.

readings. The earliest text form available, that of 9a1 and 12t3, is very close to Pesh-Isaiah and demonstrates that the Odes text was taken from Pesh-Isaiah. Influence of the Greek text can be found both in the early and in the late West Syriac recension, as well as in in the Melkite recension. The early and the late West Syriac recension have a number of shared variants, but there are also cases where the early recension agrees with the Greek whereas the late West Syriac recension does not. Sometimes both versions reflect influence from the Greek, but in a different way. Thus in 26:19, where 9a1, 12t3.8, 16t4.5, 17t5 have ܕܓܢ̈ܒܪܐ as in Pesh-Isaiah, both 9t3 ܕܥܘ̈ܠܐ and 12t2.7 ܕܪ̈ܫܝܥܐ seem to be influenced by the Greek τῶν ἀσεβῶν. These patterns of variation show the independence of the later recension vis-à-vis the earlier one,[52] and supports a model that assumes various, partly independent revisions, rather than a gradual increase of influence from the Septuagint. In some cases the Melkite recension agrees with the late West Syriac recension, both in cases where they agree with the Septuagint and in some other cases.[53] These variants show influence of the West Syriac revision on the Melkite version.[54]

3. *Conclusions*

Being part of both the Fourteen Odes series and the Nine Odes series, Isa 26:9–19 acquired a stable place in the West Syriac and Melkite Odes traditions. The East Syriac and the Maronite traditions retained a smaller selection with only three or four Odes from the Old Testament (and some from the New Testament), which did not include this chapter. Other witnesses to the liturgical use of passages from Isaiah 26 come from lectionaries and lists of scriptural readings, which do not always overlap with the section that came to function as Ode. In other Eastern Christian traditions, especially in the Coptic tradition, Isa 26:1–8 functioned as an Ode as well.

Although the inclusion of Isa 26:9–19 in the Odes series comes from the Greek tradition, the text was taken from the Peshitta. Unlike the

---

[52] Cf. Schneider, 'Wenig beachtete Rezensionen', p. 192; idem, 'Canticles or Odes', Introduction, p. iii.

[53] See e.g. above, the variant in 26:14 in table 9.

[54] Cf. Schneider, 'Wenig beachtete Rezensionen', p. 196: this pattern of agreement shows 'daß die melchitische Odenrezension laufend *noch weiter verbessert* wurde, gelegentlich nach spätjakobitischen [with references to Isa 26:9, 13] hauptsächlich aber nach griechischen Texten'.

Greek Odes, which retained the text form of the Septuagint chapters from which they were taken, the Syriac Odes reflect a development which started from the Peshitta text and which is mainly, but not exclusively, characterized by Greek influence. Our analysis of Isa 26:9–19 corroborated Schneider's claim that this influence did not increase gradually, but can be located in different revisions or recensions: an early West Syriac recension, a late West Syriac recension, and a Melkite recension. These recensions have some shared readings, but also contain some readings that show their independence.

We can agree with Schneider that the various revisions concerned not only Greek influence, but also other variations, due to various reasons. However, we did not find sufficient support for his claim that some variants should be explained as revisions towards the Masoretic Text or as influence from the Targum—which, by the way, also in Schneider's own argument appears only in some isolated remarks on individual readings.

An implication of this reconstruction is that manuscript 9t3, which in the Leiden Peshitta edition has been chosen as the basic text for the edition, does not represent the earliest attainable text type, but rather a representative of one of these recensions, namely the early West Syriac recension. Although this manuscript may be the best choice for the collection of the Odes as a whole (because of the selection of Odes it contains), for our textual analysis of Isa 26:9–19, we had to rearrange the material so as to take 9a1 as representing the earliest text type attainable, and the other manuscripts, including 9t3, as representatives of the various revisions that the text has undergone.

OF TRANSLATION AND REVISION: FROM GREEK ISAIAH TO GREEK JEREMIAH

Albert Pietersma

In a couple of recent articles[1] I have questioned Emanuel Tov's theory of translator-*cum*-reviser for Greek Jeremiah. Most recently I have done so in the introduction to Ieremias in the New English Translation of the Septuagint (NETS).[2] Especially since almost thirty years ago I publicly endorsed Tov's conclusions,[3] I have a certain feeling of unease that, due to the restricted scope of my publications thus far, I have not as yet shown adequately why I have changed my mind and now believe that Tov's theory of revision is fatally flawed.

There is no question but that Tov, now more than three decades ago, produced a book in which he organized an impressive amount of information and forged it into the most comprehensive theory of the bisectioning of Greek Jeremiah produced thus far.[4] No doubt because Tov's study is as detailed as it is, it has until recently stood the test of time rather well.[5] To re-analyze every one of Tov's examples, directly or indirectly offered in support of his theory, is certainly a daunting task.

I had hoped that renewed study of Greek Jeremiah's allegedly dual origins might become the topic of another doctoral dissertation,[6] but

---

[1] Albert Pietersma, ‘Ἐπίχειρον in Greek Jeremiah’, *JNSL* 28 (2002), pp. 101–108. Albert Pietersma, ‘Greek Jeremiah and the Land of Azazel’, in Peter W. Flint, Emanuel Tov, and James C. VanderKam (eds.), *Studies in the Hebrew Bible, Qumran, and the Septuagint Presented to Eugene Ulrich* (VT.S 101; Leiden etc., 2006), pp. 402–413.

[2] Albert Pietersma and Benjamin G. Wright (eds.), *A New English Translation of the Septuagint* (Oxford, 2007), pp. 876–881. See especially the longer version at http://ccat.sas.upenn.edu/nets/edition/.

[3] *JAOS* 99 (1979), pp. 468–469.

[4] Emanuel Tov, *The Septuagint Translation of Jeremiah and Baruch. A Discussion of an Early Revision of the LXX of Jeremiah 29–52 and Baruch 1:1–3:8* (HSM 8; Missoula, 1976).

[5] Other scholars have similarly raised questions, notably Hermann-Josef Stipp, ‘Offene Fragen zur Übersetzungskritik des antiken griechischen Jeremiabuches’, *JNSL* 17 (1991), pp. 117–128, and *Das masoretische und alexandrinische Sondergut des Jeremiabuches* (OBO 136; Freiburg–Göttingen, 1994). Further, Georg Fischer, *Jeremia. Der Stand der theologischen Diskussion* (Darmstadt, 2007), chapter 2, pp. 17–53.

[6] As Tov explains in his Preface to *Jeremiah*, his own study was initially conducted as a doctoral dissertation.

such has not as yet materialized. Yet since I translated Greek Jeremiah for NETS[7] (with Marc Saunders) and wrote an introduction to it in which *the* central problem of this book could scarcely go without comment, I decided to begin such a study on my own. This essay, however, will not be a full-blown descriptive analysis of Greek Jeremiah nor will it be another study of an individual Hebrew–Greek equivalence. Instead, I will here focus on questions of methodology.

Septuagintalists need scarcely be reminded that, within living memory, it was fashionable, so to speak, to argue for more than one translator for any given book of the Septuagint.[8] There are in fact few books which have escaped being assigned, at some time or other, to more than one translation effort. Many of the results of these endeavours have since been consigned to the dust bin of history—which is not to say that they were in vain or that all of them were wrong. On the contrary, the discipline of Septuagint Studies has learned much, and some of the theories appear to be well based.

Since this essay is a contribution to a Festschrift for Arie van der Kooij, whose 'lievelingsboek' is the book of Greek Isaiah, it would seem *à propos* to use Greek Isaiah as a bit of a launching pad to Greek Jeremiah, even though my interest here is not in bisectioning *per se* but in Tov's variation thereon.

The bisectioning of Greek Isaiah into chapters 1–39, on the one hand, and 40–66, on the other, was first proposed by Buchanan Gray,[9] whose study was subsequently refined and expanded upon by Friedrich Baumgärtel.[10] Though Baumgärtel's list of relevant items numbers forty-nine,[11] the theory has not met with enduring success. Chief among its detractors has been Joseph Ziegler, the editor of the Isaias volume in the Göttingen *Septuaginta*.[12] After conducting his own study of the problem and acknowledging that the theory as proposed by Gray and Baumgärtel has many strong points, Ziegler concluded,

---

[7] Pietersma and Wright (eds.), *New English Translation of the Septuagint*, pp. 876–924.

[8] Cf. Tov, *Jeremiah*, p. 3.

[9] George Buchanan Gray, 'The Greek Version of Isaiah, is it the Work of a Single Translator'? *JTS* 12 (1910/11), pp. 286–293.

[10] Friedrich Baumgärtel, 'Die Septuaginta zu Jesaja das Werk zweier Übersetzer', in Johannes Hermann and Friedrich Baumgärtel, *Beiträge zur Enstehungsgeschichte der Septuaginta* (BWAT 5; Stuttgart, 1923), pp. 20–31.

[11] Two shy of Tov's list of fifty-one in his central chapter.

[12] Joseph Ziegler, *Isaias* (Septuaginta Vetus Testamentum Graecum Auctoritate Academiae Litterarum Gottingensis editum 14; Göttingen, 1939; 2nd ed. 1967).

> Wenn wir das gesammte Material überblicken, so ist es schwer, die Frage der Einheit der Js-LXX zu entscheiden; die zahlreichen Sonderheiten (besonders in Js I) der beiden Teile sprechen für eine Verschiedenheit des Über(setzer)s; anderseits laufen auch zwischen I und II so viele Verbindungslinien, daß es unmöglich ist, zwischen beiden Teilen einen scharfen Trennungsstrich zu ziehen. Deshalb kann die These zweier Über(setzer)s in Js nicht in der Form aufrechthalten bleiben, wie es Gray und Baumgärtel getan haben, die die gemeinsamen Bestandteile völlig außer acht gelassen haben.[13]

It is of interest that Ziegler's concluding statement on Greek Isaiah might have been written, *mutatis mutandis*, about Greek Jeremiah, since the Gray–Baumgärtel method of cataloguing the differences between Isaiah 1–39 and Isaiah 40–66, without also enumerating the interconnections between these two blocks of text, might equally well be applied to Thackeray's study of Greek Jeremiah.[14] While, as Tov notes,[15] Thackeray recognized some links between Greek Jeremiah 1–28 and 29–(52), he is right in rectifying Thackeray's deficiency in his own study by including a chapter dealing specifically with (unique) connections between the two.[16]

Rather surprisingly, however, Ziegler fails to highlight, in his summary on Greek Isaiah, the dimension of his study with which he himself began the assessment of Gray–Baumgärtel, namely, the noteworthy translational inconsistency *within* both Isaiah 1–39 and 40–66.[17] Yet it can scarcely be argued that this aspect is incidental to a balanced translation profile of Greek Isaiah. What we have, according to Ziegler's assessment, is a translation which features a good many patterned inconsistencies in translation, namely, those which prompted the bisectioning by Gray–Baumgärtel—thus *between* Isaiah 1–39 and 40–66—as well as a great many non-patterned (contextual?) inconsistencies *within* both

---

[13] Joseph Ziegler, *Untersuchungen zur Septuaginta des Buches Isaias* (ATA 12.3; Münster i.W., 1934), p. 45.

[14] Henry St. J. Thackeray, 'The Greek Translators of Jeremiah', *JTS* 4 (1902 / 3), pp. 245–266. While earlier scholarship had noted translational inconsistency in Greek Jeremiah, as often as not it failed to support the binary split introduced subsequently by Thackeray. For example, of the 24 instances cited by Scholz 18 or 75 % do not support a 1–28 versus 29–52 split. See Anton Scholz, *Der masorethische Text und die LXX-Uebersetzung des Buches Jeremias* (Regensburg, 1875) there I. Abschnitt: 'Charakter der alexandrinischen Uebersetzung des Propheten Jeremias', pp. 12–15.

[15] Tov, *Jeremiah*, pp. 4–5.

[16] See Tov, *Jeremiah*, chapter 2: 'Important Similarities Between Jer A' and Jer B'', pp. 19–32.

[17] See also Isac L. Seeligmann, *The Septuagint Version of Isaiah. A Discussion of its Problems* (MEOL 9; Leiden, 1948), pp. 40–41.

Isaiah 1–39 and 40–66. As Ziegler demonstrated, this is a plain fact of descriptive analysis. How that plain fact is then to be *explained* may be difficult but is in any case a distinct next step. According to Ziegler, it *cannot* be accounted for by Gray–Baumgärtel's theory of bisectioning. Hence the unity of Greek Isaiah stands by default, and a new hypothesis may be in order.

Although Tov in his study of Greek Jeremiah has a chapter on connections *between* what he calls Jer a' (1–28) and Jer b' (29–52) and thus avoids the error with which Ziegler charged Gray and Baumgärtel,[18] he has no chapter on internal inconsistencies *within* Jer a' and Jer b' respectively. In this he follows not only Thackeray but, as well, Ziegler on Greek Jeremiah. Ziegler accepts Thackeray's conclusion without in any way putting it to the test,[19] contrary to what he had done in the case of the Gray–Baumgärtel theory on Greek Isaiah. All he does is to write the footnote which was to launch Tov's variation on bisectioning, namely, his revision theory.[20] Tov in turn accepts Ziegler's endorsement of Thackeray's bisectioning and with that sets out on his own course without seriously looking back. Bisectioning, therefore, is assumed to be a fact from the outset in Tov's study. All that is left is to determine the *character* of bisectioning.

As a result, to date we have no balanced translational profile of Greek Jeremiah, since a crucial component—necessitated by earlier bisectioning—is as yet missing. A probe based on doublets in Jeremiah was recently made by Tony S.L. Michael,[21] and I touch on some internal inconsistencies in my introduction to NETS Ieremias.[22] But a fully

[18] Needless to say, while for Ziegler the links between Isaiah 1–39 and 40–66 tend to negate their differences, for Tov the links between LXX-Jeremiah 1–28 and 29–52 function as a backdrop for his revision theory, in distinction from Thackeray's two-translators theory.

[19] And if he did test it, we have no published results.

[20] Joseph Ziegler, *Ieremias. Baruch. Threni. Epistula Ieremiae* (Septuaginta Vetus Testamentum Graecum Auctoritate Societatis Litterarum Gottingensis editum 15; Göttingen 1957), p. 128 footnote 1, 'Man muß Thack(eray) zustimmen (on the question of Jer's lack of unity); nur müßte noch genauer untersucht werden, ob wirklich zwei Übersetzer beteiligt waren oder bloß ein Redaktor am Werk war, der den einen Teil nur überarbeitete. Es kann nämlich beobachtet werden, daß sich in der ganzen Ier.-LXX einheitliche Züge finden, die sie von anderen Büchern abheben. Sehr fraglich bleibt, ob Kap. 52 wirklich nur ein späterer Nachtrag ist'. His *Beiträge zur Ieremias-Septuaginta* (MSU 6; Göttingen, 1958) does not broach the subject at all.

[21] Tony S.L. Michael, 'Bisectioning of Greek Jeremiah: A Problem to be Revisited'? *BIOSCS* 39 (2005), pp. 103–114.

[22] Pietersma and Wright, *New English Translation of the Septuagint*, pp. 877–880.

descriptive analysis of the book remains to be done, as a result of which a balanced explanation of the linguistic data must remain as yet a *desideratum.*

Though my earlier probes focused on specific translation equivalents, offered by Tov in support of his revision theory, here I aim to take a more methodological approach.

Given that chapter III of Tov's study is the only chapter which provides a systematic classification of data, one might reasonably label this the core of the book, designed to lay the foundation for Tov's theory of revision. Consequently, in an effort to understand how Tov arrives at his theory what better chapter to scrutinize than chapter III?

While in chapter IV Tov adds what he calls 'additional differences' (between Greek Jeremiah 1–28 and 29–52) or 'synonymous renditions', by his own admission these 'are not characterized by any particular revisional tendency'.[23] One is thus lead to infer that the differences listed in chapter IV are just that: differences between Greek Jeremiah 1–28 and 29–52, whose *revisional* character must be based upon and validated by the conclusion reached in chapter III. In other words, if the revision hypothesis is verified in chapter III, the data in chapter IV may then be drawn upon as further possible evidence, but if not, then not.

Chapter V casts the net even wider to include Baruch 1:1–3:8 (even though no Hebrew text is extant), but, as in the case of chapter IV, the *explanation* of the data must again come from chapter III, it would seem. Chapter III might therefore be regarded as foundational to Tov's theory.[24] Consequently, if the foundation in III turns out to be shaky, the edifice built thereon cannot be expected to remain standing.

According to Tov's theory, Greek Jeremiah 1–28 is approximately the first half of the Old Greek translation, while chapters 29–52 is what remains of a revision of the Old Greek. Tov posits, therefore, that both the Old Greek and the revision (labeled Jer-R by him) respectively comprised the entire book.

To be noted further is that since Tov seeks to demonstrate that Greek Jeremiah 29–52 is a revision of the Old Greek—hence a revision of a text

[23] Tov, *Jeremiah*, p. 93. His use of the term 'revisional' is of interest, since it signals that, from Tov's perspective, chapter III has indeed demonstrated sustained revision to exist in LXX Jeremiah 29–52, and that chapter III thus provides the necessary leverage for the data in IV (and V), even though revision must be assumed to have taken multiple forms.

[24] Though my interest here is in Tov's theory of revision, this implies no endorsement of bisectioning.

like Greek Jeremiah 1–28, posited to have existed as well for chapters 29–52—it is logical that the existing text of Greek Jeremiah 1–28 should serve as his point of reference, his touchstone. As the frequent notation 'passim in the LXX' indicates, the Septuagint as a whole functions as a secondary point of reference, though the notation may appear in either the first column (chapters 1–28) or in the second column (chapters 29–52) or in both at the same time.

Regarding the purpose of chapter III Tov writes as follows:

> Data provided in this chapter are intended to show how a Hebrew word was rendered in Jer a' mainly by Gk 1 [cf. LXX Jer 1–28], while in Jer b' mainly by Gk 2 [cf. LXX Jer 29–52]. We hope to *demonstrate* that the relationship between Gk 1 and Gk 2 is that of an original to its revision.[25] (emphasis added)

The hypothesis to be tested is, therefore, that Greek Jeremiah 29–52 is a revision of the Old Greek. Thus the reader might reasonably anticipate (a) a demonstration that sustained revision—in distinction from translation—does exist in Greek Jeremiah 29–52; (b) that such revision manifests a certain *trend*, i.e., it manifests a certain level of consistency and principled behaviour; (c) that such consistent revision may take a number of different forms, and (d) that a *raison d'être* for such a revision can be delineated.[26]

But before we proceed to look at the data Tov cites in support of his revision, a sideward glance might be in order. Early on in the book, Tov rightly raises the problem of how to *identify* 'revision'. In other words, if one is to *demonstrate* that text *x* is a revision—in distinction from a non-revision (e.g., a translation)—what is it precisely that one should be looking for?

Tov delineates two conditions or criteria by which to identify 'revision'. He writes,

> A given textual tradition can be considered a revision of the LXX if the following two conditions are met:
>
> (a) The LXX and the revision share a common textual basis, established by the recognition of distinctive agreements.[27]

[25] Tov, *Jeremiah*, p. 43.

[26] For (b) see '... this common denominator [of revision] is a trend towards a more precise and consistent representation of the Hebrew *Vorlage*', Tov, *Jeremiah*, p. 44.

[27] Cf. Tov, *Jeremiah*, chapter II, pp. 19–32 ('Important Similarities between Jer a' and Jer b'').

(b) The reviser retouched the LXX in a certain direction, generally towards a more precise reflection of his Hebrew source. Other revisions aim at greater clarity as well as at improvement of the Greek language.[28]

While Tov is quite correct in noting that one needs to know what it is one is looking for (i.e., revision needs to be identified before it can be recognized), what he seems to overlook is the fact that 'identification' in this case is a two-step undertaking and that these two steps should be kept distinct.

The first step has to do with identifying 'revision' as a textual phenomenon. In other words, one needs to determine whether it makes any sense to postulate that text *x* is a revision of text *y*. What conditions need to be met for this hypothesis to make sense? Tov's statement on conditions embeds two of them. That is to say, he speaks of the neccesity for

(a) the existence of at least two texts, interrelated by similarities and differences, and

(b) the existence of a text which appears to have been derived from another text, judging from certain patterned differences.

When both of these conditions—or better, pre-conditions are met—it then makes sense to take the second step, namely to identify the specifics of the revision which has been postulated. In other words, here 'identification' has to do with a given kind of revision, rather than 'revision' as a textual phenomenon. Again we can extract the following from Tov's statement:

(a) that 'revision' must have a reasonably coherent profile

(b) that this reasonably coherent profile must be in a certain direction, i.e., that there be a common denominator to the 'revisional' data.[29]

Tov, however, collapses what I have called preconditions and conditions into one, and incorporates in them precisely what they are meant to ascertain, namely, not only that it makes sense to postulate 'revision' but also the nature or profile of the revision postulated. In so doing, it would seem, he creates a circular argument. That is to say, the Hebraizing revision of his conditions appears to be the same as the Hebraizing

[28] Tov, *Jeremiah*, p. 43. Cf. chapter III, pp. 41–74 ('Differences between Jer a' and b' Probably Resulting from Jer-R's Revisions in Jer b"); chapter IV, pp. 93–103 ('Additional Differences between Jer a' and b"). I read the closing sentence of the above citation as referring to revisions *other than* the preceding Hebraizing one.

[29] Cf. Tov, *Jeremiah*, p. 44: 'It seems to us that this common denominator is a trend towards more precise and consistent representation of the Hebrew *Vorlage*'.

revision of his conclusions. But to match condition with conclusion (and *vice-versa*) he has to phrase the condition in such a way that virtually any difference in text *x* from text *y* can qualify as a Hebraizing revision. What then emerges by way of conclusion is a revision which *qua revision* is difficult to place among the biblical Hebraizing revisions known to us. This is not to say that the Hebraizing revisions we know are homogeneous and consistent, but it is to suggest that contradictions on their defining characteristic, namely, revision toward the source text, are difficult if not impossible to accommodate.

Morover, to verify the hypothesis of a Hebraizing revision for Greek Jeremiah 29–52 one needs, it would seem, a goodly number of generally agreed upon Hebraizing corrections lest, without such general agreement, 'revision' lack integrity.

That Tov's argumentation is circular is further suggested by the heading of chapter III: 'Differences between Jer a' and b' *Probably resulting from Jer-R's Revisions in Jer b*'' (emphasis added). This would appear to underscore that Tov's statement cited above, to the effect that the data in chapter III is a *demonstration*, should not be understood as a demonstration of revision. In other words, the aim of chapter III is not to test the hypothesis of 'revision' but rather to demonstrate the nature of a given revision that has been presupposed.

Tov's hypothesis of a *Hebraizing* revision clearly arises from what he sees as a logical conclusion based on Thackeray's bisectioning and his own study of connections between the two blocks of text. His argument runs as follows: since Greek Jeremiah 29–52 has patterned differences from Greek Jeremiah 1–28 but at the same time has many unique connections with it, it is not logical to posit that the two halves were done by different translators (à la Thackeray). The most logical explanation is that Greek Jeremiah 29–52 represents a revision of a text now extant only in Greek Jeremiah 1–28.[30]

The logic is compelling, to be sure, but no more compelling, I would submit, than that the patterned differences between Isaiah 1–39, on the one hand, and Isaiah 40–66, on the other, *must* mean that Greek Isaiah is not a unity.

It may furthermore be instructive to realize that if Tov's reasoning were applied to Greek Isaiah, either Isaiah 1–39 or Isaiah 40–66 would have to be labeled a revision. While it might be objected that the differences and

[30] Tov, *Jeremiah*, p. 42.

the similarities in Greek Jeremiah are more pronounced than in Greek Isaiah, that is a question of degree, not of kind.

When all is said and done, that Thackeray's bisectioning combined with Tov's chapter on similarities should have produced the revision hypothesis is fair enough. But the revision hypothesis must then be subjected to verification.

As noted Tov's verification seems circular. That is to say, the revision demonstrated to exist seems to be the same as the revision which is presupposed. Troubling is the fact that even though Tov posits a Hebraizing revision, the defining characteristic of the Hebraizing revisions/recensions we know, namely, a relatively higher degree of translational consistency is nowhere cited as a criterion for Greek Jeremiah 29–52.[31] But since in all else Greek Jeremiah 1–28 functions for Tov as point of reference, it should so function for degree of translational consistency.

A closer look at some of Tov's demonstrations may be clarifying, but one suspects that the die has been cast in advance.

Tov groups the fifty-one[32] items intended to *demonstrate* that revision exists in Greek Jeremiah 29–52 and how it can manifest itself under the following five headings:

1. More Precise Renditions. Items 1–11 (in Tov)
2. Corrections of Erroneous Renditions. Items 12–17
3. Stereotyped (literal) Replacing Non-stereotyped (free) Renditions. Items 18–41
4. Renditions Reflecting the Heb in a More Consistent Way. Items 42–48
5. Other Changes. Items 49–51.

As becomes readily apparent, Tov's classifications, rather than being informed by *descriptive analysis* of linguistic data, followed by an *explanation* of those data, are instead comprised of an admixture of description and explanation, hence the 'what' and the 'why' intertwined and in a tangle. In other words, what we see in the very labels of his classifications is a curious hybrid of descriptive linguistic information and value judgment. That is to say, whereas group 3 ('stereotyped' versus 'non-stereotyped')

[31] The issue here is not specific wording but rather the degree of one-to-one equivalency.

[32] Note that items 1 and 2 (pp. 46–48) have effectively two components, which I shall distinguish as 1a/1b and 2a/2b respectively.

and group 4 ('higher' versus 'lower degree of translational consistency') may be said to be primarily descriptive, in the sense that a given Hebrew–Greek equivalence is said to occur with a lower or higher degree of consistency in Greek Jeremiah 29–52, groups 1 ('more accurate rendition') and 2 ('correct' versus 'incorrect rendition') are patently explanatory, in the sense that the reader is not in the first instance told *what* the text is, but instead is being told *why* the text is what it is, in Tov's opinion. As might be expected, this confusion of descriptive and explanatory criteria tends to confuse the 'what' and the 'why'.[33]

Even more importantly, if Tov's demonstration is to be convincing, the various forms that revision may take should add up. That is to say, Tov's five groupings should be mutually complementary and paint a reasonably coherent picture of direction. Instead, what we see is multiple and contradictory forms that revision is said to have taken.

If the defining characteristic of Hebraizing revisions in the Septuagint is a relatively higher degree of translational consistency (than the base text)—i.e., the same Greek item for the same Hebrew—one may usefully ask how that consistency can best be measured. I would suggest that consistency can be viewed as either internal or external.

For the purposes of the present study *internal consistency* will refer to the consistency with which a specific Hebrew item (e.g. a word, phrase or construction) is rendered within a given block of text (here Greek Jeremiah 29–52). Where the same translation equivalent is employed for each occurrence of the source item, I will assign a mark of +1; where there is more than one equivalent I will assign a mark of −1, with zero reserved for instances in which no determination can be made (e.g. when the source item occurs only once).

For this study *external consistency* will indicate the degree to which a given rendering of the Hebrew item conforms to some demonstrable norm. Since, as noted above, Greek Jeremiah 1–28 functions for Tov as his point of reference (with the Septuagint as a whole as his secondary point of reference), I will use the same point of reference to measure *external consistency*. When the Hebrew item in question (e.g. a word, phrase or construction) is translated with a higher degree of consistency

[33] It goes without saying that, since the text in question is a *translation*, description of the first order has to do with mapping the translated text onto its assumed source. See, for example, Gideon Toury, *Descriptive Translation Studies and Beyond* (Benjamins Translation Library 4; Amsterdam, 1995), chapter 4 'The Coupled Pair of Replacing + Replaced Segments', pp. 87–101.

in Greek Jeremiah 29–52 than in chapters 1–28, I will assign a mark of +1; when the degree of consistency is lower in 29–52 than in 1–28, I will assign a mark of −1, with zero reserved for instances in which no determination can be made (e.g. when the degree of consistency is the same in both).

The scale I will use is the following:

−1 = not/less consistent
0 = undetermined
+1 = consistent/more consistent.[34]

The following examples will illustrate what I have in mind.[35]

1. *More Precise Renditions. Items 1–11*

Item 3 אמן

Chapters 1–28	Chapters 29–52
γένοιτο (3×) 3:19 (not in MT); 11:5; 15:11 (MT אמר); and thus generally in the Septuagint.	ἀληθῶς (1×) 35(28):6 Elsewhere renders several times אמנה, אָמְנָם and אֻמְנָם.

Tov gives the following explanation:

> While אמן is rendered in Jer a' with a verb ('let it be'), it is rendered in Jer b' with an appropriate adverb.[36]

Tov is correct in suggesting that the equivalence אמן—ἀληθῶς occurs exclusively in Jer 35(28):6. Since it occurs but once, both internal and external consistency stand at 0. The equivalence in question is unique in the Septuagint. Thus if ἀληθῶς—אמן is nevertheless to be an instance of revision, a different reason must be averred. By deciding to put it in group 1 Tov is suggesting not only that ἀληθῶς is revisional (rather than translational) but also that it is a foundational item for his theory. It is difficult to see how this is possible and how it can be said, furthermore, that the reputed replacement of a sentence (γένοιτο) is 'appropriate'. Might it

[34] I am of course not suggesting that a higher degree of translational consistency *ipso facto* spells *revision*. See discussion of specific items below.

[35] Though the headings in the parallel columns have been added and the punctuation has been adjusted, the information is that provided by Tov. Regrettably only a few of Tov's fifty-one items can be discussed here. Items 1 and 4 have been discussed elsewhere (see footnote 1 above).

[36] Tov, *Jeremiah*, p. 48.

be because אָמֵן is commonly parsed as an adverb in Hebrew?[37] Well and good, but Septuagint translators commonly render it by γένοιτο (23×), with a few (3×) transcriptions (αμην) in 2 Esdras (Ezra–Nehemiah) and Chronicles, and that fact would seem to be of greater importance than the parsing of grammarians.

While there is nothing wrong with the punctuation supplied by Rahlfs and Ziegler: Ἀληθῶς· οὕτω(ς) ποιήσαι κύριος ('Truly, thus may the Lord do.') which might then equally well have been Γένοιτο· οὕτω(ς) ποιήσαι κύριος ('May it be; may the Lord so do.'), there is equally good reason to punctuate with Swete: Ἀληθῶς οὕτω ποιήσαι κύριος ('May the Lord truly do so'), in which case γένοιτο would not work. If the translator read his source text not as two parallel sentences both expressing a discrete wish, but as a single, intensified wish, there is no reason whatsoever for positing a secondary correction. That the Jeremiah translator operated isomorphically is one thing, but that he was translationally consistent is quite another. Not least, since Greek Jeremiah 29–52 sports but a single instance, inferring a correction is rather precarious under any circumstance.

Included under group 1 are a number of structural ('grammatical') in distinction from lexical items, and it is especially these that are typically best explained contextually. I take here Tov's first example.[38]

Item 5 אחר(י)

Chapters 1–28	Chapters 29–52
Μετά (3×) 3:7; 12:15; 24:1; and *passim* in the Septuagint	ὕστερον + gen. (4×) 36(29):2; 38(31):19(*bis*); 47(40):1 (?) μετά (5×) 35(28):12; 38:33(31:32); 39(32):16; 41(34):8; 43(36):27

Tov writes in explanation of ὕστερον:

> In place of the stereotyped LXX rendition אחר(י)—μετά Jer-R used a rendition which may have been chosen because it shows the etymological connection between אחר(י) and אחרון—ὕστερος.
>
> Jer-R used ὕστερον + gen. in a sense which, according to our lexica, is not documented before the LXX.[39]

[37] See BDB 53*a*.

[38] While structural words are excellent indicators of translational difference, it is doubtful that they play as prominent a role in revision, unless the latter be highly pedantic.

[39] Tov, *Jeremiah*, p. 49.

In this case, both internal and external consistency stand at –1. Since Tov places this item in group 1 the reader is asked to believe that Tov's reviser corrected Old Greek μετά on four occasions to ὕστερον but failed to do so on five occasions.

In point of fact, the usage of the items in question is more diversified than Tov allows for. On the Greek side, several grammatical functions are being differentiated. Thus when a (temporal) conjunctive is required, μετά + articular infinitive is used (3:7; 12:15; 24:1; 39[32]:16; 41[34]:8; 43[36]:27), if for no other reason than that ὕστερον cannot be used conjunctively.[40] When a (temporal) preposition is required, μετά + acc. is used (16:16; 21:7; 35[28]:12; 38:33[31:32]; 39(32):18), again if for no other reason than that ὕστερον is not so used. When a (spatial) preposition is required (albeit typically with a figurative sense) ὀπίσω + gen. is used (2:5, 8, 23, 25; 3:17; 7:6, 9; 8:2; 9:13; 11:10; 12:6; 13:10, 27; 16:11, 12; 17:16; 18:12; 25:6, 17; 35[42]:15; 49[42]:16; 52:8), to which may be added ὄπισθεν + genitive in 31(48):2 and 39(32):40. When a comparative adverb is required ὕστερον is used—for that is how it is used in 36(29):2 and in 38(31):19(*bis*).[41] Apparently, when none of the above will do, ἐπί + accusative is used (9:16[15]).

In sum, descriptively we can say that (1) μετά occurs 5× in chapters 1–28 and 6× in 29–52; (2) ὀπίσω / ὄπισθεν occurs 19× in chapters 1–28 and 5× in 29–52; (3) ὕστερον does not occur in chapters 1–28 and 3× in 29–52; (4) ἐπί (for אחרי) occurs 1× in chapters 1–28 but not at all in 29–52. How can this fourfold rendering of אחר(י) best be explained? Differentiation based on context would seem to be an adequate explanation. Revision on the basis of the Hebrew would seem the least likely.

Other structural items cited as support in group 1 ('More Precise Renditions') are renditions of לבלתי (item 6) and למען (item 7).

The items in group 1 can be marked as: 0 / 0 = 3; 0/+1 = 11; +1 / 0 = 2b; –1 / 0 = 1b, 6; –1/–1 = 2a, 4, 5, 8; –1/+1 =1a, 7, 9; +1/–1 = 10.

[40] Cf. ὕστερον μετά + articular infinitive at 47(40):1 in most witnesses, discussed by Tov in *Jeremiah*, footnote 31, p. 83.

[41] Thus NETS translates the two verses respectively as 'later than when King Iechonias and the queen and the eunuchs and every free person and prisoner and artisan had departed from Ierousalem' and 'because later than my captivity I repented and later than that I became aware I sighed for days of shame'.

2. *Corrections of Erroneous Renditions. Items 12–17*

If 'more *precise* rendition' is given as the explanation in group 1, the six instances grouped under 2 are explained as corrections of *erroneous* renditions, though the distinction between the two classifications is debatable and in any case not descriptive. The problem that, as we have seen, arose in group 1 arises here as well. It is by no means self evident what an *erroneous* rendering is. Evidently, the label refers to the Hebrew lexeme *qua* lexeme, but the 'real' meaning of the Hebrew word may not suit the Greek context. Thus where does error end and contextual adjustment begin, and at what point does contextual adjustment qualify as exegesis? These are not rhetorical questions but questions which arise as soon as one moves beyond the level of the word. Again a few examples.

Item 12 נפץ *pi'el*

Chapters 1–28	Chapters 29–52
διασκορπίζω (9×) 13:14; 28(51):20, 21, 22 (3×), 23 (3×); cf. Theodotion in Daniel 9:7 נֵפֶּץ–διασκορπισμός.	συγκόπτω (1×) 31(48):12 BSAC′(συντρίβω rel)

Tov gives the following explanation:

> Jer-OG [cf. LXX Jer 1–28] διασκορπίζω ('to scatter') is an incorrect rendering of נִפֵּץ ('to shatter'), based upon the meaning of the root in Rabb. Hebrew ('to scatter' = Targum *ad loc.*), of which διασκορπίζω is an equivalent ([Ier] 9:16[15] 10:21 23:1, 2). Jer-R corrected this rendition.[42]

Here too internal consistency stands at 0, since the item occurs only once, and external at 0, seeing that no comparison can be made. Tov seems to be correct in at least part of his explanation, namely, that in Greek Jeremiah 1–28 נפץ 'shatter' is not distinguished from פוץ 'be scattered'. Fact is, however, that both contexts in which נפץ stands (13:14 and 28:20ff.), since they speak of humans, are inimical to 'shatter' in their Greek version. Thus reading נפץ as though it were פוץ may have been brought on by context. Moreover, translating פוץ by διασκορπίζω is scarcely limited to Greek Jeremiah 1–28 but occurs as well in Genesis (1×),

[42] Tov, *Jeremiah*, p. 52.

Numbers (1×), Deuteronomy (1×), Job (1×), Psalms (1×), Zechariah (1×), Ezekiel (8×). Tov thinks Greek Jeremiah 31:12 got it right. To be noted is, however, that συγκόπτω means more nearly 'to chop up' than 'to shatter'. It is, moreover, questionable that διασκορπίζω would fit 31:12. Statistically the Hebrew—Greek equivalence of נפץ—συγκόπτω is unique in the Septuagint.

There is, moreover, a further point to consider, namely, the Greek translation of the preceding word in the Hebrew. The Masoretic Text's וְנִבְלֵיהֶם יְנַפֵּצוּ 'and they will break their jars' (cf. NRSV) is represented in the Greek by καὶ τὰ κεράσματα αὐτοῦ συγκόψουσι 'and they will break up/chop up his mixtures' (cf. NETS). Though Ziegler reads κεράσματα and συγκόπτω respectively many manuscripts read κέρατα and συντρίβω. Ziegler may be correct in his reconstruction but it is certainly of interest that the witnesses that read κεράσματα (V-26-46-86′-544 *O*-233 Arm) read συντρίβω, whereas those that read συγκόπτω (B-S-130 A-106′*C*′) have κέρατα. Given the fact that συγκόπτω ill fits κεράσματα and that κέρας can be a container of sorts, like Hebrew נבל I, reconsidering the critical text might not be out of order.[43] But be that as it may, the point to be made here is that Hebrew נבל I ('skin-bottle / jar / pitcher') is never translated by either κέρασμα or κέρας. Instead, it has three equivalents in the Septuagint: (1) ἀσκός (Jer 13:12 [*bis*]); 1 Reg 10:3; (2) ἀγγεῖον 1 Reg 25:18; Isa 30:14; Lam 4:2; (3) νεβελ 1 Reg 1:24; 2 Reg 16:1.[44] Thus if one posits a reviser who corrected the verb of the Old Greek text (from διασκορπίζω to συγκόπτω), it is difficult not to posit that he at the same time ignored the direct object of that very verb, even though it too failed to match its Hebrew counterpart.

Another structural item included in group 2 concerns the translation of אולי:

Item 17 אולי

Chapters 1–28	Chapters 29–52
εἰ (2×) 20:10; 21:2 and further 4× in the Septuagint	ἴσως (3×) 33(26):3; 43(36):3, 7 and elsewhere Genesis 32:21

[43] Rahlfs reads τὰ κέρατα αὐτοῦ συγκόψουσιν.
[44] Not surprisingly Aquila reads τὰ νεβελ and Symmachus τοὺς κρατῆρας.

Tov gives the following explanation:

> Although אולי originally served as an adverb, at times, when "followed by another clause ἀσυνδέτως, it expresses virtually the protasis = if peradventure" (BDB, s.v.). But the majority of LXX translators, including Jer-OG, rendered אולי as 'if peradventure ...' (starting a dependent clause), making an infrequent use of אולי the basis of their main rendition.
>
> Jer-R revised the OG to ἴσως, starting off an independent sentence.[45]

Consistency for both internal and external stands at +1. Since אולי occurs only 6× in Jeremiah, the significance of its rendition in Greek Jeremiah can only be gauged in the context of the Septuagint as a whole.[46] Quite clearly it was construed in one of three ways. Most often (23×) it was rendered by εἰ/ἐάν to mark the protasis of a condition; also with some frequency (15×), it was translated as ἵνα / ὅπως / μή(ποτε) to mark a purpose clause, positive or negative (prohibition); least often (4×) it was made to function as the adverb ἴσως, three of which occur in Greek Jeremiah 29–52. How can this threefold rendering of אולי in the Septuagint be explained? Again differentiation based on context would seem to be adequate explanation. Revision toward Hebrew אולי would seem the least likely.

Since the six items in group 2 are said to be corrections of erroneous renderings in the Old Greek of Jeremiah, it may perhaps be expected that they are not common translational equivalents in the Septuagint. Yet, it bears asking just where adjusting to context ends and error begins. To illustrate I take one further item from group 2.

Item 14 התהלל

Chapters 1–28	Chapters 29–52
various (3×)	μαίνομαι (1×) 32:2(25:16) unique in the Septuagint
παρασκευάζω 26(46):9 κατακαυχάομαι 27(50):38 σαλεύω 28(51):7	

Tov gives the following explanation:

> Presumably unacquainted with the precise meaning of התהלל, Jer-OG rendered it in three different ways:

[45] Tov, *Jeremiah*, p. 55.
[46] Cf. Tov, *Jeremiah*, footnotes 56 and 57, p. 85.

1. In 26(46):9 the Heb is reflected by a "passe partout" translation ..., conforming with its context.

2. In 27(50):38 he vocalized the Heb differently from MT.

3. The rendition in 28(51):7 may have resulted from ignorance or from a different exegetical tradition ... .

Jer-R rendered the Heb correctly.[47]

In terms of consistency both internal and external stand at 0. Descriptively there is no denying that, at the word level, in three out of four cases the Greek word does not semantically match its Hebrew counterpart—hence Hatch—Redpath's dagger (†). It is equally true that each of the four passages has a different word and that all four formal equivalences are unique in the Septuagint. The question is how to explain the data.

That a reviser knew what the Old Greek translator did not is possible but is scarcely the most parsimonious explanation. Yet the item is being presented as central rather than peripheral support for Tov's theory. To be noted is that in all four instances the word chosen fits well in the context, and it is difficult to see how μαίνομαι could fit in the first three. Though Greek Jeremiah can rightly be characterized as isomorphic, isomorphism cannot be equated with translational consistency and allows for more exegesis than does literalism, which is commonly understood to equate with translational consistency.[48]

The items in group 2 can be marked as follows: 0 / 0 = 12, 13, 14, 16; +1 / 0 = 15; +1/+1 = 17.

3. *Stereotyped (literal) Replacing Non-stereotyped (free) Renditions. Items 18–41*

With group 3 Tov switches from explanation to what is more of a descriptive analysis. To speak, however, of stereotyped (literal) versus non-stereotyped (free), as he does in group 3, is not helpful if for no other reason than that all these labels are subjective and only indirectly descriptive of the text. To state but the obvious: How many occurrences does it take to make a stereotype?

Numerically group 3, as noted above, with its 24 items, is by far the largest of Tov's groups. Group 3 is also rather diverse. So for example,

---

[47] Tov, *Jeremiah*, p. 53.

[48] So Tov, *Jeremiah*, p. 41.

it includes a goodly number of structural ('grammatical') items such as prepositions (see items 21, 22, 39), articles (32), conjunctions (30, 31) which in the nature of the case tend to show more translational inconsistency than do full lexemes and tend to be less indicative of revision.

Item 38 ידע *qal*

Chapters 1–28	Chapters 29–52
γιγνώσκω (25×) οἶδα (11×) ἐπίσταμαι (4×) (43× in the Septuagint) ἐπιγιγνώσκω (2×) (53× in the Septuagint)	γιγνώσκω (17×) οἶδα (1×)

Since the second equivalence in Greek Jeremiah 29–52 occurs only once, one might mark this item with +1 for internal consistency, and since the first equivalence is standard in Greek Jeremiah 1–28, as well as in the Septuagint generally, one might mark external consistency with +1 as well. It is difficult to see, however, what is being corrected. Is the point that 29–52 has reduced the number of equivalences from four to two?

Statistically the picture is quite clear. Chapters 1–28 have 42 occurrences of ידע *qal* and use four Greek equivalents; chapters 29–52 have 18 occurrences and use two Greek equivalents. Throughout, the most common Septuagint equivalent for ידע *qal* predominates, though all four equivalencies are well attested, even the least common (ἐπίσταμαι) occurring more than 40×. Tov comments that Jer-R (cf. Greek Jeremiah 29–52) used mainly γιγνώσκω. While that is obviously true, he implies rather more than that by placing it in his group 3. The explanation for the phenomena is evidently that a reviser overlooked οἶδα in 38:34 and eliminated from his text ἐπίσταμαι and ἐπιγιγνώσκω as equivalents.

Item 25 Various

Chapters 1–28	Chapters 29–52
παρασκευάζω (5×) 6:4 = קדש *pi'el* ('consecrate') 17:22 + 12:5 = חרב *hitpa'el* ('heat oneself') 22:15	zero

Chapters 1–28	Chapters 29–52
26(46):9 = הלל *hitpolel* ('act madly')	
27(50):42 = ערך ('arrange') 27:14+	
28(51):11 = ברר *hiph'il* ('clean/polish') 4:11	

Tov gives the following explanation:

> Occurring in only six additional places in the LXX, this verb was clearly cherished by Jer-OG. The mentioned examples show that Jer-OG availed himself of this verb particularly when he felt uncertain about the meaning of the Heb. The broad meaning of παρασκευάζω made it an adequate "passe-partout" rendition.
>
> Since this general use παρασκευάζω is not found in Jer b' it was probably eliminated by Jer-R.[49]

In the nature of the case no mark can be assigned either for internal or external consistency. Since no Hebrew word is placed in the heading of item 25, it is evidently not about revision toward the Hebrew source text, even though it appears in group 3. It is thus difficult to see how item 25 can be used to demonstrate revision toward the Hebrew or for that matter to demonstrate revision of *any* kind—unless it be revision by omission.

The uncertainty about the Hebrew of which Tov speaks must refer to context rather than to the specific verbs, since all the verbs, with the exception of הלל *hitpolel*, are known to the translator of Greek Jeremiah 1–28 (see e.g. 17:22; 22:15; 27:14; 4:11). What is also clear is that since all five passages in question have to do with preparations for war, the choice of παρασκευάζω is excellent. Moreover, even though the verb is uncommon in the Septuagint, it is well known in Classical literature, including in contexts of war.

Tov *explains* the absence of παρασκευάζω in Greek Jeremiah 29–52 as 'probably' due to (secondary) revision and by his inclusion of this item in his group 3 is *describing* it as an instance of increased stereotyping. In this case and in several others like it in group 3 (see 24, 26, 29) both are problematic. By way of description all that can be said is that Greek Jeremiah 29–52 does not use παρασκευάζω. Hence the person responsible for Greek Jeremiah 29–52 apparently found no occasion for using it. Why that is so admits of several explanations and can therefore not be listed in support of a *single* explanation.

---

[49] Tov, *Jeremiah*, p. 61.

For other instances of alleged revision by omission see items 24 and 29.

Item 27 -ל חטא- ἁμαρτάνω + … (in all the obj.: God)

Chapters 1–28	Chapters 29–52
ἔναντι / ἐναντίον (4×) 3:25; 8:14; 14:20; 16:10; and *passim* in the Septuagint. dative 14:7; 27(50):7	dative (4×) 40(33):8, 8; 47(40):3; 51(44):23; and *passim* in the Septuagint. Cf. ἀδικέω + accusative for חטא ל in 44(37):18

Tov gives the following explanation:

> Since Jer-OG wanted to avoid the slightest harsh expression "to sin to (God)," he rendered the Heb with ἁμαρτάνω ἔναντι /ἐναντίον. This translation was frequently revised by Jer-R to its literal rendition.[50]

If 44:18 is ignored, internal consistency may be marked with +1 and as a result external consistency can be marked likewise with +1. Both competing constructions are, however, common in the Septuagint as a whole.

Tov labels the construction with the dative as the "literal rendition" of חטא ל. But how accurate is it to say that inflection (dative) is a more literal rendering of the Hebrew preposition ל than a discrete morpheme (ἔναντι /ἐναντίον)? Though it can scarcely be denied that ל is often rendered by the dative, there is also plenty of evidence to show that in isomorphic translations like Greek Jeremiah discrete morphemes in the source text were regularly represented by discrete morphemes in the target text. In point of fact, that is exactly what happens in Jeremiah 27:7 and 44(51):23 where ליהוה is rendered by τῷ κυρίῳ (and so *passim*. throughout the Septuagint). Moreover, throughout Greek Jeremiah one finds that Hebrew articles, *notae accusativi*, the infinitival prefix ל, personal pronouns (even when rendered superfluous by Greek inflection), pronominal suffixes, pleonastic pronouns and adverbs, prepositions, and conjunctions are all regularly represented, whether or not such representation results in standard Greek usage.

[50] Tov, *Jeremiah*, p. 62.

Item 36 יחדו

Chapters 1–28	Chapters 29–52
ἐπὶ τὸ αὐτό (4×) 3:18; 6:12; 26(46):12; 27(50):4 ἐν τῷ αὐτῷ (1×) 13:14 ἅμα (4×) 6:11, 21; 27(50):33; 28(51):38 ὁμοθυμαδόν (2×) 5:5; 26(46):21	ἅμα (4×) 30(49):3; 31(48):7; 38(31):24; 48(41):1

Though יחדו appears only 4× in 29–52, on all four occasions it is translated by ἅμα. Consequently, +1 is warranted for internal consistency. External consistency likewise stands at +1. In the Septuagint as a whole, however, ἐπὶ τὸ αὐτό and ἅμα occur about 35× each.

Tov gives no explicit explanation, but again by his inclusion of this item in group 3 he classifies it as an instance of increased stereotyping which is foundational to his theory. Statistically it is true that while יחדו occurs a total of 11× in 1–28 and 6× in 29–52, in 1–28 we find four Greek glosses while 29–52 shows but a single one, though it is unknown whether the Hebrew source text of 31(38):8 and 14 lacked יחדו or whether the Greek dropped it.

Item 30 διότι

Chapters 1–28	Chapters 29–52
ὅτι *passim* in Jer a' διότι (25×) 1:12, 15; 2:10; 3:8, 14, 25; 4:8, 15, 22, 28; 8:17; 15:20; 16:9; 20:4; 21:10; 22:4, 11; 23:12; 26(46):21, 27; 27(50):11; 28(51):5, 14, 29, 33	ὅτι *passim* in Jer b'

Tov writes:

> As in the remainder of the LXX, Jer-OG generally used both ὅτι and διότι for כי, employing διότι particularly to avoid a hiatus (see Thackeray, *Grammar*, 139). Jer-R limited himself to ὅτι.[51]

Since Hebrew כי is absent from the heading of item 30 but is nonetheless noted in Tov's comment, it is difficult to know whether the issue here is meant to be one of Hebrew–Greek equivalence or one of Greek style. If the former, the reader is led to conclude that Tov's reviser replaced διότι with ὅτι because ὅτι is the standard equivalent for כי in the Septuagint,

[51] Tov, *Jeremiah*, p. 63.

including Greek Jeremiah 1–28. Hence both internal and external consistency would stand at +1. If, on the other hand, the issue is one of preferred Greek usage[52]—as the heading suggests and Tov's comment explains—it is difficult to see how this item can be cited in group 3, since it can at most indicate a difference in translators and as such fails to support Tov's revisional theory.

Of further interest is that in Greek Isaiah διότι similarly occurs exclusively in chapter 1–39 and not in 40–66,[53] though it is not accepted by Ziegler as support for bisectioning.

Due to the diversity within group 3, including items without a Hebrew word in its heading (items 24, 25, 29, 30, 31, 41) as well as structural items (21, 22, 30, 31, 32, 33, 39, 40) translational consistency is difficult to measure. I would categorize them as follows: 0 / 0 = 24, 25, 29, 31, 32, 40, 41; 0/+1 =34; +1/−1 = 18; +1/+1 = 19, 20, 30?, 35, 36, 37, 38?, 39; −1 / 0 = 21, 22, 23, 26, 28; −1/−1 = 33; +1 / 0 = 27.

4. *Renditions Reflecting the Heb. in a More Consistent Way. Items 42–48*

With group 4 Tov continues his ostensibly descriptive classification and by his own admission there is no substantive difference between groups 3 and 4[54] since both of them have to do with translational consistency. At the same time, however, Tov comments,

> While in section (3) the revisional tendency is determined by the *character* of the rendition (stereotyped versus non-stereotyped), the renditions mentioned below (4a, 4b) are preferred by Jer-R by virtue of being the only rendition in Jer b', not necessarily more stereotyped within the LXX.[55]

Thus when all is said and done, like group 3, group 4 is indeed intended to be about increased translational consistency on Jeremiah 29–52. But the evidence presented does not seem to warrant that conclusion. Moreover, 'in a more consistent way' need *not* mean that Tov's Jer-R implements the majority equivalence of Greek Jeremiah 1–28 (see item 42), nor need it

[52] Note that Tov refers to Thackeray's suggestion with approval.

[53] Cf. Ziegler, *Untersuchungen*, p. 35 and Seeligmann, *Isaiah*, pp. 39–40.

[54] Tov, *Jeremiah*, p. 88 note 104: 'Since the tendency to represent the Heb with a stereotyped rendition ... is also a form of "translational consistency", this section incorporates *additional* forms of translational consistency'.

[55] Tov, *Jeremiah*, p. 69.

mean that Greek Jeremiah 29–52 has fewer Greek equivalents than Greek Jeremiah 1–28 (see items 43, 45, 46); in fact the opposite may be the case (44, 48). Lastly, it can also mean that Jer-R's alleged revision is rare or even esoteric in the Septuagint as a whole (43, 44, 45). No doubt, for all of these reasons Tov divides group 4 into three sub-groups:[56]

4a = item 42: two equivalents in 1–28 versus one equivalent in 29–52
4b = item 43: the same two equivalents in both 1–28 and 29–52 but with different distribution.
4c = items 44–48: chapters 29–52 differentiate when 1–28 do not.

It is difficult to see how especially sub-group 4c can be made to fit under main group 4, since, in one way or another, more often than not it reflects the Hebrew in a *less* consistent way.

I limit myself here to two examples from 4c which Tov himself recognizes to be an oddity under 4.[57] What makes 4c of special interest is that Tov labels it 'Exegetical consistency', and the notion of interpretive/exegetical activity on the part Tov's Jer-R hovers in the background throughout chapter III.

Item 44 דבר *pi'el*

Chapters 1–28	Chapters 29–52
λαλέω *passim* λέγω 1:17; 7:27[58]	1. *subject human*: λαλέω *passim* 2. *subject God or prophet*: χρηματίζω (7×) 33(26):2, 2; 36(29):23; 37(30):2; 43(36):2, 4; 47(40):2 λέγω 35(28):7 Cf. further שאג—χρηματίζω (2×) 33:16(25:30)

Tov gives the following explanation:

> The rendering of the divine and prophetic speech and the roaring of God (שאג) with χρηματίζω ('to give oraculum') in Jer b' was exegetically motivated. Jer-R was highly inconsistent in the insertion of this verb. It is noteworthy that χρηματίζω is a distinct Jer b' word within the LXX.[59]

[56] I paraphrase what they are about.
[57] Tov, *Jeremiah*, p. 71: 'Contrary to Jer-OG [cf. 1–28], Jer-R [cf. 29–52] distinguished in some cases between two meanings or usages of a word. The few examples of this group do not conform with the implication of the preceding ones'.
[58] Not noted by Tov.
[59] Tov, *Jeremiah*, p. 71.

In terms of translational consistency, item 44 must be marked as −1 for both internal and external. Just why, beginning with Jeremiah 33(26):2, we see differentiation may be explained in a number of ways, but Tov's makes good sense, since it is clear not only that χρηματίζω has become an item of interest in the book but also that its use trumps translational consistency. Moreover, as Tov notes, χρηματίζω with the sense it has here does not occur elsewhere in the Septuagint and is not mandated by Hebrew דִּבֵּר. Of further relevance is χρημολογέω ('utter an oracle') in 45(38):4 for דרש, the more since this equivalence is unique to this passage. What the relevance of this piece of exegesis is in terms of the larger context of the book, needs further exploration.[60] Here the intriguing question is whether such exegetical nuggets are restricted to Greek Jeremiah 29–52 or are attested throughout the book.

Item 45 נביא ('false prophet')

Chapters 1–28	Chapters 29–52
προφήτης (43 ×)	ψευδοπροφήτης (8 ×) 33(26):7, 8, 11, 16; 34:7(27:9); 35(28):1; 36(29):1, 8 and elsewhere Zechariah 13:2
ψευδοπροφήτης (1 ×) 6:13	προφήτης (5 ×) 34:12, 13 (27:15, 16); 39(32):32

Tov gives the following explanation:

> Jer-R endeavored, however inconsistently, to make a distinction between the real and the false prophet (both נביא), by using ψευδοπροφήτης as the main rendition of נביא—'false prophet'.[61]

Since Greek Jeremiah 29–52 renders נביא by two rather than one equivalent, the internal consistency is −1. The external consistency stands at 0.

Both Greek words occur throughout the book for the same Hebrew though not with the same distribution. As in the case of χρηματίζω in item 44, it cannot be said that ψευδοπροφήτης, chiefly beginning with chapter 33, increases translational consistency in the Septuagint as a whole, since the word is virtually unattested elsewhere including in most of Greek Jeremiah.

[60] Meanwhile see the longer version of my introduction to NETS Ieremias at http://ccat.sas.upenn.edu/nets/edition/ p. 15.

[61] Tov, *Jeremiah*, p. 72. In footnote 117 (p. 90) Tov adds *inter alia* that 'Jer-R ... introduced an element of precision into the terminology of the Hebrew book'.

Though at the purely lexical level it renders the source text more explicit, there is scarcely any contextual doubt about what the individuals in question are. There is therefore no lexical warrant in the source text for what has been done. Consequently, Tov is fully justified in identifying the use of ψευδοπροφήτης as exegetical, though unlike χρηματίζω, it occurs before chapter 33 as well, namely, proleptically in 6:13. Thus here, even more acutely than in item 44, the question arises as to whether ψευδοπροφήτης is not better explained as translational than as revisional.[62]

The items in 4. can be marked as −1 / 0 = 43, 45, 46, 47; −1/−1 = 44, 48; +1/+1 = 42.

5. *Other Changes. Items 49–51*

I take one final example from the concluding, amorphous classification and one which, again, has some interesting interpretive aspects.

Item 50 נדח, mainly *hiph'il*

Chapters 1–28	Chapters 29–52
ἐξωθέω (10×) 8:3; 16:15; 23:2, 3, 8; 24:9; 25:16(49:36); 26(46):28; 27(50):17; 28:35(51:34) and further 9× in the Septuagint.	διασπείρω (2×) 30(49):5; 39(32):37 and further Isaiah 56:8
	σπείρω (1×) 37(30):17

Tov gives the following explanation:

> Jer-OG's ἐξωθέω is a perfect rendering of the Heb. διασπείρω ('to scatter'), found in Jer b', seems inappropriate at first glance, but since in the OT הדיח is interchangeable with הפיץ ('to scatter'), this rendition should not be considered unapt. The fact that the other translators and revisers rendered הדיח similarly corroborates this point.
>
> It is difficult to determine whether Jer-R was influenced by the technical meaning of διασπορά when he replaced ἐξωθέω with διασπείρω.[63]

[62] See further the longer version of my introduction to NETS Ieremias at http://ccat.sas.upenn.edu/nets/edition/ p. 3.
[63] Tov, *Jeremiah*, pp. 74–75.

The internal consistency stands at −1 as does the external consistency.

Tov's argument seems to be that since הדיח is 'interchangeable' with הפיץ and הפיץ is often translated by διασπείρω, διασπείρω is not an unapt translation of הדיח.

By way of description, it may be noted that, in Greek Jeremiah, Hebrew נדח was regularly translated by ἐξωθέω (10×) but that on three occasions it was rendered by (δια)σπείρω.

If then, by way of explanation, one begins with the assumption that Greek Jeremiah is a literal translation (which is correct) and further assumes that literalism spells translational consistency, it follows that the three non-default (i.e., marked) renderings must derive from a second translator or from a reviser. The question is, of course, whether the latter assumption is sustainable.

Though it holds pretty much for נדח—ἐξωθέω, seeing that the former is always translated by the latter in Greek Jeremiah 1–28, the reverse is not quite true since ἐξωθέω also translates תעה *hiph'il* ('cause to wander') in 27(50):6 and דוח *hiph'il* ('cleanse away') in 28:35(51:34).[64] διασπείρω presents a slightly different picture, since in the Septuagint generally it translates twelve Hebrew words and in Jeremiah we see the following:

> 13:24 = פוץ *hiph'il*; 15:7 = זרה *qal*; 18:17 = פוץ *hiph'il*; 25:15(49:36) = זרה *pi'el*; 30(49):5 = נדח *niph'al*; 39(32):17 = נדח *hiph'il*; 47(40):15 = פוץ *niph'al*; 52:8 = פוץ *niph'al*. Thus in Greek Jeremiah διασπείρω translates פוץ 4×, זרה 2×, נדח 2×.

The first two, פוץ and זרה, occur in both halves, and the last one, נדח, only in Greek Jeremiah 29–52. This suggests that neither Greek Jeremiah 1–28 nor Greek Jeremiah 29–52 is stuck on an $x = y$ lexical relationship between the source language and the target language—which is not to say, of course, that such one-to-one linkage does not occur, but it is to say that it cannot be presupposed in any given instance.

That being the case, one might perhaps better look at the meaning of ἐξωθέω and διασπείρω respectively, instead of at the issue of lexical consistency on the translational level. Tov himself here points the way when he writes in a footnote to the switch from ἐξωθέω to διασπείρω,

[64] Tov, *Jeremiah*, p. 74 reads √ נדח in 51:34.

> Already at an early date διασπορά was used as a technical term denoting the Jewish diaspora, cf. Deut 28:25 Jer 15:7 41(34):17 Ep.Jac. 1:1. Note further that the renditions listed in the right column refer to the scattering of Israel (with the exception of Jer 37(30):17); in these cases διασπείρω denotes the 'bringing into the διασπορά'. Cf. K.L. Schmidt, διασπορά, *ThWNT* 2 (1935) 98–104 and Seeligmann, *Isaiah*, 113 on Is 35:8.
>
> It is not certain whether Jer-R was influenced by the technical meaning of the verb since 30(49):5 refers to Edom and 37(30):16 has the *simplex* of the verb.[65]

Though Seeligmann is undoubtedly correct in observing that, for Jews, διασπορά was symbolic of misery and humiliation,[66] it was not solely a negative term, as Schmidt recognizes, but a positive one as well. While διασπείρω and διασπορά have to do with scattering seed[67] and thus could have the sense of 'to throw away', it also, and perhaps predominantly, has the sense of seeding that leads to new life. Isa 35:8 spells this out rather explicitly.[68] By contrast, ἐξωθέω + cognates means 'to expel, drive away, reject'. That, however, is scarcely the whole story of Israel's (Judah's) exile, according to Greek Jeremiah.

As Tov states, it is uncertain whether the originator of Jeremiah 30(49):5; 39(32):37 had rebirth in mind, but as an explanation for the text we have it would seem preferable to a reviser who rejected a 'perfect rendering of the Heb(rew)' (so Tov) in favour of what he deemed to be a better than perfect translational equivalent.

The items in group 5 can be marked as +1/+1 = 49; −1/−1 = 50; −1/0 = 51.

Conclusions

Despite the fact that the argumentation in chapter III appears to be circular and proves what is presupposed, one may still want to ask whether the evidence presented argues at all for a Hebraizing revision (in distinction from a translation). Since Tov offers fifty-one numbered

---

[65] Tov, *Jeremiah*, p. 91, footnote 129.

[66] Seeligmann, *Isaiah*, p. 112.

[67] Not surprisingly, therefore, the standard translation of זרע + cognates is σπείρω + cognates. Cf. 37(30):17.

[68] NETS: 'A pure way shall be there,/ and it shall be called a holy way;/ and the unclean shall not pass by there,/ nor shall be there an unclean way,/ but those who have been dispersed (οἱ … διεσπαρμένοι) shall walk on it, and they shall not go astray'.

examples, to each of which translational consistency can be applied, both internally and externally, one ends up with 102 occasions for greater consistency (for lack of a better term). One may add thereto 1b(2×) and 2b(2×) (see Tov items 1 and 2 respectively) for a total of 106. Adding the respective totals from each of the five group together gives us:

Consistency	Occurrences	Percentage
+1	32	30
−1	33	31
0	41	39

The above totals are, of course, raw data. That is to say, though statistically it might look as if in 32 out of 106 instances there is evidence of a higher degree of translational consistency and thus of 'revision', upon closer scrutiny the higher degree could well be due to other causes. Yet, given the fact that the totals for +1 and −1 are virtually the same, it is not plausible to argue that Greek Jeremiah 29–52 is at all characterized by a higher degree of translational consistency than is Greek Jeremiah 1–28. Increased consistency is canceled out by decreased consistency. On that basis, therefore, there is no reason to think of Greek Jeremiah 29–52 as a revision of the Old Greek of Jeremiah—unless, at the same time, we declare it *sui generis*. Furthermore, in more general terms, it is difficult to find even a single instance, in Tov's chapter III, in which revision is a more parsimonious explanation than any other. It would seem safe to conclude, therefore, that Tov's hypothesis of revision in Greek Jeremiah 29–52 has been falsified.

As a result, in Greek Jeremiah Thackeray's theory of two translators remains standing by default, even though uncomfortably so. Given that Thackeray's two blocks of text are, as Tov has shown, interrelated by similarities and differences, he is correct in finding fault with Thackeray's theory. But since his own theory of revision, similar to the Gray–Baumgärtel two-translator theory in Greek Isaiah, fails to provide a better explanation, an explanation other than revision must be explored. Tov himself, perhaps inadvertently, points to a new hypothesis, namely, contextual accommodation and exegesis. That is to say, not only should the documented differences *between* chapters 1–28 and 29–52 be approached from the perspective of contextual accommodation and exegesis, but as well the differences *within* the so-called two halves of Greek Jeremiah. Tov deserves credit for having called attention to this aspect of Greek Jeremiah.

As noted earlier, though Greek Jeremiah can be called an isomorphic translation, typically replacing a morpheme of the source text with a morpheme in the target text, it is much less a 'literal' translation if 'literal' is understood to equate with translational consistency. Though literalism of the $x = y$ (lexemic) variety gives more scope to retroversion to the source text, literalism of the isomorphic type allows for more interpretation and exegesis. It is this aspect of Greek Jeremiah that needs more exploration. That much is crystal clear from Tov's study.

JACOB OF EDESSA'S QUOTATIONS AND REVISION OF ISAIAH

Bas ter Haar Romeny

1. *Two Questions*

In his 1981 book *Die alten Textzeugen des Jesajabuches* Arie van der Kooij discussed the Hebrew text and ancient versions of Isaiah up to the year 400 CE.[1] His interests are certainly not limited to this period, however. Therefore I think it will be permissible to write this article in his honour about a version from the first decade of the eighth century: the revision of the biblical text by the Syriac polymath Jacob of Edessa. In two important recent studies, Andreas Juckel has drawn attention to what he calls an 'earlier stage' of this version.[2] He is referring to the biblical quotations in the margins of Jacob of Edessa's revision of Paul of Edessa's translation of the hymns of Severus of Antioch. However, the editor of this material, Ernest Brooks, was of the opinion that as Jacob's full revision of the biblical text was made some thirty years later, no connection with it could be expected, 'nor, as far as I have been [able] to compare it, have I found any'.[3] Our first question is therefore: should the biblical quotations in the revision of the translation of Severus' hymns (JacS) be seen as a preliminary stage of Jacob's full revision of the biblical text (JacR), or is there indeed no connection?

---

[1] Arie van der Kooij, *Die alten Textzeugen des Jesajabuches* (OBO 35; Fribourg–Göttingen, 1981).

[2] Andreas Juckel, 'Septuaginta and Peshitta: Jacob of Edessa Quoting the Old Testament in Ms BL Add 17134', *Hugoye* 8.2 (2005) [http://syrcom.cua.edu/Hugoye]; and idem, 'Approximation of the "Traditions" in Jacob of Edessa's Revision of Isaiah', in G.A. Kiraz (ed.), *Malphono w-Rabo d-Malphone. Studies in Honour of Sebastian P. Brock* (Piscataway, 2008), pp. 227–281.

[3] Ernest W. Brooks, *The Hymns of Severus of Antioch and Others in the Syriac Version of Paul of Edessa, as Revised by James of Edessa* (PO 6.1; Paris, 1909), 1–179; (PO 7.5; Paris, 1911), 593–802. The indexes and errata are appended to Ernest W. Brooks, *A Collection of Letters of Severus of Antioch, from Numerous Syriac Manuscripts* 2 (PO 14.1; Paris, 1920), 299–310. Quotation in *Hymns of Severus* (PO 6.1), p. 6 note 3.

Our second question has to do with the textual basis of Jacob's work on the biblical text. JacR has been termed 'a curious eclectic and patchwork text' by William Wright.[4] The colophon of Genesis speaks about Jacob's use of two translations (ܡܥܠܒܢܘ̈ܬܐ): 'the one found among the Greeks and the one found among the Syrians'.[5] It is clear that the latter version was the Peshitta, but has Jacob used a Greek manuscript in addition, or the Syro-Hexapla? It was Alfred Rahlfs's opinion that Jacob used the Peshitta as his basis, correcting it with the help of the Greek Lucianic recension.[6] He saw no Syro-Hexaplaric influence in the chapter he had studied, 1 Kings 1. A completely different position was defended by Moshe Goshen-Gottstein, who thought that Jacob had produced an interrelated revision of the Peshitta and the Syro-Hexapla, with only minor traces of Lucianic influence.[7]

Recent studies by Richard Saley and Alison Salvesen have now firmly established the fact that the Peshitta was Jacob's basis.[8] It is also clear that Jacob had access to one or more Greek manuscripts. However, Saley, Salvesen, and now also Juckel leave the possibility open that he also used the Syro-Hexapla.[9] For Genesis I have already argued that it is not

---

[4] William Wright, *A Short History of Syriac Literature* (London, 1894, repr. Piscataway, 2001), p. 17.

[5] For the Syriac text, see [J.B.] Ladvocat, 'Notice d' un manuscrit oriental apporté à Paris en 1764', *Journal des sçavans* [Paris] (1765), pp. 542–555, esp. 542. The colophon of the manuscript of the books of Samuel speaks of 'those found among the Greeks', in plural; see Alison Salvesen, *The Books of Samuel in the Syriac Version of Jacob of Edessa* (MPIL 10; Leiden, 1999), p. ix, edition on p. 90, and translation on p. 67. The colophon of the Isaiah manuscript is probably lost, as the end of Isaiah is missing; see William Wright, *Catalogue of Syriac Manuscripts in the British Museum Acquired Since the Year 1838* 1 (London, 1870, repr. Piscataway, 2003), p. 39 (no. LXI).

[6] Alfred Rahlfs, *Septuaginta-Studien* 3. *Lucians Rezension der Königsbücher* (Göttingen, 1911), pp. 48–50. On this recension, which should perhaps be called Antiochene rather than Lucianic, see now also Natalio Fernández Marcos's contribution to this volume, entitled 'Is there an Antiochene Reading of Isaiah?'

[7] Moshe H. [Goshen-]Gottstein, 'Neue Syrohexaplafragmente', *Biblica* 37 (1956), pp. 162–183, esp. 165–166.

[8] Richard J. Saley, *The Samuel Manuscript of Jacob of Edessa: A Study in Its Underlying Textual Traditions* (MPIL 9; Leiden, 1998), pp. 19–20, and idem, 'The Textual Vorlagen for Jacob of Edessa's Revision of the Books of Samuel', in Bas ter Haar Romeny (ed.), *Jacob of Edessa and the Syriac Culture of His Day* (MPIL 18, Leiden, 2008), pp. 113–125, esp. 116; Salvesen, *The Books of Samuel*, p. x, and idem, 'Jacob of Edessa's Version of 1–2 Samuel: Its Method and Text-Critical Value', in Romeny (ed.), *Jacob of Edessa*, pp. 127–144, esp. 131.

[9] Saley, *The Samuel Manuscript*, pp. 121–122; idem, 'The Textual Vorlagen', p. 121; Juckel, 'Septuaginta and Peshitta', § 20; idem, 'Approximation', p. 242 with note 25. With more reservations: Salvesen, *The Books of Samuel*, pp. x–xi, and idem, 'Jacob of Edessa's Version of 1–2 Samuel', p. 137.

necessary to assume the use of this version.[10] The material presented by Juckel allows us to reconsider this question for Isaiah: did Jacob indeed use the Syro-Hexapla when producing JacS, and what did he do when he wrote JacR?

2. *The Sources*

Between 619 and 629 Paul of Edessa translated a collection of hymns by Severus of Antioch and others. This translation is known to us only through the revision made of it in 674/675 by Jacob of Edessa.[11] One of the striking elements of this revision is the fact that in addition to the biblical quotations in the text itself Jacob gives some 600 full quotations of the Old Testament and 350 of the New in the margins (these quotations are indicated by the siglum JacS in this paper).[12] Jacob's colophon makes it clear that in order to preserve the rhythm of the poetry, Paul of Edessa had added and changed words.[13] In order to show what the Greek actually says, Jacob used a system with red ink to mark Paul's additions, and interlinear notes to indicate the original expressions wherever words had been altered. For the same reason—the preservation of the original wording when the rhythm might have distorted it—he must have added the biblical quotations. As he himself states, they allow one to know 'how the proofs and testimonies from the scriptural words of the Holy Scriptures in the hymns themselves run, without variation and without addition or diminution' (trans. Brooks).

The main sources for JacS are the Peshitta and the Septuagint. It appears that about a quarter of the Old Testament readings have been translated from the Greek. Interestingly, the distribution of Peshitta and Septuagint readings differs from book to book. Thus some of the most popular books have a relatively small number of Septuagint readings: Genesis has none, Psalms only a few, and Isaiah shows a mixed picture, the earlier hymns usually quoting the Peshitta and the later ones the Septuagint. In addition to respect for what people were used to, the availability of texts may also have played a role: thus in Reigns one would

[10] Bas ter Haar Romeny, 'Jacob of Edessa on Genesis: His Quotations of the Peshitta and His Revision of the Text', in idem (ed.), *Jacob of Edessa*, pp. 145–158.

[11] For this date, see the colophon in Brooks, *Hymns of Severus* (PO 7.5), pp. 801–802.

[12] See Brooks, *Hymns of Severus* (PO 6.1), p. 6, and Juckel, 'Septuaginta and Peshitta', § 5.

[13] See note 11 above.

have expected some Septuagint readings, but I found none and, going to the New Testament, the fact that all readings of Acts are taken from the Harclean, whereas for all other books the Peshitta is quoted, should also be seen in this light.

The two complete manuscripts of Jacob's revision of the translation of Severus' hymns are BL Add 17134, which has preserved the red ink and interlinear notes, and BL Add 18816, where these features are lacking, but which sometimes adopts Jacob's corrections in the main text.[14] As the latter manuscript sometimes offers a better text than the former, BL Add 17134 cannot be seen as Jacob's autograph, as William Wright thought.[15]

Jacob's full revision of the biblical text (JacR) may be seen as a last effort to make the Greek Bible acceptable to Syriac readers. Jacob's version was a compromise between the two positions defended in Syriac Christianity: the position of Philoxenus of Mabbug, who would have liked to replace the Peshitta with a very literal rendering of the Septuagint, and that of Eusebius of Emesa, who thought that the Peshitta was reliable because the Syriac language was related to the Hebrew.[16] In addition, Jacob wanted to clarify the text to his readers. The available colophons indicate that Jacob finished the work on his revision in the monastery of Tel ʿAdda in the years 704 and 705.

JacR survives only in part in a small number of manuscripts.[17] For us, these manuscripts are a precious treasure, not so much because of their value for the constitution of the biblical text, but as a witness to the way one of the finest scholars of the Syriac Orthodox Church, comparable only to Jerome according to some, dealt with the text of the Bible and its different versions. The manuscript containing Isaiah is BL Add 14441, which has suffered some damage.[18] Small parts have been edited by Ceriani, but I base my comments here on the many verses edited by Juckel in the extensive comparative study of JacS and JacR which he gives in his second article.

---

[14] Juckel, 'Septuaginta and Peshitta', §§ 1–3, with further references.

[15] See the preceding footnote and Brooks, *Hymns of Severus* (PO 6.1), p. 6. Wright's opinion is found in his London *Catalogue* 1, p. 338.

[16] Bas ter Haar Romeny, 'The Peshitta and its Rivals. On the Assessment of the Peshitta and Other Versions of the Old Testament in Syriac Exegetical Literature', *The Harp* 11–12 (1998–1999), pp. 21–31.

[17] See Wim Baars, 'Ein neugefundenes Bruchstück aus der syrischen Bibelrevision des Jakob von Edessa', *VT* 18 (1968), pp. 548–554, esp. 548–549.

[18] See the end of note 5 above.

The Septuagint, Syro-Hexapla, and Peshitta, which are adduced here for comparative purposes, are all available in scholarly or facsimile editions.[19]

3. *The Biblical Quotations in BL Add 17134 an Earlier Stage of the Revision of Isaiah?*

As indicated above, Ernest Brooks was of the opinion that there was no connection to be expected, and indeed none actually found, between the biblical quotations in the margins of BL Add 17134 and Jacob's full revision of the biblical text. Andreas Juckel, on the other hand, indicates in his second article that he wants to 'set out the shift of Jacob's revision from the earlier to the definitive stage'.[20]

The idea that there was an earlier stage to JacR is not new. Moshe Goshen-Gottstein has already argued that such a preliminary stage could be found in Jacob's *Scholia*.[21] Alison Salvesen had to conclude, however, that although the biblical text of the *Scholia* was 'influenced by the Greek in a similar way to' Jacob's revision of Samuel, the *Scholia* and the revision 'do not relate to each other in any consistent way'.[22] She did not find a development from a less revised to a more revised text. It is my opinion that the careful research and clear presentation of the evidence by Juckel force one to draw the same conclusion with regard to the possibility of a relationship between the marginal readings of the revision of Severus' hymns (JacS) and JacR.

On the basis of a great many instances which are fully discussed, Juckel describes how in JacS Jacob either adopts the Peshitta or substitutes it

[19] The Milan manuscript of the Syro-Hexapla gives the full text of Isaiah: Antonio M. Ceriani, *Monumenta sacra et profana 7. Codex syro-hexaplaris ambrosianus* (Milan, 1874). Isaiah 27:10–65:20 can also be found in Arthur Vööbus, *The Book of Isaiah in the Version of the Syro-Hexapla: A facsimile edition of MS. St. Mark 1 in Jerusalem* (CSCO 449, Subs. 68; Leuven, 1983). The variants of two more manuscripts, London BL Or. 8732 and Add. 17213, are found in Ceriani's notes on pp. 114–139 of his facsimile. For the Septuagint, see Joseph Ziegler, *Isaias* (Septuaginta: Vetus Testamentum Graecum auctoritate Academiae Scientiarum Gottingensis editum 14; 2nd ed.; Göttingen, 1967); for the Peshitta, Sebastian Brock, *The Old Testament in Syriac According to the Peshitta Version* 3.1 *Isaiah* (Leiden, 1987).

[20] Juckel, 'Approximation', p. 230.

[21] [Goshen-]Gottstein, 'Neue Syrohexaplafragmente', p. 164, note 3.

[22] Salvesen, *The Books of Samuel*, p. xxv.

by a new translation of the Greek.[23] In cases where the Peshitta roughly coincided with the Greek, Jacob opted for the first strategy; in cases where there were too many differences, he chose the second. Though in a limited number of cases Jacob made small corrections to the Peshitta text and though his Greek renderings were sometimes influenced by the Peshitta, in general one can say that the quotations from JacS are either Peshitta texts or Syriac renderings of the Septuagint. The 'shift' is visible mainly in two innovations shown by JacR: here correction of the Peshitta becomes a major tool, and Jacob also made sure to give the Greek substitutions for the Peshitta a familiar ring as he often added the unrevised Peshitta to it in the form of a doublet or expansion. The result is indeed, as Juckel states, an approximation of the two translations.[24]

Though Juckel is right in delineating the differences of approach between JacS and JacR, it is less obvious that there is also a connection between the actual material found in JacS and the later full revision that is JacR. First of all, Juckel postulates that Jacob prepared a 'corrected Peshitta manuscript, from which he generated the definitive version of his revision'.[25] Though this is possible, the readings of JacS do not support this idea. In the two cases which Juckel presents as examples, Isa 14:11 and 29:14, JacS just gives the Peshitta without any correction. Second, we should look at the full dossier that Juckel presents. Here, those readings in JacS that just give the Peshitta are less relevant: the fact that Jacob gives a reading based on the Peshitta in JacR does not necessarily point to a development between the two sources, as Jacob could have reworked the Peshitta reading straight from a Peshitta manuscript rather than from a manuscript containing an earlier stage of the revision. We have to concentrate on Juckel's examples 1–10. In these JacS replaces the Peshitta with a translation from the Greek.

What strikes the reader of Juckel's presentation and discussion of the Greek readings in JacS is the fact that these early renderings from the Greek do not play any consistent role in JacR. If there was a connection between the earlier and the later material, one would expect Jacob to have adopted his early renderings while adding a number of Peshitta readings as doublets or expansions in order to approximate to the translations. What happens instead in JacR is that, as Juckel himself states, Jacob went

[23] Juckel, 'Septuaginta and Peshitta', passim, and idem, 'Approximation', p. 231, with the dossier on pp. 243–279.

[24] Juckel, 'Approximation', pp. 231–243.

[25] Juckel, 'Approximation', p. 232.

back to the Peshitta and corrected it on the basis of the Greek. Moreover, many times the renderings of the Greek differ from those he had given in JacS. The following are some examples:

Isa 21:3, where Jacob first translated ἐσπούδασα by ܐܬܚܦܛܬ and later by ܘܐܣܬܪܗܒܬ (in which the ܘ might come from the Peshitta, but not the verb itself).[26]

Isa 24:17, where Jacob adds a verb in JacR in order to make the text more readable (the same happened in the Bohairic version, but we should not look for a real variant here).[27] Cf. also Isa 24:19[28] and 30:18.[29]

The inconsistent relationship between JacS and JacR becomes particularly clear in Isa 24:18, where the earlier text adopted a verb from the Peshitta, ܢܬܬܨܝܕ, for ἁλώσεται, whereas JacR adopts many other features from the Peshitta, but replaces the Peshitta verb by ܢܬܬܚܕ.[30]

Comparable changes are also found in other verses, where actually also the Greek *Vorlage* seems to have been different:

Isa 24:16, where in addition to a number of different renderings which go back to the same Greek *Vorlage*, one finds that Jacob must also have read πτερύγων instead of περάτων contrary to Severus' biblical text in JacS, whereas he adopted the latter reading in JacR.[31] Here JacR also reflects the Lucianic plus καὶ εἶπε(ν) τὸ μυστήριόν μου ἐμοὶ τὸ μυστήριόν μου ἐμοί. The Peshitta is close to this but does not have JacR's singular possessive suffixes that represent μου, and the reading found in the margin of the Syro-Hexapla reflects only καὶ εἶπε(ν) τὸ μυστήριόν μου ἐμοί.

Isa 24:20, where the Greek behind the beginning of the JacS reading is not unclear, as Juckel states,[32] but rather reflects the Old Greek, while adding a doublet ܬܘܒ taken from the Peshitta. JacR reflects the Origenic and Lucianic recensions in this case.

Here and there in Juckel's examples 11–20 (where JacS gives the Peshitta), we find small variants to the Peshitta text which may or may not reflect a Greek text. In Isa 14:13, Juckel states that the reading ܐܣܩ for

[26] Cf. Juckel, 'Approximation', p. 245.
[27] Cf. Juckel, 'Approximation', p. 247.
[28] Cf. Juckel, 'Approximation', p. 248. It is not necessary to assume a different Greek *Vorlage* here for the last words of the verse, as Juckel does, as Jacob may have simply copied them from the Peshitta.
[29] Cf. Juckel, 'Approximation', pp. 254–255.
[30] Cf. Juckel, 'Approximation', p. 247.
[31] Cf. Juckel, 'Approximation', p. 246; Brooks, *Hymns of Severus* (PO 7.5), p. 694.
[32] Juckel, 'Approximation', pp. 248–249.

the Peshitta's ܐܪܝܡ, which one finds in both of Jacob's versions, 'is taken over' in the full revision from the earlier work.[33] This is doubtful: ܐܣܝܡ is a natural rendering of Greek ϑήσω, and given the fact that there are many changes in the context, it is unlikely that Jacob actually looked this word up in the earlier work.

We may conclude that what Salvesen said about the biblical text in the *Scholia* also holds good for the JacS readings: they do not relate to JacR in any consistent way, as Brooks had already noted. Of course it remains possible that Jacob now and then looked up a difficult passage in notes he made earlier, but there are no indications that JacS formed part of a large preparatory dossier that Jacob constantly consulted when making his version. Incidentally, the study of Jacob's Genesis quotations in other works, including his *Commentary on the Octateuch* and *Scholia*, has not yielded any indication that there were preliminary stages to JacR either. It is only in Jacob's *Hexaemeron*, written in the very last years of his life, that we find some biblical quotations according to JacR, as well as in one of his letters.[34] I do agree with Juckel, however, that there is a clear development in Jacob's approach to the biblical text: where he used to keep the translations separate in 674/675, he approximated them in 704/705.

Here we should, however, also bear in mind that Jacob's aim in JacS is to give the full biblical text of places quoted or alluded to in hymns originally written in Greek and citing the Septuagint. This made it necessary to replace the Peshitta by the Septuagint wherever the differences were too great. The need to present the *graeca veritas* was provided by the aim and context. In JacR, however, Jacob tried to make the Greek Bible acceptable to Syriac readers; approximation must have appeared to him the right way to reach this goal. Here he is seeking a compromise rather than the *graeca veritas*.[35]

---

[33] Juckel, 'Approximation', p. 264.

[34] The idea that Jacob was quoting JacR in his *Hexaemeron* is found, among others, in J.P.P. Martin, 'L'Hexaméron de Jacques d'Édesse', *JA* (8ème série) 11 (1888), pp. 155–219, 401–490, esp. 171–179, and in Romeny, 'Jacob of Edessa on Genesis', p. 158. Alison Salvesen has pointed out, however, that Jacob is not consistent in his quotations: 'The Genesis Texts of Jacob of Edessa: A Study in Variety', in Wido Th. van Peursen and Bas ter Haar Romeny (eds.), *Text, Translation, and Tradition: Studies on the Peshitta and Its Use in the Syriac Tradition Presented to Konrad D. Jenner on the Occasion of his Sixty-Fifth Birthday* (MPIL 14; Leiden, 2006), pp. 177–188, esp. 186, and in particular idem, 'The Authorial Spirit? Biblical Citations in Jacob of Edessa's Hexaemeron', *Aramaic Studies* 6 (2008), pp. 207–225.

[35] A different opinion is found in Juckel, 'Septuaginta and Peshitta', § 21.

4. *How to Explain Parallels between Different Versions: Methodological Issues*

Much has been written about the relationships between the Peshitta and the Targumim, and between the Peshitta and the Septuagint. In order to assess whether the Peshitta was influenced by one of these versions, a strict methodology has been developed. This methodology can and should now also be applied to the question of whether Jacob's quotations and version were influenced by the Syro-Hexapla.

First of all, one should note that parallels between two versions that disagree with the supposed *Vorlage* can be accounted for in a number of ways. A very clear survey of these is given by Percy van Keulen.[36] In short, the four main explanations are:

1. Dependence of one version on the other;
2. Use of a common source;
3. Convergence or polygenesis;
4. Chance.

In assessing the parallels between the Peshitta and Targum Jonathan, Van Keulen adopts a 'minimalistic approach'. He explains this as follows: 'there must be sound reasons to posit a form of relationship between P and TJ above the level of convergence'. This means that the minimalism is applied to the first and second explanations. In other words, following Michael Weitzman the maximum is attributed to the translator's activity.[37] Though most Peshitta specialists would now agree with this, it is good to say a little more about this.

In the past, points of agreement have often been explained as indications of dependence. This may be seen as a case of what is called 'the prosecutor's fallacy' in the parlance of juridical probability. There are points of agreement of which one can say that the probability of finding such instances if the versions are independent is tiny. The fallacy is committed if one then proceeds to claim that the probability of independence is comparably tiny. The problem is that the *a priori* odds of dependence

[36] Percy S.F. van Keulen, 'Points of Agreement between the Targum and Peshitta Versions of Kings against the MT', in Percy S.F. van Keulen and Wido Th. van Peursen (eds.), *Corpus Linguistics and Textual History: A Computer-Assisted Interdisciplinary Approach to the Peshitta* (SSN 48; Assen, 2006), pp. 205–235, esp. 208.

[37] Michael P. Weitzman, *The Syriac Version of the Old Testament: An Introduction* (UCOP 56; Cambridge, 1999), pp. 15–17, 69, and cf. 92.

of one version on the other have not been taken into account. It is true that if there is a dependency, there is a very great chance that any agreement should be explained as stemming from this dependency. However, there may be other explanations, and nowadays the *a priori* odds that one version depends on the other are considered much lower. It is, after all, natural that two translations of the same text have something in common and could combine together against the source text because of the demands of the language or a similarity in interpretation. This is all the more the case when the two versions in question are written in dialects of the same language, such as the Peshitta and Targumim. As there are no external data that prove a contact between the Peshitta and the existing Targumim, the burden of proof is on the side of those who say that there is more than such similarity, that is, that there are parallels that cannot be explained except by assuming a common source or even dependence.

Now how could one demonstrate the dependence of one version on the other in the absence of external data? Piet Dirksen stated that in order to assess the probability of the Peshitta having used Targum Onqelos at least three points should be taken into account:[38]

1. The number of cases. One would expect a translator who had Onqelos to hand to have consulted it not just in one or two verses, but in a sustained way. 'Although a small number of cases may not disprove influence, a big number would certainly help.'
2. There should be at least a few virtually certain cases of influence, otherwise one cannot move from possibility to probability.
3. The type of agreement. If the translator used Onqelos, 'we would expect him to do so in linguistically or theologically difficult passages,' rather than where the text is plain and simple.

In other words, within a larger context that shows some more points of agreement, one has to find at least a small number of cases where the two versions go against the supposed *Vorlage*, where the agreement is complicated to such an extent that polygenesis becomes rather unlikely, and in which there are no indications of a possible shared different *Vorlage*. Only if such cases can be found, can we start speaking of the probability of dependence.

[38] P.B. Dirksen, 'Targum and Peshitta: Some Basic Questions', in Paul V.M. Flesher, *Targum Studies* 2. *Targum and Peshitta* (South Florida Studies in the History of Judaism 165; Atlanta, 1998), pp. 3–13, esp. 11.

5. *The Biblical Quotations in BL Add 17134 and the Syro-Hexapla*

Now how does the methodology established for the Peshitta and Targumim and Peshitta and Septuagint apply to Jacob's versions and the Syro-Hexapla? On the one hand, it can be established that as Paul of Tella produced the Syro-Hexapla in 613–617, it is possible that Jacob had a copy. On the other hand, we know that copying this work, with its many marginal notes in Greek and Syriac, was extremely difficult.[39] We cannot therefore assume that every Syriac Orthodox monastery had a copy. The presence of manuscripts is anyway a matter of what the late David Lane called 'chance and personality'.[40] Thus the fact that Jacob is quoting the Harclean version of Acts when making his revision of Severus' hymns, and the Peshitta for the other books of the New Testament, very likely reflects the availability and non-availability of texts to him rather than a specific predilection for the Harclean in Acts, as we have noted above. So again, it is *possible* that Jacob consulted the Syro-Hexapla, but we have no external data that make it a priori *likely*.

What else do we know? First, it is certain that Jacob consulted at least one Greek manuscript. The colophons of his version are no argument here, because they may have been written by someone else (after all, they portray him as a bishop at a time when he had already left his see); furthermore, the translation 'found among the Greeks' does not necessarily refer to a Greek manuscript: it could be taken to refer to the Syro-Hexapla. The point is that his version often follows the Lucianic recension of the Septuagint as against the Hexaplaric and Syro-Hexaplaric texts.[41] Jacob could know the Lucianic readings only from direct contact

[39] See the testimony of Timothy I, Catholicos-Patriarch of the Church of the East, in his letter XLVII to his friend Sergius (*c.* 800): Oscar Braun, 'Ein Brief des Katholikos Timotheos I über biblische Studien des 9 Jahrhunderts', *OrChr* 1 (1901), pp. 299–313. For an English translation, see Sebastian Brock, *A Brief Outline of Syriac Literature* (Mōrān 'Eth'ō 9; Kottayam, 1997), pp. 245–250, and for a detailed study of the description of the copying process, Pierre Petitmengin and Bernard Flusin, 'Le livre antique et la dictée: Nouvelles recherches', in E. Lucchesi and H.D. Saffrey, *Mémorial André-Jean Festugière: Antiquité païenne et chrétienne* (Cahiers d'Orientalisme 10; Geneva, 1984), pp. 255–262.

[40] David J. Lane, 'Text, Scholar, and Church: The Place of the Leiden Peshitta within the Context of Scholastically and Ecclesiastically Definitive Versions', *JSSt* 38 (1993), pp. 33–47.

[41] See the publication by Rahlfs quoted in note 6 above, as well as Saley, *The Samuel Manuscript*, p. 119; idem, 'The Textual Vorlagen', p. 121; Salvesen, *The Books of Samuel*, p. x; idem, 'Jacob of Edessa's Version of 1–2 Samuel', pp. 135–136.

with a Greek text.[42] Second, it is also clear that Jacob had an excellent knowledge of Greek.

Given the fact that Jacob knew Greek very well and that he translated a Greek text which must have been more or less similar to the *Vorlage* of the Syro-Hexapla into the same Syriac language, it is only natural that where he and the Syro-Hexapla give the plain sense of a simple Greek sentence, the two versions will be more or less identical. Therefore those instances where Jacob, the Syro-Hexapla, and the Greek agree cannot be used to demonstrate dependence. These cases bear some weight only because of Dirksen's first point; they will never tip the scale in favour of dependence. What we have to look for are the cases where the Syro-Hexapla and Jacob together seem to go against the Greek text. When assessing the possibility of Jacob being dependent on the Syro-Hexapla, it is again safest to attribute the maximum to the translator's activity. Polygenesis will not explain every instance, however, and the fact that the Hexaplaric and Lucianic recensions often combine against the Old Greek, means that we should take seriously the possibility that Jacob and the Syro-Hexapla both go back to a Greek *Vorlage* that is different from the Old Greek.

Now Ernest Brooks stated that 'In very few cases there is some resemblance to the Syriac Hexaplar'.[43] His index of the quotations actually indicates 'Paul of Tella' as the source in only one instance, that of Job 38:4–7. Interestingly, this indication has been firmly deleted in the copy of the Leiden University Library, which bears notes probably pencilled in by Wim Baars, one of the great specialists in this field. He may have felt that it did not make sense to assume influence of the Syro-Hexapla in just one out of 600 cases (compare Dirksen's first point). The reading itself does follow the Syro-Hexapla (Syh), but not in every detail. Here are the Syh reading and the points where Jacob differs:[44]

---

[42] Many of these readings cannot be explained on the basis of the hypothesis that Jacob used the Syro-Lucianic version of Isaiah, probably made by the Chorepiscopus Polycarp at the request of Philoxenus of Mabbug, and edited in Antonio M. Ceriani, 'Esaiae fragmenta syriaca versionis anonymae et recensionis Jacobi Edesseni', in his *Monumenta sacra et profana* 5 (Milan, 1868–1871), pp. 1–40. This version is indeed based on the Lucianic text, but it also used the Peshitta, and it dealt freely with these *Vorlagen*, adding readings that have a basis in neither of them; cf. R. Geoffrey Jenkins, *The Old Testament Quotations of Philoxenus of Mabbug* (CSCO 514, Subs. 84; Leuven, 1989), pp. 20–23, 28–29.

[43] Brooks, *Hymns of Severus* (PO 6.1), p. 6 note 3.

[44] The Syro-Hexapla is quoted here according to the Milan manuscript. The text of JacS is found in Brooks, *Hymns of Severus* (PO 7.5), p. 795.

(4) ܐܝܟܐ ܗ̇ܘܝܬ ܟܕ ܡܫܬܬܣܬ ܗܘܝܬ ܐܪܥܐ. ܐܘܕܥܢܝ ܕܝܢ ܐܢ ܝܕܥ ܐܢܬ ܣܘܟܠܬܐ. (5) ܡܢܘ ܣܡ ܡܫ̈ܘܚܬܐ ܕܝܠܗ̇ ܐܢ ܝܕܥ ܐܢܬ. ܐܘ ܡܢܘ ܗ̇ܘ ܕܐܪܡܝ ܥܠܝܗ̇ ܚܘܛܐ. (6) ܥܠ ܡܢܐ ܣܝ̈ܒܠܐ ܕܝܠܗ̇ ܡܩܒܥܝܢ. ܡܢܘ ܕܝܢ ⁻ܐܝܬܘܗܝ܆ ܗܘ ܕܐܪܡܝ ܟܐܦܐ ܪܫ ܙܘܝܬܢܝܬܐ ܥܠܝܗ̇. (7) ܟܕ ܗ̣ܘܘ ܟܘ̈ܟܒܐ܆ ܫܒܚܘܢܝ ܒܩܠܐ ܪܒܐ ܟܠܗܘܢ ܡܠܐ̈ܟܐ ܕܝܠܝ.

(4) ܡܫܬܬܣܬ Syh] ܡܫܬܐܣ JacS
(6) ܟܐܦܐ ܪܫ ܙܘܝܬܢܝܬܐ Syh] ܟܐܦܐ ܕܪܫ ܙܘܝܬܐ JacS ,ܐܝܬܘܗܝ *sine obel.* JacS

(4) Where were you when I was laying the foundation of the earth?—now let me know, if you know wisdom. (5) Who laid down its measures, if you know? Or who was it that stretched a line on it? (6) On what are its bearers fastened? And who is he that cast the cornerstone on it? (7) When the stars came into being all my angels praised me with a loud voice.

Jacob's readings could be seen as corrections to Syh if he had indeed used this version: the form ܡܫܬܬܣܬ is usually interpreted as an *etpa"al* with a passive or reflexive meaning ('to be founded' or 'to settle'), which does not fit the context as one needs an active form here, ܐܪܥܐ 'earth' being the object. Jacob gives the expected *pa"el*. Syh's ܪܫ ܙܘܝܬܢܝܬܐ is probably an adjective meant to mirror the γωνιαῖον of the Septuagint;[45] it is a neologism based on the existing substantive ܙܘܝܬܐ. Jacob retains the latter form, writing 'the stone of the head of the corner'. But is it necessary to assume that Jacob used the Syro-Hexapla here? If all the readings are correct and natural renderings of a rather simple Greek text, this case certainly does not meet Dirksen's second and third criteria. There are, however, two possible problems we need to discuss:

For σύνεσιν in verse 4 both Syriac versions give ܣܘܟܠܬܐ. Ziegler notes this as a variant in his apparatus, giving a Latin translation, as the reading would have no Greek support. I think, however, that ܣܘܟܠܬܐ is not a bad translation of this Greek word at all. It is true that it is often rendered by ܣܘܟܠܐ, but in these cases there is usually a word like σοφία in the context, which forced the translator to differentiate. We certainly do not need to assume a different Greek *Vorlage* or any special connection between JacS and Syh.

The reverse is the case in verse 6, where Syh does not figure in Ziegler's apparatus, but where the reading ܣܝ̈ܒܠܐ 'bearers, pillars' would appear to reflect στῦλοι instead of κρίκοι 'rings'. Polygenesis at the translators' level could be suggested, as 'bearers' makes more sense in the context and could be inspired by Ps 74:4. As στῦλοι is attested by the Lucianic

45 For the Septuagint, see Joseph Ziegler, *Iob* (Septuaginta: Vetus Testamentum Graecum auctoritate Academiae Scientiarum Gottingensis editum 11.4; Göttingen, 1982).

recension, the simplest explanation, however, is that both Syh and JacS have used a manuscript with this reading.

In short, Job 38:4–7 is an example of a reading which Jacob certainly copied from the Syro-Hexapla if he had been consulting it regularly, but in itself this reading does not necessitate the assumption of Jacob's use of Paul of Tella's version: both Syh and JacS are correct and natural renderings of an identical and rather simple Greek text. Now what about Isaiah and Andreas Juckel's opinion?

Actually, Juckel's opinion is not entirely clear to me. On the one hand, he says that though there are agreements between JacS and Syh, the translations of JacS 'are independent renderings of the Septuagint'. In addition, he speaks of Jacob's 'refusal to replace the rejected Peshitta texts by the Syro-Hexapla'.[46] On the other hand, in his discussion of 21 Septuagint texts quoted by Jacob in JacS, he states that the 'Syro-Hexapla may have influenced his translation in a general way,' though 'special influence is hardly traceable.'[47] At this point he mentions five cases in Isaiah which might point to such 'special influence'. Let us have a closer look at these.[48]

Item 7: In Isa 25:1 JacS reads the conjunction ܘ before ܐܘܕܐ, its rendering of ὑμνήσω. Syh indeed does the same, but so does the Peshitta, which according to Juckel himself has had some influence on Jacob's renderings of the Greek.[49] Moreover, Syh renders ὑμνήσω by ܐܫܒܚ, whereas JacS and the Peshitta read ܐܘܕܐ. In fact, even if JacS and Syh had combined against all other witnesses, this variant could easily be explained as a case of polygenesis: it is an addition typical of translations and loose quotations. It appears indeed that in addition to Syh and JacS, the Sahidic translation and Cyril also read a conjunction here.

Item 11: With regard to Isa 30:18 Juckel states that the 3rd person singular with which JacS translated καταλείψετε would also be found in Syh. However, all three Syh manuscripts that have this verse have a minus: the phrase καὶ ποῦ καταλείψετε τὴν δόξαν ὑμῶν has not been rendered at all.[50] Juckel has corrected this in his second article.[51]

---

[46] Juckel, 'Septuaginta and Peshitta', §§ 6 and 8.

[47] Juckel, 'Septuaginta and Peshitta', § 14.

[48] The item numbers are those used by Juckel, 'Septuaginta and Peshitta', § 13.

[49] Juckel, 'Septuaginta and Peshitta', §§ 8, 14, 16, 20; idem, 'Approximation', p. 231.

[50] The Milan manuscript published by Ceriani, BL Or. 8732 mentioned in his notes, as well as Jerusalem, St Mark 1, published by Vööbus.

[51] Juckel, 'Approximation', p. 254.

Item 18: In Isa 64:4–8 the one JacS reading supported by Syh is also found in the Peshitta, in Greek Ms. B, and in the Lucianic recension (where also some other Greek variants are found that may have been part of Jacob's *Vorlage* in this passage).

Item 19: The reading shared by Syh and JacS in Isa 65:15 is also found in the Lucianic recension and a number of other Greek witnesses.

Item 21: The reading shared by Syh and JacS in Isa 66:17 is also found in the Peshitta.

We may conclude that none of the readings adduced by Juckel gives us reason to doubt his first statement, that the translations of JacS 'are independent renderings of the Septuagint'. No special influence can be demonstrated, and I have found no indications of what Juckel calls influence 'in a general way' either.

6. *The Revision of Isaiah and the Syro-Hexapla*

With regard to the use of the Syro-Hexapla in JacR, Juckel concurs in his second article with Richard Saley's point of view and states that the evidence is inconclusive.[52] His full discussion of twenty texts, containing a total of eighty verses, makes it clear, however, that he does reckon with Syro-Hexaplaric influence in what he calls the 'definitive stage' of the revision. In fact, there are quite a number of readings where JacR is closer to Syh, but the agreement is usually not complete, and we also find many cases where the reverse is the case, or where it is otherwise clear that Jacob follows a different source (that is, a Lucianic manuscript) for his Greek reading. The methodology outlined above will, I hope, allow us to overcome the state of inconclusiveness. To begin with, the points of agreement between Syh and JacR allow us to say that Dirksen's first requirement is fulfilled: there is a context with quite a few points of agreement. The questions are, whether we can also find 'virtually certain cases of influence' and what is the type of the agreement. In order to answer them, we need to look at those instances where JacR combines with Syh against all other witnesses. I have located four of them:

Item 9: In Isa 57:20 JacR and Syh do not reflect οὕτως,[53] but this word is actually also not attested in the Greek witnesses to the Hexaplaric

[52] Juckel, 'Approximation', p. 242 with note 25.
[53] Juckel, 'Approximation', p. 256.

recension. The minus could easily be explained as a case of polygenesis as the word is more or less redundant, though it is also possible that Jacob's Greek manuscript was influenced by the Hexaplaric recension.

Item 12: In Isa 14:3 JacR reads ܡܪܝܐ ܐܠܗܟ with Syh, reflecting κύριος ὁ θεός σου.[54] Contrary to what Juckel says, this reading is found in Greek witnesses as well (manuscripts 88 and 538). Convergence is also a possible explanation in this case. After all, Jacob found ܡܪܝܐ in the Peshitta, and if his Greek manuscript retained the Old Greek reading ὁ θεός, he might have combined these two readings. The possessive would then have been inspired by the direct context.

Item 15: In Isa 32:2 JacR and Syh do not reflect ἔνδοξος.[55] Also in the case of this minus, polygenesis is a very possible explanation, but we should note that contrary to Juckel's statement the same variant is also attested in Greek manuscripts: the 'Lucianized' 233 and the related *codices mixti* 403 and 613.

Item 19: For Isa 61:7 Juckel reports οὕτως pro διὰ τοῦτο as a reading which is supported by Syh and the Hexaplaric recension.[56] It is therefore in any case a reading not unique to Syh and JacR. However, the situation is more complicated. It appears that οὕτως as such is also the reading of the Old Greek. It is the combination with a divergent word order that is important. Here are the relevant texts:[57]

PESH ܘܪܬܐ ܬܢܝܢܐ ܬܐܪܬܘܢ ܒܐܪܥܗܘܢ
You will inherit a double inheritance in their land

JACR ܗܟܢܐ ܠܐܪܥܗܘܢ ܡܢ ܕܬܪܬܐ ܬܐܪܬܘܢ
Thus you will inherit their land a second time

SYH ܗܟܢܐ ܐܪܥܐ ܡܢ ܕܬܪ̈ܬܐ ܢܐܪܬܘܢ
Thus they will inherit the land a second time

LUC διὰ τοῦτο τὴν γῆν αὐτῶν ἐκ δευτέρου κληρονομήσουσιν

HEX οὕτως τὴν γῆν ἐκ δευτέρας κληρονομήσουσιν

OG οὕτως ἐκ δευτέρας κληρονομήσουσιν τὴν γῆν

It is clear that Syh follows the Hexaplaric recension in every detail. Apart from the second person of the verb (ܬܐܪܬܘܢ), which Jacob adopted

[54] Juckel, 'Approximation', p. 260.
[55] Juckel, 'Approximation', p. 268.
[56] Juckel, 'Approximation', p. 277.
[57] Unfortunately, constraints of the English language make it impossible to show the differences in word order in translation.

from the Peshitta, JacR stands closer to the Lucianic recension, including its reflection of αὐτῶν. The only problem is in fact the word ܗܟܢܐ: for the Lucianic διὰ τοῦτο one would have expected ܡܛܠ ܗܢܐ. Assuming that Jacob did not give a free rendering but actually read οὕτως, there are a number of options:

1. He used a Lucianic manuscript that was influenced by the Old Greek or the Hexaplaric recension,[58] reading οὕτως.
2. He used a Lucianic manuscript while adopting οὕτως/ܗܟܢܐ from Syh or a different Greek manuscript (containing either the Old Greek or the Hexaplaric recension).
3. He followed Syh while adopting in addition to ܬܐܪܬܘܢ also the possessive suffix of ܠܐܪܥܗܘܢ from the Peshitta, and removing the *seyame* from ܬܪ̈ܬܝܐ.

Though the colophon of Jacob's Samuel version clearly leaves the possibility open that Jacob used more witnesses to the Greek text, it would be hard to understand why he would go to a different source to adopt such a minor detail. The last option, use of only the Syro-Hexapla, comes with a rather complicated explanation of the three points where JacR and Syh disagree. The easiest solution is probably the first, though the possibility that Jacob was simply less precise here, rendering διὰ τοῦτο by ܗܟܢܐ, should not be forgotten either.

In short, in none of the four cases just discussed is it necessary to assume dependence. The two minuses (Items 9 and 15) are the least problematic to explain, and in the last case (Item 19) it is clear that there are many more likely options before one has to assume that Jacob consulted Syh. I admit that in the case of Isa 14:3 (Item 12), if one looks at it in isolation, the assumption of dependence on Syh is the most elegant and simple explanation, but seen in the context of the eighty verses presented by Juckel, this solution becomes rather unattractive. Here one should also bear in mind that none of these four cases actually answers Dirksen's third criterion: these are not the difficult instances where Jacob would have needed the help of an existing version.

[58] On the basis of his study of Jacob's revision of the Books of Samuel, Saley suggests indeed that he used a Lucianic manuscript influenced by Hexaplaric readings: Saley, *The Samuel Manuscript*, p. 119; idem, 'The Textual Vorlagen', p. 121.

7. *Conclusions*

The polymath Jacob of Edessa was engaged in studying the biblical text all his life. Earlier studies indicated, however, that there was no link between the full revision of the biblical text which he produced not long before his death in 708 and his scriptural quotations in commentaries and other works written before. Andreas Juckel's suggestion that the biblical quotations in the margins of Jacob's revision of the translation of Severus of Antioch's hymns would represent an earlier stage of the full revision is interesting. However, though one can indeed speak of a shift in Jacob's approach towards the biblical text, I have not found any consistent relation between the actual readings in the margins of Severus' hymns and the full revision. There were no instances where it was really necessary to assume that Jacob had gone back to the work he produced thirty years earlier. One should also bear in mind that Jacob's aims were different in the two works.

With regard to Jacob's possible use of the Syro-Hexapla, we found that Juckel's first statement about this was correct: the translations in the margins of Severus' hymns 'are independent renderings of the Septuagint'. I found no indications to support the idea of what Juckel called a 'general influence' of the Syro-Hexapla on these readings, and the possible cases of 'special influence' were not convincing either. At first sight, the full revision may seem to be closer to the Syro-Hexapla, but it appeared that there are also many readings which cannot be explained by Syro-Hexaplaric influence. Here too, there is no *a priori* likelihood that Jacob used Paul of Tella's version, and the burden of proof is certainly on the side of those who claim he did. As it is clear that Jacob knew Greek very well and that he used at least one Greek manuscript, only those readings where Jacob and the Syro-Hexapla combine against all Greek evidence are relevant if we want to find what Dirksen called 'virtually certain cases of influence'. Moreover, they should be too complex in nature to be explained from polygenesis. Such cases I have not found in the material carefully presented by Andreas Juckel.

DANS UN VASE PUR OU AVEC DES PSAUMES ?
UNE VARIANTE TEXTUELLE PEU ÉTUDIÉE EN ISA 66:20

Adrian Schenker

1. *Le problème textuel*

En Isa 66:20 le texte massorétique (TM), le grand rouleau complet d'Isaïe de la première grotte de Qumrân,[1] Symmaque,[2] et les autres traducteurs hexaplaires,[3] la Vulgate, la Peshitta, le Targûm lisent à la fin du verset l'expression בכלי טהור tandis que la Septante (LXX), appuyée par la Vetus Latina, offre la leçon μετὰ ψαλμῶν. Il semble que cette différence n'ait pas souvent fait l'objet d'une étude alors qu'elle change considérablement le sens du passage.[4] Puisque Arie van der Kooij a consacré une bonne partie de son érudition et de son intérêt personnel au livre d'Isaïe, dont il est l'éditeur dans la *Biblia Hebraica Quinta*, il aura peut-être du plaisir à une petite étude sur cette variante cendrillon, et au cas où il l'aurait étudiée (ce qui ne me surprendrait pas !) il aura peut-être également du plaisir à voir comment un collègue interprète cette variante déjà étudiée par lui-même, afin de pouvoir lui montrer avec sa grande expérience de critique textuel ce qui manque à ce présent article, qui lui est dédié avec beaucoup d'amitié.

2. *Le vase pur du TM*

L'ensemble des V. 18–20 décrit deux processions qui se mettent en mouvement à partir des extrémités de la terre habitée. V. 19 énumère les peuples et les îles les plus éloignés de Jérusalem qui n'ont jamais vu la

---

[1] Les autres manuscrits d'Isaïe découverts à Qumrân n'ont pas préservé Isa 66:20.

[2] Selon Eusèbe.

[3] Selon Jérôme.

[4] Johann Friedrich Schleusner, *Novus thesaurus philologico-criticus, sive Lexicon in LXX et reliquos interpretes graecos ad scriptores apocryphos Veteris Testamenti* 5 (Lipsiae, 1821), p. 555, la mentionne et l'explique comme une traduction métaphorique. C'est un aveu de désespoir en face de cette variante difficile à expliquer.

gloire de YHWH ni entendu parler de lui. Ils vont conduire les Israélites, exilés chez les nations, dans une procession d'offrande pour YHWH, car ils les escorteront comme on escorte une offrande, מנחה, en l'apportant à YHWH, au sanctuaire. C'est une image liturgique pour le retour des exilés, car ceux-ci seront conduits solennellement à Jérusalem, sur la montagne sainte de YHWH.

Au V. 20 la LXX a une autre leçon que le TM :[5] à la place de la *montagne* sainte, la Bible grecque évoque la *ville* sainte: τὴν ἁγίαν πόλιν. Cette différence montre, comme les précédentes au V. 18, qui ne seront pas traitées ici, et celle de la fin du V. 20, qui va être étudiée dans ce qui suit, que tout ce passage a fait l'objet de corrections ou d'ajustements, soit du côté du texte grec, peut-être au niveau de son modèle hébreu, soit du côté du précurseur du TM.[6] La première procession, V. 19–20a, ressemble à une deuxième, qui part de la ville de Jérusalem au temple. En elle, selon le TM, les fils d'Israël apportent leur offrande, מנחה, à la maison de YHWH, *dans un vase pur*. Dans la Bible grecque des LXX, les fils d'Israël apportent leurs sacrifices, θυσίας, *avec des psaumes*. Ce sont donc deux différences notables qui distinguent le TM de la LXX. V. 21 suggère ensuite une troisième procession en mentionnant les Lévites et les prêtres.[7] Car ceux-ci apporteront les offrandes et sacrifices des Israélites à l'autel où les fils d'Israël n'ont pas accès. Ce sont comme trois cercles concentriques où, à chaque fois, une procession part de la périphérie vers le centre. Le premier centre, Jérusalem, deviendra ensuite la périphérie pour le départ vers le deuxième centre, la maison du Seigneur, et celle-ci à son tour se transformera en périphérie pour le troisième centre, l'autel, qui cependant est seulement suggéré, non mentionné. Ce triple mouvement en cercles concentriques est propre à la LXX. En TM il est amorcé, mais incomplet.

Le sens de l'expression ‹vase pur› au V. 20b est clair dans le TM. Celle-ci fait partie d'une comparaison. Les nations conduisent les Israélites vers

---

[5] Déjà au V. 18 TM et LXX se distinguent textuellement en plusieurs points. Mais je n'entre pas dans une discussion de ces variantes-là. Elles mériteraient cependant d'être traitées en détail.

[6] Deux célèbres variantes concernent les expressions de l'hébreu: ‹Poul› et ‹tireurs d'arc›, פול et משכי קשת. Elles sont étudiées par Dominique Barthélemy, *Critique textuelle de l'Ancien Testament* (OBO 50.2; Fribourg–Göttingen, 1986), pp. 464–465. Elles sont d'une autre nature que celles que nous allons examiner ici et qui sont liées au symbolisme cultuel appliqué aux Israélites revenant de l'exil.

[7] Ici encore une différence: la coordination des deux termes n'est pas identique en TM et LXX. Celle-ci emploie la conjonction ‹et› alors que celui-là utilise une asyndète.

la montagne sainte sur des chars, en litière, à dos de cheval, de mulet et de dromadaire, comme les Israélites apportent l'offrande dans des vases purs au temple. Les Israélites sont en effet une offrande pour le Seigneur, V. 20a. Les moyens somptueux pour les véhiculer correspondent aux vases purs servant à amener des offrandes à la maison du Seigneur. Les deux chemins ont le même but, la montagne ou la maison du Seigneur. C'est un parallélisme qui fait du retour des exilés une procession cultuelle, une liturgie.

3. *Avec des psaumes dans la* LXX

Les offrandes sont amenées ici avec des psaumes à l'autel. Le seul parallèle explicite qui suppose un accompagnement musical des sacrifices, à savoir des holocaustes, des offrandes et des sacrifices de paix se trouve en Am 5:22–23.[8] Comme en Isaïe, l'offrande, מנחה, est traduite par θυσία. Selon Amos la musique est faite de chants, שרים, de mélodies jouées sur des instruments à cordes, זמרת נבלים, ce que la LXX rend par ᾠδαί et ψαλμὸς ὀργάνων. La musique semble avoir valeur cultuelle en elle-même, à un titre semblable que les offrandes, cf. Ps 69:31–32, puisque le rejet de la part du Seigneur s'étend simultanément aux deux, aux musiques comme aux sacrifices.

Selon la LXX de Isa 66:20 les Israélites ont la coutume d'amener leurs offrandes avec accompagnement de musique à la maison du Seigneur. On doit interpréter cela comme une procession des offrandes, accompagnée de musique, qui monte de la ville à la maison du Seigneur. La comparaison établit une ressemblance entre les Israélites, eux-mêmes une offrande pour YHWH, revenant de l'exil, véhiculés somptueusement dans un cortège triomphal qui entre dans la ville sainte, et le cortège solennel de la procession des offrandes avec musique, montant de la ville à la maison du Seigneur.

---

[8] Israel Knohl, ‹Between Voice and Silence: The Relationship between Prayer and Temple Cult›, *JBL* 115 (1996), pp. 17–34. Les passages d'Am 5:23 et d'Isa 66:20 selon LXX semblent rendre moins vraisemblable la thèse du silence complet du culte dans le temple de Jérusalem.

4. *Quelle leçon est originale ?*

Entre les Israélites qui reviennent de l'exil et l'offrande apportée à la maison du Seigneur il existe une ressemblance ou même une identité. Car les deux sont une offrande (V. 20a et V. 20b : deux fois le mot מנחה). Dans le TM, le souci de la pureté concernant la *minḥa* apportée à la maison du Seigneur va donc se doubler d'un souci parallèle concernant la *minḥa* que sont les Israélites escortés dans leur voyage à la montagne sainte. Car pendant leur retour, ceux-ci sont en contact étroit avec les nations qui les escortent en servant de guides aux chevaux, mulets, dromadaires et de conducteurs de chariots et de porteurs de litières au service des voyageurs israélites. Dans cette escorte les Israélites courent un danger de se souiller au contact avec tant de personnes qui ne se préoccupent point de pureté au sens juif. La comparaison avec l'offrande cultuelle, portée soigneusement à l'abri de toute impureté, vient rassurer les lecteurs croyants. Comme (כאשר) les offrandes cultuelles sont apportées dans des conditions de pureté parfaite au temple, de même les Israélites seront escortés dans des conditions de pureté qui les protégeront contre les contaminations possibles.

Selon la LXX, la comparaison existe de la même manière sauf que la pureté du transport de la *minḥa* n'est pas mentionnée, sans doute parce que cela va de soi. C'est inhérent à la réalité cultuelle. En revanche, la musique qui accompagne la procession de l'offrande qui va de la ville à la maison du Seigneur est signalée. Elle est festive et solennelle, comme l'escorte des exilés à Jérusalem est festive et solennelle. La comparaison porte ici sur la joie et la solennité. De part et d'autre la musique annonce la joie, la joie du cortège triomphal d'un côté, la joie de la procession cultuelle de l'autre.

Or, précisément la procession de l'offrande qui part de la ville et monte à la maison du Seigneur avec la musique n'apparaît nulle part ailleurs dans la Bible ! Elle ne peut donc pas être expliquée comme un cliché biblique importé ici par une main secondaire. Elle est au contraire singulière. En revanche, la question de pureté pour l'offrande que l'on porte est présente à la conscience biblique, cf. Ag 2:10–14 et Lévitique 6–7, et les contacts avec des étrangers impurs à l'extérieur de la terre d'Israël posent toujours problème à des juifs soucieux de la pureté prescrite, cf. Jos 22:19; Daniel 1; Esther, Tobie etc. On ne peut pas dire que Isa 66:20 serait influencé par la musique qui accompagne le culte sacrificiel selon Am 5:22–23. Cela est invraisemblable parce que là le contexte des sacrifices et de la musique est négatif. L'expression de la LXX est difficile en Isa 66:20 parce qu'elle n'est certainement pas suggérée par des parallèles bibliques. Ceux-ci n'existent pas. Elle est au contraire singulière.

5. *Un confirmatur*

Il faut ajouter, et c'est une confirmation de cette interprétation, que selon V. 20, le lieu d'arrivée du cortège des exilés qui reviennent, sera ‹ la sainte montagne du Seigneur › (avec pronom suffixe de la première personne) selon le TM, ‹ la ville sainte › selon la LXX. Dans le texte hébreu les Israélites ont pour but la maison du Seigneur établie sur sa montagne sainte. Là on porte l'offrande aux prêtres. On est dans l'espace sacré cultuel. Dans la LXX le point d'arrivée sera la ville de Jérusalem. Pour apporter l'offrande à la maison du Seigneur on devra monter de cette ville à la maison du Seigneur. Cela explique la procession qui prendra du temps et laissera ainsi la place pour faire résonner la musique pendant la montée.

Or, l'expression ‹ ma sainte montagne › ou ‹ la sainte montagne du Seigneur › est incomparablement plus fréquente que celle de ‹ la ville sainte ›. Celle-ci est très rare.[9] Mais elle existe en Isaïe même (48:2; 52:1). Mais en Isaïe comme partout ailleurs ‹ la montagne sainte du Seigneur › se rencontre beaucoup plus souvent. Cette expression figure trois fois dans le chapitre qui précède immédiatement (65:9; 65:11; 65:25). Il arrive qu'Isaïe évite l'expression ‹ ville sainte › là où il semble que le contexte la suggère (60:14; 64:14). On doit donc dire que la tournure ‹ ville sainte › est possible en Isaïe (attestée dans le Deutéro-Isaïe!), mais qu'elle est trop rare pour se glisser automatiquement dans l'esprit d'un copiste toujours exposé à l'influence d'expressions fréquentes. Au contraire, s'il y a influence d'une expression fréquente c'est bien celle de ‹ la montagne sainte du Seigneur ›.

Ajoutons que les deux leçons propres de la LXX peuvent très bien correspondre à un modèle hébreu. Ψαλμός traduit surtout des termes de la racine זמר et נגן. (En Isaïe on ne trouve pas d'autre emploi.) Le passage de ces deux leçons à celles du TM ne s'est pas fait par accident scribal. C'est une modification délibérée, de nature rédactionnelle ou littéraire.

---

[9] Neh 11:1; 11:18; Dan 9:24 (Théodotion); 3:24 (LXX, sans équivalent hébreu) et—important pour nous—en Isa 48:2; 52:1. Cf. en dehors de la Bible hébraïque 1 Macc 2:7 etc.

6. *Conclusion*

Isa 66:20 présente deux leçons de la LXX qui remontent à un modèle hébreu plus originel que les deux leçons correspondantes du TM. L'intérêt de ces leçons anciennes est double: pour l'histoire du texte biblique en Isaïe et pour l'histoire du culte sacrificiel dans la maison du Seigneur à Jérusalem.

Quant à l'histoire du texte de la Bible hébraïque, dans Isaïe aussi, comme dans beaucoup d'autres livres bibliques, on trouve donc des leçons de la LXX qui, à travers la traduction grecque, attestent un texte hébreu plus ancien que celui que le TM conserve. Ces leçons secondaires en TM n'ont pas subi un accident textuel ou scribal. Elles ont été modifiées de propos délibéré pour donner au texte biblique un profil différent, pour des motifs d'ordre théologique (ou idéologique, si on préfère) et par conséquent littéraire.[10] Cette modification a dû intervenir avant la copie du grand rouleau d'Isaïe de Qumrân que l'on peut dater vers 140 av. J.-Chr.[11]

Pour l'histoire du culte, Isa 66:20 nous laisse le souvenir d'une procession d'offrandes qui partait de la ville et montait à la maison du Seigneur et qui était accompagnée de musique! Ce fragment précieux d'une coutume liturgique a fait place dans une révision du livre d'Isaïe, conservée dans le TM, à une nouvelle leçon soucieuse de protéger la pureté prescrite par le Seigneur dans l'ultime grand retour des Israélites de leur dispersion.

---

[10] Qu'il me soit permis de renvoyer, parmi de nombreuses études à ce sujet, à Adrian Schenker, ‹Der Ursprung des massoretischen Textes›, *Textus* 23 (2007), pp. 51–67.

[11] Arie van der Kooij, *Die alten Textzeugen des Jesajabuches. Ein Beitrag zur Textgeschichte des Alten Testaments* (OBO 35; Fribourg–Göttingen, 1981), pp. 109–111.

PERSONAL NAMES IN THE SEPTUAGINT OF ISAIAH[1]

Emanuel Tov

This study deals with the representation of personal names in the Septuagint of Isaiah. It focuses on the translational, exegetical, and linguistic aspects of these names, not on the phonetic representation of the Hebrew. These names involve both personal and geographic names.[2] Our focus is the Septuagint of Isaiah, but this area cannot be separated from the other Septuagint books nor from the exegesis of the Septuagint of Isaiah in general, an area to which the honoree devoted many studies.[3]

Personal names are usually transliterated, even if they consist of two Hebrew components. As a rule, both constituents of such compound names were transliterated (e.g. 'house of …', 'mountain of …'),[4] but sometimes their first element was translated. In other cases both constituents were translated.[5]

Translators constantly struggle with the question as to what constitutes a personal name, usually to be transliterated. For example, in the case of Isaiah 8:1, 3, modern translations present a transliteration: 'The Lord said to me, "Get yourself a large sheet and write on it in common script

---

[1] Translations of Hebrew Scripture follow תנך, *JPS Hebrew–English Tanakh: The Traditional Hebrew Text and the New JPS Translation* (2nd ed.; Philadelphia, 1999). Translations of the LXX follow Albert Pietersma and Benjamin G. Wright (eds.), *A New English Translation of the Septuagint and the Other Greek Translations Traditionally Included Under That Title* (Oxford, 2007). Thanks are due to Prof. D. Gera for fine-tuning the Greek quotations.

[2] The study of geographic names in the Septuagint is somewhat neglected in the literature (see n. 22 for an early study). Thus, the bibliography of Cécile Dogniez, *Bibliography of the Septuagint (1970–1993)* (VT.S 90; Leiden etc., 1995) does not have a section devoted to this topic. On the other hand, the earlier bibliography of Sebastian P. Brock, Charles T. Fritsch, and Sidney Jellicoe, *A Classified Bibliography of the Septuagint* (ALGHJ 6; Leiden, 1973) contains sections on 'proper names', 'onomastica', and 'transliterations'.

[3] See among others, Arie van der Kooij, *Die alten Textzeugen des Jesajabuches, Ein Beitrag zur Textgeschichte des Alten Testaments* (OBO 35; Freiburg–Göttingen, 1981); *The Oracle of Tyre: The Septuagint of Isaiah 23 as Version and Vision* (VT.S 71; Leiden etc., 1998).

[4] For example, Εμεκαχωρ in Josh 7:24 (עמק עכור), ἐν Ἀραβωθ Ιεριχω in 2 Kgs 25:5 (בערבות ירחו).

[5] For examples, see Natalio Fernández Marcos, 'Nombres propios y etimologias propulares en la Septuaginta', *Sef.* 37 (1977), pp. 239–259.

'For Maher-shalal-hash-baz' ..." and the Lord said to me, "Name him Maher-shalal-hash-baz"' (JPS, all other translations similarly). However, the Septuagint translated these words ('... Then the Lord said to me, Name him "Swiftly Spoil, Quickly Plunder'").

With a computer-assisted search[6] of the Septuagint (based on the text of Alfred Rahlfs),[7] I located 27,413 occurrences of proper names in 10,912 verses in the canonical books of the Septuagint, with and without Greek endings. For Isaiah, these figures are 724 occurrences of proper nouns in 387 verses. When multiple forms of the names in the Septuagint are disregarded, we are left with 3544 different forms of personal names in the Septuagint (186 in Isaiah) representing a smaller number of names since many Hebrew names are represented by several different forms.[8] Among these 3544 different forms, words with a Hellenized ending in -ος, -ας, -ης, -ικη, -ψ, -ις, and -α, account for an average 31% of the occurrences of the proper names in the Septuagint (see below).[9] Our analysis refers to the figure that disregards the multiple occurrences of words, since frequently occurring names distort the statistics.

1. *Hellenized endings*[10]

Most names are transliterated into Greek without the characteristic case endings of Greek words. Thus, the first verse of Isaiah contains four indeclinable personal names: Αμως, Ιερουσαλημ, Ιωαθαμ, Αχαζ. One of these, Αμως, has a Greek ending,[11] but is not declinable. At the same time, four other words in that verse have Greek endings and are declinable: Ησαίας, Οζίου (nom. Οζίας), Εζεκίου (nom. Εζεκίας), Ιουδαί-

[6] The search was performed with the aid of the Accordance computer program version 7.4. See www.oaksoft.com.

[7] Alfred Rahlfs, *Septuaginta, id est Vetus Testamentum graece iuxta LXX interpretes* (Stuttgart, 1935). The text of this edition hardly differs from that of the volumes of the Göttingen Septuagint, while the apparatuses of variants differ completely.

[8] For example, the different representations of Kittim are counted separately: Κιτιαῖοι, Κιτιεῖς, Χεττιιμ, Χεττιιν, Ῥωμαῖοι (see below).

[9] All statistics are approximate only. We did not count as Hellenized the ending -ων (reflecting Hebrew words ending with וֹן-) since most words ending with these letters are indeclinable. Further, we did include words ending with -α that represent Aramaic nouns ending with *aleph* although they are not declinable.

[10] The accents and breathings of the Greek words follow the (*inconsistent*) conventions of the Göttingen Septuagint.

[11] Cf. Εἵλως, Εἵλωτος (a Helot, name of the Spartan serfs); εἰδώς participle of οἶδα, etc.

ας (nom. Ιουδαία). According to Thackeray,[12] *most* names of places and peoples reflect their Hellenized forms,[13] with a minority representing transliterated nouns without Greek endings. However, in view of the long lists of transliterated personal names in Genesis, Joshua, and Chronicles that represent their *Vorlagen* exactly with non-Greek endings, this view is very unlikely. Thackeray's view can now be refuted by computer-assisted data.[14] Thus, according to our statistics, 41 % of the proper names in Isaiah have Hellenized endings, a sizeable number, but still a minority.[15] These statistics imply that most proper names in the Septuagint represent the Hebrew/Aramaic words as such including some Hebrew/Aramaic morphemes.[16] The numbers of Hellenized endings in Isaiah, as in the other Prophetical books, are higher by 10 percent than most Septuagint books probably because the Prophets contain a greater percentage of geographic names (places, regions, people) than, for example, the historical books. In geographic names, the translators more readily added Greek endings. Similar percentages of Greek endings, usually

---

[12] Henry St.J. Thackeray, *A Grammar of the Old Testament in Greek According to the Septuagint* (Cambridge, 1909), pp. 160–171.

[13] Thackeray, *Grammar*, p. 166: '… Here (i.e., places and peoples), however, the Hellenized forms largely predominate. The translators, for the most part, had a fair knowledge of the geography, not only of Egypt, but also of other countries, and adopted the current Hellenized forms'. In n. 7, Thackeray lists the following examples: Αἰθιοπία, Ἀντιλίβανος, Ἰόππη, Καππαδοκία (for Kaphtor), Καρχηδών, Μεσοποταμία, Συρία. Thackeray, *Grammar*, p. 167 further notes: 'Rarely, apart from the later historical books, do we find places of importance like Damascus or Tyre transliterated'.

[14] For the basis of these searches, see n. 6. The statistics refer only to nouns, and not to adjectives, such as "Moabite" in Ῥοὺθ ἡ Μωαβῖτις (Ruth 1:22) and an "Egyptian maidservant", παιδίσκη Αἰγυπτία (Gen 16:1). Almost all these adjectives have Greek endings.

[15] Of a total of 724 occurrences of words classified as proper names, 289 end in -ος, -ας, -ης, -ικη, -ψ, -ις, and -α (40 %). If we focus on the individual words occurring multiple times in the Septuagint of Isaiah (168), we note that 69 of them (41 %) have Hellenized endings. Troxel presents different statistical data. According to the calculation of this scholar, 79.9 % of the 538 toponyms in that book have been transliterated in their Hebrew forms without added Hellenistic endings, while 16 % are represented by Hellenized endings: Ronald L. Troxel, *LXX-Isaiah as Translation and Interpretation. The Strategies of the Translator of the Septuagint of Isaiah* (JSJ.S 124; Leiden, 2007), pp. 190–191. Thanks are due to Prof. Troxel, who kindly showed me parts of his book prior to its publication. Similar statistics are found in an earlier study by Troxel, 'What's in a Name? Contemporization and Toponyms in LXX-Isaiah', in Ronald L. Troxel, Kelvin G. Friebel, and Dennis R. Magary (eds.), *Seeking Out the Wisdom of the Ancients. Essays Offered to Honor Michael V. Fox on the Occasion of His Sixty-Fifth Birthday* (Winona Lake, 2005), pp. 327–344, esp. 329.

[16] See the examples in n. 8 and see further in Isaiah Αιλιμ (אילים) in 15:8, Πόλις-ασεδεκ in 19:18, καὶ οἱ Σεβωιν (וסבאים) in 45:14.

approximately 30 %, pertain to the Septuagint as a whole. On the other hand, the later biblical books of Esther, Daniel, and 1 Esdras and the deuterocanonical books contain a larger number of Hellenized names than the earlier ones. In Esther and Daniel, the 61 % and 46 % respectively of such Hellenized names are either the majority or a very sizeable group.[17] For these books, Thackeray's statements are correct. Likewise, Josephus always reflects the Hellenized forms of biblical names, while Jewish Greek papyri from Egypt reflect both Semitic and Hellenized forms.[18]

Thackeray mentions the following declension groups of Hellenized names with Greek endings, also reflected in Septuagint of Isaiah:[19]

a. *Personal names*

1. Hellenized masculine names of the first declension ending with -ς, e.g. Ιωνᾶς, Μωυσῆς, Ιησοῦς.
2. Female nouns of the first declension (e.g. Λεία).
3. Theophoric names ending in -ίας (e.g. Ιερεμίας).
4. Mixed declension (partially declined) nouns in -ας, -ης, -(ε)ις, -ους, involving a nom. with -ς, an acc. with ν, and the other case endings as in Hebrew.
5. Partly declinable nouns in -ών (reflecting ון-), e.g. Σαμψών and Σαλωμών (rare).

b. *Place names*

1. Place names in -α like Γάζα declined as the first declension feminine.
2. Names of towns ending in -α like Γάλγαλα declined as neuter plurals of the second declension.
3. Place names in -ών (reflecting ון-) either declined (e.g. Ασκαλών) or not (e.g. Ακκαρών), as in most cases.

---

[17] In Job, Proverbs, and Lamentations, this percentage is equally high, but in each of these books the data are not numerous enough for a significant analysis.

[18] See Naomi G. Cohen, 'Jewish Names as Cultural Indicators in Antiquity', *JSJ* 7 (1976), pp. 97–128. Most of the names recorded in Victor A. Tcherikover, Alexander Fuks, and Menahem Stern (eds.), *Corpus Papyrorum Judaicarum* 1–3 (Cambridge–Jerusalem, 1957–1964) are of the type of Ἄβραμος such as are rare in the Septuagint.

[19] See n. 12.

c. *Names of countries*

The names of countries are represented by a variety of endings, exemplified as follows:

- -ίς עילם—Ελυμαίς (Dan 8:2); פרס—Περσίς (Dan 11:2).
- -(ε)ία בבל—Βαβυλωνία (Isa 11:11 [= שנער?]; 14:23 [no equivalent]; 39:1; Daniel passim; elsewhere Βαβυλών, incl. Isa 13:1, 19; 14:4; 21:9; 39:3; 43:14; 47:1; 48:14, 20, and the fast majority of the Septuagint verses); צידון—Σιδωνία (1 Kgs 17:9).
- -ική הדו—Ἰνδική (Esth 1:1; 3:12; 8:9; Dan 3:1 [no equivalent]).
- -αία גליל(ה)—Γαλιλαία (Joshua, 1–2 Kings, Isaiah, Ezekiel, Joel, 1 Chronicles); Ἰδουμαία (see § 5); Ἰουδαία (see § 5).
- -ίτις / ῖτις חורון—Αὐρανίτις (Ezek 47:16, 18); עוץ—Αὐσίτις (Job 1:1; 32:2; 42:17); בשן—Βασανῖτις (Joshua, Ezekiel, Minor Prophets; Joshua [also featuring a few cases of Βασαν]). גלעד—Γαλααδῖτις (Joshua, Judges, 1–2 Samuel, Ezekiel, Minor Prophets, 1–2 Chronicles);[20] מואב—Μωαβῖτις (see § 4); Χαναανῖτις (Zech 11:7 [no equivalent in the Masoretic Text]).

d. *Names of peoples*

The first two endings are the most frequent ones:[21]

- -αῖος e.g. עברי—Ἑβραῖος, אמרי—Ἀμορραῖος.
- -ίτης e.g. בית הלחמי—βηθλεεμίτης (1 Sam 16:18), גלעדי—Γαλααδίτης (Judg 10:3).
- -ιος, e.g. Ἀζώτιος—עזתי (Josh 13:3).

[20] These books also use Γαλααδ. Other books use only Γαλααδ.

[21] The endings -αῖος and -ίτης interchange, see Thackeray, *Grammar*, p. 171. E.g. 'Midianite' is represented by both Μαδιηναῖος (Gen 37:28; 37:36) and Μαδιανίτης (Num 10:29).

2. *Identifications of geographic names*

Since most translators were active in Egypt, they reflected the geography of that country well; they also were aware of several geographic identifications that were known to people living in the Hellenistic period.[22] At the same time, the translator of Isaiah turned more to transliterations than to Hellenized nouns.[23] Some examples of such identifications follow, mainly for Isaiah, leaving aside the more obvious ones.

א(ו)ן—Ἡλίου πόλις (Gen 41:45, 50; 46:20). This city in lower Egypt, already mentioned by Herodotus II.3, 7, 59, was well known for the worship of the sun god, Ra. It is mentioned in Jer 43:13 as *Beth Shemesh*.

ארם, ארם נהרים, פדן (ארם)—Μεσοποταμία (Μεσοποταμία Συρίας in Gen 33:18). This term occurs in the Septuagint from Gen 24:10 onwards. In Greek literature, it is evidenced from Polybius V.44.6 onwards (second century BCE).

אשדוד—Ἄζωτος (Isa 20:1 and passim in the Septuagint, but not in Josh 11:22; 15:46, 47 where the word is transliterated as Ασεδωθ). Ἄζωτος is the regular Greek name for Ashdod in the Hellenistic-Roman period and in earlier times. Herodotus II.157 probably refers to this city. Green points to the phonetic resemblance between Azotos and עזה.[24]

הדו—Ἰνδική (Esth 1:1 and passim; Dan 3:1; 1 Esdr 3:2).

חדקל—Τίγρις (Τίγρης). This identification occurs in Gen 2:14 and Dan 10:4. The Greek form of the river's name is attested for the first time by Herodotus I.189.

כפתר—Καππαδοκία (Deut 2:23; Am 9:7).[25] While the identification of Caphtor is not known (Crete?, Cyprus?), its identification with Cappadocia (central Asia Minor) is unlikely, since Caphtor is referred to as an island in Jer 47:4. The translator of Deuteronomy probably was misled by the similarity in sound of the Hebrew and Greek words. The Greek name is known from literary sources from Herodotus V.49 onwards.

לבנון—Ἀντιλίβανος. It is unclear why this name is used for the first Scripture occurrences of לבנון in Deut 1:7; 3:25; 11:24; Josh 1:4; 9:1 (all

[22] For early insights in this area, see Henry A. Redpath, 'The Geography of the Septuagint', *AJT* 7 (1903), pp. 289–307.

[23] See n. 15 above.

[24] Eliyahu Green in http://www.losttrails.com/herald/messages/33.shtml ('Geographic names of places in Israel in Herodotus').

[25] The Hebrew word was transliterated in the Septuagint of Gen 10:14 and it remained without equivalent in Jer 47:4.

in contexts of the borders of the land) instead of Λίβανος elsewhere in the Septuagint, from Josh 11:17 onwards. The Greek term denotes a mountain range parallel to the Lebanon. Probably the first translators considered Ἀντιλίβανος the correct identification of לבנון while the later translators chose a different one.[26]

מדי in צורי מדי—οἱ πρέσβεις τῶν Περσῶν (Isa 21:2), read as צירי מדי. The replacement of Media with Persia reflects the understanding that Persia replaced the empire of the Medes. The same rendering occurs in Jer 25(32):25, also after a reference to Elam. מדי = Μῆδοι occurs only once elsewhere in Isaiah (13:17).

נא—Διοσπόλις (Ezek 30:14, 16) and Μεμφίς (Ezek 30:15).[27] From the New Kingdom onwards, the Egyptian city Thebes was named 'the city of Amun' after the name of the city's main god; hence the references to 'No Amon' and 'No' in the Bible.[28] Its Greek equivalent was Dio(s)polis, 'city of Zeus', and therefore the identification in the Septuagint of Ezekiel is appropriate. The identification as Memphis is less apparent.

נף—Μέμφις (Isa 19:13; Jer 2:16; 46[26]:14, 19; Ezek 30:13; Hos 9:6 [מף]). This identification reflects the translators' knowledge of this city.

סבא—Σοήνη (Isa 43:3): 'I give Egypt as a ransom for you, Ethiopia and Saba in exchange for you'—LXX 'I have made Egypt and Ethiopia and Soene your exchange on your behalf.'[29] This identification (Aswan in upper Egypt) occurs only here in the Septuagint, while in 45:14 MT 'Egypt's wealth and Nubia's gains and Sabaites (סבאים), long of limb …' is rendered differently by 'Egypt has worked hard, and has the commerce of the Ethiopians, and the lofty men of Σεβωιν …' Elsewhere, סבא is transliterated as Σαβά in Gen 10:7 and 1 Chr 1:9.

סין—Σάις (Ezek 30:15) and Συήνη (Ezek 30:16). Συήνη appears also as the equivalent of סונה in Ezek 29:10 and 30:6.

צידון—Φοινίκη. Sidon is the most important city in Phoenicia and therefore this replacement is understandable. It occurs only once (Isa

[26] For an attempt to explain this equivalent, see Michaël N. van der Meer, *Formation and Reformulation. The Redaction of the Book of Joshua in the Light of the Oldest Textual Witnesses* (VT.S 102; Leiden, 2004), p. 208: '… a concern to reserve "Antilebanon" for the area promised by God, and "Lebanon" for the unconquered territory'.

[27] The occurrences of נא in Jer 46(26):25 and Nah 3:8 were not understood by the translators. See also Arie van der Kooij, 'The City of Alexandria and the Ancient Versions of the Hebrew Bible', *JNWSL* 25 (1999), pp. 137–149, esp. 142–144.

[28] See Donald B. Redford, 'Thebes', in David N. Freedman (ed.), *The Anchor Bible Dictionary* 6 (New York, 1992), pp. 442–443.

[29] Or: 'I have made Egypt your ransom, and Ethiopia and Soene the ones instead of you' (alternative translation offered by NETS [see n. 1]).

23:2), followed in the same chapter by its regular Septuagint equivalent, Σιδών (vv. 4, 12).

צען—Τάνις (everywhere, starting with Num 13:22, and including Isa 19:11, 30:4). The Greek name is mentioned for the first time in Herodotus II.66.

שנער—Βαβυλωνία. In Genesis, Shinar is transliterated as Σενναάρ (10:10; 11:2; 14:1, 9), while elsewhere Shinar is correctly identified as Βαβυλωνία (Isa 11:11) and Βαβυλών (Zech 5:11 and Dan 1:2).

תרשיש—Καρχηδών Isa 23:1, 6, 10, 14 (cf. Ezek 27:12, 25 and 38:13—Καρχηδόνιοι). The Septuagint equivalent (= Carthage, see Herodotus II.157) is the main argument for the identification of Tarshish as Carthage. This identification is by no means accepted among scholars and, in fact, a city in Spain is favored by a greater number of scholars.[30] In Isa 60:9 and 66:19, this word is transliterated as Θαρσις as elsewhere in the Septuagint (for the inconsistency, see § 5 below).

On the other hand, פלשתים was not identified by the Greek translators who either transliterated this word in the books Genesis—Joshua (Φυλιστιιμ) or provided an etymological-phonetic rendering in the remaining books, including Isa 2:6; 11:4; 14:29, 31 (ἀλλόφυλοι). Also Νεῖλος, used for the first time in Hesiod, *Theog.* 338 ff., is not used in the Septuagint. Instead, the translators represented יאר with ποταμός.

3. *Actualizations and exegesis*

More than other translators, the translator of Isaiah represented names in his *Vorlage* with exegetical renderings. This procedure reflects a rather daring intervention by the translator, to which Seeligmann devoted a sizeable segment in his monograph on the Septuagint of that book.[31] Some of these renderings represent the historical situation depicted by Hebrew Scripture with updated versions.

9:11 MT '*Aram* from the east and *Philistia* from the west—who devoured Israel with greedy mouths'—LXX '*Syria* from the rising of the sun, and the *Greeks* from the setting of the sun—those who devour Israel

[30] See David B. Baker, 'Tarshish', in Freedman, *Anchor Bible Dictionary* 6, pp. 332–333. See also the lengthy analysis of Van der Kooij, *Oracle of Tyre*, pp. 40–47.

[31] Isac L. Seeligmann, *The Septuagint Version of Isaiah—A Discussion of Its Problems* (MEOL 9; Leiden, 1948), pp. 76–81, re-published in Robert Hanhart and Hermann Spieckermann (eds.), *The Septuagint Version of Isaiah and Cognate Studies* (FAT 40; Tübingen, 2004), pp. 231–238. For a valuable recent study, see Troxel, 'What's in a Name?'.

with open mouth'. In this verse, the enemies of the time of the prophet Isaiah (Aram in the north-east and the Philistines in the south-west) were replaced in the Septuagint with those of the translator's time. The equivalents chosen are intentional, since elsewhere in the Septuagint of Isaiah ארם is rendered differently: Αραμ (7:1, 2, 5, 8) and τῶν Σύρων (17:3).[32] This is also the only place where 'Philistines' is rendered with Ἕλληνας in the Septuagint.[33] These equivalents show that the translator of Isa 9:11 referred to the enemies of his time, the Seleucid Empire in Syria, and the Hellenistic coastal cities in the west.

10:9 MT 'Was Calno any different from Carchemish? Or *Hamath* from Arpad?'—LXX '(Did I not take the country) above Babylon and Chalanne, where the tower was built? And I took *Arabia* and Damascus and Samaria.' The unusual identification of חמת with Arabia is found here as well as in Isa 11:11, where the elements of the verse appear in a different sequence in the Septuagint.[34] Usually חמת indicates the most northern border of Israel and is transliterated as Εμαθ / Ημαθ / Αιμαθ (including Isa 36:19; 37:13).[35] On the other hand, the Septuagint's translation in 10:9 may reflect an identification of חמת or Arabia different from the conventional identifications.[36] Seeligmann surmises that the translator of v. 11 refers to the Jewish diasporas of his time, which would have included Arabia.[37]

נחל מצרים—Ῥινοκορούρων (Isa 27:12).[38] Everywhere else in the Septuagint, this geographic term is rendered by its stereotyped renderings, involving φάραγξ, ποταμός, or χείμαρρος and Αἴγυπτος. On the other

---

[32] Συρία is the main rendering of ארם elsewhere in the Septuagint.

[33] See section 2.

[34] '... from Assyria—as also from Egypt, Pathros, Nubia, Elam, Shinar, Hamath, and the coastlands'. LXX: '... whatever is left from the Assyrians, and from Egypt and Babylonia and Ethiopia, and from the Ailamites and from where the sun rises and from out of Arabia'.

[35] The rendering of 15:7 נחל הערבים (valley of willows) as τὴν φάραγγα Ἄραβας is not related to this interpretation, since in that rendering it is based on a different reading of the consonants of the Masoretic Text.

[36] In this verse, Arpad is not represented in the Septuagint, and although a phonetic representation of Arpad and Ἀραβία is attractive, it is very unlikely and would not explain the equivalents in Isa 11:11. Besides, in that verse, another word is also lacking in the Septuagint, viz. Pathros.

[37] Seeligmann, *Isaiah*, p. 79; see also van der Kooij, *Textzeugen*, pp. 37–38 and Troxel, 'What's in a Name?'.

[38] MT: 'And in that day, the Lord will beat out the peoples like grain from the channel of the Euphrates to the Wadi of Egypt', LXX: 'And it shall be on that day that the Lord will fence them in from the channel of the river to Rhinocorura'.

hand, the translator of Isaiah contemporized the term as Rhinocorura (literally: the Place of the Mutilated Noses), the main border town between Egypt and Syria in Hellenistic times, known today as al-Arish.[39]

בשן—Γαλιλαία. In addition to the transliteration Βασαν (Isa 2:13 and elsewhere in the Septuagint), mentioned in §5, בשן is rendered quite unexpectedly Γαλιλαία in Isa 33:9:[40] MT 'Sharon is become like a desert, and Bashan and Carmel are stripped bare'—LXX 'Saron became marshes; Galilee and Carmel will become visible'. The parallel nouns in this verse (Sharon, Carmel) probably influenced the translator into replacing Bashan with a mountain ridge west of the Jordan.

37:38 MT 'They fled to the land of Ararat'—LXX '... but they escaped into Armenia'. The exegetical process of identifying Ararat with Armenia, not reflected elsewhere in the Septuagint,[41] but quoted by Josephus[42] may well reflect contemporary exegesis.[43]

46:1 MT 'Bel is bowed, Nebo is cowering'—LXX 'Bel has fallen; Dagon has been crushed'. Elsewhere, Δαγων represents דגון and Ναβαυ or Ναβου represent נבו (including Isa 15:2) so that the translator clearly made an effort to present a special equivalent. Bel Marduk was revered together with his first-born Nabu (thus the Masoretic Text). However, the translator may have known Dagon as a Babylonian deity alongside Bel Marduk, and against this background he may have contemporized the translation, although the full exegetical picture is unclear.

49:12 MT '(Look! These are coming from afar, these from the north and the west,) and these from the land of Sinim'—LXX '... but others from the land of the Persians'. The context of bringing people from a faraway country may have led the translator to refer to the Jewish diaspora,[44] while the identification of the Sinim remains contested among scholars.

Beyond Isaiah, note the following rendering:

---

[39] The town is named after the cutting of the noses of criminals. See Pau Figueras, 'The Road Linking Palestine and Egypt along the Sinai Coast', in Michele Piccirillo and Eugenio Alliata (eds.), *The Madaba Map Centenary 1897–1997. Travelling through the Byzantine Umayyad Period. Proceedings of the International Conference Held in Amman, 7–9 April 1997* (SBF.CMa 40; Jerusalem, 1999), p. 223; idem, in http://198.62.75.1/www1/ofm/mad/articles/FiguerasSinai.html. See also Joseph Ziegler, *Untersuchungen zur Septuaginta des Buches Isaias* (ATA 12.3; Münster i. W., 1934), p. 203.

[40] In Isa 8:23, Γαλιλαία reflects גליל.

[41] In Gen 8:4; 2 Kgs 19:37; Jer 51(28):27, Ararat is transcribed as Αραράτ.

[42] Jos. *Ant.* 1.3.6 §93 quoting from 'Berosus the Chaldean'.

[43] See Seeligmann, *Isaiah*, pp. 77–78.

[44] See Seeligmann, *Isaiah*, p. 79.

כתים—Ῥωμαῖοι Dan 11:30. In addition to transliterated names, Κίτιοι (Gen 10:4; 1 Chr 1:7), Κιτιαῖοι (Num 24:24; Isa 23:1), Κιτιεῖς (Isa 23:12), Χεττιιμ/ν (Jer 2:10; Ezek 27:6), the Septuagint of Daniel contemporized the Hebrew by representing this word as 'Romans'. The Greek word occurs only here in the canonical books of the Septuagint.

4. *Select Equivalents in Isaiah*

אדום is consistently transliterated as Εδωμ in the Septuagint from Genesis until Daniel (49 ×). At the same time, the first Hellenizing rendering Ἰδουμαία occurs in Gen 36:16[45] and afterwards often elsewhere (40 ×).[46] The following books do not seem to distinguish between the two Greek renderings: Joshua, 1–2 Kings (note the mixture of the two Greek options in 1 Kgs 11:14–16), Isaiah, Jeremiah, Lamentations, 1–2 Chronicles. Isaiah uses mainly Ιδουμαία (11:14; 21:11 [דומה]; 34:5, 6) and once Εδωμ (63:1).

אשור. The differences between the various Septuagint translators come to the fore in the renderings of this word. That Asshur was rendered in different ways can be seen most clearly through the three ways of representing the phrase מלך אשור (king of Assyria / the Assyrians): Βασιλεὺς Ασσουρ in 1–2 Chronicles (12 ×), Ezra–Nehemiah (3 ×), Jer 50(27):17, 18; βασιλεὺς Ἀσσυρίων (the only translation in 2 Kings [43 ×]) and βασιλεὺς (τῶν) Ἀσσυρίων (with the exception of 10:12 [ἄρχων], the only translation in Isaiah [25 ×]); and βασιλεὺς Ἀσσύριος ('the Assyrian king') in Nah 3:18.

1. אשור—Ἀσσύριοι. From Genesis 2 onwards, the main Septuagint rendering of the singular form Asshur is the plural Ἀσσύριοι, mainly in the phrase מלך אשור and only in the Torah and Prophets in additional contexts. The translator of Genesis distinguished between the eponymic figure Asshur whose name he transliterated as Ἀσσούρ in 10:11, 22 and the geographic unit Asshur = Assyria, as in 2:14 MT 'The name of the third

[45] The transliteration Εδωμ occurs ten times in the same chapter: vv. 1, 8, 9, 17, 19, 21, 22, 30, 32, 43.

[46] Josh 15:1; 2 Sam 8:12, 13, 14; 1 Kgs 11:1, 14, 15, 16; 2 Kgs 14:10; Amos 1:6, 9, 11; 2:1; Joel 4:19; Obad 8; Mal 1:4; Isa 11:14; 34:5, 6; Jer 25:21(32:7); 27:3(34:2); 40(47):11; 49:7, 17, 20, 22(29:8, 18, 21, 23); Ps 60(59):10, 11; 108(107): 10, 11; Lam 4:21; Ezek 25:12, 13, 14, 35:15; 36:5; 1 Chr 18:11, 12; 2 Chr 8:17; 25:19.

river is Tigris, the one that flows east of Asshur'. In that verse, he did not employ the equivalent geographic term Ἀσσυρία, but the name of the people, 'the Assyrians': 'The name of the third river is Tigris, the one that flows east of the Assyrians (Ἀσσυρίων)'. In fact, Ἀσσυρία does not occur in the translation of the canonical books,[47] although it was used in classical sources from Herodotus I.178, 185, onwards. The equivalent אשור—Ἀσσύριοι disregarding the content of the word in the context ('Assyria') is not natural in Genesis 2, nor is it natural in many subsequent verses.[48] Accordingly, it seems as if this equivalent was determined by the translator of Genesis regardless of the first occurrence of the word in Hebrew Scripture. It is not impossible that the equivalence מלך אשור—βασιλεὺς Ἀσσυρίων formed the background for the standard equivalent of Asshur in the Septuagint from its first occurrence onwards. The equivalent in Gen 2:14 is the more surprising in view of the equivalent of a geographic unit in the previous verse, v. 13 (כוש—τὴν γῆν Αἰθιοπίας). The next geographic units are transliterated (8:4 Ararat; all the names in the Table of the Nations in chapter 10; Egypt in chapter 12, often rendered in later contexts as 'Egyptians'). The rendering אשור—Ἀσσύριοι of Gen 2:14 is to recur often in the later books of the Septuagint.

When we meet Asshur again in the Torah, we read in Gen 25:18 MT 'They dwelt from Havilah, by Shur, which is close to Egypt, all the way to Asshur (באכה אשורה)'. Also this word is rendered in the Septuagint by the name of the people (ἐλθεῖν πρὸς Ἀσσυρίους). As in Gen 2:14, this rendering is unexpected not only because of its content, but also because the other geographic term in 25:18, Egypt (מצרים) is rendered by a Greek noun 'Egypt' (Αἰγύπτου).

In the third occurrence of Asshur in the Torah, in Num 24:22 'When Asshur takes you captive' we find again the equivalent אשור—Ἀσσύριοι. This time the equivalent is matched by similar equivalents in the context, both based on the Hebrew (v. 21 קיני—Καιναῖον, 24 כתים—Κιτιαίων)

---

[47] It occurs only in 4 Macc 13:9. It is difficult to know why Ἀσσυρία was not used in the Septuagint. If this non-use was intentional, possibly the translators wished to avoid a confusion with Συρία = Aram.

[48] The possibility that the phrase κατέναντι Ἀσσυρίων represents a neuter plural noun *Ἀσσύρια is attractive, since it would explain also the frequent phrase βασιλεὺς Ἀσσυρίων as well as the lack of the article in most instances. Such a neuter form, not recorded anywhere, would parallel such neuter place names as Γάλγαλα, Γέραρα, Ἐκβάτανα, Σόδομα, etc., mentioned by Thackeray, *Grammar*, p. 168. However, this option is impossible in view of the occurrence of the nominative and accusative plurals Ἀσσύριοι (Num 24:22; Isa 19:23; 30:31; 52:4) and Ἀσσυρίους (Gen 25:18; 2 Kgs 15:29, 17:6, 23; Hos 5:13, 7:11; Isa 19:23) for Asshur.

and not based on the Hebrew (v. 24 עברי—Ἑβραίους). The translation of this context is inconsistent, since the second occurrence of אשור, "They subject Asshur" is transliterated as Ἀσσούρ (v. 24).

In 2 Kings, Asshur is consistently rendered Ἀσσύριοι, almost always in the phrase 'king of Asshur'—βασιλεὺς Ἀσσυρίων (44×). This equivalent is applied in such a wooden fashion that it includes such renderings as 2 Kgs 18:11 MT 'and the king of Asshur deported the Israelites to Asshur'—LXX 'and the king of the Assyrians deported the Israelites to the Assyrians'. Similar renderings are found in 2 Kgs 15:29; 17:6, 23.

In Isaiah, the rendering Ἀσσύριοι occurs 40 times, both in the phrase 'king of Asshur' (25×) and in other contexts (17×) such as 10:5 הוי אשור—οὐαὶ Ἀσσυρίοις; 19:23 אשורה (to the land of Asshur)—πρὸς Ἀσσυρίους. In the latter verse, the translation of Asshur differs from that of Egypt (מצרים), rendered twice with the singular noun Αἴγυπτος (Egypt). In this verse, אשור is rendered with the name of the people, except for the end of the verse where the plural form of *miṣrayim* in ועבדו מצרים את אשור ('and the Egyptians shall serve together with Asshur') is matched by a Greek plural for Asshur. Isa 31:8 contains yet a different rendering (see below, Ασσουρ).

As in Isa 19:23, in Hos 9:3, 11:11, 12:2; Zach 10:10, 11; Jer 2:18, Egypt is rendered by a noun in the singular, while Asshur is represented by the plural noun Ἀσσύριοι. On the other hand, in Jer 2:36 and 50(27):17, 18 Ασσουρ is used, including in the phrase מלך אשור king of Assyria—βασιλεὺς Ασσουρ.

2. The renderings in Ezekiel are inconsistent: Ασσουρ in 16:28 (בני אשור) and 27:23; 31:3; 32:22, but in the other verses Ἀσσύριοι (23:5, 7, 9, 12, 23, in all verses except for v. 5 rendering בני אשור).[49] With two exceptions, the translator of the Minor Prophets used Ἀσσύριοι (15×). The exceptions are Ασσουρ in Hos 14:4 and Mic 5:5 (probably because of the transcription of Nimrod in the parallel phrase) and Ἀσσύριος in Nah 3:18, Mic 5:4, and Zeph 2:13.

[49] The differences are not related to the possible distinction between three different translators in this book: chapters 1–27; 28–39; 40–48. See H. St.J. Thackeray, 'The Greek Translators of Ezekiel', *JTS* 4 (1902–1903) 398–411; Emanuel Tov, *The Septuagint Translation of Jeremiah and Baruch. A Discussion of an Early Revision of Jeremiah 29–52 and Baruch 1:1–3:8* (HSM 8; Missoula, 1976), pp. 135–151. On the other hand, P.D.M. Turner, *The Septuagint Version of Chapters i–xxxix of the Book of Ezekiel* (Ph.D. diss.; Oxford University, 1970) maintains the unity of the translation.

3. Ασσουρ also represents אשור in Ps 83(82):9; Lam 5:6; Ezr 4:2, 6:22; Neh 9:32; and Chronicles (16×).

LXX-Isaiah thus reflects the main Septuagint practice of rendering אשור with the plural Ἀσσύριοι.[50] In the first chapters of Genesis, this equivalent occurs quite unexpectedly and inappropriately, possibly reflecting knowledge of the later books in that translation, which involves the further assumption that Genesis was not rendered first among the Scripture books.[51] The rendering of the singular אשור with the plural Ἀσσύριοι may be compared with similar equivalents of כוש—Αἰθίοπες (see n. 50), עילם—Αἰλαμῖται (21:2; 22:6), מדי—Πέρσαι (21:2), while most renderings of 'Egypt', 'Babel', 'Ethiopia', 'Juda' are rendered with singular forms. The translator's special approach to these nations may be shown in Isa 11:11 ἀπὸ τῶν Ἀσσυρίων καὶ ἀπὸ Αἰγύπτου καὶ Βαβυλωνίας καὶ Αἰθιοπίας καὶ ἀπὸ Αἰλαμιτῶν καὶ ἀπὸ ἡλίου ἀνατολῶν καὶ ἐξ Ἀραβίας where the Masoretic Text has only singular forms.

כוש. The eponymic ancestor כוש is transliterated as Χούς in Gen 10:6, 7, 8 and 1 Chr 1:8, 9, 10. At the same time, from the very first occurrence of כוש, designating the country, it is represented by Αἰθιοπία (Gen 2:13). Often the word is represented by an adjective designating the Ethiopians, as in 2 Kgs 19:9 מלך כוש—βασιλέως Αἰθιόπων. The latter two options are skillfully employed in Isaiah where Αἰθιοπία (11:11, 18:1, 43:3) appears alongside Αἰθίοψ (20:3, 4, 5; 37:9; 45:14). This is also the case in Ezekiel, the Minor Prophets, and Psalms.

מואב. In the great majority of its occurrences, מואב is represented by the indeclinable Μωαβ in Genesis–2 Kings, Isaiah,[52] Jeremiah, Ezekiel, Minor Prophets, Psalms, Job, 1–2 Chronicles (155×). At the same time, the Septuagint of Isaiah differed from other translations by its employ-

---

[50] This type of rendering resembles the equivalent כוש—Αἰθίοπες, but that equivalent was used skillfully (see below), while Ασσύριοι was used indiscriminately. מצרים—Αἰγύπτιοι does not provide a good parallel because of the possible confusion between the different vocalisations *miṣrayim* and *miṣrim*.

[51] Barr expressed the opinion that the translation of Isaiah preceded that of the translation of the Torah because of the lack of a consistent translation approach in the Greek translation of Isaiah: James Barr, 'Did the Greek Pentateuch Really Serve as a Dictionary for the Translation of the Later Books?' in Martin F.J. Baasten and Wido T. van Peursen (eds.), *Hamlet on a Hill. Semitic and Greek Studies Presented to Professor T. Muraoka on the Occasion of his Sixty-Fifth Birthday* (OLA 118; Leuven, 2003) pp. 523–543, esp. 539.

[52] 15:9; 16:2, 4, 6, 7, 11, 12, 13, 14.

ment of the name of the Hellenistic district Μωαβῖτις.[53] This name was used especially in the Ptolemaic administration for the regions of the southern part of the Ptolemaic province of *Coele Syria* (cf. Σαμαρεῖτις and Ἀμμωνῖτις).[54] This translator probably was inconsistent in his translation equivalents (see § 5), although it is not impossible that he distinguished between מואב as an ethnic unit (Μωαβῖτις) and Μωαβ as the eponymic ancestor. This may be the implication of Isa 16:7 'Ah, let Moab howl; Let all in Moab howl!' rendered as (οὐχ οὕτως) ὀλολύξει Μωαβ ἐν γαρ τῇ Μωαβίτιδι πάντες ὀλολύξουσι ('Moab shall wail; for in Moabitis all shall wail').

5. *Inconsistency in Isaiah*

What scholars name inconsistency in a translation implies that a translator did not have a fixed list of equivalences for each word. Inconsistency is considered a negative feature that can also be represented positively. Inconsistency often implies that a translator distinguished between the various meanings/usages/nuances of a word and by so doing he created several translation equivalents for the same Hebrew/Aramaic word. Thus, the translator of Isaiah often skillfully played with different translation options in the same context, so as to create literary variation.[55] While the distinction between inconsistency and literary variation is difficult, in the following examples inconsistency is probably involved. The most frequent representation is mentioned first.

בבל—Βαβυλών / Βαβυλωνία. See § 1.
בשן—Βασαν / Βασανῖτις / Γαλιλαία. See § 3.
יהודה—Ιουδα (5:3, 7; 7:1, 17; 9:20; 11:12, 13; 22:8, 21; 26:1; 40:9; 48:1; 65:9) / Ιουδαία (1:1; 2:1; 3:1; 3:8; 7:6; 8:8; 37:10, 31; 38:9; 44:26) / Ιουδαῖοι (19:17)
כוש—Αἰθιοπία / Αἰθίοψ / Χούς. See § 4.
כרמל—Χερμελ (Josh 12:22; 15:55; Isa 29:17; 32:15) / Κάρμηλος (everywhere else, including Isa 32:16).
מואב—Μωαβ / Μωαβῖτις. See § 4.
נבו—Ναβαυ—Ναβου / Δαγων. See § 3.

[53] 15:1, 2, 4, 5, 8; 16:7; 25:10. This form is also used once elsewhere: Jer 25:21(32:7).
[54] See Arnold H.M. Jones, *Cities of the Eastern Roman Provinces* (Oxford, 1937), p. 241. The translators thus distinguished between the noun Μωαβ(ε)ῖτης, similar to Σαμαρεῖτις and Ἀμμωνῖτις and the adjective Μωαβίτης (Moabite), as in Ruth 1:4.
[55] For examples, see Ziegler, *Untersuchungen*, pp. 32–46. For examples of inconsistency in Isaiah, see Troxel, 'What's in a Name?', p. 330.

סבא—Σοήνη (Isa 43:3) / Σεβωιν—Σαβά. See § 2.
צידון—Σιδών (*passim*, including Isa 23:4, 12) / Σιδωνία (1 Kgs 17:9) / Φοινίκη (Isa 23:2). See § 1.
תרשיש—Θαρσις / Καρχηδών. See § 2.
שומרון—Σαμαρεία (*passim*, including Isa 8:4; 9:8; 10:9–11; 36:19) / Σομορων (Isa 7:9; Neh 3:34) / Σεμερων (1 Kgs 16:24).

The above equivalents provide but a small sample of the inconsistencies in the translation of Isaiah,[56] which do not point to different translations.[57]

In sum, we found that the translator of Isaiah reflects the Septuagint system of representing personal names in the Septuagint, especially as in the Prophetical books. He is often inconsistent in his equivalents. In a limited number of cases, the translator added Greek endings to Hebrew/Aramaic words. In line with this translator's exegetical freedom, the translator of Isaiah stands out among the various Septuagint translators as someone who contemporized several geographic terms. The equivalent אשור—'Ασσύριοι takes a special place in this analysis.

[56] For similar inconsistency in other books, see צר—Σορ (Ezek 26:2, 3, 4, 7; 27:2, 3, 8 [Ezekiel α]) / Τύρος (everywhere else, including Ezek 28:2, 12; 29:18 [Ezekiel β]). שכם—Συχεμ (majority translation in the Septuagint including Judges B) / Σικιμα (especially Judges A; minority translation in Genesis).

[57] Various scholars have pointed to the possibility that Isaiah was rendered by more than one translator: Johann Fischer, *In welcher Schrift lag das Buch Isaias den LXX vor?* (BZAW 56; Giessen, 1930), pp. 2–5; Johannes Herrmann and Friedrich Baumgärtel, *Beiträge zur Entstehungsgeschichte der Septuaginta* (BWAT 5; Berlin etc., 1923) 20–31. These theories have been refuted by Ziegler, *Untersuchungen*, pp. 31–46. See also van der Kooij, *Textzeugen*, pp. 31–32.

BIBLIOGRAPHY
OF ARIE VAN DER KOOIJ

Books

Die alten Textzeugen des Jesajabuches. Ein Beitrag zur Textgeschichte des Alten Testaments (OBO 35; Fribourg–Göttingen, 1981; revised and translated version of Ph.D. dissertation Utrecht University, 1978).

Abraham, vader van / voor een menigte volkeren. Gen. 17,4–5 in het Hebreeuws, alsmede in de Griekse, Aramese en Syrische vertaling (Rede uitgesproken bij de aanvaarding van het ambt van hoogleraar in de uitlegging van het Oude Testament, de geschiedenis van de Israëlitische godsdienst en de Israëlitische letterkunde aan de Rijksuniversiteit te Leiden op vrijdag 23 februari 1990; Leiden, 1990; inaugural lecture).

The Oracle of Tyre. The Septuagint of Isaiah 23 as Version and Vision (VT.S 71; Leiden, 1998).

Books edited

With Bob Becking and Jaap van Dorp (eds.), *Door het oog van de profeten. Exegetische studies aangeboden aan prof. dr. C. van Leeuwen* (Utrechtse Theologische Reeks 8; Utrecht 1989).

With Piet B. Dirksen (eds.), *Abraham Kuenen (1828–1891). His Major Contributions to the Study of the Old Testament. A Collection of Old Testament Studies Published on the Occasion of the Centenary of Abraham Kuenen's Death (10 December 1991)* (OTS 29; Leiden etc., 1993).

With Piet B. Dirksen (eds.), *The Peshiṭta as a Translation. Papers Read at the II Peshiṭta Symposium Held at Leiden 19–21 August 1993* (MPIL 8; Leiden etc., 1995).

With Karel van der Toorn (eds.), *Canonization and Decanonization. Papers Presented to the International Conference of the Leiden Institute for the Study of Religions (LISOR) held at Leiden 9–10 January 1997* (SHR 82; Leiden etc., 1998).

With Theo L. Hettema (eds.), *Religious Polemics in Context. Papers presented to the Second International Conference of the Leiden Institute for the Study of Religions (LISOR) held at Leiden 27–28 April 2000* (STAR 11; Assen, 2004).

With Yohanan A.P. Goldman and Richard D. Weis (eds.), *Sôfer Mahîr. Essays in Honour of Adrian Schenker Offered by the Editors of Biblia Hebraica Quinta* (VT.S 110; Leiden etc., 2006).

In Press

With Michaël N. van der Meer (eds.), *The Old Greek of Isaiah. Issues and Perspectives. Papers read at the Conference on the Septuagint of Isaiah, held in Leiden 10–11 April 2008* (CBET; Leuven, 2010).

Articles

1974 'David, "het licht van Israël"', in *Vruchten van de Uithof. Studies opgedragen aan dr H.A. Brongers ter gelegenheid van zijn afscheid (16 mei 1974)* (Utrecht, 1974), pp. 49–57.

1977 'Die Septuaginta Jesajas als Dokument jüdischer Exegese. Einige Notizen zu LXX—Jes. 7', in Hendrik A. Brongers *et al.* (eds.), *Übersetzung und Deutung. Studien zu dem Alten Testament und seiner Umwelt Alexander Reinard Hulst gewidmet von Freunden und Kollegen* (Nijkerk, 1977), pp. 91–102.

1980 'Jeremia tegenover Chananja. Twee profetische visies op de vrede', *OGL* 57 (1980), pp. 22–29.

1982 'De tekst van Samuël en het tekstkritische onderzoek', *NedThT* 36 (1982), pp. 177–204.

'A Short Commentary on Some Verses of the Old Greek of Isaiah 23', *BIOSCS* 15 (1982), pp. 36–50.

1983 'On the Place of Origin of the Old Greek of Psalms', *VT* 33 (1983), pp. 67–74.

With Doede Nauta, 'Hoog(h)t, Everardus van der', in Doede Nauta (ed.), *Biografisch Lexicon voor de geschiedenis van het Nederlandse protestantisme* 2 (Kampen, 1983), pp. 147–151.

1984 'Zur Exegese von II Reg 17,2', *ZAW* 96 (1984), pp. 109–112.

1986 'A Case of Reinterpretation in the Old Greek of Daniel 11', in J.W. van Henten *et al.* (eds.) *Tradition and Re-interpretation in Jewish and Early Christian Literature. Essays in Honour of Jürgen C.H. Lebram* (StPB 36; Leiden, 1986), pp. 72–80.

'Accident or Method? On "Analogical" Interpretation in the Old Greek of Isaiah and in 1QIs[a]', *BiOr* 43 (1986), pp. 366–376.

'Das assyrische Heer vor den Mauern Jerusalems im Jahr 701 v. Chr.', *ZDPV* 102 (1986), pp. 93–109.

'Tekstkritiek en tekstoverlevering van het Oude Testament', in Adam S. van der Woude (ed.), *Inleiding tot de studie van het Oude Testament* (Kampen, 1986), pp. 87–101.

1987 'The Old Greek of Isaiah 19:16–25. Translation and Interpretation', in Claude E. Cox (ed.), *VI Congress of the International Organization for Septuagint and Cognate Studies, Jerusalem 1986* (SBL.SCS 23; Atlanta, 1987), pp. 127–166.

1988 'Symmachus, "de vertaler der Joden"', *NedThT* 42 (1988), pp. 1–20.

'On the Significance of MS 5b1 for Peshitta Genesis', in Piet B. Dirksen and Martin J. Mulder (eds.), *The Peshiṭta. Its Early Text and History. Papers read at the Peshiṭta Symposium held at Leiden 30–31 August 1985* (MPIL 4; Leiden etc., 1988), pp. 183–199.

'1QIsa[a] Col. VIII, 4–11 (Isa 8,11–18). A Contextual Approach of Its Variants', in *RdQ* 49–52 (*Mémorial Jean Carmignac. Études Qumraniennes*, 1988), pp. 569–581.

1989 'The Septuagint of Isaiah. Translation and Interpretation', in Jacques Vermeylen (ed.), *The Book of Isaiah—Le Livre d'Isaïe. Les oracles et leurs relectures unité et complexité de l'ouvrage* (BEThL 81; Leuven, 1989), pp. 127–133.

'"De tent van David". Amos 9:11–12 in de Griekse bijbel', in Bob Becking, Jaap van Dorp, and Arie van der Kooij (eds.), *Door het oog van de profeten. Exegetische studies aangeboden aan prof. dr. C. van Leeuwen* (Utrechtse Theologische Reeks 8; Utrecht 1989), pp. 49–56.

1991 'Nehemiah 8:8 and the Question of the "Targum"-Tradition', in Gérard J. Norton and Stephen Pisano (eds.), *Tradition of the Text. Studies offered to Dominique Barthélemy in Celebration of his 70th Birthday* (OBO 109; Freiburg–Göttingen, 1991), pp. 79–90.

'Zur Frage des Anfangs des 1. Esrabuches', *ZAW* 103 (1991), pp. 239–252.

'On the Ending of the Book of 1 Esdras', in Claude E. Cox (ed.), *VII Congress of the International Organization for Septuagint and Cognate Studies, Leuven, 1989* (SBL.SCS 31; Atlanta, 1991), pp. 37–49.

'Abraham Kuenen (1828–1891). De Pentateuch en de godsdienst van Israël', *NedThT* 45 (1991), pp. 279–292.

1992 'The Old Greek of Isaiah in Relation to the Qumran Isaiah Texts. Some General Comments', in George J. Brooke and Barnabas Lindars (eds.), *Septuagint, Scrolls and Cognate Writings. Papers Presented to the International Symposium on the Septuagint and Its Relations to the Dead Sea Scrolls and Other Writings (Manchester 1990)* (SBL.SCS 33; Atlanta, 1992), pp. 195–213.

'The Story of David and Goliath. The Early History of Its Text', *ETL* 68 (1992), pp. 118–131.

1993 'The "Critical Method" of Abraham Kuenen and the Methods of Old Testament Research since 1891 up to 1991. Some Considerations', in Piet B. Dirksen and Arie van der Kooij (eds.), *Abraham Kuenen (1828–1891). His Major Contributions to the Study of the Old Testament. A Collection of Old Testament Studies Published on the Occasion of the Centenary of Abraham Kuenen's Death (10 December 1991)* (OTS 29; Leiden etc., 1993), pp. 49–64.

'The Concept of Covenant (*berit*) in the Book of Daniel', in Adam S. van der Woude (ed.), *The Book of Daniel in the Light of New Findings* (BEThL 106; Leuven, 1993), pp. 495–501.

'Some Remarks on the Analysis of the Interpretative Character of Targum Jonathan to the Prophets, with particular attention to Targum Isaiah XXIII', in Irene E. Zwiep and A. Kruyt (eds.), *Dutch Studies in the Targum. Papers read at a workshop held at the Juda Palache*

Institute, University of Amsterdam (18 March 1991) (Publications of the Juda Palache Institute 8; Amsterdam, 1993), pp. 78–88.

'United Bible Societies' Policies for the New Edition of the Hebrew Bible', *JNSL* 19 (1993), pp. 1–11.

1994 'The Ending of the Song of Moses. On the Pre-Masoretic Version of Deut 32:43', in Florentino García Martínez *et al.* (eds.), *Studies in Deuteronomy in Honour of C.J. Labuschagne on the Occasion of his 65th Birthday* (VT.S 53; Leiden etc., 1994), pp. 93–100.

'Jeremiah 27:5–15. How Do MT and LXX Relate to Each Other?', *JNSL* 20 (1994), pp. 59–78.

1995 'De canonvorming van de Hebreeuwse Bijbel, het Oude Testament', *NedThT* 49 (1995), pp. 42–65.

' "And I also said". A New Interpretation of Judges ii 3', *VT* 45 (1995), pp. 294–306.

1996 'On Male and Female Views in Judges 4 and 5', in Bob Becking and Meindert Dijkstra (eds.), *On Reading Prophetic Texts. Gender-Specific and Related Studies in Memory of Fokkelien van Dijk-Hemmes* (BINS 18; Leiden etc., 1996), pp. 135–152.

'The Story of Genesis 11:1–9 and the Culture of Ancient Mesopotamia', *BiOr* 53 (1996), pp. 28–38.

'Tekstkritiek: van heldere tot omfloerste doelstellingen. Ontwikkelingen in het tekstkritisch onderzoek van de laatste decennia', *Met andere woorden* 15 (1996), pp. 31–38.

'Jeruzalem als heilige stad door de ogen van de gemeenschap van Qumran', in Konrad D. Jenner and Gerard A. Wiegers (eds.), *Jeruzalem als heilige stad. Religieuze voorstellingen en geloofspraktijk* (Leidse Studiën van de Godsdienst 1; Kampen, 1996), pp. 94–103.

1997 'Peshitta Genesis 6: "Sons of God"—Angels or Judges', *JNSL* 23 (1997), pp. 1–9.

' "The Servant of the Lord": A Particular Group of Jews in Egypt According to the Old Greek of Isaiah. Some Comments on LXX Isa 49,1–6 and Related Passages', in Jacques van Ruiten and Marc Vervenne (eds.), *Studies in the Book of Isaiah. Festschrift Willem A.M. Beuken* (BEThL 122; Leuven, 1997), pp. 383–397.

'Zur Theologie des Jesajabuches in der Septuaginta', in Henning Graf Reventlow (ed.), *Theologische Probleme der Septuaginta und der hellenistischen Hermeneutik* (Veröffentlichungen der Wissenschaftlichen Gesellschaft für Theologie 11; Gütersloh, 1997), pp. 9–25.

'Zum Verhältnis von Textkritik und Literarkritik. Überlegungen anhand einiger Beispiele', in John A. Emerton (ed.), *Congress Volume. Cambridge 1995* (VT.S 66; Leiden etc., 1997), pp. 185–202.

'Isaiah in the Septuagint', in Craig C. Broyles and Craig A. Evans (eds.), *Writing and Reading the Scroll of Isaiah. Studies of an Interpretive Tradition 2* (VT.S 70.2; Leiden etc., 1997), pp. 513–530.

1998 'The Teacher Messiah and World-Wide Peace. Some Comments on Symmachus' Version of Isaiah 25:7–8', *JNSL* 24 (*Volume in Memoriam Ferdinand Deist*, 1998), pp. 75–82.

'The Death of Josiah according to 1 Esdras', *Textus* 19 (1998), pp. 97–110.

With Karel van der Toorn, 'Introduction', in Arie van der Kooij and Karel van der Toorn (eds.), *Canonization and Decanonization. Papers Presented to the International Conference of the Leiden Institute for the Study of Religions (LISOR) held at Leiden 9–10 January 1997* (SHR 82; Leiden etc., 1998), pp. xv–xxiii.

'Canonization of Hebrew Books Kept in the Temple of Jerusalem', in Arie van der Kooij and Karel van der Toorn (eds.), *Canonization and Decanonization. Papers Presented to the International Conference of the Leiden Institute for the Study of Religions (LISOR) held at Leiden 9–10 January 1997* (SHR 82; Leiden etc., 1998), pp. 17–40.

'De canonisatie van de Hebreeuwse Bijbel (200 v. C. tot 100 n. C.)', in Konrad D. Jenner and Gerard A. Wiegers (eds.), *Heilig boek en religieus gezag. Ontstaan en functioneren van canonieke tradities* (Leidse Studiën van de Godsdienst 2; Kampen, 1998), pp. 147–163.

'Perspectives on the Study of the Septuagint. Who are the Translators?', in Florentino García Martínez and Ed Noort (eds.), *Perspectives in the Study of the Old Testament and Early Judaism. A Symposium in Honour of Adam S. van der Woude on the Occasion of his 70th birthday* (VT.S 73; Leiden etc., 1998), pp. 214–229.

1999 'The Origin and Purpose of Bible Translations in Ancient Judaism. Some Comments', *Archiv für Religionsgeschichte* 1 (1999), pp. 204–214.

'The City of Alexandria and the Ancient Versions of the Hebrew Bible', *JNSL* 25 (1999), pp. 137–149.

'The Use of the Greek Bible in II Maccabees', *JNSL* 25 (1999), pp. 127–138.

2000 'Isaiah 24–27. Text Critical Notes', in Hendrik J. Bosman *et al.* (eds.), *Studies in Isaiah 24–27. The Isaiah Workshop* (OTS 43; Leiden etc., 2000), pp. 13–15.

'The Cities of Isaiah 24–27 According to the Vulgate, Targum and Septuagint' in Hendrik J. Bosman *et al.* (eds.), *Studies in Isaiah 24–27. The Isaiah Workshop* (OTS 43; Leiden etc., 2000), pp. 183–198.

'Zur Frage der Exegese im LXX—Psalter. Ein Beitrag zur Verhältnisbestimmung zwischen Original and Übersetzung', in Anneli Aejmelaeus and Udo Quast (eds.), *Der Septuaginta-Psalter und seine Tochterübersetzungen. Symposium in Göttingen 1997* (MSU 24; Göttingen, 2000), pp. 366–379.

'The Role of the Father. A Response to Kottsieper', in Jan-Willem van Henten and Athalya Brenner (eds.), *Families and Family Relations as Represented in Early Judaisms and Early Christianities. Texts and Fictions. Papers Read at a NOSTER Colloquium in Amsterdam, June 9–11, 1988* (STAR 2; Leiden, 2000), pp. 81–82.

'The Story of Hezekiah and Sennacherib (2 Kings 18–19). A Sample of Ancient Historiography', in Johannes C. de Moor and Harry F. van

Rooy (eds.), *Past, Present, Future. The Deuteronomistic History and the Prophets* (OTS 44; Leiden etc., 2000), pp. 107–119.

'Textual Witnesses to the Hebrew Bible and the History of Reception. The Case of Habakkuk 1:11–12', in Ulrich Dahmen and Armin Lange (eds.), *Die Textfunde vom Toten Meer und der Text der Hebräischen Bibel* (Neukirchen, 2000), pp. 91–108.

'Qumran en de uitleg van de Bijbel', *Schrift* 191 (2000), pp. 147–150.

'The Use of the Bible in Dutch Church Documents on Homosexuality. Its Background and Setting', *Scriptura* 72 (2000), pp. 105–110.

2001 'H.A. Brongers', in Cornelis Houtman (ed.), *Biografisch Lexicon voor de geschiedenis van het Nederlandse Protestantisme* 5 (Kampen, 2001), pp. 91–92.

'A.R. Hulst', in Cornelis Houtman (ed.), *Biografisch Lexicon voor de geschiedenis van het Nederlandse Protestantisme* 5 (Kampen, 2001), pp. 273–275.

'The Septuagint of Psalms and the First Book of Maccabees', in Robert J.V. Hiebert, Claude E. Cox and Peter J. Gentry (eds.), *The Old Greek Psalter. Studies in Honour of Albert Pietersma* (JSOT.S 332; Sheffield, 2001), pp. 229–247.

'Textgeschichte/Textkritik der Bibel. I. Altes Testament', in *TRE* XXXIII (Berlin, 2001), pp. 148–155.

'Comments on NETS and La Bible d' Alexandrie', in Bernard A. Taylor (ed.), *X Congress of the International Organization for Septuagint and Cognate Studies. Oslo, 1998* (SBL.SCS 51; Atlanta, 2001), pp. 229–231.

'Bible Exegesis in Dutch Ecclesial Documents on Homosexuality', *Scriptura* 77 (2001), pp. 251–257.

'Tekstkritiek Oude Testament', in Erik Eynikel *et al.* (eds.), *Internationaal Commentaar op de Bijbel* 1 (Kampen, 2001), pp. 236–241.

2002 '"Coming" Things and "Last" Things. Isaianic Terminology as Understood in the Wisdom of Ben Sira and in the Septuagint of Isaiah', in Ferenc Postma, Klaas Spronk, and Eep Talstra (eds.), *The New Things. Eschatology in Old Testament Prophecy. Festschrift for Henk Leene* (ACEBT.S 3; Maastricht, 2002), pp. 135–140.

'Wie heisst der Messias? Zu Jes 9,5 in den alten griechischen Versionen', in Christoph Bultmann, Walter Dietrich und Christoph Levin (eds.), *Vergegenwärtigung des Alten Testaments. Beiträge zur biblischen Hermeneutik. Festschrift für Rudolf Smend zum 70. Geburtstag* (Göttingen, 2002), pp. 156–169.

'The Textual Criticism of the Hebrew Bible before and after the Qumran Discoveries', in Edward D. Herbert and Emanuel Tov (eds.), *The Bible as Book. The Hebrew Bible and the Judaean Desert Discoveries* (London, 2002), pp. 167–178.

2003 'Textual Criticism of the Hebrew Bible. Its Aim and Method', in Shalom M. Paul *et al.* (eds.), *Emanuel. Studies in Hebrew Bible, Septuagint, and Dead Sea Scrolls in Honor of Emanuel Tov* (VT.S 94; Leiden, 2003), pp. 729–739.

'On the Use of βωμός in the Septuagint', in Martin F.J. Baasten and Wido T. van Peursen (eds.), *Hamlet on a Hill. Semitic and Greek Studies Presented to Professor T. Muraoka on the Occasion of his Sixty-Fifth Birthday* (OLA 118; Leuven, 2003), pp. 600–607.

'Canonization of Ancient Hebrew Books and Hasmonaean Politics', in Jean-Marie Auwers and Henk Jan de Jonge (eds.), *The Biblical Canons* (BEThL 163; Leuven, 2003), pp. 27–38.

'The Interpretation of Metaphorical Language. A Characteristic of LXX—Isaiah', in Florentino García Martínez and Gerardus P. Luttikhuizen (eds.), *Jerusalem, Alexandria, Rome. Studies in Ancient Cultural Interaction in Honour of A. Hilhorst* (JSJ.S 82; Leiden etc., 2003), pp. 179–186.

'The Septuagint of Zechariah as Witness to an Early Interpretation of the Book', in Christopher M. Tuckett (ed.), *The Book of Zechariah and its Influence* (Aldershot, 2003), 53–64.

'Een canonskwestie. Het slot van het Oude Testament en het slot van Tenach—een open einde', *Schrift* 208 (2003), pp. 122–124.

'Koning Hizkia van Juda', in Robert J. Demarée and Klaas R. Veenhof (eds.), *Zij schreven geschiedenis. Historische documenten uit het Oude Nabije Oosten (2500–100 v.Chr.)* (MEOL 33; Leiden, 2003), pp. 333–340.

2004 'Old Testament Textual Criticism', in William R. Farmer *et al.* (eds.), *The International Bible Commentary. A Catholic and Ecumenical Commentary for the Twenty-First Century.* (Collegeville, 2004), pp. 216–221.

'Schwerpunkte der Septuaginta-Lexikographie', in Siegfried Kreuzer and Jürgen P. Lesch (eds.), *Im Brennpunkt: Die Septuaginta. Studien zur Entstehung und Bedeutung der Griechischen Bibel. Band 2* (BWANT 161; Stuttgart, 2004), pp. 119–132.

'Jerusalem as "the City of the Temple" in Jewish Sources from the Hellenistic Era', in Alain Le Boulluec (ed.), *À la recherche des villes saintes. Actes du Colloque Franco–Néerlandais "Les Villes Saintes", Collège de France, 10 et 11 mai 2001* (Bibliothèque de l'École des Hautes Études. Section des sciences religieuses 122; Brepols, 2004), pp. 43–52.

'The Septuagint-The First Translation of the Hebrew Bible?', *Bulletin of Judaeo-Greek Studies* 34 (2004), pp. 27–28.

2005 'La Septante d'Isaïe et la critique textuelle de l'Ancien Testament', in Adrian Schenker and Philippe Hugo (eds.), *L'enfance de la Bible hebraïque. L'histoire du texte de l'Ancien Testament à la lumière des recherchses récentes* (MoBi 52; Genève, 2005), pp. 185–198.

'Ancient Emendations in MT', in Dieter Böhler, Innocent Himbaza, and Philippe Hugo (eds.), *L'Écrit et l'Esprit. Études d'histoire du texte et de théologie biblique en hommage à Adrian Schenker* (OBO 214; Fribourg–Göttingen, 2005), pp. 152–159.

'The Septuagint of Ezekiel and Hasmonaean Leadership', in Florentino García Martínez and Marc Vervenne (eds.), *Interpreting Translation.*

Studies on the LXX and Ezekiel in honour of Johan Lust (BEThL 192; Leuven, 2005), pp. 437–446.

'Exegese', in George Harinck *et al.* (eds.), *Christelijke encyclopedie* 1 (Kampen, 2005), pp. 547–549.

'Kuenen', in George Harinck *et al.* (eds.), *Christelijke encyclopedie* 2 (Kampen, 2005), p. 1065.

2006 'Textual Criticism', in John Rogerson and Judith Lieu (eds.), *The Oxford Handbook of Biblical Studies* (Oxford, 2006), pp. 579–590.

'The Septuagint of Isaiah and the Hebrew Text of Isaiah 2:22 and 36:7', in Peter W. Flint, Emanuel Tov and James C. VanderKam (eds.), *Studies in the Hebrew Bible, Qumran, and the Septuagint Presented to Eugene Ulrich on the Occasion of his Sixty-Fifth Birthday* (VT.S 101; Leiden etc., 2006), pp. 377–386.

'MS 9a1 of Peshiṭta Isaiah. Some Comments', in Wido T. van Peursen and R.B. ter Haar Romeny (eds.), *Text, Translation, and Tradition. Studies on the Peshiṭta and its Use in the Syriac Tradition Presented to Konrad D. Jenner on the Occasion of his Sixty-Fifth Birthday* (MPIL 14; Leiden etc., 2006), pp. 71–76.

'The City of Babel and Assyrian Imperialism', in André Lemaire (ed.). *Congress Volume Leiden 2004* (VT.S 109; Leiden, 2006), pp. 1–17.

'The Text of Isaiah and its Early Witnesses in Hebrew', in Yohanan A.P. Goldman, Arie van der Kooij, and Richard D. Weis (eds.), *Sôfer Mahîr. Essays in Honour of Adrian Schenker Offered by the Editors of Biblia Hebraica Quinta* (VT.S 110; Leiden etc., 2006), pp. 143–152.

'A Kingdom of Priests. Comment on Exodus 19:6', in Riemer Roukema (ed.), *The Interpretation of Exodus. Studies in Honour of Cornelis Houtman* (CBET 44; Leuven, 2006), pp. 171–179.

'The Book of Isaiah in the Septuagint and in Other Ancient Versions', in Claire M. McGinnis and Patricia K. Tull (eds.), *"As Those Who Are Taught". The Interpretation of Isaiah from the LXX to the SBL* (SBL.SymS 27; Atlanta, 2006), pp. 49–68.

'Maarsingh, Berend', in Cornelis Houtman (ed.), *Biografisch Lexikon voor de geschiedenis van het Nederlandse Protestantisme* 6 (Kampen, 2006), pp. 177–178.

'Mulder, Martin Jan', in Cornelis Houtman (ed.), *Biografisch Lexikon voor de geschiedenis van het Nederlandse Protestantisme* 6 (Kampen, 2006), pp. 201–203.

'Das Buch Jesaja in der Septuaginta', *BiKi* 61 (2006), pp. 223–226.

'The Four Kingdoms in Peshitta Daniel 7', in Bas ter Haar Romeny (ed.), *The Peshiṭta. Its Use in Literature and Liturgy. Papers Read at the Third Peshiṭta Symposium* (MPIL 15; Leiden etc., 2006), pp. 123–130.

'Die erste Übersetzung des Jesajabuchs. Das Buch Jesaja in der Septuaginta', *BiKi* 61 (2006), pp. 223–226.

2007 'Ideas about Afterlife in the Septuagint', in Michael Labahn und Manfred Lang (eds.), *Lebendige Hoffnung—Ewiger Tod?! Jenseitsvorstellungen im Hellenismus, Judentum und Christentum* (Arbeiten zur Bibel und ihrer Geschichte 24; Leipzig, 2007), pp. 87–102.

'Moses and the Septuagint of the Pentateuch', in Axel Graupner and Michael Wolter (eds.), *Moses in Biblical and Extra-Biblical Traditions* (BZAW 372; Berlin etc., 2007), pp. 89–98.

'LXX-Isaiah 8–9 and the Issue of Fulfilment-Interpretation', *Adamantius* 13 (2007), pp. 20–28.

'The Septuagint of Ezekiel and the Profane Leader', in Henk Jan de Jonge and Johannes Tromp (eds.), *The Book of Ezekiel and its Influence* (Aldershot, 2007), pp. 43–52.

'The Septuagint of the Pentateuch and Ptolemaic Rule', in Gary N. Knoppers and Bernard M. Levinson (eds.), *The Pentateuch as Torah. New Models for Understanding its Promulgation and Acceptance* (Winona Lake, 2007), pp. 289–300.

'The Greek Bible and Jewish Concepts of Royal Priesthood and Priestly Monarchy', in Tessa Rajak *et al.* (eds.), *Jewish Perspectives on Hellenistic Rulers* (Hellenistic Culture and Society 50; Berkeley, 2007), pp. 255–264.

2008 'The Promulgation of the Pentateuch in Greek according to the Letter of Aristeas', in Anssi Voitila and Jutta Jokiranta (eds.), *Scripture in Transition. Essays on Septuagint, Hebrew Bible, and Dead Sea Scrolls in Honour of Raija Sollamo* (JSJ.S 126; Leiden etc., 2008), pp. 179–191.

'The Septuagint of Isaiah and the Mode of Reading Prophecies in Early Judaism. Some Comments on LXX Isaiah 8–9', in Martin Karrer und Wolfgang Kraus (eds.), *Die Septuaginta-Texte, Kontexte, Lebenswelten. Internationale Fachtagung verantstaltet von Septuaginta Deutsch (LXX.D), Wuppertal 20.–23. Juli 2006* (WUNT 219; Tübingen, 2008), pp. 597–611.

'Servant or Slave. The Various Equivalents of Hebrew *Ebed* in the Septuagint of the Pentateuch', in Melvin K.H. Peters (ed.), *XIII Congress of the International Organization for Septuagint and Cognate Studies, Ljubljana, 2007* (SBL.SCS 35; Atlanta, 2008), pp. 225–238.

'Isaiah and Daniel in the Septuagint. How are These Two Books Related?' in Hans Ausloos, Bénédicte Lemmelijn, and Marc Vervenne (eds.), *Florilegium Lovaniense. Studies in Septuagint and Textual Criticism in Honour of Florentino García Martínez* (BEThL 224; Leuven, 2008), pp. 465–473.

2009 'Prophetische Bücher: Einleitung'; 'Esaias: Einleitung'; 'Übersetzung Jes 1–39', in Wolfgang Kraus and Martin Karrer (eds.), *Septuaginta Deutsch. Das griechische Alte Testament in deutscher Übersetzung* (Stuttgart, 2009), pp. 1164–1165, 1230, 1231–1263.

'De Macht van het Kwaad als het Kwaad van de Macht', *Oikodome* 12 (2009), pp. 4–11.

Review article of Ronald L. Troxel, LXX Isaiah as Translation and Interpretation, *BIOSCS* 42 (2009), pp. 147–152.

'The Public Reading of Scriptures at Feasts', in Christopher Tuckett (ed.), *Feasts and Festivals* (CBET 53; Leuven, 2009), 27–44.

In press

'Rope', 'Cord', 'Tent—Rope', 'Tent—Cord', 'Thread', 'Skin', in Bob Becking and Johannes C. de Moor (eds.), *KLY. Utensils in the Hebrew Bible* (OTS 50).

'Erläuterungen zu Jes 1–39 und zu Jes 40–55', in Wolfgang Kraus and Martin Karrer (eds.), *Septuaginta Deutsch. Das griechische Alte Testament in deutscher Ubersetzung 2. Erläuterungsband* (Stuttgart)

'Rejoice, O Thirsty Desert! On Zion in the Septuagint of Isaiah' (to be published in a volume on Zion in the Book of Isaiah, by members of the Jesaja Werkplaats).

'Authoritative Scriptures and Scribal Culture', in Mladen Popović (ed.), *The Authoritativeness of Scriptures in Ancient Judaism. The Contributions of the Dead Sea Scrolls and Related Documents. Essays in Honour of F. García Martínez.*

'The Story of Paradise in the Light of Mesopotamian Literature and Culture', in Katherine J. Dell, Graham Davies, and Y.V. Koh (eds.), *Genesis, Isaiah, and Psalms. A Festschrift to Honour Professor John Emerton in his Eightieth Year* (VT.S; Leiden etc.).

'The Old Greek of Isaiah and Other Prophecies Published in Ptolemaic Egypt', in Martin Karrer and Wolfgang Kraus (eds.), *Die Septuaginta—Texte, Theologien, Einflüsse, Projekt Septuaginta Deutsch, Kirchliche Hochschule Wuppertal, 23–27 Juli 2008* (WUNT; Tübingen).

'The Septuagint of Isaiah and the Issue of Coherence. A Twofold Analysis of LXX Isaiah 31:9b–32:8', in Arie van der Kooij and Michaël N. van der Meer (eds.), *The Old Greek of Isaiah. Issues and Perspectives. Papers read at the Conference on the Septuagint of Isaiah, held in Leiden 10–11 April 2008* (CBET; Leuven, 2010).

INDEX OF ANCIENT SOURCES

DEAD SEA BIBLICAL SCROLLS

INDEX OF MODERN AUTHORS